6/16/92

The Principles of Computer Networking

25 Cambridge Computer Science Texts

The Principles of Computer Networking

D. Russell
Computing Laboratory, University of Newcastle upon Tyne

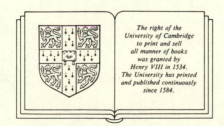

*The right of the
University of Cambridge
to print and sell
all manner of books
was granted by
Henry VIII in 1534.
The University has printed
and published continuously
since 1584.*

Cambridge University Press

Cambridge
New York   Port Chester   Melbourne   Sydney

Published by the Press Syndicate of the University of Cambridge
The Pitt Building, Trumpington Street, Cambridge CB2 1RP
40 West 20th Street, New York, NY 10011–4211, USA
10 Stamford Road, Oakleigh, Melbourne 3166, Australia

First published 1989
Reprinted 1991

Printed in Great Britain at the University Press, Cambridge

British Library cataloguing in publication data available

Library of Congress cataloguing in publication data available

ISBN 0 521 32795 4 hardback
ISBN 0 521 33992 8 paperback

To my parents

For more than I can ever know

Contents

Preface

This book is intended to cover the whole of the field of computer communications. Even with such a wide ranging ambition, there must be limits to the coverage. Roughly these are drawn at the lower end of the spectrum by assuming the properties of transmission media, and at the top end by stopping short of discussing truly distributed processing. In between, the aim has been to give an overall understanding of the principles involved.

Computer communications is such a vast and fast moving field that it is quite impossible to cover the details of any complete architecture within the confines of one book. However, that was never my intention. The real aim is to try to extract some of the *principles* that emerge in computer networking, sometimes over and over again. One prime example is the topic of flow control. The principles of flow control can be extracted independently of context, and this book devotes Chapter 4 to just that. Similarly, in Chapter 3 we look at what is at first sight a bewildering range of ways of sharing a medium. However, it soon emerges that most of their number can be reduced by asking two orthogonal questions—is the topology a bus or a ring, and is the access by contention or by token? Once these two principles have been understood, the other aspects are of secondary importance. Again, the addressing and routing principles that we discuss in Chapter 6 in relation to the techniques of providing the network service, crop up again when looking at network mail in Chapter 10, and Gateways in Chapter 15.

In overall plan the book starts at the bottom and works upwards. Thus, the early chapters through Chapter 6 explain how raw, error-prone communications media can be built into a reliable end-to-end communications service. However, the subject of communications has only just started by this time. For successful communication to take place, agreements have to be made about what the bits on this reliable pipe actually mean. This brings us to the consideration of presentation issues which are concerned with a consistent representation of the same semantic information across diverse systems. We also go into considerable detail in describing how various applications of computer connections actually work, including computer mail, terminal support, and file transfer and access. The application level tools provided by ISO, and in particular the remote operations service are explained.

As well as the "traditional" kinds of protocol with which this book is mainly concerned, a chapter is devoted to looking at so-called *lightweight protocols*, and the performance and system issues involved in the efficient implementation of communications architectures. In addition, since networks have grown so big, they need to be managed, and some of the management issues are also discussed.

Perhaps unusually, a whole chapter is devoted to Security, Authentication, and Encryption. This topic was given such treatment because the author perceives that current attitudes show a huge ignorance of what can and can't be done in this area. Computer networks are insecure, and becoming more so. However, many people either seem to be very ignorant of what can be achieved by encryption, or, naively, seem to be ready to put complete trust into encryption techniques. In 1978, Needham and Schroeder showed how, through the use of encryption techniques, two mutually unknown network entities could authenticate themselves, one to the other through the agency of a third, trusted, authentication server. This is independent of "hostile" agents observing all the messages, and inserting, corrupting, or replaying messages. Most people are very surprised by this ability, and it is surprisingly poorly known even 10 years after its first publication. On the other hand, some people put an unquestioning trust in encryption, apparently oblivious of the consistent history of broken cyphers. In addition, the interesting properties of public key encryption, together with their present disappointing position is also presented. Chapter 14 aims to give an up-to-date review of what can and cannot be done in this area.

Finally, Chapter 16 tries to summarise the need for standards, and the processes, political and technical, by which standards are produced and imposed. In addition to discussing the various political bodies that produce standards, Chapter 16 also discusses some of the techniques by which standards are described and analysed. Natural human language is inadequate and leads to ambiguity and misunderstanding, and Chapter 16 indicates some of the improved tools that are beginning to appear.

Throughout the book, the principles are illustrated by examples taken from real computer architectures. The emphasis is always on generally agreed standards, and so the examples come mainly from the ISO and ARPANET suites of protocols. The attempt has been to avoid proprietary architectures wherever possible, and the choice of the ISO and ARPANET suites is for two main reasons. One is that they are publicly and widely available, and the other is that they often have quite different approaches to solving the problems in hand. When different approaches are used on the same problem, then a careful analysis of where differences lie often illuminates the real character of the problem and reveals the principles involved.

A book like this owes much to the efforts of others. Perhaps the most help have been those with whom the author has come into contact over the long years that he has worked in designing and implementing networks. I have been privileged to encounter many luminaries, and it would be invidious to mention any individually since at least ten times as many would of necessity not be mentioned. However, I hope I may be allowed the indulgence of mentioning just two. I was privileged to know Bob Husak of the Merit Computer Network. Bob had a deep and encyclopaedic knowledge of networks at all levels, and was a good friend. His early death saddened all who knew him. In my undergraduate life as a physicist, Thomas Littlefield taught me how to get a feel for complex physical processes by employing simple mental pictures. It is an approach I have valued ever since.

Directly involved in the production of this book have been Harry Whitfield who fooled me into starting the project in the first place, and pointed out many silly mistakes, Quentin Campbell, Jill Foster, Isi Mitrani, and especially Ian Doak have read various drafts and given suggestions. From CUP, Ernest Kirkwood, Tim Bradshaw, and David Tranah have supported me during the preparation of this book.

I shall not break with the worthy tradition of thanking the typist Denis Russell for typing and revising endless revisions of the manuscript, with only the occasional hint of dissatisfaction with his lot. In addition, he typeset the text using TEX†, produced all the drawings in PostScript‡, and produced camera ready copy. Of course this leaves even less room than normal for the author to disclaim responsibility for errors. More to the point, various tools were used including text editors on several operating systems (even including UNIX§), micros, workstations and mainframes too numerous to mention, and communications systems including most of those described between these covers.

Finally, and most of all, I would like to thank my wife Marion, and the kids for putting up both with me and without me during the excessively protracted gestation period of this book. I can only hope it was worth their efforts.

---

† TEXis a trademark of the American Mathematical Society
‡ PostScript is a trademark of Adobe Systems Incorporated
§ UNIX is a trademark of Bell Laboratories

1
Data Transmission

This chapter examines the ways in which data is transmitted along communications channels or lines. The subject of data transmission is a large and complex area of electronic engineering, and a chapter of this size is intended only to give a flavour of some of the principles involved. The intention is first to describe how characters can be represented as bits, and then see how bits can be transmitted down communications channels. We shall touch lightly on Fourier Analysis and the fundamental results of Nyquist and Shannon. After a look at this theoretical basis, the chapter proceeds to examine some of the more common methods of transmitting data along communications lines. This leads to a discussion of the types of errors that we can expect to encounter. It will also be the grounding to which we shall refer when we come to discuss some of the various sorts of shared medium in Chapter 3.

1.1   Character Representation

The simplest form of communication between computers and human beings is by means of characters that are assembled into text of some sort. Other means of communication, such as graphs, sound, mice, pointing, joysticks, colour, and so on have increasingly been employed. However, in simple computer communications, text is still the most important currency.

It is normal to represent text inside a computer by choosing a set of symbols, the character set, and allocating each one to a unique number. These unique numbers are then stored in locations called bytes. A byte is a group of eight bits within a computer, and is thus capable of representing a number in the range 0 to 255 inclusive. Bytes are sometimes called "octets".

Fig 1.1 shows the ASCII character set. The letters "ASCII" stand for the American Standard Code for Information Interchange. (There are many other national and international codes that are either identical to ASCII, or are very close and differ only in the representation of a few graphic symbols. There are also others, such as ISO 8859-1 that are more extensive, and will probably replace ASCII. However, at the time of writing, ASCII is the most widely used character set of the many we might have chosen.) We can see from the table that there are 128 characters arranged in eight columns of 16. The columns are numbered 0 to 7 from left to right, and the rows 0 to 15 from top to bottom. To find the binary representation of a particular character, we multiply the column number by 16 and add the row number. Thus, for example, the letter "K" is in the 11th row of the 4th column. $4 \times 16 + 11 = 75$ (decimal) = 1001011 (binary). It is simpler to use hexadecimal numbering. Then "K" is in the Bth row of the 4th column, and we may immediately write the hexadecimal number as #4B. (#nn is the notation used in this book to denote hexadecimal numbers, base sixteen)

		0	1	2	3	4	5	6	7
0	0	NUL	DLE		0	@	P	`	p
1	1	SOH	DC1	!	1	A	Q	a	q
2	2	STX	DC2	"	2	B	R	b	r
3	3	ETX	DC3	#	3	C	S	c	s
4	4	EOT	DC4	$	4	D	T	d	t
5	5	ENQ	NAK	%	5	E	U	e	u
6	6	ACK	SYN	&	6	F	V	f	v
7	7	BEL	ETB	'	7	G	W	g	w
8	8	BS	CAN	(	8	H	X	h	x
9	9	HT	EM	)	9	I	Y	i	y
10	A	LF	SUB	*	:	J	Z	j	z
11	B	VT	ESC	+	;	K	[	k	{
12	C	FF	FS	,	<	L	\	l	|
13	D	CR	GS	-	=	M	]	m	}
14	E	SO	RS	.	>	N	^	n	~
15	F	SI	US	/	?	O	_	o	DEL

Fig 1.1.   The ASCII Character Set

The most important thing that we need to observe is the technique of representing a set of characters by a corresponding set of small binary patterns that fit into bytes. Thus, depending upon the circumstances, a given bit pattern in a byte may be interpreted either as a small integer, or as a particular graphic character. The text of this book has all at various times been represented as ASCII characters within the memory of several different computers (as well as various other representations).

There are 94 printable characters, plus the space character, in columns 2 to 7. These are the ones with the single character entry in the table. There are another 33 locations that do not represent printable characters, but have mysterious two- or three-character "names". These are the so-called *control characters*. The control characters are codes that are reserved for special functions. Thus, #0D represents the *Carriage Return*—CR function, #0A represents the *Line Feed*—LF function, and so on. These types of functions are directly related to the basic operations that are performed on simple character display devices.

For example, this text was originally typed at a simple video display terminal. On this terminal, the CR function returns the cursor to the left hand side of the screen, and the LF function moves the cursor down one line. These types of terminal and the simple means of communication that they employ are directly descended from the telex and telegraph machines that were developed over many years for sending character information over great distances. Computer communications has adopted and adapted this technology for its own uses.

In these early applications simple character machines communicated directly with each other over long distances. A typical teleprinter for example, consisted of a keyboard, a printing mechanism for printing on rolls of paper, and frequently a paper tape reader and punch for reading or punching holes in paper tape. In the early days of computing, programs were often prepared on rolls of paper tape on such machines, and then fed into the computer as ASCII encoded characters read directly off the paper tapes. Knowing this historical background makes it easier to appreciate some of the otherwise surprising aspects of character codes such as ASCII.

Codes that betray this history are such things as "ENQ"—enquire of the machine its *answerback code*. This code was a unique code on such machines as the Teletype† which was set as radial legs on a bakelite wheel, and was sent in response to the ENQ as a way of automatic self-identification. DC1, DC2, DC3, DC4 were device control codes that were sent to a device with a paper tape reader or punch, and caused this device to switch on or off.

Of course, there are many machines without paper tape equipment and thus the meanings of some of the control codes change with time. For example, DC1 and DC3 can be used to control other ancillary devices, such as cassette tapes. Alternatively, they now almost universally have the meaning not of controlling the function of an ancillary device, but of controlling the flow of the actual data. Thus, it is now the common convention that DC3 means *"Stop the flow of data to me for a while"*, and DC1 means *"OK you can start sending again now"*. Common alternative names for these control characters are "X-off" and "X-on" respectively.

The punched paper tape background neatly explains the strange character "DEL" at position #7F. The paper tapes were often prepared manually, ready for being sent automatically some time later. Human typing is notoriously error prone, and it essential that some form of

---

† Teletype is a trademark of the Teletype corporation

error correction be available. The DEL character is just that. When preparing paper tape, the operator could correct mistakes by winding back the paper tape and pressing the DEL key. This punches out all the holes, and effectively erases or DELetes the character. Thus it is important to have DEL in this place. Similarly, pieces of paper tape need a piece of blank tape at the front and the end, and it is frequently useful to have blank sections in the middle. Such blank tape shows up a binary zeros, or #00—NUL. When dealing with character data it is normal to remove or ignore NUL characters. Another example of the evolution of meaning is that the DEL character now often means not that a character has been deleted, but that the last character typed should be deleted (i.e. that there has just been a typing error).

There is another vitally important feature of the ASCII character set, and that is that it uses only half the available values #00 to #7F. Characters are usually represented in an 8-bit byte, giving 256 possible values. The other 128 values from #80 to #FF are not allocated. Fundamentally ASCII is a seven bit code. The eighth bit, #80 is used as a *parity bit*. The function of this bit is for error checking, and we shall examine parity in some considerable detail in the next chapter. However, we cannot avoid mentioning it briefly now. The idea of parity is to make the number of bits in an eight-bit byte even. Thus, our character "K" has the 7-bit binary pattern 1001011. This has 4 one-bits, and thus the number is already even, so the parity bit is 0, and the full eight bit pattern is 01001011. On the other hand, "L" has the pattern 1001100. This has three one bits, and so the parity bit must be 1 to make even parity: 11001100.

What is the use of this? Well, the assumption is that if transmission errors occur, they will affect individual isolated bits. If an eight-bit byte is received, and an error has corrupted one bit of the data, then the parity will be wrong, and the character will be rejected as in error. These days, parity is seen as a weak error detection mechanism. This is mainly because errors tend to occur in groups or bursts, and parity is only about 50% successful in detecting such errors. We merely note now that ASCII characters are still normally transmitted with even parity, and leave further discussion of error checking until the next chapter. Note that we have said that ASCII characters are *transmitted* with parity. Normally the seven bit ASCII is stored within computers with the parity bit set to zero. The parity is generated as the character is transmitted, and checked as the character is received.

We are now in a position to see how a string of text might be stored within a machine. For example the eight characters "ABC:123." would be stored in eight bytes with a hexadecimal representation of #4142433A3132332E.

In this introduction we have only looked at one way in which character data is stored inside a computer. In practice, there are several other ways of representing characters. We shall return to look at them in Chapter 8. In the meantime we should note that because there are other much more complex ways of representing much more complex abstract types than character data, then we must be prepared to handle arbitrary bit patterns. While this may seem a little obvious, several of the early communications systems were only able to handle printable characters (columns 2 to 7 in the ASCII table). This led to all sorts of trouble as new applications made increasing demands on the simple technology.

1.2 Principles of Transmission

Information is transmitted through a medium by varying some physical property of the medium in one place, and measuring the resulting changes in physical property in another place. For example, the voltage across one end of a pair of wires can be varied, and the resulting voltage or current measured across the other end. If the medium is a radio channel, then an alternating current can be caused to flow in the transmitting antenna, and the resulting electromagnetic wave is detected by using a receiving antenna and attendant receiver. The radio signal can be just switched on and off, and the transmission could then be much like a Morse-code transmission. Alternatively, the amplitude of the signal could be varied (amplitude modulation as commonly employed in broadcast medium-wave radio), or its frequency (frequency modulation as used on VHF/FM broadcast radio), or the phase of the transmitted signal can be varied (as in some of the more sophisticated data transmission modems). Again, light may be transmitted down a filament of glass by repeated internal reflections. Light is just a rather high-frequency electromagnetic wave, like radio waves, and thus all the same modulation techniques can in principle be applied. However, the only practical form at present is the switching on and off of the beam of light. There are many other forms of transmission and modulation and we only offer these as illustrative examples.

Assume, then, that we are using a pair of wires to transmit the data. Let us assume that we are using some physical property that is a single valued function of time, $s(t)$. Let us suppose we wish to transmit the single character "\". In ASCII this is represented by the hexadecimal value #5C. This is the bit pattern 01011100. If we choose to represent a binary "1" by, say, $-5V$ (volts), and a binary "0" by $+5V$, then the graph of the voltage with time might look something like Fig 1.2. (The reader is cautioned that the question of data representation is bedevilled by varying conventions concerning whether a positive or a negative voltage represents a "1"-bit.) If we choose to transmit, say, 1000

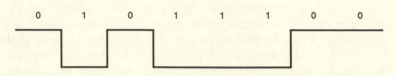

Fig 1.2.   Signal Trace For The Character "\"

characters per second, then each bit would take $1/8^{th} mS$, or $125 \mu S$.

Depending on the medium used, there is a whole wealth of detailed theoretical and practical knowledge that explains and predicts the precise way in which an input signal is transmitted along the medium to the far end. However, there is a large range of situations for which the following analysis applies (and, correspondingly, a small range of situations for which it does not).

At first sight, we might appear to need to study the various ways in which each individual waveform is transmitted. For example, a regular square wave will be transmitted and distorted in a different way from a regular saw tooth wave, which is in turn different to the distortion suffered by a regular sinusoidal wave. Indeed, each wave is distorted differently. We appear to be faced with an infinite problem—a separate study for each and every possible waveform.

1.3   Fourier Analysis

Fortunately, there is a simplification that can be made for linear channels. A linear channel is one for which the output signal is proportional to the input signal, or *linear* in the input signal. Thus, although a linear channel may distort an input signal, a saw tooth for instance, if it is fed with a signal twice as large, then the resulting signal will be exactly the same distorted shape, but twice as large. This is closely true for methods that are used for the transmission of analogue signals. Of course, this is no accident. The linear property is so desirable that it is a necessary part of analogue channels.

When a channel is linear, it is possible to analyse the signal propagation in terms of a *Fourier series*. Under certain constraints Fourier showed that any signal can be represented as the sum of an infinite series of sine waves. There are many standard texts that cover this way of representing signals. When a signal is represented as a Fourier series, there is a series of signals starting from low frequencies and increasing in frequency. In general, the slowly varying parts of a signal are represented by the low frequencies, and the quickly varying parts of a signal are represented by the high frequencies. Beyond a certain point the *amplitude* or size of the higher and higher frequency components starts to decrease. This is when the representation of the

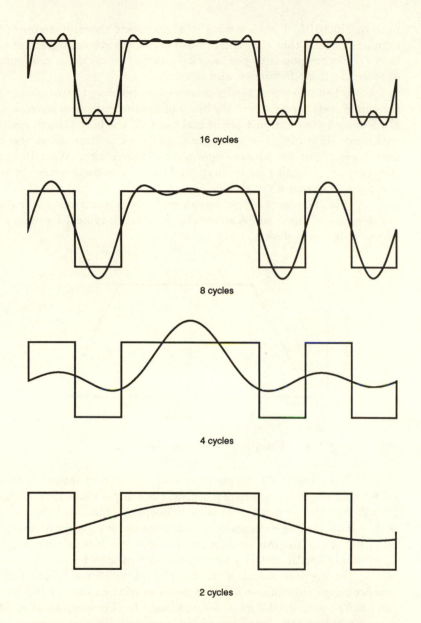

16 cycles

8 cycles

4 cycles

2 cycles

Fig 1.3.   Fourier Approximation to a Bit Pattern

signal is essentially complete. The series is said to be *converging*.

For example, in Fig 1.3 we see the effect of including more and more frequencies in approximating more and more closely to a simple bit pattern 01000101. The increasing frequencies are shown in terms of the number of cycles that the signal makes across the whole pattern of bits. One cycle corresponds to the base frequency, two cycles to a frequency of twice the basic frequency, and so on.

When we stop at the frequency corresponding to two cycles then the sum merely shows where the block of three consecutive zeros occurs. For four cycles we can just about make out all the bits, though perhaps with some difficulty. For eight cycles the Fourier sum shows the bits quite clearly, but the square edges are not very sharp. With 16 cycles the edges are becoming fairly sharp, and this sharpness increases as more and more frequencies are added.

With Fourier analysis, we can analyse our communications channel in terms of these single sinusoidal signals. A typical frequency response diagram is shown in Fig 1.4.

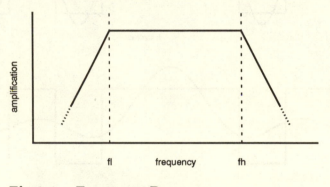

Fig 1.4.   Frequency Response

Fig 1.4 shows a flat response over a large mid range which tails off for high and low frequencies beyond the central band. Such a graph is exhibited by audio channels such as telephone lines and "Hi-Fi" amplifiers. On telephone channels the flat response is roughly between 300 and 3100 Hz. This provides the familiar channel with some detectable distortion but with perfectly acceptable performance for human conversation. On the other hand, a "Hi-Fi" audio amplifier will have a much broader range covering as much as possible of the range of the human ear—20Hz up to 20,000Hz is not unusual. In this way, an attempt is made to reduce the distortion of the reproduced signal to below that detectable by most listeners.

Square waves, such as our bit patterns, always have an infinite if converging series. Thus, some of the frequencies in the signal will be higher than fh for any real channel. In Fig 1.3 we showed the effect of truncating the series at certain values. As the number of terms included becomes greater, the goodness of the fit improves. In practice, of course, the series will not be truncated, but the higher terms lying above fh will be progressively attenuated.

Conversely, the attenuation of low frequencies, below fl, will cause a reduction in the faithfulness in which slowly varying features are represented by the Fourier series. Just as wavelengths of the same order (and shorter) as a bit duration are required to represent single bits, so also wavelengths as long as (or longer than) a bit duration are required to represent consecutive runs of bits of the same value.

1.4 Noise

Apparently we could compensate for a cutoff frequency fh that is too low by inserting an electronic amplifier that amplified differentially above fh in an attempt to compensate for the fall off in the basic channel. However there are fundamental limits to the extent in which we can compensate by using this trick. The limit arises because whenever a signal is present, there is always a certain amount of noise.

Noise comes in many forms. Of course, there is the obvious interference caused by switches, motor cars, fluorescent lights and so on. This tends to be very erratic and bursty in nature. Such interference can often be prevented by shielding. Much more fundamental is the noise in the channel caused by the motion of the individual electrons. This is caused by the fundamental physics of the electronic circuits. All electronic circuits generate some of this noise, and any amplifier will amplify this noise along with the signal that is of interest.

Thus when a signal is injected into one end of a channel, a mixture of signal and noise comes out of the other end. Should the signal coming out of the channel be too low, then we can amplify it, but we will also amplify the noise. If the signal is weaker than the noise, then it will be lost in the noise as surely as the noise of a cough in the cheers of a football crowd. This ever-present background noise is of fundamental importance.

1.5 Limits of Data Transmission

There are two fundamental laws that describe the amount of data that can be transmitted on a communications line, and how this is limited both by frequency response and noise. Nyquist derived the result that limits the signalling rate of a perfectly noiseless channel, and Shannon extended this result to account for the effect of noise.

Nyquist looked at a perfectly noiseless channel, but one that was limited in bandwidth by a filter that let through frequencies up to a sharp cutoff ($F\ Hz$). If the received signal is then carefully examined, it is only necessary to sample the signal $2F$ times per second. More frequent sampling would not add any more information. Of course, remember we are talking of perfect theoretical samples—the experimental error of an actual real measurement is ignored. The more frequent samples are pointless because they could only add information about signals with a frequency higher than F, and these, by definition, cannot get through the channel because of the perfectly sharp cutoff filter.

If the signal can have a number B different levels, then Nyquist's theorem states that the maximum data rate r is given by

$$r = 2F \log_2 B \quad \text{bits per second}$$

For example, if we have a perfect channel that can transmit signals of 0, 1, 2, 3 volts, and is limited to 1 kHz, then the maximum data rate is $2 \times 1000 \times \log_2 4 = 4,000$ bits per second. Note here most especially that there is a basic signalling rate which is $2F$. This is called the *baud rate*. However, each signal can be at one of four levels, giving the possibility of sending $log_2 4 = 2$ bits of information. This gives the *bit rate*, and *is not in general the same as the baud rate* despite the almost general sloppy confusion of the two even by many people and companies working in the communications field, who should know better.

Shannon extended Nyquist's work to allow for the presence of noise. For a perfectly noiseless channel, we have seen that the frequency cutoff limits the baud rate. However, the bit rate can be increased without limit by increasing the number of levels sent, B. We can see subjectively that when the levels become numerous enough (i.e. "close" enough) that the noise in the channel starts to interfere with them, then the noise will limit the value of B, and thus the achievable bit rate. The important measure here is the signal-to-noise ratio. This is the ratio of the signal power (not amplitude) to the noise power. If S is the signal power, and N the noise power, then the signal to noise ratio is S/N. Rather than a straight ratio, this is usually expressed in terms of the logarithmic measure, Bels, where

$$R = \log_{10} \left(\frac{S}{N} \right) \quad \text{Bels}$$

Thus $R = 1$ Bel means that $S = 10 \times N$, and $R = 2$ Bels means $S = 100 \times N$. Since this is obviously a somewhat powerful ratio, a more common measure is deciBels (dB). $R = 10dB$ means $S = 10 \times N$, and $R = 3dB$ means that $R \simeq 2 \times N$.

Shannon's major result is that for noisy channels with bandwidth f and signal-to-noise ratio S/N, the maximum data rate, R, is given by:

$$r = f \log_2 \left(1 + \frac{S}{N} \right) \quad \text{bits per second}$$

This expresses a limit to the number of levels that can be used to squeeze higher bit rates out of the basic baud rate. This is a fundamental limit and cannot be circumvented by any devious means of averaging over time or increasing the number of levels.

For a typical telephone voice channel with 3000 Hz bandwidth and S/N of $30dB$, this gives a maximum data rate of $30,000$ bits per second. Looking back at Nyquist's result, we see we can sample the channel at a maximum baud rate of 6000 samples per second. To attain the maximum bit rate from this then $log_2 B = 5$, and thus we need to use $2^5 = 32$ levels. The fundamental noise in the channel means that extra levels will not help us since we will not be able to use them because of the uncertainty in measuring the levels that is caused by the noise. It is well known that noise can be averaged out over longer periods, and thus we might try to increase the number of levels by making them last longer and thus average the noise over a longer period. However, we have then reduced the baud rate itself, and thus not increased the resulting bit rate.

It should be remembered that the Shannon limit is a maximum. Actual practice is very short of this. Simple techniques on a voice grade line, e.g. frequency shift keying that we shall look at presently, yield only a few hundred bits per second. There are standardised techniques that routinely yield 1200 to 2400 bits per second, but this is significantly more expensive to implement, and only becoming available at a modest price in the late 1980s. Some equipment will work at up to 9600 bits per second, but it is very sophisticated and correspondingly expensive.

Having looked at the major elements of the theory, let us see how it is applied to real situations. So far in this chapter, we have seen how it is useful to analyse a signal in terms of its Fourier transform, or constituent frequencies. We have looked at the major results of Nyquist and Shannon, seen how the bandwidth of a channel limits its baud rate, and how the signal-to-noise ratio limits the corresponding bit rate. We shall now briefly look at some practical ways of using a real telephone channel. Again, this section is a rapid visit to some of the "tourist attractions" of the subject rather than an exhaustive study.

1.6   Real Data Transmission

The most obvious way of sending our eight-bit byte is to take the eight bits, one by one, and send, say, -5 volts for a binary one and $+5$ volts for a binary zero. (It may seem slightly more natural to use an encoding something like $+5$ volts for a binary one, and 0 volts for a binary zero. However, it is the convention that the voltages are "inverted".) If we have a continuous wire, then this method can work quite well over limited distances. However, as the distance increases, the signal will be reduced by losses in the wire, and eventually an amplifier will have to be introduced to boost the signal. In this way, the signal may be transmitted considerable distances. However, there are some snags with this method. Firstly, a long run of consecutive zeros or ones will cause low frequency components to be produced. These will pass through a continuous wire (that has no low frequency cutoff—it will transmit a continuous current) but will not pass through a telephone channel because of the cutoff below 300 *Hz*.

There are several techniques for avoiding this problem. One that is commonly used is to encode the ones and zeros not as constant voltages, but as constant tones or frequencies. Thus, for example, a binary one could be transmitted by sending a tone of 1200 *Hz* and a zero by sending 1600 *Hz*. The receiver consists of two filters. Each such filter accepts a narrow band of frequencies around 1200 and 1600 respectively. Behind each filter is a detector circuit that looks for the tone coming in through its filter, and outputs a voltage when it detects the signal is present.

(This method of transmitting a signal by using it to change some property of another signal is called *modulation*. The modulated signal is the *carrier signal*. Switching between two frequencies or tones in the way we have described is called *frequency shift keying*. There are many other methods of modulation, and we shall meet some of them later in this book. Sending a signal directly without using it to modulate another signal is termed *base-band transmission*.)

We have just described a very simple form of *modem*, that is, a *MOD*ulator *DEM*odulator. This method of encoding binary 0 and 1 with two frequencies is called frequency shift keying. This method of transmitting data is used with a system shown schematically in Fig 1.5.

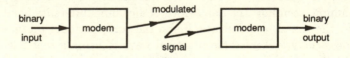

Fig 1.5. Modems

As we mentioned above, the input signal typically swings between +5 and -5 volts. This is fed into a modem that modulates the signal, or changes it into a form that is suitable to be transmitted on the medium that is being used. The signal is received at the far end, demodulated, or converted back into the binary form, and given to the user.

With this method we have solved several of the problems of sending binary signals down a communications line. However, one vitally important problem remains. The output signal will closely mimic the input signal. However, how is the receiver to turn this signal into a correct sequence of bits? Obviously it must look at, or *sample* the signal and turn $+5V$ into zero bits, and $-5V$ into one bits, but the question is, when should it decide that the last bit has just finished, and the next bit has started? The receiver must sample the signal at the right times otherwise the received information will be misinterpreted. For example, if the receiver sampled at twice the rate at which the transmitter sent, then every bit would effectively be duplicated. If it sampled at half the rate, then alternate bits would be missed. Two extra pieces of information are needed—when to start sampling, and how often to sample, i.e. the phase and frequency with which the sampling is to be performed. In computing, this regular sort of indication of the moment to sample the value of a signal is usually referred to as a *clock signal*.

1.7   Asynchronous Communication

In asynchronous communication the clock signal is obtained as follows. The eight bits of the byte are framed by two extra bits, a start bit and a stop bit. The start bit is a zero and the stop bit is a one. The group of ten bits is then sent as shown in Fig 1.6. Note that Fig 1.6 shows the ones encoded as a *mark* or -5 volts, and zeros as a *space* or $+5$ volts. The normal idle state of the line is mark, -5 volts. Thus, the signal is "upside down" and back to front, since the rightmost bit is transmitted first, and thus appears on the time graph at earlier times, on the left of the picture.

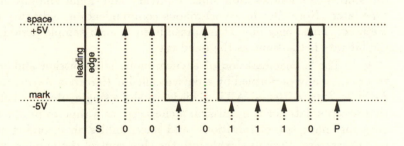

Fig 1.6.   Asynchronous Transmission

The transmission of bits rightmost or least significant first is almost universal outside the IBM world. Naturally, (:-) † IBM transmits the bits leftmost first, as well as using different codes to represent the

---

† This symbol, (:-), indicates that the writer has his tongue in cheek, and is explained in Chapter 10 in network mail

same letters, but that is a tale for Chapter 8 when we discuss presentation issues.

In Asynchronous communication it is important that the start bit is a transition from the normal idling state (*mark*). In this way the leading edge of the start bit can be seen, and this sharp edge is available to synchronise the receiver's clock for the rest of the character time. In between characters, the receiver constantly looks for this edge.

The bit timing or rate is a matter of agreement between the sender and the receiver. There are many common rates starting from the lowly 110 or even 50 bits per second, and on up through 150, 300, 600, to 9,600, 19,200 and beyond. There are also some less common intermediate bit rates at 7200, etc. The receiver maintains an internal clock that runs at sixteen or more times this agreed bit rate. Thus for 9,600 bps the clock may run at 153,600 ticks per second. When the receiver sees the leading edge of the start bit, it starts a counter running at this tick rate. It waits for 8 ticks (half an expected bit time) and looks at the signal again. If all is well then it should be looking at the middle of the start bit. If the input is still at the space level, then the receiver starts to assemble an eight bit byte. It does this by sampling the input signal at the expected mid-point of each succeeding bit, that is at every 16th tick of its clock. Finally, it looks for the stop bit. This should be a *mark* level. If not, then a *framing error* has occurred. It is important that the stop bit is of opposite polarity to the start bit, the idle line state. This ensures that the leading edge of the start bit can be seen properly whether the following start bit comes immediately after the stop bit or follows after some arbitrary additional amount of idle time later. Note that in asynchronous communication, only two levels are used. Thus, only one bit is transmitted in each sample period, and the bit rate is the same as the baud rate.

The implementation of asynchronous transmission and reception is normally performed by a device called a *Universal Asynchronous Receiver Transmitter*—UART . This is usually a single integrated circuit that accepts data for transmission a character at a time to produce the outgoing mark/space transitions, and unscrambles an incoming signal into characters. Various signals into the chip control the number of bits per character, the bit rate, number of stop bits, etc. We shall return to the UART later in this chapter.

Let us look at what this scheme gives us. Firstly, each start bit causes a re-synchronisation of the receiver's clock and so each byte can follow the last end-to-end, or can be isolated by an arbitrary amount of idle time. Thus this scheme is eminently suitable for transmitting single characters as they are typed. Asynchronous communication is widely used for connecting simple character terminals to computers. The bursts of output to the screen, perhaps 2000 characters in a group, can be handled as well as the single hesitant keystrokes from the keyboard.

The other important advantage is that the receiver's clock is repeatedly re-synchronised by the recurring start bits in the data. Thus the clock has to stay synchronised to, say, $1/3$ of a bit in 10 bits, some 3%. Such a tolerance is quite easy to achieve in contrast to keeping bit synchronisation over perhaps 10,000 bits by dead reckoning.

This sort of communication is called *Asynchronous Communication* because the two ends do not need to synchronise their clocks and keep them synchronised over long periods. The clocks are repeatedly readjusted every character. As mentioned above, this method is commonly used for simple terminal connection (often referred to as *dumb terminal* or *glass teletype*). Such communication is widely available, and it is often the only form of communication available in practice across a variety of small machines. Thus, this form of communication is often used to communicate between micro-computers of dissimilar types in the absence of any other common form of communication. When modems are used the speed is limited by the operating speed of the modems— 300, 1200, or 2400 bps. However on local connections where the so-called *null modems* (that we shall study later in this chapter) are used, speeds of 9,600bps, or 1000 characters per second are routine, and 38,400 bps is common.

There are many variations on the asynchronous theme. Besides various speeds, various numbers of bits per character can be sent, and the number of stop bits may be 2 or even 1.5! One of the bits may be a parity rather than a data bit, and the parity may be even, odd or always one or zero.

Many computers automatically recognise the speed of a newly connected terminal. The terminal is connected to the computer by some means, and then the terminal user types some character repeatedly, carriage return for instance. The host machine then sets its receiver to a certain speed and listens to the incoming signal. On looking at the received bit pattern, it attempts to work out what the speed actually should be, and switches the receiver to that speed.

> **Exercise 1.1**   Design an algorithm to perform automatic speed recognition on incoming carriage return characters.

1.8   Synchronous Communication

In synchronous communication a long block of data rather than just a single character is transmitted. The byte boundaries are no longer so significant, and it is the record boundaries, the beginning and end of the block of data, that become more important. In this form of communication, the bit rate of the incoming signal is not derived by a combination of start bits and dead reckoning, but the rate is derived from the incoming signal itself. Thus the signal contains not only the data bits themselves, but also the clock rate.

There are many ways in which this can be done, but we shall only look at some of the more common ways. One common method is called *phase encoding*. In phase encoding, a tone is transmitted at some fixed frequency. The changes, from a one to a zero, or vice versa, are encoded by a jump in the phase of the tone.

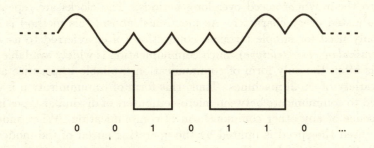

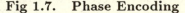

Fig 1.7.   Phase Encoding

In Fig 1.7 we see three and a half cycles of the tone. After one cycle of the tone, at 2π (radians) the signal suddenly departs from the basic sine curve, and the half-cycle is inverted. This is the equivalent of a phase shift of the signal of π (that is a shift to the right or left by an angle of π, or 180 degrees. In the scheme, this corresponds to a change either from a 0 to a 1, or from a 1 to a 0. In the diagram we show the transmission of the six bits 0010110 during the three cycles of the basic signal. The phase shifts, and thus the bit changes, occur at 2π, 3π, 4π, and 6π. Note the very important property of the technique—the basic clock rate is twice the frequency of the basic tone, and thus it can be obtained directly from the signal itself along with the data bits. Thus the receiver can stay in continuous synchronisation with the transmitter.

We note that this method of modulation uses the maximum baud rate of two samples per cycle of the base frequency (assuming the frequency is the maximum possible for the channel). There are several ways of increasing the number of levels that may be sent in this way. The phase of the wave may be shifted by other subdivisions of the 360 degrees—four values spaced at 90 degrees, or eight at 45 degrees are not unusual. In addition, the amplitude may also be changed. In this way, the bit rate may be increased until the noise in the circuit, or the expense and complexity of the circuitry limit the achievable data rate.

In practice it is common to use not just two phase values, but perhaps four or even eight. If we use eight then on each half cycle we can shift the phase by any of eight different amounts. This can be detected at the receiver, and the eight values can be used to transmit three bits. Thus, *V.22-bis* modems work with a modulation rate of 600 baud, but a bit rate of 2400 bits per second.

Note that not only must the receiver keep up with the incoming rate of bits, as in asynchronous communication, but the transmitter must also keep up a stream of bits at the bit rate. This is in contrast with asynchronous communication where the transmitter need only supply bits a byte at a time. We shall return to this problem later when we discuss the framing of blocks of data.

1.9   Signal Encoding

We have now encountered two kinds of signal encoding, asynchronous encoding and phase encoding. In asynchronous transmission, we have seen how a signal varies between two states, the mark and space states, and the way in which this signal represents or encodes the data bits, and a certain amount of the timing information. Thus, the receiver needs to know the *approximate* bit rate, and then from the way in which the signal varies the precise bit rate and the character or byte boundaries can be deduced. The start and stop bits are carefully arranged to ensure that the bit rate can be derived from the signal.

In the case of phase encoding, the signal carries the bit rate in terms of the length of a half-cycle of the signal, and the data in terms of the shifts in the phase of the signal. In this case the receiver does not need to know the incoming bit rate, even approximately, since it can deduce it from the incoming signal. On the other hand, the byte boundaries must be determined by some other means as only a bit stream is defined. Indeed, the incoming signal only defines when the data bits *change*, and thus the polarity of the first bit must also be defined by some external means. Both the bit polarity and the record boundaries are most commonly represented by the *bit-stuffing* method described later. This is another structure that is overlaid on top of the bit stream encoded by some such means as the phase encoding method described above.

There are many other ways in which data bits are encoded in signals, and we only have space to examine some of the more common ones. In general, binary data is a series of bits. The bits will be transmitted one by one, and in general we will take a certain time, say b, to receive (or transmit) each bit. This binary data can in general be represented by two simultaneous signals, one—the *clock*—to indicate the arrival (or departure) of each bit, and the other to represent the binary value of the bits themselves. Thus, for example, the bits 00101110 can be represented by the simultaneous clock and data signals in Fig 1.8.

(From now on we show logic 1 as the higher value in the diagram as opposed to the inverted convention that applies particularly to asynchronous transmission.)

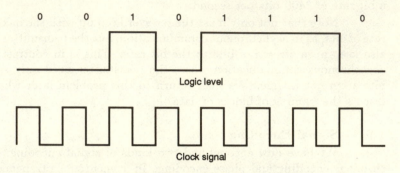

Fig 1.8.   Bit Values and Clock Signal

It may seem surprising that there are many ways in which such simple information is encoded into signals. One class of codes is the *Non-Return to Zero*—NRZ pulse codes. This slightly odd name indicates that the signal stays constant—does not return to zero—during the bit period. There are three NRZ codes, *NRZ-Level*—NRZ-L, *NRZ-Mark*—NRZ-M, and *NRZ-Space*—NRZ-S. These are shown in Fig 1.9. With NRZ-L two signal levels represent the bits directly—perhaps the most obvious encoding method. With NRZ-M and NRZ-S it is a *change* in signal level that corresponds to one bit value, and an *absence* of a change that corresponds to the other bit value. NRZ-M and NRZ-S are complements of each other. Note that with NRZ-L the signal level corresponds directly with the binary value, whereas both NRZ-M and NRZ-S suffer the polarity indeterminancy that was mentioned earlier concerning phase encoding.

It is quite beyond the present text to discuss all the pros and cons of the various NRZ codes. However, we can remark that none of them provides a clock determination as part of the code. Thus, for NRZ-L, consecutive bits of the same value are indistinguishable from one bit (of the same value) transmitted for the whole period. Similarly, for the two other NRZ codes, consecutive alternating bits are indistinguishable from one bit covering the same time. So, for NRZ coding to be useful, the clock signal must be supplied or derived by some other means outside this particular set of encodings. (See the discussion on clock recovery below.)

Of the three codes, NRZ-L is the most common, but NRZ-M is met frequently, and is usually known as NRZI for *Non-Return to Zero, Invert on ones*. The choice of whether bit values should be represented

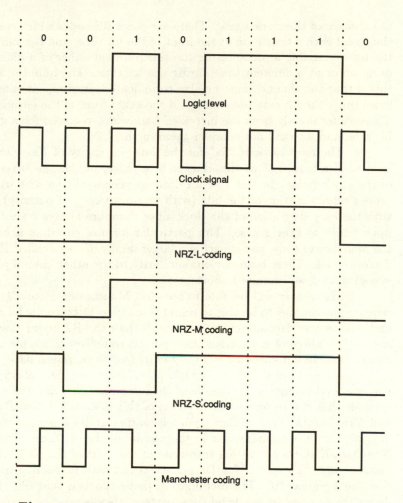

Fig 1.9. Various Data Encoding Methods

by levels or by transitions is also influenced by the fact that it is more reliable to detect transitions in the presence of noise than to detect a level.

Another class of codes is the *Return to Zero*—RZ class of codes. These codes are essentially a combination of the level encoding of NRZ-L with the clock signal. However, some of these still manage to provide a signal from which a clock cannot reliably be derived. As an example, unipolar RZ is the logical *and* of NRZ-L and the clock signal. This produces a cycle of the clock signal for a binary one, and the absence of any pulse for a binary zero. The obvious problem with this is that a long sequence of zeros would cause a loss of clock synchronisation due to the absence of the clock signal. There are other RZ codes which encode the signal with a transition at the front of the bit time, and the value of the bit by sending a pulse during the time interval either of a different duration or at a different time during the bit time. The implication of this is that the channel must be able to indicate transitions at three or more times the bit rate (depending on the exact form of the encoding). These suffer mainly from the increased bandwidth required for a given bit rate, and we shall not consider them further.

The most obvious "fix" for the data sensitivity of *Unipolar-RZ* is to send a zero, not as the *absence* of a pulse, but as the *inversion* of the clock pulse. In this case all data sequences will be sent with a proper representation of the bits (with no uncertainty of polarity) and with the easy derivation of the clock since there are always transitions upon which to synchronise. This particular form of encoding is called the Manchester code, and is part of a larger family of codes called *Phase Encoded*—PE. There is an obvious similarity to the other kind of phase encoding that we examined above.

The reader will be able to see that Manchester encoding only requires the channel to be able to signal transitions at twice the bit rate, and is thus less demanding on bandwidth than the RZ codes that we saw require three or more transitions per bit to deliver a reliable clock signal. Manchester encoding is widely employed to represent data.

As we have shown in Fig 1.9, Manchester encoding always involves a level change in the middle of the interval. There are two useful symbols that can be formed in violation of this rule, called *Non-Data-J* and *Non-Data-K*. Each of these symbols starts out like a regular "0" or "1", but there is no transition in the middle of the bit-time. Thus, a Non-Data-K starts out with a transition at the start of the bit interval, like a regular "1", and a Non-Data-J starts out with no leading transition like a regular "0". The usefulness of these signals is that since they do not correspond to any valid data pattern, they cannot be produced by any data signal. Thus, they can be used to signal special conditions, such as the boundaries of a packet—that is they may be used for framing. We shall encounter this use when we discuss the *token ring* in Chapter 3. However, they must be used in moderation. Extensive use of these symbols can result in the loss of synchronization, since the Manchester code plus these two signals has actually become a *NRZ* code, and thus suffers from the problems of that code family. However, we shall see that the Token ring uses these symbols in pairs only, and only in the starting and ending delimiters. Thus, by this parsimony, the inherent problems of full *NRZ* codes are avoided.

1.10 Clock Recovery

We have seen above that data can be encoded in various ways. One of the critical aspects of an encoding method is that some form of clock recovery must be possible. Some of the encodings achieve this by using rather large amounts of bandwidth. For example, Manchester encoding has a signalling rate—the *baud rate* of twice the bit rate, and some other RZ codes are even more profligate with transmission bandwidth. This is acceptable if bandwidth is not a critical factor, for example on local dedicated links. Asynchronous communication is sometimes criticised because of its use of two bits per character for data framing and clock synchronisation. However, two per character, or 25% is not bad compared with some common methods.

When bandwidth is very much at a premium, various complicated methods have been employed to use NRZ signals to supply both data and clock reliably. The advantage of NRZ codes is that since they only change at the bit boundaries, they only need a baud rate of the same frequency as the bit rate. The trick is to avoid the long sequences of similar data that result in constant NRZ signals and loss of synchronisation. In IBM's *Binary Synchronous Communication*—BSC, long sequences of zeros are avoided by inserting dummy characters to break up such sequences. Such characters are control characters, like SYN, and can thus be extracted from the data stream at the receiver. The more recent method of framing blocks by means of *bit stuffing* that we shall meet later also avoids the transmission of long seqences of ones, and thus leaves the door open for NRZ encoding to be employed. So we see that by inserting either special characters or special bits depending on the data pattern, the most efficient encoding methods may be used.

As a final sample of the rich field of data encoding we shall mention the 4B/5B code that is used in the *Fiber Distributed Data Interface*—FDDI. This is a particular kind of ring network that we shall meet again when we discuss local area networks. At the moment it is of interest as an illustration of a particular encoding method. Briefly, data bits are taken four at a time, and encoded into a five bit group. Thus the design data rate of FDDI of 100 Mbps is achieved with a 125 Mbaud compared with the 200 Mbaud that would be required by Manchester encoding. The savings are substantial, since the technology needed to transmit on fibre at 200 Mbaud is five or ten times the cost of that required for 125 Mbaud.

The coding scheme takes the 32 possible combinations of five signalling elements and allocates 16 of them to represent the 16 possible sets of four bits. Of the others, it allocates eight for special control functions (such as framing packets, indicating idle line states, etc), and the other eight are invalid. The resulting signalling bits are then transmitted using intensity (or amplitude) modulation and NRZ-M encoding, where a one bit is signalled by a change in the light intensity on the fibre, and a zero by a constant light intensity. The codes for the 16 data patterns are chosen such that there are at least two transitions for each five signalling bits (and thus the clocks can stay in synchronisation). In this way the 4B/5B encoding achieves a well clocked signal plus the useful additional special non-data symbols for a modest 25% overhead in bandwidth (the same as asynchronous communication). The cost is of some modest complexity. However, since this method is the subject of standardisation across an expectedly large market, the complexity will be implemented in off-the-shelf logic chips of a low cost.

1.11   Data Coding and Modulation

Before leaving the topic of encoding, we should mention the relationship between data encoding as just described, and modulation. Data coded in the ways just described is transmitted in this form only for limited distances. This might be on the cable between a modem and a terminal for a matter of a few metres or possibly a few hundred metres. Alternatively such types of codes are used between components on a printed circuit board—a matter of up to a few centimetres. At the other extreme, a modem is used to *modulate* some medium, such as a telephone line or a radio wave, and transmit the signal a matter of many kilometres. The so-called *Local Area Networks*—LANs—frequently use the encoded signal directly on the medium without modulation, and such modes of transmission are often referred to as *base-band*. Base band transmission is used only over limited distances, such as the few kilometres maximum of the typical LAN. However, the picture is not always as "simple" as that and sometimes modified LANs can use modulated transmission to convey the signal across the medium.

1.12   Modem Signals

Telecommunications systems are constructed on a modular basis. We have seen briefly how modems change the logic levels into a form suitable for transmission on a voice grade circuit. Now we shall look at the interfaces and devices that make such a system work. For asynchronous communications we have seen that UART is usually employed. This device interfaces on the one side to the modem and on the other side to the parallel bus in the computer. The scheme employed looks like Fig 1.10.

This figure is symmetrical. At either end we have some internal computer bus that works with parallel data and control. Typically this bus has eight-bit parallel data, and several parallel control lines. The control lines carry such signals as "next output byte is ready", "next

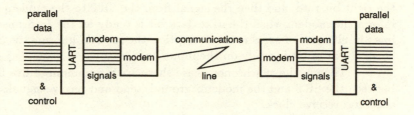

Fig 1.10.   Modems, and Parallel and Serial Data

input byte is ready", "last output byte has gone", "set UART speed", and so forth. The precise nature and meaning of the signals will depend on the type of computer, and the maker of the UART. However, the most important fact is that it is a byte-by-byte interface. The function of the UART is to turn this sequence of bytes into a sequence of bits on the modem interface. The UART is usually implemented as a single integrated circuit or "chip".

In operation, the UART will be initialised from the attached computer bus by means of the appropriate signals. Let us suppose that the UART and the modem have agreed that both are ready to function, and that a single eight-bit byte has been transferred from the attached computer into the UART. The UART transfers the byte into an internal holding register. It then sends (Fig 1.6) a start bit, the data bits, and the stop bit. These are *clocked* out onto the single line at the rate that the UART has been set up with. This transmitted signal requires just two wires, the signal and a reference ground signal. At the receiver, the modem decodes the signal and presents the incoming data across two wires again, the incoming signal and the reference ground. The receiving UART looks at or *samples* the incoming signal and presents the assembled bytes, eight bits at a time, into the attached machine.

With two simultaneous channels, one in and one out, just three wires are needed, receive data, transmit data, and common reference ground.

With synchronous transmission the setup is similar except that a *Synchronous Receiver Transmitter*—SRT replaces the UART. The important difference in this case is that the SRT does not work in isolation in determining the transmission speed, but works closely with the modem. There are two common cases. The modem may take over all responsibility for the transmission rate. In this case, an extra clock signal from the modem to the encoding device pulses as the modem expects the next bit from the SRT. It is the responsibility of the SRT to keep up with this data rate. An alternative is for the SRT to take the responsibility for the bit rate. The modem will be switched to approximately the right bit rate, and then the signal from the SRT to the modem will inform the modem when the next data bit is ready on the transmission line. In all cases of synchronous reception the modem informs the SRT when the next bit is ready on the input line.

Thus in the synchronous case there are a minimum of five lines between the SRT and the modem: ground, send and receive signal, and send and receive clock.

1.13   Other Modem Signals

We have looked at some of the basic signals between the modem and the attached computer device. There are many more that may be employed depending upon the particular circumstances. These signals have names that sometimes give a clue to their meaning, and they are usually referred to by a two- or three-letter abbreviation. The signals between the modem and the computer constitute the interface that is commonly referred to as *V.24* or *RS232C*.

The signal *Data Terminal Ready*—DTR is the signal from the computer (the *Data Terminal* in the jargon) to the modem (the *Data Set*), telling it that the Data Terminal is ready, and that the Data Set should connect itself to the communications line. The corresponding signal from the modem is *Data Set Ready*—DSR.

Before sending data, the terminal is supposed to send the modem the signal *Request to Send*—RTS. The modem's response is *Clear to Send*—CTS. Originally this was used with half duplex or two way alternate communication. Two way alternate modems can send data either way along the joining wires, but only one way at a time. The computers using such modems had to "turn the line round" at the appropriate moments, somewhat like the radio operator's "over" operation. This was achieved by alternate ends raising and lowering the RTS signal. The CTS indicated that the channel was turned round and ready to go. The delay involved in the modems settling down could be a large fraction of a second for long circuits. More recently, some devices that plug in in place of modems (such as simple printers) use the CTS signal as a simple way of controlling the flow of data. (We shall return to this topic in Chapter 4 when we consider flow control.) However, most modern modems are full duplex, and the RTS and CTS signals are no longer used in this way but merely asserted at the start of the data connection.

Other signals from the modem include *Carrier Detect*—CD and *Ring Indicator*—RI. V.24 refers to CD as *"Data channel received line signal detector"*, and to RI as *"Calling Indicator"*. The full V.24 recommendation includes 43 possible signal lines (plus shield ground) and a further 12 lines for transfering dialling digits if automatic dialling is being used. Some of the signals implement second channels parallel to the first (usually used for supplementary control), and so on and so forth. We shall study some of these signals in later parts of this chapter.

The signals between the modem and the computer constitute the interface that is commonly referred to as *V.24* or *RS232C*. This is essentially the set of *interchange circuits* between the *Data Terminal Equipment*—DTE and the *Data Circuit-terminating Equipment*—DCE. This is a considerable introduction of jargon all at once, so let us examine the topic in slightly more leisurely detail.

The interface has been standardised by the CCITT—a body we shall describe in more detail in the chapter covering standards. The number of the standard is V.24. This is almost identical to the US domestic standard RS232C, and the two terms are often used interchangeably. The standard is expressed in terms of Fig 1.11.

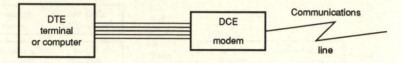

Fig 1.11. Interchange Circuits

Note that this diagram is just a part of one end of Fig 1.10. The DTE is the computer interface, or interactive terminal, and the DCE is the modem that interfaces to the communications line. V.24 specifies 55 interchange circuits, but luckily only a small number of these are in common use. The interchange circuits are usually connected through standard 25-way D-type plugs and sockets. The signals are shown schematically in Fig 1.12, which shows the most common interchange circuits, and the pins associated with them on the 25-way plug and socket.

The signals are represented by small voltages in the range $\pm 5V$ to $\pm 15V$. The receiver has a resistance to passing current. Via Ohm's law of resistance, this controls the amount of electrical current, and thus power that the source of the voltage must supply. This resistance is in the region of $3k$ to $7k$ ohms. The source must generate between $+5V$ and $+15V$ for a logic 0 and $-5V$ to $-15V$ for logic 1. The source typically has a low source resistance of around 300 ohms, and drives about $+8V$ and $-8V$. Receivers that trigger on a $3V$ threshold give a good immunity against noise. On the interchange circuits, logic 0 and 1 are used to send and receive data, and on all the control signals a logic 0 means on or true, and a logic 1 means off or false.

1.14 Automatic Answering

As an example of one of the more complex uses of the interface signals, let us look at the sequence for answering an incoming call on

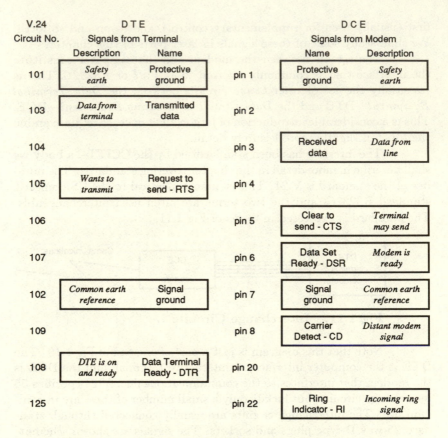

V.24 Circuit No.	DTE — Signals from Terminal			DCE — Signals from Modem	
	Description	Name		Name	Description
101	*Safety earth*	Protective ground	pin 1	Protective ground	*Safety earth*
103	*Data from terminal*	Transmitted data	pin 2		
104			pin 3	Received data	*Data from line*
105	*Wants to transmit*	Request to send - RTS	pin 4		
106			pin 5	Clear to send - CTS	*Terminal may send*
107			pin 6	Data Set Ready - DSR	*Modem is ready*
102	*Common earth reference*	Signal ground	pin 7	Signal ground	*Common earth reference*
109			pin 8	Carrier Detect - CD	*Distant modem signal*
108	*DTE is on and ready*	Data Terminal Ready - DTR	pin 20		
125			pin 22	Ring Indicator - RI	*Incoming ring signal*

Fig 1.12.   The Principal V.24 Signals

a dial-up port. When the call comes into the port, the ring indicator, pin 22, changes in time with the ring signal just like the ring from an ordinary telephone. If the computer wishes to answer, then it turns DTR (pin 20) on. This causes the modem to "pick up the phone", and it then transmits a responding tone back to the other end of the telephone connection. The modem at the other end responds with a suitable tone and the two modems are then in communication. This is indicated by a signal from the modem from pin 8 (*Carrier Detect*—CD). Detection of the data carrier from the far end is the way in which the DTE monitors that the connection is still intact.

If CD disappears for more than a short instant, then the computer will normally drop the call by turning DTR off. Whenever either DTE wishes to transmit data it must turn RTS on and wait for CTS to come on. Most modern modems are full duplex. This means that they can transmit data both ways simultaneously. It is normal practice with such modems to keep RTS on continuously, thus keeping both channels open all the time. The RTS–CTS handshake is primarily of use for two-way-alternate modems that take it in turn to use the channel exclusively.

We have described only ten of the 55 interchange circuits in V.24. The function and presence of the other 45 signals depends on the type of modems that are in use. For example, some modems provide a second channel separated from but parallel to the first. This channel has its own duplicate set of signals: RTS, CTS, CD, etc, each with its own pin assignment.

We have seen earlier that with asynchronous communication, the signal is received with no explicit bit timing, and how with synchronous communication the bit timing may be extracted from the signal even for long sequences of similar bits. This received bit timing is passed across the DCE–DTE interface by other signal lines. Thus, pin 24 allows the DTE to tell the modem the times when a new bit is present on pin 2, and thus the rate at which the modem is to transmit them. An alternative method is to allow the modem to control the precise transmission speed, and in this case pin 15 transmits the clock signal back from the modem to the DTE to tell it when to present another bit on pin 2. With synchronous modems, the incoming clock rate is always signalled from the modem to the DTE on pin 17.

There is a host of other signals, such as signal quality detection, set programmable data rate, etc. These are less often used, and we shall not mention them further.

It is important to note that for a specific type of modem, a specific set of signals is required. Conversely, a specific DTE also expects to communicate using a specific set of pins. For simple everyday use, pins 1 to 8, plus 20 and 22 are used. If the modems are on either end of a fixed line, and there is no dial-up or switched element, then Ring Indication (pin 22) is not needed. If the communication is synchronous, then pin 17, and either pin 15 or 24 will be used.

1.15   Null Modems

We have talked at some length about the use of modems for communicating over long telephone lines, and we have also examined the interface between the modem and the DTE. For communication over a limited distance it is not necessary to use modems at all, and it is possible instead to use the voltages of the V.24 interface directly. The V.24 signals can be used directly over distances of 100 metres or more, and it is common practice to use the signals directly within a building.

Of course, pieces of equipment usually come complete with the D-type connectors that expect to be plugged directly into modems using a simple cable. D-type connectors are the standard 25-pin plugs and sockets that are used in these applications. If we plug two such pieces of equipment together, omitting the pair of modems, then the equipment will not work. However, some simple reconnection will enable the connection to work. For example see Fig 1.13.

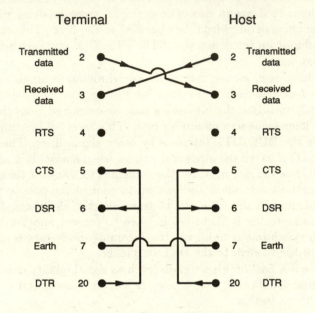

Fig 1.13.   A Simple "Null" Modem

The absolute minimum is that the transmitted and received data should be cross-connected, and the common reference grounds should be connected together. In our diagram, DTR is connected at each end back to DSR and CTS. This means that each end always "thinks" the line is connected whenever it asserts the outgoing pin 20, and this is quite independent of whether the other end is active at all. This diagram shows the minimal *null modem*. Only the send and receive data signals are "real", and all the others are fakes to satisfy the requirements of the two pieces of DTE equipment.

The question of the protective grounds is much more complex. Sometimes they are not connected together as the pieces of equipment are normally earthed separately. Indeed, the differences in ground potential can cause problems when interconnecting over long distances, and the general problems of earth loops are notorious. Another problem is that of safety, and the various attendant regulations. In general, this is a very complex area, and no general guidance can safely be given except to seek professional advice. This is particularly true when considering wires between buildings.

Despite or perhaps because of the small number of interconnecting wires, null modems of this type are widely used. However, if a truer picture of the far end is required, and two more interconnecting wires are available, then DTR at each end can be cross-connected with DSR and CTS at the *other* end. The advantage of this arrangement is that if either end is switched off, or the cable connecting the two DTEs together is broken, then the DTEs at either end are informed by the disappearance of the signals DSR and CTS.

A more deluxe form of null modem is the cross-connection of DTR at each end with just DSR at the other, and in addition the cross-connection of RTS and CTS at opposite ends. This is generally only necessary if the DTE uses the RTS-CTS pair in any non-trivial way. Generally RTS is kept constantly asserted. However, if RTS is pulsed with some expectation that CTS will respond (for example, either DTE thinks it is driving half-duplex, or two-way-alternate modems) then a successful null modem may need this extra interconnection.

The CD line is often used to monitor the presence of a signal on the communications line. If the DTE does monitor this signal, then null modems can provide it by connecting it to the DTR or preferably the RTS signal. These can be looped either from the same end, or from the opposite end. Obviously the signal is more meaningful if taken from the opposite end of the null modem.

Many DTEs are designed to connect only to fixed rather than dial-up modems, and so do not need the RI signal. However, if a dial-in modem is being simulated, then the RI can be supplied from the DTR signal.

It is fairly common to construct synchronous null modems. In these, the send and receive clock lines are cross-connected.

1.16   Local Loopback or Cross-Connection?

We have discussed the various ways in which null modems can be constructed by "faking" input signals from output signals. For some signals, such as the data lines, the input signal at one end of the connection must obviously be taken from the output signal at the other since it is difficult to think of many applications, beyond testing, for null modems that merely loop the transmitted data signal back into the received data signal. However, we have already noted that DSR and CTS can be obtained either by local loopback from DTR, or by cross-connecting with the DTR signal from the far end. Other things being equal, this gives a more realistic simulation of a real pair of modems since if one end is inoperative and does not assert DTR, then the other

learns of this via the failure of DSR and CTS. In general, it is better
to connect input signal lines from one end with output lines from the
other.

However, things are of course not always equal. If the null
modem is operating over a few metres, then the extra wires required for
the extra signals are inexpensive, and easy to supply. If, however, the
null modem is operating over perhaps a hundred metres, and especially
if there are many such modems operating together, then interconnecting
wires may be at a premium. In this case, there may be strong economic
or logistical reasons for wanting the minimum number of interconnecting
end-to-end wires in the null modem.

> **Exercise 1.2** Consider the design of a synchronous null modem.
> Is it possible to loop back the send and receive clock lines at one
> end, or must the clock lines be carried end-to-end? What are the
> implications of trying to simulate modems that control the transmit
> clocking rate in preference to the DTE being in control?

In some environments, very large numbers of terminals and computers are connected together by null modems. Indeed the asynchronous
V.24 interface is the nearest approximation to a common communications interface in the late 1980s. It is often the only common communications interface to be had across a diverse population of micro
computers.

1.17   Plugs and Sockets

Despite the apparently mundane level of the subject, it is worth
mentioning plugs and sockets.

The 25-way D-type connector is quite excessively expensive and
bulky, especially in large numbers. Many sites find it advantageous
to use other forms of plugs and sockets for intermediate wiring. Of
course, terminals and many micros often come complete with the D-
type connector, and it is clearly right to use the sockets as supplied.
However, host interfaces often come with expensive panels containing
blocks of eight or sixteen sockets on a panel. Considerable savings in
money (perhaps more than 20% on a large installation) and space can
be made by purchasing the interfaces with more economical sockets.
The use of telephone-style modular jack plugs is very attractive and
the jacks are much more convenient to install and operate. However,
this advantage needs carefully to be weighed against the fact that many
pieces of equipment come ready supplied with D-type connectors.

In practice, plugs and sockets cause a quite disproportionate
amount of inconvenience. With the normal operation of Murphy's Law,
plugs always need plugging into plugs, and sockets into sockets. This
is made more likely by the convention that both modems and terminals

normally have sockets, and are expected to be joined together by a single cable with a plug on either end. If the cable is too short, and two cables are needed, then the plugs on the ends of the two cables will of course not plug into each other. In the author's laboratory, one of the most useful interconnectors is a length of 25-way ribbon cable that has two D-type plugs and two D-type sockets joined onto it. This allows instant resolution of sexual problems with plugs and sockets.

Murphy's Law is not so easily circumvented, though. With the use of null modems, transmit and receive are always the wrong way round, and another supply of crossovers is also needed that pass through all 25 lines of the D-type connector except that send and receive data are crossed over. Some temporary connections look like Christmas tree decorations.

Careful design, and strict discipline are necessary to prevent this sort of mess from escaping the development laboratory and infesting the production environment.

1.18   Originating Dialled Calls

We have explained how a computer can accept incoming calls by "listening" to the ring signal, answering with DTR, and monitoring the progress of the call with CD.

Calls may be initiated either manually or automatically. Manual calls are placed by people dialling computers. The person listens, and when the modem at the computer end replies with the modem tone (as the host end turns on the DTR) the person switches his end of the line over to the modem, and the two modems can then communicate.

Automatic calls do not require the intervention of a person. V.24 includes the definition of signals that control an *Automatic Calling Unit*—ACU. This allows the DTE to pass dialling digits across the interface and into the calling unit. Note that in addition to the signals between the DTE and the modem, there is also another set of signals— actually twelve more lines—to control the ACU.

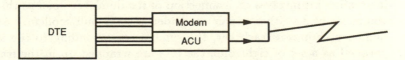

Fig 1.14.   Modem With Automatic Calling Unit

An alternative packaging of the same function is the so-called *intelligent modem*. In this device, the ACU is integrated as part of the modem, and only the ordinary, non-ACU, modem control signals connect the DTE and the modem. The ACU itself is controlled by means of the data on the transmit line, pin 2. Thus, the "intelligence" inside the modem monitors the transmit data.

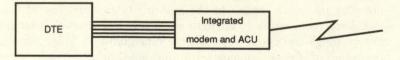

Fig 1.15.   Modem With Integral Calling Unit

Special commands on this data line are picked up by the microprocessor inside the modem and are used to control the dialling of outgoing calls.

At first sight this seems more complicated than employing the parallel set of ACU control lines. However, the elimination of the parallel ACU control signals is precisely the advantage—an "intelligent modem" can be plugged into a standard modem port that implements only ten or less of the full 25 signal lines, and the dialling can be controlled by software alone, merely by sending the appropriate codes down the data line to the modem. While the modem itself is slightly more complicated, it can be used with any standard modem port with no change to the hardware. Clearly though, the modem does need appropriate supporting software.

1.19   Character and Record Structure

So far we have discussed various common forms of modulation, and have looked in particular at both asynchronous and synchronous communication. In asynchronous communication, each character, usually eight bits, has a special framing sequence of start and stop bits. In between each such framed character can come an arbitrary pause or gap when no data is being transmitted. Thus, the most common application of asynchronous communication is the support of bursty communication.

Perhaps the epitome of this is the support of the *dumb terminal*. Typically, this involves the connection of the dumb terminal to the host computer using either a pair of modems, or a null modem. As the human user presses each key, the symbol corresponding to the key is encoded as a set of eight bits, the bits are wrapped up in the framing bits, and the whole frame is sent to the computer. The computer will usually send back or *echo* the same character, an "a" for an "a", for example. However, from time to time the host will respond with several characters. For example, "carriage return" will often cause the echoing of both "carriage return" and "line feed". More extremely, if "carriage return" signals the end of a user command, the computer may output a small response ("OK" for example) or a large one (perhaps the listing of a file) before waiting for the next command. Similarly, interactions with screen-based editors can be very varied and asymmetric in nature. At the one extreme a single typed character may change one character on the screen, at the other it might cause one or several screen scrolls or refreshes. For our present purposes, the importance of such discussions is that traffic is very varied and intermittent, with perhaps seconds or minutes between keystrokes, or it might be very busy, with a screen full of perhaps 2000 characters or more transmitted within as little as a second. Asynchronous communication spans this range of use very well.

On the other hand, synchronous communication is usually arranged to transfer whole blocks or records of information at a time. These blocks or packets of information are usually at least several characters long, and are typically a few hundred characters long. With synchronous communication, it is important that we have a way of finding the beginning and end of each of the packets transmitted.

The earliest schemes for delimiting packets used special control characters. Thus, we might choose STX (see Fig 1.1) and ETX to frame blocks of data. To send a block of data then, we would first transmit an STX, then the block of data characters, and then a final ETX. The receiver could then scan the incoming data stream, and pick out the blocks of data by scanning for the STX and ETX characters.

One characteristic of synchronous communication is that we must continue to transmit data—we cannot just pause between characters or synchronisation will be lost. It is quite possible that we shall not always have data to transmit, and thus an idle character has been defined, SYN (for SYNchronous idle). In between data blocks, we can send SYN characters to keep the modems busily in synchronisation.

Thus to send two packets "ABC" and "XYZ" interspersed with short non-data pauses, we might transmit:

SYN SYN STX A B C ETX SYN SYN STX X Y Z ETX SYN SYN

and so on. This scheme works well while only character data is to be sent. However, computer systems frequently wish to send more general data, such as binary numbers, object code, graphical data and so on. The problem arises when the binary data to be transmitted contains the block framing characters STX and ETX themselves. So, if we need to transmit a packet containing a byte with the value #03, the ETX character, we shall have a problem. Suppose, for example, the record to be sent contains the three bytes P ETX and Q. If the transmitter sends

STX P ETX Q ETX

then what will the receiver see? Clearly, the most obvious reception will be the packet with the single character P.

One might try to fix up the receiver's algorithm by adding a rule something like *"If ETX is not followed by either STX or SYN, then take it as a data byte rather than as a terminating ETX"*. This would clearly work in our example, and give us the correct received block P ETX Q. However, this sort of scheme rapidly runs into other problems. It will not be long before the sequence of data (as opposed to control) P ETX STX Q needs to be transmitted. Obviously this is less likely than just a straightforward ETX in the data, but in purely random data it will occur with a chance of something like 1 in 65,000 times. For a line operating at 9,600 bits per second, this is about once per minute. Clearly we need a less vulnerable mechanism.

The common way of achieving this is by some sort of escape mechanism. We can construct such a mechanism by choosing a further special control character *Data Link Escape*—DLE. The mechanism works as follows. Every character that has a special function must be preceded or flagged by a DLE character, otherwise it is just plain data. Thus, to transmit our problem block P ETX STX Q we merely frame it with DLE STX and DLE ETX and transmit it:

DLE STX P ETX STX Q DLE ETX

The receiver now looks for DLE STX and DLE ETX as the block markers. Since the ETX and STX from the data are not flagged by DLEs then they are passed through as data.

Doubtless the new problem has been spotted by many readers— what about DLEs in the data, and in particular pairs of data bytes such as DLE ETX etc? This is solved by the further rule *"On transmission, double DLEs coming from user data, and on reception, replace double DLEs by a single data DLE"*. Thus, the data packet N DLE ETX M will be transmitted as

DLE STX N DLE DLE ETX M DLE ETX

It is easy to see that the receiver will not now be confused by the pair of DLEs since the double DLE means one data DLE, and thus the following ETX is not special and is just another data byte.

We now have a method that can transmit arbitrary data. In the jargon this is referred to as a *transparent channel* because the channel cannot be "seen" by the data—that is does not change any of the data.

Exercise 1.3   Write a simple program that takes in a series of tokens: the 26 letters of the alphabet, and the symbols STX, ETX and DLE. The program should output a properly framed record. For example, when supplied with N DLE ETX M it should output the sequence shown in the example above.

Exercise 1.4 Write a second program that takes the output of the first program, and reproduces the original data record by recognising and stripping out the delimiters. Make this program emit some suitable message for invalid input (e.g. for DLE followed by anything other than the proper control characters, or data outside a DLE STX—DLE ETX bracket).

Exercise 1.5 Put the above two programs together so that the output of the first is taken as the input for the second, printing both the intermediate and final results. Exercise the combination with various inputs.

Exercise 1.6 The DLE escaping rule states that control characters such as "STX" and "ETX" should be prefixed by "DLE" when they are actually functioning as control characters—delimiting the data blocks—but when they appear as part of the data they have no "DLE" prefix. Would it be possible to invert this rule so that control characters delimiting data stood by themselves, but control characters occurring within the data were flagged with "DLE"? What advantages or disadvantages would there be for such an arrangement?

1.20 Bit Stuffing

There is another very common form of delimiting blocks or frames. We have just looked at character oriented DLE insertion. Now we can compare this with the evocatively named *bit stuffing* method. In this form of communication the data to be transmitted is considered not as a string of characters, but as a string of bits. A special sequence of bits, called a *flag sequence* comes at the start and end of each block, or between consecutive blocks. This special sequence is the eight bits 01111110—zero, six ones and another zero. To avoid the possibility of data containing the same sequence, we "stuff bits" into the transmitted bit stream, and remove the stuffed bits from the received data.

Thus, a block of data is transmitted by sending the flag, and then the data, bit by bit. The transmitted data is examined, and if five consecutive one bits are seen, a zero is inserted or stuffed into the transmitted bit stream (whether or not the next bit would have been a zero anyway). The receiver examines the data following a flag. After five one bits it examines the next bit. If it sees a zero, then the bit must have been stuffed and is discarded. If it is a one, then this must be the terminating flag.

Thus, the data sequence 01111110 is transmitted as

01111110011111101001111110

The data has been wrapped inside flags, and a zero bit has been stuffed after the fifth data one in sequence.

Exercise 1.7   Do exercises 1.3–1.5 again, but this time taking in an arbitrary sequence of bits, producing a framed and stuffed packet on the line, and finally unwrapping and unstuffing the received data packet.

Exercise 1.8   Using the above program, consider the form of the "stuffing rule". Why should bits be stuffed always after five one bits? Why can't you stuff only if the next bit would be a one, and not bother if it is a zero?

Such bit-oriented framing can work with arbitrary bit strings of any number of bits long, unlike the character-oriented framing, sometimes now called "DLE-stuffing", which can only work with whole numbers of characters. However, in practice, almost all communication is with blocks of eight-bit bytes or "octets".

1.21   Errors

Finally in this chapter, we shall briefly mention errors. All earthly endeavours are subject to errors, but in communications we have to be aware of them all the time. All telephone users are aware of the clicks and bangs, dialling tones and crosstalk that can occur from time to time. Most such errors are easily detected as such in human conversation, even crosstalk with another telephone call usually causes amusement rather than real confusion. In human conversations we can recover from such errors by such means as *"Pardon, would you repeat that, please?"*, etc.

The situation is different in computer communication. Computer data usually contains a minimum of redundancy for efficiency's sake. In addition, only binary data can be received—no intermediate non-binary form that is clearly doubtful—you always get zeros and ones even though they may be all wrong. What we need to do is to build in mechanisms that can distinguish reliably between received packets that are uncorrupted, and those that have been changed by errors. Having detected the corrupted packets we have to recover from the errors, and obtain correct data. This error detection and recovery is the subject of the next chapter.

2
Error Detection and Recovery

This chapter examines the ways that are commonly used to detect transmission errors, and to recover from them. Parity and checksums are examined in some detail, as are the basic error recovery mechanisms. Some time is taken in discussing the concept of an acceptable error rate. This concept is rarely recognised, let alone discussed, and yet it underlies most engineering decisions in this area.

The various error recovery mechanisms include the general forms of forward and reverse error control. Reverse error control procedures are the subject of extensive study both because of their wide use and in order to illustrate their surprising complexities. There is a final brief mention of the method of recovering from errors by the remote procedure call style of working.

2.1   Error Detection

In the last chapter we discussed the various ways in which data could be corrupted during transmission. For the purposes of this chapter we shall assume merely that the data, during transmission, will be subject to corruption by some means. We shall examine ways of detecting such errors, and then show how to recover from such errors.

When we were looking at character representation in the last chapter, we encountered the concept of parity. The ASCII character code derives from the earlier telegraph and related codes. In these codes each character was encoded as a separate group of bits and transmitted down the communications channel independently of every other character. If we are to detect errors in this process by some automatic method, then the obvious place to do it is at the character level. Parity provides a mechanism for doing just this.

To recap on the implementation of parity—each group of bits has an extra parity bit added. The value of this bit, zero or one, is chosen so that the number of bits in the group is always even for even parity (or odd for odd parity). With ASCII transmission the convention is that the parity is even. Thus, for example, the seven bit code for "a" is 1100001. There are an odd number of bits in this, so we must add a parity bit of 1 in the most significant bit to make the even parity "a" 11100001. Similarly, "b" has the even parity code 11100010. On the other hand the code for "c" is 01100011—the 7-bit code has an even number of ones, and so the parity bit is a zero. At the receiver, the parity of incoming characters is checked. All characters with correct even parity are accepted as correct, and all those with odd parity are rejected as being in error.

> **Exercise 2.1**   Choose an 8-bit pattern with odd parity. Write down the set of all the original ASCII characters that could have been changed into it if just one bit is in error.

> **Exercise 2.2**   Choose an 8-bit pattern with even parity. What character does it represent if there has been no error? If there have been two separate bits corrupted, what group of characters could the original 8-bit pattern have represented?

2.2   Hamming Distance

We are studying how we can take a block of data bits and produce another, bigger block of bits containing some redundancy that allows the detection or correction of errors. The block of data bits is usually referred to as a *data word* and the bigger block containing the redundancy is the *code word*. The use of the term "word" does not imply any relationship with the other use in computers as meaning a "word in memory", and will in general be of a quite different size.

In discussing parity above, we have seen how any single bit error will result in invalid parity, and how a second bit error will result in a correct parity again. We can see that we have divided the 256 possible combinations of eight bits into two sets—those with even parity and those with odd parity. A one bit change in any code moves it to a code in the other set, and vice-versa. Here we have seven-bit data words, and adding the parity gives eight-bit code words.

Hamming studied the properties of errors in 1950. He defined a mathematical concept now called the *Hamming Distance*. The Hamming Distance between two codewords is the number of single bit changes that must be made to convert one codeword into the other one. Thus, for example, the Hamming Distance between the binary numbers 10 and 01 is two, since both bits must be changed. If we look at the set of even parity codes, then the shortest distance from one member to another member is 2. Conversely, for eight-bit codes there are eight odd parity codes at a Hamming distance of 1 from each even parity code.

2.3   Error-Correcting Codes

The parity code is only an error *detecting* code. Sometimes we may wish not merely to detect errors, but to *correct* them also. One of the simplest error correcting codes is a two-dimensional form of the parity check. The bits to be transmitted are arranged into a notional rectangular array. We then add parity bits for each row and column of

```
b  b  b  b  b  b  b      P
b  b  b  b  b  b  b      P
b  b  b  b  b  b  b      P
b  b  b  b  b  b  b      P
b  b  b  b  b  b  b      P
b  b  b  b  b  b  b      P
b  b  b  b  b  b  b      P

P  P  P  P  P  P  P
```

Fig 2.1. A Simple Error Correcting Scheme

bits, as in Fig 2.1. In this way we have both a horizontal parity check for each row, and a vertical parity check for each column. It is easy to see that if we get a single bit error anywhere in the data, then this will show up in both the corresponding horizontal and vertical parity checks. The intersection of the row and column with the bad parity indicates the bit that needs to be corrected.

Exercise 2.3   Consider what would happen if there were two errors. Consider the two cases:
   a) the two errors are in different rows and columns,
   b) the two errors are in the same row (or column).

Hamming used his concept of distance to give more insight into error detecting and error correcting codes. He also invented an ingenious error correcting code for single-bit errors that uses the minimum number of extra checking bits. Let us assume that we are taking a set of m data bits, and forming a codeword of n bits. The usual way of doing this is to add k bits (where $k = n - m$) to the m data bits as extra checking bits. Parity checking is the simplest example of this ($k = 1$). However, in general the n bits in the codeword can have any suitable relationship to the original m data bits.

For example, we could take each m-bit data word as an m-bit integer, and form code words by squaring the integer. In this case $k = m$. On decoding, only codewords that are perfect squares would be correct. The point of this particular example is merely to illustrate that the $n + k$ bits of the codeword do not necessarily contain the data bits as a subset.

Considering all the 2^n possible bit patterns in the n-bit codeword, only some smaller number can be valid, and usually only 2^m combinations are valid. Each of these 2^m combinations should preferably be separated from each other by the maximum possible Hamming Distance. This is because we wish to maximise the number of single-bit changes—errors—that are needed to convert one valid codeword into any other valid codeword.

Hamming used a geometrical analogy where an n-bit code word is represented in n-dimensional space by one of the vertices of a hypercube. The Hamming Distance between two codewords is then the shortest distance along the edges of the hypercube between the two corresponding vertices. Put in these geometrical terms, we must try to distribute the valid codewords at maximum Hamming Distance apart on the vertices of the hypercube.

We can see that if we can manage to space all the valid codewords at a distance d from each other, then all errors of $d-1$ bits or less will be detected. Similarly, if we can assume that there will be less than $d/2$ bit errors in any codeword, then we can correct all such errors by assuming that the nearest valid codeword was the original codeword before corruption. Conversely, for a given pattern of errors we need about twice the number of check bits to correct for errors rather than just to detect them.

We have seen how parity allows the detection of all single-bit errors. In Hamming Distance terms, this is because all the correct parity codewords are at the optimum distance of 2 from the nearest of their correct parity neighbours, and thus the density of the packing is the greatest possible. Thus parity is the optimum way of detecting single-bit errors. Hamming devised a way in which single-bit errors could be corrected. This is also optimal in that the minimum number of extra bits is used.

2.4   Hamming Single-Error-Correcting Code

The problem is to design an error-correcting code for m data bits by adding k check bits to form an n-bit codeword. Each of the valid 2^m codewords will have n invalid but correctable codewords at distance 1. These are the codewords with a single-bit error. This makes a total of $n+1$ code words that are unique to this one valid message, and all of these codewords must be further than 1 away from all the other codewords associated with the other $2^m - 1$ messages. This means that there are a total of $(n+1)2^m$ valid or correctable codewords. Clearly, this must be less than the total possible number of codewords, 2^n. Thus

$$(n+1)2^m \leq 2^n$$

Substituting $k = n - m$, we get

$$m + k + 1 \leq 2^k$$

For a given number, m, of message bits, this gives a bound on k, the minimum number of check bits needed to correct single-bit errors. Hamming devised a scheme that achieves this limit, and also gives an immediate and simple indication of which bit is in error. To do this he numbered the bits in the codeword from 1 to n. Then, taking each bit in turn, the number of its position was represented as a binary number, that is as a sum of powers of two. He then used one parity bit for each power of two. Thus, for example, take the bit in position 6: $6 = 110$ (binary), and thus the bit in position 6 is included in the parity check for 2 and 4, but not for 1. Similarly, the bit in position 9 is included in the check for 1 and 8, but not for 2 or 4. He allocated the parity bits themselves to the positions 1, 2, 4, 8,... etc, and the data bits to the remaining positions, 3, 5, 6, 7, 9, 10,...

Let us take an example, using even parity. Suppose we wish to encode an ASCII character "K" = 1001011. Take a codeword as in Fig 2.2 and allocate the seven bits of data to bits 3, 5, 6, 7, 9, 10, 11 (avoiding the parity positions):

		1		0	0	1		0	1	1
1	2	3	4	5	6	7	8	9	10	11

Fig 2.2. Hamming Code: Data Bits Assigned

We see that avoiding the parity bit positions, we need to use up to bit position 11. Now we shall calculate the parity bit positions. Bit 1 is the parity over positions 3,5,7,9,11, and must be set to 1 for even parity, Fig 2.3.

1		1		0	0	1		0	1	1
1	2	3	4	5	6	7	8	9	10	11

Fig 2.3. Hamming Code: First Parity Bit Assigned

(Note that with this arrangement of parity bits, the value of bit 1 does not depend on the value of any of the other parity bits. This is true of all the parity bits.) Similarly, bit 2 checks positions 3, 6, 7, 10, 11 and is set to 0; bit 4 checks bits 5, 6, 7 and is set to 1; and bit 8 checks bits 9, 10, 11, and is set to 0.

1	0	1	1	0	0	1	0	0	1	1
1	2	3	4	5	6	7	8	9	10	11

Fig 2.4. Hamming Code: All Parity Bits Assigned

Now, suppose that the codeword is transmitted, and suffers an error in, say, bit position 6—Fig 2.5. If we calculate the various parity bits, we find that bits 1 and 8 are OK, but bits 2 and 4 are wrong. $2 + 4 = 6$, the index of the bit in error.

The bound on the number, k, of check bits for a given number, m, of data bits is given by the equation above. In our example we see

1	0	1	1	0	1	1	0	0	1	1
1	2	3	4	5	6	7	8	9	10	11

Fig 2.5.   Hamming Code: Error in Bit 6

that $k = 4$ gives $m \leq 16 - 1 - 4 = 11$. We have used seven of the possible 11 bits in this case. However we have enough check bits to cover code bits up to 15. With 15 code bits we would have $15 - 4 = 11$ data bits. Thus Hamming's method allows the achievement of this limit providing we choose to use all the data bits that are available.

Exercise 2.4   Encode the ASCII character "p" using an odd parity parity Hamming code rather than the even parity code used in the example. Corrupt one bit, and check that the error correction correctly indicates which bit to correct.

Exercise 2.5   Write a program to accept a character and generate a Hamming codeword for it. Write another program to take the output of this program and check that it is correct.

Exercise 2.6   Modify the encoding program in exercise 2.5 so that just one bit is corrupted. Modify the receiving program to take this incorrect codeword and correct the error.

2.5   Burst Errors

We have looked at the use of parity in error detection. Parity is a useful way of checking for errors when we can be reasonably sure that errors will be single-bit errors, and will be well separated, one from the next. Both parity checking and Hamming correction rely on errors being isolated single-bit errors. Of course, life is not like that.

Even if errors really were single-bit errors and occurred randomly, chance would ensure that from time to time a codeword has more than one single-bit error. In this case both parity checking and Hamming error correction would fail. However, life is even worse than that, since there is a strong tendency for errors to occur in bursts. The likelihood of this is seen when we consider electrical interference. Suppose that switch gear, perhaps, or lightning emits interference that corrupts data on a communications link. If the interference lasts for several bit times then it will most likely invalidate a block of several bits. A simple parity check has only a 50:50 chance of detecting such a burst of errors, and a Hamming code would fail completely.

Exercise 2.7   Re-do exercise 2.4, but this time corrupt two bits. What is the result of applying the error correction process?

The effect of burst errors may be alleviated by transmitting data in a different way. The block of data bits can be arranged conceptually

in a rectangular array—the characters are arranged in rows, each with
its parity. Then the bits are transmitted column by column. In this way
any burst errors will appear in the received array smeared down a column
rather than across a word, and so (assuming the burst is shorter than
a column) each burst will affect only one bit per word. This trick can
be used either with parity checking or with Hamming code correction.
However, while it reduces the effect of burst errors, it does not stop the
occurrence of multiple errors due to chance.

> **Exercise 2.8** The same effect of limiting the damage of burst
> errors by transmitting the data in a non-sequential order, may also
> be achieved by transmitting the data in the normal sequential order,
> but assigning the parity bits each to a non-consecuitive set of bits.
> Work out the details for such a method.

2.6 Checksum Error Detection

There have been several methods devised for detecting multiple
bit errors. One of the simplest is to take each byte of a block as an 8-bit
binary number, and add it into an 8-bit accumulator. Carries out of
the most significant bit are lost—that is the summation is done modulo-
256. After transmitting the block of data, the value of the accumulator
is transmitted. At the receiver, the value of the last byte is checked
against the data, and errors should show up as a difference. In practice,
the check is made slightly easier by first taking the two's complement
of the value in the accumulator before transmitting it. In this way, the
receiver can sum over both the data and the check byte and expect zero.

The advantage of this checksum over a simple longitudinal parity check is that the effect of the carries during the 8-bit additions "mixes
up" the bits. Thus, a data bit in one column will influence the checksum in several columns because of the carries into more significant bit
positions. Very roughly, we might expect a random burst of errors to
affect the resulting checksum randomly, and thus we should have a 255
to 1 chance of detecting any error.

2.7 Cyclic Redundancy Checks

In the late 1950s another class of error checking code, the *Cyclic
Redundancy Check*—CRC was introduced by Prange. These codes were
analysed by Peterson in terms of polynomials in 1961. This type of check
is now almost universally employed, and we shall study it in some detail.

The operation of a CRC is best introduced as a block diagram
of a piece of hardware implementing the check—Fig 2.6. In general
the hardware is a shift register k bits wide with several exclusive-OR
operations and a feedback loop from the right-hand side. The diagram
shows a specific example with a 16-bit checksum and implementing the

standard CCITT CRC. The register is initialised to zero and then the bits are fed in from the left one by one. As bits are shifted out of the right end of the register, they are fed back and exclusive-ORed at certain positions both with the data being shifted along the register, and with the data entering from the left. When all the m message bits have been fed in, the data is followed by a set of k zeros. At the end of all this the contents of the register form the checksum. This k-bit checksum is then transmitted following the data. The receiver can obviously perform the same calculation and compare its result with the one received, and thus detect transmission errors.

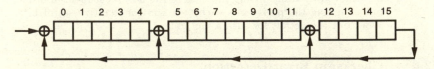

Fig 2.6.   Calculating CRCs With a Shift Register

There are two main attractions of such an apparently complex form of checksum. Firstly, the shift register with feedback is easy to implement in hardware, as the diagram illustrates. Secondly, as we are about to see, the method can be analysed by a straightforward if somewhat mathematical method. There is a widespread myth that, while checksums might be cheap and efficient to implement in hardware, they are slow and expensive to implement in software. Indeed, there seems to be a trend to use the additive type of checksum in host-to-host applications where the checksum must be calculated in software. Later on we shall examine the efficient algorithms that are available to calculate CRCs by software. These have been available in the literature since at least 1971 (Boudreau and Steen), and there seems little point in using the inferior additive type of checksum in most circumstances.

2.8   CRC Analysis

Peterson (1961) analysed the CRC codes by noting that the operation was the same as the division of polynomials in a slightly unusual algebraic system. The m message bits are taken as the coefficients of a polynomial in a dummy variable X with degree $m - 1$. Thus, for example, a message 11010100 is associated with a polynomial $1 + X + X^3 + X^5$. The feedback loop is represented by another polynomial. The one in the Fig 2.6 is represented by $1 + X^5 + X^{12} + X^{16}$. This latter is called the *generator polynomial*. As a final part to the specification of the algebraic system, the coefficients are all modulo-2. Thus $1X^a + 1X^a = 0$, $0X^a + 1X^a = 1X^a + 0X^a = 1X^a$, $0X^a + 0X^a = 0$, and $-1X^a = 1X^a$. In this system, we see that addition is the same as subtraction, and both are the same as the exclusive-OR operation. Multiplication of a polynomial by X is the same as shifting the original coefficients by one bit. Looking back at our feedback diagram, the effect of shifting a bit out of the shift register and feeding it back into the rest of the register is the same as adding in the generator polynomial, which in turn is the same as subtracting it in modulo-2 arithmetic. An example should make this all clear. Look at the generation of the CRC for a message of #D4 done by long division (NB that this is the reverse of the normal layout, with the higher powers of X on the right hand side):

```
0000 0000 0000 0000 1101 0100
      100 0010 0000 0100 01
    ──────────────────────────
    0 0100 0010 0000 1001
    1 0000 1000 0001 0001
   ─────────────────────────
   0001 0100 1010 0001 1
   1000 0100 0000 1000 1
   ──────────────────────
   1001 0000 1010 1001        =#90A9
```

    Careful examination of this division and comparison with the shift register method should convince the reader that the two are the same mathematical process. Note that the long division divides by the 17-bit pattern, with the one corresponding to X^{16} in the rightmost position. In the shift register this is performed by implication with the rightmost bit shifting out of the 16-bit register, and the remaining 16 bits corresponding to the powers of X from 0 to 15 (or rather, just the one bits), being implemented by the exclusive-OR gates in the feedback loop.

    The value of this new algebra is that the normal theorems of algebra still apply and can be used in analysing the properties of certain manipulations, as we shall now see.

    We have the message polynomial $G(X)$ and the generator polynomial $P(X)$. We have divided $X^k G(X)$ by $P(X)$ and obtained the quotient $Q(X)$ and remainder $R(X)$. The actual code word transmitted corresponds to the polynomial

$$F(X) = X^k G(X) + R(X)$$

Since we are using modulo-2 arithmetic, $+R(X) = -R(X)$, and thus if the receiver calculates the checksum over the received $F(X)$ he should get zero.

    Exercise 2.9   Calculate the checksum by long division for the message #0C18 using the same generator polynomial.

Exercise 2.10   Write a program to generate checksums for an arbitrary hexadecimal input string using the same generator polynomial. Implement the long division bit by bit in a software loop.

2.9   Back-to-Back Blocks

It is possible in real systems for a receiver to miss the delimiter between two blocks sent one after another, or for the sender to miss sending the delimiter. Whatever the actual reason, in practice we do sometimes get two otherwise perfectly good data blocks and their checksums concatenated together. If two blocks are transmitted with correct checksum, and then concatenated together, the checksum over the combined block will be zero. Thus the CRC will not detect this particular sort of error. A small modification of the basis of the CRC calculation picks up this sort of error too. Consider the message

$$X^k \times G(X) + X^{(m-1)} \times L(X)$$

where

$$L(X) = 1 + X + X^2 \ldots + X^{(k-1)}$$

The term $X^{(m-1)} \times L(X)$ is the equivalent of initialising the shift register to all ones before starting the CRC calculation. Again we divide by $P(X)$ to get $Q(X)$ and $R(X)$, such that

$$Q(X) \times P(X) + R(X) = X^k \times G(X) + X^{(m-1)} \times L(X)$$

We then transmit the message, followed by the ones complement of $R(X)$, i.e.

$$F(X) = X^k \times G(X) + R(X) + L(X)$$

At the receiver, we compute

$$M(X) = \frac{X^k \times (F(X) + X^{(m-1)} \times L(X))}{P(X)}$$

This is equivalent to initialising the register to all ones, and then processing the codeword F(X) as normal. Now,

$$M(X) = \frac{X^k(X^k \times G(X) + R(X) + L(X) + X^{(m-1)} \times L(X))}{P(X)}$$

$$= \frac{X^k(Q(X) \times P(X) + L(X))}{P(X)}$$

$$= \frac{X^k \times Q(X) + X^k \times L(X)}{P(X)}$$

The remainder is just the right term. This is a fixed value independent of the message polynomial $M(X)$. For our generator polynomial $1 + X^5 + X^{12} + X^{16}$ this evaluates to #F0B8. Thus, if there is no error we expect to end up with this "magic pattern" depending only on the generator polynomial we are using. More especially, if we concatenate two blocks together and calculate the checksum over the whole combined block, the result will not be the right magic number, and the procedure will thus detect and reject the concatenated blocks. This is the method actually used in the calculation of the checksum for HDLC link level error control as used in X.25.

> **Exercise 2.11** Using the unmodified method, if two blocks are concatenated together with a byte of zero between them, what is the overall checksum? What difference does it make using the modified method?

> **Exercise 2.12** Note that (for error free transmission) the final sum is independent of the value to which the *transmitter's* register is initialised, and is dependent on the initialisation of the receiver's register only. Show this by
> a) Reviewing the mathematics above
> b) Considering the implementation in terms of shift registers and feedback loops.
> Since the final magic pattern is independent of the transmitter's initialisation of the shift register, why do you think that it is set to ones? (Hint—a common transmitter fault is to "stick" at the start of a block and send a sequence of ones or zeros.)

2.10 Error Analysis

If a transmission error occurs, then the resulting code word H will be made up of the correct code word, F together with some error bits E, where

$$H(X) = F(X) + E(X)$$

Since $F(X)$ is divisible by $P(X)$, we can see that if $H(X)$ is not divisible by $P(X)$ then $E(X) \neq 0$ and thus some error has occurred. On the other hand, if $H(X)$ is divisible by $P(X)$, then $E(X)$ is divisible by $P(X)$. This implies that either $E(X)$ is zero—no error—or that $E(X)$ is non-zero but still divisible by $P(X)$. Peterson showed that the polynomial $P(X)$ needed to have certain simple properties to detect various classes of error. For example, if $P(X)$ contains more than one term, then all single bit errors will be detected, and all polynomials with the factor $1 + X$ detect all odd numbers of errors. There are extensive studies that show the efficiency of CRCs in detecting very wide classes of errors, and lead to the high confidence in which cyclic codes are viewed. For further information on this see the comprehensive work by Peterson and Weldon.

2.11   CRC Computation by Program

So far we have discussed the implementation of checksums by hardware in a shift register. Exercise 2.10 shows that a straightforward bit-by-bit calculation is very easy in software. However, it also demonstrates how expensive it is too. Even if software has direct access to a hardware register of the appropriate size, and shift, branch on carry, and exclusive-OR instructions, the tightest machine code loop will take half a dozen instructions or so to process each bit. This means that even a modest data rate of 1000 characters per second will tax the power of all but the most powerful microcomputers. A high-level language program that must implement the shift register as an array of bits, and must implement the shifts and exclusive-OR operations as software loops scanning over the elements of the array will be impossibly slow. For this reason, there is a strong tendency for checksums only to be done in hardware. If some sort of software check needs to be done, as in the ISO transport service for example, or the ARPANET *Transmission Control Protocol*—TCP, it is common to specify an additive sort of sum as it is believed to be less expensive

There is, however, an efficient way of calculating the checksum byte-by-byte. In fact, the method allows the inclusion of any group of bits at once (up to the size of the checksum), but the best tradeoff is probably byte-by-byte. To illustrate how this is done we shall examine the operation of the shift register over several bits. Let us start at some intermediate step, t, when the register contains some intermediate value, and look at the values generated for steps $t+1, t+2$, etc. The new bits coming in are labelled b_{t+1}, b_{t+1}, etc. R_t denotes the register at step t, and r_n refers to the nth bit in the register R. We shall consider the 16-bit checksum, though the method obviously generalises to a checksum of any size. Thus:

$$R_t = \{r_0, r_1, r_2, \ldots r_{13}, r_{14}, r_{15}\}$$

Let $f_0 = r_{15}$, the rightmost bit of the register at time t that will be fed back at the next stage:

$$
\begin{aligned}
R_{t+1} \quad = \quad & \{b_{t+1}, \quad 0, \quad 0, \quad \ldots \quad 0, \quad 0\} \quad (a) \\
+ \quad & \{0, \quad r_0, \quad r_1, \quad \ldots \quad r_{13}, \quad r_{14}\} \quad (b) \\
+ \quad & \{f_0 p_0, \quad f_0 p_1, \quad f_0 p_2, \quad \ldots \quad f_0 p_{14}, \quad f_0 p_{15}\} \quad (c)
\end{aligned}
$$

The register at $t+1$ is made up of three parts. First is the new bit that gets shifted in, part (a). Next, the bits from the step before shifted right, part (b). The final part, (c), is the feedback loop. It consists of the bit shifted out of the right hand side $f_0 = r_{15}$ multiplied by the generator polynomial. This is equivalent to the conditional feedback loop. Progressing to the next step, let $f_1 = r_{14} + f_0 \times p_{15}$, the bit that will be shifted out of the right-hand end of the register and fed back:

$$
\begin{array}{llllllll}
R_{t+2} & = & \{b_{t+2}, & b_{t+1}, & 0, & \cdots & 0, & 0 & (a) \\
& + & \{0, & 0, & r0, & \cdots & r_{12}, & r_{13} & (b) \\
& + & \{0, & f_0p_0, & f_0p_1, & \cdots & f_0p_{13}, & f_0p_{14} & (c_1) \\
& + & \{f_1p_0, & f_1p_1, & f_1p_2, & \cdots & f_1p_{14}, & f_1p_{15} & (c_2)
\end{array}
$$

Again the three parts (a), (b) and (c) express the new bits shifting in, the original register shifted right, and the feedback. In this case there are two parts to the feedback, one each from the two steps so far. If we progress to the next step, we can define

$$
\begin{aligned}
f_2 &= f_1p_{15} + f_0p_{14} + r_{13} \\
&= (r_{14} + r_{15}p_{15})p_{15} + r_{15}p_{14} + r_{13}
\end{aligned}
$$

It is left as an exercise for the reader to write down R_{t+3}.

Clearly, the expressions for the feedback loop, f_n, are getting increasingly more complex due to the way in which the loop is feeding back into itself. In practice, most polynomials are fairly sparse so that many of the terms f_n are zero. However, the most important point is that the new data bits coming in from the left will not start to effect the feedback loop until they have shifted the full width of the register. Further than this, if we look at the effect of shifting in i new bits (where $i \leq k$, the number of bits in the checksum), we see that the sum is still made up of the same three parts—the new bits, the old bits shifted right, and the feedback, which depends only on the rightmost i bits of the original register. We can exploit this to add in a block of i new bits to the checksum in one compound operation rather than a number of steps proportional to the number of bits being added. We take the rightmost i bits of the checksum, and calculate the feedback, shift the leftmost i bits right by i bits, and add in the i new bits. The first of these steps—the calculation of the feedback loop—is quite complex because of the recursive nature of f_n. However, if we choose some reasonable value of i, then we can calculate the k-bit feedback for each of the 2^i possible combinations of the i bits once and for all and store it in an array.

For example, suppose we are working with a 16-bit checksum, and want to calculate the checksum by adding in one data byte at a time. We first calculate the 16 bits that the feedback loop generates for all 256 possible combinations of the right-hand eight bits of the old checksum, and store this in an array of of 256 16-bit registers. Then, for each byte added to the checksum, we take the existing checksum and form a new checksum by summing (modulo-2):

1) the feedback array indexed by the rightmost eight bits of the old checksum.
2) the old checksum shifted right eight bits (i.e. its left byte moved to replace the right byte, and the left byte replaced by zero)
3) the new byte of data in the leftmost eight bits

Not only is this a small set of steps per byte, rather than per bit, but it is also a set of byte operations rather than bit operations. These are usually much more accessible, particularly with high level languages. Even the exclusive-OR operation can be implemented by table lookup if necessary for efficiency.

Exercise 2.13   Write a program to calculate CRCs by the above method. Compare its results, and performance, with those from exercise 2.10.

Exercise 2.14   Extend the above program to calculate the CRC using the 32-bit polynomial $X^{32} + X^{26} + X^{23} + X^{22} + X^{16} + X^{12} + X^{11} + X^{10} + X^8 + X^7 + X^5 + X^4 + X^2 + X + 1$, again working byte-by-byte. Consider the pros and cons of doing more bits at a time, say 12 or 16 or 32. (The polynomial given is that used in the standard local area networks for Ethernet, token ring, and token bus that we shall encounter in the next chapter.)

2.12   Choice of Method

We can see that we now have a range of ways in which a CRC type of checksum can be calculated. Clearly, the most efficient in terms of resources is implementation in hardware. However, we shall see in Chapter 12 the need for software end-to-end checks. In addition, the the available hardware may not implement checksums. In software, we may implement bit-by-bit shifting and feedback, or the more powerful byte-by-byte method. Generally, the latter is to be recommended. However, in special cases, the bit-by-bit shifting method may be more appropriate. Some years ago the author wrote a small loader program that read the data from a communications line and loaded it into the computer's memory. Since the loader had to sit in a small read-only memory chip, space and simplicity were of the essence, and since the machine was unable to do anything else while the loading was taking place, machine efficiency in terms of machine cycles used was unimportant. Bit-by-bit shifting was the method of choice here.

Some machine architectures provide special instructions or hardware to calculate checksums. For example, the IBM 3705 communications controller has special hardware to implement the IBM checksum, the DEC VAX has a special instruction to generate checksums for blocks of data, and the DEC PDP11 has a special device that can be plugged into the Unibus, the KG11, that can be used for CRC calculations.

2.13   Forward and Reverse Error Correction

We have seen the ways in which parity and checksums can be used to detect or to correct errors. It is generally easier to detect errors than to correct them, and requires less overhead in terms of check bits. However, if we merely detect errors in a received packet, what can we do about it? It would seem much better to use an error correcting code to correct the errors and then proceed to use the packet of good data than merely to know that the received packet is faulty. This method of error correction is normally termed *forward error correction*. However, there is an alternative. The receiver of a bad packet of data can simply ask the sender to send the faulty packet again and hope that the packet gets through OK the second time. This is termed *reverse error correction* because of the reverse flow of messages requesting re-transmission.

2.14   Reverse Error Correction Protocol

We shall try to design a simple error recovery protocol that can operate between a sender S and a receiver R. *A protocol is a set of messages and the rules for exchanging them.* This is the first of many protocols that we shall encounter. We have several aims in designing this protocol in the way that we do. Rather than presenting a finished work of art and discussing its functional beauty, we shall try to simulate the way in which we might design such a protocol had we not at first understand all the issues. By starting with what might seem an obvious solution, stumbling up some blind alleys and showing how the protocol design fails to work in certain cases, we hope to give the reader a better understanding of those issues. Making mistakes and learning from them is a powerful way of arriving at an understanding of a problem, and we hope to simulate some of that process below.

The sender will send a series of data messages to the receiver. Each of the messages will have some sort of error checking attached to it, probably a CRC. We shall assume that every now and again random errors are detected by the receiver. We shall first attempt a protocol in which the receiver sends messages to the sender to accept or reject (ask for a retransmission) of each packet as it arrives. Let us define the messages that the receiver can send back to the sender; an acknowledgement that the last block was received without error, ACK, and a negative acknowledgement, NAK, indicating that the last block was in error. Let us then attempt to recover from errors as follows. The sender S will send a series of messages $M_1 M_2 M_3, \ldots$ It sends each one, and then waits for a response from the receiver. The receiver R looks at each message as it arrives. If the checksum indicates that a block was OK then it sends back an ACK. If the block was in error then it sends back a NAK. When S receives an ACK it proceeds to send the next message, and when it gets a NAK it re-sends the last message. The principle is that since the errors are random, then if we send and re-send a message enough times it will eventually get though without error.

2.15   Parallel Exercise

To achieve the fullest appreciation of the amazing complexities of even a simple protocol like this, it is important to examine its operation under realistic conditions. Users may be tempted to try to gain experience by running programs under some simulation environment in, say, two processes in a time-sharing system. It is wise to avoid this route if possible because it is extremely difficult to simulate realistic modes of failure. Almost by definition, only the errors that the designer thinks of are designed in. The important thing about realistic failure modes is that they are almost infinitely varied and surprising. A reasonably realistic environment can be set up by taking two microcomputers and connecting them together via an RS232 link and a null modem as described in Chapter 1. Errors may be introduced by momentarily unplugging the link and then plugging it back again. For best effect the bit rate should be set as low as possible since it is highly desirable that the momentary break in the link should corrupt just a few bits rather than a whole block.

The following parallel exercise will lead the reader through the steps examined in the text. Packets flowing in each direction should be framed with a DLE, STX, etc. type of mechanism. Inside the packets, the control should be a one byte value, and all packets should contain a CRC in the last two bytes.

2.16   Protocol Representation

When sending data from S to R, we shall at first merely need to add a checksum, and then frame the packet transparently as described in the last chapter. Thus, if we have a data packet "ABC" to send, we first calculate the two checksum bytes CS, and then frame the packet with a DLE, STX, etc type of framing. Thus, the packet on the transmission line will be

DLE, STX, A, B, C, CS, CS, DLE, ETX

(Plus any extra DLEs inserted for transparency.) Note that the checksum may be any binary pattern depending on the other bytes in the block, and thus the DLE insertion may need to take place in the checksum as well as in the data. The data on the return leg will be only the two messages ACK and NAK. Together with the checksum, these become the seven character block

DLE, STX, ACK, CS, CS, DLE, ETX

and similarly for NAK.

> **Exercise 2.15** Implement the two ends of the simple protocol described above. Set a transfer going and introduce errors by interrupting the connection. Observe the behaviour of the protocol. Does it work? Does it hang up, transmit corrupted data without recovering, lose packets, duplicate packets, lock up and fail to proceed, or fail in any other way?

2.17   Protocol Evaluation

The protocol we have designed does not always work. This is because in constructing the simple protocol above we have made several implicit assumptions that are not necessarily valid in practice. Firstly, we have implicitly assumed that all the data packets will get through—they may be corrupted, but something will get through. The somewhat severe method of introducing errors that we have used means that whole data messages or whole acknowledgements may sometimes get lost. In this case then the whole protocol will lock up. Thus, if a data message is lost then the intended receiver of the packet (either S or R) will wait forever. A similar hang up will occur if a single bit error corrupts either the beginning delimiter, DLE STX, or the final delimiter DLE ETX. In this case the start or end of the packet will be missed, and the receiver will wait for a properly framed packet forever. The hangup can also be caused either by an ACK or NAK being lost or corrupted.

One solution for the hangup problem is to implement a *timeout*. When a data packet has been sent from S a timer is started. If an acknowledgement, either an ACK or a NAK has not been received after the specified period, then some recovery action must be taken. The type of action depends on what type of message has gone missing. If the data packet has been lost, or a returning NAK has been lost then the packet needs to be retransmitted. However, if an ACK has been lost, the retransmission of the data packet will result in that record of the data being duplicated.

Knowing what to do next is easy with a "bird's eye view" of what has just gone wrong. Unfortunately, neither end has such a view; each end has a limited and different view of what is going on. Thus, if a data packet is lost in transit then the transmitter cannot know this directly, and neither can the receiver. They can only infer the loss from other events, or from the lack of events. Thus, the transmitter may infer that the transmitted packet has been lost because it has not been acknowledged within a certain time. However the actual reason for the absence of an acknowledgement might well be the loss of the ACK packet itself, or of a rejecting NAK packet. Similarly, the receiver may infer the loss of a transmitted packet if one does not arrive within a specified period. However, it may merely be that the transmitter has no data to send.

The complexities of protocol design arise in a large degree from this uncertain process of inference from incomplete data. Designing a good protocol is partly a matter of deriving the best inference from an event, and partly a matter of designing the responses based on this inference so that the desired result is eventually achieved, even though the inference was not necessarily the whole truth of the matter.

In the final analysis, the inferences are used to develop the protocol rules, but the inferences themselves are irrelevant. What matters is what result the protocol rules produce in the face of the actual events.

Returning to the problem of recovery from lost blocks, one solution to all this that might spring to mind is to create a new message from the sender *"Did you get my last message"*—DYGMLM. This should just elicit a repeat of the ACK or NAK from the receiver. If the receiver has just sent an ACK or a NAK, then it can just repeat it. However, if it has not received any block it should send a NAK to get the sender to retransmit the last block. The problem here is how can the receiver know that it has just missed a block? The receiver's knowledge is insufficient to implement this bird's eye view strategy. It is possible to design complicated ways of using timeouts, etc so that the receiver can respond with some confidence that it has just missed a block.

The receiver could get a new packet type *"Which was that message that I may or may not have just missed"*. However, it is better to anticipate the question. All the data blocks sent can be labelled— A and B are sufficient for our purposes—and then we can extend the DYGMLM to include A or B as a parameter. With these simple extensions, the DYGMLM question can be simply answered.

Thus, after sending a packet labelled x (either A or B), and timing out after a fruitless wait for a response, the sender can transmit DYGMLM,x. The receiver remembers the label of the last packet that it received correctly. It compares this remembered label with the label on any DYGMLM query. If they are the same, then an ACK is transmitted, and the S end can proceed to the next message. If they are different, then a NAK is the correct response, whereupon the S end retransmits the data packet that has been lost.

The value of the timeout is important. For any communications setup there is a round trip delay time. This is the time for a block to be transmitted, received, the far end to respond, and the transmission time on the return leg. Clearly, this time will vary depending on various factors, including the block length, transmission speed, the length of the communications line, and the response time of the computers at either end. It is necessary to set the response timeout great enough so that the lack of response when it expires is not merely because the message has not yet had time to return. If the timeout is too short, then this can in itself cause duplicated packets.

Exercise 2.16 Explain how.

It is usual to set this time to a value of several or many times the round trip time. In principle, there is no upper limit to this time, but in practice it needs to be low enough so that the delay caused by a lost packet and consequent timeout and error recovery are not excessive.

2.18 Protocol Representation Again

Life is now becoming more complicated. We not only need ACK and NAK messages from the receiver to the sender, but we also need both data and DYGMLM messages from the sender to the receiver. To separate all these messages out, the usual technique is to allocate two fields at the start of each and every packet. Let us allocate a series of opcodes, say DATA = 1, DYGMLM = 2, ACK=3, and NAK = 4. The two labels A and B can be represented by 0 and 1. For simplicity, let us allocate the opcode to the first byte of each packet, and the label to the second (though we could easily pack the two fields into the eight bits of the first byte).

Thus, a data packet labelled A with data A B C becomes "1, 0, A, B, C". We then add the two checksum bytes CS, and the framing DLE STX and DLE ETX to get

DLE, STX, 1, 0, A, B, C, CS, CS, DLE, ETX

(plus any inserted DLEs for transparency). Each of the other three message types has a similar format, except for the absence of the data field. Thus DYGMLM,A is represented as

DLE, STX, DYGMLM, A, CS, CS, DLE, ETX

and similarly for B.

Exercise 2.17 Implement this new extended protocol on the two linked micro computers. Does the protocol lock up now? Are there any errors?

Our protocol is still not perfect. It now recovers from any *single* short isolated burst of errors that cause the corruption or loss of any one packet. Thus, an error in a data packet will be recovered by a

NAK response; a lost data packet or ACK response will be recovered by a DYGMLM sequence, and an error in a DYGMLM sequence cannot happen if we are assuming isolated errors.

In showing that the protocol recovers from errors in or loss of any single packet we have uncovered its weakness—what happens if we get two errors together? This may sound extreme, but if there is a chance of 1 in 100 that any one packet is corrupted, then we can expect every 100th corrupted packet to be immediately followed by another corrupted packet. Indeed, life can easily be worse than this as we have pointed out that errors often hunt in packs or bursts rather than being randomly distributed.

Let us look at the possible effects of a group or burst of errors. Suppose a DYGMLM gets corrupted. The receiver has no idea what type of incoming packet has just been corrupted. Remember that each end has only a limited and incomplete knowledge of what we can see from our advantageous position. The only possible response to an error is a NAK, and so it will NAK in response to every DYGMLM block that suffers a transmission error. Consider, then, the sequence:

- A message is sent from S and received OK by R.
- The receiver responds with an ACK
- The ACK is lost.
- The sender sends a DYGMLM
- The DYGMLM is corrupted in transmission
- The receiver replies with a NAK
- The sender sees the NAK, thinks this means that the data was corrupted rather than the DYGMLM and re-sends the data packet.

The result of all this is that we get duplicated data because of the wrong interpretation of the misleading response seen by S. In addition to the problem of duplicated data, there is the problem of what the transmitter S is supposed to do when it gets corrupted control messages from R.

To avoid the duplication of data blocks, there is a simple strategy that can be pursued. The receiver can keep track of the packet labels: A, B, A, ... Whenever it receives a block with the "wrong" label, then it can discard it as a duplicate. However, it should respond with an ACK to persuade the transmitter to proceed with the transmission of the next block. This is an example of the receiver telling a "white lie" to the transmitter. Strictly there has been an error—the duplication of a data block. However the receiver can correct this by merely discarding the block, and rather than confusing things by complaining, it merely gets on with the job.

Exercise 2.18 Implement this change in the behaviour of the receiver.

The protocol now manages to avoid the duplication of packets. However, we still have not worked out a satisfactory action for the transmitter to take when it gets corrupted packets from the receiver. Rather than elaborating the protocol, this is a good time to make it simpler. Instead of needing the DYGMLM message, we can now use the data messages themselves to perform this action. The use of the labelling scheme at the receiver to eliminate duplicated blocks means that we can now overload the meaning of the data blocks. Thus, rather than sending the DYGMLM message, the sender S can merely re-transmit the data block again and again each time the timer expires until it gets an ACK (with the right label) in response. It then proceeds to the next block. Since the receiver will discard duplicates, the re-sending of the data block anticipates a NAK response to the DYGMLM. And since the arrival of the duplicate block gets an ACK response, then the effect is the same an an ACK response to the DYGMLM. The sender can now also respond to an error in a packet from the receiver by re-transmitting the data packet.

The protocol is now:

- The sender sends each packet together with its label
- The receiver replies appropriately with ACK or NAK
- If the sender gets an ACK it proceeds to the next packet.
- If the sender gets a NAK, an error in a received packet, or times out waiting for a response, it re-transmits the data packet
- The receiver discards duplicate packets, but still responds with an ACK.

Thus we see that we now have a complete list of actions to take in all circumstances by both ends.

Exercise 2.19 Implement this protocol. How does this protocol perform now?

Exercise 2.20 Devise and describe a sequence that causes the receipt of the same data packet twice.

2.19 A Minimal Link Protocol

The protocol became simpler when we allowed properly for the corrupted packets from the R to S. Indeed, it is possible further to minimize the protocol by eliminating the NAK response. In this case the protocol reduces to the sender repeatedly sending a packet until it eventually gets an acknowledgement. The duplicated packets will be eliminated by the operation of the label. However, the NAK is not completely redundant. It serves the purpose of speeding the recovery from lost packets in those cases where an error can be detected, since a NAK response and a resend of the packet in error will proceed faster than a resend because of a timeout.

We shall meet several variations on this error recovery protocol in this book. Sometimes it is possible to speed the recovery from errors with a NAK response, but sometimes, as with the TCP protocol in Chapter 6, it is not possible to use the NAK mechanism, and the only recovery is by timeout and retransmission.

2.20   A Real Link Level Protocol—The HDLC Family

Now that we have looked at the basic problems of error recovery on a point-to-point link, we are ready to look at the way in which a real link level error recovery protocol works. We are about to describe the workings of the *High level Data Link Control*—HDLC protocol that is used on X.25 point-to-point links. Variations of this same protocol are called *Synchronous Data Link Control*—SDLC in the IBM world (and it is from the original SDLC that the protocol family is derived), or IEEE 802.3 link level control in the world of local area networks. There are many other flavours of basically this same protocol. The details change, but the basic principles are all the same, and we shall not distinguish the differences. We shall describe the two main features of the protocol— the notion of connection and the state of the link, and the concept of multiple outstanding frames or window operation.

2.21   The Notion of State

Implicitly and unremarked, an extra notion has crept into our protocol, and that is the one of *state*. We have seen how the sender and receiver use alternate packet labels A, B, A, ... to avoid the problem of duplicate packet reception. We can express this by saying that both the sender and the receiver have two possible states, A and B. The sender is either in "send the next packet with label A"—state or "send the next packet with label B"—state, and correspondingly for the the receiver. We avoided duplicates by having the receiver discard packets labelled B if it was in the state "expecting next packet labelled A" and vice versa. This works fine if both the sender and receiver start in the corresponding states, and we have implicitly assumed that they will both start in the A-state. Our duplicate discarding action was a device to keep the two states in lock step by recovering from the case where the receiver's state had advanced (by receiving a frame successfully), but the senders had not advanced (because of the loss of the ACK).

Suppose, however, that the two states lose synchronisation for some other reason. The most likely, apart from software error, is that one or other machine at the end of the link is restarted. Clearly, there will be a problem if the machines start up with the state undefined. However, even if the state is always well defined at the start of operation, it can become unsynchronised if the two ends of the link are restarted independently.

As an illustration of this, assume that the sender has just received an acknowledgement of packet labelled A, and so both ends of the link have moved on to state B. If at this point the receiver "crashes" and re-initialises, it will now be in state A. The sender will meantime have been trying to send the frame labelled B. Eventually, the receiver will be ready and will receive the B-labelled frame. It will compare the label B with its expected label, A, and see that they disagree. According to our protocol, it will discard the frame as a duplicate, but reply ACK. The sender will see the ACK, assume the packet has been received correctly, and proceed to the next packet. From then on, the two ends are in step, and will work correctly, but the first frame has been lost because of the lack of synchronisation at the start.

In order to avoid this problem it is usual for a link to have two *phases*, commonly called the *Connected Phase* and the *Disconnected Phase* for reasons that should become obvious. There is then a special part of the protocol to ensure that the two ends enter the connected phase together and synchronise their states at the same time. As an illustration of this we shall briefly sketch the connection part of the HDLC protocol.

When either end of a link is first started, it is in the disconnected phase. When disconnected, it will neither transmit nor accept data. Five messages are used to manage the transition between the two phases. We shall call them *Connect, Connect Accept, Disconnect, Disconnect Confirmation*, and *Disconnected Mode*. When one end wishes to go from the Disconnected Phase to the Connected Phase, it sends the *Connect* command. The receiver of the Connect command has two options. If it is also willing to become connected, then it replies with the *Connect Accept*, but if it wishes to remain disconnected it can reply with the *Disconnected Mode* message. If the call is accepted then both ends enter the Connected Phase and also synchronise their states. Similarly, either end may initiate a *Disconnect* and respond with a *Disconnect Confirmation* in order to become disconnected again.

How does this protocol handle such misfortunes as one end crashing and restarting when a link is working away merrily? One end thinks it is still talking to the other end (which has perhaps been mysteriously quiet for a while)—i.e. it is still *Connected*—while the crashed end has come up in the Disconnected Phase, and is about to send inappropriate replies to the other end.

HDLC provides several strategies for dealing with this. The most effective is for one end first to ensure that both ends are in the Disconnected Phase before attempting to move to the Connected Phase. To achieve this, the first step when (re)starting is to emit a *Disconnect Request* message, and wait for a reply. If the other end was already disconnected, then it will respond with *Disconnected Mode* to indicate this. On the other hand, if it was still connected, as in our example, then it would emit a *Disconnect Confirmation* and move into the Disconnected Phase. One way or the other, the two ends of the link achieve an agreement on being in the *Disconnected* phase. Once this solid baseline is agreed the two can then initiate the connection by exchanging *Connect* and *Connect Accept* messages.

Note that while this resynchronisation of the states ensures that no new packets are lost after the reconnection of the link, there is no way of handling the loose ends that are left over from the previous severing of the link. In particular, if a message has been sent along the link, and received correctly, but the link failed before the sender received the appropriate ACKnowledgement, then there is no way that the sender can know whether the packet got through, and there is no way that the receiver can know whether the sender got the acknowledgement. There is then the possibility that the packet will be duplicated because the sender will make other arrangements for the delivery of the packet, not knowing that the receiver is going to deliver the packet anyway. Resolution of this problem is the responsibility of higher levels of protocol.

Now that we have described the concepts of being connected and disconnected, we can face the question of what to do if repeated attempts to transmit a frame in the face of errors fail to get the frame through. Just as a suitable retransmission timeout value is chosen, so also is a maximum number of retransmission attempts. If this is chosen as, say, 10, then after 10 successive retries without success, the assumption is made that some fairly permanent problem has arisen, and the disconnection procedure is commenced. Despite the transmission problems, an attempt is made to transmit the *Disconnect Request* to enter the disconnected phase. Again, 10 attempts will be made (or less if the attempt gets through and is acknowledged). Eventually, the *Disconnected* phase is reached. Before communication can be resumed, the two stations will insist on exchanging *Disconnected Mode* messages before embarking on the reconnection process.

2.22   Multiple Packets—Windows

The final elaboration on the link level protocol that we shall consider is the use of multiple outstanding packets. Later in this book we shall return several times to the question of why we should wish to

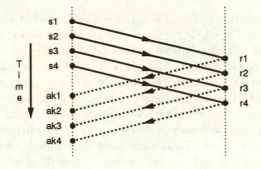

Fig 2.7. Multiple Outstanding Packets

use multiple packets across a link rather than just sending one packet at a time and waiting for its acknowledgement. For the time being we shall merely observe that there is a delay between sending a bit at one end of the link and receiving that same bit at the other end. If the signal is transmitted at, say, $2/3$ the speed of light, then the delay t seconds across a link of length l metres is

$$t = \frac{1}{0.66 \times c} = \frac{1}{200,000,000}$$

If the bit rate is b bits per second, and a frame is f bits long, then the transmission time, T, for a frame is $T = f/b$ and thus the ratio of the two is

$$\frac{t}{T} = \frac{lb}{200,000,000 f}$$

By making $lb > 200,000,000f$, we can see that the last bit will have been transmitted before the first bit arrives at the receiver. By making the length of the circuit and the bit rate high enough in comparison with the frame length (and the speed of light) we can make the link "store" more and more frames. Indeed some early computers actually stored data in a similar way to this except that the mode of transmission was sound waves in a tube of mercury rather than electromagnetic waves.

Now, if the circuit can store a frame or three, then only sending one frame at a time and waiting for the response means that most of the time the sender will be idle while the bits meander to the other end and the ACK saunters back. The utilisation of the link will be correspondingly small.

Exercise 2.21 Calculate the ratio t/T for links that are 10 metres, $100m$, $1Km$, $1000Km$, $72,000Km$, and $100,000,000Km$ each for bit rates of 300 bps, $9,600bps$, and $1,000,000bps$, all for frames 1000 bits long. Comment on the implications of the figures.

One solution for this problem is for the sender to send not just one frame at a time, but a whole series of frames, and not to expect acknowledgements immediately, but some time later. In Fig 2.7 we see a sender sending a series of packets 1, 2, 3, 4 ..., the receiver getting them several *packet times* later and immediately acknowledging them, and the sender receiving the acknowledgements several further packet times later. After a time (more than we have shown) there is a full overlap with the sender sending packets and receiving the acknowledgements some several packet times later. Such a mechanism is called a *window mechanism*. The reason for such an odd name is that if we view the sender's sequence of packets as an infinite series, 1, 2, 3, 4, 5, ... then we can imagine a conceptual "window" onto this sequence of width w. The sender will be prepared to send w packets before getting an acknowledgement. Thus, if packet n has just been acknowledged, then the sender will be prepared to send up to packet $n + w$.

The number w is limited since there is a possibility that packets not yet acknowledged, i.e. "inside the window" will be lost due to transmission errors, and will have to be re-transmitted. Thus, up to w frames must be stored against this eventuality. The number w is agreed upon in some sort of way. This may be because of the definition of the specific protocol being used, because of some administrative agreement (e.g. entry in a form) when the service is being set up, or perhaps as a negotiation in the protocol. We shall meet all variations of this theme in this book.

In order to tie up the various acknowledgements with the corresponding frames to which they refer, all the frames are numbered, and numbers in the acknowledgements refer explicitly to specific frames. Really, this is just an extension of the A, B, A, ... labelling. Indeed, clearly we cannot allocate an unlimited space for the numbering scheme, and it is normal to allocate a fixed small number of bits for the numbers. Two popular choices are three bits and seven bits giving numbers modulo-8 and modulo-128 numbering schemes respectively. With modulo numbers, the numbers cycle from 0 up to $modulus - 1$ and back round through 0 again. Thus, for example, three bits gives the sequence 0, 1, 2, 3, 4, 5, 6, 7, 0, 1, 2, 3, 4, ... and so on ad infinitum. The TCP protocol uses 32 bits to represent its very large window—modulo-4,294,967,296.

On a point-to-point link, the packets must keep in the same order, and thus acknowledgements may be combined together. So a receiver need not acknowledge each and every frame, but could merely acknowledge, say, frame 2 and then frame 4. The implication of acknowledging frame 4 is that frame 3 has also been received correctly. Similarly, if the last acknowledgement was for frame 5, then acknowlediing frame 2 implies (modulo-8) that frames 6, 7, 0, and 1 are also being acknowledged. Thus, the frames are transmitted in order from the sender, and the receiver from time to time sends back an acknowledgement of the last frame it received correctly.

More specifically, it is usual for the sender to keep a variable called the *send state variable*—N_s, and the receiver to keep a *receive state variable*—V_r. Both of these variables—or states—are initialised to zero by the connection process just as, with our labelling scheme, the two ends agreed to start using the label A. As each frame is transmitted, it is labelled with N_s. At the receiver, V_r is compared with each incoming frame that is received safely without checksum error. If the label is the same, then the frame is accepted and V_r is incremented modularwise. If not, then a frame has been lost and some recovery action will be taken.

The receiver emits acknowledgements by sending a message back to the sender from time to time saying *"I am next expecting frame numbered V_r"*. The receipt of such a message acknowledges all frames with numbers less than V_r, and allows them to be released. Note here that a possible ambiguity must be resolved. For example, with modulus 8, $n + 8 = n$. The implication of this is that the window size used on a link must always be less than the modulus, since if this is not the case, then the acknowledgement message becomes ambiguous. As an illustration of the case which many beginners get wrong, consider (moduluo-8) that eight frames numbered 0 through 7 have been sent—that is 8 outstanding frames. If a message comes back saying *"My next expected frame number is 0"* then what does this mean? Does it mean *"I've received all 8 and I'm expecting more starting again with frame numbered 0 (again)"* or does it mean *"I didn't get any at all, and I want you to retransmit the first packet, numbered 0, followed by the rest"*? Only by allowing at most *modulus* -1 (here 7) frames outstanding can this ambiguity be removed.

How then does this window protocol recover from transmission errors? There are two mechanisms. The retransmission method that we described with our alternating label protocol still applies, but there is a new mechanism that relies on detecting a gap in the sequence numbers. When the receiver detects a checksum error, then the packet in error is discarded, and no further action is taken. When a data packet arrives with a valid checksum, its sequence number is compared with the expected number, V_r. If the two are the same then the frame is accepted, otherwise it is assumed that an intermediate frame has been lost. In this case the receiver discards the data in the frame (though the control information is still valid and can be used) and requests the sender to retransmit the missing packet of data. This request is made by sending a reject packet with the expected number: REJ, V_r. This has the dual function of acknowledging packets up to $V_r - 1$, and requesting the sender to back up and retransmit packets starting with that numbered V_r.

We can see that if errors are mostly single isolated errors (that is affecting one packet only, there may be multiple bit errors), and if corrupted and thus discarded packets are followed by further data packets, then this mechanism will detect and attempt to recover most errors by requesting the retransmission.

However, there is a subtlety that we omitted. (Let us use modulo-4 numbers for the sake of a briefer illustration.) Suppose that the transmitter has had frame 2 acknowledged, and it then sends frames 3, 0, 1. During transmission, an error causes frame 3 to be discarded, and then the correct (checksum OK but invalid sequence number) receipt of frame number 0 causes a REJ,3 to be sent. When it gets this frame, the transmitter will back up and retransmit all three frames 3, 0, 1 again. However, after the REJ, 3 in response to frame 0, the receiver will see the original frame 1, also with a sequence error. It will thus send another REJ, 3, thus causing the receiver to get two REJ,3 messages for the same error, and is likely to (re)transmit 3, 0, 1, 3, 0, 1 in quick succession.

Clearly, there have been some redundant retransmissions. Even worse than this we are in danger of entering a continuous false sequencing error loop causing the link either to lock up or to perform very badly. The way out of this is to introduce another rule *"Only one retransmitting event may take place at once"*. In other words, once a receiver has sent a reject to cause a retransmission, no further rejects may be sent until the next packet in sequence has arrived and cleared the rejecting state.

While the reject mechanism can be expected to recover most individual errors, it cannot handle some other types of error. One of these types of error is when a transmission error causes the frame to be discarded, but the frame is not followed by another. When this happens no further frame arrives whose sequence number may be compared with V_r, and thus the reject mechanism cannot be activated. The other type of error that the reject mechanism fails to handle is caused by the restriction that we needed to make of only one outstanding reject event at once. This means that if the REJ message itself is lost, or the retransmitted packet is itself corrupted, then the reject mechanism will lock up.

The solution to both of these problems is to fall back on the timeout and retransmit on the part of the transmitter whenever a transmitted frame remains unacknowledged for some time. Clearly, this is the same mechanism that we used with the simple alternating label scheme, A, B, A, ... The same considerations apply to the choice of the retransmission timer—that it should be big enough that all chance of delayed acknowledgements still arriving has passed and retransmission is the only recourse left. The mechanism also meshes in with the reject mechanism in that the eventual successful retransmission of an outstanding rejected packet will clear the reject condition and re-enable the reject mechanism.

Thus, we see that HDLC has two reject mechanisms. The sequencing check and reject response should allow the rapid recovery of most errors, and the timeout and retransmission mechanism is a slower but more comprehensive fallback mechanism for the more complex failures.

> **Exercise 2.22** Why are there two reject mechanisms, and not just one?

2.23 Querying the Send State Variable

HDLC allows a variation on the timeout and resend method of error recovery. Either end of an HDLC link can request from the other the value of its send state variable. In effect, this is saying *"tell me the next frame number you expect from me"*. A request of this kind can be used to find out whether and frames that are unacknowledged have actually been received safely and are merely unacknowledged (or the acknowledgement packet has been lost), or have truly been lost and need retransmission. When one end gets such a request from the other end it must reply immediately. Of course, such a request, and its response are subject to loss just like any other packets. Only one such request must be outstanding at one time. The sender can repeat the request, but only after either a successful response to the last request, or the expiration of a suitable timer. If the response indicates that data packets have been lost, then the sender can retransmit them.

> **Exercise 2.23** What are the advantages and drawbacks of on the one hand timing out and resending the unacknowledged blocks directly, and on the other hand first requesting the other end's V_r to see whether the resend is necessary?

2.24 Remote Procedure Calls

There is another way of looking at the simple error recovery protocol that we have just devised. This is as one form of *Remote Procedure Call*—RPC. An RPC is just the same as a normal procedure call except that the action does not take place "locally"—the parameters are exported to a remote location, the procedure is executed there, and the results are returned.

For example, suppose a process can write a record into a local file (ie no networking is involved) by calling a procedure $Write(Buffer)$. To write a series of records, the process might execute the piece of pseudo-code:

```
do i := 1 to n
    Write(Buffer[i]);
end do;
```

With a remote file we must use a remote procedure call. The write procedure is elaborated somewhat to include the label (A, B) and a result indicating a success or failure of the attempt. The write causes the emission of the data buffer together with its label, and the procedure then waits for the response. The procedure returns with a result of "success" if an ACK is received, or with "failure" if a NAK comes back, or the timer expires with no response. Thus the write procedure looks something like:

```
procedure Remote_Write(Buffer, Label, Result);
begin
    Output_Data_To_Line(Buffer, Label);
    Await_Reply_Or_Timeout();
end;
```

and the piece of program to use it looks something like

```
do i := 1 to n
    cycle
        Remote_Write(Buffer[i], Label, Result);
    until Result = Success;
    end cycle;
end do;
```

Thus, with RPC we export the parameters, and wait for a positive acknowledgement. We keep on trying until we eventually succeed. The algorithm in the server side is:

```
cycle
    Wait_For_Incoming_Packet();
    if CRC_Is_OK()
    then
        if Incoming_Label = Expected_Label
        then
            Put_Record_Into_File();
        end if;
        Respond(ACK);
    else
        Respond(NAK);
    end if;
```

end cycle;

We have described one of the intermediate versions of the protocol that we derived above, but from a different conceptual viewpoint. The advantage of the RPC-type of protocols is that they are simpler to understand and to implement. However, we shall see that they are a subset of the range of possible protocols. Most of the non-RPC protocols are significantly more complicated both to understand and to implement, but there are sometimes compelling reasons to use the more complicated protocols.

2.25   Forward or Reverse Error Correction?

In this chapter we have looked at both forward and reverse error correction. In forward error correction we add enough extra redundancy so that we are able to correct all the likely errors in the data. In reverse error correction, we add enough redundancy so that we are able to detect all the likely errors in the data, and then we use recovery procedures to cause the correct packet to be re-sent. Under what circumstances should we use one approach or the other?

The advantage of reverse error recovery over forward error correction is primarily that the CRC codes provide an extremely powerful method of detecting errors with the minimum of overhead. Remember the arguments concerning Hamming Distance and the extra bits required for correction compared with detection. When an error is detected, then a whole packet has to be retransmitted. However, provided that the error rate is reasonably small, then the traffic due to the retransmission is small and the impact on the throughput of the link is modest. For forward error correction a much larger amount of redundancy has to be added to correct for the same set of likely errors, and this has to be added to every packet. The result is that the extra checking information has a larger impact on the throughput of the link than the occasional retransmissions incurred for reverse error correction.

The problem with reverse error correction is usually that on the occasions when an error does have to be repaired, there is at least a round trip delay, and if the timeout part of the recovery protocol is activated there is a delay of many round trip times. For many applications this does not matter. As long as most packets are delivered quickly, the odd exceptional delay during error recovery can be tolerated, and for short links up to a few kilometres, the round trip time is likely to be very short anyway. However there are some exceptions to this. Some applications are very time critical and cannot tolerate such delays, even occasionally. In addition, some links, especially via satellites, have exceptionally long round trip times of about 0.24 second. In these cases it may well be advantageous to put up with the extra overhead of an error correcting code so that errors may be corrected without incurring the delay in resending the packet.

Perhaps the most extreme example of round trip delay is when data is transmitted from a deep space probe. In this case the delay may be hours, and it is normal to rely entirely on highly redundant error correcting codes not only because of the very long round trip delay, but also because the retransmission may not be possible anyway.

2.26   Acceptable Error in an Imperfect World

We have examined various ways of detecting errors and recovering from them by both forward and reverse correction. To a first approximation it is usual to think of a raw communications medium as error prone, and to think of the data stream after error correction as being error free. While this simplification is sufficient in many cases, it is important to remember that it is only a simplification. As always, the real world is more complex.

At the one extreme there are some applications whose absolute accuracy is not of the ultimate importance. For example, digitised voice can withstand the odd crackle—perhaps fortunately for telephone users. In any case, with digitised voice it is more important to deliver a section of speech even with crackle than to delay delivery while a good packet is retransmitted. Timeliness is more important than the absolute in accuracy. Digitised, raster scan pictures will not usually be useless if one pixel is out of place. The text of computer mail can withstand occasional errors, and my typing accuracy when entering the first draft of this book was considerably lower than many communications lines. Thus we can see there is a large class of applications where a substantial error rate can be tolerated. Most of these applications could run over many raw communications media without error detection or correction.

In the middle comes a large class of applications where errors in just one bit can cause the complete collapse of an application. For example, if we transfer the source text of a computer program, the corruption of just one character is likely to invalidate the whole program. An error in the control data for a numerical milling machine might cause the piece to be chopped in half. An error in the coordinates for a graph plotter can start the pen off on a trip to Mars—or at least to the edge of the paper in that direction. In these applications it is quite normal to apply full error detection and correction procedures. The assumption here is that the raw error rate of the communications line is too high. This may or may not actually be true. The raw error rate of a telephone line is extremely varied in practice, and is decreasing rapidly with the introduction of new telephone technology. The practical rate may be once every few minutes or once in a week, and a dedicated private line may be much better than this. This is probably more than adequate for plotting graphs, but whether it is adequate for a milling machine depends on the value of the piece.

At the other extreme come the applications that have very demanding requirements on accuracy. As someone once remarked when listening to a nuclear reactor engineer's somewhat nonchalant attitude to computer reliability *"If a sugar cube factory hiccoughs and gives birth to a sugar cube a metre along the edges, who really cares? But if a nuclear reactor hiccoughs and pulls out the control rods rather than dropping them in, who's left to care?"* Even with the error detecting power of the checksum, there is still a possibility of a residual transmission error, and in Chapter 12 we shall see how other types of system error can creep in.

In the novel *"Mother Night"* Kurt Vonnegut describes the minds of some of his madder characters as being like a machine with the odd missing cog—mostly the mechanism works flawlessly, but now and again a missing cog causes a frightening disorientation. This analogy certainly describes the activity of some computer systems when fed with faulty data.

When the consequences of an error are not merely serious, but potentially catastrophic, then the likelihood of such an error must be reduced to an extremely low rate. Note however, that the word is "reduce" not "eliminate". No precaution, however extreme, can eliminate *all* possibility of error. All we can do is to take more and more precautions to reduce the probability to some level that is perceived to be sufficient. If two computer systems are pointing guns at each other and each is programmed to fire second, then eventually and inevitably—given enough time—one will mistakenly think that the other fired first and shoot back in error. The likely delay, depending on the setup, may be days, years, or many times the age of the Universe, but it cannot be infinity.

The whole point of this little sermon is that error detection and recovery procedures are used to reduce the error rate of a channel to an "acceptable" level depending on complex tradeoffs between cost and the needs of the application. The level need not be the same for everyone, and is rarely properly quantified. The only people properly qualified to assess the level are the users, as they are the only ones who can properly evaluate the consequences of a given error rate on their application.

This last point leads to a final philosophical consideration. In engineering a communications medium it is normal to reduce the error rate of the raw medium by using some form of error detection and recovery. With its overhead, such a reduction in error rate reduces the available bandwidth of the channel. This bandwidth is being traded for a reduced error rate. However, given such an "improved" channel, an application may find that the error rate is much lower than it needs, and that the bandwidth that it could have used for other more productive purposes has been "spent" unnecessarily. The application cannot trade in the reduced error rate for increased bandwidth. This is an argument for giving the application the maximum possible "unimproved" bandwidth, since it can always trade in some bandwidth for a reduced error rate if it so wishes. An alternative, that has the same effect is to let the application choose the error rate versus bandwidth tradeoff that it wishes to make. While some transport services have a *quality of service* parameter that is meant to allow this type of choice, the underlying facilities to support this properly are much less common.

2.27   Summary

This chapter has looked at various ways in which transmission errors may be detected and corrected. Either forward or reverse error correction is possible, but we have seen that reverse correction is more common. The bulk of this chapter has been concerned with the techniques for detecting such errors by adding a specific kind of redundancy—the CRC—and with the design of a suitable protocol for recovering from the errors so detected. We shall meet elements of this recovery protocol several more times in later chapters.

3
Shared Media

This chapter deals with the various forms of shared media. Shared media are very common in networking, particularly in local networks, though much of the basic theoretical work for contention access was done for sharing a radio or satellite channel. This chapter covers the two main types of shared topology—the bus and the ring—and the two main kinds of medium access control—by contention and by token—and shows how these two principles are orthogonal. The principles of most forms of sharing a single medium are covered in this chapter. Sharing a medium is mostly about access control. The buzzphrase for this is *Medium Access Control* and this layer of networking is referred to as the *MAC-layer*.

3.1   Why Share a Medium?

We have seen in the previous chapters how data can be transmitted across a link between two machines as in Fig 3.1(a). As a network becomes more complex, in Figs 3.1(b) and (c), we can see that the web of wires and interfaces becomes rapidly more complex. For full interconnection of n machines the number of wires required is $n \times (n-1)/2$, and the number of interfaces is twice that, each machine needing $n-1$ interfaces. This number rapidly gets out of hand, even for small numbers of machines. Such a rat's nest of wire and sheer number of interfaces is quite impractical. Fortunately, it is also quite unnecessary too.

Fig 3.1(d) shows the same set of machines as Fig 3.1(b). However, there are many less links in the network. In contrast to Fig 3.1(c), communication between any two machines may take a varying number of "hops" from a minimum of one hop (eg from A to C) up to a maximum of three hops (eg from D to E via C and B). Any machine may still communicate with any other, but sometimes the communication involves some of the intermediate machines, B and C, that switch data for their neighbours.

We shall study networks of this type in Chapter 5. The main subject of the present chapter is the study of an alternative way of joining a set of machines together by sharing a single medium.

Fig 3.1(e) shows another way of joining the same set of five machines together. The diagram shows a generalised "shared medium". The immediately obvious characteristic of such an arrangement is that each machine has a single interface to the shared medium. This is inde-

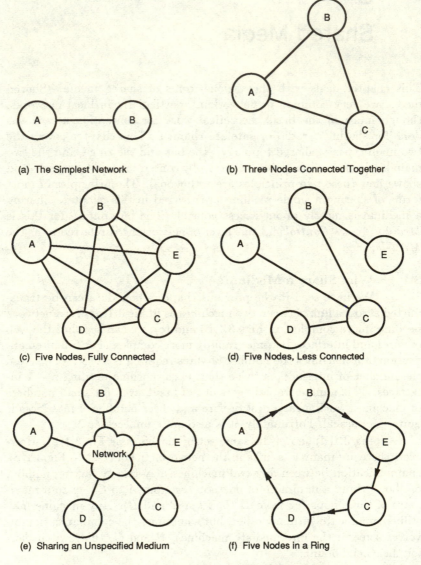

(a) The Simplest Network

(b) Three Nodes Connected Together

(c) Five Nodes, Fully Connected

(d) Five Nodes, Less Connected

(e) Sharing an Unspecified Medium

(f) Five Nodes in a Ring

Fig 3.1.   Various Network Configurations

pendent of the number of machines attached to such a shared medium. Any node may talk to any other, and no node needs to switch or handle the traffic for other nodes with which it is not communicating directly.

Clearly, sharing a medium in this way has many desirable attributes, and we shall now proceed to study in some depth various ways of sharing a medium amongst a set of machines.

How, then, can we share the medium? There are several ways of classifying the methods. We shall classify according to the way in which a machine gains access to the medium, and use the loose headings of *Time* and *Frequency Division Multiplexing*, (TDM and FDM), *Contention*, and *Token*. However, we shall also see that the division is not always quite so straightforward as one might at first expect.

3.2   Time and Frequency Division Multiplexing

There are two "traditional" ways of sharing a channel among several users that are both very widely used, especially in the telephone world. These are called *Time Division Multiplexing*—TDM and *Frequency Division Multiplexing*—FDM.

Fig 3.2 shows an abstract representation of TDM. Here we see a set of stations S_1 to S_n on the left hand side, the shared medium in the middle, and a set of receivers R_1 to R_n on the right. There are two notional commutators, one at each end. These are ganged together so that the commutators scan together round their sets of communicating stations. Two rotary switches with the appropriate connections would make a simple if crude time division multiplexing system. As the commutators scan round connecting pairs of stations S_n and R_n together, the current pair gets a short time during which they can communicate. With our ganged switches, we could imagine 10 stations on one switch being connected to 10 receivers at the other switch, and the switch moving one click per second, giving each pair of stations 1 second in every 10.

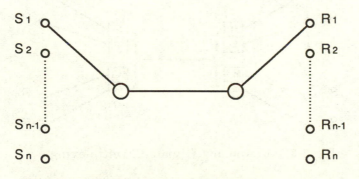

Fig 3.2.   Time Division Multiplexing

A modern implementation of TDM is unlikely to use a real mechanical arm as the commutator. One way of implementing the notional commutator is to structure each scan of the commutator as the sending of a single data packet. In the packet will be a sample of one bit from

each of the sources. For example we might wish to multiplex a number
of 1200-bps channels down one 64,000-bps channel. We could choose
to group 50 1200-bps channels together, and then every 1/1200th of a
second we could sample all 50 channels to construct a 50-bit packet.
On the 64,000-bps channel we have 53.33 bit times for each bit on the
1200-bps channels, which leaves us barely room to mark the beginning
and end of the 50-bit packet on the 64,000-bps channel. This packet is
then sent down the line where the corresponding commutator breaks it
up and distributes the bits, one per 1200-bps channel.

Fig 3.3 illustrates FDM. The basis of FDM is that a data signal
can be sent not just in the base band, using channel frequencies from
0 up to the highest frequency level, but by using any similar "band"
of frequencies as we saw briefly in Chapter 2. The usual device for
achieving this is a modem, and we saw in Chapter 2 how a modem
might be used to transmit a $9600bps$ signal down a $3000Hz$ voice grade
line. If we have a channel that is capable of carrying a much greater
bandwidth, say $100KHz$, then it is possible to take 25 such channels, shift
the frequency of each one, and fit them into the available bandwidth.
For example, channel 1 would carry 0 to $3KHz$ (unshifted), channel 2
would occupy 4 to $7KHz$ (Shifted by $4KHz$ and leaving a gap of $1KHz$),
channel 3 would occupy 8 to $11KHz$, etc. At the receiving end, a battery
of "unshifters" would produce the original 0 to $3KHz$ signals. Such is
the common technique of FDM that has been used for many years to
multiplex telephone voice grade channels onto high grade trunk lines.

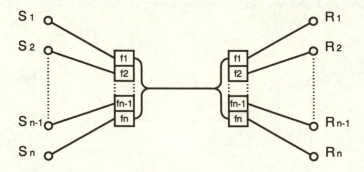

Fig 3.3.   Frequency Division Multiplexing

Of course, people using telephone lines can only generate and
hear frequencies on the normal auditory range and thus frequency shifting is needed to move the signals to the appropriate channel for FDM.
Modem technology is not always limited in this way. Many modems
are in fact made to work only on voice grade telephone lines. The
multiplexing onto high grade trunk lines is done by the normal tele-

phone techniques of shifting the frequency band at each end as we described above. However, modems can be made to generate the shifted frequency band directly. Such modems are often termed "frequency-agile modems", because they can agilely be switched from one working frequency to another. Using sets of such frequency-agile modems we could implement the FDM channel of Fig 3.3. For example, the pair of modems communicating using channel 3 could be set up to communicate using the frequency band 8 to $11KHz$ directly. This eliminates the frequency shifting step in Fig 3.3. Perhaps more importantly, it enables the FDM function to be distributed.

Implicit in Fig 3.3 is the physical grouping of the frequency shifting function at the two ends of a point-to-point wire. With frequency agile modems we have the ability distribute this FDM function. This is exploited to great effect when using *Cable TV*—CTV technology. Large networks, up to the size of a town, can be constructed using the highly developed CTV technology. This has a huge raw bandwidth. For data communication purposes, this bandwidth can be split up into many FDM channels using pairs (or larger sets) of frequency agile modems sharing the same channel. The modems need not be grouped together, but can be distributed across the cable in the places where they are needed. Though we shall later criticise the efficiency of FDM in terms of wasted bandwidth for bursty channels, a CTV cable has such huge bandwidth that wasting some of it may not be important in some circumstances.

Of course one of the most familiar versions of FDM is the everyday broadcast of radio and TV signals.

To a first order approximation both TDM and FDM give the user a very similar service. They both allow a large bandwidth channel to be shared by several channels with smaller requirements. There are many boxes on the market that provide just this service, and they are popular for exactly the reason that it is often cheaper to buy bandwidth in bulk and then to split it down into the chunks that are required, than it is to buy the smaller channels individually.

Of course, the user must need the smaller channels in the right configuration so that the TDM or FDM technique can be used, and we have seen briefly how FDM is perhaps more flexible here, at least in the context of cable networks and frequency agile modems.

Both TDM and FDM split the available channel into n subchannels, each getting approximately $1/n^{th}$ of the raw bandwidth (ignoring the small wastage in separating the channels). The primary objection to this is that the division is static. Many uses of such channels, particularly data channels, are bursty in nature. The subchannels must then be allocated so that they can supply sufficient bandwidth in the busiest periods, with the result that much bandwidth is wasted most of the time when the traffic is much lower or even zero. Silence may be golden, but it is just as expensive on the telephone as full-duplex gossip. The rest of the techniques described in this chapter have two main aims. One aim is the dynamic sharing of bandwidth between multiple users. This is based on the same principle as traditional computer time sharing, that by evening out the bursty, and uncorrelated demands of users, a more efficient system can result. The second aim is to remove the geographical constraints of TDM, and to a lesser extent, FDM. Thus the medium will reach the physical locations of the people wishing to communicate, and the stations will be able to communicate freely with each other as they need to, rather than being constrained by the underlying technology.

3.3   Contention Access

Contention sharing of a medium is really a very familiar method in everyday life. When a group of people occupy a small room, and several of them wish to talk to others, then what sometimes happens is that a person, A, wishing to speak just goes ahead and speaks. Often, this attempt to speak is successful, and the statement is made by the speaker, and heard by the recipient, B. The next message may be from the recipient, B, back to A, or may be from any other person C to person D.

It can sometimes happen that two people, A and B, both start speaking at the same time, and thus each interferes with the speach of the other. What might happen then is that both speakers stop talking, and then have another try a few moments later. In such cases, usually one of the two speakers restarts first, and is not re-interrupted by the other one.

One further rule often (well, sometimes) observed is that whenever a person hears another person speaking, he desists from starting to speak until the other's speech has stopped.

Of course, this is a simplistic view of what actually happens in a room full of people wishing to converse. In reality, people use eye contact, interrupt each other, shout, or use that remarkable human ability to filter out the one voice that is of interest from the babble of the others. However, our simple model is a reasonable approximation to the way in which a contention access protocol works. The important part is that the people (machines) that wish to talk (send messages), do so in a fairly unstructured way. They compete for the use of the medium. There is a likelihood that messages will "collide" sometimes, and when this happens there are methods to detect that sort of error and to recover from it. There may be additional rules or ways in which the likelihood of messages colliding can be reduced, such as waiting for a quiet period before trying to get a word in edgeways. Methods of this general type are called "contention" methods for the contentious way in which access to the medium is gained.

The simplest form of contention access is usually referred to as *Simple Aloha*. The term "Aloha" is used because the method was originally used on the Aloha Network in the early 1970s. On the Aloha Network, a group of stations shared a single radio channel to provide access for terminals distributed across the Hawaiian Islands to a central computer.

When a terminal attached to a station has a line of input ready it transmitted it in a packet on the radio channel. If there was no other transmission from another station that overlapped with its transmission then the packet was likely to get through (ignoring the effect of static or other interference). However, if another station also transmitted a packet in such a fashion that it overlapped in time, even by as little as one bit, then both packets were totally destroyed. The packets are said to have "collided". When this happened, both stations would wait for a randomised time and then retransmit. The hope was that the retransmissions would eventually succeed in missing each other.

On the Aloha Network, each interactive terminal was attached to a minicomputer, and this controlled the access to the shared radio channel. All of the stations communicated with a central controller, the *Menehune*. The Menehune controlled the communication with the central host, and some other services, and also communicated back with the other stations on the radio network. Two separate radio channels were used. One channel was shared by all the stations sending into the central Menehune (the *in-* or *up-*channel), and the other was used by the Menehune to broadcast to all the other stations (the *out-* or *down-*channel). Since only the Menehune transmits on the down-channel, there is no contention on this channel. The interesting channel is the up-channel which all stations share and compete for.

The term *Aloha Access Method* has come to be generally applied to any method in which access to a shared medium is made in this random contention fashion. The essential character is that the packets are sent "blind" without first "looking" at or "listening" to the medium in order to take avoiding action. Collisions are detected by listening to the broadcast channel. The Menehune will broadcast an acknowledgement. If such an acknowledgement fails to arrive then a collision has occurred (or, just possibly, the packet has been lost for other reasons), and recovery will be attempted. Recovery is done by delaying for a randomised time and then trying again.

The Aloha access method is particularly appropriate for a satellite channel, and a large number of theoretical studies of satellite channels controlled by variations on the Aloha access method were published in the 1970s. We shall see below that the efficiency of the access to a shared radio channel can be greatly improved by first listening to the channel to see whether another packet is in the process of transmission. However, with a satellite channel this procedure is not possible because of the long round-trip delay up to the satellite and back down again.

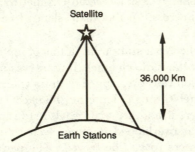

Fig 3.4.   Earth Communication via Satellites

Satellites used for communication are usually in geosynchronous orbit. The use of geosynchronous orbit was first suggested in 1945 by Arthur C. Clarke who is now better known in science fiction circles. Satellites in low orbits travel around the Earth in about 90 minutes. Using such a low and fast moving satellite is a substantial problem in interception—somewhat reminiscent of picking up an invading warplane with a searchlight. Clarke observed that all satellites obey Kepler's laws of motion, and in particular that the period of revolution is proportional to the radius of the orbit to the power $3/2$. Thus, by choosing a large enough radius the orbital period can be increased to match the rotation time of the Earth. A satellite in equitorial orbit at an altitude of 36,000 km will appear to stand still in the sky. More importantly, once a directional radio aerial has been pointed at the satellite, then it need not be moved again, unlike the sophisticated and expensive steerable aerials that were needed for the first low orbit satellites. As a bonus the high orbit means that the "footprint" of the satellite—that area of the Earth's surface in direct line of sight—is very large.

Such communication satellites are used regularly for long haul point-to-point circuits. Many readers will have used them for long distance telephone conversations and been mildly disturbed by the long delay introduced into the conversation, and few readers will not have seen live international TV pictures "beamed via satellite". We are interested in sharing a broadcast satellite channel amongst several computers at a scattered set of ground stations. The usual arrangement is that, just as on the original Aloha radio network, many users share an "up" channel to the satellite, and the satellite broadcasts down to all ground stations on another channel. The satellite has replaced the Menehune. However, the replacement is not exact. The Menehune is an active part of the Aloha network, and broadcasts explicit acknowledgements of incoming data. On the other hand, the satellite is little more than a mirror in the sky. It takes the bits it receives on the up-channel and retransmits them on the down-channel. It does not check the packets for validity. That is the responsibility of the transmitting ground station. It must listen to the "reflected" signal and check its own transmitted packet.

The parameters of the system are important—or, more precisely, their relative values are. With an altitude of 36,000 km, the round trip delay is about 0.24 seconds. If a channel rate of 24,000 bits per second is used, and packets are the original fixed length of 888 bits, then each packet takes 0.037 seconds to transmit. Put another way, if a station transmits packets end-to-end up to the satellite, then by the time the first bit of the first packet arrives back down on the broadcast channel, the station will be part way through transmitting packet seven. The circuit is about 6.5 packets "long". Clearly, it is no use first listening to the down-channel to see if anyone else is transmitting a packet—the information is far too far out of date. Note, the important fact is not the absolute values of the physical parameters, but that the round trip time is several times the transmission time for one packet. The same ratio could be achieved for any values of the path length and packet length if the bit rate is suitably chosen, and vice versa. In addition, the curvature of the Earth means that a transmitting station can't first listen to the up-channel either.

3.4   Throughput

Let us examine the throughput of the Aloha channel. Most studies of the Aloha channel have assumed packets of a fixed length. This fixed length has an associated transmission time, that is usually referred to in Aloha circles as the *slot-time* for reasons that will presently become clear. It is usual to measure the traffic in the normalised terms of packets per slot. Let us denote the successful (average) traffic by S, and the total traffic (successful, plus all the colliding packets) by G. Clearly, we can successfully send at most one packet per slot, and so the maximum value of S is 1. Most of the work in this field is aimed at getting S up as near as possible to 1. When collisions occur more than one packet will have been sent in a slot, and thus the total offered traffic, G, is unbounded.

Subjectively, we would expect that when the total traffic, G, is low ($G \ll 1$) there should be few collisions, and thus $S \simeq G$. Conversely, when the traffic is very high ($G \gg 1$) then there will be many collisions, and most of the traffic will be retransmissions ($S \ll 1 \ll G$).

To develop a more specific model, let us assume a large population of users, N of which have packets ready either to send or to re-send. Each of the N ready stations will transmit its packet with probability s per slot-time. The total traffic G is the number of packets transmitted by the N ready stations during one slot:

$$G = Ns \tag{3.1}$$

As a packet arrives at the satellite, there is a danger period during which another packet may be arriving also, and may overlap this packet. The overlap may be very large, or only one bit. Overlap of any amount is always fatal, and leads to complete packet destruction. Looking at Fig 3.5, we see that as packet A arrives at time t, there may already be packet B arriving. If the time is measured in units of slot-time, then any packet whose arrival started after time $t-1$ will interfere. Similarly, any other packet C that starts to arrive while A is still arriving, ie up to time $t+1$, will also cause packet loss. Thus, any other packet arriving during the two slot times from $t-1$ to $t+1$ will corrupt the packet A.

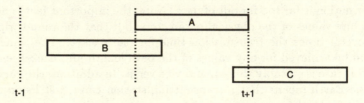

Fig 3.5.   The Collision of Two Aloha Packets

We can now calculate the probability that during one slot-time just one station chooses to transmit and during the critical window of length two slots, no other station chooses to transmit.† The single transmission happens N ways with probability s, and the $N-1$ other stations each desist with probability $1-s$ in each of the two slot times, giving

$$S = (Ns) \times (1-s)^{2(N-1)} \tag{3.2}$$

Now, if we make N large, and s small, but keep the product Ns $(= G)$ to order 1, then we can convert Eqn 3.2 into

$$S = Ge^{-2G} \tag{3.3}$$

---

† We assume that the stations become ready to transmit independently of each other—i.e. that this is a "Poisson process"—see e.g. Mitrani (1987)

Exercise 3.1   Show this

The plot of Eqn 3.3 is shown in Fig 3.6, labelled "Pure Aloha". The maximum value of S in Fig 3.6 is $1/2e \simeq 0.184$ for $G = 0.5$. Clearly this figure seems somewhat modest—a mere 18%. However, this is obtained for a remarkably simple control procedure—if the packet collides, just try again after a randomly varying interval.

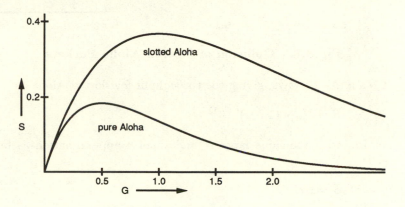

Fig 3.6.   Aloha: Throughput Versus Offered Traffic

It was soon observed that there was a conceptually simple way of increasing the throughput of the channel. This is achieved by dividing time at the satellite receiver into equal periods, each one a packet time long. These are called slots, hence the term *slot time* introduced earlier. The ground stations constrain the start times of the packets so that they will only arrive at the satellite aligned with these slot boundaries. In this way, the partial collisions in Fig 3.5 are converted into either "full" collisions, or absence of collisions. This is illustrated in Fig 3.7 where we see that packets A and B become ready during slot 0. Instead of being transmitted immediately, they are both delayed until the start of slot 1, and transmitted as A' and B'. They arrive together, and completely destroy each other. However, they have both left slot 0 untouched, and thus not corrupted any packet being transmitted there. Packet C becomes ready to transmit during slot 1 and thus misses its start. It is transmitted for the start of slot 2 and suffers no collision. Subjectively, we see that collisions are "concentrated" leaving more "room" for successful single slots.

The effectiveness of slotted operation is seen in our simple mathematical model. The chance of the single transmission is Ns as before, but now the chance of all others desisting for the single slot window is

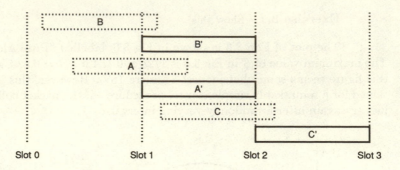

| Slot 0 | Slot 1 | Slot 2 | Slot 3 |

Fig 3.7.   Collision of Slotted Aloha Packets

$1 - s$ in $N - 1$ ways, giving the throughput for slotted Aloha as

$$S = Ns \times (1 - s)^{(N-1)} \tag{3.4}$$

Which, with the same large N and small s approximation as before, gives

$$S = Ge^{-G} \tag{3.5}$$

The plot for "slotted Aloha" is also shown is Fig 3.6. Here the maximum throughput is $1/e \simeq 0.368$ for $G = 1$, twice that of "pure" Aloha.

> **Exercise 3.2**   Assume a satellite in synchronous orbit 36,000 Km above the earth's equator at 75° W. Assume Earth's radius 6000 Km. Assuming the parameters of the original Aloha system (at the end of the last section), calculate the difference in the path length between the satellite and Miami, Florida (25°52′ N, 80°15′ W) and the satellite and Seattle (47°41′ N and 122°15′ W). Express this in terms of slot time.
>
>   Propose a practical method for synchronising Miami and Florida ground stations so that they can transmit on slot boundaries.

We have analysed the Aloha system in terms of throughput S and total channel traffic G. What is perhaps more important from the point of view of a specific station is the time that it must take in transmitting and retransmitting a packet before it gets it through the channel successfully. A measure of this is the ratio of the total number of times the packet is transmitted (successful plus retransmissions) to the successful transmission: G/S. Rearranging Eqn. 3.5, the expected number of (re)transmissions per packet is

$$E = \frac{G}{S} = e^G \tag{3.6}$$

Not surprisingly, E increases exponentially with the total channel traffic.

The blocking time or wait time for access to the channel can be derived from the throughput by assuming that each of the N ready stations gets an equal share of the throughput S. This gives a wait time W, where $W = N/S$.

Now let us look at the stability of the Aloha channel. To get a feel for this we must add a little more detail to the model. The most usual model is the one in which each of the contending stations has a terminal with a human user. The human "thinks" for a randomly distributed time, and then types a line. When the line has been entered, the user's thought process is "blocked" or suspended until the line has been transmitted successfully (and presumably the user gets some sort of response), upon which the user's "thinking" mode resumes. While this is clearly a somewhat unrealistic model of a person, let alone a computer, it has been widely used in theoretical studies and numerical simulations. The most important feature of this model is that as the user's access time increases because of the busyness of the channel, so the traffic that he generates reduces because his "thinking block" increases. Thus, there is a feedback between the traffic in the channel and the offered load. We shall now study the conditions under which this is sufficient to prevent the channel from becoming overloaded.

Assume that for a certain channel, we have a total number of terminals, M, and that the probability of the terminal user's thinking time expiring is p per slot. The number of "blocked" terminals is our previous number N, (sometimes referred to as the "backlog"). Thus we can write the input rate i packets per slot, at which new packets become ready to transmit as:

$$i = (M - N)p \tag{3.7}$$

The plot of this is a straight line, sometimes called the *load line* shown in Fig 3.8. The input rate is Mp when no stations are blocked, and this drops to zero when all M stations are blocked. By definition the system is constrained to operate only along the load line except during transient statistical variations.

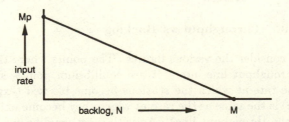

Fig 3.8.   Load Line: Backlog vs Input Rate

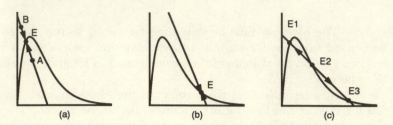

Fig 3.10.   Stability Depending on Offered Traffic

Let us now add the plot of Eqn 3.4. The plot of slotted Aloha in Fig 3.6 shows the throughput, S as a function of G the total traffic, or attempts per slot. Remembering that $G = Ns$, and with the same limit as $N \to \infty$ and $s \to 0$, we get:

$$S = Ge^{-G} = Nse^{-Ns} \tag{3.8}$$

Fig 3.9 shows the plot of throughput S against the backlog for various values of the retransmission parameter s. As we expect, the maximum achievable throughput is about 38% in all cases, but that this occurs at differing values of the backlog, depending on s (derived from the value of $G = 1$ and $G = Ns$). As s decreases, the retransmission time is longer, and the backlog increases. Combining the two curves, we get Fig 3.10 which shows the load line and the achievable throughput together.

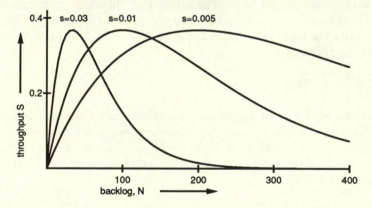

Fig 3.9.   Throughput vs Backlog

Let us consider the various figures. The points where the load line and the throughput line intersect are equilibrium points, since at these points the rate at which the stations become blocked (expressed by the load line) is the same as the rate at which they become unblocked (expressed by the throughput line). As with most equilibrium points, the interesting question is are they stable?

Consider a point A on the load line as shown in Fig 3.10(a). Here, the rate at which stations are becoming blocked (the load line value), is less than the throughput achievable for that backlog (shown by the throughput curve). Thus we can expect that the net result is that the backlog will reduce. If the backlog reduces, the system's operating point moves along the load line with reducing backlog, and increasing input rate until the equilibrium point E is reached. This is shown by the direction of the arrow on the load line.

On the other hand, at point B, the rate at which stations become blocked exceeds the throughput. The backlog will increase, and the feedback through the blocking mechanism will move the operating point back towards E.

By this analysis we see that the point E is a stable operating point of the system. Small statistical variations that push the system away from E will be counteracted by the inherent stability of the system.

Note the properties of this equilibrium point. The backlog is small (and thus also the access time), and the throughput is only slightly below the theoretical maximum.

Now apply the same arguments to the equilibrium point in Fig 3.10(b). Again we see that the point is stable. However, it is clearly much less desirable, since the throughput is small and the backlog (and thus access time) are both large. Much of the channel capacity is spent in the unproductive process of corrupting and retransmitting packets.

The case in Fig 3.10(c) is more complex. Here we see that we have three equilibrium points, $E1$, $E2$, and $E3$. Applying our analysis, we see that the points on the load line with backlog greater than $N2$ will tend to move towards $E3$, while those with backlog less than $N2$ will tend to move towards $E1$. Thus we have two stable equilibria, $E1$ and $E3$, and these are desirable or not as the similar equilibria in cases (a) and (b) are or are not themselves desirable. The other equilibrium point $E2$ is unstable in the sense that the smallest disturbance will result in the operating point then moving further and further in that direction along the load line until it reaches either point $E1$ or $E3$. Equilibrium at point $E2$ is just as unstable as a pencil stood on its point.

How will such a system work in practice? Clearly we would like it to operate around point $E1$, and indeed, since $E1$ is stable, there is some hope that we might be able to continue in this fashion. However, the problem is that all such systems are statistical, and all statistical systems suffer fluctuations in load. Such fluctuations in load are compensated in situations (a) and (b) by the basic stability of the system. Thus statistical fluctuations may push the operating point anywhere along the load line. However, the operating point will then tend always to move back to the stable equilibrium point. However, in (c), once the statistical fluctuations drive the operating point beyond $E2$ it progresses inexorably towards $E3$, the stable overload position. Thus the system will flip mode "spontaneously" from $E1$ to $E3$, and stay in this new locally stable mode. Clearly there is a theoretical possibility that further statistical fluctuations will flip the mode back again. However, if the mode flips from $E1$ to $E3$ once per hour, and stays there for an hour, then the behaviour is hardly acceptable.

How, besides faulty design, might we operate with a situation other than (a)? Remember that the load lines have two main parameters; M the total population of users, and p, a measure of the traffic producing potential of a single terminal. The load lines in Fig 3.10 are all drawn with the same characteristic user at a terminal (i.e. p-value), but with different total populations, M. Situation (c) may have twice the total population of situation (a). Thus economic considerations—sharing the cost of the channel among more users—may drive us towards a bistable system as in (c).

Such a situation is not always a disaster. Kleinrock and Lamb have made calculations for realistic channels. One such channel will support about 110 users in the monostable equilibrium mode (a). However, it will support twice that number in the bistable mode (c). They have also estimated that the specific system would operate around the desirable point $E1$ for about two days on average before flipping into mode $E3$. If manual intervention, e.g. restarting the channel every other day, is acceptable, then a considerable financial advantage can be gained. Mitrani (1987) gives an alternative analysis of the same phenomenon.

However, there are other ways to stabilise such a system. Looking at Fig 3.9, we see that by changing s, the traffic generated by a station, we can move the the throughput curve out. Thus we can see that each of the stations could monitor the parameters of the channel and in particular, they could measure the rate at which packets are corrupted. This in turn gives a measure of the throughput of the channel. The system could operate normally with large s, and then switch to a smaller s when the onset of overload was detected. Note that this is in effect a voluntary reduction of the load offered by the stations.

An alternative is that a station could alter the parameters of the load line at the onset of overload. Thus, by decreasing p, the arrival rate, the load line could be hinged down around M until the overload had dissipated.

Note that decreasing p is shedding load by stations directly (in that stations throttle their data generation themselves), while decreasing s is shedding load indirectly (in that more stations become blocked and thus stop "thinking"). The two methods are much the same in effect in that overload is avoided by (temporarily) throttling back the offered traffic. We shall meet this concept of throttling back the offered traffic again when we look at the Ethernet.

3.5 Other Aloha Disciplines

Many variations of the basic Aloha scheme have been proposed. The main aim of such schemes is usually to increase the maximum throughput. One such scheme is a combination of TDM and slotted Aloha. Each of the M stations is allocated every M^{th} slot, and all stations keep track of all M slots each time they come round. If the channel is very busy with all M stations using their own slot in the M-slot cycle then the channel is operating as a pure TDM channel. Each station can be thought of as using a subchannel. For example, station 42 would use slot 42 of cycle 1, slot 42 of cycle 2, and so on. The throughput is close to 100% with no collisions. The channel can be thought of as divided up into M subchannels, each subchannel consisting of a series of slots, one from each cycle of M slots. However, if one station falls idle and fails to use its slot on a cycle, then the corresponding slot becomes available for contention on the next cycle. Any other station with more data than can be handled using its own subchannel can see that this subchannel has become idle, and can attempt to seize it by transmitting in the next slot. If there is no collision, then that station has seized the subchannel, and can continue to use it. However, if there is a collision, then all stations other than the normal owner of that subchannel must desist from using that subchannel until they see it idle again. In this way, we see that the normal owner can regain control of its own subchannel with only one lost slot. Other stations can seize the subchannel, but the contention process, if two of them are trying, is a somewhat longer process because of the necessity of giving the normal owner the priority. Perhaps "borrowing" a subchannel is a better term than "seizing".

Note that channel access time would be large if every station waits for its own slot every time. This is acceptable if the channel is heavily loaded, but objectionable under lightly loaded circumstances, where pure Aloha gives the shortest access time. Thus some channels work in a hybrid mode, switching from pure Aloha to this reservation Aloha mode when a given traffic threshold has been reached.

Observe the tradeoff between complexity and the efficiency of use of the channel. It is not always better to use the most sophisticated protocols. Imagine, for example, that one wishes to design a channel serving 2400 stations, of which a maximum of 600 would be simultaneously active, each generating a 1000-bit packet every minute. One might choose to build a reservation Aloha system running on a 10kbps channel at near 100% throughput. Alternatively, a much simpler pure Aloha channel could handle the same traffic if the channel is 100kbps.

Although this might "waste" 90% of the raw channel capacity, it is quite possible that the cost of extra bandwidth might be saved by the much simpler control and lack of need for synchronisation at each of the 2400 ground stations and the absence of any need to allocate the 600 in the active subset to one of the subchannels. The price of efficiency can sometimes be too high.

Several other variations on the basic method of driving the Aloha channel have also been proposed.

3.6   Aloha Models

In our analysis of the Aloha scheme. we have assumed a large population of stations and made some rather simplistic assumptions about the behaviour of the users of those stations. Much work has been done on sophisticated Markov models (see, e.g. Mitrani, 1987). Even with such models, it is often still necessary either to make drastic simplifications or to resort to simulation, or both. However, though the detailed numerical results differ, the results are generally similar. Whilst the reader who needs a deeper understanding of Aloha channels should certainly study these works, he should treat the numerical results of such Procrustean models with some care. All models of a real system can be criticised in some measure, and our aim is a functional understanding of the system rather than a detailed quantitative model which will of necessity be much more complex and beyond the scope of this book.

3.7   Aloha Summary

The Aloha channel is a contention channel access method that can be used under circumstances when the sender cannot tell until long after the event that a particular packet that he is sending will collide with another. This is because the round-trip delay time is much longer than the duration time of a packet. Listening to the channel to see whether it is safe to transmit is like looking at the rings in a tree trunk to see whether this summer is a warm one—the information is too far out of date to be useful.

We have examined the throughput of a channel and seen how this decreases rapidly with approaching channel saturation, and how the small access time for quiet channels increases rapidly at the same time. We have briefly looked at stability, and seen how saturation can be avoided mainly by throttling the offered load in some way or other. We have also looked briefly at one of the ways of making such a channel operate under heavy load with very few collisions.

3.8   Carrier Sense Multiple Access

In the Aloha channel we have emphasised that a collision is

only detected after the event, sometimes long after. Now let us look at a different type of channel where we can do much better than this. When talking in a crowded room, we remarked that a speaker could wait for others to cease speaking before beginning himself. Such a technique can be used with advantage on a medium where the the end-to-end delay time is less than the transmission time for a packet. In other words, under conditions where hearing a packet on the medium is some sort of assurance that it is still being transmitted.

What sort of channel has such a character? One obvious example is packet radio. With packet radio, a group of stations is spread over a geographical area of diameter a few tens of kilometres. A radio signal takes about 300μS to traverse an area 100 Km across. If the rate of the channel is 10 Kbps, then 1000-bit packets will each take 0.1 seconds to transmit. Thus we can say that the packet is about 300 "times as big" as the radio area, or put another way, our 100 Km radio area is about "three bits across". (Assuming that the bit rate is the same as the signalling rate.)

Let us imagine, then, that a station in this area has a packet to transmit. If it first listens to the channel it will hear what any other station is transmitting with a delay of at most three bits. Thus, if the channel is quiet, then the station may start to transmit with a high probability that the packet will not collide with another. This initial sensing for the already present carrier signal of another station gives the method its name *Carrier Sense Multiple Access*—CSMA†. We see that the collision "window" has shrunk from something the size of a packet (or two packets with pure Aloha), down to a small fraction of that—corresponding to the end-to-end delay time. Thus contention for the channel only takes place during the short time at the start of the packet. Once transmission is past this window, and its signal has started to reach all other stations, then it has seized the channel, the transmission is safe, and all other stations will be deferring any output until the channel goes quiet again. When the channel becomes quiet, there are several ways in which the waiting packets can be transmitted. We can choose to transmit immediately the channel becomes quiet. If there is a collision, then the colliding stations will wait a random time and try again. This technique is called *1-persistent CSMA* because the probability of transmission is 1 whenever the channel is idle. The main problem with this strategy is that if two packets are waiting, then they will both collide—always—and require retransmission.

---

† Despite the fact that the method is most frequently encountered with local area networks such as the Ethernet that employ baseband signalling and thus do not actually involve a carrier as such.

One variation on this is *p-persistent CSMA*. In this case a station transmits with probability p when the channel is found to be idle, and with probability $q = 1 - p$ waits for one packet (or slot) time. Clearly, this reduces the probability of two packets colliding immediately after another packet has been transmitted that we noted in 1-persistent CSMA. The final variation on the theme is *non-persistent CSMA*. In this version, the station senses the channel, and transmits if the channel is quiet. However, if the channel is busy, it does not continuously sense the channel, but waits for one slot time before repeating the process. Since the sensing of the channel is not continuous, the packets do not tend to be transmitted immediately after another one, and the tendency for collision after another packet is reduced. Note that non-persistent CSMA is *not* the same as 0-persistent CSMA.

We shall not derive the expressions for each of these methods. Under certain assumptions, Tobagi (Kleinrock and Tobagi, 1975) has derived the equations:

$$S_1 = \frac{Ge^{-G}(1+G)}{G + e^{-G}} \tag{3.9}$$

$$S_n = \frac{G}{1+G} \tag{3.10}$$

$$S_p = \frac{Ge^{-G}(1+pGx)}{G + e^{-G}} \tag{3.11}$$

$$\text{where} \quad x = \sum_{k=0}^{\infty} \frac{(qG)^k}{(1 - q^{k+1})!} \tag{3.12}$$

Fig 3.11 compares persistent CSMA, non-persistent CSMA, pure Aloha and slotted Aloha.

3.9   Ethernets

Clearly the CSMA protocols are a great improvement on the Aloha protocols as we might expect from our earlier discussion. However we see that there can still be a significant waste of bandwidth. With all the CSMA protocols, there is the small window when two (or more) stations may start to transmit before they see the start of the other's transmission. In a way that is directly similar to the analysis of pure Aloha, this window is of length twice the end-to-end delay time across the medium (in the worst case). With packet radio, once a station starts to transmit, the transmitted signal completely swamps any signal that might be coming from another station. Thus, once the transmission starts the station will continue right to the end of the packet, ignorant of the transmit status of any other stations. Should collision occur, then

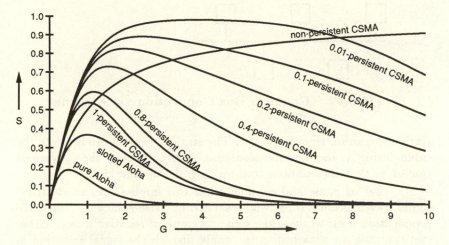

Fig 3.11. Channel Throughput: Aloha and CSMA

the collision will waste a whole packet time since none of the stations can know about the collision and abort the wasteful transmission.

However, not all shared media are like this. With carefully designed cable systems, it is possible for a transmitting station to see a disturbance generated by another station transmitting at the same time that is similar in magnitude to the applied signal. In this way it can detect a collision, and we can abort the wasteful transmission. Such a system is termed *Carrier Sense Multiple Access with Collision Detection*—CSMA/CD for short. Mostly it is known informally as "Ethernet", the name assigned by the originators, Metcalfe and Boggs.

Metcalfe and Boggs described the Ethernet in a paper in 1976. It was a local CSMA/CD network that had been in use at the Xerox Palo Alto Research Center (PARC) for some time. The original Ethernet spawned a later joint standard network definition adopted by the companies of DEC, Xerox and Intel, and this was later followed by the IEEE 802.3 and international ISO 8802 standards. The method is now the most widely followed standard for local area networks. Though there are differences between the variations of Ethernet, the principles are the same, and we shall not distinguish between them here.

An Ethernet is constructed by joining a set of stations onto a common piece of cable as in Fig 3.12

If any of the stations transmits onto the cable, then after a suitable interval to allow for the transmission of the signal, all the other stations will be able to hear the transmission. Each station first operates in the CSMA mode—it listens to see whether the cable is busy before it starts to transmit. The collision detection mechanism works while the

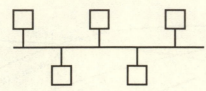

Fig 3.12.   Common Bus Connection via Ethernet

station is transmitting the packet. The station continues to listen to the cable during its own transmission, and is able to detect the distortions caused by the other stations transmitting at the same time.

Let us pause and consider what this implies. As an electrical signal travels down a wire, it is weakened by various factors. The cable propagation itself weakens the signal because of resistive losses. Other stations that are attached to the cable disturb the signal resulting in the signal being weakened and reflected. The cable may have joins, or be made up from segments out of different batches of cable, or from different suppliers, and so on. All this means that careful specification of the network cable must keep these distortions and losses within strict limits so that a signal of a certain minimum strength can reach the furthest extremity of the network and still have enough strength left to be detected reliably when colliding with the stronger transmitted signal of another station.

Unless collisions are to be detected, it is sufficient that the signal from another station be sufficiently strong compared with the noise level so that the data can be extracted reliably. With the Ethernet the requirements are more severe than this. The signal from other stations, under worst case conditions, must be strong enough so that its disturbance of the locally transmitted signal can be detected reliably. This is a much more severe constraint. There is some parallel with being able to detect a whisper across a quiet cathedral, and listening for the same whisper when a choir boy is standing a few feet away and singing at the top of his voice.

Thus we see that the Ethernet CSMA/CD mechanism should produce a more efficient access method than the plain CSMA without the CD. We can develop a simple variant of the pure Aloha analysis to demonstrate this. We can see that the Ethernet will operate in two modes. First comes a contention period when perhaps several stations will try to seize the medium by transmitting a packet. Once one station has transmitted for a sufficient time and no collision has occurred, then we know that all other stations that are ready to transmit will hold off because they will be seeing the packet already being transmitted. The original station can be said to have seized the medium, and there will be no further transmissions until the transmission of the current packet is complete. There will in general be several attempts to seize the medium before one is successful. Thus we can see the activity as several short bursts of contention activity separating organised periods when one station has seized and is using the network—Fig 3.13.

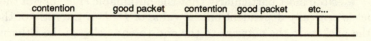

Fig 3.13. Contention and Transmission on Ethernet

If we consider in detail what happens in a contention period, we see that it is analogous to the pure Aloha that we discussed earlier in section 3.3). After a packet starts to transmit, it may be interrupted by any other packet that has already started to transmit elsewhere on the network, and whose signal arrives after some transmission delay. As with the pure Aloha analysis, let us define our slot time as the minimum end-to-end delay across the Ethernet cable. Thus, our hopeful packet may be corrupted by any other packet that started transmitting up to one slot time previously. Conversely, as our own packet travels across the network, it may be corrupted by any other packet that starts transmission before it arrives at the station. This event may happen up to the one slot time into the future.

As with our Aloha analysis, we take a population of N stations with packets ready to transmit, and assume a probability of transmission of s (per unit slot time). The successful single transmission happens N ways with probability s, and the other $N - 1$ stations each desist with probability $1 - s$ for each of two slots. This gives the probability of success as

$$S = Ns \times (1 - s)^{2(N-1)} \tag{3.13}$$

Which for large N but finite Ns becomes

$$S = Nse^{-2Ns} \tag{3.14}$$

To derive the Ethernet efficiency, we need to find the relative size of the contention period and the period during which the slot has been seized and is transmitting data uninterrupted. If S is the chance of some station seizing a contention slot, then $1/S$ is the average number of contention slots before a successful seizure. We have seen that the maximum value of S is $1/2e$, and thus the average number of such contention slots is $2e$. If each packet is P slots long, then the upper bound on the channel efficiency is

$$E \leq \frac{P}{P + 2e - 1} \tag{3.15}$$

The -1 in the denominator reflects the fact that the last of the $2e$ slots in the contention period is the successful one, and part of the transmitted packet. Sometimes the contention is done only with a preamble, and only when the contention slot has been seized successfully is the data transmitted. In this case, the -1 disappears from the denominator.

Note most particularly that the obtainable efficiency of the Ethernet is critically dependent on the value of P. P is the ratio of the size of the packets in the network to the end-to-end delay of the Ethernet. If P is 1 then the network will work in pure Aloha mode and the maximum achievable E is about 18%. By increasing the value of P sufficiently, E can be pushed arbitrarily close to 100%.

When a collision occurs the station schedules a retransmission. The retransmission time is increased with each subsequent collision. This has the valuable effect of stabilising the channel by effectively throttling back the offered traffic when the traffic is too high. In terms of our study of the stability of the Aloha channel, this is similar to reducing the retransmission parameter s. The algorithm for increasing the retransmission time, or "backing off" is expressed in terms of the slot time. For the nth retransmission attempt, the delay before attempted retransmission is an integral number of slot times chosen randomly from the range 0 to 2^{n+1}. This has the effect of halving the probability of retransmission (per slot time) after each unsuccessful attempt to seize the Ethernet medium.

3.10 CSMA Summary

We have seen in this section how the simple contention access of the Aloha channel can be improved if some means can be found of first detecting an existing transmission before starting a new transmission. This has been likened to the improvement in accident rate when driving a car with your eyes open. The most important application of this medium access method is the Ethernet, and Ethernet is commercially the most popular local network at the time of writing.

3.11 Rings

We now come to the study of ring-shaped media. Let us consider a set of machines that we wish to network together. We could join them all together in a ring with point-to-point links. Suppose the links all operate in one direction only as in Fig 3.14. Thus, data would only travel in the direction A to B to ... to E to A. Therefore, for machine B to send to machine C, the data is just sent down the link directly from B to C. However, if machine C wishes to reply, it does *not* send it back along the link directly to B since the link operates only in the opposite direction. Instead the data is sent forwards along the ring to

D. Station *D* sends it onto *E* and so on until the desired destination *B* is eventually reached.

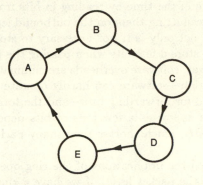

Fig 3.14.   A Ring of Five Nodes

Clearly, such a ring is a somewhat unusual animal in terms of the point-to-point networks discussed earlier. However, this ring does have one considerable merit—it is extremely simple. Each node has only to inspect each packet received from the single source. Either the packet is for itself, or it must be passed on to the next station in the ring through the single outgoing link. This is the extreme in simple routing. On the other hand, there are some obvious drawbacks. All of the network, i.e. all the stations have to be operational. Any single node or link failure means that only forward communication with those stations this side of the break is possible. No backward communication at all can take place. Such partial communication, at most one way between any two stations, is absolutely useless for most applications. It is for this reason that for some time rings had a reputation for fragility. However, we shall later see solutions to this problem, so let us put it to one side for a while, and study the detailed operation of various types of ring network.

There is a further problem with the store and forward ring as described above. That is that the delay experienced by a packet that has to go round most of the ring to reach its destination can be quite large. As the packet traverses each link, it is subject to propagation and transmission time delays. In addition each station will store the packet in internal buffers, and do significant processing to examine each packet before queueing the packet for onward transmission.

There are two ways of reducing this delay. Firstly, and most obviously, local rings run at very high bit rates, typically 1 to 100 million bits per second or more, and the physical extents of rings are usually fairly restricted, perhaps to a building or a group of buildings. This combination of speed and short distance keeps the propagation and transmission delays quite small.

Secondly, the ring protocols can be carefully designed so that the lowest level protocol can be implemented in dedicated hardware, and the hardware can operate much of the time by reading in bits from the input leg of the ring, and retransmitting them on the outbound leg with only a bit or two delay. Thus, not only is it not necessary to store full packets, it is only necessary to store a few bits when passing the packet on to another station. In this way, software overheads are eliminated for all but the source and destination—software can hardly operate in the sub-microsecond range required for forwarding bits—and the total ring delay from end-to-end may be as low as a few tens of bits depending on the type of ring. This is often much shorter than many packets in transit.

It is important to grasp the implications of the ring operating at the bit level rather than at the packet level. If we have a ring that is 1 Km round, operates at 10 Mbps, and the signal travels at $^3/_4$ the speed of light, then the wire will store 44 bits. Say we have 10 stations, each of which has a 3-bit delay, then the stations store 30 bits, and the total ring storage is 74 bits. So, for one of the types of ring that we shall study in detail, the slotted ring, the 74 bits is less than two slots, and the ring will carry one complete slot. On the other hand, with the token ring, the 74 bits will not even store an empty packet—the header, delimiters, checksum, etc are more than 74 bits. Thus a token ring must expect a single packet to more than fill the ring, with the start of the packet coming back to the transmitting station before the packet has finished transmitting—and sometimes even before the header has been completely transmitted! Thus, the packet "fills" the token ring in a similar way to which the Ethernet packet "fills" the Ethernet medium.

3.12   The Slotted Ring

This is often called the Cambridge Ring, as it was developed in its present form mostly at the University of Cambridge. The fundamental way in which the slotted ring works is to have one or more circulating "slots" or minipackets as shown in Fig 3.15. (The diagram shows the original 38-bit minipacket. Later versions have more bits, but their function will not concern us.)

bits

1	1	1	8	8	8	8	1	1	1
strt pkt	full/ emty	Mon passd	destination	source	data	data	response	parity

Fig 3.15.   A Slot on the Cambridge Ring

The slot continually circulates round the ring, with the left-most bits in the diagram being transmitted first. Suppose one station wishes to send to another. It must wait for and use an empty slot. As each start bit passes, the eager station copies the start bit out on its transmit side and then immediately follows it with a "full" bit. It then looks to see if it was a full or empty bit that it received. If the bit was already full, then some other station has already claimed the slot, and the station must bide its time waiting for another empty slot and merely copy data past for others. If, however, the bit indicated "empty" then the station can proceed to transmit its waiting data. It transmits the destination address, source address (its own), the data fields, zero response bits, and parity. We shall discuss the monitor bit later.

Each station continuously monitors incoming slots for those destined for itself. Whenever such a slot is found, a decision is made about the data. If an input buffer is free, then the data can be copied to the buffer and the response bits set to "accepted". If no station copies the data, then the response is left as zero. (The two other values are discussed below). Note that the order of the bits means that only a one bit needs to be stored at the station at any one time.

When the slot returns round the ring to the sender, the sender marks it empty, and the slot can then be used by other stations down stream. The slot is always marked empty after use even if the station has further data to send. This is so that other stations get a chance to transmit, and the operation of the ring is "fair"—that is no station may "hog" the ring bandwidth.

Clearly the protocol is in some senses "inefficient" in that much of the raw bit rate is used to carry other than data. In each 38 bit slot, only 16 bits are available for data. This is a utilisation of 42%.

Exercise 3.3 Compare this figure of 42% with the 18% and 37% throughput for pure and slotted Aloha. Would you use the judgemental words "good", "bad", "high", "low", etc? Why?

In addition, even on an otherwise quiet network, any pair of stations can only use one third of the minipackets. Thus any pair of stations can use a mere 14% of the raw bandwidth of the ring. (Other pairs of stations can of course use the empty slots, making up the rest of the 42% available for data.) This seems fairly low. However, we should not forget that the raw bit rate of local networks is typically very high, and rings can in general easily be made to operate at faster bit rates if necessary. A modest fraction of a lot is still quite a lot.

Let us look more closely at the function of the response bits. Each station has a source selection register. This 8-bit register can be set to

- 0 : reject everything
- 255 : accept from any source

• 1 to 254 : accept only from that source

This facility is used by the protocol that often sits immediately above the minipacket level, and is used to provide a multi-byte packet interface for higher level protocols. The source select register is first set to receive from any other source on the ring. When the first minipacket arrives, the higher level packet is started, and the source select register is set to receive only from that source. The data in the larger packet is then sent minipacket by minipacket. On completion of the larger packet, the source select register is set back to 255, and the larger packet is processed. Thus, if a third station attempts to send to a station that is in the process of receiving a larger packet, then the hardware response bits will indicate this. The response bits have four possible values, which mean:

a) Accepted by destination—can send next minipacket.
b) Rejected—Find something else to do
c) Busy—Probably a temporary buffer shortage, try again soon.
d) Unmarked—He's not responding. Maybe not switched on or broken.

The busy status is of most interest here. It allows the efficient mixing of stations of different complexity and speed. A typical Cambridge Ring has two sorts of station. One is a very simple "programmed" interface. In such an interface, the host computer is given a single minipacket interface. When a minipacket arrives the station copies it off the ring, puts it into a holding register that is available to the host machine, and then requests an interrupt. The host will have to read the single minipacket by software intervention before the next one can be received. Since such responses to interrupts are via software intervention, the process can be quite slow. Should another minipacket arrive along the ring before the host software has read out the last one, the hardware can fend it off temporarily with the busy status. Another kind of interface is a *Direct Memory Access*—DMA interface. Here the response to the incoming minipacket may be by hardware or by dedicated microprocessor. The response time will be much faster, and the actual data rate is quite likely up near the possible throughput of the ring station. Such a DMA station would typically have the multi-byte packet level protocol built into the dedicated hardware or microprocessor. We discuss these two general types of interface further in Chapter 12.

With the low level flow control we can have the possibility of a high performance DMA interface sending to a low performance programmed interface. Such a combination can be expected to be working for much of the time in a receiver busy mode. However, it is important to distinguish between busy and rejected. In the busy case, it's probably not worth doing anything else but trying again several times. In the rejected case the likely delay until a successful transmission will be much longer. Thus slotted ring interfaces are typically built with hardware that persists in trying to send a minipacket several times in the face of busy signals before giving up. Persisting, of course, does not violate the "fairness" algorithm—the slot is released after an unsuccessful try, and the next free slot claimed and used for the re-try. However, we should not forget that the re-trys will occupy some of the otherwise potentially useful 42% of the bandwidth.

3.13   The Monitor Station

Let us now turn to the maintenance aspects of the slotted ring. One of the most important aspects is the maintenance of the slot structure. The bit error rate on local networks is very low, perhaps one in 10^{10}. However, minipackets may become corrupted for a variety of reasons. In addition to transmission errors, the electronics of the stations themselves may make errors, power may fluctuate, stations may be turned off, etc. It is important that the regular supply of empty slots should not disappear otherwise the ring will stop. If a full slot is generated, and not removed for any reason, then it will circulate indefinitely unless steps are taken to remove it. This recovery is performed by the monitor station.

The monitor station is a special station that must be present on all slotted rings. It is the monitor that generates the slot pattern in the first place, and which monitors the slots as the ring is running. On power-up the monitor station decides how many minipackets the ring should contain. This may be either by simply having the number set by some external means, or by some sort of sizing process. There are various detailed specifications concerning the startup, and the transmission by the monitor station of specially formatted minipackets ("full", but with a null destination address) that we shall not describe. The ring may "contain" one or more slots—that is, the "length" of the ring must be at least one minipacket. It is the responsibility of the monitor station to ensure this, if necessary by inserting extra delay or storage into physically small rings. After startup, the monitor station generates the slot structure—a set of empty slots—on the outgoing side, and takes various measures to ensure its maintenance in the face of various errors. The monitor station also performs various other maintenance functions on the ring.

As it transmits each full slot, the originating station sets the monitor pass bit to one. The monitor looks at all full packets as they pass. If the monitor pass bit is one, then this is the first time past. The monitor changes the monitor pass bit to zero, and just passes the slot on.

If the sending station removes the full packet in the normal way, then all is well. If, however, the packet is not removed, then it will circulate round to the monitor station a second time. This time the monitor sees that a full slot is passing that has zero monitor bit, i.e. it has passed before. This is obviously a lost packet, and the monitor removes the packet, and sends out a new empty slot. Note that since the bits are at the front of the packet, the removal algorithm implies the storing of only a few bits—not the full slot.

Another function often performed by the monitor station is that of logging of errors. Every station generates and transmits even parity in every minipacket. This is quite independent of the parity of the incoming packet. It also checks the received parity on every packet. Thus if it sees bad incoming parity then the origin of that parity must be either that section of the ring immediately upstream (and including its own parity checking circuits), or the upstream parity generating circuits. The station must then generate a parity error message in the next available empty slot. This message has a source address of the detecting node, and a destination address of zero, and full bit set, and monitor pass zero (in contrast to the normal setting). The logging function logs such messages, and the monitor removes the slot because of the setting of the monitor pass bit. Thus all link-by-link errors should get logged.

Let us look at the utility of this. Firstly, the mechanism does *not* do any detection or correction for the two stations that might be using the data field of the slot. The users of the two stations must decide whether the error rate provided by the ring is sufficient for their purposes. Many might decide that it is. One bit in 10^9 is one bit in twenty minutes of flat-out ring operation. For an interactive terminal this is a single character in months or years of typing. Other applications may be less forgiving, and require a higher level error detection and recovery. However, the ring parity mechanism does not provide this.

The ring parity mechanism is for monitoring the health of the ring. It allows the monitor station to build up a picture of the low level error rates, and is operational all the time that slots are circulating, whether or not they are being used for data transmission. It is commonly observed with electronic equipment that before serious errors occur there is frequently a preceding period when normally infrequent errors gradually increase. Monitoring of such errors can be a powerful maintenance tool, allowing pre-emptive replacement of components that are about to go badly wrong. In addition these replacements can take place during scheduled maintenance periods rather than allowing the fault to become hard during peak operation, as it surely will if left.

3.14 Slotted Ring Summary

We have examined the basic slotted ring operation. We have seen how the slot handling protocol ensures fairness between the stations, how the monitor station maintains the slot structure in the face of various ring errors, and how the parity operation allows the monitoring of ring errors at a low level, segment by segment. In addition the multiple values for the response field in the minipacket allow not only the sender to know whether the receiver got the packet, but also provides an elementary flow control that allows ring stations of widely different speeds to interwork successfully.

3.15 The Token Ring

Let us now look at a related, but significantly more complicated type of ring, the token ring. The ring we shall describe is essentially the ring standardised in the IEEE 802.5 standard, that was in turn largely based on the earlier ring developed in the IBM Zurich research labs. There have been many earlier research token rings, but we shall not describe them.

The major difference between the slotted ring and the token ring is that in the slotted ring there is a fixed slot structure with a small field in which data can be sent. The the length (in bits) of the total number of slots in use at any time must be smaller than the length of the ring. With the token ring a much bigger block may be sent. In this case only one block can be in transit round the ring at any time, but that block may be very large, and may be much longer than the ring. In other words, a station must be prepared to accept the returning header of the packet that it is still transmitting. However, we shall see that the fundamental operation of the token ring is otherwise very similar to that of the slotted ring. This particular token ring has a set of maintenance facilities built into the ring operation that is even more extensive than the slotted ring.

On the token ring a block of data is sent framed by a *starting delimiter* at the front and an *ending delimiter* and *frame status* at the end. The access to the ring is regulated by a single *token* which gives the ring its name. The token is represented by a bit in the *Access Control*—AC field near the start of the block of data on the ring (see below). Before transmitting data, a ring station must *claim* the free token. While in posession of the token, the station may transmit data packets, but must eventually release the token by transmitting an empty packet with the token bit set in the AC field round the ring to make it available to other stations. The function of the token is much like that of the full/empty bit in the slotted ring, but the packet size is variable, and the sizes of packets and the control fields in the token ring are much larger than in the slotted ring.

In the slotted ring, the size of the ring is adjusted so that it is at least "one slot big"—i.e. that the last bit has been transmitted from a station before the first bit of the same slot arrives back round the ring. If necessary, the monitor station must insert extra delay to ensure this on physically small rings. Very large slotted rings may have enough delay to "contain" several slots. However, with the token ring this is no longer possible since the variable size of the data field means that a packet is almost always "bigger" than the ring. Thus the ring station must expect to receive the start of the data packet it is transmitting before it has finished transmitting the end. Indeed, in contrast to the slotted ring there is no possibility of filling very large rings with several packets, because the operation of the protocol forbids multiple tokens quite independently of ring size.

When a station wishes to transmit data, it looks for a passing starting delimiter, and then follows it with an AC field with a zero token bit. If the bit that it just received already indicated "claimed" then the token was not acquired, and the station must wait until the next time round.

If the attempt to claim the token was successful, the to- and from-addresses are transmitted, followed by the information field, checksum, ending delimiter, and frame status. Clearly, the basic operation is just the same as the slotted ring, though the fields are quite different in format and size.

Token Ring Packet Format

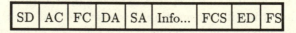

| SD | AC | FC | DA | SA | Info... | FCS | ED | FS |

SD: Starting Delimiter
AC: Access Control
FC: Frame Control—control or data
DA: Destination Address
SA: Source Address
Info: Information
FCS: Frame Check Sequence
ED: Ending Delimiter
FS: Frame Status

Since the frame can be of variable length and possibly quite large, it is easier for transmission errors to cause synchronisation with the frame structure to be lost. Thus, the token ring has a special way of marking delimiters. All data on the ring is encoded using the differential

Manchester encoding described in Chapter 1. We noted there that this method allowed the transmission not only of 0 and 1, but also two "bit violations" called *Non-Data-J* and *Non-Data-K* (J and K for short). Both the starting and the ending delimiters are special octets containing:

$$\boxed{J\ K\ x\ J\ K\ x\ y\ z}$$

(Note carefully, that J and K are transmitted in pairs to maintain the absence of the DC component.)

For a starting delimiter, x, y, z are all zero:

SD: $\boxed{J\ K\ 0\ J\ K\ 0\ 0\ 0}$

For an ending delimiter, $x = 1$ and y and z are used to transmit control information that we shall consider later.

ED: $\boxed{J\ K\ 1\ J\ K\ 1\ I\ E}$

I: Intermediate Frame

E: Error

The access control field is also one byte long:

AC: $\boxed{P\ P\ P\ T\ M\ R\ R\ R}$

PPP: Priority

T: Token Bit

M: Monitor Passed Bit

RRR: Reservation

The fields in the access delimiter are used in a very similar way to the corresponding ones in the slotted ring. When a station has a packet to transmit, it inspects the passing data for the distinctive starting delimiter. It then uses the token bit in the access control field in just the same way as the slotted ring full/empty bit is used. (We shall describe the use of the priority and reservation fields in some detail later.) The FC byte indicates the type of the packet—control or data. The following source and destination addresses are similar to the slotted ring (except that they are much bigger), and there is a potentially very large and variable sized data field. The protective checksum, FCS, completes the data field, and the frame is completed by the ending delimiter (ED) and frame status (FS) fields.

FS: $\boxed{A\ C\ r\ r\ A\ C\ r\ r}$

A: Address Recognised

C: Frame Copied

r: Reserved (no function defined yet)

The FCS field on the token ring is not used in quite the same way as the parity bit in the slotted ring. In the slotted ring correct parity is always transmitted by every station, and parity errors on the receive leg are logged as errors specific to one section of the ring. On the token ring the end of the information field is detected by recognising the ending delimiter complete with its deliberate bit violations. By this time the FCS field may well have been transmitted on the outgoing side, so the opportunity of regenerating a correct field has been lost. Instead of this the error bit in the ending delimiter is set. By this means, a station can detect whether this error is "new". If the receiver detects an FCS error and the error-detected bit has not been set, then the error is a new one, and points to an error in the immediate upstream section of the ring—just like the parity bit in the slotted ring. An FCS error together with the error detected bit already set means that this is not a new error, but one that has occurred upstream of the next ring station upstream. (The other possibility of a correct FCS with the error bit set is very unlikely. It is possible that an invalid packet may have had a second corruption that made the FCS again valid, but while possible, it is extremely unlikely, and it is much more likely that the ending delimiter itself has suffered the transmission error.) Thus we see that the FCS itself provides a true station-to-station error check—unlike the slotted ring where such station-to-station checks are pushed to a higher level. The combination of FCS and the error-detected bit allows the continuous segment-by-segment monitoring of the health of the ring in a way that is very similar to that provided by the parity mechanism in the slotted ring.

The reporting of the health of the ring is specified slightly differently for the token ring. A slotted ring station must try to transmit error packets for all parity errors. However, this is not required of token ring stations. Both token and slotted ring stations report breaks and send appropriate signals along the ring. These messages originate at the station immediately below the break, and contain its address. Thus the monitoring station can report the location of the break immediately and thus enable correct action to be taken.

3.16   Token Ring Priority

The token ring has a priority mechanism. The intention of the scheme is that when the ring is heavily loaded, it will be possible for priority traffic to pre-empt ordinary traffic. Three bits in the access control field contain a priority in the range 0 to 7. Each packet to be transmitted has an associated priority. For example, regular data might have the default priority, 0, real time process control might have priority 3, and emergency alarm data priority 5. To transmit each packet, the station must use a free token with a priority less than or equal to that of the packet. If such a token passes by, then it is used to transmit the frame. However, if the token has higher priority than the waiting packet, or the token is held by a station that is transmitting data, then the transmission cannot take place. The transmitting station will use the reservation mechanism to request a suitable free token.

When the ring is lightly loaded, and particularly when there are periods when no station has data to transmit, then a free token of priority 0 will circulate round the ring. As each station wishes to transmit data then it can seize this free token and transmit its data— of whatever priority. However, if the ring becomes busy enough that stations start to become ready to transmit while the ring is still in use by another station, then the waiting stations will use the priority bits in the passing access control fields to request that a token of the appropriate priority be generated as soon as possible. As the transmitting station removes the packet from the ring it examines the reservation field. If this indicates that a higher priority token is required, it stacks the old priority, and generates a token with the higher level priority. When this token has been used and returns round the ring, the station absorbs it, unstacks the old priority, and generates a new token at this new level. In this way, the stations co-operate to give priority access to the ring. We shall now study the somewhat complex details of this mechanism. Since the scheme is complex, we shall look at it in several stages of increasing detail.

Assume the packet of a certain priority is waiting at a station for transmission. The station scans the passing data for an access control delimiter. If this is a free token, and the priority of the token is less than or equal to the priority of the waiting packet, then the token is claimed by turning on the token bit, and transmitting the waiting packet, followed by the FCS, etc. It then waits for the completion of the reception of the incoming packet as it comes round the ring. As the AC field arrives, it transmits a new token, and then removes the incoming frame—the one it transmitted—from the ring.

This simple scheme gives no priority access unless the circulating token has non-zero priority, and implements the "fair" access of the slotted ring. This can be seen in Fig 3.16.

Suppose the free token is circulating with priority 0, and had just left ring station *D* and was about to arrive at *A* when each station has a packet become ready for transmission at the priority levels 1, 3, 2, 4

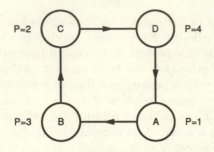

Fig 3.16.   Token Ring Priority

at the stations A, B, C, D. Station A will claim the incoming token, flip the token bit, and transmit the packet. The destinations of the packets are irrelevant to the present discussion as the packets always complete a full circuit of the ring before being removed by the originating station. Note that the access control field will contain the pre-existing priority field. This need not be the same as that of the packet being transmitted, and in this case it is zero rather than 1. However, this does not matter as the token is not free and may not be claimed by any other station.

All the other stations will see the busy token passing by and will thus not be able to transmit. Station A waits to see the incoming frame header, and then transmits the free token. Finally, it transmits the end of frame, and goes back to repeat mode. If the transmitted token is at the original priority, then it will be immediately seized by station B, and used to transmit its priority 3 packet. The token is then released to C, used by C, and so on round the ring. Clearly, the ring is still being used in strict round-robin fashion with no priority operation at all. The ring is operating in the "fair" mode of the slotted ring.

What we need is some way for a station to generate a ring token that can only be used by the highest priority waiting packet. This will bypass the lower priority stations and cause the priority mechanism to operate. How can a station that is about to generate a new token know to generate one of the right priority? The reservation bits in the access control field provide a mechanism to do this. As a claimed token is transmitted, its reservation bits are set to the binary value zero. As each waiting station sees a busy token pass by, it compares the reservation value with its own waiting priority. If its own priority is higher, then it replaces the field with its own value. Thus, when the AC field has made the full ring circuit back to the original transmitting station it will contain in its reservation field the maximum waiting priority at any other ring station. Thus, when it generates the new free token it knows the right value to put into the priority field.

Exercise 3.4   Why is the AC field not included in the checksum?

Thus, in our example, the AC field on the information frame transmitted by A will have a busy token bit, and a reservation field of zero. Station B will see the busy token. It compares the following reservation bits with the waiting priority of 3. Since $3 > 0$, the reservation field is set to 3. Station C compares the new reservation value 3 with its waiting value of 2, and leaves the field unchanged. Station D will replace the reservation field of 3 with its waiting priority of 4. Station A removes the incoming frame from the ring, but remembers the reservation field. Station A now has to transmit a token. Since the requested token priority is 4, it must remember the old priority. It puts this old value, 0, onto its stack, and generates a free token with priority 4. This new token cannot be used by either of stations B or C, and station D gets to use the ring before they are allowed to. Station C transmits its priority 4 packet. As the packet goes round the ring, the eagerly waiting stations B and C change the reservation field and station D receives reservation 3 from its circulating packet. Station D is now finished with the token, and generates a new token with priority 4. It cannot drop the ring priority as it is not the stacking station. The free token passes round to station A—the stacking station.

The original station A knows that a returning free token with priority 4 is the one it generated, and it must be prepared to lower the priority. It sees the reservation field of 3, and thus transmits a new token with priority 3. This is used by station B to transmit its packet. Station C is still trying to transmit its priority 2 packet, and sets the reservation accordingly. Station C transmits a new free token with priority 3, which comes round to the stacking station again. The reservation field still indicates that there is a station requesting a priority (2) higher than the stacked priority (0), so the ring priority is dropped to 2. Station C uses this to transmit its packet. This time the reservation field remains at zero since there is no station left to transmit. The free token generated by C is received by A. The reservation field is now the same as the stacked priority, so the stacking station can cease to stack. It pops the old priority, generates a priority zero token, and ceases to have special function.

In this somewhat extended example of priority operation above, station A remembered the old priority as it issued new free tokens at various higher priorities. Note that a station only becomes a stacking station when it issues a new free token at a higher requested priority. A station does not become a stacking station merely by seizing a free token, even if the packet it transmits has a priority higher than that in the seized token. Thus in our example, all the stations seize the token, but only station A actually alters the ring priority. In addition, station

A only becomes the stacking station *after* it has transmitted its first packet, and discovers a reservation field on the incoming access control field. Note also that it is quite possible for packets arriving in the correct order to cause several stations in turn to become stacking stations, each raising the priority progressively higher than it was last time (as opposed to merely changing the priority several times during a single stacking episode as in our detailed example). Indeed, the stacking requirement may be recursive at the same station, and the required storage is truly a stack rather than just one old stored value.

> **Exercise 3.5** What is the maximum stack size required at a station?

We have now seen how the priority system works. Why do we need such a complicated system? In a substantial network that is very busy, there are at least two possible design requirements. It may be that all stations are seen as equally important. In this case, all stations would run at equal priority, and on a saturated ring would get an equal share of the bandwidth, and equally poor response time. However, there may be certain applications that are seen as more important. It may be that certain time-critical applications are on the ring. In this case, the priority scheme would allow this set of stations to get a very rapid response rather than waiting for their "fair turn". However, it should be noted that this scheme is a strictly pre-emptive scheme rather than a bandwidth-sharing scheme. In other words, if there is sufficient traffic at high priority to saturate the ring, then the lower priority traffic will have to wait indefinitely.

> **Exercise 3.6** Imagine a small ring with a few stations operating at priority zero. Contrive an arrival sequence of packets at the stations that will cause first station *A* to stack and raise priority to 1, then station *B* to stack and raise priority to 2 (while *A* is still stacked!), then station *A* to stack and raise the priority to 3 (while *B* is still stacked, and *A* itself is stacked "under" *B*).

> **Exercise 3.7** On the token ring, bits within bytes are transmitted most significant (left-most) bit first. When a station is unable to transmit a waiting packet and is comparing the reservation field on the ring with the waiting packets priority, ready to decide whether to change the reservation field upwards, how many bits must it store before transmitting the whole field? Three, one,...? If the order of bit transmission were reversed, would this make a difference? For right-first transmission, can you think of a minimal change in the protocol that would require minimal storage in the blocked station?

> **Exercise 3.8** Design a slotted ring protocol with a priority mechanism similar to that on the token ring, but with only two levels, 0 and 1. Describe an example of it in operation.

3.17   Token Ring Errors

The main device used by the token ring to handle errors is the maintenance of a number of timers. If the timers expire, then the stations abandon various operations and return to merely repeating data on the ring.

When hard errors are detected, for example no input signal from the upstream leg, a station becomes a "beaconing" station. That is, it starts to transmit a continuous series of packets downstream. The address in these packets allows the quick identification of the failing segment.

The token ring has the concept of a monitor station. However there is no single station that is designated the monitor as on the slotted ring. In normal operation, one station is the active monitor, and this transmits an *I'm here* frame periodically. All other stations are in *Standby Monitor* state. If the *I'm here* frames don't arrive for a certain period, then all the standby stations attempt to become the active monitor by transmitting a *Claim Token* frame. (This can happen at ring startup time, or whenever the ring has restarted after some error, or the monitor station has been powered off, etc). If no other station is trying to become the monitor at the same time, then the attempting station will get its token claim frame back and becomes the active monitor. However, if several are trying at the same time, then each will see the other's claim token frames. In this case, the station with the higher address drops its claim in favour of the other(s).

The function of the active monitor is mostly to check for circulating frames that have not been removed by the sender, in much the same way as on the slotted ring.

3.18   The FDDI Ring

The *Fiber Distributed Data Interface*—FDDI ring is another kind of token ring. FDDI is designed to be a very fast ring that can have considerable physical extent. The ring is intended to operate on optical fibre at a data rate of 100 Mbps but with fibre lengths of up to 2 Km between repeaters, up to 1000 repeaters, and a total fibre length of up to 200 Km.

The FDDI ring has many interesting properties, and it includes in its design many of the desirable diagnostic and reconfiguration facilities that we have seen are available with ring media. However, we shall pick out two aspects of FDDI for particular mention. These are the detailed role of the token, and the capacity allocation mechanism.

Exercise 3.9   Calculate the minimum length of a packet in bits that will just fill a maximum sized FDDI ring with the parameters above.

We see immediately that the basic parameters of the FDDI ring mean that the capacity can only be used if either excessively long packets are transmitted, or if more than one packet is allowed on the ring at once. FDDI allows multiple packets from multiple sources to be in transit at the same time, but achieves this using just one token.

When a station has data to transmit, it waits for a token to come past, and captures it. It then transmits several packets on the ring. The receiving station(s) copy the packet from the ring, but let it circulate back to the sender. The sender is responsible for removing the packet from the ring. The receiver(s) copy the data from the ring, and indicate that the packet has been recognised and copied by setting the appropriate bits in the ending delimiter just as the 802.5 ring signals the same information in its frame status field. However, the sending station does not retain the token, it transmits it immediately following the packets it has sent out. In this way the token circulates hard up against the preceding data and allows the ring to be kept busy. This is in contrast to the IEEE token ring in which there is the requirement to retain the token until the starting delimiter of its own transmitted packet has returned. It is this that is "turned back into" the access token. In this way the IEEE ring will start to run with the ring sometimes idle when frames are being transmitted that are "smaller" than the circumference of the ring even when there is traffic ready to go. However this will not be so likely because of the smaller size and slower speed of the IEEE ring.

> **Exercise 3.10**   The IBM token ring conforms with the IEEE 802.5 token ring described in previous sections. Later versions of this ring have a feature called "early token release" whereby a free token can be transmitted immediately following the end of a transmitted packet— the requirement to wait for the returning starting delimiter has been removed. In what circumstances will this be helpful?

The FDDI ring has a mechanism for allocating traffic fairly amongst the stations while still maintaining the full utilisation of the ring if there is sufficient traffic in total, and even if most of that traffic comes from a small subset of the stations using the ring. It does this by allocating a *Target Token Rotation Time*—TTRT. This is allocated by means of a management protocol amongst the stations, and is the same for all stations. In addition to this, each station has a "share" or *Synchronous Allocation*—SA. The various synchronous allocations are set so that

$$\sum_i SA_i + D_{Max} + F_{Max} + Token\ Time < TTRT$$

Here D_{Max} is the propagation time for a circuit of the ring, F_{Max} is the transmission time for a maximum length frame, and *Token Time* is the transmission time for a token.

Each station measures the time between receiving tokens in a token rotation timer TRT. On receipt of a token, this is transferred to a token holding timer, THT, and TRT is reset to zero and starts running again. At this point the station may transmit frames (as long as it has frames to transmit):

1. It may transmit synchronous frames for a time SA_i.
2. After transmitting any synchronous traffic, THT is set running. The station may continue to transmit asynchronous data as long as $THT < TTRT$.

We see that in this simple way, all stations are guaranteed a part of the total bandwidth via the synchronous allocation, but that any station may take up the remaining slack if it has anything to send. Note that this can result in the token rotation time exceeding the target for a time, but that this condition is transitory.

> **Exercise 3.11** Consider an FDDI ring that is idle with no traffic being sent. Ignore D_{Max}, F_{Max}, and the *Token Time*, suppose that each of three stations has a synchronous allocation of three slot times, and that the TTRT is 12 slot times. If each of the stations suddenly has an infinite supply of data to send, trace the way in which each of the stations changes its TRT, and how many synchronous and asynchronous frames does it transmit in the first few cycles of the token?

The FDDI ring also has a priority structure that is cast in terms of eight priority timer thresholds for each station. The station can only transmit asynchronous traffic in a priority category as long as THT is less than the threshold for that category.

> **Exercise 3.12** When discussing time and frequency division multiplexing in section 3.2 we remarked that a kind of distributed frequency division multiplexing could be constructed on a cable network by using frequency-agile modems. To what extent can the various kinds of slotted and token ring that we have discussed be considered as a kind of distributed time division multiplexing?

3.19 Other Types of Ring

We have examined the operation of the slotted and token rings in some considerable detail. However, the reader should be aware that we have omitted various details from our description. Rather than supplying them now, we refer the interested reader to the relevant standards. Now we shall briefly describe several other types of ring to highlight important similarities and differences.

The first of these other types of ring is the register insertion ring. With the slotted and token rings a station wishing to transmit must wait for a circulating token or slot so that it may access the ring. With the register insertion ring the packet is made ready in a shift register at the station. The shift register must be made exactly the same size as the packet. The packets may all have to be the same size as the fixed shift register, (somewhat like the slotted ring) or the register may be adjusted (electronically on the fly) to the size of the packet—packets can be made to fit a fixed register either by chopping long ones into pieces, or by making short ones bigger with padding. Once the packet is ready in this register, the station scans the data passing through the station on the ring. When it spots the boundary between packets on the ring, it switches in the shift register. Thus the ring has instantaneously become bigger by the size of the shift register. The bits are shifted out of the register and onto the ring, at the same time being replaced by data shifting in from the ring—Fig 3.17.

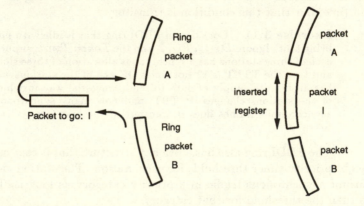

Fig 3.17.   Register Insertion Ring

The shift register is now part of the ring, and remains so until the data transmitted has rotated right round the ring and is back in place in the shift register. At this point, the packet is removed by switching out the shift register, and returning the ring to its original shorter state.

Exercise 3.13   Outline more details of a register insertion ring. Pay particular attention to the need for an easily recognisable packet boundary. What method might you use to detect the return of the packet to the shift register? How would you recover from a ring failure that made the returned packet unrecognisable? Do you see a use for a monitor station? How would you maintain the record structure on the ring when no station was actively transmitting data?

3.20 Contention Rings

We shall look briefly at two contention rings. In the first type of contention ring, the operation is much like the operation in slotted and token rings. However, the main difference is in the way that tokens are generated at startup time and regenerated when they are lost. In normal operation, the token circulates, and is claimed by stations with a waiting packet in the usual way. However, if a station has a packet ready to transmit, it will wait only a limited time for a free token. If no free token arrives during that time, then the station merely stops waiting and sends the packet anyway. When the packet has traversed the ring it is removed by the sender, and a free token transmitted in its place. Successful operation requires some more elaboration of this protocol to handle unusual events, for example, two stations trying this at the same time. It will be seen that the Ethernet device of backing off, and retransmitting again at a random time later handles this conflict nicely.

Thus we see that a contention ring of this sort handles token loss in a way that is very similar to the Ethernet access method. This allows the generation of the first token when the ring is started up (and is thus empty) and the regeneration of lost or corrupted tokens. The control is completely distributed. There is no static or dynamically allocated monitor station, except in the transient period when one or more stations is generating a new token. However, the normal operation of the ring with a circulating token that is claimed by stations wishing to transmit.

The second type of contention ring differs from the first in that when there is no traffic on the ring, then the ring is empty. There is no circulating token. When a station has a packet to transmit, it first listens to the ring. If the ring is silent, then the station transmits the packet onto the ring, and then follows it with a free token. It then removes the packet and the free token as the they return round the ring. In this way, access time for the ring is very small when the ring traffic is low because there is no need to wait for a token. If two stations start to transmit simultaneously, there will be a clash, and both stations will back off and retransmit at randomly delayed times in Ethernet fashion. The remaining case is when the station wishes to transmit, and finds the ring already busy. This can be expected to happen when the traffic is fairly high, or by chance when a second station becomes ready to transmit as another's packet is passing on the ring. It is here that the utility of transmitting the free token following the packet is seen. Remember that the first station to transmit sends a packet followed by a free token. The second station will watch the packet go by, and wait for the following token. It sees this, transmits its own packet, and again appends a free token. Thus, we see that when the ring is very busy (and any initial contention period has settled down), the free token is seized in turn by the busy stations to transmit their packets. The ring is again working like a "normal" (non-contention) token ring. Clearly, each station removes its own packets from the ring, and then inspects the following token. If it is free, then it is removed, and the ring becomes available for contention access. If the following token is claimed, i.e. it is the header for a packet on the ring, then it must be passed through, together with any following free token. The free token is only removed by a station removing its own packet, and seeing the immediately following token. Clearly, lost or corrupted tokens can be recovered by a timeout contention mechanism as used in the other type of contention ring.

On comparing the two types of ring, we see that they are very similar, except in their behaviour under light load. Under light load, the necessity to wait for the circulating token in type 1 contention rings will introduce a small delay. This access delay will not be present with type 2 rings operating under light load. However, balanced against this is the fact that type 1 contention rings only use contention to recover from error conditions, and in particular to recover from lost tokens. On the other hand, type 2 will tend to suffer contention at moderate traffic levels. The resulting loss in bandwidth must be set against the overhead in waiting for the constantly circulating token used in type 1. Under heavy load the two types of rings will operate in a very similar way with the token being passed from station to station. The type 2 ring will rarely operate in contention mode when the load is heavy.

3.21   Ring Summary

We have now covered the wide range of ways in which ring-shaped media may be shared. Typically the access is controlled by a token, and we have seen the several ways in which the token is used to control the traffic. The most important variation is that the relative "size" of the typical ring packet compared with the size of the ring requires a different token management protocol in order to maintain a high utilisation. We have noted that the topology of the ring allows the rapid location and isolation of errors, and we shall see later in the chapter on management that the perceived weakness of rings—that all of the ring is one large "point of failure" can be eliminated by careful topological design.

Rings are often supposed to be synonymous with token access, but we also saw that ring access could be controlled by contention methods. We now complete the circle, so to speak, by introducing the concept of the token bus.

3.22   Token Bus

The final type of medium sharing that we shall examine in some detail is the token bus. The token bus is topologically the same as the Ethernet. All stations are joined together by a single passive wire, and each station taps onto the wire. As with the Ethernet, any transmission by any station will be heard by all the other active stations connected to the bus. However, instead of all the stations competing for access in Ethernet fashion, access to the bus is regulated by the passing of an access token among the stations. Thus, the operation is an interesting mixture of the bus topology exemplified so far by the contention networks, and the regulated token access that we have so far found associated with ring networks.

The normal operation of the token bus is logically similar to that of the token ring. Stations are organised into a logical ring, and they pass an access token from one station to the next in the logical ring. As each station receives the token it may use it to transmit its waiting packets, and it must then pass the token onto the next station in the logical ring. Note the use of the word "logical" here. The stations are arranged into a logical ring in contrast to the rings we have seen so far which are physical rings. In a logical ring the token is passed from station to station in order of the station numbers. When the token reaches the highest numbered station, it is passed onto the lowest numbered station. The order of the numbers, and thus the passing of the token has absolutely nothing to do with the physical location of the stations, but only to do with their logical order. This is in contrast to the physical rings, where the token is passed in strict physical order, and is quite independent of the numbers or addresses assigned to the stations. Further, we should remember that in real physical rings, the stations talk only to the next station downstream, and listen to the next station upstream. Communication with stations further away on the ring is always through the agency and "goodwill" of intermediate stations. In contrast, on bus networks, including the token bus with its logical ring, every station talks to every other one, and can hear every other one. We shall now examine how the logical ring comes into existence, and is maintained in the face of errors.

As with all local networks, every station must be assigned a unique address. In addition, the token bus has a "slot time". This is similar to the slot time that we defined when we were looking at the Ethernet. The slot time is the maximum time that any station must wait for a response from any other station. Thus it includes both the maximum distance delay across the network, and back, plus the maximum response time within the stations at either end, plus a safety margin.

The process of logical ring establishment starts with initialisation. This is triggered at all or any of the stations by an inactivity timer. This indicates that the bus has gone quiet for too long, perhaps because of loss of token, or because the first bus stations have just been switched on. When this happens a regulated contention system comes into action. The aim of this is to choose from amongst the eager waiting stations, that one which has the highest address. The algorithm used is to take the 48 bits of the station address and sort the station addresses using two of these bits at a time. Each competing station emits a *Claim Token* packet with a data field that has length 0, 2, 4, or 6 slots. The length is chosen in increasing order, depending on the value of the two bits from the address that are currently being used as shown in the table.

Address bits selected	Data length in slots	Delay in slots before responding "Set-Successor"
11	6	0
10	4	1
01	2	2
00	0	3

After transmitting the appropriately sized claim token field, a station waits for one slot time (to allow for the end to end delay and the uncertainty in the other stations starting) and then listens. If it hears silence, then no other station of higher priority is competing in the initialisation contest. However, if there is not silence, then another station (or more) is transmitting a longer claim token packet, and thus has a higher priority in the claiming contest. Assuming unique addresses, this process will eventually result in exactly one station "winning" the contest and claiming the token.

Having won, the victorious station must now build a logical ring from all the waiting stations. It does this by issuing a *Solicit-Successor* packet. This packet specifies an address range from itself downwards. There will in general be several stations ready to join the ring, and that are ready to respond to this frame. All of them will respond with a *Set-Successor* packet. The token holder sees this contention as a noise burst, and must resolve the contention. To do this it issues a *Resolve-Contention* packet. When they see this frame, all the hopeful joiners respond with further *Set-Successor* frames. However, this time they first delay a time that is 0, 1, 2, or 3 slot times before transmitting the *Set-Successor* response. This delay is determined similarly to the data length in the initialisation phase. However, here the order is reversed so that stations with higher values transmit first, thus again giving the higher numbered stations the priority by allowing them to transmit sooner this time rather than longer as in the initialisation phase (see table above).

The listening token holder will either hear a single valid response, or will hear two or more responses, possibly interfering with each other. In the first case, the single successor has been found. In the second case the contention must be resolved further, and the token holder sends another *Resolve-Contention* frame. On the second and successive *Resolve-Contention* events, two things happen. Firstly, each station will have been looking during the previous delay period. If it heard some other station transmitting, then it does not transmit, thus deferring to their higher priority. Secondly, at each *Resolve-Contention* event, a further two bits of the address is chosen to select the delay. This process eventually results in the selection of a single successor, which is the highest numbered station less than the token holder. This process is repeated until eventually a complete ordered set of stations is constructed.

During the operation of the logical ring, stations may join or leave the ring. As each station in the logical ring is about to pass the token to its successor, it first opens a window in which a limited set of new stations may join the ring. To do this, it issues a *Solicit-Successor* frame to invite any new station in the gap between it and the next ring member to join. Normally, there will be no new member, but occasionally there will be a single response from a new station joining the ring. Very occasionally, two or more new stations in the logical gap in the ring will try to join, and the full blown contention mechanism will be invoked. Stations may leave the logical ring by just ceasing to operate. There is a mechanism whereby a station that passes the token onto the next station listens to see if the destination station makes use of the token. If there is no activity on the bus, the station tries sending the token again (in case of transmission loss). On the second failure an attempt is made to bypass the station by sending to its successor. Such an error recovery mechanism can obviously be used to omit a station that has just been switched off. Alternatively, a station that wishes to leave the ring can wait for the arrival of the token. It then can emit a special packet to its immediate neighbours in the ring telling them about its leaving. The neighbours can then talk to each other directly without invoking the error recovery procedure.

3.23   Token Bus Summary

With the token bus, we see that the normal operation is that of a logical token ring. However, there is a somewhat complex protocol to handle the initialisation of the logical ring, and to maintain its integrity during operation when stations join and leave the ring. Despite this complexity, token buses do operate satisfactorily, especially in manufacturing environments, where the priority mechanism is attractive. In addition, the complex initialisation can be completed in quite a short time.

3.24   Summary

We have now covered the total spectrum of shared media. We have discovered that there are two main *orthogonal principles*: that access can be managed by contention or token, and that the topology can be either bus or ring shaped in nature. These two principles can then be combined in a variety of ways. In addition we have seen how contention access can be made very efficient when the physical parameters of the system enable carrier sensing to be used resulting in the simple and very successful Ethernet. Contention access control is a very simple mechanism to implement, but we have seen that token access allows the implementation of a priority structure. Contention access admits of the possibility of indefinitely delayed access because of its statistical nature, but token access can give guaranteed access within predictable times even under heavy load. However, this difference is only likely to be important in practice when the medium is moderately or heavily loaded. Under light load, contention access will be more immediate than token controlled access. On the other hand, when we consider topology, rings have very desirable diagnostic and maintenance properties and suitable designs scale very well to higher speeds and larger sizes where carrier sensing becomes less efficient. It seems likely that the present dominance of the simpler contention bus networks will give way to the more complex, but more scalable and more maintainable token ring types of network in the future.

4
Flow Control

"We apologise for the late arrival of this train, which is due to us following the train that is in front of us."
—British Rail Guard

One preoccupation of computer people is to make things go faster, so at first sight it seems a contradiction that one of the major elements of communications technology is flow control, the more so since many computers are much faster than most of the communications devices attached to them. Flow control is, as the very name implies, the controlling or restricting of the flow of data in a suitable manner. Some writers refer to flow control as "pacing".

The fundamental need for flow control is easily perceived, as is demonstrated by the instant appreciation of the humour in the above quote, but the subtleties and complications that are uncovered when we go beyond simple use are remarkable.

4.1   Examples of Flow Control

To illustrate the need for and some of the techniques of flow control, we shall examine a series of examples. These are of increasing complexity, and each is related to the last.

- A Remote Printer

A computer system has a distant printer connected by a simple communications line. If the printer is capable of printing, say, 100 characters per second, and the communications line can transmit 120 characters in a second, then there is clearly a likelihood that the computer will sometimes send data down the line faster than the printer can print it. Some method of limiting this overrun of data is clearly needed.

- Matched Speed

A simple way of avoiding the problem of data overrun from which the previous example suffered is to match the communications speed with that of the printer. This is commonly done with computer terminals that print "hard copy" on paper. For example, primitive electronic typewriters can print at 10 characters per second. These are often attached to a communications line that runs at 10 characters per second. Since the two speeds are the same, the typewriters can keep up.

- Varying Speeds

If the teleprinter of the previous example could always keep up the 10 characters per second, then there would be no problem. However, some operations take longer than the $1/10$ of a second that printing a normal character takes. The most important of these is the carriage return operation. The control character that causes the teleprinter to return its printing mechanism to the left-hand side of the paper takes just one normal character time to transmit, but depending on several factors, the time for the action to be performed may take up to three character times. During the second and subsequent character times, other characters may arrive. Since the carriage is in the wrong place, the character is printed then and there, wherever it might be, rather than on the left hand side that hasn't been reached yet.

The common method of allowing for this unfortunate effect is to send a control character that does not make the printer mechanism try to do anything. Favourite choices for such a "fill" or "idle" character are *null* and *delete*. Thus the computer knows about the characteristics of the particular printing mechanism which it drives, makes certain calculations about the times required for the various operations, *carriage return, line feed, page/form feed*, and so on, and sends down the appropriate number of fill characters to allow for these times. An alternative tactic is actually to use a timer in the sending computer and refrain from sending anything during these critical times. Which of the two strategies is chosen will depend mainly on implementation constraints or efficiency considerations inside the sending computer.

Even for such trivial types of operation, the code within the driving computer may already be quite complex. The same piece of code may easily have to cover ten or twenty different types of printer, and respond differently for up to half a dozen special operations on each of them, possibly allowing for how far the carriage has to travel in the particular case in hand, and allowing for various combinations of carriage return and line feed.

Mercifully, the need for such dead reckoning techniques has essentially disappeared due to the appearance of terminals with much improved characteristics. Fortunately also, the kinds of terminals used in the examples above are now only museum pieces. However, much of this type of behaviour is enshrined in the X.3 set of international protocols described in Chapter 7.

- Receiver FIFO

One attempt to obviate this tedious need to send fill characters is to provide a mechanism that is faster than the communications line, together with an internal *First-In, First-Out*—FIFO buffer. A very popular arrangement is to have a mechanism that can print at, say 45 characters per second, but driven from a 30 characters per second line. The carriage return function on such a device still takes much longer than one character transmission time, $1/30$ second. However, during such a slow operation incoming characters are accumulated in the buffer. When the slow operation is complete the fast mechanism will consume characters at the high rate of 45 per second until the buffer is empty. It will then print them as they arrive, 30 per second. This results in the at first disconcerting effect of a spurt of fast character printing at the start of each line.

Clearly, it is possible deliberately to outwit such a machine by sending a sufficient proportion of slow operations that the buffer overflows, but in normal use such overflow is unlikely. Such buffers are in any case usually augmented by explicit flow control as described below.

Even with voluntary flow control by dead reckoning or with an internal FIFO buffer, we may get data overrun. The most obvious circumstance is when the paper jams or runs out on printing devices, or when a user wants time to peruse the screen of a video terminal. If data is not to be lost in these cases there must be some mechanism for the recipient to stop the flow.

- On/Off Flow Control

The most common way of achieving this effect is to allocate two control characters for the task. As described in Chapter 1, characters can be divided into two groups, the printable characters, and the control characters. If we allocate two control characters for the "X-on" and "X-off" functions, (DC1 and DC3 in Fig 1.1) then we may use them as follows. When the receiver decides that it is nearly "full up" with characters, it may send an X-off character to the sending machine. The understanding is that the sender will then refrain from sending further characters. It is the receiver's responsibility to decide when it is ready to receive further data, and then send an X-on character. The X-on and X-off are simple flow control messages which mean, respectively, *"You may send me data"* and *"Please stop sending data"*.

Obviously, such a system allows for the paper jam to be rectified, or for the user to pause output while he reads the video screen. It also allows terminals with an internal buffer to prevent the sending computer from overflowing the internal buffer. In this case the X-on/X-off flow control is usually activated at "high water" and "low water" marks in an attempt to keep the level of data in the internal buffer within bounds, and thus run the attached mechanism at optimum speed.

- DTR Flow Control

Sometimes a logically equivalent method of flow control is used. Terminals are mostly connected by a standard multi-way plug that can be plugged directly into a modem. This plug can transmit many signals besides the straightforward data signals as we saw in Chapter 1. In particular, the *Data Terminal Ready*—DTR line may be interpreted as the analogue of the X-on/X-off signal.

• Microprocessor Printer Control

Perhaps the ultimate variation on this theme of increasing function comes with the introduction of the dedicated microprocessor controlling the printing or display mechanism. Such microprocessors are able to perform various optimisations with printing mechanisms. For example, multiple consecutive spaces can be combined into a single fast skip, the next line may be printed backwards, saving the slow return back to the left hand side, and so forth without limit. In the case of video displays, the micro may implement anything from a simple roll up of text on the screen, through inserting or deleting lines or characters and complex local editing, up to a full blown programmable or "soft" terminal with text scrolling, line re-entry, and full screen based editing. Again it is possible to implement all this on top of a link that has only simple X-on/X-off flow control, and most of it has appeared on the market in just such a guise.

4.2   Record Oriented Flow Control

The series of illustrative examples has so far been presented in terms of character flows: streams of characters flow across some medium and various strategies are used to control this character flow. Many of the same ideas can be applied to control the flow of records or packets. Clearly, if the sequence of characters was replaced by a sequence of packets, then we could have an X-on packet, etc, and the algorithms could work just the same. After all, a record or packet is just a longer string of bits. It is just this difference—that a packet is a longer string of bits than a character—that both makes different flow control strategies desirable or necessary, and also allows such different strategies. Since packets are longer it is less likely that the receiver will be able to store a large number of them compared with a similar number of characters.

Packets may have structure, and it may be that the receiver wishes to control the flow of different classes of packet differently. Lastly, it is this internal structure of packets that means that flow control messages may be more complicated than the simple on/off protocols we have so far examined, and makes it possible to do flow control in more complex and interesting ways.

We shall now proceed to examine some examples of more complex flow control involving packets.

• Multiple remote printers.

If, instead of the single printer attached to a communications line, we have a small remote computer driving two printers, as in Fig 4.1, we see the types of signal the two computers need to exchange.

Clearly, as we anticipated above, a simple stream of characters is insufficient. When characters arrive at the remote printing station, there

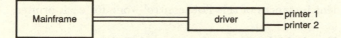

Fig 4.1.   Driving Two Printers Down One Line

needs to be some indication of which printer they are supposed to be printed on. Such information is not present in a simple character stream, and must be provided by some means. The usual method is to structure the stream of characters into records, or perhaps use a transmission medium that naturally involves a record structure. Then each record will contain a region at the front that contains some control information. This kind of field is frequently called an *opcode* (for *op*eration *code*). In our case, we might use a single byte to indicate for which printer the record is destined. This is an elementary form of addressing.

Each of these two printers will require some sort of flow control for precisely the same sort of reasons that individual printers in the earlier examples have needed flow control. Let us provide it in a simple and crude fashion by providing a simple pair of X-on and X-off packets. Then the driver computer will have some pool of buffers to hold the packets it receives from the host computer. When it decides that it wants the host to stop, it sends the X-off packet, and when it decides it wants more, it sends the X-on packet. This scheme or protocol will indeed stop the host overrunning the printers, but it is a very unsatisfactory way of driving the printers. The problem is that the protocol is completely unselective. Should one printer be very busy, or, still worse, broken, then the driver computer has no way of communicating this to the host. It can only stop the flow completely. It can't say *"Stop the flow of packets for the first printer, but keep sending it for the second one"*. Not only do the demands of individual printers vary for all the sorts of reasons we have discussed at length above, but the demands of printers vary independently of each other.

Fortunately, the fix is fairly obvious—the flow control messages need to identify the printer to which they are referring: the X-on and X-off messages need to contain the address bytes that identify the destination printer in just the same way as the output records do. We have now expanded the protocol—the vocabulary available to the receiver—so that it can now selectively control the flow for each of the printers.

It is useful to look at this in terms of layers. At the bottom layer we have a medium that transmits a flow of records. On top of that is another layer that uses this record structure and a header byte to provide two independent flows—i.e. to multiplex two flows on top of a single flow. The topmost layer consists of a simple stop/go flow control protocol between a client and a server. Note that there are two independent instances of this flow control—one for each printer.

4.3   Bandwidth, Throughput, and Delay Time

Before proceeding further with the study of flow control mechanisms, we shall deviate for a moment to examine the concepts of bandwidth, throughput and delay time, and the way in which these are inter-related.

We have come across the concept of *bandwidth* before when we were discussing various transmission techniques in Chapter 1. Bandwidth is concerned with the transmission of information by some means. For our purposes here, we shall define bandwidth as the rate at which information can be transmitted through an interface—Fig 4.2.

Fig 4.2.   Bandwidth of an Interface

Throughput is concerned not with an interface, but with communication between two entities. Each of the entities has an interface to a shared communications medium. The throughput is the rate at which the two entities can send bits end-to-end across the communications medium—Fig 4.3.

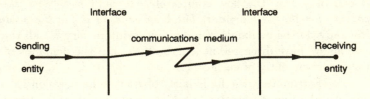

Fig 4.3.   Throughput End-to-End

Well, what is the difference between the throughput and the bandwidth—why aren't the two just the same? In some cases they are. If the speed of both of the interfaces and of the communications medium is the same, and the sender just sends continuously, then the throughput is the same as the interface bandwidth.

The throughput starts to deviate from the bandwidth, downwards of course, when we start to consider the effects of flow control protocols. We shall see that this is so even when the receiver is not deliberately using the flow control protocol to stem the flow. Even when the user is operating the flow control mechanism in such a way as to promote maximum flow, then many protocols still cause the throughput to drop below the raw bandwidth apparently available at the interface.

We shall take an everyday, yet somewhat extreme example. Imagine two executives who wish to communicate about some matter. For some reason the to and fro conversation must be conducted by letter. As each of the executives dictates the latest letter to her secretary she is using an interface (dictation), that operates at perhaps 10 characters per second (say 100 words per minute). However, depending on the nature of the communication, the letter will be of limited size. Imagine our executives typically write about 1000 words, say 5,000 characters. Such a letter will be dictated in less than 10 minutes. Each letter will take a day or three to reach the recipient, and some further time before a reply is prepared. If each letter takes just one day, then we see that the throughput of the discussion is 5,000 characters per day, or about one character every $17 1/4$ seconds. The difference is clearly due to the fact that the dictation interface to the secretary operates for less than 10 minutes per day thus reducing the "efficiency" well below 1%.

The problem with conducting such a conversation by letter is the *delay time* involved in delivering the letter. If some other means of sending the letter could be found that managed immediate delivery, then the throughput of the conversation would be much higher. One example of such a means might be to send the letters by FAX, or to use two linked teleprinters with the executives standing over their secretaries operating the machines. Much the same effect could be had by conducting the conversation by telephone. Some of the details change in this case, but the essential point is that the delay time has been eliminated, so increasing the throughput up towards the level of the raw bandwidth of the interfaces being used.

If we think of our executives in terms of entities using a communications medium, then we can see that the reduction of the throughput was because of the protocol being used: each entity sent one small message, and then waited for a replying message from its peer entity. The nature of the conversation means that the protocol cannot be changed. The throughput can only be increased by decreasing the delay time. Using faster interfaces with higher bandwidth has no effect on the communication since the time traversing the interface is negligible compared with the overall delay time.

Let us look at another example that is concerned with computing media. A full reel of magnetic tape may contain 2700 feet of tape recorded at 6250 characters per inch. That is well over 100 million characters. The mounting of such a tape on a tape drive in say 10 seconds might be viewed as the passing of 10^8 characters across an interface in 10 seconds, say 10^8 bits/sec. (Let us ignore the time taken to position and read the tape.) A boy on a bicycle could carry such a tape a comfortable 15 miles in an hour, and achieve a throughput of 10^8 characters in 3600 seconds, a still impressive 300,000 bits per second. This is comparable with the speed of the more expensive communications links, and many computer telecommunications links are tens of times slower.

And yet, even such a vast bandwidth would not be at all adequate for the humblest interactive terminal, since it is accompanied by a quite unacceptable delay time. If every character typed in, or even every input line, was individually recorded on a magnetic tape, and dispatched on a one hour's trip by boy powered bicycle, then the user of the interactive terminal would get little work done—his throughput would be abysmal even if he had the dedication to continue. What has changed is the size of the parcel of data. This has dropped from the 10^8 characters of a full tape to the few typed characters on the terminal. The potential throughput cannot be exploited because of the transactional nature of the terminal interaction. Indeed, the terminal's throughput would increase enormously if it were attached to the most modest of telephone lines capable of transmitting a mere 10 characters per second. The difference of course would be that the end-to-end delay time would now have dropped to be comparable with his typing speed for one character, and the throughput has correspondingly risen. Note that the new raw bandwidth is a mere 10 characters per second, 3,000 times smaller than before. Yet because the delay time has dropped his throughput has risen from a few characters per hour with the bicycle to a few characters per second with the slow communications line, a 3,600 times increase.

4.4   Flow Control Mechanisms

Having examined at some length the relationship between bandwidth, throughput, delay time, and flow control mechanisms, we shall now alter the focus of the study, and examine various flow control methods. The prime aim of these methods is to increase the throughput. In general the underlying idea is to have sufficient packets in transit so that the effect of the delay time is nullified, and yet the flow is kept under control.

4.5   M and N Pacing

A concept introduced in the ARPANET is that of "M and N pacing". The original type of flow control on ARPANET was a simple token at the message level. The ARPANET message could be up to 8063 bits in length. A receiver indicated its willingness to receive the next message by sending a *Ready For Next Message*—RFNM (pronounced "rufnum" by the the initiates). The ARPANET may chop the message into "packets", and one message may be split into up to eight packets. Thus a RFNM is a permission to send up to eight packets. The splitting up of the message into eight packets was done for several reasons, but of interest here is the fact that each packet could be transmitted independently. Thus, each of these packets may be scheduled for retransmission from one node to the next before the following packet has been received. It was quite possible for the first packet in a long message to be completely received at the destination before the last packet had started transmission from the sender. Clearly this reduces the end-to-end delay time considerably for long messages. The receiver could not send the next RFNM until the last packet of the last received message has arrived. Thus, for each message in a long transfer, there is a time equal to the transit time of the RFNM plus the transit time of the first packet when the receiver is not receiving data from the network. The throughput is thus reduced considerably from the apparently available bandwidth.

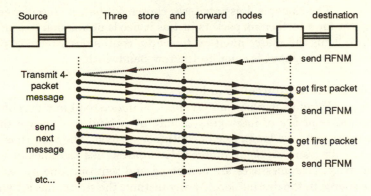

Fig 4.4.   "RFNM" Flow Control

Fig 4.4 illustrates this process for a simple example. The messages are all four packets long. The "network" is two host interface machines with an extra intermediate stage. We assume that the hosts communicate instantaneously with these interface machines. Thus the packets are stored in three store and forward machines and transmitted down two comparatively slow communications lines.

The M and N pacing technique attempts to allow complete overlap between consecutive messages. The technique works in terms of packets rather than the larger messages. The receiver requests the source to transmit N packets. When the receiver has received M packets, it sends a further request for N packets. After this, it sends a request for a further N packets after receiving each further N packets.

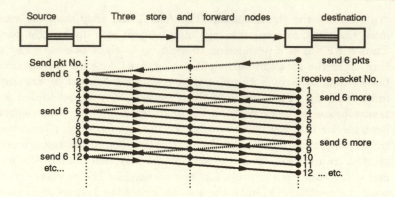

Fig 4.5. M and N Pacing

Fig 4.5 illustrates the same physical setup as the previous illustration of RFNM flow control. However, here the flow is controlled by N and M pacing. The example uses $N = 6$ and $M = 2$.

The example illustrated was chosen so that the receiver gets the request for a further six packets just as it needs permission to send some more. Thus the source manages to send a continuous stream of packets and the throughput is equal to the raw bandwidth.

4.6   Flow Control Windows

Window mechanisms can best be understood in terms of a long ordered sequence of messages. It may be helpful to envisage them as lines printed on a long piece of continuous paper. They are thus shown in the diagrams as being ordered downwards, like the lines of text on this page. The messages are numbered and sent out, one by one, from the source to the destination. At any instant, the sender has a "window" onto this sequence of messages (strip of paper), and has permission from the receiver to send any message within this window. So if the window extends from n to $n + w - 1$, then the sender may send any of the w messages numbered from n up to $n + w - 1$ inclusive.

```
trailing edge of window :    |—  message  n
                             |—  message  n+1
                             :     ...
                             :—  message  n+w-2
leading edge of window :     |—  message  n+w-1
```

Fig 4.6.   Flow Control "Window"

Flow control messages will be sent from the receiver from time to time. These will have the effect of saying

"I have now got messages numbered n to n + m − 1 inclusive"
and imply that

"I am now ready for you to send me the messages numbered n + m to n + m + w − 1 inclusive."

In other words, as the receiver acknowledges the receipt of a block of messages at the trailing edge of the window (top in the diagram), the window moves or slides "downwards" or "forwards" in the ordered sequence, and allows those messages that have just been passed by the movement of the trailing edge of the window to be sent. The process of moving the window forward by m is illustrated in Fig 4.7.

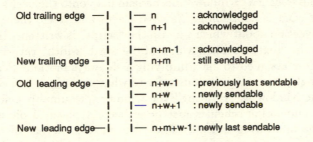

```
Old trailing edge — |    | — n          : acknowledged
                    |    | — n+1        : acknowledged

                    |    | — n+m-1      : acknowledged
New trailing edge — |    | — n+m        : still sendable
Old  leading edge — |    | — n+w-1      : previously last sendable
                    |    | — n+w        : newly sendable
                    |    | — n+w+1      : newly sendable

New  leading edge— |    | — n+m+w-1 : newly last sendable
```

Fig 4.7.   Advancing a Flow Control Window

In general, the receiver and sender will have different windows onto the sequence of messages. This is caused by the time delay that the control messages suffer just like the data messages do. When the receiver sends the message to update the window, there will be a time before the sender of data gets this message. The aim of the window mechanism is to have the window sufficiently large that the sender may continue to send: the "height" of the window allows multiple outstanding messages.

4.7   Windows and Cyclic Numbering

It is usual to implement a window mechanism in terms of cyclic or modulo numbers. For example, a three bit field may be reserved, allowing numbers in the range 0 to 7. With such cyclic numbers, the window mechanism operates in exactly the same way. All the numerical comparisons are just the same except that they are done in modulo arithmetic.

The one limitation introduced is that the maximum window size must be *less* than the modulus of the numbers involved—thus in our example with 3-bit numbers, the modulus is 8, and the maximum window size is 7. There is a very simple reason for this. Just imagine for a moment that you wished to use a window size of 8 with modulo-8 numbers. Then because of the way in which modulo arithmetic works the sender would find that it was always valid to send data: with a window size of 8, records 0 to 7 inclusive are able to be sent; with moduluo 8 arithmetic, records 8, 9, 10, etc are numbered 0, 1, 2, etc, and thus can be sent too—the desired flow control has disappeared.

Exercise 4.1   Compare this restriction with the similar restriction in error recovery protocols in Chapter 2.

4.8   The Mental Picture of a Window Mechanism

There is general confusion about the precise way in which the elements of the so-called "window" mechanism map onto the user's mental picture of what is happening. As with stacks and trees, there is no universal convention about which way up the "script" is written—the diagram shows the "text" upside down, and the word "width" rather than "height" is often assigned to "w", implying a sideways motion. Perhaps most confusingly, many descriptions refer to what we have called sliding or moving the window as "rotating" the window, presumably referring to the cyclic numbering schemes just described. A physical picture of that would be interesting indeed! Thus, the mental picture of a real physical window is only vaguely useful as a representation of what is really going on.

4.9   Implications of Window Mechanisms

The window mechanism as just described is an abstraction of several "real" mechanisms—that is parts of protocols that are used in actual operating communications networks. These actual instances of window mechanisms usually occur in combination with other features of the protocol, and often interact with these other features in complex ways. We shall return to some consideration of this presently.

The essence of the window mechanism is that the size of the window is fixed. This size may be implicit in the protocol (e.g. the number's *modulus* $- 1$), agreed by some administrative procedure, or derived by an analysis of the availability of buffers. Frequently it is is quite outside the control of the implementor of the protocol. This may give rise to problems. The worst such problem is that the receiver must normally be prepared to accept a "window full" of data. In our case this is w buffers for the w messages constituting a "full" window. For small windows this may not be a problem, but if a large window is specified, or required for performance, then the number of buffers required may be embarrassing. Depending on circumstances, a statistical approach may be used: many tasks each receiving data to be put onto disc files may share a pool of buffers. The pool of buffers could be large enough to satisfy the peak demands of a subset of the tasks, but not of all of them. Such techniques are very good at handling statistically random variations, but fail for common-mode variations. In our example, this technique would handle surges on individual file server tasks that were not correlated with surges for other servers. However, if all servers were held up at the same time, say by a transient disc error necessitating recovery action that held up all disc users, then the fact that all servers would simultaneously require an exceptional number of buffers could well lead to a global buffer shortage.

Such statistical considerations apply to many types of flow control. However, the main objection to the window mechanism as such is that the window size is fixed, and thus cannot be varied to accommodate varying or various circumstances.

As an example of varying circumstances, let us imagine a protocol for transferring bulk data—moving batch jobs for example. On a lightly loaded machine at night it may be appropriate to have a large window size. This will allow many records to be simultaneously in transmission across the network and thus make best use of both network and host resources. However, if the same transfer were to take place in the busiest period of the day, such as mid-afternoon, then a small window size may be more appropriate. This is because buffers in the machine are much more likely to be in short supply due to other activities. Likewise, the network, and any of its internal buffers, will also be in demand, and multiple packets in transit will yield lower dividends.

As a converse example, some applications exist where a large window size will never be of use. Perhaps the most obvious is a simple enquiry/response system. In such a system at most one record is sent in any one direction before a response is sent back. If such a system is implemented on top of a lower level of protocol that contains a window mechanism then inefficiencies can result: clearly, if a statistical pool of buffers is used then there is much beneficial sharing. However, if a simple minded implementation has allocated a maximum window size pool of buffers, say seven, then most of them will never be used—$6/7$ in our example.

Finally, the mechanism may react with other protocol elements in unfortunate ways. Many protocols, including X.25 (see Chapter 6), have a "RESET" function. The effect of this is to discard data in transit, set the connection back to some well known state, and make sure the two ends synchronise on this RESET at the same point in the call (i.e. can resume from the same fixed point in the conversation). The effect of RESET generated by the network is to pass the buck up to the higher levels of protocol, effectively saying *"I'm in a mess, you sort it out from this point"*. Alternatively, a network user can call for a network reset to sort out problems too. Such a facility can be used in several ways, but the one of most interest here is to recover from congestion, or buffer shortage problems. The interaction with flow control is in the setting of the call back to the initial state. The initial state of X.25 is with the flow control window fully open. Thus, after a RESET the receiver must be prepared to accept a window full of buffers. Now, if the receiver has just been short of buffers and called a RESET to recover from that shortage, then a "window full" of buffers is the last thing that it wants. However, if it's right out of buffers, RESET might be the only thing it can do.

4.10   Credit Mechanisms

The credit mechanism can be viewed as a generalisation of the window mechanism, though it is normally presented as a completely different form of flow control. With a credit mechanism, the receiver does not acknowledge data at the "bottom" edge of the window, but instead requests the transmission of new data that was previously just above the top edge of the window. The protocol no longer concentrates on the bottom edge of the window and implies the top edge by an agreement about the size of the window, but now talks only in terms of the top edge of the window. Nevertheless, it is still useful to think of this protocol in terms of a window.

The receiver keeps a note of the last record that it has received and can issue credit allowing the sender to send up to that record plus some number. This number can be thought of as the window size. It should be noted that the receiver's window size is completely under the control of the receiver, in that it can open it just as much as it wants by issuing new credits. In this way it can adapt the window size to changing conditions by controlling the rate at which it issues credit. Note, however, that it usually cannot revoke credit once it has been issued. (One counter example to this is the most complex version of the ISO Transport Protocol.) This is not usually a problem, though, since incoming data always tends to close up the window. With a credit mechanism, the "RESET" has the effect of revoking all credit, thus closing the window firmly shut instead of leaving it gaping wide open as in X.25.

As with the fixed window protocol, the sender sees a varying sized opening depending on network delays. However, since the opening now also depends on the size of the window at the receiver's end, it is at least possible to adjust the receiver's window in an attempt to keep the sender's window slightly ajar, rather than being stuck with the parameters as given.

There are two main variations on this credit flow control depending on how the credits are represented. The most obvious variant is that the receiver sends credit messages to the sender containing just a number of credits. The sender then may implement a send algorithm by keeping an integer which is initially zero. When it receives credit, it adds this to the integer, and it decrements the integer each time a record is sent. Flow is controlled by the sender only sending when the integer is non-zero. There is no need for the sender to number the records as sent. An implication of this method is that it is only useful when used on top of other layers of protocol that ensure that records are not lost or duplicated.

The other variant is to send credit in terms of sequence numbers. The credit messages are then an invitation to send up to a specified number, and the data records sent in response are numbered. Such a representation is more useful than the cumulative credits described above if it is used within a layer of protocol that does not have an assurance of delivery. Clearly, a repetition of a credit message couched in terms of sequence numbers will not cause problems but repetition of credit messages of the straight credit type would cause the flow to be incorrectly controlled.

> **Exercise 4.2**   Compare and contrast this method of sending credit with the uses of the sequence numbers in HDLC described in Chapter 2.

4.11   Credits and Sliding Window Protocols

The perceptive and devious reader may have noticed enough similarity between the straightforward fixed window mechanism, and the credit mechanism just described to suggest that he could operate a sliding window protocol to have the same effect as the credit protocol. Indeed, if there is a limit to the possible accumulated credit, then the two methods can be seen to be almost exactly the same—the updating of the trailing edge of the window in the sliding window protocol, with its implied movement of the leading edge of the window is exactly the same as the explicit advance of the leading edge by the credit messages.

With a modest perversion, the fixed window protocol can be operated with a window size that exceeds the fixed window size. If a sending implementation was prepared to accept "acknowledgement" messages from the receiver in advance of that record actually being sent, then the sending window could be opened arbitrarily wide. The sender could accept such advance acknowledgements and accumulate them against the time when records could be dispatched. It might even call such advance acknowledgements "credits".

So what are the real differences? The first is that the initial opening of the window is under the control of the receiver with a credit mechanism but it is defined as wide open with the fixed window mechanism. This initial condition may well be crucial in some implementations and in some conditions.

The second difference is more subtle, and depends on interaction with other elements of the protocol of which this mechanism forms a part. In X.25, a window mechanism operates at two different levels and is used for two quite different applications. At the link level, the window mechanism is used mainly to acknowledge the safe receipt of frames of data (and is not really directly concerned with flow control at all). As we have seen, blocks are numbered modulo-8, and a maximum of seven data blocks may be sent until the first is acknowledged. When an error is detected, the error recovery procedures cause the sender to back up to the first of the blocks in error and re-send it. Thus, until the trailing edge of the window is advanced past them, the sender is not free to discard blocks that remain in the window. In this case, the acknowledgement message serves two functions. It allows the copies of those records acknowledged to be released by the transmitter, so freeing resources in the sender, and it also allows further records at the leading edge of the window to be transmitted. Clearly there is an interaction here between the two uses of the acknowledgement message—implicitly to allow further data flow, and explicitly to acknowledge safe data receipt.

Thus, when evaluating a window mechanism, we need to have a clear picture of the significance of the edges of the window. If only the leading edge is important, then there is close equivalence with a credit mechanism apart from initial conditions. If the lower edge is really significant (as in TCP), rather than just being present (as in X.25 level 3), then there are further differences as we shall see in the next two chapters. (TCP and X.25 are discussed in Chapter 6.)

4.12   Do We Really Need Flow Control?

This chapter has been devoted to expounding the need for flow control and the techniques used in implementing it. However, we have seen an example in the remote procedure calls of Chapter 2 where the flow control is implicit, and we shall encounter the blast file transfer protocol in Chapter 12 where flow control is deliberately dispensed with in the quest for increased throughput. However, it is a fact that flow control is essential for most applications that rely on an ordered flow of data along a connection between two entities.

4.13   Flow Control in Real Life

In our analysis of flow control so far, we have concentrated on fairly simple models of what is going on. In particular, we have entirely ignored the fact that "real networks" carry traffic for other people too—they are not just standing idle to transmit our traffic.

Just how important this factor might be is very difficult to estimate. In a local area network that has a "raw bandwidth" of 10 megabits
per second, and connects half a dozen lightly loaded systems together,
it is extremely unlikely that there is ever any real contention for the
medium. In such a network, it is a close approximation to the truth to
ignore completely the effect of any other traffic.

Somewhere near the other extreme stand public data networks.
At busy times, the delay on these networks increases substantially, and
may be irritating even for the slow human interactive user.

Let us examine the sort of interaction that we might expect
between heavy traffic and window flow control protocols. We shall again
take a simplified model as illustrated in Fig 4.8.

Fig 4.8. Simplified Model Network

In Fig 4.8 we see two hosts connected to two different nodes on a
store and forward network. We shall again assume that all the links are
of the same speed. As we have seen above, we might expect to maximise
the throughput of the data flow from A to B by arranging that at all
times there is one packet in transit on each of the intermediate links.
We might do this by an end-to-end window mechanism. In our example,
the size of the window will have to be three for the forward direction of
transmission, plus a further three for the acknowledgements travelling
in the reverse direction. The two hosts might then expect the network
to be giving a throughput equivalent to the raw bandwidth of each of
the links.

However, a more realistic picture is shown in Fig 4.9. Here we
see that instead of just one single pair of hosts exchanging data, our
more realistic model has three pairs of nodes exchanging data. Each
flow of data travels on separate links from its originating host to node
1, then shares the link from node 1 to node 2 with both the other flows,
and finally travels on to its destination host, again by a separate link.

Since the link from node 1 to node 2 is shared between the
three pairs of hosts, it is not possible for each of them simultaneously
to be allocated all of its bandwidth. Also, it is unlikely that any pair of
hosts has any explicit knowledge of the behaviour of other hosts in the
network.

Let us imagine that each pair of hosts agrees to maximise the
throughput of their exchange of data by using a window mechanism,
and that they choose a window size of 6 that is derived from a model

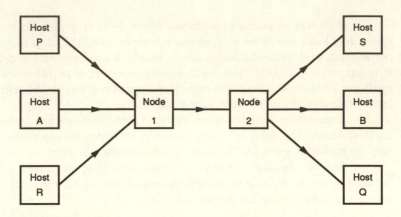

Fig 4.9.   More Realistic Model Network

like Fig 4.8.   In this case, each pair of hosts will have six packets in transit at any one time, a total of 18 for the three connections. There can only be a maximum of 14 packets in transmission on the network shown in Fig 4.9, and thus at least four of the 18 packets must be stored somewhere. Presumably this will be mostly in the internal queues of the two nodes, awaiting transmission on the bottleneck link between the two nodes.

Actually, the situation is much worse that that.   Only rarely can all the links be busy. Since the middle link is the bottleneck, then (assuming fairness in operation) it will carry traffic for each pair of hosts for only one third of the time. So, on average, each of the host-to-node links will only be in operation for one third of the time in either direction (assuming all links are the same speed), and only three packets will be in transmission in either direction, leaving 12 packets to be queued for transmission on the centre link. The capacity of the various network links is not in some sense "in balance" with the offered load.

Thus we can see that in the case of this congested network the window mechanism has been only modestly effective in increasing the throughput. However, worse than that, it has had the effect of considerably increasing the network congestion. The effect of the large window size has been counter-productive. Since a total of six packets can be in transmission, using a window size of more than 2 merely increases congestion without increasing throughput.

Though our model of Figs 4.8 and 4.9 is now much more realistic in that it allows us qualitatively to understand the dramatic impact of other traffic on the shared link, it still falls far short of an adequate model from which quantitative figures can be derived. In a real network many more variables must be accounted for. The packets of data between hosts are often, though by no means always, wildly variable in size, and the contra-flowing acknowledgements are usually shorter. Actual networks incorporate links of various speeds. X.25 links from networks to hosts are typically in the range 2400 to 9600 bits per second, and between nodes are typically 9600 to 64000 bps. (though all these speeds are rising rapidly). Most variable of all is the "other" traffic. This may vary slowly with the time of day, and quickly with individual bursts of traffic. Few networks are sufficiently large that traffic can really be said to average out, and the traffic itself is fundamentally "bursty" in nature rather than being of the random distribution so often found in simulation models—"bags" of mail, or the burst of activity as staff save files just before going home are very non-random in nature.

In such a complex world, what can the conscientious network subscriber or operator do? Pairs of subscribers might be able to adjust the window size gradually up and down and note the effect of this on the throughput. They should always attempt to use the smallest sized window that gives an improvement over the next smallest one. In this way, they are achieving maximum throughput with minimum congestion to the network. However, for this to work, the variations in observed throughput must be due to the changes made in the window size rather than in other variables, such as someone else sending a bag of computer mail along one of the shared links. One might also imagine two pairs of subscribers trying to minimise their window sizes at the same time, and the variations in throughput observed by each pair being influenced just as much by the changes in window sizes being made quite independently by the other pair as by the probing changes made by the observing pair.

In addition to some sort of sophisticated algorithm to achieve a stable window size, the users would need a protocol to communicate the necessary information end-to-end. Many windows are not actually end-to-end across a network, but across the user to network interface only (e.g. X.25 without the D-bit set—see Chapter 6). Thus such subscribers cannot influence the internal network congestion directly anyway. Possibly the only practical way in which windows can be adjusted in practice is "manually"—the parameters are adjusted manually from time to time and crude long-term observations are used to evaluate the effectiveness of the changes.

There is more scope for network operators to tinker constructively with the parameters. Mostly, their ability to tune the network lies in their opportunity to observe the traffic patterns in the network from their bird's-eye view. It is then within their power to relieve congestion by the installation of inter-node links with higher bandwidth where this is required. It is also possible for the network that is becoming congested to stop the traffic coming in until some of the congestion has cleared.

In this way the network is able to reduce the effective bandwidth of the incoming links. We can see that this is similar, in a way, to increasing the internal bandwidth in that both are methods of putting the internal and external bandwidths into some sort of "balance".

However, flow control "in the large" has problems of its own in that deadlocks may occur. We shall examine this in the next chapter.

The final, and perhaps the most complex tool available to the network operator is that of tariff structures. The rates for the use of resources often has a time element: the rate at peak times being higher than at quieter, less busy times. This has the dual effect of moving some traffic out of the peak times, and of making those who generate the peak traffic, and thus necessitate the installation of equipment that is under-utilised the rest of the time, pay for the extra equipment necessary.

The complexity of the situation has now truly gone beyond mathematical analysis since it now incorporates value judgements and budgetary considerations by both the providers and the users.

5
Network Routing and Congestion

In this chapter we examine the various issues involved in supplying the basic network service. Mostly these issues are to do with routing data through the network and delivering it to its intended destination. We shall see how the route of a particular packet is determined both from its destination address and also from the topology and traffic in the network itself. We shall look at the problem of deadlocks, and how we can either recover from a deadlocked situation or avoid getting into it in the first place. We also compare and contrast the two main approaches to the provision of network service—datagrams and virtual calls. Finally we examine the issues of broadcasts and multicasts, and how these relate to local and wide-area networks. This chapter gives a grounding in the internals of networks in preparation for the discussion of the network service in the next chapter.

5.1   Network Addresses, Routes and Topology

So far in this book, we have looked at the various ways that data is transmitted either along point-to-point links or across shared media of various flavours. We have seen how errors occur, and ways of detecting transmission errors and correcting them. It is now time to look at the ways in which these basic elements may be combined together to form the systems that are commonly called "Computer Networks", or often just plain "Networks". In this chapter we shall be concerned with some of the issues involved in the varying topology of networks, of identifying network users by means of addresses, and of finding routes across a network to the desired destination.

Fig 5.1 is a schematic view of a network with a set of users attached to it in some unspecified way. We shall assume that the users of the network are attached to it in order to send data to each other (other reasons have been known, such as keeping up with the Joneses), and that the data will be passed across the network in packets. In this very schematic view, it should be noted that a "user" is a very general term, and includes individual terminal users on simple terminals and large multi-user mainframes servicing several hundred terminals.

For a packet of data to reach the intended recipient, the recipient needs to be identified in some way. The technique for doing this is to assign each and every network user a unique address. The reader may wonder why the user is not identified by a "name". We shall return to

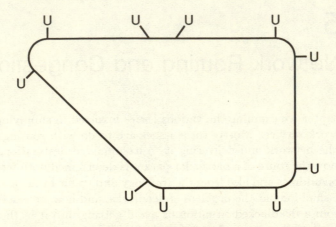

Fig 5.1.   A Network With Some Attached Users

this point later. Suffice it for now to say that the users are assumed to be located "in the same place" (whatever that means), and thus can be reached at the same "address" all the time. To lawyers, we are clearly not talking about persons "of no fixed abode". The sender of the packet of data attaches the appropriate address to the packet in some way before sending it out onto the network. The address is used by the network in order to deliver the packet, and the recipient uses the address to accept only packets intended for itself.

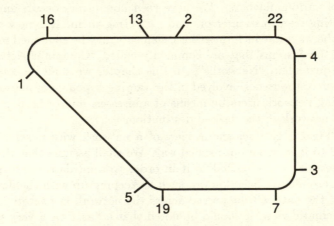

Fig 5.2.   Unique Network Addresses

Fig 5.2 shows the same network as before, but now each of the users has been allocated a unique number. We shall see presently that this *identifier* or *address* might have various forms, but for the time being we need only remark that it must be unique. The packets are each labelled with a destination address, and this is used as the means of delivering each packet to its intended recipient.

5.2   Datagrams and Virtual Calls

Having introduced the notion of an address, we now need to establish the twin concepts of the *datagram* and the *virtual call*.

In its simplest form the datagram is an individual unit or packet of data together with a destination address. This is shown schematically in Fig 5.3.

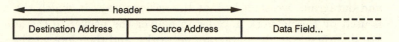

Fig 5.3. A Simple Datagram

Datagrams are sent out onto the network one by one, and the network will interpret the destination address and try to deliver the datagram in some way. The network will operate on a "best effort" basis—that is, it will usually manage to deliver the datagram, but it may lose datagrams sometimes, or the datagrams may be delivered in a different order from that in which they were sent, be delayed by varying amounts, or even be duplicated, corrupted, or misdirected. There is a parallel here between a datagram service and the telegram service (from which the word "datagram" derives), or a postal service. Telegrams or letters may be delivered out of order or delayed. They may also be lost (but are rarely duplicated!).

A virtual call service parallels a telephone call. Firstly, an association is established between two users, one of which calls the other. Once the call has been established, the two users exchange data along the virtual call or connection, and then finally one or other initiates the disconnection of the call. These three phases of *call establishment, data transmission*, and *call disconnection* parallel the telephone phases of calling and answering, conversation, and hanging up. In general terms, the virtual call type of service also differs from the datagram service both in that the destination address is only needed in the initial setup phase, and also in that the flow of data is supposed to be in order, and not have any duplicates or gaps.

A simile that may help to fix the two concepts is that of a postal chess game. When two players engage in such a game they exchange letters, each one containing one move. The postman who delivers the letters considers them to be individual entities, which have no association, one with another. Each letter is merely one more item in today's mailbag. On the other hand, the chess players know differently. Each of the letters is to them one more step in a carefully ordered sequence. The letters in this simile correspond to the datagrams, while the chess game corresponds with the virtual call.

This simile also introduces the useful notion that a virtual call can be built on top of the datagram service, and we shall return to this notion later. The other valuable idea introduced is that both the postman's view and the chess players' views are equally valid from their own perspectives. The postman's view is no more and no less valid than that of the chess players.

Now that we are armed with the notions of address, virtual call, and datagram, we shall look at the various ways in which the address is used by the network in order to deliver the packet to the addressee. We shall first consider datagram networks, and then look at the slightly different issues involved in virtual call routing.

5.3   Routing Datagrams

The way in which datagrams are routed depends on the topology of the network. The easiest type of routing is the degenerate case of the shared medium. In Chapter 3 we examined in some depth the various ways in which several users could share a medium to communicate with each other. The medium could be either a ring or a bus, and the access to it could be either by means of a token or by contention. However, all shared media have the common property that every packet is received by every user of the network. Thus, we see that there is no problem in working out a route—everything is broadcast everywhere. Routing becomes merely the degenerate task of each of the receivers ignoring all the packets not meant for itself.

We can think of shared media solving the routing problem by brute force, and this brute force approach can be extended significantly further. Fig 5.4 shows two shared media joined together by means of a *bridge*.

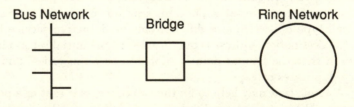

Fig 5.4.   Bridging Dissimilar Networks

A simple bridge receives every packet that arrives from either network, and retransmits it onto the other network as soon as possible.

This is again a brute force approach in that the bridge is merely matching or "bridging" the two dissimilar technologies of the two networks. It is taking no filtering action and packets are forwarded to the other network independently of whether the destination is that side or not. The bridge is merely acting at the "Media Access Control" level on each side, and is commonly referred to as a MAC-level bridge.

Clearly, such a simple MAC-level bridge will work, providing that the traffic on the two networks is sufficiently low that both of the networks and the bridge can handle the total traffic without becoming overloaded. Such a MAC-level bridge may be performing several functions. Firstly, it is, in our case, connecting two dissimilar types of shared medium together—"bridging" from one to the other. Another function that it may often be serving is that of a long distance connection. Shared media (with the exception of radio channels) are typically limited to a few kilometres in size. On the other hand bridges can use long distance high speed links to join two local networks together.

It is important to note that the addresses used on a set of bridged local networks must be chosen from a single set of addresses. There must be no conflicts. If there are conflicts, with any address being used on more than one network, then the networks must remain separate networks that are joined together by a gateway rather than a bridge. Gateways are discussed in Chapter 15.

A bridge of this brute force type is very useful. However, there is a very simple refinement that makes it much more useful. Datagrams have the source address as well as the destination address on them. If the bridge monitors each source address, then it can build up a picture of where every source address is, and it can use this picture as a way of deciding whether or not any given packet needs to be transmitted on the other side. Thus, at start-up time, the bridge has no knowledge of where any address is, and it copies all packets through to the other side. However, as each address transmits its first frame, the bridge monitors the source address, and learns on which network that address is. Thus, from then on it will know whether or not to forward packets sent to that address.

Such a simple device is very valuable, since it allows bridges to be used to segment a large network and to keep local traffic from flooding the rest of the network unnecessarily. Thus, for example, a group of machines in a department that do 90% of their communications with each other (perhaps to a local file server, or suchlike), and only 10% with the rest of the network, can be put on their own local segment, and joined to the rest of the network by such a bridge. In this way, not only can the overall load on the network be reduced, but private local communication is kept safer from the prying of users on the rest of the network.

We can see that we can extend the use of such simple bridges to fairly elaborate structures. The extension to a tree of networks joined by bridges is a straightforward extension of this setup. However, we immediately run into problems when we introduce cycles into the connection. Consider Fig 5.5.

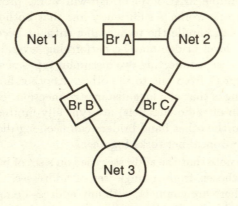

Fig 5.5.   A Loop of Bridges

If we "switch on" the setup in Fig 5.5, then all the bridges will be in a complete state of ignorance about where any address is. The first frame transmitted onto the network will be passed through all the bridges, and copies of itself will circulate round the network endlessly.

Exercise 5.1   Why?

Rather than investigating this particular type of setup further, we shall look at the very similar problems involved in a network of store and forward nodes connected by point-to-point links.

Fig 5.6 shows a network with the same geographical spread of users as in Fig 5.2. However, rather than the network being a shared medium of some sort, it consists now of a set of five "nodes" A to E connected by a set of point-to-point links. Each of the network users is attached to one of the nodes by means of an HDLC link (for example), and the links between the nodes are themselves point-to-point links too. To send a packet across the network it is first sent down the link from the user to the nearest node. In each node, the controlling program examines the destination address on the packet, and uses some algorithm to choose the next link down which to send the packet onward towards its destination.

We note that the addresses of various network users are scattered randomly across the nodes. Thus, if we are a network user attached

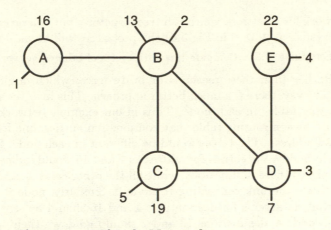

Fig 5.6.   A Simple Network

at address 13 for example, the route to destination addresses 3, 4, and 5 are quite different, whereas the routes to destinations 4 and 22 are very similar.

How can we implement a network like Fig 5.6? One possible way would be a Monte Carlo approach, or perhaps the drunkard's walk: once the datagram was in the network, we could choose a link at random down which to send the packet next. Though this would eventually work it would be clearly very inefficient. A very similar method has been christened the "hot potato" method. In this, the packet is sent out on the route with the shortest output queue, independently of its actual destination. We might be tempted to try the brute force method of broadcasting the datagram across all nodes. As the datagram arrives at each node it can be retransmitted to all attached nodes. Obviously the data would get to its destination very quickly. Indeed we can see that the method is very similar to the linked shared-medium networks that we studied earlier in this chapter. Here the node corresponds to a single shared-medium network, and the point-to-point links to the bridges between the networks (working without filtering).

The problem with this simple appeal to brute force is that the duplicated datagram would reach all other destinations in the network too, generating a large volume of redundant traffic, and worse than this, the volume of traffic would grow exponentially as each copy of the datagram produced multiple copies of itself as it arrived in each node, and the copy sent back to the originating node also produced multiple copies, and so on recursively. One way of attempting to patch up this broadcast method is to introduce a rule that as a datagram arrives at a node down a specific link, it is only rebroadcast on the other links out of that node, and not back along the link from which it arrived. Such a rule will work for a network which is a tree structure, but wherever there are cycles (such as B, D, C in Fig 5.6) the procedure will break down.

Exercise 5.2   Compare this with cycles of bridged networks.

Rather than these methods of brute force, which don't work very well anyway, there is a much better approach. This involves setting up a "routing table" in each node. Thus in our example network, each node would have a routing table that contains ten entries, one for each destination address. The tables would be different in each node. So, for example, in node A the entries for addresses 1 and 16 would indicate the specific links to those destinations, while all the other eight destinations would indicate the link connecting to node B. Similarly, node B would indicate that datagrams for destinations 1 and 16 should be sent down the link to node A, destinations 13 and 2 should go down their specific links, 5 and 19 should go to node C, and the rest to node D. The routing tables for all five nodes can be constructed in a similar way.

In constructing these routing tables, we have merely taken the topological diagram in Fig 5.6 and worked out the shortest route from wherever we are to the given destination. Then the first leg of that route is the entry in the routing table. So, while it is possible to get from B to E via C, the shortest route is directly via D. We have chosen the "best" route using the assumption that the "best" means the smallest number of links en route. There are other ways that are sometimes used for choosing the "best" route, such as trying to avoid particularly busy links, but we shall not be concerned with them here.

We can imagine that as networks get larger and larger, the maintenance of the routing tables becomes progressively more difficult. Thus, if we take a network with a hundred nodes and a thousand subscribers (actually a fairly modest network), then we will have to keep a routing table with a thousand entries in each of the hundred nodes—100,000 entries in all—and each time a subscriber joins the network, or moves his connection, or leaves the network, all 100 tables must be updated.

Such maintenance is required because we have not imposed any order on the allocation of the addresses. Consider instead the relabelled network in Fig 5.7. Here we see that the addresses have been allocated in a two-tier manner. Thus, all users on node D have the first part of their address 6, and no other users attached to other nodes have 6 as the first part of their address. The address is in two hierarchically related parts—a node number and a line number. Thus, when trying to figure out the route to a specific destination, the algorithm goes something like:

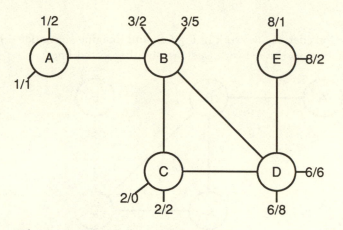

Fig 5.7. Two-Tier Addresses

if *Destination_Node_Number = My_Node_Number*
then

      – packet is in the right node: look up the
      – destination in the line table

else

      – packet is still in the wrong node: look up
      – the next segment of the route in the node routing table.

end if

The advantages can immediately be seen if we go back to the network of 100 nodes and 1000 users. Instead of every node needing to maintain a lookup table with 1000 entries, each node has one lookup table with 100 entries to find the destination node, and another with 10 entries to reach the ten locally attached users on this node. Furthermore, when new users join the system, only the local lookup table needs to be modified. The node routing tables need only be changed on the much less frequent intervals when the basic node topology changes.

> **Exercise 5.3** Consider the further structuring of our 100 node and 1000 user network so that the nodes are divided into ten "regions" of ten nodes each. What further advantages are to be gained by such a scheme? Are there any disadvantages?

5.4   Dynamic Routing

So far we have considered only static routing tables in the sense that we have implicitly assumed that the routing tables would be constructed manually by some clerical process. However, it is fairly straightforward to construct an algorithm that will allow the nodes automatically to update their routing tables in response to changes in the network topology.

Consider the network in Fig 5.8, and imagine that node E is not yet connected to the network as shown by the dotted line.

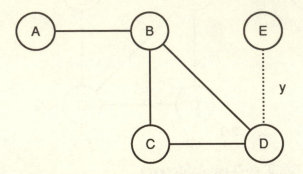

Fig 5.8.   Routing Table Modification

Nodes A, B, C, and D are all connected, and have up-to-date routing tables—that is, they will all have correct entries for nodes A, B, C, and D, but no entry for node E. Now imagine that link y becomes active. At this point, nodes D and E each tell the other the list of nodes to which they have routes (including themselves). Clearly, E will learn that it can use the new link to get to A, B, C, and D. More interestingly, D will learn that it can now get to the new node E. To make this knowledge generally useful, it must tell nodes A, B, and C the news. It can do this by sending a copy of its new updated routing table to nodes B and C. Node B will get the extra information about E, update its routing table, and then send the new routing table onto its neighbour A. A will in turn update its table, and the whole network now knows how to get to E.

Note that there are some as yet unstated subtleties about this algorithm to avoid an explosion of duplicated update messages. Firstly, only when the routing table has been changed are the neighbours informed. If this were not the case, then every update message that arrived in a node would cause a further set of update messages to be sent out, one on every output link. Each of these would update a destination node, and cause a similar further multiplication of update messages, and so on recursively. Thus the number of update messages would diverge exponentially.

We have also. omitted one further subtlety. As the message about the new attachment of node E arrives from D at B and C, we assumed that B and C would be sensible enough not to tell each other about the route to E. We have again fallen into the trap of our bird's-eye view. Down on the ground in B and C they have no such overall knowledge, and we need some extra information to stop messages endlessly flying around the loop B, C, D in both directions constantly updating the route to E.

Exercise 5.4 Follow the messages, starting at D to B and C and convince yourself of this.

With our bird's-eye view we can see why the messages do circulate endlessly. There are two routes from B to E—one directly via D and one indirectly via C (and similarly from C). Indeed, there is an infinite set of routes from B round the DC-loop and back again to B in either direction an arbitrary number of times. The dumb algorithm has merely shot off setting them all up for us as dumb algorithms are wont to do! Clearly what the algorithm is *not* doing is to pick the *shortest* route for us.

We need a further piece of information—the *length* of the route from "here" (wherever we are) to the given destination. So, rather than just passing a routing table from node to node that is merely a list of the possible destinations, the length of the path to that destination must be passed also. Thus, when E joins, D will see that its distance to E is one "hop". It will tell B and C, which will then get distances to E of two hops. B tells both A and C about the three-hop route to E. And C also tells B about its three-hop route to E. Of these three messages, only the new route to A will be useful. Both B and C will ignore the new routes to E since they already know a better one, so their routing tables are not updated, and the algorithm terminates.

There is another device to help limit the unnecessary spread of packets around the network. When the arrival of a routing message in a node causes the successful update of the routing tables, then the new routing information does not need to be sent back down the route from which the message arrived. It is self-evident that any destination in that direction has a shorter route to the new destination, and so the sending would be a waste of time. However, this is only a small improvement on the algorithm. One of the main points of interest, as we shall see later, is that this is an important part of the algorithm when packets are broadcast by reverse routing. Indeed, updating routing tables is a very specific application of broadcasting.

Clearly, the method of dynamic routing is very important both in that it automates a serious clerical maintenance problem, and in that it allows a network to adapt its routing tables to exploit alternate routes when a network link fails.

Exercise 5.5 Follow the revised algorithm manually, and convince yourself that it terminates, even when there are alternative routes available.

Exercise 5.6   Write a simple program to simulate the algorithm for a fixed number of nodes, but with the user able to type in new connections or the severance of existing connections. Simulate Fig 5.8. Convince yourself that the algorithm both terminates and chooses the best route.

Exercise 5.7   Use the program above to simulate link failures in Fig 5.8.

Exercise 5.8   Suppose Fig 5.8 is fully connected, and all routing tables are up to date. If link y fails, follow the various routing table updates, in particular the establishment of the alternate route from C to E via B and D.

The method of dynamic routing that we have described rests on at least one basic assumption—that every node knows its own correct identity, and that every node has a different identity. One possible way in which this assumption may be invalidated, besides the obvious one of an administrative mix-up, is that a machine fault may corrupt one identity into another. Then there would be two nodes on the network with the same address, both of which would be trying to establish a universal set of routing tables pointing to itself. This would clearly cause general chaos in the table entries concerned. This kind of error has occurred on at least one large network.

Exercise 5.9   Consider what ways you might employ to avoid or reduce the possibility of hardware or software errors causing this kind of corruption. What organizational arrangements could be made to stop human error causing such a confusion?

5.5   Load Balancing

We have examined the way in which routing tables may be dynamically adjusted to find the shortest route (smallest number of hops) across a network. Similar techniques have been used to balance loads on a network. Thus, if there were, for example, two alternate long distance routes across a network, and each had the same number of hops, then a load balancing algorithm would attempt to choose the quietest route. Much theoretical and practical work has been done, particularly on the ARPANET (Kleinrock 1976).

In their simplest forms, such algorithms are quite similar to the dynamic routing algorithm that we have described above except that instead of a number of hops, some other measure, for example, estimated delay, is carried in the routing update message. More elaborate schemes may involve maintaining routing tables that indicate two or more possible routes to the same destination that have similar delays. By choosing from a set of similarly delayed routes, perhaps at random or by a round robin, the traffic on the routes may be balanced.

One of the problems with such schemes is that to be useful, they must react fairly quickly to transient traffic problems. To do this, the routes must be updated rapidly, which in turn involves the frequent sending of the updating messages. Unfortunately, the messages themselves then add significant or even large extra traffic to the network and thus increase the very network delays whose minimisation was the aim of the exercise.

5.6   Re-Routing

With dynamic routing, whether of the reconfiguration type, or of the faster load balancing type, a series of datagrams that started in one order can be shuffled because of changes in the route, or because different load balancing routes of slightly different delay were chosen for consecutive datagrams. This re-ordering is one of the characteristics for which users of datagram networks must be careful to allow.

> **Exercise 5.10**   Show how a series of packets flowing from **A** to **E** in Fig 5.7 can get re-ordered if the link **B-D** goes down and an alternate route comes into use.

> **Exercise 5.11**   How might link failures in Fig 5.8 result in duplicated datagrams?

5.7   Congestion and Deadlock

The schemes just described allow for the efficient routing of datagrams in a store and forward network as long as the traffic is sufficiently low that congestion does not become serious. Once congestion does become serious, then there is a growing danger of deadlocks. The simplest type of deadlock may be illustrated by considering the two-node network in Fig 5.9. (Note that in this section we are showing one full-duplex physical connection as two simplex connections in each of which the flow of data is strictly one way only. This is to emphasize that the flows in the two directions are quite independent for the purposes of this section.)

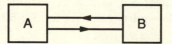

Fig 5.9.   A Simple Deadlock

Suppose that the two nodes **A** and **B** each have a finite set of buffers, and that in each case all the buffers are full with packets to send to the other node. In order for node A to be able to send to node B, node B must be able to find a free buffer in which to put the incoming data. To do this, it needs to free one of the buffers that are queued for transmission to A. Of course, the converse is also true. Thus we have the classic deadlock: to progress, each node needs the other to progress first. Sometimes this is known more floridly as the "deadly embrace".

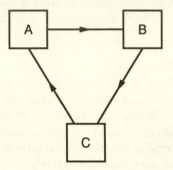

Fig 5.10.   A Multiple Deadlock

The deadlock can show up in other forms too. Thus, with a three node network in Fig 5.10, all three nodes have all their buffers full. Node A is waiting to send to node B, B to C, and C to A. In general, if we have a set of n nodes, then there is the possibility of a deadlock involving a cycle of up to n nodes, each one waiting for the next in the cycle.

Thus we see that flow control deadlock occurs when there is a set of links in the network along which flow is stopped because of congestion. In addition, this particular set of links involved in the deadlock is arranged in a directed topological ring such that the congestion at each source can only be relieved by a relief in the congestion at the next node in the ring. Note again that in this section we are taking each "link" to be one uni-directional flow between nodes. So, flow must be stopped in a set of links, *and* those links must be arranged in a loop.

One way of detecting such a deadlock from our bird's-eye knowledge of the whole network is to form a dependency matrix. In this, when node x is waiting for node y, we insert a 1 in row x, column y. All other positions are zero. Thus, the dependency matrix for Fig 5.10 is in Fig 5.11.

We would not expect a node to wait for itself, and thus the diagonal of the dependency matrix should be zero. If we now multiply the matrix by itself, the result is the second order dependency matrix— an entry in position (x, y) shows not the direct dependency of x on y, but the indirect dependency through one other node. Moreover, the

$$
\begin{array}{c}
 \\
A \\
B \\
C
\end{array}
\begin{array}{ccc}
A & B & C \\
\left(\begin{array}{ccc}
0 & 1 & 0 \\
0 & 0 & 1 \\
1 & 0 & 0
\end{array}\right)
\end{array}
$$

Fig 5.11.   The dependency matrix D for Fig 5.10

value in the position shows the number of different ways in which this
dependency occurs. Fig 5.12 shows this for our example.

$$
\begin{array}{c}
A \\ B \\ C
\end{array}
\begin{array}{ccc}
A & B & C \\
\left(\begin{array}{ccc}
0 & 1 & 0 \\
0 & 0 & 1 \\
1 & 0 & 0
\end{array}\right)
\end{array}
\times
\begin{array}{c}
A \\ B \\ C
\end{array}
\begin{array}{ccc}
A & B & C \\
\left(\begin{array}{ccc}
0 & 1 & 0 \\
0 & 0 & 1 \\
1 & 0 & 0
\end{array}\right)
\end{array}
=
\begin{array}{c}
A \\ B \\ C
\end{array}
\begin{array}{ccc}
A & B & C \\
\left(\begin{array}{ccc}
0 & 0 & 1 \\
1 & 0 & 0 \\
0 & 1 & 0
\end{array}\right)
\end{array}
$$

Fig 5.12.   The dependency matrix D^2 for Fig 5.10

The reader should go through Fig 5.12 deriving by matrix multiplication, and then convince herself that its physical interpretation is
consistent with Fig 5.10. The next stage is the cube of the dependency
matrix, Fig 5.13. Here we see that the cube of the dependency matrix for
our example has non-zero values on the diagonal. This indicates that
A is waiting indirectly on itself to move via a link through two other
nodes, and similarly for B and C.

$$
\begin{array}{c}
A \\ B \\ C
\end{array}
\begin{array}{ccc}
A & B & C \\
\left(\begin{array}{ccc}
0 & 1 & 0 \\
0 & 0 & 1 \\
1 & 0 & 0
\end{array}\right)
\end{array}
\times
\begin{array}{c}
A \\ B \\ C
\end{array}
\begin{array}{ccc}
A & B & C \\
\left(\begin{array}{ccc}
0 & 0 & 1 \\
1 & 0 & 0 \\
0 & 1 & 0
\end{array}\right)
\end{array}
=
\begin{array}{c}
A \\ B \\ C
\end{array}
\begin{array}{ccc}
A & B & C \\
\left(\begin{array}{ccc}
1 & 0 & 0 \\
0 & 1 & 0 \\
0 & 0 & 1
\end{array}\right)
\end{array}
$$

Fig 5.13.   The dependency matrix D^3 for Fig 5.9

In general, if we take the dependency matrix, and raise it to
increasing powers, then either non-zero elements will appear on the diagonal and there is a "transitive closure" which indicates a deadlock,

or the matrix will become all zero indicating no dependencies of the corresponding length anywhere in the network.

Interesting though this method is in understanding deadlocks from our position in the crow's nest, it is of little use down in the confined world of the node. The node's view of the world is limited to itself, and what little it can surmise about its neighbours. In particular, when congestion is impending, it is that much more difficult to probe the rest of the network.

Clearly, deadlock is a condition to avoid. There are two ways of avoiding the condition. The first is to try to detect the deadlock when it has happened and then break it, and the second is to avoid getting into the deadlock in the first place.

One of the simplest and most effective ways of detecting an incipient deadlock is for each node to monitor the number of datagrams within its own storage. Whenever the total number of datagrams approaches the total storage available, then the inclination would be to stop the inward flow on some or all of the inter-node links. We have seen above that this stopping of flow is a necessary (but not sufficient!) condition for that node being involved in a deadlock dependency cycle.

Having detected a local indication that a deadlock may be about to involve this node, there are several possibilities of avoiding deadlock. If more buffers can be found, then inward flow can be allowed to continue, and thus we might allow flow to continue by stealing a buffer that is already full, and re-using it for the newly arriving data—in other words, throwing away a perfectly good datagram before it has been sent on its way.

At first this may seem to be a grossly irresponsible thing to do. After all, the only task in the life of a switch in a datagram network is to receive datagrams and send them out again along other links. If we start throwing them away, then surely we are giving a worse service than we would in persisting in trying to deliver them? A little thought should reveal the error in this way of thinking. If we hang onto the datagrams and become completely congested and deadlocked, then the datagrams in them will never be delivered. As far as the users of the datagrams are concerned this is worse than the odd one being thrown away. At least if some get through, there is the chance of error recovery procedures being brought into play to re-send the packet, but if a deadlock occurs then the channel has become completely inoperative.

A similar strategy is to allow a node to fill up, and then to set a timeout. When the timeout has expired a deadlock is assumed to have just started, and a set of datagrams is discarded and the buffers reused to accept new incoming data. The number of datagrams to discard may vary from one to perhaps all. Usually the ones to choose are those that have been resident for the longest. However, there is another variant on the process that has more general use than the local breaking of suspected deadlocks.

Later we shall see how virtual calls are built on top of datagram networks. One of the more difficult processes with such networks is to make sure that when we try to recover from errors by retransmitting a datagram, we do not get the datagram that we assumed was lost turning up much later, and causing duplicate data such as we discussed in Chapter 2. A very powerful aid when implementing such protocols is the specification of a maximum lifetime within the network. Providing such a lifetime is implemented correctly, the two ends can time out and retransmit secure in the knowledge that if the timeout is longer than the permitted lifetime of the datagram, then duplicates cannot occur. This timeout can also be used in the intermediate nodes as a way of breaking a deadlock. Thus, if a datagram is queued for an outbound link, its lifetime timer will still be running. If the lifetime timer expires while it is still queued in a node, then the datagram should be de-queued and destroyed—that is, the buffer used to accept another incoming datagram. It can be seen that such a mechanism serves the dual purpose of helping the higher level protocols to avoid duplicated datagrams, and also of breaking deadlocks.

We can see then that we can either avoid deadlock even starting by refusing to run out of datagrams in the first place, or we can live slightly more dangerously by hanging onto the datagrams even into a complete local congestion, and then breaking the deadlock if no movement starts after a period of stagnation. Alternatively, the datagram lifetime also breaks deadlocks as well as helping higher level protocols to function properly. However, while the lifetime mechanism may be very attractive, enthusiasm for this mechanism should be tempered by the fact that the implementation may be difficult and somewhat approximate.

In 1980 Merlin and Schweitzer invented an ingenious way of avoiding deadlock. Suppose the maximum distance across the network is d hops. If we then allocate $d + 1$ buffers in each node, numbering them 0 to d, then by ensuring that after n hops the packet is in a buffer numbered n, we can show that the possibility of deadlock is eliminated. We can see this by examining what other packets a given packet can be waiting for. Since at each move from one node to the next, a packet must move to a buffer in a higher numbered set, it can only be waiting, if at all, for a packet in a higher set. No packet in a higher set can ever be waiting for a packet in a lower set, and thus no cyclic dependencies can exist.

We can visualise the sets of buffers as a multi-layer vertical sandwich, with the buffers in set n being represented by the nth slice of bread. Packets can only move upwards through the sandwich, and so can never be waiting for packets coming down in the opposite direction.

In the terms of our dependency matrix, the rows and columns of the matrix must now represent not just the nodes, but the $d + 1$ buffers within each node. The matrix thus becomes $d + 1$ times bigger. If we arrange the new rows and columns so that the buffer numbers increase with increasing row and column number, we can see that all the dependencies must be above the diagonal, and thus the possibility of a transitive closure is eliminated.

Merlin and Schweitzer developed their method much further than the outline that we have presented. However, there is one aspect that would give some problems in practice, and this is the precise means by which the flow control is communicated. Consider Fig 5.14. Suppose that node X has a buffer in class n free. How does it communicate this to the adjacent nodes that may send? If it sends a message to all of them, then it may well get several messages for the one free buffer. One possibility is for X to poll each of the other nodes that may wish to send. The nodes either respond with a packet, or with a polite refusal. Clearly the problem with this approach is the cost of the polling in terms of link bandwidth CPU resources, and delay.

Another possibility is for the nodes that wish to send to ask for permission to send to a buffer numbered n. Thus, X will have to keep a list of requests from each of the expectant senders. Then when a buffer becomes free, it can send a go-ahead to one of the nodes that wishes to use the buffer. Again, this has an overhead in that a request must be sent before any buffer may be sent, but this is less than is likely with polling.

Each of these approaches to implementing the Merlin-Schweitzer deadlock avoidance scheme has a significant overhead in terms of packets transmitted across links, and in terms of complexity and other resources. Merlin and Schweitzer themselves suggest that if their method is implemented, then it should only be activated as the likelihood of deadlock approaches with increasing buffer occupation, and that when traffic is lighter the method should not be active.

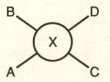

Fig 5.14.   Selective Flow Control

Datagram networks should be designed and sized in such a way that they can handle most of the traffic most of the time. On the occasions when the traffic starts to overwhelm the network, then the network sheds load and avoids deadlock by discarding datagrams. This should happen only in cases when unusual statistical events combine by chance to cause unusual loads. Care must be taken to allow for common mode overload situations. For example, a mass enemy attack might cause a military network to have an extremely "unusual" level of traffic from many points all at the same time. It would be more than embarrassing if such a network were forced to discard datagrams to avoid deadlock under such situations. At a more mundane level, a worldwide financial crisis, or a mid-air emergency in an aircraft are two other possible common mode overload situations that should be allowed for.

Having said all this, there are means to deal with certain overload conditions that we shall examine in Chapter 12 when we look at performance issues.

5.8   Virtual Call Networks

The issues that we have just discussed concerning deadlock and discarding datagrams are some of the main affairs that are cited as reasons for constructing networks on the *Virtual Call* principle. We shall look at the principles involved, and then ponder some of the pros and cons of the two approaches. In the next chapter we shall examine important examples of each of these methods of constructing networks.

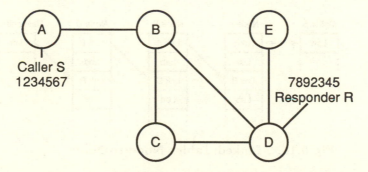

Fig 5.15.   A Virtual Call Network

Fig 5.15 shows a simple network with user S attached to node A at address 1234567, and user R attached to node E at address 7892345. Suppose S wishes to establish a virtual call to destination R. A call request packet is sent to node A specifying the requested destination and a label "Lsa" by which it wishes to identify this virtual call in future.

The point of specifying the label Lsa is that S may wish to maintain several virtual calls, and Lsa distinguishes which one in future messages. Lsa is unique on the link between S and A. In X.25, Lsa is the "*Logical Channel Identifier*".

Thus, the call request packet is

"*Connect to 7892345 from 1234567 using label* Lsa"

When the call request packet arrives at node A a control block will be allocated for the new virtual call. Amongst the information stored in this control block will be the label Lsa, and an identification of the link back towards S. Then A will examine the destination address "7892345", and work out the next link in the chain by means of routing tables that are equivalent to the routing tables that we used earlier to deliver datagrams. It identifies the link to B as the next step in the route. Next, a label is chosen for use on this link to B—Lab, which is unique on this link, and enters both the new label and the new link in the control table for the virtual call. Finally, a new, modified connect packet is sent onto B:

"*Connect to 7892345 from 1234567 using* Lab"

It is important to see that the label for the virtual call changes as the call progresses step-by-step, and link-by-link through the network. The process is repeated, with the allocation of the control block, the resolution of the next leg of the route, and the allocation of the next link, until the destination is finally reached.

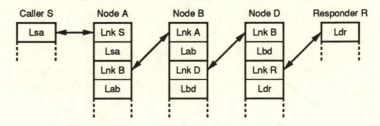

Fig 5.16.   Linked Tables Node-to-Node

Note that we now have a string of control block pairs linked together by means of the *(link identifier, link label)*-pair through each link. When the recipient at address 7892345 eventually replies with a *Call accept* packet, the route has been resolved once and for all, and the links from control block to control block do not need to be re-established. In particular the long addresses such as 1234567 and 7892345 do not need to be re-interpreted.

Once the connection phase is complete, then any link along the chain of control blocks that represents the virtual call knows the virtual call by means of this *(line, label)*-pair. This is one of the prime advantages claimed for the virtual call arrangement—that the full addresses are only needed in the call setup phase, and during the data transfer phase only the much shorter call labels are required. This is a twin advantage, since the shorter labels save bandwidth on the communications links, and the labels can be used as a simple lookup mechanism for the control blocks—perhaps even used as an index into an array—whereas the address on a datagram needs to go through a possibly complex analysis to yield a route. We shall return to this point below.

In the call setup phase it is normal not only to allocate control blocks in each node, but also to allocate some buffer resources. Thus, a call request packet may specify a maximum window size to be used across the network. As each node allocates its control block, it can also allocate a number of buffers equal to the maximum window size (in each direction) for each virtual call. For the default window size of 2 in X.25, four buffers would be dedicated to the virtual call control block in each node on the route. If a *Call_Request* arrived in a node and it was not possible or desirable to allocate the full complement of buffers, then the node could revise the window size downwards accordingly. Since the *Call_Accept* packet will also carry an indication of the window size agreed (with possible downward revision) along the whole route, the node-by-node allocation can be re-adjusted.

By pre-allocating buffers like this at call setup time it is possible to avoid the deadlock problem completely. Thus, if we allocate enough buffers to each virtual call for a worst case then we can know that it is impossible to get more packets in this node than this allocation, and if we make sure that the total allocation across all virtual calls through the node does not exceed the total number of buffers, then that node can never be short of buffers, and thus can never be part of a deadlock chain. (Unfortunately, X.25 is not quite so well behaved as this in that some packets are not subject to the window allocation—see the next chapter.)

Thus, virtual calls can improve the link efficiency by reducing the amount of addressing information transmitted with most packets, improve processor efficiency by reducing the amount of network address processing, and avoid the possibility of deadlocks.

With a virtual call being set up as a list of control blocks on a fixed route through a set of nodes, we can see that all packets must follow the same route. This one fact in itself predicates most of the important differences between virtual calls and datagram services. Thus, because all the packets on a virtual call follow the same fixed route, they cannot arrive out of order, but must arrive in the same sequence that they were transmitted. Again, if each of the inter-node links has a sufficiently low error rate (probably as enhanced by an HDLC-type of error recovery protocol), then the virtual call should deliver ordered data with a similar high reliability.

It is worth noting here that the end-to-end reliability of a virtual call depends in reality on more than the sufficiently low error rate of the links involved. In particular, there is also a significant probability of error in each of the systems involved in the virtual call. We shall return to this topic more detail in Chapter 12.

Any failure of a link or node should be noticed by neighbouring links or nodes, and all the virtual calls affected can be identified by searching through the control tables. The calls can be cleared by sending a *Disconnect* message to the user at the end of the call away from the point of failure. Thus, to a first approximation, a virtual call is expected to deliver received data without loss to a high level of reliability, or to fail completely if any link on the route fails. (For a closer approximation, see the description of the RESET function in X.25 in the next chapter)

The datagram service is rather different in that there is no assurance of these properties. However, many datagram networks deliver ordered datagrams (unless there are load balancing alternate routes, or errors occurring) without loss to a similar level of reliability as a virtual call network as long as they are not operating close to capacity and discarding datagrams to alleviate congestion.

The virtual call approach seems to offer an advantage over the datagram service in that, by allowing the possibility of pre-allocating a maximum set of buffers along a route, it can make deadlocks impossible. However, it would do this by a massive over-commitment of resources. In our example of allocating four buffers in every node for a window size of 2 in each direction, we are allocating a total of four times the number of nodes along the route of the virtual call. If the average length of the virtual call in a network is, say, 4 or 5 nodes, then four or five times as many buffers are being allocated overall as there will ever be packets in the network even in the worst possible case. Even with the present plummeting cost of memory, this is indeed an expensive solution. A reasonably engineered datagram network will be able to avoid congestion for the vast majority of the time by allocating a considerably smaller number of buffers than this and relying on statistical variation to make the average demand for buffers per call to be much less than a window full. When statistical extremes strike and a momentary overload causes buffers to be lost, then error recovery procedures allow the lost packets to be recovered. However, the incidence of discarded packets can be reduced to negligible levels with much less than a full window allocation per connection.

There is a common myth that virtual call networks do not suffer from this sort of congestion. *"If there are too many calls"* the argument goes, *"then later calls will be rejected at setup time. Once the call is connected, then there can be no congestion problem. On the other hand, datagram networks often suffer from congestion and thus from lost packets."* The author remembers a very frustrating weekend trying to use international X.25 networks to call back home and leave an urgent message. It was easy to get connected, but once connected, I'd just get logged in and start to compose the message when the call was cleared with the reason "congestion". The people at the information number were all very sympathetic, but not at all helpful, and each useless call cost me lots of money at intercontinental rates. *"Of course, there must have been a fault"* is the apology. Surely, but both forms of network— datagram and virtual call—will function correctly when properly engineered. There is no fundamental flaw in either way of doing business.

Of course, here we have implicitly assumed that even a datagram network will in fact be used to support connections, perhaps with a protocol such as TCP described in the next chapter (and thus that directly or indirectly—via a window mechanism—there is a bound on the traffic). If this is true, then our assumptions may be largely correct. However, there are some applications that do not follow this strictly sequential model. One is the blast protocol that we discuss in Chapter 12. In this a whole file is sent quickly as a series of datagrams without flow control, and any scrambling is undone by numbering the records at the file access level. Other applications may be of a transactional nature where, for example, a management task may periodically ask all of a large set of destinations a simple question such as *"What temperature does your sensor register?"*. Neither of these examples maps particularly well onto a virtual call model, but are more suitably implemented on top of a datagram service. However, their extremely bursty nature poses problems in the design of the supporting network.

Datagrams are disordered when network routing adapts to alternates, when load balancing alternate routes are employed that have slightly differing delays, or perhaps when errors in intermediate switches cause faults. Avoiding this problem is one of the big advantages claimed for virtual call networks—their data remains sequenced. However, this type of "failure" can also be viewed as the big strength of the datagram approach. It is precisely at the point when datagram networks disorder datagrams that the corresponding virtual call network will disconnect the calls going through it. Is it better to receive data out of order and with gaps, or to lose the connection completely? Only the user can really make this final choice, though if only a virtual call service is available, then the choice has been imposed upon her.

Finally, we have noted that with virtual calls, the address is only needed at call setup time—during the rest of the time, a simpler and much shorter call identifier or "logical channel identifier" may be used. Undoubtedly this is an advantage in that the logical channel identifier is shorter than a full-blown address, and thus occupies less communications bandwidth. Nevertheless, the falling cost of bandwidth mitigates this advantage.

The other advantage of the short logical channel identifier is that a full-blown address of perhaps 12, 20, or more digits may involve some complex processing to turn it into a route, whereas a short logical channel identifier can probably be used as a direct lookup index to obtain the control table. Using the logical channel identifier after the initial call setup must be an advantage. This is again true, but just how much of an advantage it really is depends strongly on the structure of the address. We have seen how addresses may be arranged hierarchically with great advantage for deriving routes. If the addresses are appropriately structured, then only a small part of them—perhaps little more than the number of bits in a logical channel identifier—need to be processed at any one stage. Even if the addresses are not structured in such a convenient manner, it is possible to use programming techniques such as caching all the "active" addresses and using hash lookup techniques to increase the efficiency of processing.

It is likely that the use of a short logical channel identifier will retain the edge over the full-blown address, but the gulf between the methods is narrower than some commentators claim.

5.9   Hybrid Networks

Many so-called virtual call networks are in fact hybrid networks in the sense that on the periphery they give a virtual call interface, but internally the individual packets are handled as datagrams. Thus, the communications subnetwork in the middle is a datagram network, and has all the advantages of a datagram network in terms of adaptability in the face of failures. On top of this an end-to-end virtual call connection is provided by the sort of protocol that we shall study in the next section. Perhaps the archetypal example of this type of network is the Canadian Datapac Network (Cashin 1976, Clipsham 1976, Twyver 1976). Externally this provides an X.25 service, and it is indeed from Datapac that the international X.25 standard derives. Many of the advantages of the two approaches are combined in such a hybrid network.

Fig 5.17 shows the general arrangement. Here, the link from the user to the network is a virtual call interface—X.25 in the case of Datapac. Through the network itself, the data is carried on datagrams.

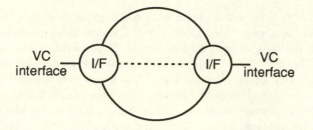

Fig 5.17.   Virtual Calls Over Datagrams

Thus, the user will get the sequenced data that is associated with the virtual call service, but integrity of the virtual call is not dependent on the vulnerability of the linked list of control tables as in Fig 5.16, and the network can adapt to errors using the full datagram recovery abilities. Here we see X.25 as the true interface protocol. Indeed, on Datapac, the "standard window" of 2 was only across the X.25 interface and a separate window of 3 operated end-to-end across the datagram subnetwork. The result of all this was that the total window from end-user to end-user was actually 7 rather than the 2 that it appeared to be at first sight.

5.10   Broadcasts and Multicasts

So far in this chapter we have looked at the issues involved in routing data from a single source address to a single destination address. There is another type of addressing that is referred to as "broadcasting" where a packet is sent, not just to one other address, but to all other addresses. A slight variation on this is when the packet is sent, not to everyone else, but to a subset of the other network users. This is called a "multicast". The issues of multicasts are sufficiently close to those of broadcasts for us to ignore the differences.

Broadcasting is done by attaching a special destination address to a packet and then sending the packet out across the network. The special address is recognised by all destination addresses, and received by all of them.

At first this may seem to be a rather odd form of communication. However, there are several types of application where this broadcast form is useful. One is advertisement. The familiar broadcast media, radio, TV, and newspapers, carry advertisements for both commercial and public service. In addition the dissemination of information via news programs, weather forecasts, and so on is at least as important as their function as pure entertainment. Because of the nature of the broadcast, the information reaches destinations that the sender never even thought of.

Similarly, a broadcast on a network can be used to advertise a service, such as a name lookup service. A name lookup service can come up on a network address and advertise *"The name lookup service is at address 14159265359"*, rebroadcasting the message at some suitable interval. Any other network user thus learns where such useful services may be reached without having to have an inbuilt knowledge of the location of important services, and all the operational problems of inflexibility that this can bring. This method has the huge advantage that the addresses of critical services, such as the name lookup service, need not be well known, but may be changed or the service may even be duplicated without incurring the awkward operational problem of altering the inbuilt address in all the users.

Another useful type of application of the broadcast mode is as a network-wide posting or poll of some event or reading or suchlike. Thus, a network management broadcast might periodically update the clocks in a network from a standard synchronised clock, or it might interrogate the value of some counter of interest—counting checksum failures for instance. We have already seen the utility of one particular form of broadcast—keeping routing tables up to date.

Having established some uses for broadcasts, let us look at some of the implications of this type of working. Firstly consider addressing and routing. For broadcasts we need a special address that will be recognised both by the routing mechanism and by all the destinations. Typically, this may be all zeros or all (binary) ones, or any other special and easily recognisable pattern. This is recognised by all the intended destinations. The routing must be such that the packet is duplicated and directed to all the required destinations. We saw in Chapter 3 that with most shared media, all packets reach all destinations anyway, and thus little further action needs to be taken beyond perhaps ensuring that the mechanism in ring networks of marking a received packet as having been received does not inhibit its further reception at other ring stations.

When we look at two shared media that are joined by bridges, we can see that the simple strategy of copying everything through to the other side is exactly what we need for broadcasting. Indeed, if we use bridges that monitor source addresses to do selective forwarding, then we must be careful that they still forward broadcasted packets. However, this should automatically follow from the fact that the destination address used for broadcasting should never be used as a source address, and thus the gateways should never be fooled into thinking that they "know where the broadcast address is". Of course, to make absolutely sure, the gateways could be aware of the broadcast address and forward broadcast packets accordingly. Clearly, cycles of bridges will cause problems, just as with non-broadcast packets, and we shall treat this problem in the context of a mesh store and forward network as we did earlier when considering non-broadcast packets.

Life becomes more interesting when we consider a mesh store and forward network (Dalal and Metcalfe 1978). Consider our basic network as in Fig 5.7. Suppose a broadcast packet is inserted into the network at node D. This will be forwarded to all destinations by sending copies of it down the links to E, C and B. At E the packet is delivered to the attached addresses 8/1 and 8/2. At C it is delivered to attached addresses 2/0 and 2/2. The copy sent from D to B is delivered to 3/2 and 3/5, and also sent on to A. So far so good. But we have omitted two necessary parts of the algorithm. Firstly, the packet should clearly be sent from D to B, but when it arrives in B, it should not be sent back again to D. How can our broadcasting algorithm achieve this? The trick is to use the normal routing tables in each node together with the "From" address. A broadcast packet should be sent away from its source, and thus the (forward) routing table is used to send the packet to all other destinations away from the source destination.

There is another necessary flexuosity. When a copy of the broadcast datagram arrives from D at both C and B, it will be re-broadcast along all links from both C and B. Thus, it will be sent from C to B and also from B to C, with the result that both will get a second copy of the datagram. Again we can use the from-address and the routing table to eliminate these duplicates. We compare the route by which the datagram arrived with the route to its source address. If the two are not the same, then the packet may be discarded as a duplicate (even if it actually arrives before the "proper" one).

Exercise 5.12 Compare and contrast the routing of broadcast datagrams with the updating of routing tables.

Exercise 5.13 Would there be any point in a destination AC-Knowledging the safe arrival of a broadcast datagram? Does the concept of a "broadcast virtual call" make any sense to you?

5.11   Source Routing

In this chapter we have concentrated on the most commonplace type of network where the data is *addressed* to a specific destination, and the *route* to that destination is derived from the address by the network itself. The advantage of this method is one of binding and of division and distribution of function. The network is responsible for the function of deriving the route from the address, thus relieving the network users of this task. In this way the users do not need to have a knowledge of the topology of the network, and do not need to keep this knowledge updated nor manipulate it in any way. Indeed, on most such networks there is no direct way in which users can control the network route in any way. (The TCP/IP suite of protocols does provide a way of specifying a route for exceptional reasons such as security, but that is unusual.)

However, there are some circumstances in which so-called *source routing* is useful. By *source routing* we mean the mechanism whereby the network user does not specify an *address* for the destination, but the *route* to get there. In this way the function of deciding the route is not performed by the network. As we have suggested above, this may be because the user has some specific reason for choosing the route, like avoiding untrusted paths in the network, but another possible reason is that the network may not be able to derive the route from the address. At first this seems rather surprising. We are used to computers of ever increasing power, and in this chapter we have described mechanisms for performing this function that are widely and successfully used.

One example should convince the reader that the notion of source routing should not be discarded. Recently, Haas and Cheriton (1987) published a specification for an extremely high performance wide-area network, *Blazenet*. Blazenet is intended to exploit the potential of optical fibre technology to transmit at gigabits per second over long distances. The proposal is for a wide-area network consisting of long-haul, point-to-point fibre optic links connected by fast switches. The switches must themselves operate extremely quickly, and the authors suggest that they should be implemented using "photonic" implementation. This will allow the data to be switched from link to link at full speed. One snag is that while photonic implementation may be very fast, photonic logic cannot yet be very complex, and the traditional derivation of route from address is not practical to implement. Haas and Cheriton suggest that each packet should have a header with a sequence of *hop-selects*. As the packet arrives in each switch, the first hop-select field is used to choose the next link to the next switch. This list of hop-selects constitutes a *source-route* that is constructed by some means outside the Blazenet subnetwork because of the inability of the network itself to perform the routing derivation function.

5.12   Summary

This chapter has examined the internal issues involved in constructing a network out of suitable collections of point-to-point links and shared media. The primary issues are those of finding a suitable route from source to destination, and of avoiding the problems of deadlock. The frequently emotional issue of whether to operate the network by giving the users a *datagram* or a *virtual call* interface has been examined. The reader should now be armed with sufficient understanding of the internal issues of providing a network service so that she can progress to the next chapter with its description of the network service itself, and the kinds of protocol used to provide that service.

The reader should be warned that many of the same, or similar principles of addresses and routes that we have introduced in this chapter will reappear only slightly changed in Chapter 15 on gateways.

6
Network Service and Interface

In the last chapter we expounded the principles involved in actually constructing the network itself out of the constituent pieces. In this chapter, we build on that knowledge to describe the *interface* to such a network service, and we relate the characteristics of the service provided at the interface to the underlying network. This is done by detailed examination of the two most important network services, X.25 and TCP, together with their protocols. This is followed by an overview of the ISO transport service. Finally we give a brief summary of ISDN facilities. At the end of this chapter the user should have a good knowledge of the principles of network interfaces in general, and of the three most important actual services in particular.

6.1   X.25

X.25 is one of a set of standards produced by the international body, the CCITT. The same standard is blessed by ISO as IS 8208. (Chapter 16 describes standards bodies in more detail.) X.25 is far and away the most important networking standard. We are about to describe the workings of X.25 in some detail. However, it should be recognised that the standard itself is large and extremely detailed. The CCITT definition of X.25 (1984) covers 187 large pages of fairly small type, plus another 46 pages covering the HDLC-type of link layer that we have already described. Clearly only the bones of the standard can appear in a general treatise like this. On the other hand it should be said that much of the bulk of standards documents is quite rightly concerned with ensuring compatibility down to the most mundane level of detail, such as order of transmission of bits. Since this book is concerned with principles we are able to take a cavalier attitude to such nit-picking detail.

It is essential to realise that X.25 is primarily a definition of an *interface* to a network. It does not define how a network works internally. Thus, in Fig 6.1, we see a simple abstract network.

There we see that the network users are labelled "DTE" and the network interfaces are labelled "DCE". This labelling is the terminology used by the CCITT to distinguish between the end controlled by the network supplier (the *Data Circuit-terminating Equipment*—DCE) and that operated by the user (the *Data Terminal Equipment*—DTE). X.25 is the standard that defines the protocol across the link between the DTE and the DCE for public packet switched networks. Two things should be

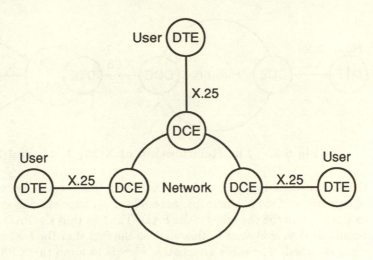

Fig 6.1.   The Basic Role of X.25

noted carefully from this diagram. Firstly, X.25 is defined by the people who operate the networks†, and so it is not basically a peer-to-peer protocol, but has various elements of a master (DCE) to slave (DTE) relationship. The other thing to notice is that it is essentially an interface definition—X.25 has nothing to say about the internal construction of the network, such as the implementation of routing, that we discussed in the last chapter. So the question of how the internal switches work, or even whether they actually exist, is a completely open question.

Indeed, it is even an open question just how other people might attach to the network. It is usual for a network to offer the same interface to all its subscribers, and indeed, X.25 is far and away the most common choice as suggested in Fig 6.1. However, it is entirely possible to offer a different protocol interface on the same network. A prime example of this is the X.28 protocol. We shall discuss this way of supporting simple character terminals in the next chapter. However, for our present purpose, X.28 is a protocol that defines how a simple character terminal such as a display screen with keyboard talks to a logical entity called a *Packet Assembler-Disassembler*—PAD. That is, the PAD interfaces between the X.25 *packet* network on one side and the *character-by-character* world of the simple terminal on the other by constructing or assembling packets from characters and vice versa—Fig 6.2.

There are two conceptual views of such a network—both of which are equally valid. One is that Fig 6.2 shows an X.25 network

---

† Public networks are often run by the national Postal, Telegraph and Telephone Authority—the PTT.

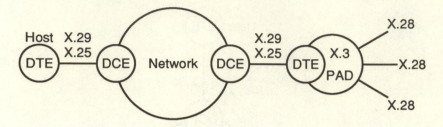

Fig 6.2.   The Relationship of X.25, 3, 28, and 29

that has a single type of interface—X.25. On this network are two types
of subscriber. One is a multiple access host—a time-sharing system for
example—and the the other is the PAD. The fact that the PAD supports
terminals is as irrelevant to this view as the fact that the host may have
discs attached. The other alternative view is to lump the X.25 network
and the PADs together as one conceptual network as in Fig 6.3.

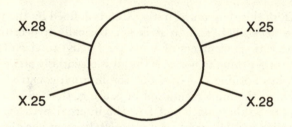

Fig 6.3.   An Integrated Network View

The new integrated network now has two different types of interface, X.25 and X.28. The two interfaces are quite different, though
they are related in very well-defined ways via the X.3 standard (see the
next chapter). Indeed it is precisely such a combined service that most
public networks supply, and the main use of public networks is still to
connect dumb terminals to time sharing X.25 hosts.

This may appear to be a perverse way of visualising the network,
but there do exist networks that provide exactly the services shown in
Fig 6.3, but which internally have a quite different structure from that
shown in Fig 6.2. In particular, the internal network protocol may be
quite different from X.25, and the PAD may be interfaced directly to
this internal protocol rather than using X.25 at all.

However, though X.25 grew up as an interface from a user to a
network, it has been widely pressed into service as a user-to-user protocol. With the earlier versions of X.25, and their concentration on the
asymmetrical master–slave, DCE–DTE relationship, this meant that a

prior agreement on which end was which was necessary. However, this need has been recognised in the 1984 version of the protocol. As well as in the traditional interfacing role, the 1984 version can also serve in a peer-to-peer relationship. That is, it can either be used as a network-to-user interface, or as a symmetrical user-to-user interface across a link. In order to recognise this, the 1984 version talks about DTE to DXE working—the "DXE" is meant to denote either "DCE" or "DTE"; that is the protocol can work either in the earlier master-slave way, or in the symmetrical peer-to-peer way across a link. Peer-to-peer working is not important in the context of public X.25 networks run by the PTTs, but is vitally important in other environments, particularly where X.25 is used as the network service between two peer entities across a local area network.

6.2   The X.25 Protocol

X.25 is built on top of a single point-to-point link. This link connects the user to the network, and is run with an error correcting protocol. Strictly, X.25 specifies a specific variant of the HDLC protocol on the link. However, the packet level of X.25 that we are concerned with here is quite independent of the details of the way in which the link is run. All that is required is some way of passing the packets across the link between the user DTE and the DXE with adequate reliability, and some indication of when the link fails so that both the user and the network can clear down the X.25 connections.

X.25 provides a virtual call service, and allows the multiplexing of many virtual calls over a single link. We have discussed the concept of the virtual call in the last chapter. However, though we implicitly alluded to the need for multiplexing, we did not look at the concept explicitly. Multiplexing allows the X.25 user to run multiple virtual calls with many users over the single X.25 link. The classic example of this is when a time sharing host is attached to an X.25 network by a single X.25 connection. There may be many X.3 PADs also connected to this network, and many of the terminals attached to the various PADs may each have a virtual call to the time sharing host, each operating quite independently. Indeed it is common for such an arrangement to attach several hundred terminals to a host via a single X.25 link.

This multiplexing of virtual calls is achieved by allocating a label to each virtual call on the X.25 link. This label is called the *Logical Channel Identifier*—LCI.

6.3   Packet Format in X.25

Fig 6.4 shows the general format of X.25 packets. The first four bits constitute the *General Format Indicator*—GFI. Essentially, this

byte

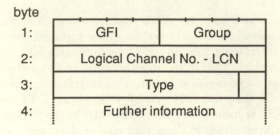

Fig 6.4.   The General Format of X.25 Packets

defines how the rest of the packet is laid out. There are two main variations on this format concerned with whether a flow control window of 8 or 128 is allowed. We shall encounter the meaning of some of the other bits in the GFI later. However, we shall be concerned with the basic layout for a window size of 8. The two fields Group and LCN together constitute the 12-bit *Logical Channel Identifier*—LCI. The 4-bit group field is sometimes used as a way of segmenting the full possible range of 4096 logical channels into 16 groups of 256 logical channels. So we may have some such arrangement as *"Outgoing calls will be in groups 1 and 2, incoming calls on groups 3 and 4, and permanent calls in group 5 only."* and so on and so forth. These groups are mainly of implementation or administrative use, and do not affect the principles of X.25, and so from now on we shall treat the logical channel identifier as a single 12-bit number.

The third byte contains the *packet type*. There are various types possible here as shown in Table 6.1. In Fig 6.4, the rightmost bit is labelled specially. The reason for this will become apparent when we look at the various packet types in more detail.

6.4   Call Connection in X.25

Virtual calls, including those in X.25, have three main phases. First the call is set up. If the setup is successful, there is a data transfer phase, and then finally the call is cleared or disconnected.

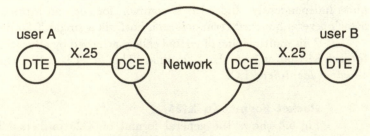

Fig 6.5.   The Basic Model

From DTE to DXE	From DXE to DTE	8 7 6 5 4 3 2 1
Call Request	Incoming Call	0 0 0 0 1 0 1 1
Call Accepted	Call Connected	0 0 0 0 1 1 1 1
Clear Request	Clear Indication	0 0 0 1 0 0 1 1
Clear Confirmation	Clear Confirmation	0 0 0 1 0 1 1 1
Data	Data	x x x x x x x 0
Interrupt	Interrupt	0 0 1 0 0 0 1 1
Interrupt Confirm.	Interrupt Confirm.	0 0 1 0 0 1 1 1
Receive Ready	Receive Ready	x x x 0 0 0 0 1
Receive not Ready	Receive not Ready	x x x 0 0 1 0 1
Reject	Reject	x x x 0 1 0 0 1
Reset Request	Reset Indication	0 0 0 1 1 0 1 1
Reset Confirmation	Reset Confirmation	0 0 0 1 1 1 1 1
Restart Request	Restart Indication	1 1 1 1 1 0 1 1
Restart Confirm.	Restart Confirm.	1 1 1 1 1 1 1 1
Diagnostic	Diagnostic	1 1 1 1 0 0 0 1
Registration Rqst.	Registration Rqst.	1 1 1 1 0 0 1 1
Registration Conf.	Registration Conf.	1 1 1 1 0 1 1 1

Table 6.1 Packet type Identifiers in X25

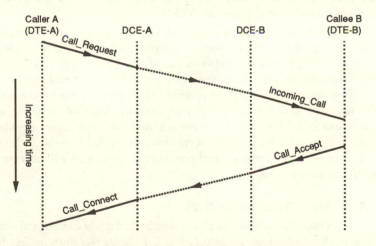

Fig 6.6. Call Establishment Time Sequence

The call setup and clearing is best understood with a specific example. In Fig 6.5 we see an X.25 network with two users **A** and **B**. Let us follow the steps by which user **A** establishes a virtual call to user **B**. First, **A** chooses a new LCI with which to identify the call. The LCI has a local significance between DTE **A** and the corresponding DCE on the X.25 network, and it has no relationship with LCIs in use at B or anywhere else. Indeed, B may be thousands of miles away on a different continent. Thus, user A chooses an LCI that is not in use on that X.25 link. It constructs a call request packet with a header as in Fig 6.4, a type of 00001011 from table 6.1, and the requested destination address, its own address, and some other parameters. This sent across the X.25 interface to the DCE. The time sequence involved is shown in Fig 6.6, where the time increases downwards from the top—in the way that text is read, rather than up from the bottom as is normal in graphs.

The DCE at A then communicates in some unspecified way with the DCE at the destination using whatever internal protocols are appropriate. This causes the DCE at B to generate an *Incoming_Call* packet to send to the corresponding DTE. This packet is similar to the original *Call_Request* packet, but, most importantly, DCE B must choose a new LCI that is locally unique on its own X.25 link to user B. When the incoming *Call_Request* arrives at B, the user decides whether to accept the call. If it decides to proceed, then it will generate a *Call_Accept* packet. So that everyone knows which of the many different virtual calls is being accepted, the local LCI must be used in this call accept packet. When the DCE at B receives this accept packet, it communicates suitably with the other DCE at A, and this DCE will then emit a *Call_Connected* packet to the original caller at DTE A.

Note that we have looked at this from our usual advantageous position up in the clouds, and explained events in terms of two users communicating with the network using the same X.25 interface protocol. However, as we have noted above, the X.25 protocol applies to one interface only, and it is quite possible that user B may be connected to the network by an entirely different means. All that actually matters when using X.25 is that the network and the user agree on the X.25 protocol on the interface. However, visualising both ends of the virtual call at once is the more natural conceptual view, and will correspond to actuality in many cases.

6.5   Data Transfer in X.25

Once the call has been established, data is exchanged using the data packet type from Table 6.1. Fig 6.7 shows the data packet format. We see from the table that the data packet type is the one and only type with a zero in the rightmost bit, and so this allows the other seven bits to be used for the three fields the *receive sequence number*—P(R), the *more data bit*—M, and the *send sequence number*—P(S). Since these seven bits may be any pattern, it is necessary to detect that these seven bits have this different meaning by first examining only the rightmost bit. The rightmost bit can be thought of as an escape. In addition to this, the leftmost bit of the GFI has also been pressed into service as the Q-bit—the data qualifier bit.

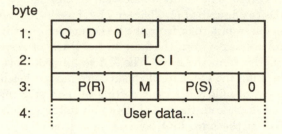

byte

| 1: | Q D 0 1 | | |
| 2: | L C I | | |

3: P(R) | M | P(S) | 0

4: User data...

Fig 6.7. The Format of X.25 Data Packets

The two 3-bit numbers P(R) and P(S) are used for flow control as we shall see presently. Since they are three bits long, these two numbers cycle modulo-8 allowing a flow control window size of up to 7. However, some applications require a larger window size than this, and for these applications there is another format of X.25 packets that allocates seven bits to these numbers, thus allowing the numbers to cycle modulo-128, and the window size to be up to 127. This other format is controlled by the third bit in the GFI—if it is 1 then the longer numbers are allocated and the format of several of the packets changes. However, since the principles are the same, and only the details have been changed to confuse the beginner we will not mention this alternative format further.

On any X.25 link, the packets will be limited in size by prior agreement. The "standard size" for the packets is for a data field of up to 128 bytes long, though "nonstandard" sizes from 16 through 4096 bytes may be agreed. Whatever the agreement, it is likely that the X.25 user may wish sometimes to send his data in longer logical records. X.25 allows him to do this by taking his long logical packet and sending it as an X.25 *complete packet sequence* or *M-bit sequence*. Thus, if the logical record is 365 bytes long, and the maximum user data field is 128 bytes, then the user can send two full packets of 128 bytes, plus a third remaining fragment of 109 bytes. The first two will be sent in data packets with the *M-bit* set (*M* for *More data*), and the last one is sent with the *M-bit* clear (for *completed packet sequence*). Thus, one *complete packet sequence* as indicated by the *M-bit* is one logical record.

We can see that it is possible within X.25 for two communicating users to have different maximum packet sizes. The complexity of the rules for whether packets may or may not be combined or fragmented as they pass from one such user to the other is one of the reasons for the size of the X.25 specification.

The *Q-bit* is a simple provision of two logical streams of data on the same connection. Thus, each logical record may be marked, or qualified by the Q-bit. The main application of this facility is in controlling X.3 PADs (as described in Chapter 7). Thus, logical records without the Q-bit are user data to or from the PAD, and records with the Q-bit set are control messages from the host to the PAD, or responses from the PAD to queries from the host. The X.3 set of protocols must be almost unique in using the Q-bit mechanism since most other higher level protocols choose to build such multiplexing of data streams into the user data field itself. Indeed, the use of the Q-bit in the X.25 header is strictly a violation of the pure ISO layering model used in OSI. In addition, we shall see when we discuss X.3 that the use of the Q-bit has some functional shortcomings because of the way in which the flow control of the two streams is not independent. However, the widespread importance of X.3 ensures the continued use of the Q-bit mechanism for many years to come.

When using the Q-bit it is important to ensure that the value of the Q-bit is constant across all the packets constituting the logical record in the M-bit sequence.

6.6   Flow Control in X.25

X.25 flow control is by means of a fixed window mechanism. We have discussed many variations on this theme in Chapter 3. In X.25, flow control is in terms of data packets. Each data packet is labelled with a sequence number, P. As we have seen, the sequence numbers are modulo-8. Two such numbers are packed into the type byte as shown in Fig 6.7.

Each virtual call has a window size specified by some means or other. The size may be arrived at by negotiation when the call is established or by default. Whatever is the means of deciding, the window size stays fixed for the rest of the call. Each packet is numbered with the send sequence number P(S). The receiver, at either end of the X.25 link, moves up the bottom edge of the flow control window by sending the received sequence number of the next record expected to arrive at the bottom edge. This number, P(R), may either be sent piggybacked on the data flowing in the opposite direction as indicated in Fig 6.7, or in one of several other packet types, including RR and RNR packets. In addition to controlling the flow by the window mechanism just described, flow may be turned on or off by the two packets *Receiver Ready*—RR and *Receiver Not Ready*—RNR. Either end of the X.25 connection may request the other to stop transmission irrespective of the state of the flow control window by sending an RNR packet. The flow may be restarted by sending an RR packet.

In Chapter 4 we observed that the fixed window method of flow control allowed less precise control of the flow than the related credit type mechanism. This is particularly true whenever the mechanism first starts up (when the call is first established) or is restarted (after a RESET for example). At this point, the receiver must be ready to accept a "window full" of data. The overlayed RR–RNR-type of on–off mechanism also allows the control of the flow of data on the virtual circuit. However, there is a round-trip delay from sender to receiver and back, so the sender of the RNR packet cannot rely on it stopping the flow until some unspecified time has elapsed. Since several virtual calls may be multiplexed across a single HDLC link, the queuing of RNR packets behind packets belonging to other virtual calls on the same link, and the possibility of HDLC-level flow control also operating independently, make the RR–RNR mechanism one of dubious utility.

However, we can note in passing that the RR packet can be used as a convenient way of advancing the flow control window in the reverse direction should there be no suitable data packets on which to piggyback the P(R) values. Perhaps the saving feature of all this is that the default window size is 2. Large window sizes (particularly those up to 127 that are available with the extended format) could rapidly run into problems with such mechanisms unless generous quantities of buffers were allocated.

We can see that the flow control of X.25 is remarkably similar to the frame numbering and RR–RNR mechanisms in HDLC. However, the similarity is misleading and potentially confusing. In HDLC, flow cannot properly be controlled by not acknowledging frames at the lower edge of the window and thus not rotating the window. If HDLC frames remain unacknowledged, then the sender will eventually time out and disconnect the link. The receiver must acknowledge frames that have been sent, and must stop flow as necessary with RNR. Thus, in HDLC, the RR–RNR mechanism is the only genuine form of flow control. The HDLC window is not a proper form of flow control, but is only an aspect of the error control mechanism. On the other hand, in X.25 the window really *is* a form of flow control. Moving the window is not primarily acknowledging packets, but permitting new ones to be sent. (However, see the discussion of the D-bit mechanism below.) In X.25, packets can remain "unacknowledged" indefinitely, and so both the window and the RR–RNR mechanism can be used to control data flow.

Obviously, X.25 was inspired by HDLC. However, the window mechanism has not made the transition gracefully. A fully controlled window as we shall see in TCP, is much to be preferred. However, TCP had the benefit of being designed some years after the original version of X.25 in the mid 1970s.

One of the criticisms of X.25 is that some of the functions of X.25 duplicate those of the lower HDLC layer on top of which it lives. Indeed there seems to be no real need for flow control at the HDLC level if that at the X.25 level is operating. Some X.25 implementations never invoke the link level HDLC flow control at all, and rely entirely on the X.25 packet level flow control.

Exercise 6.1   Is it possible to run X.25 with no flow control at the X.25 packet level, but relying entirely on the flow control at the HDLC level (the opposite of that just described)? In what circumstances would this be possible, and in what circumstances would it not be possible?

In our description of X.25 flow control we have carefully avoided discussing whether or not the flow control takes place across an X.25 link between the DCE and the DTE, or end-to-end between the DTEs at either end of the virtual call. However, it was implicit in our earlier insistence that X.25 was primarily an interface protocol, for one end of an X.25 call, that any flow control must have significance only between the DTE and the DCE at either end of the X.25 link. This was certainly so for Datapac where one window operated across the X.25 link, another end-to-end across the datagram subnetwork, and a third across the X.25 link at the other end. However, a large number of the early X.25 implementations assumed that the flow control was not just across the interface, but end-to-end across the virtual call.

When X.25 was revised, it had to take account of this unfortunate diversity of interpretations. Thus, in Fig 6.7, we see that the GFI contains the *D-bit*. This D-bit stands for *"Delivery Confirmation"*. When the D-bit is set, the advancement of the bottom edge of the window at the DTE coming from the other end implies not just that further flow is permitted at the top of the window, but also that packets that have just been acknowledged by the passing of the bottom edge of the window have actually arrived at the other end of the virtual call. However we should note that the "overloading" of the window mechanism with this delivery confirmation meaning means that the confirmation of delivery with the window mechanism also enables data flow, as far as the window mechanism is concerned.

In order to confirm delivery and still restrict data flow, the X.25 RR and RNR packets must be used. However, since they are merely on–off controls, and the width of the X.25 window is not dynamically alterable during the X.25 call, we see that the introduction of the delivery confirmation interacts in an undesirable way with the flow control. There is a parallel here with interaction between confirmation and flow control in the case of the HDLC window.

There are other ramifications of the D-bit mainly to do with its interaction with other aspects of the X.25 protocol, but we shall not discuss this further.

6.7   Expedited Data in X.25

We shall now describe briefly two other operations that can take place in the data state. One is that a small amount of urgent data can be transferred along the virtual call independently of the normal flow control. Thus, even if the flow of normal data on the virtual call is stopped, the *expedited* data that is carried on the *interrupt* packet will get through. Expedited data may overtake previously transmitted ordinary data, especially if flow control is delaying its flow, but can never be overtaken by ordinary data transmitted later. The amount of data on an interrupt packet is limited to 32 bytes, and in addition, only one interrupt packet can be sent at a time. This is enforced by requiring an interrupt packet to be acknowledged before another can be sent. As a side issue, we can note that the expedited packet is an extra packet outside the flow control window. If the X.25 network is to avoid the possibility of deadlock by allocating enough buffer space for the worst case (see last chapter), then this must be allowed for in addition to the size of the flow control window.

6.8   RESET in X.25

The other operation that may take place during the data state is the RESET. The RESET operation is an attempt to recover from various error situations such as the detection of the loss of a packet, a protocol violation, an error in an implementation, or a desire by higher level protocols to return to some well-defined state.

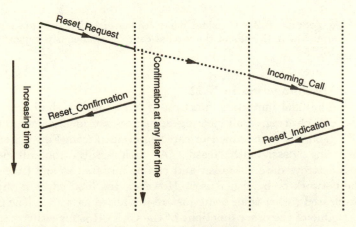

Fig 6.8.   User Requested RESET

The RESET operation causes flow control to be re-initialised, packets in transit to be discarded, and so on. There are two main types of RESET. One is when a user requests a reset. In this case the RESET is propagated to the far end of the connection. The RESET confirmation from the other end is propagated back, and the RESET is complete. The other type is when the network detects an error and RESETs the call by sending a RESET indication to both ends of the connection. The RESET is complete when both users have responded with the RESET confirmation. By comparing Figs 6.8 and 6.9 we can see that only the originator knows where the RESET started, unless diagnostic information is carried in the packet itself.

Note that the RESET confirmation in the case of the user requested RESET is not tied to any precise point in time. In particular, the DCE may choose to respond with the RESET confirmation immediately upon receiving the initial RESET request from the DTE, or it may choose to wait until some considerable time later when the reset percolates across the network, and is responded to by the other end. This is indicated in the time axis on the left of Fig 6.8.

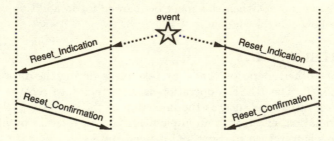

Fig 6.9. Network Requested RESET

Exercise 6.2 Consider what sequence should take place if both users, at both ends of the virtual call, simultaneously request a RESET.

6.9   Disconnection in X.25

The final important function of X.25 that we shall describe is that of call clearing. Call clearing sequences are identical to those of RESET, and the time sequences can be obtained from Figs 6.8 and 6.9 by replacing "Reset" with "Clear". As with RESET the call clearing process destroys data in transit and can be initiated at any time either by the network or by either user. However, the final effect is that the call is cleared rather than being just re-initialised as with a RESET.

One of the other functions of the CLEAR is for either a user or the network to refuse a CALL REQUEST.

6.10   Connections Over Datagrams—The ARPANET TCP

So far we have looked at the X.25 protocol as the most important way of providing a network service. As we have seen, virtual calls
are multiplexed across a point-to-point link by virtue of the logical channel number. The other main approach is to provide a basic datagram
service to the end-user, and for end-users to use a protocol on top of
this datagram service to give a virtual call service. As we have said, this
virtual call service can look exactly like X.25, and is the way some X.25
services are actually implemented internally in the network. However,
we shall look at the ARPANET TCP/IP set of protocols as the most
important real example of virtual calls on datagrams.

The ARPANET *Transmission Control Protocol*—TCP is the
protocol invented by the ARPA community for use on the ARPA network. Its use, though, is much wider than the ARPA community since in
the mid-to-late 80s TCP is the *de facto* standard protocol that is used on
the vast majority of local networks connecting mixtures of "super-mini"
computers, such as the DEC VAX class of machine, and high powered
personal workstations such as Suns and many other types of machine.
The only other rival sets of protocols are the proprietary Xerox XNS set
of protocols, the ISO transport class 4 protocol, and X.25. Of these, the
XNS and ISO class 4 protocol are very similar to TCP in concept, and
we have covered X.25 earlier in this chapter.

TCP implements a connection-oriented service that lives on top
of a datagram service. We have already looked at some of the characteristics of a datagram service—that data can be delivered out of sequence,
lost, duplicated, delayed by varying amounts, corrupted or delivered to
the wrong address. To produce a reliable virtual call service on top of
such a service, we need to be able to recover from these irregularities.
Firstly, we shall consider the general principles involved, and how they
vary significantly from a link protocol like X.25, and then we shall use
this as a background for a more specific exposition of TCP.

6.11   Sequence Numbers in TCP

The function of TCP is to open and maintain a connection between two entities, transfer data, and then finally to clear the connection
down. While the connection is in progress (and indeed while it is being
set up), datagrams may be corrupted and shuffled in the ways in which
we have just described. In order to recover from these errors, TCP uses
a sequence numbering scheme. The TCP service provides a two-way
simultaneous flow of data—full duplex. Each flow of data has an associated independent sequence number—each and every byte of data is
numbered in ascending order. In effect, each byte is transmitted individually from the sender to the receiver and acknowledged individually

by the receiver. Should a byte be lost in transit, then the sender will wait for a certain time for an acknowledgement, and then retransmit the byte, and will persist in this until the byte is finally acknowledged or the connection is abandoned. (Actually we shall see that TCP bundles both the bytes that are sent and the acknowledgements returned together into packets, but let us ignore this efficiency consideration for the time being).

At the receiving end the sequence numbers are used both in order to send acknowledgements and also to re-order data that is received out of sequence. Flow is controlled by the receiver sending messages back to the sender indicating the maximum sequence number that it is prepared to receive. In the terms of the discussion of flow control in Chapter 4, this is the window type of flow control with an independently variable "front edge". Alternatively, it can be viewed as a credit type of flow control mechanism. It is definitely not a fixed window of the type found in X.25.

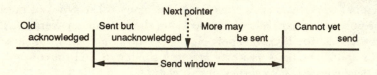

Fig 6.10.   The Sender's View

The mechanism works by the sender and receiver maintaining similar but different views of the data flow. The receiver maintains a flow control window. This is defined by a pointer to (i.e. the sequence number of) the next byte of data expected from the other end, and the width of the flow control window. Data will arrive in datagrams in various sized segments, anywhere from one byte upwards in length. The segments also contain the sequence number of the first byte in the segment. These sequence numbers are used by the receiver to re-order the data, discard duplicate data, etc. If there are gaps in the data, then the receiver may queue the arriving segments "on one side" until the missing segment finally arrives.

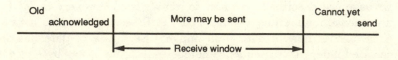

Fig 6.11.   The Receiver's View

As the segments of data arrive successfully, the "next" pointer is moved up. Depending on the chosen strategy, the "receive window" may be kept a fixed size, or perhaps a completely independent "front pointer" is maintained.

From time to time, the "Next" pointer and the "Receive Window" are transmitted from the receiver to the sender. This action is a dual one. The "Next" pointer, by moving forward through the sequence, acknowledges those bytes that it passes, and the "Receive Window" value, taken with the updated "Next" pointer moves the notional "Front" pointer forwards. The movement of the "Front" pointer gives permission for more data to be sent, and may be viewed as either a variable window or a credit type of mechanism, though the definition of TCP consistently refers to it as a window.

The sender's view is slightly more complex. The sender will also have a window, and may send data sequentially from the bottom edge to the top edge. However, at any time the sender will only have sent as far as some intermediate point in the window. Thus, it maintains the three data pointers: "Unacknowledged", "Next", and "Front". In addition, once data has been sent, it may not be discarded until it has been acknowledged by the far end. Should the data remain unacknowledged for some time, then the sender may assume that it has been lost, and will retransmit all the data between the "Unacknowledged" and "Next" pointers. When the acknowledgement messages arrive from the receiver, the values of "Next" and "Receive Window" from the incoming segment are used to update the "Unacknowledged" and "Front" pointers. Note that as the "Unacknowledged" pointer is updated, then data stored in case of the need for retransmission may be discarded, and retransmission timers may be cancelled. As the "Front" pointer is moved, any data held up can now be transmitted.

> **Exercise 6.3**　Compare and contrast this method of error recovery with that in HDLC (Chapter 2). Are there good reasons for the differences? Could a single protocol replace both without any disadvantages?

6.12　Connection Management in TCP

The other main area of TCP is the management of the connection process. The mechanism was presented in a paper by Dalal and Sunshine (1978). At the simplest we might expect a simple handshake as in X.25 would be sufficient. Thus, the entity wishing to establish a connection could send a *Call_Request* to the other party. The other party could then reply either in the affirmative, or may simply reject the advances of the caller. Thus, it would seem that a simple request–response sequence would suffice. In many circumstances, this would indeed be all that was required. However, we have seen how datagram services may corrupt data. One of the more challenging problems that may be caused is when a packet is unduly delayed. When such a delay is combined with a computer that "crashes" and restarts, then the scope for confusion is considerable.

As an illustration of this, consider an example. Caller **A** emits a *Call_Request* to a callee **B**. While the *Call_Request* is wending its way to **B**, **B** is deciding what to reply, and the reply is dawdling back, machine **A** crashes, loses all memory of what it was doing, gets restarted, and decides again to call **B** by emitting another *Call_Request*. After emitting this second *Call_Request*, the next message it gets is the orphaned reply to the earlier *Call_Request*. We have now the situation where the remaining debris of an earlier call has got mixed up with the first attempts to establish a new call, and the confusion may have dire consequences.

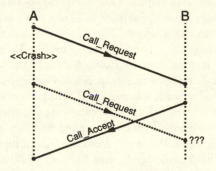

Fig 6.12.   Crash and Restart During Connection

Dalal and Sunshine devised a mechanism whereby this confusion could be avoided by making the handshake slightly more complex. The fundamental device is to choose a new, unique identifier that can be attached to the call request packet. A suitable method is to time stamp with a resolution small enough so that no two call request packets from the same starting point can ever contain the same time. The point of specifying a time stamp is that it is something that should not be corrupted by the machine crashes and thus produce accidental duplicate values. Any reliable source of unique stamps would do equally well.

Thus, the *Call_Request* carries the time stamp and the *Call_Accept* will carry this unique brand back. On receipt back by the instigator of the call, the stamp is checked, and if it does not agree with the original value sent out on the *Call_Request*, then remedial action is taken.

The actual mechanism is slightly more complex still, and to see the reason for this we must glance back at the sequence numbering system used to control the data flow and to recover from errors.

Just as there is a chance that a crash and restart of a system may confuse the reconnection process, there is also a chance that delayed data segments may disrupt the data phase of a properly established call. As an illustration, suppose that the connection had just established and begun transmitting data. Byte 42, say, was in transit when one end of the connection crashed. For some reason, byte 42 may have got delayed in the network while the crashed machine restarted and reconnected, and then again started to transmit data. At this point, byte 42 suddenly arrives from its hiding place. Without some safety mechanism, this dilatory byte could cause complete disruption of the correctly re-established connection.

The mechanism is again to use a unique label for each data byte so that the delayed byte from the earlier connection will be seen for the orphan that it is, and promptly and properly thrown out onto the street. Rather than attach a second label to each byte in addition to the sequence number that we have already seen the need for, the sequence number itself is also used as the unique label. To achieve this, the sequence numbers are not started from the perhaps obvious 0 or 1, but are started from a new unique point for each connection. In this way, any new connection will have sequence numbers that are different from any remaining wreckage of old liasions, and the old wreckage can be divined and discarded.

In TCP, the unique starting point is called the *Initial Sequence Number*—ISN. Since this is unique, this ISN is also used as the unique stamp on the call request packet, and is returned on the call accept packet. As a final intricacy, TCP is defined so that it is capable of being used in a completely symmetrical manner, with each end deciding on its own sequence number that it will use in sending to the other end. Thus, the establishment of a connection involves each end emitting a *Call_Request* to the other end that specifies an ISN, and receiving a *Call_Accept* confirming the ISN from the other end. Fig 6.13 shows a call being established in a fully acceptable manner with the exchange of four messages and the establishment of two different ISNs for use on the two independent flows of data on the connection.

Of course, while this is a possible sequence, and illustrates the symmetry of the protocol, such crystalline symmetry is very unlikely in practice, and a much more usual sequence is not for two users actually to establish a connection in this way, but for one user to wait for incoming calls, and the other to make the active connection request. Such a sequence is shown in Fig 6.14.

In this sequence, we see that the call request from A arrives at B complete with the ISN that is to be used both in acknowledging the *Call_Request*, and, after being updated, the data that follows.

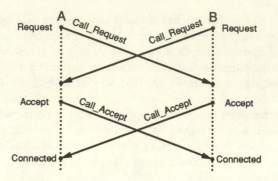

Fig 6.13.   Symmetrical Call Setup

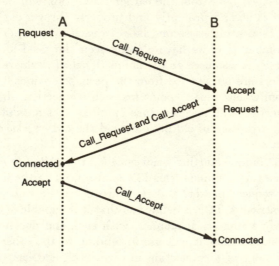

Fig 6.14.   Asymmetrical Call Setup

The response is a combined packet indicating both a *Call_Accept* and a *Call_Request* in the same packet, together with two sequence numbers—the acknowledgement of the one in the original *Call_Request* packet, and the specification of the ISN that B will start from when sending to A. The final packet acknowledges the receipt of this second sequence number. Since this is the most usual sequence and involves the exchange of three packets, it is called the *"three-way handshake"* despite the fact that four logical messages are exchanged.

Now that we have seen how the ISNs allow us to verify a valid connection sequence, the question arises about what to do when an invalid sequence is detected. In TCP the device is called the RESET. (TCPs RESET function should not be confused with the quite different

RESET function in X.25.) When either end of the connection receives a packet that it decides is a clear violation of the protocol, i.e. not intended for the current connection, it should send a RESET. If there is some uncertainty about the matter, then a RESET should not be sent.

For example, if a packet arrives that is merely outside the window, then this may be merely be exceptionally delayed data and should not result in a RESET. On the other hand if there is no connection, then anything but a RESET should elicit a RESET response.

More specifically, there are three main groups of errors:

a) No connection yet—not even a LISTEN. Any incoming packet except a RESET should elicit a RESET. In particular, a *Call_Request* to a port that is not yet started should be rejected with a RESET.

b) If the connection is not yet completed, then any acknowledgement of something not yet sent causes a RESET. In this way, orphaned *Call_Accepts* are dealt with.

c) Once the connection is set up, then acknowledgements for things outside the window do not cause a RESET, but instead an empty segment is sent with a restatement of the current send sequence number and receive pointer and window. (Otherwise delayed duplicates could cause connections to be severed.)

A RESET takes its sequence number from the incoming packet that was in error.

When a RESET arrives, the receiver checks to see whether its sequence number refers to any sequence number in its transmit window. If it refers to sequence numbers outside its transmit window, then it ignores the RESETs as referring not to something that it has just done, but to some debris from an earlier misfortune. If the RESET does refer to something within the transmit window, then in most cases the connections are aborted. The exceptions to this are when the receiver is LISTENing for an incoming connection, or has just been in the LISTENing state and has responded to an incoming call request. In these cases it merely returns to the LISTENing state.

6.13   Call Disconnection in TCP

In X.25, when we start to clear a virtual call by one end emitting a *Clear_Request* in one direction, then not only will there be no more data flow in that direction, but any data flow in the opposite direction is uncertain, and will very soon be disrupted by the final dismantling of the virtual call. Indeed, there are no sequence constraints on the time when the *Clear_Confirmation* is returned to the disconnecting end, and when the *Clear_Indication* is delivered to the far end. In Fig 6.8 we indicated that this may not be in strict time sequence after the other end responds to the clear indication, but may be immediate, and before the indication has even been delivered to the other end. The *Clear* operation is disruptive of data in transit, and may overtake data going in the same direction, and arbitrarily disrupt data in the reverse direction. The users of an X.25 connection (the two protocol entities) must normally come to some agreement that the two-way data exchange is complete, and all data of importance has been delivered before hanging up the call. In addition, X.25 gives no assurance that previously transmitted data will be delivered (except as indicated by the D-bit) if a disconnect is initiated. The X.25 *Clear* is a disruptive breaking of the virtual call.

TCP's approach to disconnection is different from that of X.25 in both these ways. The disconnect or *Close* is a logical marker that follows the data, and keeps its place at the end of the segment in which it is transmitted. Thus, it is not disruptive, and no defence action against the disruption needs to be taken. Not only does the *Close* not destroy data, but each of the two data flows on the duplex TCP connection can be closed independently. Thus, if A and B are exchanging data, A can decide that it has finished sending to B and send a *Close*. However, B can still continue sending data to A, and of course, A must keep updating its receive window and notify B of this to acknowledge the receipt of the data, and the further movement of the forward edge of the window that is necessary to allow the flow. Eventually, and independently, the reverse leg from B to A will be closed too.

6.14   The Actual TCP/IP Protocol

Now that we are equipped with the general notions of how TCP works, let us examine some of the practical details.

Firstly, we have talked about assigning unique ISNs to each of the two directions on a connection. In practice, TCP allocates a 32-bit integer to contain each of the sequence numbers, and the TCP specification makes some comments and suggestions about strategies for choosing ISNs and the possible consequences of some of these strategies. Some implementations may validly conclude that the full blown checking for orphaned packets is overkill in the circumstances in which they will operate, and for the levels of reliability that they expect to achieve. Such implementations may merely choose the same ISN each time.

This choice is a deliberate tradeoff between the ultimate in security, and the awkwardness of attempting to use a unique ISN each time. An alternative strategy is to estimate the *Maximum Segment Lifetime*—MSL. This is a combination of the specified datagram lifetime, the response time of any other TCP implementation, and a safety factor for implementation and operational errors. Any segments emitted (or rather reactions thereto) may be expected to reappear out of the network at any time until MSL has elapsed, and they have all drained out of the network. Thus, an implementation may choose to stay silent for a period of MSL after it has started. It can then be sure that all previous traffic from previous incarnations has gone from the network, and that any new ISN that it chooses will be unique, even if it merely reuses the same ISN that it used last time.

We can see that in some circumstances, the simple initial strategy of ignoring the problem altogether is merely the asymptotic extrapolation of the strategy of staying silent for the period MSL. The original TCP specification chose 2 minutes as a "reasonable" engineering choice for MSL across the ARPANET. Since the ARPANET is a large, complex, long haul network, such a choice was reasonable. However, TCP is often used on closed local networks, such as a single Ethernet. In such circumstances a realistic estimate of MSL will probably be only a few milliseconds. Since few machines can crash and restart faster than this, and in any case the scope for shunting datagrams into a siding is that much less, it is reasonable to assume that when a TCP starts up that MSL must have already elapsed since any previous incarnation.

Of course, implementors should be careful about such assumptions. The implementation may work superbly while the original assumptions are still valid, and in such cases the assumptions, buried in code, are forgotten until one fine day when the local Ethernet with its millisecond delay is gatewayed to the actual Internet...

For deluxe military strength implementations (TCP was, after all, developed in the military research community in the USA), the TCP specification suggests binding the allocation of ISNs to a local time-of-dayclock. The effect of this is to increment the low order bit every 4 microseconds. With this method, the ISN generation will cycle in about $4\frac{1}{2}$ hours. Since the ISN is bound to an external clock it can be assumed to be undisturbed by machine crashes, and since it cycles in a time much longer than the MSL, this method will ensure unique ISNs.

6.15   The Internet Protocol

TCP is defined on top of an underlying *Internet Protocol*—IP. IP allows datagrams of various lengths to be sent across a mixture of diverse networks that together make up the Internet. The IP datagram contains 32-bit source and destination addresses, and allows for the fragmentation and reassembly of datagrams at intermediate steps on the journey across the Internet should this be necessary.

Fig 6.15 shows the internet datagram layout, and Table 6.2 gives a brief description of the fields.

The IP service allows a large datagram to be specified that is up

◄──────────────────32 bits wide──────────────────►				
Version	IHL	Type of Service	Total Length	
Identification			Flags	Fragment Offset
Time to Live		Protocol	Header Checksum	
Source Address				
Destination Address				
Options				Padding

Fig 6.15.   Internet Header Format

Version	Format of the header.
IHL	Internet Header Length in 32-bit words.
Type	Type of service—defines quality of service desired: priority, delay, throughput.
Total Length	Length of this datagram, including header and data.
Identification	The sender assigns this to aid in assembling the fragments of a datagram, and distinguish them from otherwise similar fragments of other datagrams.
Flags	● May or may not fragment ● Last fragment in a sequence of fragments.
Fragment Offset	Offset from start of original datagram (in units of 8 bytes).
Time to live	Maximum lifetime of datagram in the Internet.
Protocol	Identifier of higher level protocol.
Header Checksum	Checksum over the header only. This includes fields that change, and must be changed when they do.
Source Address	32-bit Internet Address.
Dest. Address	32-bit Internet Address.
Options	These allow the control of routing, e.g. for security, the specification of security levels, the recording of routes, and time stamping.

Table 6.2 Fields in the IP Datagram Header

to 65535 bytes long. Clearly, this may be too long for many applications, or intermediate networks, and thus the datagrams may be fragmented and reassembled. The original "meta-datagram" may be fragmented on an 8-byte boundary, and the fragment offset is used to identify the fragments. The *Last Fragment*-flag identifies the final fragment, and thus, together with the other data in the IP header, defines the total datagram length. At the destination, the fragments are reassembled using these fields, together with the identifier, protocol, and address fields. Once the first fragment has arrived, there is a strict time limit within which the last fragment must arrive, otherwise the whole datagram is discarded. This time is of course the remaining time in the *Time-to-Live* field.

The IP fragmentation and reassembly mechanism should not be confused with the sequence numbers used at the higher TCP level. Although superficially similar, the two mechanisms are quite separate and independent, and serve different functions.

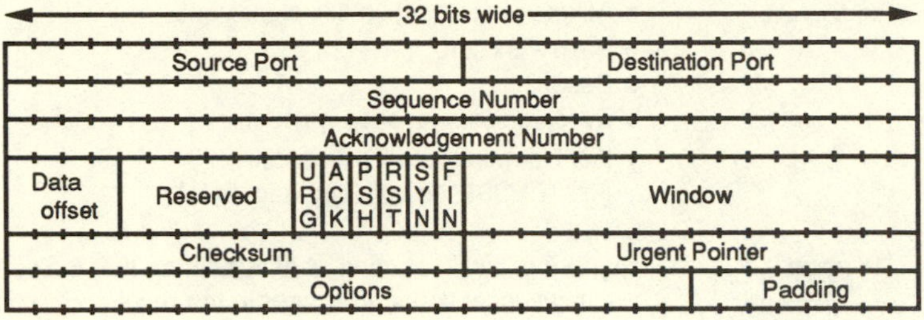

← 32 bits wide →		
Source Port		Destination Port
Sequence Number		
Acknowledgement Number		
Data offset	Reserved	U A P R S F R C S S Y I G K H T N N	Window
Checksum		Urgent Pointer
Options		Padding

Fig 6.16. TCP Header Format

TCP uses the IP service to send the segments of data. Each segment is sent with a header as shown in Fig 6.16.

Source Address		
Destination Address		
Zero	PTCL	TCP Length

Fig 6.17. TCP Pseudo-Header Format

Further explanation is in order concerning the way in which the abstract packets that we called *Call_Request, Call_Accept* and so on are mapped into the actual header shown in Fig 6.16. TCP connection establishment is defined using the term *SYN* for *SYNchronise Counters*. Thus, what we have called *Call_Request* is, in TCP-speak a *SYN*-packet, i.e. a packet with the *SYN* flag set in the header, and the sequence number set to the value upon which the sender wishes to synchronise with the receiver. The *Call_Accept* packet becomes an ordinary acknowledge carrying the sequence number back to the caller. (Well, actually one more because the *SYN* is, for some reason, deemed to occupy the first data byte.) If the handshake is the normal three-way handshake as in Fig 6.14, then the abstract *Call_Request* and *Call_Accept* combined packet is represented by setting both the *SYN*-bit and the *ACK*-bit in the same packet, and filling in both sequence and acknowledgement numbers.

Source Port	16-bit port number
Destination Port	16-bit port number
Sequence Number	Number of first byte in this segment
Ack Number	Number of next byte expected in the reverse direction.
Data Offset	Number of 32-bit words in this TCP header
6 Control Bits:	• Urgent pointer Field is significant
	(We have not described this concept in TCP)
	• Acknowledgement field is significant.
	• Push Function.
	• Reset.
	• Synchronise sequence numbers.
	• FIN No more data from sender.
	(i.e. "CLOSE" follows last data byte).
Window	Number of bytes, starting at ACK pointer, that the sender of the segment is willing to accept in the reverse direction.
Checksum	16 bit additive checksum over the whole of the header, and the data.
"Pseudo Header"	This is a 96-bit notional header that is prefixed to the real header. The pseudo-header contains the source and destination addresses and the protocol field. In addition the "TCP length" is the total length across the TCP header and data fields. This pseudo header is not carried anywhere, except implicitly in the IP header, but is computed. Since the pseudo-header is included in the header checksum, it adds an extra element of redundant checking on the segment.

Table 6.3 Fields in the TCP Header

6.16   The ISO Transport Service

We have looked at X.25, the quintessential network service, and at TCP/IP the transport service of the ARPANET. Clearly, the two are fairly similar services in that they support a connection between two entities across a wide-area network. The most important difference between the two is that on the ARPANET the approach has been taken that TCP will provide a connection end-to-end between the two communicating entities. All that is required of the underlaying network is that it be able to send internet datagrams according to the internet protocol, IP. This has been carefully designed so that it can be used end-to-end across a whole series of heterogeneous networks. (We shall return to this theme of joining dissimilar networks together to form an internetwork when we study gateways in Chapter 15.) On the other hand, X.25 is principally either an interface protocol to a network, or a protocol across a single network. X.25 does not sit so easily as an internetwork protocol (though its extended addressing capability, 40 digits in the case of the

1984 version compared with only 16 on the earlier version, means that it can be used as an internetwork protocol given the proper management of the address space).

For this and other reasons, the ISO model designates that layer four should provide a transport service end-to-end much in the same way as that provided by TCP. This transport service is supported by a fairly complex transport service protocol. The purpose of this service, compared with the underlying network service is to provide various enhancements. However, the protocol allows for various optional enhancements to be negotiated. We shall look at the functions of this protocol in outline.

Underlying networks are of three types depending upon their error rate:

A: The error rate of the underlying network service is low enough, and needs no improvement

B: The undetected error rate of the underlying network service is low enough, but it sometimes reports errors (e.g. via a RESET) that need recovery

C: The error rate of the underlying network service is insufficient. It is assumed that both error detection and recovery are needed

The protocol provides five operating modes, or classes that allow all three types of network service to be accommodated. In addition, there are mechanisms that allow several transport connections to be multiplexed over a single network connection (such as an X.25 virtual call) and thus spread the duration charges that are often imposed on such network connections across several transport connections to the same network location. On the other hand, some network connections do not provide sufficient throughput, and so the protocol allows the use of several virtual calls in parallel to support the one transport connection. This not only increases the available throughput, but also allows some redundancy as insurance against network failures.

The five classes of transport protocol are:

0: Simple
1: Basic error recovery
2: Multiplexing
3: Error recovery and multiplexing
4: Error detection, recovery and multiplexing

There are no really new principles involved in this protocol compared with those we have studied so far. The novelty of the protocol is primarily in the combination of several such features in these increasingly complex classes.

Class 0 essentially says that the underlying network connection is good enough—Type A above—and needs no enhancement. For example some X.25 networks provide a service that is just about good enough to be used for an interactive terminal session. Any errors that occur, such as a RESET will be converted into a disconnection of the transport service connection. No other enhancement is performed.

Class 1 is a modest improvement over Class 0 to accommodate networks of type B. It will recover from reported network errors such as RESET or premature DISCONNECT, but will not try to detect errors that the network layer does not report. The data is sent in numbered packets across the underlying network connection, and a copy is kept until an acknowledgement is received. When the network connection signals an error (for example an X.25 RESET) then a recovery or resynchronisation procedure is initiated that causes lost packets to be retransmitted.

It is possible to use the flow control of the underlying network providing this is of the end-to-end type (as provided by the D-bit option in X.25). Otherwise functions provided in the protocol itself must be used. The flow control in this protocol separates out the acknowledgement of data and the permission to send more data in the way that TCP does and X.25 fails to do. Obviously the use of the delivery confirmation of an underlying network service such as X.25 would destroy this separation.

In addition, Class 1 allows the transport connection to be reconnected using another network connection should the first connection fail. Class 1 transport service would be a considerable improvement on the service that is commonly provided by present-day public utilities.

Class 2 assumes a network of type A whose quality of service is adequate. However, it allows several transport connections to be multiplexed together, and for packets from several different transport connections to be combined together in one network packet. In this way network duration charges may be shared amongst several transport connections, and packet charges may be reduced if several transport service records can share the one network packet. To achieve this multiplexing, the records for the individual transport connections need to be marked with a connection number (called a destination reference in the protocol, its function is much like the logical channel identifier in X.25). In addition, each of the multiplexed connections must maintain its own flow control so that each flow can be separately regulated.

Logically, Class 3 is a combination of the error recovery functions of Class 1 and the multiplexing functions of Class 2.

Class 4 enhances the functions of Class 3 by detecting errors due to the network service being insufficiently good. It does this by adding a checksum to each and every record sent, and checking it at the receiver, In addition, records may arrive out of order, and the receiver may need to put them back into sequence. A little thought should convince the reader that these types of errors are those to be expected of a datagram service. Indeed, the error recovery and flow control procedures of this class of the transport protocol show an interesting resemblance to the corresponding elements of TCP. One of the bigger differences is that the data is referred to in terms of records rather than the individual bytes as used in TCP.

Once we recognise that Class 4 of this transport protocol is essentially working with the assumption of a datagram network service, then the transmission of the individual datagrams via different routes becomes a simple concept to grasp. Thus this class naturally lends itself to recovering from all sorts of network errors, not only those that can be accommodated by Classes 1 and 3. In addition, since the datagrams can be sent down parallel virtual calls or across parallel links or networks, then the way is open for increasing the throughput of a transport connection by using several network connections or just several network routes in parallel. Indeed, this class of protocol has been used successfully in local area network operations with no network layer at all (since the routing of the local network, such as an Ethernet was sufficient) and no link-level error recovery (since the error recovery in the transport layer provides an adequately low error rate). Of course, the absence of network level addressing means that this scheme cannot be extended beyond a single local network. To extend beyond a single local network, there is an ISO connectionless network service, with corresponding protocol that parallels the ARPANET IP protocol that we looked at earlier. This protocol provides the fragmentation and reassembly facilities of the IP protocol, together with sufficient addressing capability for full internetworking. ISO transport protocol calss 4 together with the ISO connectionless network protocol provides an analogue of TCP/IP working.

6.17   ISO Transport across Heterogeneous Networks

There are (as ever) two opposing views on how to extend such operations to internetworks consisting of a combination of local and wide area networks. One is to use the connectionless network layer together with ISO transport class 4 connections on top of it as described above. The other is to use X.25 (1984) as the network layer with class 0 (or possibly higher) on top. The point of using the 1984 version of X.25 is that the extended addressing available, together with the global registration of appropriate addresses will allow this network service to be used end-to-end. One of the big advantages of the use of class 4 transport service is the use of end-to-end checksums, whereas X.25 will tend to use step-by-step checksums on individual links. With end-to-end checksums, the resulting quality depends almost exclusively on the reliability of the end systems, whereas the step-by-step approach is subject to the lowest reliability of any intermediate step. We return to this subject in Chapter 12 when we discuss system issues and system complexity.

The two views on the combination of class of transport protocol together with type of network service have adherents that are, very roughly, the European Community with Class 0 over X.25, and North America with Class 4 over connectionless network service. These are the chosen routes to ISO Open Working for these two camps. Unfortunately, since the ISO model not only defines the transport service to have end-to-end significance, but defines the protocols themselves to be end-to-end. In principle, then, the two classes of protocol cannot interwork. Beneath all the pseudo-religious argument of virtual call versus datagrams, the point of it all seems to have been forgotten—the poor user who just needs open interconnection to get her work done.

Fortunately, the ultimate power of the user as paymaster has managed to bring some pragmatic sense back into the matter. Though the ISO model defines the end-to-end significance of the service and protocols, the detailed *semantics of the service* are what matter. In this case, transport services can be joined together by careful sequencing of the connection establishment primitives. The result is that two transport connections *can* be joined in series and also preserve the service semantics. In this way the user service—the point of the exercise after all—can be gatewayed between the differing camps. The details of the model are violated in principle, but only in such a way that does not actually impact any services in practice.

6.18   The ISO Transport Checksum

It is worthwhile briefly describing the checksum used by class 4 of the ISO protocol. Since it is expected that the transport service will be implemented in software in the end systems the designers provided a checksum that could conveniently be implemented in software. Arithmetic is performed with byte-sized integers (in the range 0 to 254, modulo 255), and ones complement arithmetic (so that minus zero (255) is the same as zero). A record is considered as an array of n bytes a_i for i from 1 to n. Two extra checksum bytes are added to the record at positions $n + 1$ and $n + 2$ and are calculated so that both

$$\sum_{i=1}^{n+2} a_i = 0 \quad \text{and} \quad \sum_{i=1}^{n+2} ia_i = 0$$

Exercise 6.4   Find an efficient algorithm for calculating the two checksum bytes for records that are to be transmitted. It should not be necessary to use multiplication while looping over the bytes calculating the checksum, but only at the final stage of the process.

Exercise 6.5   Would this kind of checksum detect additional leading or trailing zeros, or two records concatenated together?

In view of our earlier investigation of fast methods of implementing cyclic redundancy checksums in Chapter 2, and the wealth of analysis supporting this type of redundancy, the reader may wish to consider whether he thinks this novel type of checksum as specified for class 4 operations is a wise choice.

Thus, we see that the ISO transport protocol uses a wide range of techniques that we have encountered earlier to enhance the basic network service to the level specified by the transport service user. This can vary from very close to no change through various levels of error correction and multiplexing up to an elaborate protocol that will provide a good quality of service in the face of severe network errors, and is also capable of using several network services in parallel for performance or redundancy.

6.19   ISDN

Telephone services are mainly concerned with the provision of voice transmission. This can be achieved by a fairly modest analogue channel that is switchable on demand according to the wishes of the caller. There have been many changes in the technology of telephone services for a whole variety of reasons. In particular, rather than the circuit being analogue end-to-end it is normal for the speech to be digitised and for the vast majority of the transmission between exchanges to take place with purely digital signals. At the same time, there has been a huge growth in the use of telephone circuits for the transmission of data. Since the service delivered to the customer is analogue, then the normal way of transmitting data is to use modems to convert the digital signals in the computer or terminal into the analogue signals that must be transmitted along the telephone wire. At the exchange, these analogue signals are digitised and switched between the exchanges. Clearly this is not an ideal situation. Indeed, this can be seen by the fact that a modem on a voice circuit typically runs at 2400 bits per second or less, and it takes a very expensive modem to work up to 9,600 bps. On the other hand, a voice circuit on a high capacity inter-exchange link is allocated 64,000 bits per second.

For this, and many other reasons, the whole of the telephone system is being revised, and a system called *Integrated Services Digital Network*—ISDN is being introduced. ISDN is no less than a completely new architecture for the telephone system. With the size of the telephone system worldwide and the investment in it, there is clearly no way the whole system can be instantaneously replaced, and one of the important aspects of ISDN is the way in which it will coexist with the existing traditional systems, and indeed have to interwork with them. If getting an ISDN phone meant that the subscriber couldn't call non-ISDN phones, then the take up would be very small!

The fundamental key to ISDN is that the digital stream is taken right out to the telephone set itself. In addition, a single telephone will have several channels of data. ISDN defines several channel types: the B-channel is a 64kbps digital channel for encoding a voice analogue signal or sending data; the D-channel is 16 or 64 kbps for signalling and control; and the H-channel is 384, 1536, or 1920 kbps. These (and other) channels will be supplied in various combinations. Two of the most important are the *Basic Rate* which is 2B+D, and the *Primary Rate* which is either 23B+D or 30B+D. The basic rate is that supplied to ordinary telephone sets, and the primary rate is meant to fit in the standard offering "wideband" link. Thus 23B+D fits in the North American T1 link, and 30B+D fits in the European 2.048 Mbps channel.

One 64,000 bps channel allows a voice channel to be digitised into 8-bit sample 8,000 times per second. Thus, the basic rate allows the possibility of a voice channel, a simultaneous 64,000 bps data channel, and a 16,000 bps control channel all on the same twisted pair that was used for *Plain Old Telephone Service*—POTS. These three channels are transmitted along the wires, in both directions, in 48-bit packets sent every 250 μS. This gives a gross bit rate of 192kbps. Each of these 48-bit raw packets, contains two 8-bit blocks of bits from each of the two B-channels, and four bits from the D-channel. The other twelve bits in the frame are concerned with maintaining synchronisation, and various other functions. Note, that despite the underlying frame structure, the three channels are actually raw bit streams. There is no error checking or correction.

6.20   Signalling System Number 7

The format and content of packets sent on the control channel are defined in the CCITT SS # 7. This system has evolved from earlier signalling systems, and is being shaped to fit into the ISO communications model. In particular, the lower layers resemble X.25 with an error correcting layer 2. SS# 7 is concerned with telephone signalling (establishing calls and routing messages) and with system management (congestion, trunk utilisation and suchlike). For more detail about this and many other aspects of ISDN the reader is referred to the *IEEE Journal on Selected Areas in Communication* Vol SAC-1 May 1986.

6.21 Facilities on ISDN

Having got the standardised bit pipe to every telephone, together with the signalling system for use on the special channel, what facilities does the user actually get? Well, as a replacement for simple POTS, the user will get the vastly improved quality of the digital channel together with the advantages of the separate signalling channel. For the simplest use, this will mean "merely" faster call setup time. However, the separate signalling channel allows not only the elimination of intrusive dialling tones or squeaks on the auditory channel, but also permits a much richer dialogue between the user's telephone and the exchange. New facilities, such as callback when free, displaying the telephone number of the incoming call on the telephone before the call is answered etc become possible. These require both the exchange to understand and provide these facilities, and also the user's telephone to interface with them and provide some suitable interface with the user. Already such facilities are starting to revolutionise the service available to users even though the user interface is often pretty dreadful.

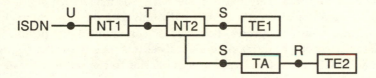

Fig 6.18. The Various ISDN Services

However, perhaps the most exciting possibilities arise because of the several other interfaces defined by the CCITT. Fig 6.18 shows the heirarchy of possible interfaces that can be built on top of the basic service. CCITT specifies four primary access points R, S, T, and U. We see that the ISDN connection of type U comes into the most basic box, the NT1. This allows the most basic type of service to be provided at point T—transmission only. This may be enhanced by the facility NT2. This is usually a customer PBX, though it may in the future be a box that is aimed at providing facilities other than switching. This provides the S access point. This is the point at which the new breed of ISDN terminals will be connected. This includes the telephones with the new ISDN facilities, and also new devices like fast FAX devices and suchlike. The other type of device to use the S point will be the TA box. The function of the TA box is to use the S point type of service to supply various kinds of service that are currently supplied by other means. This includes the present X-series and V-series of interface standards. In this way the large existing investment in modems and other equipment will be protected, and may be allowed to wither away rather than needing to be killed off.

6.22   ISDN and Computer Communications

We see that ISDN will not only replace the voice telephone network with a much improved service, but the availibility of the underlying digital service directly to the customer will vastly improve the utility of the service for the information technology user. The standardisation of the various interfaces together with the deregulation of PTTs in some countries, will allow the provision of completely new services. These services will involve the implementation of complete stacks of protocols including application level protocols within the new devices themselves. The services will be managed both by the PTTs, and also by third party value-added companies. That ISDN will be a revolution cannot be doubted.

However, ISDN has sometimes been touted as the universal panacea for all network problems. In particular, PBXs with ISDN facilities have been suggested as the solution for all the communications needs of a company or a University. In the early 70s many such organisations would have pounced on an ISDN with universal 64 kbps channels as a wonderful solution beyond their wildest communications needs. Much effort was spent in developing slow speed campus networks to provide an X.25-X.28-sort of service that was inferior to the services that will be available from ISDN.

However, times have moved on. ISDN services for computer communications into the home, or to casual and irregular connections elsewhere promise to be a wonderful advance, and the new ISDN services will be very impressive. However, Campus networks already typically run at a channel rate of 10 Mbps, and even then need partitioning so that local traffic on one part of the network does not spread unnecessarily across the whole network and swamp it. Already FDDI is being installed and is running at 10 times that rate (See Chapter 3), and several development projects are investigating both local and wide area networks running in the gigabit per second range. (See, e.g. Haas 1987). The story has been consistent in the sense that whenever networking has provided more bandwidth, computer applications have been found for it. This includes the use of networks for moving files and accessing filestores, paging virtual memory, accessing remote super computer facilities, including manipulating graphics remotely in real time, and on and on. The only limit on what is useful is what is available at a reasonable cost (whatever "reasonable" means).

In addition, ISDN services are dominated by the provision of a switched circuit. Such a circuit is of fixed bandwidth, and the capacity is allocated to the connection whether it is used or not. However, computer communications are extremely bursty in nature, varying from very high demands over short periods to long periods of very low or zero activity. Indeed, it is this very bursty nature that predicates most packet switching. Providing switched ISDN circuits cannot be an efficient way of supporting such traffic. Of course, if the cost is low enough, then the fact that some bandwidth "goes to waste" is as inconsequential as the fact that most machine cycles on personal computers do not do "useful work".

Modern use of wide-area networks is still dominated by slow-speed terminal access and mail, and ISDN services will make a large impact in that area. However, ISDN is only just starting to appear, and by the time it is widely available the major use of networks will certainly have moved beyond simple terminal access to the more demanding bulk data transfer which is already the main use of fast local-area networks. Already wide-area networks are providing ever faster transmission speeds. Thus, while it is clear that ISDN will be immensely valuable for all sorts of applications, it can only supply one *part* of the overall communications needs of the computing community, particularly of the more advanced community of research computing in industry and research. This is particularly true in the local "campus" environment where even in countries that still have PTT monopolies, ISDN will have to compete directly with fast local networks for the higher performance applications.

6.23 Summary

The previous chapter looked at how a network service could be built from the component services across links or shared media. This chapter has rounded off this study by looking in some detail at the various ways in which such a network service can be made available to the network user. We have also summarised the ISO Transport Service.

The new ISDN services have been reviewed. They partly fit into the theme of this chapter, but in addition to the network service that fits into the theme of this chapter, ISDN services also supply point-to-point links at the low end, and complete applications bundled ready for the user at the other extreme.

The provision of this end-to-end transport or network service marks an important point in the study of networks. Below this service we are concerned with all the "traditional" telecommunications issues of modulation, transmission, addressing, routing, etc. All these complex issues are targeted at one superficially simple service—providing a reliable "bit-pipe" between two network users. As we have seen, not only are there several layers of services cooperating to provide this service, but there may be diverse kinds of media and protocols all working together in series or parallel to give the required service. Conversely, above this bit-pipe we shall see that the uses to which this transport service are put are similarly diverse, and there are again several cooperating layers involved.

Sometimes this has been likened to an "hour-glass" with diverging protocols and services both above and below the conceptually simple transport service. The reader should expect a sea change in the character of the protocols and services that we shall proceed to study. Below the transport service the protocols are concerned with providing the bit-pipe on a variety of media and in a variety of configurations. Above this bit-pipe, transmission and connectivity end-to-end are taken for granted, and the problems of data representation, heterogeneity, data semantics, and various other computing issues related to dispersion and diversity become the issues to be tackled.

7
Terminal Support

This chapter starts with a discussion of the two main ways of supporting simple character terminals remotely across networks. On the way we encounter several of the various different ways of representing data in a communications environment. We then proceed to describe full-screen terminals with form-filling capabilities, and finally outline the protocols X and NeWS that are used to support bit-mapped terminals across high speed networks.

So far in this book we have studied the problems associated with moving data across networks—the transport service and below. This chapter marks the start of our examination of higher level concepts. However, we have not entirely finished with the issues involved in the lower levels, and shall return to them several times in later chapters.

7.1   Supporting Simple Character Terminals—Triple-X

Through the early chapters of this book we have looked fairly closely at the various ways in which a simple terminal can be supported on a point-to-point link. We have looked at the basic ways of representing characters in terms of eight bit bytes, and of transmitting these bytes asynchronously. With very simple terminals it is common to have an arrangement something like Fig 7.1.

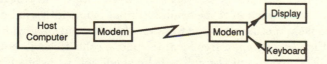

Fig 7.1.   Dumb Terminal Attachment

Here we see a dumb terminal attached to a host computer by means of a pair of modems. The dumb terminal is shown as a pair of separate devices connected to the modem. A keyboard is the input device to the computer and the display is the output device. The display is usually a video display screen.

The implication of this type of arrangement is that all data typed at the keyboard is sent to the host computer, and only the host computer writes on the terminal's display. This may trouble some people who have used such devices and seen that as they press the keys on the keyboard, the corresponding character appears on the screen. Of course, what happens is that the pressing of the key generates the ASCII bit pattern which is sent down the communications line to the host computer in the ways that we have described earlier. When the host receives the representation of the character, it considers what to do with it, and usually echoes the character back along the reverse path, resulting in the apparent direct connection between the keyboard and the display. However, sometimes the "echo" is more complex. For example, a carriage return character often causes the "echoing" of a carriage return and line feed sequence, or, if it is the terminating carriage return for a command to the computer, then the "echo" may well be the response to the command—a few lines of information perhaps, or possibly the listing of an extensive file of data.

In Fig 7.1, we show a dumb terminal attached to a host computer using a pair of modems and a communications link. The communications link may be very short, or very long, and may be a fixed leased line or dial-up on the public switched telephone network. Huge numbers of terminals are connected to host computers in this way. In addition, one of the most important types of program for microcomputers is the terminal emulation program which enables the microcomputer to be used in place of a simple terminal.

When we described asynchronous communication in Chapter 1 we commented that this form of communication was very suitable for connecting simple terminals to computers, particularly as it could handle single isolated characters that are separated by long variable pauses. This is precisely the pattern that we expect typed input to follow. Sometimes single keys are pressed with long intervening pauses, and sometimes an expert typist will pound out text. Even with the fastest human typist only a small fraction of the available input bandwidth will be used, and it is unlikely that a very large fraction of the output bandwidth will be used either. For cheap or free local telephone calls, this will not matter much. The expense of the call will be small and is justified by the immediate response that is available.

However, as the distance increases, the cost of the telephone call becomes increasingly important, and once the call crosses international borders, the cost skyrockets. It then becomes increasingly evident that the utilisation of the now expensive link is very low, and something needs to be done. In addition to this, as the length of the circuit increases, the likelihood of transmission errors increases, particularly for dial-up circuits.

The X.3 PAD is an attempt to address this problem. Essentially, the X.3 PAD is constructed by taking much of the terminal support function out of the host (the upper diagram in Fig 7.2) and putting it in a box at the other end of an X.25 connection (as in the lower diagram in Fig 7.2). (See also the last chapter.) The PAD gets its name from its function of bridging between the packets of the X.25 network on the one side, and the character terminal access on the other. It is a *Packet Assembler Disassembler*—PAD.

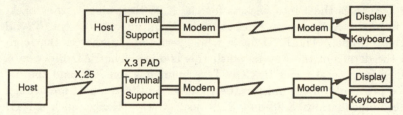

Fig 7.2.   Using X.25 to Link Terminals

The effect of such an arrangement is to allow the PAD to be moved much closer to the user's terminal, and thus the dedicated circuit between the two modems is very short. Most of the total circuit from terminal to host is now the X.25 connection between the PAD and the host. Since the X.25 circuit is a packet switched circuit rather than a dedicated circuit, the links along the X.25 circuit are shared amongst many users, and thus the cost is shared and is less than that of a dedicated circuit. Of course, while a saving is made by using the multiplexed X.25 link, a new cost has also been introduced. This is the introduction of the new element, the PAD, and the complex protocol, X.25, that must be handled. The expectation is that the savings incurred in shortening the dedicated circuit will more than compensate for the extra costs introduced.

Of course, the utility of the X.3 PAD solution is also increased by considering e.g. Fig 6.3 in the last chapter. There the typical X.25 network has a mixture of a large number of X.25 hosts and X.3 PADs. In general, any user of any PAD may establish a virtual call to any host. Two terminals on the same PAD may be talking to two quite different hosts at the same time, and the one terminal can call a different host each and every time it is used. Thus, a telephone call to a local PAD in the user's city will enable her either to call another local host in the same city, or a host across the country, or on the other side of the world. Of course, the X.25 charges will vary according to the destination, but they will usually show a considerable saving compared with a direct call through to the host using direct dialling. In addition, while public X.25 networks usually have PADs that are only reachable by using modems and the public switched telephone network, private X.25 networks often have terminals permanently connected to the PADs using null modems and fixed wires. Such an arrangement gives the terminals very flexible switching between the available hosts and avoids the speed limitations commonly imposed by the public switched networks and the modems employed.

Let us examine this most widely available terminal service. As we have indicated above, the PAD takes characters in from the terminal and assembles them into packets for the X.25 side, and it takes packets from the X.25 side and disassembles them into characters to send to the terminal. The PAD has a whole series of parameters that control the details of the way in which this is done. The PAD function is defined in general terms in CCITT recommendation X.3, and the detailed protocols on the links to the terminal and to the host are defined in recommendations X.28 and X.29 respectively. Hence, such a PAD is sometimes referred to as a "*Triple-X*" PAD in honour of these three recommendations.

In general, the PAD disassembly function is the simpler of the two. The PAD takes the packets sent out from the host, breaks them down into the individual characters, and sends the characters to the terminal with hardly any change. The exceptions to this simple picture are that sometimes extra line feed characters are inserted after carriage return characters, sometimes carriage return and line feed sequences are inserted into the character stream to "wrap" long lines into narrower displays, and sometimes extra "idle" characters are inserted after slow functions such as carriage returns to allow the carriage of a paper printing terminal to return to the left margin of the paper before further printing characters arrive.

The treatment of input data is much more complex. Incoming characters are assembled in a buffer until a decision is made that the input buffer is complete, and may be sent to the host as an X.25 packet. This forwarding decision can take place depending on the time elapsed since the arrival of the last character, the character last typed (i.e. was it a "line terminating" character), or buffer being full. In addition, input characters may be "echoed" back to the terminal's display (together with similar insertion of line feeds, nulls, and line wrapping), and the input buffer may be simply edited ("*Delete the last character I typed*", "*Junk the line and start over*", and "*Redisplay the line—I've lost track of what I've done*").

The operation of the PAD is controlled by a set of parameters. These may be changed and interrogated from the host via the X.29 protocol or from the terminal via the X.28 protocol. The X.28 protocol is a simple command-response dialogue with the terminal user. When the user wishes to talk to the PAD rather than to the host she types a special character to escape from data transfer mode to PAD command mode. This character is itself controlled by one of the PAD parameters.

Tables 7.1 and 7.2 show the PAD parameters. As the standards

Parameter   Decimal Value, and Function

1   Escape to PAD mode
           0—off
           1—DLE
           32–126—corresponding graphic character

2   Echo
           0—no echo
           1—echo

3   Data forwarding characters:
           0—none
           1—any alphanumeric
           2—the CR character
           4—ESC, BEL, ENQ, ACK
           8—DEL, CAN, DC2
           16—ETX, EOT
           32—HT, LF, VT, FF
           64—other control characters not shown above

4   Idle timer delay
           0—off
           1–255—Timer in 1/20ths sec

5   Flow control—terminal to PAD
           0—no flow control
           1—PAD emits X-on and X-off to control terminal input data.
           2—Same as 1, but applies to PAD command mode too.

6   PAD output messages
           0—no messages
           1—messages other than *prompt* in standard format
           4—*prompt* messages in standard format
           8–15—messages in non-standard format

7   Action on break
           0—ignore
           1—send an *interrupt* packet
           2—*reset* the X.25 connection
           4—send an *indication of break* message
           8—Esacpe to PAD mode
           16—discard output (set par 8 = 1)

8   Discard output (see parm 7)
           0—normal output
           1—discard output

9   Padding after carriage return
           n—send n padding characters.

10   Line folding
           0—no line folding
           n—after n graphic characters insert CR/LF.

11   Speed—read only
           ●sense the bit rate of the terminal.

12   Flow control—PAD to terminal
           0—no flow control
           1—User can send X-on and X-off to control PAD output.

Table 7.1.   The Twelve Mandatory PAD Parameters

Parameter	Function and Values
13	Linefeed insertion after CR 0—No LF insertion 1—Insert LFs after CRs sent to the terminal 2—Insert LFs after CRs sent to the host 4—Insert LFs after CRs echoed back from the PAD to the user.
14	Padding after LF n—insert n padding characters after an LF.
15	Editing—on or off 0—off 1—Input line editing is active. (Forwarding on packet full and idle timer change.)
16	Character delete character
17	Line delete character
18	Line redisplay character
19	What the PAD emits or "echoes" when editing an input line 0—nothing 1—printing terminal assumed 2—display (video) terminal assumed 8 or 32–126—sends character specified
20	Echo Mask—Controls echoing of input characters 0—off all characters echoed 1—don't echo CR 2—don't echo LF 4—don't echo VT, HT, FF 8—don't echo BEL, BS 16—don't echo ESC, ENQ 32—don't echo ACK, NAK, STX, SOH, EOT, ETB, ETX 64—don't echo editing characters as specified in parms 16, 17, 18 128—don't echo of all other control characters not mentioned above, plus DEL
21	Parity treatment 0—no parity checking or generation 1—check parity 2—generate parity
22	Page wait 0—no page wait n—wait after n linefeeds

Table 7.2.   The Ten Optional PAD Parameters

are revised and developed, the number of parameters is increased. The table summarises the 1984 version of X.3. However, only the first 12— those in Table 7.1—are mandatory. Despite this, many PADs in the real world either implement fewer parameters than this, or sometimes pretend to implement certain parameters, but actually lie about the values. At the other extreme, many PADs implement values beyond those in X.3. As time passes the number of official parameters in X.3 is bound to increase. Each parameter has a numerical value in the range

0 to 255, and can thus be stored in one eight bit byte.

X.3 PADs are normally used in one or other of two main modes either simple character-by-character forwarding, or line-by-line forwarding, possibly with input line editing.

To understand the operation of the terminal we shall think of the terminal as two completely separate parts—a display and a keyboard. The display may be either a simple paper printer, or a video screen. The terminal may be either a custom designed terminal or a microcomputer running a terminal emulation program. All keystrokes are sent to the PAD as individual characters. On arrival, the characters are stored in the PAD's internal buffer. Quite separately, and independently, the PAD may be sending characters to the terminal's display. On the other side of the PAD—the X.25 connection to the host—data packets may be sent from the PAD to the host, and received from the host by the PAD. Both the connections from the PAD—to the host and to the terminal—are said to be *full duplex*—that is, data may flow both ways quite independently.

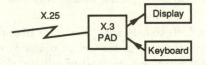
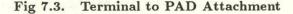

Fig 7.3.   Terminal to PAD Attachment

If a host wishes to take full control of a display, for example to implement a screen-based editor, then it will probably try to arrange for each and every character to be forwarded from the PAD to the host as it is typed in. Setting echoing off via parameter 2, and setting parameter 3 to 127 will cause most keystrokes to be forwarded to the host in their very own packets. (The exceptions are the non-alphanumeric characters, such as the period and the ampersand for which specific forwarding cannot be specified.) If this is not sufficient, then the PAD needs to be set to forward on timer (parameter 4). This does indeed give the host complete control over the screen, since only the host writes onto the screen and all the user keystrokes must first be forwarded to the host for processing.

However, the cost is twofold. Firstly, a complete packet is used for each input character. When networks charge by the packet rather than by the character, this can be very expensive. But even if networks are free, wide area networks frequently have round trip delays of several seconds to cross the network, be processed by the host, and be echoed back across the network again to the terminal. Seeing your individual keystrokes echoed with a delay of several seconds is a disturbing experience. Not only is this round trip delay a problem, but allocating a whole packet to each and every input keystroke can cause serious network congestion. As a modest optimisation of this, parameter 4 may be set for an idle timer delay. When this is active the PAD waits for the specified interval to see whether another keystroke will arrive before deciding to forward the packet. Only when the input has been idle for a time is the packet forwarded. In this way the packet fill is increased. However, there is a conflict between choosing a small enough time for the echoing to be timely, and a large enough time for bunched characters to share packets to a significant extent. In any case, the round trip delay to the host and back is unchanged.

The other main way of operating the PAD is line by line. The PAD is set up so that the input characters are stored in a buffer until some data forwarding character—most commonly carriage return—is entered. At this point the line is forwarded to the host. While the buffer is accumulating the input keystrokes, the characters are usually echoed to the display (parameter 2 = 1) so that the typist can see what is going on. To achieve this sort of operation parameter 3 should be set to the value 2 to indicate that carriage return means send the line to the host.

There are various extra frills to help with this mode of operation. For example, parameter 13 allows the optional insertion of line feeds after input carriage returns. A fairly primitive method of editing the input line is provided via parameters 15 to 18: with input line editing enabled (parameter 15), parameters 16 and 17 specify a keystroke—usually a control character—that deletes the immediately preceding character, or deletes the whole line ready to start over again. Parameter 18 allows an incomplete (i.e. not yet sent) line to be re-displayed on the terminal to see what it looks like now after whatever editing has been applied to it. It is useful if the terminal operator has lost track of the editing of the input line—all too easy on some systems.

Finally, parameters 7 and 8 allow the host to control the action when the user presses BREAK on her terminal. This action may be anything from ignoring the BREAK (parameter 7 = 1) to discarding and resynchronising output. (If parameter 7 is 21 then a BREAK causes parameter 8 to be set to discard output, and the host must then re-enable output by restoring parameter 8 when all the data in transit has been discarded.)

Most of the other parameters deal with cosmetic aspects, such as the suppression of PAD messages, the insertion of padding characters after CR or LF for slow printing terminals, the folding of long lines at the right hand side of the display, flow control to and from the PAD, and so on.

X.3 provides a rather crude way of controlling a terminal. It is adequate for line-by-line mode, or, with the caveats about cost and performance expressed above, for the full control of a simple video terminal. However, there are some severe limitations. For example, in line-by-line mode, the parameters are inadequate to handle properly the cases where an echoed input line straddles the right margin of a display. If characters are deleted across such a margin, then the line redisplay function is often needed to be sure about what is going on. In addition, should a buffer be forwarded because it is full, then the line editing functions suddenly become unable to correct the fragment of the complete input line that has just been sent (i.e. forwarded) across the network.

One of the most notable omissions from the definition of X.3 is any guidance on what should happen if data arrives from the host while the PAD is composing and echoing an input buffer. Some PADs choose just to mix up the characters in the output stream. Thus, if the PAD is outputting data from the host, and the user types a character, then the output and the echoed input will be interleaved, character by character. The result is a rather odd display, and is probably as good a reason as any for the existence of the input line redisplay function. Another strategy for handling this conflict is the so called "polite typeahead". In this approach, the echoing is held up until the completion of the printing of an X.25 complete packet sequence from the host. As we saw in the last chapter, a complete packet sequence is a series of packets all but the last of which has the more data bit set. Such a sequence can normally be assumed to be a complete piece of text from the host—often a line. Once the echoing of input has started, then further output from the host is held up until the input buffer has been forwarded, and the input line is complete. The effect of this is usually the interleaving of input and output line by line rather than character by character. Most people find this mode preferable to character by character interleaving.

However, there are some dangers with polite typeahead. For example, accidentally touching the space bar can cause the start of assembly of an input buffer, and the locking up of output. Since the echoed space is not often glaringly obvious, the terminal session can mysteriously "freeze". A way of limiting the resulting damage is to build in a timeout, but now the implementation is starting to become disproportionately complex. In addition, your author for example likes sometimes to type most of the next line while waiting for the computer to finish processing the last. Usually it is prudent to wait for the completion of the output messages from the last line before finally sending the new line by pressing the return key. With "polite typeahead" this method is invalidated because the incomplete input line blocks further output until it is completed. For these sorts of reasons, I tend to call this "rude typeahead" to the consternation of some colleagues.

Some hosts with locally attached terminals provide a form of typeahead called "interlocked". In this form of typeahead, input is buffered, but it is only echoed when the host is eventually ready to accept input. The result of this is that the script of a terminal session is not disordered by the user typing ahead, but is kept in "proper" order as accepted by the host. Unfortunately, X.3 does not provide such an option. Another widespread concept ignored by X.3 is that of an "end-file" signal. This is a signal that is typed in by a user to signal end of input—for example, the end of text when composing a message, or the end of the source text when entering a computer program.

The protocols X.28 and X.29 respectively define the way in which the PAD interacts with the character terminal and with the X.25 host. X.28 defines the exact format of the various messages and responses between the user and the PAD. X.29 specifies the details of the way in which the host sets or interrogates the PAD parameters. X.29 is a very simple and straightforward protocol. The requests to change PAD parameters, or to interrogate them are transferred as sets of byte pairs—the index value and the value itself. The vector of byte pairs is prefixed with a one byte operation code and is transferred as a complete X.25 packet sequence with the Q-bit (qualifier bit) set. There are three main messages from the host to the PAD—*set parameter*, *read parameter*, and *set and read parameter*—and one from the PAD to the host—*parameter indication*. (There are also a few error messages defined.)

Though a simple and very widespread protocol, there are two criticisms of Triple-X that we shall make at the moment, and we shall make a philosophical criticism later when comparing the philosophy of X.3 with other ways of supporting simple terminal access. The first criticism is that the PAD may only *respond* to queries from the host—it can never originate the parameter indication messages. On the other hand, the terminal user can, by entering "PAD recall" mode and using the X.28 protocol, change any of the PAD values. Thus, if the value of some parameter, such as the line folding width, is important to the host, then it must keep polling the PAD to find out whether it has changed. We have a trade-off between the frequency of polling being high enough so that a change is noticed within a reasonable time, and being low enough so that the traffic generated by the polling is not unduly expensive.

The second criticism is the fact that the "control messages"—the messages used to control the operation of the PAD and change and interrogate its parameters rather than to communicate directly with the terminal—are mixed in with the data and separated only by the Q-bit. This means that they are subject to the same flow control, and the consequence of this is that if terminal output is paused—stopped in page wait for example—then the PAD messages will be held up behind the data on the X.25 link. Thus, if the host uses X.29 to read some PAD parameter, and receives no reply for some period, it cannot be sure whether the delay is because of the interaction with the data flow control, or whether the PAD is not going to reply at all. Of course, all true X.3 PADs *should* reply. The problem is that the real world contains many "defective" or non-conforming PADs, both those run privately and those run by various pubic utilities around the globe. Working in the real pragmatic PAD world means relying on hardly anything. Separate flow control for data and control should always be provided in a protocol design to alleviate this sort of problem.

Despite or perhaps because of the low level of support that is offered, X.3 PADs are widely available across the world. Traffic between X.3 PADs and their hosts is probably still the major use for X.25 networks. However, hosts providing terminal access using X.25 and X.29 access need to be aware of possible variations in PAD implementations. Not only are some of the parameters optional, and some PADs defective, as we have mentioned above, but some PADs lie and cheat about their parameters. Often this is done by the PAD implementors because some hosts make remarkably stupid use of the X.3 parameters. However the result of such well meaning fiddling is often even worse confusion on the part of hosts that are trying to make sensible but unusual use of the parameters. PAD support using X.3 in the real world is an art, and the less use that is made of the X.3 parameters, minimal though they are in some respects, the more successful is the service likely to be.

> **Exercise 7.1** Should a host that wishes to operate in line-by-line mode normally set parameters 16, 17, and 18 (the characters to delete characters and lines and re-display lines)? Consider the extreme cases when a) all the PAD users are fairly local—on a research park run by one company, and b) the PAD users are widely scattered across many other institutions—each PAD user uses several different hosts each of which has its own way of doing things.

7.2 Virtual Terminals—TELNET

In looking at X.3 we have seen that most of its function is aimed at the minutiae of the support of real physical terminals: at the details of line wrapping, idle insertion, buffer forwarding conditions, line editing, and suchlike. It is very much assumed that the users of an X.3 service will have a real physical terminal, perhaps even a genuine Teletype or a functionally similar device, that is attached to the PAD either by a fixed or by a dialup line. We have seen that the parameters are usually set up either for character-by-character working, or for line-by-line entry, and with the details usually controlled by the host.

Most of the parameters are really of no interest to the hosts at all, and it is normally most prudent if the host leaves as many as possible unchanged (quite contrary to the actual way in which many hosts seem to change as many as possible).

The TELNET protocol that is used on the ARPANET takes the diametrically opposed view. In TELNET the notion of a *Network Virtual Terminal*—NVT is central. The NVT is a simple abstract terminal that merely responds to the printable ASCII characters, plus the carriage return and line feed characters. All the grungy details of idle delays, how to delete erroneously entered characters and so forth are deemed to be strictly local and private affairs for the terminal end, and no business of the host. The actual terminal may not be an ASCII terminal at all, but perhaps the very different IBM 2741 type of terminal for instance.

The great value of this approach is that of abstraction—of hiding all the irrelevant detail. Of course there is a problem in that no real terminals look like an NVT, and so some "intelligence" must be used between the real actual terminal and the connection to the host. Thus the abstract NVT may be a local minicomputer with an attached terminal, or a microcomputer running an NVT emulation program. Very commonly the NVT is implemented as a process running on one host that has a through connection to another remote host (which is the model described in the defining document). Thus, a user may be logged into his own machine by whatever method is deemed appropriate. At some stage she will then invoke some talk-through program to connect to the remote host. The program needs only to implement the simple abstract NVT. This is a considerably simpler task than implementing a talk-through program that pretends to be a full-blown X.3 PAD.

Let us look more closely at this concept of an abstract terminal. The TELNET NVT is an extremely simple device, amounting to little more than a stream of ASCII characters plus a break signal. However, TELNET is not limited to such a simple model. There are four basic protocol messages that allow the two ends to negotiate more complex behaviour. These are the messages DO, DON'T, WILL, WON'T. These messages each have a parameter indicating an option that is being negotiated. Such an option may be as mundane as setting tab stops, or as elaborate as agreeing to implement a data entry terminal similar to the IBM 3270 that we shall meet later. Thus, suppose that an option is known as "3270" and one or the other end wishes to start using this option. It would send "DO 3270" along the connection to the other end. The other end has the option of accepting the request with "WILL 3270" or refusing it with "WON'T 3270". Similarly, the host may send the request "DON'T 3270" to cease using this option and drop back to using the basic NVT. As well as requesting the other end to use an option, either end may volunteer that it will use an option. It does this by emitting an unsolicited "WILL 3270" and the other end can accept or reject the offer with a "DO 3270" or a "DON'T 3270". Notice the symmetry of this arrangement. There is no constraint on the time ordering of a DO-WILL exchange. Either end may initiate the exchange or the DO and WILL may cross in the network. The final effect is the same. The symmetry is similar to that for the exchange of messages when clearing down an X.25 or a TCP connection. The negotiation is also symmetrical in the sense that either end can ask the other to perform some option, or may volunteer to perform the option itself.

Note the symmetry of the NVT model despite the fact that the terminal to host arrangement is usually deemed to be quite asymmetrical, and Triple-X is itself very strongly asymmetrical. The value of the symmetrical NVT approach is that it allows peer-to-peer communication rather than the more limited master-to-slave relationship. All TELNET implementations are able to work with each other using the basic NVT with no options. No options need to be implemented since any options that are not implemented can be refused with the "WON'T" reply. Only those options desired need to be implemented. In this way, the simple basic NVT and the negotiation mechanism allow TELNET implementations to range from very simple to extremely elaborate, and all still interwork. In addition, the negotiation mechanism allows the protocol to be infinitely extensible by the process of registering more and more specialised extensions to the basic protocol. At the same time it should be remembered that the basic NVT is extremely simple because of the elimination of the non-essential details by means of the process of abstraction.

The contrast with the Triple-X approach is quite striking. Of course, it is tempting to draw conclusions about which approach is "best". Rather than such a simplistic approach, we shall note that the two approaches have grown out of rather different conditions. The Triple-X approach does indeed expect that real dumb terminals will be attached to a PAD using modems and dial-up connections, and this is often closely approximated in practice. In such an environment something will have to see to such mundane details as idle characters, what happens at the right margin, etc. This is not to say that the Triple-X model is either perfect, or the only possible one. But it is to a large extent an appropriate one. The fact that the growth in the use of microcomputers as terminals obsoletes some of the X.3 parameters is an accident of history rather than a criticism of Triple-X.

The ARPANET TELNET protocol grew up in a different environment where the most common use is for host computers to be attached to the individual end-user by means of a directly attached terminal. TELNET is then primarily used to call from host to host when the user wishes to call through his local host to some other more distant host. In this case, as we commented above, the strong abstraction of the TELNET NVT approach, leaving low level terminal support strictly in local hands, is much more appropriate. Of course, as with all generalisations, the above is not universally true. On the one hand X.29 is, of necessity, used when connecting through from one host to another that provides only a host-end X.29 service and on the other hand there are some PAD-like boxes with directly attached terminals which provide a TELNET service through to remote hosts.

What we are now starting to see are the beginnings of the issue of presentation. With the basic TELNET NVT a simple abstract ASCII terminal is defined. This can in reality be mapped to and from other representations. Thus, for example, the actual real terminal might be an IBM 2741. (In practice, this is now very unlikely, since there are few IBM 2741 terminals left in service. However, the example is used because the contrast in function is still striking and instructive.) This terminal does not work using the ASCII code, but instead uses a special transmission code unique to the 2741. So, to display the three characters "Abc" the hexadecimal codes 41 62 63 would be transmitted—rightmost bit first—to an ASCII terminal. To drive a 2741, the four codes 62 7C 64 67 are sent—leftmost bit first. Not only does the 2741 have a different code for each character, but the codes are actually six bits (plus odd parity) rather than the 7-bit ASCII codes. A similar number of printable characters is achieved by having shift characters, such as the code 7C shown above—shift to lower case. (We assumed the terminal was in upper case to start with.) This allows most codes to represent either of two graphic characters depending on the shift. There are other differences between ASCII terminals and 2741s such as the fact that a 2741 is a half-duplex terminal—either the printing element is being driven from the host and the keyboard is locked, or the keyboard is both transmitting to the host and operating the printing mechanism and output from the host is suspended. Indeed, there is (or was) a whole family of 2741 terminals that differed from each other in various ways, and a family of 1050 terminals that were similar, but different too. Even further, all of these had exchangeable golfball typing elements, and full general support needed to be able to accommodate this type of variation too.

That most of this tribe is now obsolete is a relief for those whose job it is to support terminals. The point of raking up this piece of computer archaeology is to illustrate the point that simple character terminals whose only job, after all, is to print or display less than a hundred different graphic symbols can be and actually have been implemented in an amazing variety of different ways. This general topic has now come to be referred to as "presentation" since it deals with the various ways in which information is presented to or by a machine.

With the basic TELNET NVT there was but a single presentation of the NVT data. It may be necessary to map this to or from other representations from time to time to support actual real terminals, but the fundamental meaning of the data is the same—in this case a particular letter of the alphabet. When options are negotiated with the WILL, WON'T, DO, DON'T mechanism, the interpretation of the data stream may change completely. To illustrate this we will take an example of both kinds of function.

We have seen briefly how the basic stream of ASCII characters may need to be altered if the real terminal is an IBM 2741. There is another common mapping requirement for a change in character codes. Right at the start of this book we looked at the structure of the ASCII code. Unfortunately, this is not the only character set used in computers. IBM mainframes use another set of codes for representing characters, the *Extended Binary Coded Decimal Interchange Code*—EBCDIC. This is shown in Fig 7.4. EBCDIC is an eight-bit code, and since it does not use any of the eight bits for parity the code has 256 possible values. Thus, for example, the three-character message "Abc" that we looked at before is represented by #41 62 63 in ASCII, but by #C1 82 83 in EBCDIC. Thus, if an EBCDIC host wishes to print these three characters "Abc" on an ASCII terminal it must be sure to send the ASCII codes and not the EBCDIC ones.

	0	1	2	3	4	5	6	7	8	9	A	B	C	D	E	F
0	NUL	DLE	DS		Sp	&	-						{	!		0
1	SOH	DC1	SOS			/			a	j	~		A	J		1
2	STX	DC2	FS	SYN					b	k	s		B	K	S	2
3	ETX	DC3	WUS	IR					c	l	t		C	L	T	3
4	SEL	RES	BYP	PP					d	m	u		D	M	U	4
5	HT	NL	LF	TRN					e	n	v		E	N	V	5
6	RNL	BS	ETB	NBS					f	o	w		F	O	W	6
7	DEL	POC	ESC	EOT					g	p	x		G	P	X	7
8	GE	CAN	SA	SBS					h	q	y		H	Q	Y	8
9	SPS	EM	SFE	IT					i	r	z		I	R	Z	9
A	RPT	UBS	SM	RFF	¢	!		:								
B	VT	CU1	CSP	CU3	.	$	,	#								
C	FF	IFS	MFA	DC4	<	*	%	@								
D	CR	IGS	ENQ	NAK	(	)	_	'								
E	SO	IRS	ACK		+	;	>	=								
F	SI	ITB	BEL	SUB	|		?	"								

Fig 7.4. The EBCDIC Character Set

The normal way of doing this is to arrange a lookup or translate table. Thus, to translate an EBCDIC message into an ASCII one we need a table with 256 one-byte entries. In each position we put the ASCII code that corresponds to that EBCDIC entry. Thus, in position #C1 (starting from 0) we would put the value #41, since #C1 is *EBCDIC-speak* for "A", and thus the corresponding *ASCII-speak* value of #41 needs to be substituted for it to represent the same abstract concept, "A", in the other language. We need to have entries for all 256 possible EBCDIC codes. Then to translate from EBCDIC to ASCII we can take the EBCDIC bytes one by one, use them to index the translate table, and obtain the corresponding ASCII. Similarly, to translate from ASCII to EBCDIC we need an inverse table. Thus, for translating the character "A" position #41 in the table must contain #C1.

Comparing Figs 1.1 and 7.4, we can that a large number of the printable characters have representations in both ASCII and EBCDIC. Even many of the control characters are simply mapped between the two codes. However, there are several problems. One such is the question of what should be done with such symbols as the EBCDIC cent symbol, #4A, which has no corresponding graphic in ASCII. There are two common strategies here. One is to take all the doubtful EBCDIC symbols, such as the cent symbol and the blank entries in the EBCDIC table (such as the range #51 to #59) and turn them all into the same ASCII character. Either the space character or the "?" symbol are two common choices. The other strategy is to observe that the parity bit can be pressed into service to extend the ASCII character set. Strictly it ceases to be ASCII once eight bits rather than just seven are used to represent data. However, there are several standard 8-bit code tables that include most of the ASCII character set as a subset. The most important of these is probably ISO 8248. If this extension is accepted, then a full 256 combinations are available. The main importance of this is that each and every EBCDIC symbol can then be translated into a different "extended ASCII" character.

Of course, whether the extra characters in the extended set actually "mean" anything is another question, the answer to which depends on the context in which the characters are interpreted. For example, if the 128 extra characters are sent to most ASCII terminals they will merely be interpreted as the same as the existing 128 characters with the other parity—not very useful in most circumstances. However, one big advantage of translating every EBCDIC character to a different extended ASCII character is that the process is a *reversible* one, and thus no information is lost in the process. Such a consideration is worthless if the eventual destination is an ASCII printing terminal, but it may well be that the codes will eventually be turned back to EBCDIC again, and if this is the case then the original information can be completely reconstructed. If the other method of converting all doubtful EBCDIC values to question marks is pursued, then the characters that have been translated to question marks cannot be distinguished one from another. Information has been destroyed and the original bytes cannot be recovered.

There is no absolute best choice for the translation—8-bit ASCII or folding all the doubtfuls into one new character. If a printing terminal is the destination, then the folding approach is a good one, but if the reverse translation at some future time is a possibility then the reversible mapping should be used. Perhaps one of the better compromises is that a reversible translation should normally be chosen. At the destination then, just before printing, either the reverse untranslation can be done, or all the extended non-printable characters can be turned into question marks, or whatever the appropriate choice is. The point of this approach is that just as information is not actually destroyed until the last possible instant, so the freedom to choose various final ways of treating the data is also preserved.

Thus we have seen that by using some such representation as the TELNET VTP it may be necessary for either end of the connection to translate to or from the agreed data representation on the connection. It may be that an EBCDIC host is talking to another EBCDIC host using ASCII on the connection. Providing that a reversible mapping is used then no information is lost. However, clearly there is a pair of translations to be performed, which is to a small extent wasteful of resources. Within the TELNET specification it is possible to negotiate a binary option. With this, the two end users agree to use the raw data as is with some private agreement as to its meaning. Clearly, two EBCDIC hosts could agree to this to avoid the intermediate ASCII stage and the dual translation overhead.

7.3   Screen Based Terminals

However, there are fundamentally different ways of handling terminals, and correspondingly different kinds of protocols that can be used. As an illustration, we shall look at the Virtual Data Entry Terminal. Simple terminals merely display a sequence of characters much like a typewriter types on paper. Indeed many of the early computer terminals were electric typewriters that had been modified to receive and transmit asynchronous data in some form—for example the IBM 2741. More recently paper printing terminals have been almost entirely replaced by video display terminals where the display is a television like screen. Indeed, we mainly assume such a type of terminal in most of this book.

One of the simpler ways in which video terminals deviate from a simple command-response model is embodied in the data entry terminal. In everyday life much information is gathered by getting people to fill in forms, credit application forms, tax forms, visa applications. The range seems endless. A form provides a simple visual mechanism for prompting the filler for a list of specific information. The data entry terminal is a translation of this idea into computer terms. Just as the line-by-line interactive terminal session can be thought of in terms of alternating permission to write on the bottom line of a continuous roll of paper, so in screen mode working with a data entry terminal, the session can be thought of in terms of alternating access to the whole rectangular screen.

The normal sort of sequence is for the application to lay out the screen with a form, the keyboard operator to type the appropriate data into the unprotected fields, and for the computer system to check the data, and then either prompt the user to correct erroneous data, or act upon correct data. Notice the alternation of control between the computer controlling the whole screen, then the user having control of the device, then the computer again. Such operation is typically termed "two-way-alternate", or sometimes "half-duplex" to distinguish it from the full-duplex operation that is typically possible with simple ASCII terminals. One way of thinking of this is to consider that a notional access token is passed back and forth. Only when the operator or the host computer has possession of the token can she access the display.

The seminal influence in this area was the IBM 3270 terminal. This has a screen typically of 24 rows of 80 columns, though many other shapes and sizes have been produced. The screen can display characters, but in addition it may be divided into "fields". A field is a consecutive set of characters. Each field has a set of attributes. These attributes are typically things like "protected", "highlighted", "numeric only" and so on. these allow the screen of the terminal to be laid out like a form—a hospital patient registration form or airline seat reservation form perhaps. Thus, the computer application program will lay out the screen with a set of fields with various attributes. Some fields will contain data that is for the terminal operator, and some will contain blanks into which the terminal operator will enter the required data. For example there may be a protected field containing the text "`Telephone number:`" followed by a field with twelve or fourteen blank spaces in which the operator will be expected to enter the appropriate number. The field for the telephone number will be unprotected. Depending on the expected use of the field, it could be either numeric only, or it may be open for any text if hyphens or "X" is sometimes expected. Filling in the unprotected fields on such a form is logically the same as filling in a paper form, except that the computer system may be expected to take some immediate action online—checking the validity of the data and then acting upon it.

The operational details of the 3270 are highly specific to the device itself (though most things from IBM are of such importance in the marketplace that they form their own *de facto* standard). Not only are the character codes in EBCDIC, but there are very specific ways of specifying the attributes of the fields. Many otherwise fairly "dumb" ASCII terminals have had similar facilities grafted onto them, and of course the details of the implementations are as varied as the manufacturers. In an attempt to alleviate the problem of every application program having to know about every different terminal, there have been several attempts to define a standard abstract virtual data entry terminal. The idea is that the application programs need only know about the abstract virtual terminal, and that the terminal end of the network connection should map from the virtual terminal onto the real physical terminal. The ARPA TELNET *Data Entry Terminal Option* defines just such a terminal. A whole series of commands allows the manipulation of the fields on the screen, and the placing of the cursor. A very similar abstract terminal is defined in the Euronet *Virtual Terminal Protocol*. We shall briefly describe this protocol as an example of this general class of virtual terminals.

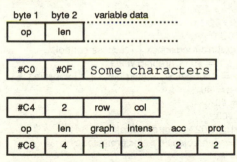

Fig 7.5. Euronet Item Encoding

A Euronet VTP stream is made up at the lowest level as a series of *items*. Each *item* consists of a set of bytes. The first byte is the *item code* followed by the length of the item data, and the the data itself—Fig 7.5. The same diagram shows the encoding for the text item "Some characters", and a cursor positioning item. To set the attributes of a field that starts at the current cursor position, an attribute item is sent, followed by a list of attributes. There are two possible types of attribute in this protocol—graphic rendition and access control. The figure also shows the item encoding for this.

The items are placed end-to-end in a block with a block header. The block contains two important markers. One is the end message marker, and the other is the YrTurn marker—the equivalent of the access token that we described before. Table 7.3 gives a fairly complete definition of the Euronet VTP in Backus-Naur form.

```
<block>::=<DEVT block> | <Conn/disc block>
<Conn/disc block>::=#02 <conn/dis command>
<DEVT block>::=<Type block header><Type item list>
<Type>::= text | control | param
<Type block header>::= B8 B7 B6 B5 B4 B3 B2 B1
B4 B3 B2 B1    : 0 no EOM; 1–15 EOM(n)
B5             : 0 not your turn; 1 your turn.
B7 B6          : 0 text; 1 control
               : 2 parameter; 3 reserved
B8             : 0 no extension; 1 reserved for extension
<item>::=<item code><data length><0–127 bytes of data>
<text item>::=<text-segment> | <newline> | <pos>
             | <next-u-field> | <list-of-attributes>
             | <delete-attribute> | <erase-unprot>
             | <delete-all> | <extension>
<text-segment>::=#C0 n <n characters>
<new line>::= #C1 0
<pos>::= #C4 2 X Y
<next-u-field>::= #C5 0
<delete-attribute>::= #CA 0
<erase-unprot>::= #CC 0
<delete-all>::=#CD 0
<attribute>::=<graphic rendition> | <access control>
<graphic rendition>::= #01<graphic value>
<graphic value>::=<normal> | <invisible> | <intensified>
<normal display>::= #01
<non display>::= #02
<intensified>::= #03
<access control>::= #02 <control value>
<control value>::=<unprotected> | <protected>
<unprotected>::= #01
<protected>::= #02
<extension>::=<text norm mode> | <text insert mode>
             | <text delete> | <unprot posn>
<text normal mode>::= #D0 0
<text insert mode>::= #D1 0
<text delete>::= #D2 n
<unprotected posn>::= #D3 2 F# C#
```

Table 7.3.   Elements of the Euronet VTP

Fig 7.6 shows an example protocol sequence and the resulting screen display. Note that the attributes apply to positions later *on the screen*, rather than later in the sequence of protocol elements.

If the following protocol sequence was sent to a terminal

```
(YrTurn, Em),
(DEL-ALL),
(POS,10,3),
        (ATTR,(GR,Norm),(AC,Prot)),
        (TextSeg,"Identifier:"),
(POS,21,3),
        (ATTR,(GR,Norm),(AC,Unprot)),
(POS,10,5),
        (ATTR,(GR,Norm),(AC,Prot)),
        (TextSeg,"Password:"),
(POS,21,5),
        (ATTR,(GR,Non-Display),(AC,Unprot)),
(POS,21,5)
```

it would produce the display:

```
            Identifier:MyName

            Password:    _ _ _ _ _ _
```

Fig 7.6.   Protocol Example and Resulting Screen

As is shown, the user can type "`MyName`", then a tab to next field key, then "`Shazam`" (not displayed, but shown in the picture as an underline) and finally the "ENTER" key. The "ENTER" key causes the emission of only the fields that the user could possibly have modified—the unprotected fields. Thus, in our example a possible sequence might be

```
(YrTurn,Em),
(Next-Unprot-Field),
        (TextSeg,"MyName"),
(Next-Unprot-Field),
        (TextSeg,"Shazam")
```

There are two main points to note about this protocol. The first is that its interpretation is quite different in principle from a simple ASCII or EBCDIC stream. The contents of the text fields will be sent as ASCII characters, but all the opcodes, lengths, row and column numbers, attributes, and so on are not bytes that can be meaningfully interpreted as ASCII. Sending a data stream that is intended for a Euronet virtual terminal to an ASCII terminal will produce only gibberish.

The second main point is to underline again the two-way alternate notion of this type of terminal as embodied in the YrTurn token. With the simple ASCII terminal, we saw that the data displayed on the screen was a mixture of data output from the host application and data echoed from the keyboard. There were several ways of mixing these two streams of characters, including character-by-character and line-by-line. The result will be a mixing of data on the screen that will be variously jumbled depending both on the strategy and on the respective times at which the user and the host send data. With full-screen applications this approach is not viable, and the discipline of an access token has been introduced. Explicit control of this token by the host and the user enables a much closer control of screen formatting to be achieved. In this way the screen can be used in new ways that are not possible in the undisciplined world of X.3, basic TELNET (without any negotiated options) and similar character terminal protocols. With screen access not controlled by a token, the only formatting that is really possible is a simple typewriter-like progression, line-by-line like the text on this page, with the two ends taking it in turn to alter the screen. However, the combination of the access token, plus the ability of the host machine to restrict the complete freedom of the user in modifying the screen allows the screen to be managed in very complex ways.

Perhaps the most widely known of these is the splitting of the physical screen up into several "windows", and this is the next major topic of this chapter.

7.4   Supporting Bitmapped Terminals—X and NeWS

Following the early work of Englebart, the development of windowing systems at Xerox PARC, and the commercial success of the Apple Macintosh, user interfaces based on *Windows, Icons, Menus and Pointers*—WIMPs have become one of the most fashionable topics both in Computer Science and in Computer practice. One of the best summaries of this work is by Goldberg (1988). WIMP interfaces to computer systems are the new user-friendly successors to command line interfaces, and we must assume that the reader has at least a vague idea about the way in which these interfaces appear to the user.

Most of the early work concentrated on having the interface implemented all in one machine, usually a powerful personal computer. The window would mostly be associated with its supporting process in the same machine, and any networking would be performed in some ad-hoc manner. Recently however, two rival windowing systems for use in a networking environment have appeared that can each claim to have at least pretensions as a de facto standard. One is the *X-windows* system that is associated with the Project Athena at MIT, and the other is the Sun *NeWS* system.

We shall now describe both these window systems, and explain in outline how they allow the support of sophisticated window support over a network. Here we must add perhaps even more caveats than usual. Window support is a very large and complex subject, and several books have been written on it (see, e.g. Hopgood 1986). The supporting software is large and complex, and the documentation is voluminous. In addition, these systems are the subject of rapid evolution, and it is with no little trepidation that your author includes reference to such quickly evolving topics in the comparitively static medium of a book. However, the topic is of such vital importance that the absence of its treatment would be glaring indeed.

7.5   The X-Window System

The X-Window System (or just "X") was developed at MIT (Scheifler and Gettys, 1986). The idea is that a single server supports a set of multiple overlapping windows on a display screen in front of a user. The user has the usual WIMP keyboard and mouse (and possibly other devices). The server is also connected via a high speed network to several hosts from which the user obtains service. The user's screen is divided into several rectangular windows, and each window forms the interface between the user and a service. In some ways, this is like having multiple terminals sharing the same screen. However, there is more to it than this. One of the immediate benefits is that text may be *cut* from a window attached to one application and *pasted* into a window attached to another application. In other words, the separate windows are integrated together into one facility that is more than just the sum of the separate windows.

In their paper Scheifler and Gettys describe many of the design considerations that went into X. Some of the important points are that the *clients* are freed from most of the device dependence on various specific displays. In essence, a client works with an idealised terminal and the server is responsible for realising that abstract virtual terminal on the real hardware. However, the X terminal is still a bitmapped terminal. In the supporting protocol, the co-ordinates are in terms of pixels on the actual display—they are integers. On the other hand, the client is not responsible for painting every pixel individually across the network. Instead, X provides a rich set of primitive actions, such as displaying characters, defining fonts (many fonts come ready supplied), and drawing and filling various geometrical shapes. In addition, a client can control various attributes of the windows.

X works with one notional *server* for the user, and a set of *client processes* with which the user is interacting—see Fig 7.7. In some ways this is the inverse of the more usual *client-server* relationship, where the user as a client obtains services from servers. In X the server is at the user end, and the *application processes* are the *clients* using the server to display and manage windows.

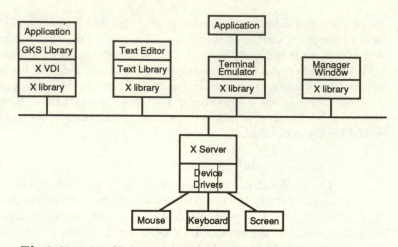

Fig 7.7.   An X Server and Several Clients

In X, windows are meant to be very cheap entities, to be used as the basic building blocks for user interfaces. The goal is to make the windows usable for such things as individual items in menus, or for buttons. The server may deal with hundreds of such elementary items for a single screen. Implementors find such windows a powerful construction tool.

Windows are organised hierarchically. Thus, an application might have a window allocated to it, and it may then divide that window into multiple sub-windows, for buttons, menus, scroll bars, and the like. Alternatively, an application may choose first to divide its window into two or three main windows and pass these onto sub-processes, and then for the sub-processes to decompose these second level windows into scroll bars, buttons, etc.

In order that a window, including all its subwindows, may be moved around as a whole, the co-ordinates of sub-windows are relative to the containing parent window. Thus, the movement of a containing window has minimal effect on the processes associated with the windows that it contains.

X supports resisable, overlapping windows. Applications have to be able to work with windows of various and varying sizes—though, of course, sometimes there is a minimum size for a window to be useful for a specific application. The fact that windows may overlap means that sometimes windows are obscured by others "in front of" them. This means that output to such areas of these windows will not be displayed on the user's screen until the windows are rearranged to reveal such obscured areas. When a window is exposed by such rearrangement in the server, the exposed area must be refreshed.

In X the decision was taken that the server would not be bound to maintain the obscured area of a window. The argument goes that the potential storage, especially for multi-coloured windows, would be too much to expect of all servers, and that the client would be expected to refresh the window across the network. Thus, the server will, from time to time, generate "exposure events" and send them to the client, indicating that the client should refresh that part of its window. In the meantime, the server fills the region with a background pattern that has been specified by the user.

Of course, such refreshment involves network traffic. In X various design decisions have been taken in trading off between network traffic, storage required in the server, and the complexity of both the protocol and the server implementation. These trade-offs have been taken assuming that the protocol will be operated across a very fast local network operating at a throughput per user of perhaps $0.5 Mbps$, with a round trip delay time of a few tens of mS. Thus it was reasonable for X to assume that the substantial network traffic involved in re-writing part of an obscured window could take place within a very short time. In addition, the model of echoing user keystrokes across the network from the host is also reasonable in such an environment. However, while X would *work* across a wide-area network, the lower throughput and longer round-trip delays would alter the *feel* of the user interface substantially, making it much more sluggish—not to mention the effect of any volume related charges on the bills that would eventually have to be footed on a commercial network!

Having said that servers are not *required* to be able to refresh exposed areas of windows, the X model *allows* server implementations to maintain the obscured parts of overlapped windows if the implementor so decides, and then it can redisplay the contents when the area is exposed without generating an exposure event to the client.

It is worth noting that X servers are required to be able to service several client processes simultaneously without allowing one client to interfere with the operation of the others. This means that the protocol must be mostly *asynchronous*. That is, the server must be able to process the requests from the clients one by one, and requests should not normally involve an interlocked interaction with the server which, in the mean time, locks out other clients. X mostly achieves this aim, but there are some explicit occasions when the protocol allows a client to *grab* server resources. The normal asynchronous operation means that the model of remote procedure call with its implied synchronisation and interlocking of the two ends is not suitable as the model of interaction in X. This is one of the ways in which X departs rather fundamentally from the "V" system from which it is partially derived. Indeed, this is true of many asynchronous communication protocols.

When a simple character terminal is being emulated in an X window, the characters typed by the user are displayed by the client maintaining the window. The client can control which of a whole range of *events* about which it should be notified. This can include the press and release of various combinations of keys—not just SHIFT keys—and also the notification of when the mouse pointer crosses the boundaries of specified windows, and when mouse keys are pressed or released. It is up to the client process owning the window to decide how these events are processed, and what the response should be. Thus, since the client is in control, the response can be anything that the implementor of the client decides.

As an interesting example of this, consider the tracking of the cursor. The cursor is displayed by the server, possibly even by the hardware of the display upon which the server is implemented. The actual visual display changes depending upon what was decided by the creator of the window, and the server will switch the visual representation as the "hot spot" moves from window to window. This, together with notification of the boundary-crossing events is sufficient for much cursor support—the cursor does not need to be tracked from the client process across the network.

However, there are times when this is not sufficient. For example, when a window is being re-sized or perhaps a graphics package wishes to allow the user to "drag" an object across a window, either a "rubber band" window outline or a "shadow" of an object may be tracked in real time from the client. This can be performed by the client going into a special mode, *grabbing* the cursor—which causes the frequent emission of positional information from the server to the client—and redisplaying the outline. This mode of operation also locks out other clients from updating their windows, and their requests are queued. In addition, other windows will not be notified, even if the cursor strays into what would normally be their territory and would normally cause boundary invasion messages. This kind of operation is both network intensive and intrusive in the sense that the updating of windows in the server by other clients may be obstructed.

As a final point in this cursory look at X, there are interesting demarcation areas. We have just seen how clients can sometimes interfere with the operation of others in special circumstances. Similarly, in principle more than one process can be involved in intercepting one event. Window managers are implemented by certain sets of events being intercepted and acted upon by a window manager, and others by the clients. Thus, window positioning and re-sizing will typically be handled by a window manager, and other events, such a typed input and clicking on certain buttons, by the client. In addition, it is typically the window manager that controls how the keyboard input is redirected to different clients depending on such things as the position of the cursor, or whether the mouse button has been clicked in a certain window.

Clearly, there is scope for conflict between the clients and each other, or between clients and the window manager. The base X protocol does not resolve this kind of conflict, and it is left to higher levels to provide such a policy. This can be done by accessing X only through a higher level library of routines. Indeed, this is the normal mode of access to X for at least three reasons:

- Such access allows the resolution of such policy decisions by the use of a higher level set of primitives.
- The use of such a higher level set allows an overall style of working to be attained. X deliberately eschewed making any such policy decisions and concentrated on providing the basic tools.
- The use of such a higher set of primitives frees the programmer from needing to hande all the gory details of the X protocol, and thus simpler and clearer programs can be produced more quickly. (Rosenthal 1987)

This is fine as far as it goes, but it allows the possibility of widely differing windows coexisting on the user's screen—one might have a close box to click, another a pull-down menu, and a third a chord of keys to be pressed together—all for the same function. None is necessarily "better", they are just different, and thus cause a loss in user convenience in exactly the kind of user interface that is supposed to be so good. The big lesson of the Apple Macintosh user interface is not just that a WIMP interface is good, but that a *consistent* WIMP interface is even better. The combination of a consistent library of routines, and a design philosophy, allows this to be achieved in X too.

X has very quickly become widely used to support WIMP terminals over a network. This is due to a combination of factors. The system was developed by a small team, and is obtainable in source form, essentially free. Porting to a wide set of environments is actively encouraged, and user reactions have been taken into account. The wide adoption by both commercial companies, and academia has ensured that X has become, in a very short interval, the de facto standard for this type of terminal support across networks.

7.6 NeWS

The SUN Microsystems *Network Extensible Window System—*NeWS (sic) has many similarities with X (Sun 1986). Multiple overlapping windows are connected to various remote processes across a network. The windows support bitmapped text and graphics, mice, and colour. The communication is carried on top of a simple reliable two-way byte stream such as TCP. Thus much of the above description concerned with the external appearance of X applies also to NeWS. However, the fundamental mechanism is radically different.

NeWS is based on the page description language PostScript (Adobe 1985). PostScript is the most important way of describing pages for laser printers. This book has been produced using TEX to typeset the text, and then the output was turned into PostScript and used to drive an Apple LaserWriter. The diagrams were hand-programmed directly in PostScript and combined with the PostScript derived from the TEX. PostScript allows the placement of text and pictures in arbitrary ways on the page. Images may be scaled and rotated in various ways, even to the extent of using the outline of a character as a clipping path for another image. In addition, PostScript is a complete programming language. For example all the *calculations* for the illustration of Fourier analysis in Chapter 1 were performed *in the printer itself* by specifying the algorithm in PostScript as part of the picture definition rather than specifying the coordinates of the curves as the pre-calculated output of some other process. Similarly, the exponential curves describing the Aloha and CSMA throughput in Chapter 3 were also calculated by the printer. PostScript is one of the most powerful ways of describing graphical shapes available.

In NeWS, the PostScript model has been extended in various ways. The NeWS server can support multiple lightweight processes, and new processes can be "forked" dynamically from operating programs. These processes are used to support "objects" that implement arbitrary functions. Changes in the multiple-window environment, with mouse, buttons, and keyboard are represented by events. These events, or messages are passed amongst the objects within the NeWS server, and within the various client processes on the various communicating host systems.

PostScript has the concept of a single "page" upon which opaque "ink" of various shades (black to white, and coloured) is painted. There is no concept in PostScript of being able to "read" the page. This is a potential problem in a multiple-window system since sometimes items like pull-down menus are implemented by effectively reading the bits, storing them elsewhere while the menu is displayed, and then moving them back when the menu disappears. NeWS handles this type of operation by implementing multiple "canvasses". Each of these arbitrarily shaped canvasses—they may even have holes—can be painted with ink, and then the several canvasses may overlap each other. When moved, the exposed parts of the canvas will be revealed without the need for repainting.

There are a number of libraries of routines provided that allow for the support of windows, menus, and cursor following. In addition an object-oriented programming interface is provided, including a class structure and simple inheritance.

PostScript is an interpreted language, and it is possible to send pieces of PostScript code as messages to objects, and thus dynamically alter or extend the behaviour of objects in an arbitrary way. And despite all this late binding and flexibility so typical of an interpreted language like PostScript, NeWS runs very quickly.

7.7   A Comparison of NeWS and X

It is perhaps the point that pieces of program may be added to the functionality of objects that marks the most fundamental difference between NeWS and X. X provides a very rich set of primitives, but it is essentially static. Fundamental changes to the function of the server can only be made by reprogramming the server. Of course parameters can be changed, and window managers altered, but the fundamental *protocol* remains the same, and thus also do the fundamental operations of the server. Thus, for example, the client has no way of saying "*Well, I want rubber-banding to work this way, and I'll get the server to do it for me*". There is no mechanism to instruct the server to take on such a function, and thus the operation must be done across the network from the client. However, with NeWS, a suitable definition of the function can be expressed in PostScript, sent to the server to be combined with a new object, and then any arbitrary function can be done in real time, within the server, and with no intervening interaction across the network with the client.

The other big difference between NeWS and X is in the abstract model of the screen. In X the screen is a rectangular array of pixels, and even the coordinate system is described in terms of fairly small integers of pixel displacements. Of course, there are higher level primitives in the protocol, to express characters, or fonts, or line drawings, but the model is still an idealised form of the type of screen that is commonly available. On the other hand, PostScript has a model where the displacements are real numbers, and can be arbitrarily scaled and transformed, as can the coordinate system to which they relate.

Finally, the interface to X is a fixed set of primitives that ultimately correspond to the fixed set of protocol elements. This is contrasted with NeWS, in which the interface is by means of an interpreted language.

As of the time of writing, X has by far the most support, in that it is available essentially free, and is backed by a large range of computer manufacturers. On the other hand, NeWS is a proprietary product from Sun Microsystems. However, the licence fee is modest, and Sun would like to see the wide adoption of NeWS by various companies, in the same way as their *Network File System*—NFS has become widely adopted. It seems clear that X will dominate the market for the near future, but that NeWS, or something similar, should supercede it because of its clear technical superiority. However, in computing, as in life, excellence does not always prevail.

7.8   Summary

We have seen how various kinds of terminal support are implemented across networks. This varies from the simplest character terminals that are supported by Triple-X or TELNET through data entry terminals with a full screen, field oriented format (though still firmly character terminals), to full support of multiple window bitmapped displays using the most sophisticated graphical techniques.

Along the way, we have encountered various aspects of data representation in different systems, and some of the problems of mapping this from system to system. It is this problem of preserving the information content of data as the data moves from one system to another with differing representations for the same abstract object that constitutes the subject of *presentation* that we shall study in the next chapter.

8
Presentation

The focus of this chapter is the data representation itself—a topic now generally referred to as "Presentation". Firstly several examples of the problems of moving data between differing systems are examined. The chapter closes with the introduction of the general purpose *Abstract Syntax Notation 1*—ASN.1 that will be used in following chapters.

8.1   Data Representation

In the last chapter we looked at several different methods of terminal support across a network. We found that different types of terminal had various ways of representing the same graphic character. This problem is much more extensive than mere character sets—tiresome though these might be. We now look at the differing ways in which some types of data are represented, and the problems that this poses for communicating in the diverse and varied world of computing.

We have already seen the necessity of mapping between ASCII and EBCDIC representations. However, if data is to be passed between a computer that uses the EBCDIC character set, such as an IBM mainframe, and one that uses the ASCII character set, such as a DEC VAX, it is not always appropriate just to translate it from EBCDIC to ASCII. Suppose that the data is actually a series of binary integers. If this is the case, then doing the EBCDIC to ASCII translation is a useless exercise. Of course, a reversible translation will do only repairable damage—the damage is repairable by merely doing the inverse translation, providing that it is realised what has happened.

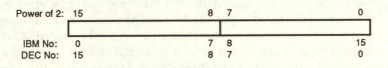

Fig 8.1.   16-Bit Integer Encoding

It might seem then that for integers, it is merely a matter of sending the bits unmolested (i.e. untranslated), and all will be well. However, even for such simple entities as binary integers there is a set of pitfalls for all but the most wary. One is the order of transmission of bits in a byte. Consider Fig 8.1. Here we see a 16-bit integer that will occupy two bytes.

In the figure the integer is shown in the normal order with the higher or more significant order bits on the left. The powers of 2 are shown on the top of the diagram. Different machine architectures have different ways of numbering the bits. As an example of two contrasting ways, we shall take the IBM 370 and the DEC PDP11 architectures. Not only do these two machines use EBCDIC and ASCII respectively, but they number both the bits and the bytes in different ways. Thus, the 370 numbers the bits from the left to the right (most to least significant) starting at 0, while the PDP11 numbers them from right to left (least significant to the most significant), also starting at 0.

At the byte level, this means that the bits in a byte are transmitted left to right from an IBM machine, and right to left from a PDP11 machine. If we transmit data from an IBM machine and receive it in a DEC machine, then we have to allow not only for the possible differences in codes if it is character data, but even if the data is a series of byte integers, we need to be aware of the different order of transmission of the bits. Unless this is allowed for the bits in the bytes will be effectively reversed.

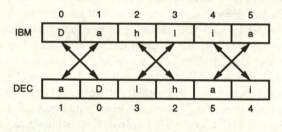

Fig 8.2.   Word Encoding

Having got the bits in the byte sorted out, we are still left with problems of byte ordering. With IBM machines the bytes are also numbered from left to right, like the bits but the converse is true on DEC machines. Thus, with a two-byte word (a halfword on an IBM 370), the leftmost, or most significant byte is transmitted first, while on a DEC machine, the rightmost or least significant byte is transmitted first. So if we have a series of bytes to move from an IBM machine to a DEC machine, we may need to take the byte ordering into consideration in different ways depending on the meaning of the bytes. We shall give some illustrative examples.

a) If the bytes are a series of 8-bit integers, then as we transfer them we need to take the bytes one by one and allow for the bits being serialised and re-assembled in reverse order. We either need to agree to reverse the bits before transmission or after reception.

b) If the bytes make up a series of 16-bit integers (halfwords on the IBM 370 or words on the PDP11), then we also need to swap the bytes too. Consider Fig 8.2. We see that as the bytes are serialised in the opposite order, then the bytes get assembled in reverse order—just like the bits.

Again, the two parties need to agree on who does the swapping— either before or after the transmission. Interestingly enough the DEC PDP11 architecture includes a byte swap instruction for convenience in swapping the high and low bytes in a 16-bit word.

c) If the two machines are exchanging character information, first the data will need to be translated from ASCII to EBCDIC, and then it will need to have the bits in each byte reordered. Usually this is done in one combined translation operation with a translate table that combines both the code change and the bit reversal. The bytes will not need reordering in this case since as with the byte integers, there is no association of the bytes together into higher order structures.

From these three simple examples, we see that the transfer even of simple integer or character data across a network is fraught with complications. The two ends have to agree on the precise format of the data on the communications line, and then decide how to map to and from this format and their own internal format. Thus, with simple integer data, there has to be an agreement both on the number of bits in an integer, and on the order in which these bits are transmitted along the communications line. On the other hand with character data, an agreement has to be struck about which end translates into the other's code, and then in which order the bits and bytes (=characters) are to be transmitted.

We have illustrated these problems of the representation or the presentation of data in terms of the differences between IBM 370 and DEC PDP11. There are many other possible examples, including machines with 6-bit characters or 36-bit words. We have considered only positive integers. Negative integers may be stored in either ones-complement or two's complement form. As for floating point numbers— the details are preferably not mentioned in polite company. Ours were merely specific examples from a very wide range of actual practice. We have explained the solution to the difficulty as being for one end or the other to take the responsibility of matching the representation used at the opposite end. In this way all the work is concentrated in one place, and one of the two participants in the conversation has no work to do.

Another approach that is often taken is that rather than each connection involving a bilateral agreement that the communication will be in terms of the actual concrete representation of one of the parties, a general abstract representation should be used for communication, and each communicating party should map to or from this representation. The approach of using a generally agreed standard representation in which to exchange data has several advantages. One is to solve the N^2 problem. The N^2 problem arises because in order to ensure that it can communicate with any other type of system, every one of N different types of system has to implement the mapping from its own representation into that of the other $N - 1$ systems. Thus, $N^2 - N$ implementations need to be done, and the problem is said to be of order N^2. If however, all N systems agree that when they communicate they will use just one abstract representation, then each of the N types of system only needs to implement the one mapping—giving a problem of order N.

Standardising on methods of communication is the subject of Chapter 16, and so we will not pursue the standardising topic itself here. However, we have seen examples of this approach in the TELNET NVT and in the Euronet VTP. For simple character transfer, the most likely abstract representation is a stream of ASCII characters. Indeed, it is not unusual for one IBM machine to send character data to another using an ASCII character stream as the abstract representation on the network link. Put like that, it does seem daft for an IBM machine to translate data from EBCDIC to ASCII, transmit it to another IBM machine, and then for them promptly to be translated back to EBCDIC in the destination machine. Of course, proprietary IBM networks do not work in such a way, and use EBCDIC throughout. However, if a general agreement on some particular standard, such as using ASCII on communications links has been achieved, then the need for the two communicating entities to negotiate which representation to use is eliminated. It is a fact of life that ASCII in its various guises is a non-proprietary international standard, and in various forms is used in a multitude of applications, whereas EBCDIC is a de facto standard used mainly by IBM or those manufacturers that explicitly wish to look like IBM machines. If an agreement is made to use ASCII, then each IBM machine must have its interface to this common standard. Given that, it can communicate freely with all other implementors of the same standard. It is then probably easier to continue to use this standard, than to recognise the special cases when EBCDIC could be used end-to-end.

We see then that there is a need to agree carefully on the precise way in which an abstract entity such as a character or a letter of the alphabet is transmitted across a network using a set of bits. With the ISO OSI model such considerations have been assigned to the presentation layer. The purpose of this layer is to agree between the two entities on the format of the data passed between them, and to provide a suitable syntax for representing all the likely useful forms of data. This is done both by having a register of possible representations, and of having some especially powerful types of representation, such as the ASN.1 notation (that we shall meet later) that are capable of very wide application.

An alternative approach is for the two ends to agree to use only characters when communicating. Thus, if only the printable ASCII characters are used, then the techniques for transmitting them between various machines, including mixed ASCII and EBCDIC machines, are well understood.

At first this may seem a somewhat restrictive approach. What about all those richer types of data rather than just mere character strings? To respond at the most fundamental level—any data can be represented by a bunch of bits—zeros and ones—and thus in principle only the two characters "0" and "1" are needed. Of course, this would be hideously inefficient, and in some sense it is no solution at all since it does not face the problems of bit and byte order, etc. We need an abstraction away from such mundane bit order problems that are specific to particular types of machine. A much more useful and productive method is to use the sort of input/output conventions that programs have used for years. Thus, we might use the sort of conversion that is involved in a FORTRAN FORMAT statement. For example, a 16-bit integer could be converted into decimal digits using "I6" format, and the resulting spaces, sign, and digits could be transmitted along the link to be converted back to binary data at the other end. Here we are relying on the convention that "-32766" has the same meaning whether expressed in EBCDIC or ASCII, whatever the size of the word in which it is stored (assuming the word is big enough), and in whatever order the binary bits and bytes of the binary word are stored. We are relying on the convention that -32766 is always written in that way, and never as 66723-, or any of the other possible jumblings of the symbols that might be imagined. We are also relying on the digits being decimal, and not perhaps octal, or hexadecimal. Since the conventions here are very strong, in contrast to the case with the eccentric diversity of the internal binary formats in computers, then we can consider this as a higher level abstract representation where all the detail is taken for granted. Alternatively, we can take the combination of the characters "-32766" and the format item "I6" as an abstract specification of the value in question.

One of the major advantages of such character-only protocols is that they can be relied on when used over connections that are really only meant for supporting terminals. It is a fact that a very large number of connections in the world are intended to support character terminals only, and the components supporting the connection have a depressing habit of corrupting, discarding, and adding characters outside the normal printable ASCII set. The connections are certainly not transparent. This is particularly true when microcomputers are attached to mainframes using terminal access links. If the data is encoded as printable characters only, then such corruptions can be circumvented.

In addition to our example of character representations of numbers, binary representation in terms of hexadecimal can transfer arbitrary bytes across a character-only network. Since two characters are needed for each byte, twice as much network traffic is needed as when transmitting straight binary data. However, this cost is less that the tripling of data that we saw might be necessary to transmit 16-bit integers as decimal digits.

As well as the delights of FORTRAN-style FORMAT conversion, we shall mention two other interesting data representations that are in terms of all or nearly all printable characters. The first of these is the so called *Simple Screen Management Protocol*—SSMP (Hunter 1985). SSMP has the concept of a rectangular screen of characters that we encountered with data entry terminals. The protocol has various primitives concerned with writing characters, defining fields where the user may modify data (something like the unprotected fields on data entry terminals), scrolling up or down a certain subset of the screen lines, splitting and combining screen lines, and so on. The details of this protocol are beyond the space we have available here. However, of interest to us now is the way in which these primitives are encoded. It was a fundamental part of the design that the protocol should be usable across a triple-X terminal access network between an application program in a host, and a user's personal computer running a special program. To this end, the vast majority of the protocol had to be in printable characters only with no special binary patterns to transfer. In this way the vagaries of networks, and particularly of various mainframe and micro operating systems, strange front-end processors and so on were accommodated. To take a simple example, to set the cursor to the row and column position n, m, the character sequence

$$= Bn, m;$$

is sent. In this, the "=" indicates the start of a primitive, the "B" identifies the set cursor function, "n" and "m" are strings of decimal digits specifying the coordinates in the normal way, "," is the parameter separator, and ";" signals the end of the primitive. Clearly, there are many other letters representing the the other primitive functions, each with its own parameter layout. The important point for the present discussion is that by a careful choice of characters and layout, a representation has been achieved that completely avoids doubtful characters, such as

"DEL", "NULL", "DC1", that can be swallowed or generated by transmission systems, or which might produce undesirable side effects such as
stopping the flow of data. At the same time, a simple yet sophisticated
control of a screen character display terminal can be achieved. Much
of this book has been entered and partly formatted at one time using a
screen editor that uses SSMP to control a screen in a very sophisticated
way, and yet few binary codes beyond the printable character set are
needed.

There is a further example of the representation of a still more
complex screen, yet still using only printable ASCII characters. This
is the PostScript language that we met in the last chapter when describing NeWS. There we commented that PostScript and NeWS were
perhaps the most sophisticated of all data representations, and yet the
representation is entirely in the form of ASCII characters.

8.2   Compression and Encryption

Two other aspects of presentation that are very important are
data compression and encryption.

Data compression is a fairly obvious desideratum—other things
being equal it is clearly better to transmit less data than more. Commercial networks usually charge for network use both by data volume
and by duration time, and the trend is for the volume related charges
to become more important in relation to the duration time. Even if the
network is "free" it is still advantageous to reduce the volume of data to
be transmitted. All networks have to be paid for at some time or other,
and if users of a "free" network contain their demands on the network
by using compression, then the dreaded day when funds must be found
to enhance the network to enable it to carry more traffic is deferred.

The other advantage in compressing the volume of data during
transmission is the corresponding improvement in effective throughput
and delay time. All network connections will be limited in some way,
and the limit is often much less than the rate at which computers could
otherwise exchange data. If the actual data is first compressed, then the
limit will apply to the compressed volume of transmitted data rather
than to the original volume of raw computer data.

Let us look at some of the common forms of data compression.
One of the earliest forms was used on the HASP spooling system that
controlled remote card reader and printer systems on IBM mainframes
in the late 1960s and the 1970s. It was observed that the vast bulk of
such data was printed text, and not only that, but it was often program
source and listings, or tabular output data. Particularly in a card oriented environment this means that large parts of such data consists of
sequences of spaces, followed in frequency of occurrence by sequences of

asterisks, hyphens, and suchlike. The sequences of spaces are obvious from the white space between columnar text—the other characters appear in long sequences when they are used, for example, to form "pretty print" boxes around headers.

The idea was that the sender would detect such sequences of identical characters and send a short compressed record instead of the long sequence of characters. Thus, each record sent to the printer, or read from the card reader was not represented as a sequence of characters, but as a sequence of record fragments that were referred to as "strings". Each string started with a *String Control Byte*—SCB. In the SCB the first three bits have special meaning.

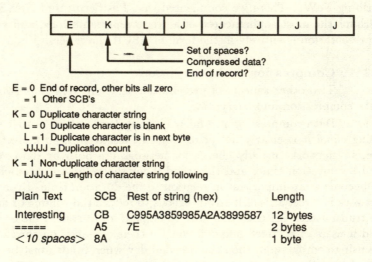

E = 0 End of record, other bits all zero
    = 1 Other SCB's

K = 0 Duplicate character string
    L = 0 Duplicate character is blank
    L = 1 Duplicate character is in next byte
    JJJJJ = Duplication count

K = 1 Non-duplicate character string
    LJJJJJ = Length of character string following

Plain Text	SCB	Rest of string (hex)	Length
Interesting	CB	C995A3859985A2A3899587	12 bytes
=====	A5	7E	2 bytes
<10 spaces>	8A		1 byte

Fig 8.3.   SCB Encoding and Example Coded Strings

The first bit, E, is an end of record marker. For some reason this is defined to stand in a byte of its own, with all the other fields zero. The next bit, labelled K indicates whether this is a compressed string. If K=0, then this is a compressed string of one of two types indicated by the L-bit. If L=0 also, then the record implicitly represents JJJJJ space characters. JJJJJ is a 5-bit number giving a range of 0 to 31 spaces. The space character is not itself transmitted. This special form exists because space is the character that occurs most commonly in groups, and so this short notation has been defined especially for it. On the other hand, if L=1, then the character itself is not a blank, and follows immediately after the SCB itself. For uncompressed text, K=1, and the six bits LJJJJJ give the length of the text following as a number 0 to 63.

Exercise 8.1   Write a routine to take a string of plain text and encode it as a series of SCBs. Write another to decode a given string of SCBs.

Exercise 8.2   What criteria would you use to decide whether to use a compressed SCB for a series of bytes rather than just using the uncompressed SCB form? How would you decide whether the use of processor time was justified? Under what circumstances could this form of compression be expected always to produce expansion rather than the intended compression?

There are several variations of this HASP technique. Some do not have a special recognition for space, but all are similar in principle. Another related technique is that of truncation. Thus, if all the data is assumed to be printable text, it is often acceptable to truncate any trailing spaces on a record. This is particularly helpful when data from a file with fixed length records is sent for printing or is displayed on a simple terminal. In these cases, sending trailing spaces is almost always a waste of time since the destination will at best discard them, or at worst waste time chuntering a printing element across a page only to return to the left margin at the end of a line without making any marks on the paper. Of course, similar considerations apply to filing systems too. It is still not unusual to find program source stored as "card images"—80 character fixed-length records—even though punched card handling equipment has, thankfully, become something to be seen only in museums. Many years ago studies showed that a wide range of text that had been read in from 80-column cards could be stored in varying length records, i.e. with trailing spaces truncated, with an average length of less than 40 characters. (The cards obviously didn't contain sequence numbers in columns 73 to 80, but then few did in practice.) Similar economies can often be made when transferring printable data across networks.

Of course, truncating trailing spaces is not always a safe operation. It may be that the original records were truly variable length, and that the trailing spaces were not merely surplus garbage but important information. A simple but true anecdote illustrates this nicely. Some years ago a certain compiler occasionally complained about undeclared variables, when the variables had clearly been properly declared. The fault was capricious in that a small change in the program text would make it disappear. The problem only occurred when the identifier in question contained a double "a" character. It turned out that the first pass of the compiler turned the program text into an internal set of tokens, and this set of tokens was then written out into an intermediate file. The internal form of the letter "a" was #40—a space character in EBCDIC. From time to time such "spaces" happened to fall at the end of a record written out to the intermediate file. The file routines helpfully truncated the "useless" double trailing space to leave only single spaces, and thus economise on file space. Thus, the identifier "aa2zy" might be converted to "a2zy" if the internal representation of the initial "aa" fell at the end of a line in the intermediate file. This story nicely illustrates the need for a proper appreciation of the true semantic meaning of data before any suitable decision can actually be taken about its proper handling.

A more sophisticated approach to compression can be seen in the TELNET byte macro option (Crocker and Gumpertz 1977—RFC 735). TELNET has the facility of being able to specify that any particular 8-bit byte should be expanded into a particular string of characters. Thus, for example, the text of this book could be scanned for frequently occurring words, such as "thus", "protocol", or "the", and the few most common could be allocated to a macro-byte. We might choose "%" to stand for the three characters "the", "$" to stand for "macro-byte", and "*" to stand for "string" and from %n on we could transmit % one $ instead of % four characters that we needed to send before. Clearly, this is potentially a very powerful mechanism. % problem is in choosing % right *s to be candidates for representation as $s—remembering that % possible number of $s is strictly limited. In addition, once %y have been chosen, it is necessary to scan % data to be transmitted in order to recognise % text *s that are eligible for replacement and change %m to $s. It would be quite easy to expend more resources in % extra processor power necessary for performing % * recognition than might be saved in network resources transmitting % data.

However, there are some pragmatic ways of anticipating likely candidates for assignment as macro-bytes. It may be that by some means an implementor knows that one particular use of the TELNET connection will be to transfer one particular type of data. This may be a protocol stream that will contain a particular set of keywords very frequently, or perhaps it may be PASCAL source programs. In this case it may well be possible to choose 50 or 100 keywords for assignment to macro-bytes, and thus achieve a useful compression of the data stream. A similar technique, of storing BASIC programs in terms of tokens representing keywords in the language is widely employed.

The logical extension of the macro-byte technique is to analyse the transmitted data in terms of a set of commonly occurring sequences of characters. Thus, English text may be analysed in terms of a dictionary of words plus some punctuation. In turn, these words are analysed according to their frequency and allocated to a sequence of numbers of various lengths (in bits). Thus, supposing the most frequent words were *"the"*, *"of"*, *"and"*, *"to"*, and *"a"*, we could allocate them to the binary numbers 0, 1, 10, 11, 100, and so on. Of course the problem with this scheme as it stands is that given the sequence of bits such as "10" we cannot tell whether this represents *"of the"* or *"and"*. There are two possible solutions. One is to use Huffman coding (Huffman 1952, or see, e.g. Hamming 1980). In this scheme the codes are chosen so that no one complete code is the same as the start of any other, and thus the decoder knows immediately when the end of a code has been reached in the bit stream. Another possibility is to use *non-data* "bits" or "bit violations" such as those mentioned in Chapter 1 to mark the word boundaries. In one way or another, we can use the least number of bits for the most common words and gain considerably in data compression. However, we have also gained considerably in complexity, both in the initial analysis to determine the most advantageous assignment to the binary numbers, in the processing necessary to analyse the text in terms of these numbers, and in the mechanism necessary to pack the numbers together for transmission. It is not clear that many applications justify this type of approach.

In addition, there is a practical difficulty with the use of minimum redundancy codes. With comparatively sparse codes, such as English text coded as straight ASCII bytes, the odd single bit error will corrupt at most one character, and the corruption is as unlikely to be critical as is the single isolated keying error of the human typist. However, with minimum redundancy, a single bit error may well invalidate the rest of the data being transferred. Thus, the damage is by contrast unlimited, just as with compressed data using counts, a single bit error in the SCBs count field will invalidate not just the current string, but also all those following. We see then that the reliability requirements for the use of compressed data are more stringent than for simpler data. One might expect this when redundancy is removed and the "meaning" of every bit is increased.

8.3   Encryption

We shall discuss encryption extensively in Chapter 14. However, we need to mention it briefly now because of the interaction between compression and encryption. When sensitive data is being passed between computers, it is sometimes desirable to encrypt it so that it cannot be understood by recipients for whom it is not intended. We shall see that one of the essential properties of encryption is that sequences of identical plain text characters should not be encrypted as identical encrypted characters, otherwise the code is open to some rather simple types of attack by means of frequency analysis. Indeed, many of the forms of attack on cyphers consist in looking for patterns of some sort and relating them to expected patterns in the underlaying message. To guard against this, encryption methods are designed to hide the patterns in a message. On the other hand we have just seen that compression often takes the form of looking for patterns in the data—repeated characters or frequently occurring words—and expressing the patterns in some more compact form. Thus, there is little prospect of achieving useful compression after encryption has taken place. In any case, it seems that some of the most successful forms of compression are to be achieved by working as closely as possible to the application. Fig 8.4 shows the curve of Aloha throughput, and the PostScript program that generates the picture. Even though the program is well commented, and laid out for readability, rather than compactness the reader should be able see that the expressive power of PostScript gives great potential for compressing information by representing its logical patterns rather than by generating a raw list of coordinate data.

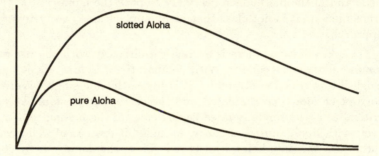

```
% work in mm rather than the native "points"::
/mm {72 25.4 div mul} def

/Helvetica findfont 7 scalefont  setfont % set font for labeling

0 38 mm moveto 0 0 lineto 90 mm 0 lineto stroke    % draw the axes

0 0 moveto                               % start of "pure" Aloha
0 0.02 3                                 % loop - small steps for G
{dup dup -2 mul 2.71828 exch exp mul     % calculate the function
   100 mm mul exch 30 mm mul exch        % scale the co-ordinates
   lineto                                % add the line segment
 } for stroke                            % end of the loop; draw it
14 mm 12 mm moveto (pure Aloha) show     % and label it

0 0 moveto                               % same for "slotted" Aloha
0 0.02 3
{dup dup neg 2.71828 exch exp mul
   100 mm mul exch 30 mm mul exch
   lineto
 } for stroke
26 mm 32 mm moveto (slotted Aloha) show
```

Fig 8.4.   Pictures and their PostScript Representation

Both of these considerations show clearly that compression of data must always take place before any encryption. Indeed, some forms of compression form a reasonable first attempt at encryption, at least as far as the casual listener or opportunist eavesdropper goes.

8.4   Abstract Syntax Notation 1—ASN.1

A little earlier we referred to the use of FORTRAN FORMATs as one way of specifying the relationship between internal machine representations of program values and external machine independent forms such as character strings. We shall now pursue this simile as a way of introducing *Abstract Syntax Notation 1*—ASN.1.

With FORTRAN formatted I/O, a set of program variables to be output is matched with a FORMAT statement and converted to a stream of printable characters by means of a WRITE statement, or for input, a READ statement uses a FORMAT statement to convert between an input character stream and a list of variables. For example, to output an integer J and a floating point number X, the fragment of FORTRAN

```
100     FORMAT(I6,' ',F8.2)
        WRITE(6,100) J, X
```

might produce the following (where "s" stands for a space to make the layout explicit)

```
sss-66sssss3.14
```

and to input three integers, the program fragment

```
200     FORMAT(I2,I4,I3)
        READ(5,200) J, K, L
```

would convert the string 123456789 into the three integers 12, 3456, 789. Note that the FORMAT statement controls the mapping between the external forms of the data—the printable characters—and whatever internal forms the FORTRAN variables take. Thus, the integers may be represented by any number of bits (as long as the number is sufficient), and data could be passed between a machine that had 16-bit numbers, 32-bit numbers, 41-bit numbers, decimal representation or whatever by agreeing to use the same FORMAT statement to convert between the idiomatic internal format, and the widely agreed external set of characters.

The function of the FORTRAN FORMAT statements is to define the mapping between the external character representation of data, and the internal representation within the computer's idiosyncratic structure as FORTRAN variables. The function of ASN.1, together with the *Basic Encoding Rules* is much the same—to define the relationship between the meaning of the abstract entities and their representation while being transmitted in a canonical, machine-independent form.

When the X.400 series of recommendations for message handling systems was developed for the 1984 cycle of the CCITT, there were several of the upper layers of the ISO model that were not fully developed. One of these was the presentation level. Since this was obviously very important for message handling, X.409 was developed as a general way of specifying "Presentation Syntax and Notation". X.409 was seized upon as an extremely valuable tool for all sorts of high level applications, and we shall meet it again in several applications later in this book. ASN.1 is essentially a re-editing of the text of X.409 to fit in with the ISO style, and in the 1988 version of the CCITT recommendations, the updated version was adopted as one of the X.200 series of recommendations in recognition of its extended role as a general protocol tool rather than being specific to mail, and X.409 was then withdrawn. ASN.1 is also the ISO international standard IS 8824, and the basic encoding rules for ASN.1 are contained is IS 8825.

ASN.1 defines a generalised set of standard notations for data types, each with a standard representation or encoding. For example, the standard types include strings, integers, and Booleans, and the standard representations define how each of these is in turn represented on the communications line as a series of bytes (or "octets" in the jargon). It is possible to use these types to build other more complex types corresponding to records or structures in programming languages. The standard notation for the types corresponds loosely to FORTRAN FORMAT statements (or the elements that make up those statements, such as "I6") and the standard representations correspond to the rules for converting between an internal representation of this format item and the external sequence of characters, e.g. 123456 for item I6.

However the FORTRAN simile should not be stretched too far. X.409 is much more flexible in its expressive power than is FORTRAN formatted I/O, and we shall shall now look at a few of the elements of ASN.1 that go beyond the FORTRAN simile. ASN.1 uses a Backus-Naur notation to describe the various permissible forms. There is a set of built-in types, such as Boolean, Integer, BitString and OctetString. Then variations on these types can be defined, and in particular they can be grouped together into more complex combinations. Each value of each type is represented as a triple—an identifier, a length, and the contents.

A Boolean value, for example, may be true or false. This is represented by three octets (or bytes). The value of false is #01 01 00. The first byte, #01, indicates that this is a Boolean value, the second byte, #01, is the length in bytes of the rest, and the final #00 byte indicates the value false. For true the last byte must be non-zero, and so a suitable representation of true would be #01 01 FF. (We shall drop the "#"-notation for the rest of the chapter, and assume hexadecimal when describing byte values.)

Integers are fairly similar. For example, the integer 256 (decimal) would be represented by 02 02 01 00. Here the identifier is 02, and so is the length. The binary representation is 01 00. ASN.1 (or, more precisely, the companion *Basic Encoding Rules*) is very detailed in specifying the order of the bits and bytes so that there should be no scope for different interpretation of the received protocol elements in the way we have seen in diverse computer systems.

In many computer languages, there is the concept of *enumerated types*, or *identifier lists*. The hackneyed example is type colour = (red, green, blue). In ASN.1, the corresponding construction is that of a Named-NumberList. The example of colour might then become INTEGER {red(0), green(1), blue(2)}. Here we have explicitly assigned specific integer values to particular identifiers. Thus, the value "red" would be encoded as 02 01 00.

With a programming language like PASCAL it is not normally necessary to know the association between particular values of enumerated types and their internal representation, since there is no way directly to access the internal representations of an enumerated type. The sort of time it becomes important to know these values is, for example, when constructing mixed language programs—FORTRAN with PASCAL for example—or when setting up record declarations to map on to a pre-existing external structure, such as a record in a file or a message in a communications protocol. In this case the normal approach is to consult some extra compiler information to determine how enumerated types map onto binary representations, and then to arrange the declarations accordingly. The program then becomes dependent on the particular compiler used. The explicit association of identifiers with numbers in ASN.1 avoids having to resort to such privileged information.

Bit strings consist of zero or more bits. They are packed in bytes from the left. The number of unused bits in the rightmost byte is put into the first octet. Thus, binary 10101 is encoded as 03 02 03 A8. The first 03 identifies this as a bit string, the next 02 is the length of the rest in bytes. The next 03 indicates that the final three bits in the last byte are unused, and the A8 indicates the five bits 10101 in the leftmost five places in the final byte.

A similar form is the octet string. This is less fussy about trailing unspecified bits than the bit string, and thus there is no initial byte to indicate the unused bits in the last byte, and any trailing bits left unspecified are assumed to be zero. This gives a slightly shorter representation for strings that are a whole number of octets long. In this notation, the hexadecimal value ACE can be sent as 04 02 AC E0.

Finally in the basic types, a null indication is represented by the sequence 05 00 (05 = null, 00 = length of the absent contents).

So far we have described some of the simple built-in types. Now we shall describe some of the ways of building on these primitive types to form other types that are tailored to the particular application. The first byte, the identifier byte, has more structure than we have indicated

so far. If the bits, from the left, are designated ccf54321, then we have
seen various of the built-in types with particular values of the rightmost
bits, but with "ccf" all zero. We shall meet the meaning of the first
two bits "cc" presently. The identifier form bit "f" indicates a primitive
form when zero (as in all the examples we have seen so far) or, when
one, the constructor forms that we are about to discuss. A primitive
form is one where there is no internal structure. A constructor form is
one where the contents are a series of constituent data elements. These
data elements may be formed either from the primitive built-in types we
have discussed so far, or even recursively from other constructor forms.
There are various types of constructor.

One form of constructor is the sequence. This is an ordered
set of zero or more elements. This corresponds to the record type of
PASCAL. As a simple example, a type may be defined as

SEQUENCE {madeofwood BOOLEAN, length INTEGER}

Then the value {madeofwood true, length 62} can be encoded as

        30 06 01 01 FF 02 01 3E

This may conveniently be displayed as

Seq	len	Contents			– contents are the two
					– elements below
30	06				
		Bool	Len	Contents	– the first element
		01	01	FF	
		Int	len	Contents	– the second element
		02	01	3E	

Note that the identifier has the constructor format bit set, plus the identifier code of 16 decimal indicating a sequence. The example we have
given is a particularly simple one. However, it is possible to have OP-
TIONAL elements, and, unlike the PASCAL variant record, the optional
elements need not always be at the end of the list. This may in some
cases lead to ambiguous representations—that is it may not be possible
to tell from a received record which elements have been omitted. PAS-
CAL takes great care that the programmer is not able to write down
structures that are nonsense. ASN.1 might be termed *Structures for Real
Programmers*, in that it is quite possible to specify sequences that are
ambiguous. The onus is on the designer of the sequence not to specify
structures that can be ambiguous.

There is also the SET type. This is very similar except that
the members are no longer ordered. Again there is the possibility of
ambiguity if the notation is used incorrectly. As an example of the SET
type, consider the definition

SET {bredth INTEGER, bent BOOLEAN}

Then the value {bredth 7, bent false} can be encoded as

31 06 02 01 07 01 01 00

Note that since the order of a set does not matter, an equally valid representation is

31 06 01 01 00 02 01 07

with the elements interchanged. Here the receiver will be able to tell which is which from the different type representations. This is why one of the restrictions on the SET type is that if the constituent types are to be easily distinguished one from another then they must all be different.

The other principal way of generating new types within ASN.1 is by the process known as Tagging. Before we proceed to describe this process, we need to describe the class bits on the front of the identifier. These two bits are used to specify the four classes Universal, Application-Wide, Context-Specific and Private. Universal types are widely useful types, independent of particular sorts of application. Good examples of these are the Booleans and integers with which we started this description. Application-Wide are generally useful only within one type of application. For example, some application, such as a file security protocol, might define a type to represent file names, or another to hold passwords. The class for such specialised types might be Application-Wide since they might be useful across the file security application, but not understood by any other applications such as a funds transfer protocol, or a TopTenQuery protocol. We mentioned above that SET types had restrictions on all the types being different so that the different elements that were present could be distinguished, one from another. Sometimes new types may be generated by the tagging method we are about to describe merely to satisfy this need. In this case the types may only have meaning within the particular SET and so the class would be context specific. Finally, the Private class is reserved for devious uses by inventive designers determined to prove their originality and cleverness at obfuscation.

We are ready now to describe the generation of new types by the method of tagging. A new tagged type is defined from an existing type by specifying the new class and identification number, and the pre-existing type in terms of which it is being defined. The resulting type may be either explicit or IMPLICIT. In addition to a formal specification in terms of another type, there is frequently some informal text that further refines the definition. Let us take a couple of examples. Suppose we do actually want to represent file names and passwords for our fictitious file security protocol. For passwords, we may well wish to transfer just the printable ASCII characters that the user has typed at a keyboard. Thus, a possible representation might be

[APPLICATION 27] OCTET STRING

and an accompanying piece of text would explain that *"Only the printable ASCII characters can be transferred, and these are each represented by seven bits packed into a single octet."* As a specific example, the password "Sesame" would be encoded as the following:

7B 08 04 06 53 65 73 61 6D 65

This is best understood by breaking it down. The representation contains an outer part containing the newly defined tag, with its class and number. Thus, the class is APPLICATION (cc = 01), and the form is constructor, since this new tagged type "contains" another type. The last five bits contain the specified type number (there is an escape mechanism if five bits are not sufficient), and the length occupies the next byte as usual. Contained within this type is the octet string that we have met before, complete with its opcode and length.

```
op   len    contents
7B   08

          op   len    contents
          04   06     53 65 73 61 6D 65
```

Clearly, this is rather long winded compared with the original form of octet string, since we have gained both an extra opcode and an extra length byte. Another way of generating tagged types is by means of the IMPLICIT form. The above form is said to be explicit since the base type items in terms of which it is defined appear explicitly within it. In many applications, this will be unnecessary, since, for example, whenever the password opcode (27) appears, it will always be obvious that the contents have the form of the octet string. Thus, the alternative form might be to specify the password as

[APPLICATION 27] IMPLICIT OCTET STRING

with the same accompanying caveat as before. Our previous example of "Sesame" would then be encoded as the following:

5B 06 53 65 73 61 6D 65

Here "cc" still indicates the APPLICATION class, and the identification number is 27 (#1B). However, since the form no longer contains the Octet-String opcode the form bit has reverted to primitive rather than constructor. The length follows, and the contents is the ASCII string as before. This is now IMPLICIT since the explicitly contained Octet-String has been lost, and the type of the value as a whole is implicit in the newly defined opcode. In other words, with an Octet-String a receiver has a chance of decoding the meaning of an incoming string since the Octet-String is a universally known type. However, with a new form, such as our password type, the meaning is more narrowly known. To interpret such a string, the receiver needs the type definition. This second case corresponds to the FORTRAN I/O statement, where a FORMAT statement is needed to make sense of a bunch of incoming characters.

The method of generating tagged types is surprisingly powerful. One of the most useful of the types defined in ASN.1 is the IA5String. This type is defined by

IA5String ::= [UNIVERSAL 22] IMPLICIT OCTET STRING

"IA5" stands for the *International Alphabet Number 5* which for most practical purposes is the same as ASCII. Thus, this new type "IA5String" comes with some text specifying that only the 7-bit representations of IA5 are allowed rather than the full 8-bit freedom.

Lest this tagging seem to be merely a cosmetic exercise, let us take a simple example. Suppose we wish to transfer a set of names for a person and the person's parents. It may be that the names of the parents are unknown, so we can make these items OPTIONAL. We can construct all the names as tagged IMPLICIT IA5Strings, but we choose different identifier numbers for each. Since we do not specify the type, it defaults to the most common case, context specific. A suitable structure to hold the three names might then be:

Parentage ::= SET
    { subjectName [1]IMPLICIT IA5String,
     motherName [2]IMPLICIT IA5String OPTIONAL,
     fatherName [3]IMPLICIT IA5String OPTIONAL
    }

Note that since this is a SET, the three names may appear in any order. We have made the subjectName mandatory, but the other two names optional. The distinct identifier numbers allow the three names to be uniquely identified in whatever order they are received, or whichever of the optional parental names is omitted.

Finally, we will comment that this notation contains various wrinkles to avoid the problem of built-in limitations that plague other protocols and computer systems in general. Repeatedly in computer systems a design choice is made to allocate, for example eight bits for a parameter. *"Nobody will ever need more than 256 values of this parameter"* says the designer, and just a few years, or even months later the horrendous problems of increasing the size of this field without breaking all the existing applications may well take more effort than all the original design effort in the first place. Anyone who has looked at the problems in moving the IBM 360/370 architecture from 24-bit addressing to 31-bit addressing as part of the move to XA architecture will have a keen appreciation of this sort of problem. The thought of moving the IBM 360/370 architecture beyond 31 bits is just too painful to contemplate. Two such limitations of this nature have been designed out of the ASN.1 *Basic Encoding Rules* representation from the start.

We have seen that five bits in the identifier byte have been allocated for different identifying numbers. Despite the qualifying effect of the class bits, it would not be difficult to devise simple examples of tagged types that exhaust this range. Thus, a generalised and unlimited escape mechanism has been built in. Values in the range 0 to 30 decimal (as all our examples have been) are encoded as themselves. The value 31 is an escape. In this case the actual value is stored in one or more following octets. Each of the following octets is marked. Bit 8 of the last one is zero, and bit 8 of all the others is 1. Thus, if the ID code was binary 10110010101111001, then it would be encoded in the four bytes

    ccf11111 1 0000101 1 1001010 0 1111001

(we have shown bit 8 of each extension byte separately from the other seven bits of the ID code for clarity).

The length is the other part that has an unlimited range. This is achieved by using three different forms: short, long, and indefinite.

The short form is used in preference whenever the length to be encoded is up to 127 (decimal). This is just encoded as a 7-bit binary number with the top bit set to zero. This is the form that we have encountered so far.

The long form is for use when the length is more than 127, and can accommodate numbers that can be *represented* within 126 bytes. The numbers are represented as a binary number packed into contiguous bytes. All leading zero bytes are removed to produce the shortest number of bytes. The length of this number, in bytes is then put into a leading byte with the top bit set. Thus, the length 255 would be encoded as

    10000001 11111111

and the decimal number 16,777,215 would be encoded as

    10000003 11111111 11111111 11111111

Note that the limit on the number of bytes in the long form number is 126 (plus the leading byte itself). This means that a leading byte may have the value 11111110, but not 11111111. This latter value is reserved for future expansion! The limit of 126 bytes gives truly astronomical possibilities. However, the indefinite form gives the possibility of exceeding even this. This form may only be used with constructor forms, since it allows the length of the constructor to be specified not as an explicit length, but as the sum of all the elements forming the construction. In this form, the length field is specified as

10000000

The implication of this is that the total length of this construction is the sum of the lengths of the constituent elements. Thus, the end of the list of elements is marked by a special End-Of-Contents item EOC. This has the representation:

EOC	Len	Contents
00	00	absent

It will be perceived that not only is this an escape that allows truly unlimited lengths but perhaps more importantly it allows the construction to be sent as it is constructed. If the length always needed to be sent at the front, then the whole item might need to be constructed before *any* of it could be sent. An obvious application might be a message, where the construction consists of several header strings (sender, destination, etc) followed by the body of the text. The indefinite form allows this to be sent as it is constructed. The short or long form would require a complete knowledge of the length at the start of the process.

8.5 General

This chapter has shown some of the problems of moving data between diverse machines while retaining its meaning. The all-purpose tool that has appeared is ASN.1, and we have looked in some detail at how ASN.1 works. ASN.1 grew out of X.409. Its data representation powers are considerable, being comparable to those in PASCAL, but they are more directly related to the Xerox Courier, and the SUN external data representation (XDR) work. ASN.1 is strictly a definition of an abstract syntax. The actual transfer syntax—the bits and bytes—are described by the Basic Encoding Rules, and these two come as separate international standards (IS 8824 and IS 8825). However, the term "ASN.1" is often used to embrace both aspects. ASN.1 is being used in the definition of all ISO applications level protocols, and we shall meet it several more times in later chapters.

9

File Transfer and Access

After terminal access, one of the most frequent applications of computer networks is that of transferring files. We shall now consider some of the issues that have particular importance in this context.

We have seen that with terminal access there are wide differences in the way in which hosts wish to drive terminals, and a similarly diverse set of ways in which terminals are capable of working. Just as hosts have radically different views about what they expect from a terminal, so they also have radically different views of what files look like. We have already seen some of the gruesome detail of bit and byte ordering, EBCDIC versus ASCII, various integer sizes and so forth. In this chapter, we shall take it as read that file transfer and access protocols will be involved with this level of mismatch, and proceed to look at some of the higher levels of mismatch that also have to be faced when files are transferred between differing machines, and their varied operating systems.

9.1   File Structure

One of the first problems to be encountered is that different systems have radically different ideas of file structure. For example, many systems, including Unix and MS-DOS, view a file as a single linear sequence of characters much like the stream of ASCII characters that would be sent to a simple ASCII terminal. Differing applications may view this linear sequence as just that—an array of characters—or they may interpret certain embedded characters as line delimiters. Thus, if such a file is to be interpreted as text, then it is normal to have new line indicators at appropriate boundaries to format the text. Alternatively, another application may view such a file as a sequence of binary information. In this case the actual values of the bytes may represent values of data types other than text characters—integers, say, or executable object programs. The fact that certain bytes just happen to contain the "newline" value is purely incidental. The file may well have a record structure, but it is quite likely to be based on a count stored at the front of each logical record, or a fixed format perhaps, or a directory at the front of the file, or in another associated file, etc.

Another common organisation of files at this level is to have the operating system support a record structure directly. In this case, each record will usually correspond one-for-one with a line in a source program, a line of text in a message, or a line of output destined for a printer. The majority of IBM mainframe operating systems have a structure of this sort. Depending on the details of the representation, the records may be of a fixed length, or they may be variable up to some maximum. They may deliberately be designed to represent the operations of real physical devices, sometimes those that have (or should have) disappeared in the dim and distant past. For example, 80-byte fixed length records are very likely to be rooted in the antiquity of card readers, and 133-byte output records are often on their way to a line printer. There is a parallel with operating systems with character string file structures. These were often conceived in an environment containing Teletypewriters rather than card readers and line printers. One of the advantages of such file organisations that has sometimes been claimed is the ability to send the file to be printed by the teletypewriter with virtually no change. Perhaps operating systems, like people, are prisoners of their history.

The important point of difference between character stream files and record-oriented files is that the records of record-oriented files are logical entities in themselves—they are not obtained by scanning the individual data bytes in the file to look for line delimiters, that is they are not dependent upon the contents of the file. The records may contain any characters at all, including newline characters, and yet they remain just a single record. Record structures may come in many varieties. The records may be fixed length as we have indicated, perhaps mimicing some real device, or they may be of varying size up to some maximum. The size may be specifiable when the file is created, or it may be built into the implementation—for example by the designer's choice of a one or two byte field to hold the length. In addition to this there are wide variations in the way in which the records may be accessed. At the simplest level, the records may be purely sequential, and can only be accessed from the beginning by reading through the sequence. Thus, a file with this structure is fairly similar in function to a file stored as a character sequence with embedded newline characters. The next variation on this scheme is for the records to be numbered sequentially. This number may be used to access a specified record directly as an alternative to sequential access from the front. Character string files sometimes have a similar facility where a particular byte may be accessed by means of its index. However, if a particular line in a character string file has to be accessed, then it is normally necessary to read from the front counting the newline delimiters. The only way to avoid this is to maintain a "line index" giving the offset in the file of the front of each such record. Maintaining this is much the same as maintaining a record-oriented file.

The next order of difference is the ability of the various file types to be updated. Character string files may sometimes be updated by overwriting one sequence of bytes with another of the same length. It is not really possible to replace one string with another of a different length without rewriting at least the tail the file. With record-oriented files the updating is often more flexible. If the records are all of the same size, then it is usually possible to replace one record by another. However, if the records are of variable sizes, then the possibilities are strongly implementation-dependent. If the implementation relies on the records being stored sequentially, then the restrictions will be much the same as for character string files. However, if the actual records may be stored in random fashion with an index that points to the actual records (giving the file its structure) then it may well be possible to replace one record by another of a different size (by allocating space for the new record, altering the index pointers appropriately, and releasing the old space). Depending on the structure of the index, it may also be possible to insert new records between two old ones, or remove an old record without disturbing any other records on either side.

Finally, there are some differences between files at a more subtle level. For example, most filing systems allow the storage of records of zero length. This might correspond to a blank line between paragraphs in a message for example. In a character string file this would be represented as two consecutive newline indicators. In a record-oriented file this might correspond to a record of length zero. However some record-oriented files allow the deletion of a record by writing a record of zero length in that place in the file. The implication of this of course is that such a file cannot store zero-length records, and thus some other representation must be found for a blank line. In the case of text files for instance a line of length 1 containing a single space character is a suitable representation, whereas it would be inappropriate if the file contained binary data.

While there are some ifs and buts, record-oriented files and character string files compare roughly as discs to tapes. Direct access to particular places is much easier for record-oriented files than for character string files. For small files of a few thousand lines the difference may not be severe, and indeed it may actually be less work to rewrite a small character string file in its entirety than to update one record in a similar sized record-oriented file. This is because of the overhead in maintaining the index in the record-oriented file. However, for files of increasing size the difference widens. In other words the extra overhead in maintaining the index for a record-oriented file is compensated for by the need only to access the one record rather than to scan through a large section of uninteresting file. Thus for applications that tend to deal in "small" files the character string file may be more appropriate, while for large files there may be more merit in the record-oriented approach. However, our task here is not to claim the merits of one or the other kind of file organisation but to point out the differences in file system semantics that file transfer between systems needs to be able to accommodate.

9.2   File Transfer Protocol

Let us suppose then that we are designing that part of a file transfer protocol that is to be used to communicate file structures between various combinations of filing systems. Sometimes it will be used to transfer between two systems which both have the character string style of file, sometimes it will be used to transfer between two systems that have keyed direct access files, and sometimes it will be used to transfer a file from a character string file structure to a record-oriented structure or *vice versa*. How can we handle such a diversity of combinations? One possibility might be to choose the type of file at one end or the other of the transfer as the type of file to be transferred, and then it would be the responsibility of the other party to map to or from that file type to its own kind of file in some suitable way. This approach is of course very successful when the two parties to the transfer have the same system. In this case, the mapping is a null operation at both ends, and the transfer becomes the fairly simple problem of representing the file in some suitable way on the communications line, and transferring the data across the transport service. When a large population of similar machines, say Unix, or VM/CMS machines wish to communicate together this is a very effective method.

The problems, as ever, start to appear when the communicating machines are of different sorts, and have different kinds of file structures. The truly astounding variation in file types makes it very likely that for any chosen type the other party to the transfer would be unable to do the mapping because that particular one mapping, out of all the possible mappings, was actually unavailable.

The unavailability may be for various reasons. It might just be that the implementors of the connection to the Gargleblaster system had never heard of the Beeblebrox filing structure, and thus there was no provision for it in the FTP implementation. Another possibility is that if the chosen representation of the file on the communications link has certain semantic implications that cannot be implemented in the foreign filing system, then the mapping cannot be done in principle. The implication is that the representation on the link is chosen because its semantics are necessary to the transfer, and thus if the semantics cannot be represented across the mapping, then the transfer is pointless.

Perhaps an example is in order. Suppose that the representation on the link is that of a record-oriented file structure with keys. The keys may contain some of the file information, such as a social security number, and thus it would be pointless to transfer the file unless the semantics of the keys could be maintained. If the destination file structure could only be a character string file with no possibility of random access of the individual records, then there would be little point in transferring the file. In particular cases, it might be possible to represent the keyed file structure, for example by putting the social security number at the beginning of each "record" (sequence between newline characters). However, if the sequential file could not support direct record access, then the exercise would still be pointless. In any case, severe practical difficulties might arise if either the data, or the keys, or both, could contain binary data such as numbers. Now and again these would certainly produce the newline character by accident and destroy the intended file structure. It is certain that some sort of representation *could* be devised, even if it was merely the log of the transfer syntax put into a file, but whether it could in general be put into a form that was in practice actually *useful* in the destination system is seriously in doubt.

9.3   File Types

A modification of outlook that is intellectually fairly modest, allows the design of protocols that are actually useful in practice. Instead of an unlimited and indefinitely expanding set of targets that is just the union of all real filing structures, we can choose a smaller set of abstract filing structures, and combine this with some mechanism that allows the selection of a suitable one of these structures for a particular transfer. The trick is to choose a set that is rich enough to accommodate all the "genuinely different" structures, but that is simple enough that a large set of the possible hosts can have an attempt at implementing some of them. *"Some of them?"* you may ask *"Aren't we back in the same boat if the two entities choose disjoint sets?"* Yes, we are, but there is another aspect to this. There is a negotiation phase where the two ends agree on the representation to use. Commonly, this takes the form of an offer/response exchange before the start of the file transfer proper.

Thus, one end, probably the initiator, may offer to use transfer forms A, P, Y, or Z, and the responder chooses one out of this list, say Y. The offer list is chosen subject to two constraints. One is of course which of the forms in the protocol definition have been implemented. Another is which of the forms in the definition is perceived to be appropriate for the semantics of the data. If the data is readable text, then the presentation level forms would indicate that the data on the link is character data in a particular code. Either ASCII or EBCDIC code may be offered. At the file structure level, the possibility of a character string format might be offered, or perhaps a series of records would be another option—with the inbuilt implication that an ascending sequence of record keys would retain the order of the records. Transferring text records and then scrambling their order is a pointless exercise. Another necessary aspect of the negotiation phase is that of record sizes. It is all very well starting to transfer a piece of text, and then finding, part way through, that a line with a 100 characters has just arrived, but that the recipient can only store a maximum of 80 characters in a line.

Of course, it may not be possible to transfer a particular type of file from one machine to another in principle. Just having a set of abstract representations and a negotiating mechanism doesn't make it possible successfully to transfer direct access files into a system that does not support that type of file organisation. However, if we have chosen the set of file structures successfully, then it is likely that there are many fewer possibilities. In other words, the number of different abstract file types should more nearly match the number of fundamentally different file organisations, rather than having 57 varieties of character string files, another 57 varieties of record structured files. In other words we are, as usual, using the device of abstraction to escape the mundane details of specific implementations.

As a lowest common denominator it is universal that all computer systems have some way of being able to store printable text in either ASCII or EBCDIC (or some code easily mappable to these character sets). The actual data may either be stored as a character string file or as an ordered set of records. An FTP must always have this type of file organisation as one of its options as a basis to fall back on if all else fails. Indeed, many common file structures that we are actually interested in transferring can be represented in some similar form. An obvious example of this is source text for programs. Mail messages also form a growing body of data to be transferred far and wide between computers, and much computer mail is represented wholly as characters. Character data, together with pragmatic rules for its interpretation are the *lingua franca* of communications in the late 1980s. Indeed, some FTPs, such as the NIFTP and the ARPANET FTP provide little else but character or binary transfer.

Thus far we have talked in rather general terms about the file representation used by the FTP on the link, and that a set of options may be presented by one party, and one of the options selected by the other party to the transfer. A more general model is the concept of a virtual filestore. Just as we found it helpful to think about various terminals in terms of an abstract virtual terminal, so it is useful to think about file transfer protocols in terms of a virtual filestore. It is then possible to think about a range of transfer protocols in terms of variations in this virtual filestore. Thus a range of different files can be mapped onto this virtual filestore. The description of the real file is in terms of various attributes.

9.4   ISO File Transfer Access and Manipulation Protocol

The time has come to illustrate the general notions that we have been discussing by referring to a particular file transfer protocol. Historically, two of the most important file transfer protocols are the ARPANET FTP and the "Blue Book FTP" or NIFTP protocols. We have not chosen them because they are rather old protocols, and so do not address some of the questions that we have been discussing. In addition, they tend to lump together many of the other topics, such as session and presentation issues, together into the one protocol. This is not surprising in view of their age, and is no criticism of them in their own historical context. However, we shall instead take the much newer ISO *File Transfer, Access and Manipulation*—FTAM protocol. This is of increasing importance, and it addresses most of the issues of file transfer that we wish to discuss.

FTAM has at its centre a virtual filestore which contains zero or more virtual files. These files are mapped in some way onto real files in the real filestore of an actual machine. The virtual files have a tree structure that is built up recursively of *File Access Data Units*—FADUs. The idea is that the tree structure may be parameterised in various ways so that it may be mapped closely onto the various sorts of files about which we have been talking.

In the description of the virtual filestore, the file access structure is defined in terms of the ASN.1 as shown in Fig 9.1. There are several interesting points to be noticed about this definition. Firstly, its recursive nature allows the whole file to be identified with an outermost FADU. The internal structure of this file may optionally be of various structures because of the optional structure of the "Contents" production, which may either be directly a DataUnit, or may recursively be another structured subtree—another FADU. At the bottom, the DataUnit is left as "EXTERNAL". This means that some mechanism outside the FTP process itself needs to be used to decide the details of its encoding. The sort of issues to be decided for this are those that we looked at in the last chapter: is the data characters, or integers, or colours of the rainbow, or social security numbers, or dividend forecasts, or Swiss bank account numbers, or octane ratings. . . ?

9.5   Virtual and Real File Structures

How does this generalised structure map onto the types of file we have been looking at? The byte stream file might be mapped in either of two ways. We might decide that the whole file is one DataUnit

```
FADU ::=        SEQUENCE
                {faduIdentifier [0] IMPLICIT FADUIdentifier,
                    contents Contents
                }

Contents ::=    CHOICE
                {leaf [1]IMPLICIT DataUnit OPTIONAL,
                    nonleaf [2]IMPLICIT Nonleaf
                }

Nonleaf ::= SEQUENCE
                {du [0] DataUnit OPTIONAL,
                subtrees [1] SEQUENCE of SEQUENCE
                    {arcLength [0] INTEGER DEFAULT 1,
                        FADU
                    }
                }

FADUidentifier ::= identifier Identifier

Identifier ::= CHOICE
                {name [1] GraphString,
                    number [2] INTEGER
                }
DataUnit ::= dataUnit [0] EXTERNAL
```

Fig 9.1.   FTAM Virtual File Structure

(and internally it is likely to be represented as one long string of octets). The tree is then particularly simple, being but a single leaf. Another closely related alternative might be to interpret the internal structure by scanning for the newline markers and mapping these into a sequence of individual data units of similar form to the above. Then each of these data units becomes its own simple subtree or FADU. The FADU identifier is most naturally an integer, being the number counting from the start. (Though there is room for creative individuality here with possible consequent general confusion, since the integers could start from 0 or 1 depending on one's personal prejudice, or the identifiers could be chosen as the names of flowers from this year's seed catalogue.) The whole file has become a two-level affair, with the lowest level data units being wrapped up as FADUs and then packed together in a single sequence to make up the complete file.

When we look at a real filing structure that has records, then it is natural to go straight for the two-level tree structure, with the lowest level data units corresponding to the records in the file. If the file has associated keys of some sort, then these will naturally be represented as the identifier, either as a string of characters (the name) or as an integer. However, we shall see presently that different mappings may often be needed.

When preparing to transfer a file between two virtual filestores, it must be recognised that the virtual filestores must be mapped into real filestores at the participating hosts. Thus, only certain variations of the general tree structure will actually be allowed in the virtual filestore at a particular machine. It is pointless transferring a file with, say, a recursive internal structure to a particular host if, when it gets there, nothing useful can be done with the file because no useful mapping to or from the real filestore can be performed. This kind of restriction is handled by applying a set of constraints to the file transfer.

So, before transferring a file, a suitable set of constraints must first be negotiated. The kinds of constraints that may be applied are such things as the maximum depth of the tree structure representing the file and the maximum length that each actual data unit may have. This should prevent a file transfer starting, only later to realise that the recipient virtual filestore was unable to receive the file properly because its host system imposed some limit on the virtual filestore through the necessary mapping to the real system. Thus, we might expect that a record-oriented system would choose a simple single-level tree to transfer a file to another similar record-oriented system, and that a byte stream system might choose either a single-level structure, or a single-leaf structure to exchange files with another similar system.

Unfortunately, this is not the whole story, and there are all sorts of possibilities for different interpretations. We have already seen how a byte stream system may choose either a single leaf to transfer the contents of a file, or a single-level tree. Similarly, a record-oriented system may more naturally choose a single-level tree, or it may in some circumstances need to hide its record structure in order to talk to a byte stream filing system.

9.6   Document Types

Imagine what would happen if we tried to transfer a file between a record-oriented system and a byte stream system. The record-oriented system might offer to transfer a record-oriented virtual file (i.e. with a length from root to leaf of 1). If the intended recipient refused, insisting that only a zero length was acceptable, then the sender would have a choice. Either the transfer could be abandoned, or the sender could accept the zero-level transfer, and map its record-oriented file into a flat file by concatenating all the records in the real file together with newline characters sandwiched between them. FTAM deliberately can only talk in terms of transfers between virtual files in virtual filestores, and cannot be used to talk about the mapping between virtual filestores and real filestores. Thus, it cannot be used to help in the decision of whether the fallback mapping in this case is a useful one. In some circumstances, such a mapping would be very useful, in others completely useless.

FTAM copes with this problem by relying on a set of *document types*. Thus, we might have a document type "simple text". This would be used to transfer files that normally represented simple straightforward text of the sort that people often type directly into a computer, or display on a simple printer. In systems such as MS-DOS this would be represented as a simple stream of characters with embedded carriage return characters to indicate new lines. In an IBM mainframe operating system such as MVS, this same abstract entity might well be represented as a series of records—one per line—with the characters themselves as EBCDIC codes, and the newline breaks being represented as a combination of the record structure itself and ANSI carriage control characters in the first character position in each record. Other document types might be "FORTRAN Source", "Credit Rating Report", "Cylinder Temperature Measurements", "TEX Source" and so on. It would be up to each system to decide on the correct mapping from the abstract document type into an actual representation in the real operating system. However, since the document type itself indicates much of the abstract semantics of that type of document, the mapping becomes much less susceptible to alternative ambiguous interpretations.

Fig 9.2.   Simplest Virtual File—a Single Leaf

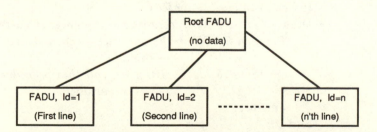

Fig 9.3.   Virtual File With Single Level Tree

When we look at the examples of access structures for files as shown in Figs 9.2 to 9.4, we see the increasing complexity from the simple

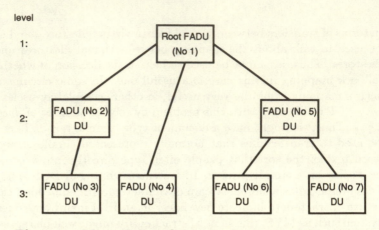

Fig 9.4.   More General Access Structure

byte stream file, through a flat file which is a series of records, to a more general tree-structured file. Note that it is possible in the general case to have a data unit stored either at a leaf or at an intermediate node. In addition, the arc lengths are by default 1 (see the ASN.1 definition of a Nonleaf, but that some arcs can be longer. In our example, the arc from the root node number 1 to the FADU node number 4 is of length 2. Our more general example also shows the FADUs labelled with a number. When the overall file labelled 1 is sent, the constituent FADUs are sent in a well-defined order. This order is generated by "walking the tree from left to right". This can be thought of as applying a recursive procedure to the recursive ASN.1 definition of the file access tree. This procedure may loosely be defined as

> **procedure** *Send_Fadu(Fadu)*
> **begin** *− − any node may possibly contain a DU to send* ::
>   *send(any contained Identifier and Data_Unit);*
>   **if** *Fadu.contents = nonleaf*
>   **then** *− − this FADU contains a sequence of subtrees*
>   **for** *each FADU in the sequence − −each subtree "left*
>   *− − to right"*
>   *Send_Fadu(FADU); − − call this procedure*
>   *− − recursively*
>   **end for;**
>   **end if;**
> **end procedure** *Send_Fadu;*

This simple ability to define a unique way of walking the tree is very important. Though many record-oriented files may have keys (i.e. FADU identifiers) that have an implicit order (such as sorted in ascending numerical order, or alphabetic order on the "name") such ordering is not essential, and it may well be important that the ordering of the file be maintained across the transfer independently of the values of the keys. Indeed, the key values may possibly themselves be null, or otherwise non-distinct. This ability to define a simple unique order of transmission is the primary reason for the hierarchical virtual file structure being chosen. It is recognised that this structure is inadequate for some files (though overkill for many others) but the more general network form has no simple walking algorithm, and thus does not lead simply to a unique way of retaining order during the file transfer.

9.7 File Access

We have tended so far to look at the FTAM protocol entirely in terms of transferring the contents of the file. Before we proceed to look at the other aspects of file transfer, we shall mention briefly those aspects of FTAM concerned with accessing files. File access is different from file transfer in that parts of a file may be accessed rather than the whole file. Thus, an editor might work remotely on a file, accessing only those portions of the file that are required. This type of access obviates the need to transfer the whole file across the link. The difference may be minimal for small files, a brief memo for instance, but may well be dramatic for, say, a small alteration in the text of a book.

FTAM allows (virtual) files to be accessed at the level of the File Access Data Unit. Remember that the FADU may correspond to the whole of a byte stream file, a single record in a record-structured file, or a subtree in some more complex file structure, and of course all files are represented in total by the root FADU. When file access or transfer is in progress, there is a notion of a pointer that moves around the file access tree. The access parts of FTAM allow this pointer to be moved, either forwards or backwards in the tree walking sequence, or the pointer may be moved directly to search for a specific FADUidentifier. Since this identifier will probably map onto the record key in a real direct access filing system, this allows direct access on the corresponding real file. It will be seen that attempts at doing direct access on byte stream files may be prevented (if so desired) by choosing the appropriate virtual file to present to the network connection.

In addition to being able to move around the file structure, several other basic operations are provided for in FTAM. These are such operations as insert, replace, erase and extend.

9.8 File Transfer "In The Large"

Now we have looked in some considerable detail at the elements of the FTAM protocol concerned with file structuring and data transfer and access, we shall back up and consider the operations pertaining to whole files, and to the file transfer activity as a whole. In general, file transfer takes place between a source and a destination, and at the behest of a third party. In the general case, this third party need not be situated at either the source or the destination of the transfer.

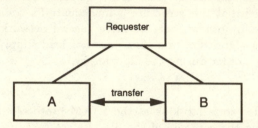

Fig 9.5.   General Picture of a File Transfer

Thus, we might in general expect that the requester of a file transfer operation would need to communicate with two agents, A and B which will each perform one end of the file transfer process. Indeed, one of the first major FTP protocols, the ARPANET FTP, has this sort of notion as the basis of its definition. The implication of this kind of model is that the control and synchronisation of the two agents performing the transfer is performed over a separate network connection path from the actual data transfer itself. The protocol is thus split up into two parts: the control protocol is carried on top of a terminal-like connection using the TELNET protocol, while the data transfer itself takes place on a transport type of connection supported by TCP. This method does have some structural advantages in separating out two logically separate flows, but it had the disadvantage of incurring the expense of maintaining several connections where, as we are about to see, one will do, and of needing some coordination in establishing the appropriate network of connections to perform the transfer.

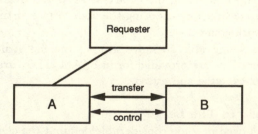
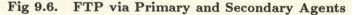

Fig 9.6.   FTP via Primary and Secondary Agents

Fig 9.6 shows a more common arrangement. Here, the requester communicates directly with only one of the agents involved in the transfer. This agent then communicates with the other agent along a single link, multiplexing both the control information and the data itself. We see that this has eliminated one of the network connections, and with that the need to synchronise the establishment of the triangle of connections, and the cost of the extra connection. The debit side of this approach is the need to multiplex the control and transfer data on the link between the two transfer agents. However, this method of managing the file transfer is so advantageous that it has been used in all cases other than the original ARPANET case.

Given this model, it is normal to concentrate still further on the transfer itself, and to ignore the connection between the requester and the agent that operates on the requester's behalf. There are good reasons for ignoring this other link. One of the most important is that the most common arrangement in practice is for the requester actually to be in the same system as his primary file transfer agent. Thus, the link between them might not be a network link at all, but may perhaps consist of running an application program within an already established terminal session or of submitting a batch job to a background request queue. In this case, the link is not a network link, and defining a specific network protocol that must be used would be adding a considerable and quite unnecessary burden.

There are in addition several other ways in which a requester may communicate his wishes with a prospective agent. This may be by establishing a terminal connection with the system where his intended agent resides, or it might involve some such process as sending a message. Herein lies the other important reason for not defining a network connection between the requester and his agent as part of the file transfer protocol. Many file transfer processes are initiated by some process between the requester and his primary agent, and then the actual process may take place some time later while the original requester (if she is a human) is doing something else. Insisting on a "live" connection with the requester while the transfer is in progress would place quite unnecessary and irksome time constraints on the process.

Thus it is normal to assume that the requester communicates her desires, and supplies any necessary parameters to her agent via some separately specified user interface. The file transfer process itself is then defined independently of this. Thus, we have the final situation shown in Fig 9.7.

Here the requester's agent resides in the same system as either the source or destination file, and uses a single connection to transfer either to or from a remote file. Thus, the file transfer protocol must

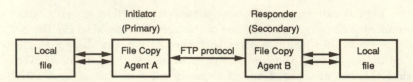

Fig 9.7.   FTP via Initiator and Responder Agents

be asymmetrical in at least two orthogonal ways. Not only is there a source and a destination for the file, but there is also an initiator (the requester's primary agent) and a responder. The file transfer may either be from or to the initiator.

The file transfer process itself requires various pieces of information to proceed. The fairly obvious ones are the names of the files in the two systems, plus some tokens for establishing the necessary authority for accessing the filing system. Most operating systems (beyond the simplest systems used on personal computers) require some sort of authorisation of individual users before they are allowed access to a system. This type of authorisation is needed for two main reasons. Firstly, resources will be consumed for any access and it is usual for these to be billed to an account in some way. Secondly, most filing systems have some form of access control. Apart from the owner, a file may usually be permitted for various forms of access to other users. Thus, whether the file to be accessed belongs to the requester of the transfer or to someone else, she will need to identify herself, or some account which she can use in order to access both files involved in the transfer. This is done in various ways on various machines, and so a fairly flexible set of identifiers and passwords is usually allowed for in a file transfer protocol. Note the asymmetry of the protocol in this respect. It is assumed that the initiator and the requester have come to some agreement about access to the "local" files—that is, the files in the system in which the initiating agent resides. This agreement is arrived at locally, probably by the requesting user "signing in" or "logging on" to the local machine. The tokens are those provided by the requesting user to pass to the responding system in order to access the file there.

In addition to the structure and contents of a file, files as a whole have certain properties or attributes that are important for FTP. The file name is one of the obvious ones. Different filing systems have wide ranging conventions for this, and so it is important that the protocol should be capable of carrying any conceivable possibility. It is particularly important that an FTP agent, that must of necessity reside in a specific system, must not impose any local constraints on filenames that are for use in foreign systems. Thus, if an agent existed in an operating system that supported only upper case alphabetic names of at most eight characters, then such a restriction imposed on remote file name references would very severely compromise the open interworking possibilities. Again, a particular file might have very specific limits imposed on the type of access (in addition to specifying those who are allowed to access the file at all). These might be "read only", "replace existing records only but don't change the file structure", "only add new records, possibly only at the end", and so forth. In addition, selective constraints on actions might include restricting those who could change certain attributes, particularly the access attributes themselves. The variations in this area between different operating systems is such that only some of them can be expected to appear in any generalised FTAM protocol.

Several other attributes may be of interest in file management. They include the identity of the creator and owner of the file, the last reader, and the last modifier, and the time and date of the corresponding events. In addition, the size of the file and the size to which it might need to be expanded in the future are prudent things to ascertain when negotiating to set up the transfer.

In order to transfer a file using the ISO FTAM, a number of nested regimes are established. A particular regime is established during a specific phase when a certain protocol exchange sets up the extra context required for the regime.

In the first place, a connection between the FTP initiator and the FTP responder must be established. In the jargon, this is the so-called *application association* i.e. an association between two application programs, the FTP agents, for the purpose of transferring the file. This *application connection regime* is set up by the protocol exchange that takes place in the *application association establishment phase*. There is nothing in this phase that is specific to file transfer except perhaps the identification of file transfer agents rather than agents of some other kind, and other connections or associations between application processes use much the same procedures. These procedures are such things as establishing authorisation to use communications resources, and the establishment of the accounting processes necessary for this. Since these types of service are used for all such application associations rather than just for FTP, they are being extracted and standardised. They are commonly referred to as *Common Application Service Elements*—CASE, and we shall return to them in Chapter 11.

Within the application regime, there is a file store management phase. Next comes a file selection phase. This either creates a new file or identifies an existing file to which operations in the contained regimes will apply. The file selection phase establishes the file selection regime. A file management phase comes next. This allows, for example, the attributes of a whole file to be either read or changed. The file management phase does not establish a nested regime.

Inside all these regimes we are at last able to open the file. The file must be open in order for its contents to be accessed. While it is open, that is during the file access regime, the data access operations may take place. These operations act upon the FADUs that we encountered earlier. Each FADU may in general be very large, and may consist of a large number of constituent presentation units. However, the file operations themselves, such as location of a particular position (FADU) in the file, or the reading, writing, or changing of a unit can only take place in terms of a complete FADU.

This whole process may be visualised as a series of nested program scopes as in the following informal piece of program:

> **begin** $<$ *Application_Association_Regime* $>$
> *A general CASE establishment*
> *Then as yet unspecified filestore management phase*
> *may take place*
> **begin** $<$ *File_Selection_Regime* $>$
> *This starts when a specific file is either*
> *created or selected*
> *Then some file management may take place*
> *for example attributes may be read or altered*
> **begin** $<$ *File_Access_Regime* $>$
> *The selected file is opened to access*
> *its contents*
> *A particular FADU may be located*
> **begin** $<$ *Data_Transfer_Regime* $>$
> *Data, i.e. FADUs are transferred*
> **end** $<$ *Data_Transfer_Regime* $>$
> *The selected file is closed.*
> **end** $<$ *File_Access_Regime* $>$
> *The selected file is de $-$ selected or deleted.*
> **end** $<$ *File_Selection_Regime* $>$
> *The application association is terminated.*
> **end** $<$ *Application_Association_Regime* $>$

The piece of pseudo-code above attempts to show the nesting of the regimes, and the way these are related to the phases. The phases (periods when a particular type of protocol exchange takes place) generally occur at the beginning and end of the regimes, though some of the management phases may not in themselves establish another nested regime.

9.9   Checkpoint Recovery

Most file transfer services have facilities for checkpoint and re-transmission recovery. At first, this seems like an amazing thing to put into a file transfer process. After all, we have seen that there are facilities for error recovery at nearly every level in the stack of communications protocols and services. This ranges from the simple retransmission of a frame at the data link level, through end-to-end retransmission, re-establishment of another network connection if one fails, and even session re-establishment. Why do we need yet another error recovery mechanism? Are the designers of network services paranoid? Well, network service designers may well be paranoid, since networks have the habit of failing in ever more inventive ways in order to thwart the intent of the designers.

Some types of network failure are sufficiently severe that no amount of technical work can prevent them. Examples of this may be the catastrophic failure of a gateway, the failure of the power supply, or perhaps the taking of some machine out of service for regular mainte-nance. It is not unknown for some machines even to be switched off for extended periods through a long holiday. Sometimes it is possible for file transfers to be scheduled to avoid the planned activities, but there will always be some failures of this type in even the best run establishments.

So, despite the best efforts of the designers, the network con-nection between two users—or file transfer agents in our case—is not perfect. If it is sufficiently good, then the FTP error recovery will not be needed. However, if failures do occur with sufficient frequency that they cannot be ignored, then some account has to be taken of them.

Well then, if a file transfer is interrupted, why not just re-start it, and send the complete file again? Why add all this extra recovery mechanism, when such a simpler method is available? In many cases this is by far the best solution. Particularly for small files, it will be much easier, and probably cheaper (because of the absence of the recov-ery mechanism) merely to reperform an aborted file transfer. Suppose, though, the file is a very large one—an industrial database perhaps, the source for a new computer operating system, or the income tax records for the occupants of a large city, then if it is three-quarters complete when it fails it would be very wasteful in both time and money to re-start it from the start of the data rather than from some more recent checkpoint. It may not even be possible to schedule a very long transfer and be sure that it would be complete before the next scheduled inter-ruption. Suppose a multi-megabyte file transfer would take 40 hours, and one of the machines involved has scheduled maintenance at 6.00 am every morning.

Thus, we see that some applications have a need to recover at the file transfer level from interruptions in the file transfer process itself. We can at the same time see that many applications do not need such levels of sophistication, and should not be burdened with the overhead involved in either implementing or handling the protocol for such recovery. Thus, error recovery mechanisms of this sort should be optional, and their use negotiated at the start of the transfer process.

This type of error recovery is implemented in terms of the commitment protocol. Again, this has been identified as something that will be of use not only to file transfer, but also to many other applications of networking. It is thus one of the other services that has been identified as belonging to the CASE development. (See Chapter 11.)

9.10   Summary

File transfer involves much more than moving the data bits from one machine to another. It is vastly complicated by widely varying data structures and representation both at the level of the data itself, and at the higher levels of file structure. We have examined the issues involved by taking ISO-FTAM as our exemplar. FTAM uses an abstract, high-level virtual file description, and defines its protocols in terms of this model. It also goes further than this and attempts to resolve some of the possible ambiguities of mapping this file structure into various real files by a set of *Document Types* to associate the semantics of file types with specific representations in terms of the virtual file. We have also looked at some of the issues involved in the manipulation of files as entities, and in managing the file transfer process itself.

10
Network Mail

So far in this book we have looked at the various ways in which computer networks are used to allow terminals to connect to machines, and to allow file transfer and access. Ranking closely after terminals and files, computer mail is another major application of computer networks and computer conferencing is also becoming fairly common. As a way of introducing network mail, we shall first look at computer mail on a single shared computer system. This will allow us to outline the basic characteristics of computer-based mail, and will form the background that we need when discussing network mail.

There are many traditional methods of communication without the use of computers. Readers will be familiar with the use of the telephone, sending memos, writing letters, preparing reports, calling meetings, visiting individuals, or attending conferences. In a broader sense, papers are written to publish and document research and related development, and books such as this one are written to disseminate information. These methods of communication all have their advantages and disadvantages. For example, the telephone can be extremely useful as a rapid method of communication, but it can also be extremely frustrating trying to call someone who is out, leaving her a message to call back, and then you yourself being out when the call is returned. The recent explosive growth of cellular telephone services has alleviated some of the problems of access where the expense is justified. However, one of the main problems of the telephone is its intrusiveness for the receiver of the call. Letters or memos are a slower form of communication that have a very strong advantage over the telephone in that they can be stored in the in-tray of the recipient until she is ready to process them. The recipient is in control of the receipt of such messages in a way that she is not with incoming telephone calls—letters and memos are less intrusive than telephones.

One severe problem with the telephone is the time difference when used across large differences in longitude. Even coast-to-coast across the USA reduces the intersection of the working day of the would-be caller and callee, and there is almost no overlap between the normal working day of Europe and the West coast of North America. Letters are even slower over such long distances, and it is perhaps in this area where computer mail, and network mail in particular, shows to best advantage.

10.1   Computer Messages

Suppose that some community of people shares a computer system. One of the most obvious examples is a group of people using a time-sharing computer. The group may perhaps be research workers on a common project, administrators for some computerised database, or members of a commercial company. If such a group uses a shared facility regularly—typically using the computer system at least once per day—then there is probably a need for them to communicate with each other because of some shared interest. That interest may be the computer system itself, or it may come because of some entirely different shared interest, in Chinese cooking perhaps, or safety regulations. A *Computer Based Message System*—CBMS will allow such a set of people to exchange messages by means of their computer terminals as part of the service that they get from the time-sharing computer.

Typically, this service appears to each user in the form of an abstract "mailbox" that she has available in the computer system. By the use of suitable commands to the computer system, perhaps in the form of running some special mailing program, she can interact with her mailbox and manipulate the message in various ways. As she logs into the computer for each interactive session, she is told of the existence of any new messages in her mailbox which she has not yet seen. When she wants to see the messages she can run the mailer program that allows her to receive her messages, read them, and reply to them. She can also originate messages by running the same mailer program when she feels the need to do so. When she sends messages they are put into the recipient's mailbox. If the system supports it, the recipient may be told of the arrival of such new messages.

In addition to this one-to-one type of sending, many mailing systems support extensions in terms of lists of recipients. Thus, mail may be copied to various recipients in addition to the primary one. This is the parallel in traditional mail of sending a letter to Tom, and carbon copies to Dick and Harry. In addition, mail may be sent not just to a specific person, but to a group of people—such as "The Turbine Designers" or "The Christmas Party Committee". We shall see how these concepts of mailing lists expand the user's perception of network mail, and how they are allowed for in the protocols.

The details of the facilities available to the user vary, but it is usually possible to direct incoming messages into computer files, and incorporate the contents of existing files into outgoing messages. The facilities may be very sophisticated, including a complex filing system that allows the messages to be filed and cross-referenced for future retrieval. The user interface may range from a few basic commands to receive and send messages up to a screen-based system with icons, pointers, mice, and suchlike good things. What is of interest to us from the network point of view is that users are in control of the message flow. They may be told of incoming messages in their mailbox as they log into the system, or even as the messages arrive they may get notification. However, it is the user who decides when to look into the mailbox. The user is in control. This as a much less intrusive process than the shrill tones of the incoming telephone call.

Another important characteristic of these mailing systems is their immediacy. When one user sends a message to another user of the same machine then the message is usually immediately available. The recipient may become aware of the incoming message within seconds if she is logged into the system. At the other extreme, she may be on vacation, and it may be a week or two before the recipient finally sees the message. However, the normal mode of operation is that most recipients will receive their messages within a few hours if they are frequent computer users.

Computer-based mail, then, shares the timescale of seconds to days with letters, memos, and telephone calls. This is in contrast to published research papers and books which have lifecycles of 6 months upwards. Computer mail is also in the same group as letters in its interactive qualities and by virtue of the normally small group of recipients. Published papers are somewhat less interactive, and books tend fairly severely to be one-way communication. Computer mail also has some novel properties not shared by the other media. One of the most important of these is that since a computer message contains readable text and resides within a computer, then it may be used to transfer not only readable messages for people, but also computer programs or other machine-readable data.

We see then that computer mail has certain properties that make it similar to but different from telephone and postal communication. For the sorts of communities that we have just described it has proved extremely useful. Computer networks have allowed such mailing systems to be expanded in two interesting ways. The first way is that the wide-area terminal access that we have looked at allows the community of users of a single computing system to be spread far and wide. It is now cost-effective for a user to use computing resources on the opposite side of a large country or an ocean. Indeed, wide-area networks often, but sadly not always, have a flat charging rate that is distance independent even across countries of continental extent. Thus, if a computer is outside the reach of a local phone call, then the access cost is independent of distance. This is true even if public utility networks are used. Once the user is on one of the several large national and international private networks, whether within a research community or a business community, then the charge is often free of the huge artificial rate increases imposed by public utilities at national boundaries. The result of all this is that the community of users of a computer system may actually be spread over several thousands of miles. For users of such networks, the "Global Village" is a present reality.

We can now see that the very fact that terminal access has allowed such a geographical spread of the "community" has altered the very nature and utility of the messaging system itself. It is now the case that the computer message system is probably the preferred means of sending messages within such a community rather than the more traditional ways. If the two parties to a communication are both logged into the system at the same time, then the conversation can be almost immediate, and yet the same system allows the storage and queuing of messages that is so useful over such a widespread community. One such system that the author uses has a set of users that is spread across the USA, Canada, and the UK. Normally, messages may be stored for up to several hours or days for the recipient. This is particularly useful when someone in Europe is communicating with someone on the Pacific coast of North America. However, should the two users be logged into the system at the same time, then an interchange of messages can take place in real time. The author has both observed and participated in such exchanges several times. Indeed such exchanges are not at all unusual.

However, the utility of electronic mail can be spread even further by using networks in another way. As well as allowing terminals to access remote machines, networks also allow computers to communicate and send messages one to another. Thus, for example, a person may wish to communicate with colleagues who normally use other machines. A physicist at one university may have more need to communicate with another physicist at another university abroad than with, say, a biologist in an office across the road. Of course, wide-area terminal access allows this to happen in principle. Two people may agree to use a specific machine on which to exchange messages. Then each of them will obtain authorisation to use the machine and will call in regularly to check mailboxes. The problem is that allocation of such facilities to "foreigners" may not always be administratively convenient, to put it mildly, and the cost of regular international calls to poll for messages can be expensive. Even worse is the necessity for a user of several mailboxes to poll several different places for her mail. Such an arrangement is more satisfactory from several points of view if it is made symmetrical. Thus, the sender can contact the other remote system directly to send the message. This eliminates much needless and expensive polling. However, it is not very satisfactory as it requires that each sender learn a new operating system for each new correspondent.

Fortunately, the need to have access to, to learn, and to use more and more systems can be eliminated by arranging for the local mailing systems on each machine to deliver mail not just to local mailboxes, but to remote mailboxes too. Thus, just as we send a local message to "`Phyllis Quot`", then we may send a message remotely to "`Marmaduke Pertwee at Nosey Park`". In the latter case the message system detects the qualifying "`at Nosey Park`" and instead of searching locally for "`Marmaduke Pertwee`", makes special arrangements for the message to be dispatched for the distant "`Nosey Park`". Typically, this may mean putting the message into some local "mailbag" and arranging for its dispatch across the network. Sending such messages across the network is the process of network mail that we are working ourselves up to study, but before we delve into the discussion we shall briefly look at what change in user service this has bought us.

Thinking of our two physicists wishing to communicate, we can see that each of them now only has to deal with his own local computer system. There is no need to be concerned with all the logistical and administrative problems of using a remote mailing system. The remote user will be seen merely as someone who has an extra address associated in some way. Outgoing messages will need the address attached to them so that the system can deliver them, and incoming messages will typically be stamped with the originator's address both so that she may be properly identified, and so that any replies may be properly returned.

In outline, what happens is that the message is converted into a specific format and sent out from computer to computer across network connections until it reaches its destination. We shall look at the ARPANET mailing protocol *Simple Mail Transfer Protocol*—SMTP for a specific example. Suppose that a researcher `Adam Douglas` working at `Rackminster Park` wishes to send a message to `Darin Mustang` at `Warminster College`. Following the discussion above, he would send to

```
Darin Mustang @ Warminster College
```

The local mailing system would see the destination by spotting the "`@`"-symbol and immediately recognise that it should not be looking locally for a `Darin Mustang`, but should be trying to work out how to deliver messages directed to `Warminster College`. Assuming that this college is known to the mailing system, it will put it in a mailing bag ready for the next time a delivery to Warminster is made. This delivery may take place immediately, or it may take place some time later—at a fixed time of day perhaps. In the ARPANET environment a TCP connection is made at some time between the mailing systems at Rackminster Park and Warminster College. Suppose that because of the pending message from Adam Douglas, the Rackminster Park mailing system initiates the call. The dialogue on the transport connection would be something like the following:

```
Party  Message

Rack:  MAIL FROM:<Adam Douglas@Rackminster Park>
War:   250 OK

Rack:  RCPT TO:<Darin Mustang@Warminster College>
War:   250 OK

Rack:  DATA
War:   250 Start mail input; end with <CRLF>.<CRLF>

Rack:  'See, here's the workbox, little wife,
Rack:    That I made of polished oak.'
Rack:  He was a joiner, of village life;
Rack:    She came of borough folk.
Rack:  .....
Rack:  <CRLF>.<CRLF>
War:   250 OK
```

Let us look at this sequence. The command "MAIL FROM..." tells the receiver that a new mail transaction is starting. During each connection several transfers can take place. This command marks the start of a new transfer. The command specifies who the mail is from. The reply allows the mail receiver either to accept the proposed transfer, or to reject it. All replies have a number (250 in this case) and some text. The numbers have a structure to which programs may easily react, while the text is for transmission to human readers. All commands have specific responses, and the response must be received before the protocol progresses to the next step. The protocol is very deliberately designed in this lock-step manner, with commands and responses in strictly alternating sequence.

The next command is "RCPT TO...". This specifies the intended recipient of this message—Darin Mustang. Having established the sender and receiver for the message, the Rackminster mailer indicates that it is going into the data transfer state with the "DATA" command. This is accepted with a specific response. One of the parameters of the response is a specification of the sequence that should be used by the sending mailer to indicate the end of the message. This is normally a line containing a single full stop.

On receipt of the positive response the body of the message is sent followed by the terminating line. While we have shown only text in our example, the message is actually more complex, and has a header that we shall discuss presently. When the message has been sent, the receiver replies with the "250 OK" message. This means that the receiving mailing system has accepted responsibility for the message. Roughly this means that it will either deliver the message to the destination mailbox, pass the message onto a further mailer, or return a failure message addressed to the original sender (via the "FROM:.." field of the "MAIL..." command) if something should go wrong. The implication of this is that the receiving mailer has stored the message in non-volatile memory.

All this is very straightforward for our simple case. Let us look at some possible variations on the theme. Firstly, the originating mailing system may not have any knowledge of a requested host (the "@ Warminster College" in our example). In this case the originating mailing system needs to communicate back to the requesting user. This is a local matter, and it takes place in whatever the approved local way is. The next possible failure is that the destination refuses to receive any mail from that particular sender (by refusing the initial "MAIL..." command), or it may disclaim all knowledge of the intended destination. Again the user will get notification in some local manner from his mailing system.

However, once the responsibility for the message is accepted by a non-local mailing system, then the mechanism for informing the original sender that something has gone wrong is for a message to be sent back to the user (using the information in the "MAIL FROM..." command) and containing some explanatory text. Thus, we see that the retention of the address back to the originator of the message is important not just to allow the eventual human recipient to reply to the message, but also to allow the various automata along the route to send back failure or information messages to the originator should something go wrong. The need for this becomes more apparent if we consider a more complex example than just two communicating mailing systems.

For example, it may be that the two installations in our example cannot communicate directly, but only through a third party. The third party must be able to relay mail that is not intended for itself. Thus, suppose that Warminster College is connected to a private X.25 network. For reasons political it is not allowed direct connection to a public network. However, Rackminster Park has the good fortune to be connected to a public data network, and thus has direct worldwide connections. To get from one network to the other messages must be sent through a relay that is connected to both networks. Suppose this interconnecting gateway is called "O'Brien". Then the simple conversation that we had before will take place not between Rackminster and Warminster directly, but first between Rackminster and O'Brien, and then later between O'Brien and Warminster. The conversation itself will be identical in both cases, but the meaning of the commands and responses is now subtly different since they sometimes refer to non-local senders and recipients. So we see that naming a host does not necessarily mean that the transfer can or will take place in one step. In general the message is passed from host to host until the final destination is reached. The way in which the possible route is worked out may be very simple or it may be very complex—the transfer may be a single use of one transport service connection, or it may be many uses of separate transport connections. In many ways this is a reincarnation of the low-level routing issues that we encountered when discussing the internals of the network service in Chapter 5. At each step the intended destination is re-examined, and the next relay is chosen by using various criteria.

SMTP has various extra messages that may be used to help with the forwarding process. For example, a receiving host may not actually be able to deliver the message locally to the intended recipient mailbox, but it may know that the recipient may be reached at a mailbox somewhere else (perhaps the user is visiting somewhere else, or has moved, and has directed the mailing system to forward her mail). It may volunteer to forward the mail with a response

```
251 User not local; will forward to <New-Dest>
```

Alternatively, it may refuse the message and throw the ball back into the sender's court with

```
551 User not local; please try <New-Dest>
```

As we have said before, a major application of network mail is the sending of mail to mailing lists. These are lists of people who have a common interest of some sort. This might be perhaps Laser Printing, Local Area Networks, AIDS Research, you name it. Typically such mailing lists are arranged around a moderator. Interested people send messages to the moderator, who "vets" them according to relevance, legality, and good taste and then sends them to everyone on a mailing list. This may be simply a set of people in a file. Thus, the moderator may have a file in her system that contains perhaps several hundred entries such as

```
Fred_Cheney@Fee-John.EDU
John_Mortimer@Fie-Jack.AC.UK
```

and so on. Each approved message is sent out using all the names in the list. It may be that some of the names are actually further mailing lists. Thus, a message may arrive at some intermediate destination, addressed to "Printing-Fanatics". This may be a further list that is expanded in a similar way to the original list. The complete list is thus a tree of mailing lists that branches at the individual places where it encounters another mailing list. (Of course if the "tree" develops cycles due to mailing lists pointing to each other, then messages will multiply exponentially without limit. This kind of error is quickly noticed.) The need for such a multi-level fanout is clearly related to the economy in sending a message on a link once rather than several times. However, the SMTP does encourage the sending of messages once with several recipients since the RCPT command allows several recipients for a message to be negotiated one by one before embarking on the message transfer itself.

In addition to the SMTP protocol that is used to transfer messages from host to host across a transport connection, the messages themselves have a very specific format. This loosely corresponds to the envelope on a normal letter that has the recipient's address, and possibly other information such as a return address, a postage stamp, a cancelling stamp (that is supposed to indicate the place and time of postage but is invariably illegible), perhaps a customs declaration and so on. The contents of an envelope, the letter itself, is a matter of agreement between the sender and the recipient. In the same way, an ARPANET message contains a header and is followed by the contents.

The reader should be careful of the terminology. The traditional "envelope" physically contains a letter and has addressing and suchlike information written on the outside. Computer messages on the other hand consist of two parts—a header and a body. The header consists of, or contains, the addressing and suchlike information, and the body contains, or just is, the message itself. The correspondence of the header with the envelope is thus close rather than exact, and in particular, the meaning of such words as "contains" are subtly changed.

The header consists of various sorts of information that are of assistance in delivering the message, returning error indications to the sender, or reporting the progress of the message through the system. An ARPANET message is a piece of text. The first part of the text is a header containing a list of fields each with a leading keyword. Following this header, and separated by a blank line is the body of the message. We shall examine the possibilities by looking at some examples.

```
Date:   Mon, 1 Dec 86 16:33:42 GMT
From:   Russell Godber <russ@uk.ac.ncl.cheviot>
To:     George Malcolm <CJ42@uk.ac.ncl.styhead>

Hi George,
        Just to remind you about the project meeting
on Thursday.  Don't forget that we want a
progress report on the Gargleblasters.
-- Russ.
```

This is an example of a fairly minimal message. The header contains just three fields. The "To:" and "From:" fields contain an address in two forms. The first is a fairly informal name that is primarily for the human reader. The second between the angle brackets (<>) is a precise machine-readable specification of the sender's mailbox. The other field "Date:" contains the date and time in a fairly formal way. Thus, it is both easily parsed by a machine, and also understood by a human reader. Note that both the date and the time are present, together with the time zone. The text of the message is a simple reminder to a colleague. In early versions of the protocol it was possible to drop the "To:" field from the message, since that information is carried in the SMTP protocol that transfers the message. Fortunately, few mailing systems were so parsimonious, and later versions of the protocol insist on the destination being specified.

Let us look at some more examples. We shall show only the headers. The contents are left to the imagination of the readers.

```
Date:        26 August 1985 00:20:26 PST
From:        Bob <RLH@TreeTown>
Sender:      Tom---Bob's secry
Reply-To:    Handy Badpoor <JJJ@Take-A-Break>
Subject:     Source required for Pink Flamingoes
To:          Joe and Jim <Burg@CCMU>
cc:          Higher Management <Boss@Redwood>
Comment:     Please reply - this matter is urgent
             and overdue.
    ...
```

Here we see a message sent from a particular person to another. However, there is a "Sender:" field in addition to the "From:" field. The "Sender:" field indicates that the person who actually sent the message was Tom, but that the message was sent on behalf of Bob, as indicated in the "From:" field. This sort of device is useful if (as indicated in our example) the message was sent on the instructions of one person to another—by Bob instructing his secretary, Tom in our example. Just to complicate matters, any replies are supposed not to be sent to either Bob or Tom, but to Handy Badpoor at the mailbox address indicated. This may be because Bob and Tom will be away, and they have persuaded Handy to handle the replies for them.

The subject field gives some indication about the contents of the message. This is usually a summary of the contents of the message typed in by the sender, and may be used in several ways in addition to being read by humans. As an example of the other ways in which this field can be exploited, one message system used by the author allows the incoming messages to be displayed as a list of senders and subjects. The recipient can then choose to view the more interesting looking messages first, or all those messages on the same subject together. The system also allows the messages to be filed automatically in a database and indexed by keywords that appear in the subject. For example, all messages with the word "`Flamingo`" in their subject might be grouped together. The "`Cc`" field specifies a list of the other people to whom the message is being sent. Many systems use the subject and sender fields to group and sort messages in various ways.

```
Date:           12 Feb 87 00:20:26 MST
From:           Rolling Christmas <PArtist@GSB>
Subject:        Medieval Banquets
To:             Ralph <Uncle@Agricultural>
ReSent-Date     11 Feb 87 23:37 PST
ReSent-To:      Lyn@UNCAM
ReSent-From:    Sailor Ralph <Uncle@Agricultural>
Comment:        Snakepit's latest escapade!
Received:       from Agricultural by Farne via PSS;
                12 Feb 87 07:59:24 GMT
    ...
```

Here some new fields have appeared. These particular ones indicate that a message was sent from Rolling Christmas to Sailor Ralph. Ralph immediately sent it on to Lyn. The "`ReSent...`" fields are a trail of the message through the various places it has visited. These extra fields that are added as the message traverses the networks are extremely useful for tracing the message back when things go wrong. The particular route shown is a comparatively simple one. It is not at all unusual to get messages that have been relayed through five or ten different machines, quite apart from the network switches used implicitly by the transport service links. In addition, careful examination of the "`Date:`" fields indicates that the message completed the trip in about 40 minutes, since the MST and PST time zones are seven and eight hours "behind" GMT respectively.

It is beyond our scope to examine all these fields exhaustively. However, there are fields that allow the message to be marked as being a reply to a certain earlier message or can refer to certain other messages, indicate that the body of the message is encrypted and so forth. There is a truly rich set of such fields.

10.2   Forwarding, Relaying and Address Structures

We have already had a need to discuss the relationship between addressing and routing in connection with routing datagrams through a network in support of the network service. Perhaps the most complex addresses are to be encountered with network mail. A really full exposition of this subject would take many chapters and so we can give only an inkling of the true complexity here. The problem is multi-fold, and has many causes. One is that there are several disjoint mail networks that overlay each other. They all have different syntax for their addresses, and are joined in several usually rather arbitrary places. Since the address structures are quite different, then a message has to be routed through a specific gateway using an address that gives a specific route that binds it to passing through specific machines rather than the preferable hierarchical structure that leaves the binding to the route to the time of transmission.

Even within one network, particularly a network as large and complex as the ARPA network, the sheer size of the network means that addressing information cannot be maintained in a single local database. It has become necessary to break the network down hierarchically. All this leads to remarkably complex addresses. There are moves in progress to change this complex arrangement into a single hierarchical structure covering all networks. Indeed, during the time this book was being written, large changes have taken place, and most readers should never need directly to use the routing mechanism we shall now describe. However it is still presented as an illustration of the important principles involved.

Let us look in more detail at an ARPA-style address. A simple form is

`Fred@Destination`

Such an address is deceptive in its simplicity. All we have to do is to look up "`Destination`" in some index to obtain a network address for a transport service call. The call is placed to the mail server process at that network address, and the message is sent using SMTP. This is the way that mail used to be sent on the ARPANET.

As time went on, two things happened. One was that several other mail networks grew up beside the ARPANET. There are several of these, but some of the larger ones are CSNET, UUCP, BITNET/EARN, and JANET. All these are non-commercial networks. At the same time there has been a rapid growth of mail networks whose existence is purely commercial. Of course, people wish to send mail to all these other networks. The way that has grown up is to have a set of gateways joining these networks. For example the gateway between ARPA and JANET used to be run by University College, London. (This has now changed, but the principles remain the same.) Its ARPA address was `UCL-CS.ARPA`. Thus, to send a message from ARPA to a user "Ford Prefect" at JANET address `UK.AC.NCL.MTS`, the following might have been employed:

> Ford_Prefect%UK.AC.NCL.MTS@UCL-CS.ARPA

What this means is *"send the message to the ARPANET address* UCL-CS.ARPA*"*, the gateway to JANET. When the message arrives at the gateway, the destination "Ford_Prefect%UK.AC.NCL.MTS" is examined. This is recognised to be an onward address on JANET. The "%" is used to separate the destination from the user, and the address is converted at the gateway to

> Ford_Prefect@UK.AC.NCL.MTS

We see that the message has been routed through a specific gateway. This is fine while there is but one gateway. However, should there be more than one gateway, the fact that the message route has been specified through one particular gateway excludes the possibility of using any other gateway. We shall re-examine some of the issues here in the chapter on gateways. However it should be said that this technique of overloading the onward routing of a message onto the "recipient" is a fairly powerful one. Some of the messages that eventually stagger into the author's mailbox have a truly impressive list of gateways specified in their return path. A fictional, but realistic address might be

> Distant_Cousin%Second_Gate%Final_Gate%Last_Host@First_Gate

For this technique to work, it is important that the recipient field be left strictly alone by the mailing systems en route. Thus, messages destined for CSNET frequently have a whole series of exclamation marks in them, while such marks are not used in ARPA addresses.

> Charmion_Davis%visor!cramer!isocron@CSNET-GATE

If ARPA insisted that these !-marks not appear, then this would stop the exchange of messages with CSNET. Fortunately, mail networks pass such foreign notation through precisely in order that interworking can take place.

For this technique to work when sending a message through a series of gateways, the source and destination addresses have to be manipulated as each gateway is traversed so that the return route may be constructed. We return to this subject later in the chapter on gateways.

10.3   Domain Structure

The snag with maintaining very large networks is that it is very difficult to maintain the index for looking up the destination address. If the index is maintained somewhere centrally and then copies are sent out periodically, there is a gap between the centralised index being updated and the distributed copies being updated too. The solution is simple—distribute the index more often. But, as the index gets bigger then the cost of distributing it increases because of its size. In addition, the number of places that want their own copy increases at the same rate, so the total update traffic goes up as the square of the size of the index. If we argue that the rate of change will also increase linearly with the size of the index, then the maintenance of an absolute fidelity will cause the frequency of distribution also to increase at the same rate. The total network traffic just to maintain the index may thus increase with the cube of the size of the index.

In addition to this, we have briefly mentioned the problems with binding a route to a specific gateway too early. Thus, if there are two gateways, it would be advantageous to use alternate gateways when one gateway had a problem, or was taken out of service. Likewise, it would be useful to exploit a new gateway as soon as it becomes available, rather than several months later when the senders get around to updating the destination for a particular person which they have put into some file somewhere and just use regularly without thinking.

The usual solution for such problems is to split the total index hierarchically. Thus, the addressing space becomes not merely a flat space but a series of nested domains. Each of the domains then becomes more manageable and if the directory lookup function is stored on an easily accessible yet easily maintainable server, then it becomes possible to exploit new gateways in a timely fashion. As an example, consider Fig 10.1, which is taken from the ARPANET documentation.

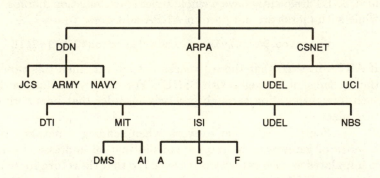

Fig 10.1.   The ARPANET Domain Organisation

An address in this tree structured space might then become something like "`B.ISI.ARPA`" or "`UDEL.CSNET`". (Note here that the most significant part of the address—the "larger" domain—comes at the end of the address, and thus the address must be processed from right to left rather than left to right. In this it follows the fairly traditional way of addressing written letters with the most important part of the address on the lower lines, and the more local parts on the upper lines. There is some disagreement on whether this, or the reverse order is "right", and futile arguments are used to support one form or the other. For the final definitive judgement on Big-Endians versus Little-Endians the reader is referred to Swift (1726).

Suppose that we have a domain-structured address such as

```
A_Person@B.ISI.ARPA
```

The treatment of this address depends on where the address is being processed. Should the message originate within the CSNET domain, then the final part "ARPA" will be recognised as indicating another domain. In other words, a *wildcard* kind of match will be performed by matching "<anything>.ARPA". No attempt is made to process the less significant part—the "B.ISI"-part—and the wildcard match will result in an address of a gateway that gets closer to the ARPA domain. When it passes through the gateway, the address is re-evaluated. If we assume the one gateway gets to ARPA (in principle, a chain of gateways might be needed depending on the topology, and on the routing tables) the higest level domain, the network domain is correct, so that resolution of the next part "ISI" will be sought from the address server. Actually, the whole address will be processed by the server, but this time the match will be of more than just the ARPA-part. This server will resolve this part, and will essentially indicate another server where resolution of the next part, the B within the ISI domain, can be performed. So we see that address resolution servers will be allocated to nodes within the domain tree. It might be that the servers used in series can reach the final intended destination (as is the case within ARPA for our example), or it might be that they merely denote a temporary staging post (as when the message is sent across CSNET to the ARPA gateway). Note that the actual route is resolved at the time that the message is sent. Thus, if there are two gateways between CSNET and ARPA, then the most appropriate one can be chosen by the initial address server rather than at some earlier time when the sender first finds the initial route that works, and never bothers to change it, even when a more appropriate gateway comes on stream.

Exercise 10.1 Consider an hierarchical address scheme a) with a single global directory, and b) with directories attached to nodes of the tree.

What differences in traffic patterns would you expect? (Consider both the query traffic and the update traffic.) Would it be advantageous to duplicate any of the servers? What drawbacks would there be with such duplication?

Though we have described an hierarchical domain addressing system in terms of separate physical networks with gateways between them, and given ARPA and CSNET as our prime example, the structure is more flexible than this. The domain structure may be purely administrative, and need not actually map directly onto real networks at all. To take an example, in the UK, the academic community which consists of Universities and government funded research bodies, maintains a separate physical network called JANET. An hierarchically structured naming service has grown up in association with this. On the front of these addresses (the most significant part) comes a qualifier "`UK.AC`" standing for the "UK Academic Community". To a good approximation, this is currently equivalent to "JANET". Within this the various universities have their own domains within which sub-domains and eventually hosts or services are registered. Thus, "`UK.AC.DUR.MTS`" indicates a particular service, MTS, at the University of Durham that can be reached by calling a particular X.25 address on JANET. However, it is quite conceivable that the JANET network could be discontinued, and all University services attached directly to a new public X.25 network run by a commercial carrier such as Mercury and supplying the majority of the commercial X.25 traffic in the country. The access to `UK.AC` sites would then be by a mechanism that is shared by many public commercial services. However, it would still be convenient to group all the `UK.AC` sites together in the same hierarchical domain system. The network addresses would have a different pattern, but the administrative structure of the academic community would be unchanged.

Another aspect of this domain system is that several new domains have been added alongside the topmost domains in Fig 10.1. For example, `CD` for Canada, `EARN`, and the `UK.AC` we have already referred to. The various networks each need to recognise the extra "foreign" domains and route the messages through the corresponding gateways. The result is that as far as the user goes, the various networks have to a large extent been combined into one larger whole, and considerations of explicit gateway routing have disappeared with the attendant benefits for the user.

We see that the domain concept has been used in two very different ways—both as a way of dividing up the original ARPANET that had grown too big, and as a way of uniting different networks together into a logical whole. The main objection to this arrangement is that the domain organisation of Fig 10.1 did not anticipate the need for a top level of "`USA`", and some object to whole countries being in some way sub-divisions of the USA. However, as the world moves towards the acceptance of ISO addresses as described later in this chapter, even this virility objection will disappear.

Of course, desirable though such an hierarchical arrangement is, the changeover from the old arrangement to the new one is a gradual procedure, and necessitates a long period of several years of overlap during which the two styles of address must coexist.

We will return to the consideration of domain structured addresses when we look at directory services in the next chapter.

10.4   Other Mail Networks

So far in this chapter we have looked at the characteristics of network mail systems and the protocols to support them. We have concentrated primarily on the ARPANET model as being one of the biggest mail networks. However, there are many other mail networks in existence, and the reader may wonder why we have hardly mentioned them at all. Partly, it is a matter of time and space. An exhaustive study of many networks would take a lot of space. In addition, this book is concerned primarily with principles—laying a foundation with which the reader may proceed to understand the idiosyncrasies of particular or even peculiar mail networks. Even ignoring this aim, the coverage of the ARPANET mail protocols should give a moderately good coverage for many networks since the protocols are actually widely used outside the ARPANET. The SMTP protocol is often used to transfer messages from one system to another independently of whether the ARPANET transport protocol (TCP) is used.

Even where SMTP is not employed, the ARPANET specification for the content of the messages—the specification of the header fields—is still often used. It is not unusual to find messages formatted in the ARPANET fashion, but transferred between hosts using, say, a file transfer protocol in place of SMTP. Some "Mail Networks" do not have an identifiable physical network at all, but may be merely an administrative agreement to exchange mail using a specific set of protocols—perhaps including some of the ARPANET protocols. The MAILNET network, during its brief life, was an example of such a mail network. The physical network used was a combination of dial-up telephone links and X.25 calls across public national and international data networks.

Another network that transfers many messages is the BITNET, NETNORTH, EARN network. This "network" is based on IBM machines that exchange files bilaterally using proprietary IBM protocols on point-to-point links—often leased lines. Depending on addressing information, the file may be forwarded through several machines to its final destination. A semi-informal mail system has grown on top of this by passing messages in some of the files in a format that is in the same spirit as the ARPANET message format, but actually of several differing forms. The network has grown from the original BITNET in the

USA, not only by non-IBM computers implementing the same set of protocols, but also by other countries implementing the protocols too (NETNORTH in Canada, and EARN across Europe, the middle East, and Africa), and gateways to most of the other major mail networks, including ARPANET, CSNET, UUCP, and JANET. Messages are usually delivered very quickly—often within minutes, but sometimes very slowly—as one year end when a certain gateway machine was shut down from before Christmas until after the New Year with consequent chaos caused by returned messages. Here again, there is no corresponding identifiable communications subnetwork since some of the links are leased and some are shared with other functions, or even use X.25 virtual circuits.

10.5   X.400 Mail Systems

Many of these mail networks are "research" networks "only". They are not open to public, and particularly not to commercial users. There are many informal agreements between the organisations running these networks that each will handle non-commercial traffic to and from the other network on the basis of *"I'll send your mail if you'll send mine"*. Much of the time this works amazingly well, and the author has sent and received literally thousands of messages using such networks and the gateways between them. However, this is not an entirely satisfactory state of affairs. One problem is in knowing when a marginally commercial message shouldn't really be sent using such networks. Another is that there is apparently a very large commercial market available, and to supply such a market, international standards are needed as well as a network run by public carriers, so that commercially confidential information can be entrusted to appropriate bodies.

In addition, message traffic needs not only to send readable text, but also various other forms of data. Often source programs are exchanged via messages, and even binary object programs may be sent. However, character-based message protocols tend to be somewhat cavalier with binary data, and strategems such as translating bytes into hexadecimal representation first and attaching high-level checksums and suchlike are necessary to make this type of traffic reliable. Message systems need to solve the problem of other data types—voice, teletext pictures, and new types not yet anticipated.

This is why the X.400 series of protocols were agreed by the CCITT in 1984 and 1988. X.400 is being adopted by a wide range of public and private networks, and will undoubtedly completely supersede the older mail protocols.

As usual, there is a range of jargon to learn. The main functional elements of the system are illustrated in Fig 10.2.

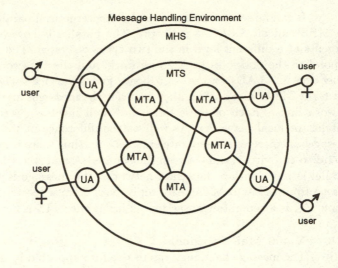

Fig 10.2.   The X.400 Message Handling Environment

The total conglomeration is referred to as a *Message Handling Environment*. This includes all the elements of the system plus the users who (or that) use the system. The users interact with the message handling system by means of interactions with *User Agents*—UAs. The X.400 recommendations define the internal workings of the *Message Handling System*—MHS, but they do not define the interaction between the users and the UAs. This is in recognition of the fact that such interfaces will often be part of an operating system. Indeed the "users" may be inanimate automata that send messages to others of their kind, or to humans. In addition, the user interface is the place where many vendors may wish to add value to the system by adding useful filing and cross referencing facilities for example, or by constructing a particularly simple and "friendly" interface. UAs correspond roughly to the mailboxes that we talked about when describing the ARPA messaging protocols.

The point of the whole conglomeration, then is to allow users to send and receive messages via their own friendly UA. To do this the messages are shifted between the source and destination UAs via the *Message Transfer System*—MTS. This core system consists of a set of *Message Transfer Agents*—MTAs that are interconnected in a mesh. We see that there is a nested hierarchy of systems. The core system is this MTS that consists of co-operating MTAs. Around the MTS is connected the set of UAs, and this makes up the total MHS. The total Message Handling Environment is made up of the MHS, the users, and the interfaces between the users and the MHS.

It can be seen that there is a striking structural parallel between the MHS and an X.3/X.25 network. The parallel is however between elements at a different level in the two types of system The MTAs correspond to the nodes of the X.25 network, and the UAs correspond to either the X.3 PADs or the X.25 hosts giving service. The links between the MTAs along which they transfer the messages are themselves network links. Each of these links may well involve a series of X.25 switches or local networks. As well as the difference in the levels, the messages themselves are separate entities, and thus there is no notion of an end-to-end virtual call between the source UA and receiving UA. The parallel is more with a datagram network—the message is transferred in toto from MTA to MTA. Any reply back from a receiving UA to a source UA is a separate transaction as far as the MTS is concerned.

10.6   X.400 Mail Protocols

The message handling system itself is supported by several protocols that allow the constituent entities to interact to supply the message service. Consider Fig 10.3. There we see that the UAs talk end-to-end using the P2 protocol. Inside the MTS the MTAs talk to each other using protocol P1 to exchange the messages. This corresponds loosely with the ARPA protocols SMTP (cf P1) to transfer the messages across a link, and RFC822 (cf P2) to define the header format.

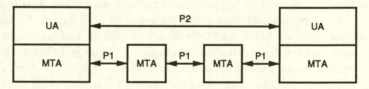

Fig 10.3.   Some of the X.400 Protocols

We have encountered the ASN.1 notation in Chapter 8 in the context of presentation syntax. ASN.1 originates from X.409, and was developed to describe the protocols and data structures in the X.400 series of protocols. We shall look at a little of its application in this area. However, even the description of the single protocol P1 in X.411 takes six pages of ASN.1 notation plus another 17 pages of mixed ASN.1 notation and text. The whole X.400(84) series of recommendations is 266 pages—and that includes references to other standards! We can thus see that a complete decypherment is beyond the present tome, and we shall have to be satisfied with a few illustrative examples.

The messages making up P1 are *Message Protocol Data Units*— MPDUs. MPDUs come in two classes—one containing a user message, and the other containing either a delivery report or a "probe". A "probe" is a request to another MTA for information about whether a message can be sent successfully in this direction towards a UA. This range of possibilities is expressed in ASN.1 as

```
MPDU ::= CHOICE{ [0] IMPLICIT UserMPDU, ServiceMPDU}

ServiceMPDU ::= CHOICE{[1] IMPLICIT DeliveryReportMPDU,
                       [2] IMPLICIT ProbeMPDU
                       }
```

Thinking back to the way ASN.1 is represented via the Basic Encoding Rules we thus see that an incoming MPDU may be examined for a leading "opcode". Depending upon whether this is 0, 1, or 2 we can recognise this MPDU as one of the three basic types of *Protocol Data Unit*—PDU. The UserMPDU transfers a user message, but with a header containing some information pertaining to this transfer between MTAs:

```
UserMPDU ::= SEQUENCE {UMPDUEnvelope, UMPDUContent}
```

that is, a header part and a content part in strict order. The UMPDContent is just defined as a string of octets, that is, arbitrary bytes. We shall return to this later. The envelope contains a set of fields:

```
UMPDUEnvelope ::= SET {
              MPDUIdentifier.
              originator ORName,
              original EncodedInformationTypes OPTIONAL,
              ContentType,
              UAContentID OPTIONAL,
              Priority DEFAULT normal
              PerMessageFlag DEFAULT{},
              deferredDelivery [0] IMPLICIT Time OPTIONAL,
              [1] IMPLICIT SEQUENCE OF PerDomainBilateralInfo
                       OPTIONAL,
              [2] IMPLICIT SEQUENCE OF Recipientinfo,
              Traceinformation
              }
```

That is, the envelope consists of a set of fields, each of which gives some information. Since this is a set, the order is not important, and the fields must thus be distinguishable one from another by means of their structure. One of these fields, the MPDUIdentifier is defined by

```
MPDUIdentifier ::=[APPLICATION 4] IMPLICIT SEQUENCE
              {GlobalDomainIdentifier,
              IA5String
              }
```

We are now nearly at the leaves of the tree of productions, since

```
GlobalDomainIdentifier ::=[APPLICATION 3] IMPLICIT SEQUENCE
                           {CountryName,
                            AdministrationDomainName,
                            PrivateDomainIdentifier OPTIONAL }

CountryName ::=          [APPLICATION 1] CHOICE
                           {NumericString,
                            PrintableString}
```

and similar productions for the other two fields.

We thus see that the detailed syntax of the MPDUs is built up by a very precise definition of the allowable fields. This is not to say of course that the syntax of other messaging protocols is necessarily poorly defined. Indeed, the syntax of the ARPANET messaging protocols is also very precisely defined using another variant of BNF productions.

It is instructive to examine another pair of productions in this protocol:

```
ORName ::=              [APPLICATION 0] IMPLICIT SEQUENCE
                           {StandardAttributeList,
                            DomainDefinedAttributeList OPTIONAL}

StandardAttributeList ::=SEQUENCE
                           {CountryName OPTIONAL,
                            AdministrativeDomainName OPTIONAL
                            [0] IMPLICIT X121Address OPTIONAL,
                            [1] IMPLICIT TerminalID OPTIONAL,
                            [2] PrivateDomainName OPTIONAL,
                            [3] IMPLICIT OrganizationName OPTIONAL,
                            [4] IMPLICIT UniqueUAIdentifier OPTIONAL,
                            [5] IMPLICIT PersonalName OPTIONAL,
                            [6] IMPLICIT SEQUENCE OF OrganizationalUnit
                                OPTIONAL}
```

These two productions define the main structure of an O/R name—the name of the originator or recipient of a message. The reader may remember that we made passing reference to the varied structure of names in the ARPANET and other environments which exchanged mail. The problem is that the various hierarchically related parts of the address had to appear in a specific order, and different people or organisations had different ideas about which order was best—Big-Endians and Little-Endians. This way of defining names as a structure avoids the problem of becoming embroiled in futile discussion since all of the constituent parts are labelled (as tagged types). In fact, the grammar does define that they appear in a specific sequence (since SEQUENCE rather than SET is used in the production). However, the definition does not rely on this order since the elements are all separately labelled (tagged). The first two entries, CountryName and AdministrationDomainName are also tagged (in further productions of the grammar) in such a way that they too cannot be confused with other elements.

We said above that the UMPDContent, the content of the P1 user PDUs, was just defined as a string of bytes. This string of bytes is transported across the MTS from MTA to MTA using only the P1 protocol to reach its destination User Agent. This string of bytes is passed uninterpreted, and its contents are none of the business of the MTAs making up the MTS. In fact X.400 defines that these contents should be the end-to-end PDU's between UA's. They are the messages complete with their headers that make up the P2 protocol. There are some relationships between the P2 PDUs and the P1 protocol carrying them. However, it is important that these relationships should not be exploited. The reason for this is that the two protocols should be kept quite separate. This allows the protocols to be developed separately—for example to try out a new P2 protocol independently of P1 (or vice versa). One obvious variant might be that the P2 PDU's might be encrypted on a bilateral peer-to-peer basis between UAs without disturbing the P1 protocol used within the MTS.

The messages themselves are passed end-to-end from UA to UA using the protocol P2. Mainly, this defines the format of the header and body of the message. It is worth looking at a few of the main constituent productions of the definition:

```
UAPDU ::= CHOICE{[0] IMPLICIT IM-UAPDU,
                 [1] IMPLICIT SR-UAPDU
                 }
```

i.e. there are two sorts of UAPDU—PDUs exchanged by User Agents—and inter-personal messages or Status Reports. The IM-UAPDU is a SEQUENCE {Heading, Body}, and the Heading is defined by

```
Heading ::= SET{
    IPMessageId,
    originator         [0] IMPLICIT ORDescriptor OPTIONAL,
    authorizingUsers  [1] IMPLICIT SEQUENCE OF ORDescriptor OPTIONAL,
    primaryRecipients[2] IMPLICIT SEQUENCE OF Recipient OPTIONAL,
    . . .
    subject            [8] CHOICE {T61String} OPTIONAL,
    . . .}
```

Here we have shown only five of the possible fifteen fields. The first field is a structure that contains the ORName in the form that we described for the P1 protocol, and a printable string. The other fields are obvious corollaries of the fields in the ARPANET message format. The message body is perhaps slightly more structured than might at first be expected:

```
Body     ::= SEQUENCE OF BodyPart

BodyPart ::= CHOICE{[0] IMPLICIT IA5Text,
                    [1] IMPLICIT TLX,
                    [2] IMPLICIT Voice,
                    [3] IMPLICIT G3Fax,
                    [4] IMPLICIT TIF0,
                    [5] IMPLICIT TTX,
                    [6] IMPLICIT Videotex,
                    [7] NationallyDefined,
                    [8] IMPLICIT Encrypted,
                    [9] IMPLICIT ForwardedIPMessage,
                    [10] IMPLICIT SFD,
                    }
```

Without going through these in detail, we can see that this description of the contents allows the possibility of mixing a large variety of formats for the data to be passed in the body of the messages. Though this is allowed, and the tags allow the recipient to sort out which kind of data constitutes the message, sending, say, a Videotex message does not ensure that the recipient can necessarily interpret the contents. The sender must first ensure that the recipient can handle the type of message body. However, this does address one of the points that we made in the introduction to X.400—that an ever increasing diversity of information types is being transferred by message, and some recognition of this in the protocol is a very useful step. One of the other interesting fields is the ForwardedMessage. This is a recursive definition that may include a complete forwarded message (which may itself contain a forwarded message (which itself ...)).

We shall not describe the format of status report PDUs, but merely note that these are the means by which UAs communicate information concerning such things as whether, when, and why a message was delivered to its intended recipient, forwarded as directed, and suchlike.

Our simple model above has assumed that the UAs and the MTAs know to whom they are talking. In other words, the possibility of a fake entity masquerading as a MTA and "stealing" messages destined for some other recipient, or of generating fake messages is not really addressed. It is assumed that this area of security is controlled by other means. For example, the MTA's would probably have a list of the addresses of other MTAs, and would check them against the reliable network addresses supplied by the communications subnetwork. It would also be common for UAs to be implemented within the same computer operating system as their nearest MTA. In this way the protocols P1 and P2 would be sufficient for the construction of a complete messaging system. However, X.400 recognises that some, possibly many, User Agents will be implemented within personal microcomputer systems. Such systems are likely to connect with their local MTA via an occasional dial-up telephone connection or X.25 call. Such connections are not so susceptible of checking by means of network address and so a further protocol, P3 is defined by which a UA may communicate with a remote MTA. P3 allows the UA to LOGON to the remote MTA, (requiring an identifier and password), SUBMIT and have DELIVERed messages, perform various other management processes across the link such as change parameters, probe for the possibility of delivering messages, receive NOTIFIcations about previous failures and, finally, LOGOFF.

X.400 recognises that message services will be supplied by various organisations such as public carriers or PTTs, or private organisations. The service supplied by these organisations may be a publically available service, such as public carriers or PTT's traditionally supply, or such as the newer commercial companies are now able to market. The service may be restricted to some sort of community like the ARPANET military/research community, or the JANET academic/research community, or they may be completely private to a company, such as the very large "internal" networks operated by, for example, DEC or Ford. X.400 allows for "management domains" of one or more MTAs, possibly with some UA's. Typically, a message may traverse several management domains before reaching its destination UA. X.400 classifies management domains into "administration domains" (those domains that are run by public carriers or PTT's) and "private domains" (those run by other bodies). It is recognised that messages will often traverse both public and private domains.

10.7   Conferencing

We have looked at computer messaging systems in some depth. Another aspect of human communication with the aid of computers is computer conferencing. There is no generally accepted definition of computer conferencing, but one school of practise takes many of the activities that go on in real human conferences and uses a computer to organise analogous operations within a computer. Such systems typically support several "conferences" and individual persons may become observers or perhaps full participants of each conference. People may start a "discussion"—which roughly corresponds to something between a formal presentation with a question session at the end on the one hand,

and an informal discussion among a small group of people in the bar on the other. However, all members of the conference will be able to see the discussion, and respond to it, or perhaps "forget" this particular discussion if it is not of interest for some reason. Conferences often benefit from a moderator or chairman to guide the discussion if some specific target is to be achieved.

The sender may have noticed a resemblance between conferencing and exchanging messages. Indeed, the main difference seems to be in the way in which the individual contributions may be organised and manipulated by the recipient-cum-participant. The simplest mailing systems merely allow the sequential receipt of messages, and perhaps their filing for future reference. Such systems are not suitable for much more than simple person-to-person dialogue. More complex mailing systems allow messages to be filed automatically in folders and operations on folders to be performed such as filing according to keywords in the subject field, etc. Sometimes it is possible to search the folders according to certain criteria—for example, the appearance of some keyword. This sort of mailing system is getting quite close in function to a conferencing system given a set of mailing lists that correspond to the membership lists of conferences, and the distinction is less clearcut than before.

Few mailing systems support the complete set of organisational tools that are expected of the more sophisticated conferencing systems. However, there is no generally agreed distinction between the two types of system, and consequently fierce arguments about the differences tend to take place, including in these mail/conferencing systems themselves.

The reader can expect no resolution of this question in this tome. However, it should be noted that extensive discussion does take place at present via the medium of message systems and mailing lists. Several megabytes per day are sent out on such mailing lists. Each such list corresponds with a conference. A discussion is identified by the same subject field on a set of messages. Typically, users may participate in a discussion by replying to one of the messages. This picks up the subject field and sends the message back to the moderator of the list. She vets the message and re-sends it out to the full mailing list for everyone to see. If a recipient becomes tired of seeing some discussion then she may instruct her mailer to discard all future messages with that particular subject field.

Whether this is an adequate substitute for full-blown conferencing depends on the quality of the user's mailing system and the user's own proclivities, but that such methods are widely used and useful is undeniable.

10.8   Human Factors

So far we have introduced network mail and conferencing, extolled their virtues, and described the technicalities of the protocols. However, there are some problems with computer-based communication that are sometimes ignored. Perhaps the most severe are those of human behaviour patterns. The successful use of computer communication depends strongly on the community of users checking their mailboxes regularly. This is usually most successful if the users are regular users of the host time-sharing system anyway. Then a moderately well written mailer usually ensures that such systems are extremely successful.

This success has sometimes lead to the enthusiastic installation of similar mailing systems to serve a less homogeneous community of users. For example, suppose that a company sees the success of such a mailing system amongst its technical staff who regularly use a time-sharing system anyway. They may be tempted to introduce the system as a primary company-wide communications system. The problem is that the employees who do not use the computer system regularly must now learn how to use the computer system, at least enough to log in and then run the mailer program. Even if this hurdle is surmounted, they then need to log in to check their mailbox regularly. If they only get very occasional messages, then the trouble of checking the mailbox daily may well not be seen as worthwhile to receive the odd message once a week or perhaps even less frequently. In addition, such novices are likely to find user-to-computer interfaces much more daunting than regular computer users who are used to having to put up with such abominations. Since many of the other potential correspondents will be suffering from the same problems at the same time such introductions are likely to fail unless managed either very skilfully or very forcefully.

Another problem that is frequently encountered with computer communication is sometimes referred to as "flaming". What seems to happen is that a ferocious argument arises for no apparently good reason, and the combatants tend to go way beyond the normal bounds of civilised debate. Violent personal abuse is not at all unusual. To observers, and those caught up in such a battle, this is often quite surprising and even shocking.

One of the most important reasons for this is that computer communication feels like informal friendly discussion. Indeed, this is one of its great virtues when conducted properly. However, it is lacking some of the essential ingredients of such discussions. The only channel of communication is what people type, and, being informal, they often dash off a reply without thinking about it sufficiently carefully. The potential for misunderstanding is all too great, particularly when the participants in the discussion are thousands of miles away from each other, and may well never have even met. Other checks and balances of normal conversation—the smile or the tone of voice indicating that the speaker is not serious, the grunt of agreement or derision, laughter, the expression on the face of the listener indicating incomprehension or indignation—are missing in computer communication today. This is because it is strictly typed text. As we have seen, X.400 is starting to admit of other data types, and there are various "multi-media" mailing systems that allow drawings and voice to accompany the message text, but we still have some considerable way to go to match the richness of human communication in the coffee room or the bar.

In addition, it must be said that some participants can be very opinionated and even immature—though such conditions are hardly the exclusive province of computer communications.

There are two ways in which the problem may be reduced. The most important is by participants learning from past experience. After all, computer communication is just a new social medium, and participants need to learn the required social skills. Now that many participants have indeed learned these skills, there is a noticeable transfer of these skills to new participants, just as there is in other social situations in which people find themselves.

Another vital touch is the reintroduction of a new channel of communication. We have commented on the lack of the normal visual symbols, such as smiling, and the way in which the data types of X.400 may offer some possibility of their reintroduction in the future. One such channel has been introduced by the low-tech device of the symbol :-). This symbol, known variously as the *smiling face* or the *tongue-in-cheek-symbol*. The convention is that when this appears in some message, the writer is not necessarily completely serious. This simple symbol may well have saved more bouts of high blood pressure than any other short sequence of letters in recent history.

10.9   Summary

In this chapter, we have explored various aspects of network mail—what it is, how it looks in general terms, and how it is implemented both using the widely implemented ARPANET protocols and the newer X.400 protocols. Finally, we have briefly mentioned computer conferencing, and the human factors which are so important in this kind of network application.

11

Application Level Services

As well as the standards for all of the lower layers, sets of standards are also being developed for the application layer itself. The actual conceptual structure of the application level is still being developed as this is being written. However, the general approach is to consider the application entity that participates in a communication as a collection of elements or *Application Service Elements*—ASEs. Thus, there may be one ASE that is concerned with the setting up of the connection (or *"Application Association"*) with the other corresponding application entity. Another may be concerned with ensuring that a bank account gets debited exactly once (rather than zero or two times in the face of errors at some critical moment). Still another may be concerned with ensuring that the part number that has come from the other entity is a valid part number, and requesting a correction from the originator if the part number is invalid, or if the part is no longer held in stock. It will be seen that some of these elements, such as establishing and releasing a connection are common across many diverse uses of networks and so are called *Common ASEs*—CASEs and others are specific to particular applications, and are thus *Specific ASEs*—SASEs. The present trend is to try to standardise CASEs as being of general utility, while it is unlikely that SASEs will ever be extensively standardised because of their more specific nature. Clearly, the categorisation of an ASE as a CASE or a SASE is somewhat arbitrary.

11.1 CASE Standards

As examples of CASE standardisation, we shall examine the association control CASE (formerly known as "Kernel CASE") and *Commitment, Concurrency, and Recovery*—CCR. The CASE Kernel is very simple, being merely the recognition that to make use of network services, two application programs ("entities") need to establish some sort of connection. Since the word "connection" implies connection-oriented working rather than connectionless working, the more neutral term "association" is used, leading to the term "Association Control" for work in this area. Thus, the CASE Kernel is concerned with the general services that are required in establishing and managing such associations at the application level. Obviously such services are of general utility, and have been standardised under the CASE grouping in order to avoid the wasteful duplication of work with all the different applications developing different ways of performing the same function.

The CCR standardisation is more complex. The reader may well remember the discussion in the early part of this book concerning error recovery, and some of the problems that we encountered in ensuring that records were transferred correctly exactly once—without omission or duplication. This general type of problem recurs at the very highest level—the application level. As examples of this, consider the transfer of a computer mail message from one machine to another, or the debiting or crediting of a bank account. Suppose that the two application entities have established the appropriate presentation connection. If application A sends a mail message to application B, and then the presentation connection fails before an acknowledgement is received, how can it know whether the message arrived or not? Similarly, if A initiates a credit or debit to a bank account managed by B, and again the connection fails, how can A know whether or not the transaction was successful? In both examples, wrongly assuming the operation was successful may result in the operation never being performed at all, and wrongly retrying the operation may result in the operation being performed a second time (or more, if further errors occur during the retry). If we review the ways that we examined of recovering at the link level, we can get some clues for ways of making the performance of application-level operations reliable *exactly once* operations even in the face of wide classes of errors.

A powerful concept is that of *idempotency*. An operation is said to be idempotent if each and every one of its applications is equally potent or effective—that is, gives the same result. For example, writing a specific record into a file at a specific position is an idempotent operation, since the second or the forty-second successful application of the same operation gives the same resulting file. However, *adding* or *appending* a specific record to the end of a file is not idempotent since the nth successful operation will add the nth copy of the said record to the file.

The designer of an individual application protocol may make all its operations idempotent by careful design and may then use this property to achieve the exactly-once state by repeating the operation until a positive acknowledgement is finally achieved. The reader will see that the repitition of the operation until an acknowledgement is received achieves "at least once" semantics, and since the operation is idempotent, the final effect is equivalent to "exactly once" semantics.

However, designing idempotent operations is not in general a simple task. In our link-level protocol we suggested that rather than transferring *"another record to add to the file"*, we could transfer *"record n of the file"* (which follows our explanation of the term above). Extending this concept to updating bank accounts would not be easy—how could we perform the nth update to a bank account, and what if two different requestors each simultaneously tried to do the nth update to the same account? In the link level case we saw that numbering records was a way of making them idempotent and thus eliminating duplicates. Providing that careful protocol design eliminated the problem of duplicates by relying on the sequential nature of a simple , or by relying on a limited lifetime of the packets, then again the problems of duplicates could be eliminated. In connectionless operation the numbering scheme has to be extended substantially, but the principles remain the same.

The CCR protocol extends these notions. The operation is two-phase. In the first phase the initiator requests the respondent to *"commit"* to a specific operation. Thus, in the example of debiting a bank account, this means that a *"commitment"* will be made that a certain debit will be possible in the future. This might mean checking the account for the requested funds, and then reserving the requested funds to ensure that they will be available in the future when the actual debit is made. While no actual debit from the account is made yet, other debits will not be allowed in the interim if they would invalidate the commitment. Now, this may all sound very well, but how has this made us more immune from certain classes of error? The point is that the initial request from the initiator, and the commitment from the respondent are each *uniquely stamped.*

We shall first explain this in the connectionless terms that we used earlier when discussing exactly-once semantics. With the initial request, the initiator uses some unique stamp. This may be a sequence number, or the date and time, or some other unique mark. This is combined with the unique identification of the request originator. There are two uses of the word "unique" here, and we need to be more specific. Request originators are application entities. All application entities in the world (or universe, or whatever grandiose word that we wish to use) must be uniquely and unambiguously identifiable by some sort of name. In OSI the specific term is *Application-Title.* This is the handle that allows application associations to be set up in the first place. For each such entity, some internal mechanism must then be used to generate an identifier unique *within that entity* for the purposes of distinguishing one operation from all others. Suitable sources of such identifiers are counters of some sort that are protected from crashes of the computer system, such as a counter on disc, or a date and time. The combination of this and the Application-Title gives a globally-unique identifier.

Thus, the requester emits the request with the unique identifier, and also ensures that once this request is initiated, a suitably protected record is made. It is essential that once a sequence is started, it will be progressed. A record is typically made on disc, and not kept in volatile memory so that if a system crash intervenes then the process can be restarted, or backed up to the last checkpoint. The uniquely stamped request arrives, and the recipient records it, and checks to see whether it can be honoured. The response is either with an offer of commitment or a refusal. Once the offer of commitment is made, then the respondent must be prepared either to proceed to the completion of the commitment, or to roll back the commitment—i.e. cancel the operation.

Why might we need something so elaborate? One of the model situations that has been presented to justify such a protocol is a guest checking into an hotel. The CCR could be used to check her credit card or bank account for the expected cost of the stay, and also to reserve that amount. The actual debit—the completion of the commitment—will be done as the guest checks out the next day or the next week.

During this time, the respondent may allow other operations depending on the nature of the committed operation and the cleverness of the implementation. Thus, in the banking account, it may allow other debits or commitments providing that the account does not become overdrawn. However, there is no explicit requirement for this within the CCR protocol. The bank account *could* remain locked—all other requests being queued waiting the completion. However, this latter option would probably not be acceptable in our hypothetical case of a guest checking into an hotel, though it might be acceptable if the two operations were a linked credit in one account and corresponding debit in another that were expected to complete within seconds.

In mentioning the transfer of funds as two linked individual transactions, we have included the "concurrency" aspect of this protocol. Thus one "master" may initiate several linked operations, and require a successful offer of commitment for all of them before proceeding with any of them. Thus, one might imagine that a process that is organising the insurance on a communications satellite may wish to spread the risk around. Thus, it might take the $100,000,000 requested, and try to pass the risk onto others in chunks. Only when it had offers of commitment from perhaps 20 other organisations for $5,000,000 each would it decide to accept the risk. Should it get offers from 18 others and not be able to place the last $10,000,000, then it could roll back all the offered commitments and send a refusal to the original requester. Thus, we see that the CCR protocol allows a complex negotiation amongst several parties to be combined into a single large atomic action. Either all the actions are eventually successful, or none are.

We still need to look at the recovery from errors. These are not errors of the communications medium, but are errors caused by one or other system "crashing" sometime, and losing some information in "volatile" memory. Assuming that the originator has established a unique request identifier in some safe queue of jobs, on a disc file somewhere, then it will emit the request. If it crashes before the request is emitted, then eventually it will reissue the request, and it will periodically reissue the request until it receives either an offer of commitment or a refusal.

At the recipient, incoming requests will be processed, either as a complete request in itself, or involving some interaction with the originator. As part of the process, the respondent will either reject the request, or decide to offer a commitment, and store some information about the commitment. This will include enough information to maintain the commitment itself (such as the amount of debt committed for example) and will also include the unique identification of the request. All this will be recorded again in some "safe" storage. If the same request is repeated—perhaps because the response was lost—then the unique identifier allows the recipient to see that this is the same request. In this way, any repetitions of the request are made idempotent—the unique identifier is serving the same function in achieving this as the sequence numbering at the link level, or as the time and date stamping in the RPC with remembered state.

Eventually, the initiator must decide either to revoke the commitment with the rollback function or to accept the commitment with *Order Commitment*. In either case the specific atomic identifier is again used. Here again, the use of the unique identifier achieves idempotency. A commitment may be ordered several times, and it will only ever be achieved the once because the local implementation will ensure the atomicity that is required. Should the commitment acknowledgement be lost, then a repeat of the commitment request will eventually result in its getting through.

All of this process has been described in connectionless terms, where the actions at the initiator (or master or superior) and at the respondent (or slave or subordinate) are tied together with the unique identifier. In the OSI case, the ability of a session to survive crashes of one or other end of the session connection by re-establishing a transport connection is exploited to replace most of the use of the unique identifier. In addition, the several synchronising tokens supplied by the session service are used to represent the start of the action, the offer (or refusal) of commitment, the request for the commitment to be honoured or revoked, and the request for a restart of the whole process.

We have described this CASE CCR protocol in terms of exactly-once semantics. As we have said before, nothing in this life is perfect, and this protocol does not actually provide *perfectly* once-only semantics, except under certain assumptions. The protocol will actually recover from certain classes of error as it is supposed to, but it is as important to realise the limitations of *any* technique as it is to understand its virtues. The protocol has been described in terms of two co-operating processes that keep persisting, in the face of "crashes", in trying to complete or abandon the atomic action. Thus, it is assumed that each of the parties will indeed resume after a crash. Of course there might be all sorts of reasons why the procedure will not be resumed ranging from the mundane bug to the dramatic burn-down-the-building type of fire, earthquake or flood. In addition, the recording of certain information "in a safe place", in particular when the subordinate commits to an action, is usually described in terms of recording information on disc rather than in volatile memory. Those who have spent long nights repairing the wreckage to a filing system left by a disc crash may be less inclined to view this as a "safe" place than others. As always, things are better or worse, safer or less safe by degrees. What the CCR protocol is giving us is a technique for improving the reliability of an action from that of a computer process to that of a disc file. Should this improvement not be enough, then other techniques for recording the checkpoints can be devised—such as recording the information twice on two different disc spindles perhaps, or twice on two different systems in concrete bunkers on two different continents. The technique is the same. The degree of improvement depends on the implementer and the requirements that she is trying to meet.

11.2   Remote Operations

As yet another important example of an application protocol that has been factored out and made into a generally useful tool is the *Remote Operations Service*—ROS. This originated with the X.410 recommendation *Remote Operations and Reliable Transfer Server* that was defined as part of the 1984 Message Handling work by the CCITT. This was identified by ECMA as having wide utility in the work on distributed systems that ECMA was studying, and has been adopted by both the CCITT and ISO as a generally useful tool for specifying applications level protocols.

ROS is closely related to the remote procedure calls that we meet in other places in this book. The basic idea is that an application entity in one location desires the performance of an operation of some sort by a peer application entity in some other system. It does this by sending a formalised message to the other entity requesting the action, and giving some parameters for the action. The entity may then wait for the completion of the action, probably getting either some results or a failure message. Possibly there may be no response at all to the request and the initiating entity may proceed immediately the request has been dispatched. In this way it is very similar to the remote procedure call type of operation that has been the basis of many research and of some production network architectures. A remote procedure call is just the same as a normal, or local procedure call except that instead of the procedure call being executed within the local environment, the procedure call is exported in some form, complete with its parameters, and executed in a remote system. The results of the procedure call—either a normal result or an error indication—are then returned to the calling system. The primary difference is that with ROS it is possible to specify a remote operation that never has a response, not even an error message, and thus the initiator and responder are not necessarily interlocked by the single thread of control from initiator to responder and back as they are with RPC. That is, with RPC the initiator must always wait until the signalled response from the responder, whereas with ROS it is possible to specify operations with no response.

The basic template for defining new remote operations is

```
<name of operation> OPERATION
        ARGUMENT <type of operation's parameters>
        RESULT <type of operation's results>
        ERRORS <list of possible errors>
            ::= <operation code>
```

and each returning error has possible accompanying information:

```
<name of error> ERROR
        PARAMETER <type of information with this error>
            ::= <error code>
```

To allow freedom in defining operations without parameters, results or errors, the corresponding parts of the template are optional, and similarly the error message's parameters are also optional.

As an example of such an operation, suppose we have a remote name server to which we can send a name as an IA5 string, and expect to receive an X.25 address in response. We shall assume that the possible errors are that the number is unknown, or that the service is temporarily unavailable. In the latter case an estimate, in minutes, until the time when the service will again be available is supplied as a parameter.

```
requestX25Number OPERATION
        ARGUMENT destinationName IA5String - - Look up this name
        RESULT Digits
        ERRORS {nameUnknown, serverTemporarilyUnavailable}
            ::= 1

nameUnknown ERROR
            ::= 2
```

```
serverTemporarilyUnavailable ERROR
    PARAMETER estimatedMinutesTillAvailable INTEGER
    ::= 3
```

Given these definitions in ASN.1, the rest of the ROS protocol is defined. The ROS protocol is very simple. It uses just four Protocol Data Units:

- Invoke send the request to the responder
- ReturnResult brings back a result if there has been no error
- ReturnError if there was an error
- Reject used if there was a protocol error—a violation of the ROS protocol itself, or of the particular definitions within this particular ROS protocol.

The actual encoding of the ROS PDU's is defined by the definitions:

```
OPDU      ::=   CHOICE {[1] Invoke, [2] ReturnResult,
                      [3] ReturnError, [4] Reject}
Invoke    ::=   SEQUENCE {invokeID INTEGER, OPERATION,
                      argument ANY}
ReturnResult ::= SEQUENCE {invokeID INTEGER, result ANY}
ReturnError ::= SEQUENCE {invokeID INTEGER, ERROR,
                      parameter ANY}
Reject    ::=   SEQUENCE {
                      CHOICE {INTEGER, NULL},
                      problem CHOICE {
                          [0] IMPLICIT GeneralProblem,
                          [1] IMPLICIT InvokeProblem,
                          [2] IMPLICIT ReturnResultProblem,
                          [3] IMPLICIT ReturnEerrorProblem
                      }
                }
```

plus further definitions for the four classes of problems.

This formal definition specifies that each PDU will have a leading opcode of 1, 2, 3, or 4 specifying the type of PDU. Most PDU's then have an invocation ID, and this is then followed by specific information from the specific protocol definitions. The fact that most of the ROS protocol is already defined means that the designer at the application level only needs to design the application specific part as a series of ASN.1 definitions. Once this is done then the protocol is complete and there is no further protocol design to be done. Of course, the actions of both of the peer entities need to be programmed, but this is a matter outside the protocol in any case. We can see then that the ROS environment takes much of the chore of designing irrelevant detail out of the hands of the protocol designer, and he is left with the application-specific part of the protocol design. ROS is very widely used as a tool in a very wide range of application level protocols.

11.3   Upper Layer Architecture

The early forms of communication were comparatively unstructured. For example, HASP multi-leaving mixed up many concepts that we now treat quite separately, and some concepts such as network-level routing were not even present. This is not a criticism of HASP—as one of the earliest communications systems, its foresight in developing new concepts and its success in terms of "market penetration" and data shifted are unrivalled. However, as time progressed, it became necessary to develop and separate many of the common communications facilities into separate identifiable layers. This evolution is still proceeding as this is written in the late 1980's. The concepts pertaining to the lower layers of link-level, network-level and end-to-end transport connections are reasonably well agreed—though there are of course substantial groups that cling to differing opinions about certain aspects. Essentially, a transport connection gives an end-to-end bit pipe that operates with a specified bit error rate that is deemed to be adequate for the application in hand. This bit pipe may (depending on the options of the transport service) recover from various network failures, may make use of multiplexing for a cheaper connection, or may split the traffic over several network connections if increased throughput is required. On the other hand, the higher levels of protocol deal mainly with quite different concepts. They take the reliable bit-pipe as given and mould it in various ways in order to make of it a more useful service for communications at the higher level.

We have been considering some of the issues involved in the higher layers by looking at the two main types of terminal support, file transfer and access, and mail transfer. In particular we have identified "presentation"—the representation of abstract data items such as integers or character strings—as one of the important issues. We have also seen that some applications wish to exchange tokens to control their conversation, for example when accessing a shared data structure associated with screen mode terminals. The work in developing the ISO OSI model of open communications has identified many issues in this area. As this is written, there are still many issues left to resolve, but many are quite clear in principle, and thus we shall take some time to look at these principles.

When all is said and done in communications, the name of the game is to allow two (or more) computer processes to co-operate in some task. The tasks may be many and varied, such as driving a user terminal, transferring a file or a job, accessing several bank accounts, ordering parts and negotiating transport for them and the best price on the deal, managing a credit card transaction from the time a guest first books into an hotel until the time that she leaves several days later, operating a remote milling machine, and on and on. Since the one architecture is expected to cover all these diverse possibilities, it should not be surprising that the whole architecture is complex and contains many features that may be essential for one sector of the market but irrelevant for another. For this reason, many of the facilities, particularly at these higher levels, are optional and are open to negotiation. Let us start then with the general case of two application processes that wish. to communicate and examine how the various diverse requirements are catered for in the structure (or "architecture") of the layers above the transport layer.

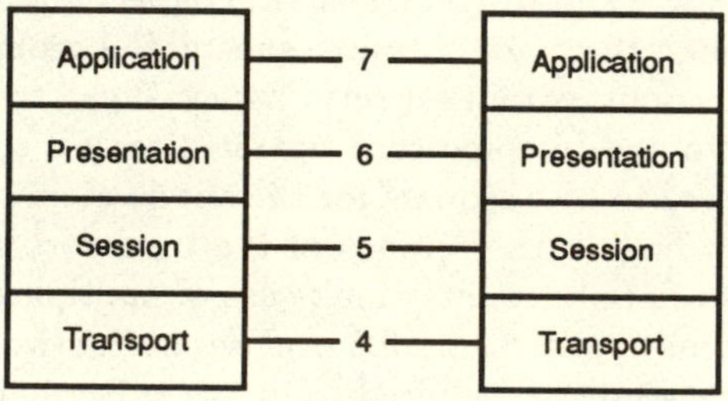

Fig 11.1.   The Four Upper OSI Layers

The ISO model of communication has three layers above the bit pipe that is provided by the transport layer. It is envisaged that *Application Entities*—processes within a computer—will communicate using the transport layer. We have studied the various issues involved in presentation in some considerable detail. These allow two entities in radically different computers to communicate using one or other of various sets of *Abstract Syntaxes* for the communication. It is the business of the presentation layer to supply the appropriate facilities for selecting and using the appropriate syntaxes. Let us now look at the facilities supplied by the session layer.

We have seen that while some sorts of connection, such as those supporting "dumb terminals" work in "full duplex" with the two flows of data taking place independently, other sorts of connection impose more order on the data stream by employing tokens to control and regularise the access to a shared resource, such as a display screen. This control of the dialogue by the exchange of tokens is one of the duties assigned to the "session layer". In the simplest case no tokens are employed, and the conversation is free-running in both directions—"full duplex". In other cases the application may make use of session level tokens. (Actually, the application layer can only use the services of the presentation layer, but let us ignore this distinction for the sake of simplicity for the present.) The tokens may be as simple as exchanging a single token for access to a single resource—"two-way alternate" or the application may be more complex as in the case of the CCR (Commitment Concurrency and Recovery) protocol that we shall deal with presently.

Another service that may be supplied by the session layer is concerned with the missmatch of the duration of the interaction time between application entities at the top level, and the duration normally expected to occur at the transport layer. Typically, two application entities may interact (participate in an *Application Association*) to perform some task. This interaction may last for a short time and involve moderately intensive activity, such as transferring a small file. In this case it is natural to employ a single transport connection. Other interactions may be more varied in nature. For example, a group of suspicious characters could arrive in a restaurant, and since the proprietor is anxious to ensure that they are able to pay before leaving, she might insist on checking their credit cards. She could estimate the bill, and make a reservation with the credit card company for the appropriate amount of money before the diners are served with their first drink. This is the start of the application association—between the restaurateur's intelligent credit card processor and the credit computer on the other side of the globe. The next interaction is two hours later when the merrymakers are finished and the bill is totalled up. The two computers co-operate in the debiting of the precise amount of money. The Application Association has lasted two hours, but it is natural to map this onto two shorter transport connections—one for the original credit check and reservation of money, and the other for the settling of the final bill. The session layer performs this kind of mapping of one application association onto the appropriate set of transport connections.

Note that, once again, we seem to have duplicated the functions that occur at the lower levels. The transport layer may also map a single transport connection onto several network connections. This may happen for a couple of reasons at the transport layer—the network connection may be insufficiently reliable and the transport layer may be improving the reliability by re-establishing broken network connections, or the duration charges on network connections may be high and the transport layer may be economising by clearing the network connection during times when the transport connection is idle and not passing data. The reasons at the session layer are different. In the credit card case it is plain to the application that the next transaction is likely to be some considerable time later when the meal has been eaten. One can easily devise more extreme examples, such as checking into an hotel on the basis of a credit card, or an application association between a bank account and a gas utility, say, that lasts as long as gas is supplied, but only becomes active once a month or once a quarter when the account is paid. The point is that a transport connection is useful during periods of activity, and during the rest of the session it can be cleared. Another reason for clearing a transport connection might be if one or other machine "crashes" or is taken out of service for a time. An hotel's credit card computer might be shut down for maintenance each Friday morning at 5.00 a.m. Clearly, the long term sessions for each of the residents that have promised to pay with credit cards cannot be lost, but must be resumed on the other side of the computer maintenance, or machine crash.

Talking of crashes leads on to the other session layer function—checkpointing. We have seen how file transfers may be interrupted by a failure of either the communications medium or of one of the two participating computers. We said then that in some circumstances there were compelling reasons to go back and resume the transfer from some well known checkpoint rather than starting over. Such a checkpointing requirement is not limited to file transfer, and so the general checkpointing facility is built into the session layer.

How then are these services made available to the application layer—or those processes in the application layer that wish to make use of them? The ISO model is strictly layered—each layer may make use only of those services immediately below. Thus, the application layer may make use only of the services of the presentation layer immediately below, and it cannot use the session services at all. The solution is essentially to pass the majority of the session services straight through the presentation layer, Fig 11.2.

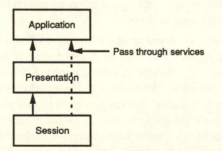

Fig 11.2.   Session and Presentation Services

Thus, to a large extent, the services of the session and presentation layers are just presented to the application layer "side by side" rather than the one being nested within the other, or being logically contained within the other in some way. While this may sound a little like sticking slavishly to the original model when this is actually unnecessary, there are good reasons for the services of the session layer to be handled by the presentation layer. We have seen how the representation of data (the main job of the presentation layer) can be a very complex and sophisticated process. In general, the syntax can be changed from time to time by agreement between the two applications and their two application entities. We have also just pointed out that one of the services of the session layer is a checkpoint/restart service. Suppose that a session layer checkpoint is established, and then a little later the presentation entities negotiate a change in the presentation syntax. If the session is then restarted back at the last checkpoint the presentation entities will be out of step with the session unless they are aware of the roll back to the checkpoint. For this reason, all the session services are passed to the presentation layer. This inspects them, and then passes them on to the application layer. Some of the services, such as the session service S-TOKEN-GIVE are just passed through directly as the presentation service element P-TOKEN-GIVE, and no further action is taken. However, if the session service initiates a roll back to a checkpoint, then the presentation service notes this, and rolls its own state back to this point too.

Thus we see that while the character of the interaction of the session and presentation layers is different from that of the lower layers, yet there is still a necessary hierarchical relationship for some of the services.

11.4 Directory Services

An extremely useful general concept is that of a *name* that refers to some object. It is difficult to imagine human language without nouns. In computer programs, names appear in the form of *identifiers* which are used to refer to locations in computer memory. The programmer writes her program in terms of the identifiers (and other language constructs) and the compiler manages the mapping of these names onto computer memory and registers thus relieving the programmer of a mass of detail irrelevant to the programming task in hand. In networking, we have already come across many such naming operations.

For example, in Chapter 5 we saw how the network service involves network *addresses* which are resolved into *routes* across the network itself. If some of the network involves shared media, then part of the overall network routing involves the choice of particular addresses of entities attached to that shared medium. When looking at mail in the last chapter, we saw that people and institutions were referred to by *mail names* and *addresses*. These names, and the addresses in particular, need to be resolved into network addresses for the MTAs to be able to pass the mail involved onto the final destination. This resolution of mail addresses into the network address of the next MTA in the chain is performed by routing tables, and we saw how the mail addresses were formed into an hierarchical structure so that the address could be processed piecemeal according to the *domain* structure.

There are several advantages to this kind of naming that we mention in the various places in this book. One of the important points is that of *late binding*. By late binding we mean that the information is only actually used or bound when it is actually needed. In the mail case there are multiple levels of this binding: from the mail address to the several network addresses through the MTAs, from the network addresses to the several routes through the actual networks themselves, from the routes across the networks to the actual hardware addresses on the shared local media, and even further, if we wish to labour the point, to the actual buffer locations within the switching machines that handle the packets in transit. If there were no late binding, and the sender of the message had to bind all this information to a message as she typed it in before sending it, then there would be no computer mail ever sent, just as, were the sender of a letter required to name the postboxes, delivery vans, postmen, and the detailed route (*"turn left at the end of the road, and after the pink house..."*), then few letters would ever get sent.

When looking at mail systems in Chapter 10, we saw how the mail address of the recipient could be processed in several stages. Thus, a message for a different *domain* would have effectively only the most important part—the domain specification—resolved in the first domain. This would yield a network address for a mail gateway to the next domain. Then the message, complete with the *complete* mail address of the recipient would be transferred to the mail gateway and stored there. There the complete address is again parsed, and another onward address is used for the next leg. Note here that the mail transfer is not (necessarily) performed across a single network between two MTAs, but may take many steps. In addition, the high-level network protocol involves the transfer of the mail address itself. At each of the MTAs this mail address is reprocessed, and results in a different network address across the next network.

The X.500 (or IS 9594) standard defines a directory service that is superficially similar to the ARPANET scheme. X.500 supports a *Directory Information Base*—DIB that is tree-structured along the lines of the ARPANET domain scheme. The intention is that the leaves of the tree will contain information about *objects* that exist outside the DIB itself, such as people or services.

The DIB is made up of directory entries. The entries corresponding to nodes in the tree point on either to other nodes, or, eventually, to leaves. Each entry has a set of data whose content is constrained by what X.500 refers to as a *schema*. This is roughly what computer languages call a system of type declarations, and is expressed in ASN.1. The tree, like the ARPANET tree, is designed to be stored in a distributed fashion, with different branches of the tree being administered by different organisations. These organisations control both the type and the content of the entries under their jurisdiction. Each entry has a *distinguished name*. This is an hierarchically structured entity which consists of the distinguished name of the node that points to it together with an extra piece of information that denotes that entry as opposed to others attached to the same node.

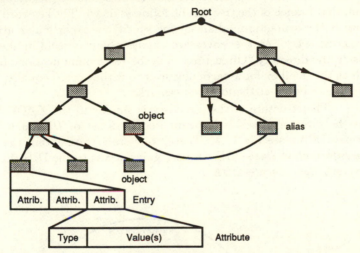

Fig 11.3. The X.500 Directory Information Tree

Logically, there is intended to be a single tree as in Fig 11.3. There is a notional root, and from that root the tree branches to nodes corresponding to countries. Within countries, there will be further divisions, for example, "the Academic Community" or "Government", or a large company. Within each of those will be further divisions. At each node, the administration of that node decides how the node branches further to the more qualified levels. It is anticipated that this will primarily develop along administrative lines within the organisation concerned.

Rather than an ordered notation with dots to separate the parts, X.500 has a keyword and value type of notation to indicate the name. Thus, we might have a hypothetical name

C=GB, G=UK.AC, I=Newcastle, D=Brewing, CN=Broughton

Here we have the "keywords" or attribute types C for country, G for grouping, I for institution, etc ...

> **Exercise 11.1** Though the keyword approach allows some freedom in the ordering of the elements of an X.500 name, complete freedom can only be had if the keywords are unique, not just at one level or node, but at every level. Construct an hypothetical tree where the same name in keyword-value notation means two different things depending on the order of application of the keyword-value pairs in climbing the tree. What constraints do you think should and/or could be imposed in choosing the keywords?

Each entry has a schema as mentioned above. For intermediate nodes, this essentially defines the pointers onto the further branches, or sub-trees. The entry contains several attributes, and by specifying one of them, that branch of the tree can be followed down. The keyword notion above is the syntactic mechanism for specifying a particular attribute at a node entry. At the leaves are entries about objects in the world outside the directory. Often these may be telecommunications objects, such as the mailbox for a particular user, but they could equally well be the price of beans at the local supermarket.

The structure of the directory is similar to the X.400 MHS in that the directory itself is implemented by a set of *Directory Service Agents*—DSAs, see Fig 11.4. These co-operate to maintain the *Directory Information Base*—DIB. A user gains access to the DIB through a *Directory User Agent*—DUA.

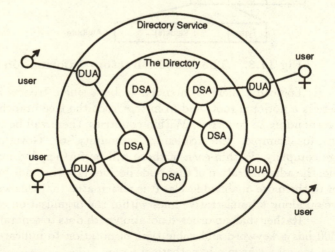

Fig 11.4.   The X.500 Directory Functional Model

Since there is only one logical tree, this implies that the information obtained is independent of the location of the directory user. Thus, the information must have global significance. In other words, information such as *"The mail address of X"* may be stored, but *"The route to X from here"* cannot be stored, since the route depends not just on *X*, but also on *here*, and *here* depends on the location of the enquirer. Thus, *within* the one name space, this kind of directory cannot be used for routing, and can only yield the one consistent answer to the same question independently of location. Note that an item such as *"The route from X to Y"* is different in kind from the above, and could, at least in principle, be stored in such a database. Any addresses stored in such a database need to be absolute addresses, at least throughout the space served by that directory. Thus, in the ISO case, when there is supposed to be only one global DIB, then any addresses had better be globally significant. The ISO *Network Service Access Point*—NSAP addresses have this property of universal uniqueness. Conversely, network routing or mail routing (through MTAs) must be done by some other means.

The X.500 specification recognises that such a single global database will be implemented on several DSAs. The DIB is split up into management domains as indicated above, and it is also divided amongst various DSAs. The management domains need not correspond to the DSAs, though it seems likely that many of the administrative domain boundaries will correspond with the physical boundaries of the DSAs. The standard envisages that enquiries of the directory by a DUA may be handled in various ways. The DUA will be able to contact the directory in various places by calling a DSA that is prepared to handle DUA enquiries. If the DSA can answer the query directly, then that is the end of the matter. However, if it does not have the information, then it has two main methods of finding the information. The first is to make an ongoing call to another DSA within the directory to find the information, and return it to the enquiring DUA. This might involve a single call if the location of the information is known, or it might involve climbing the tree to higher authorities, and then descending again to the appropriate DSA, possibly in another country. All this might take several separate calls. The alternative is to just return information to the DUA that enables it to perform essentially the same actions on behalf of the user. The ARPANET Domain system refers to these two modes as "recursive" and "iterative" methods of servicing the requests.

The X.500 directory is meant to be used in various modes. Firstly, there is the simple operation of giving a fully specified hierarchical name of an entry and requesting either a specific piece of information, or perhaps the whole entry. This mode might be used to retrieve, say, the current mail address of a well known person. Slightly more complex is the operation of "browsing" where the name of a non-terminal entry is given, and a list of all the entries below is requested. In support of this general kind of operation there are facilities for the user to specify filters on the kind of information that will be returned, and limits on the resources that the Directory will use (and, possibly, charge back to the user's account). There are also certain access controls so that some of the information will be accessible only to particular users.

In addition to the simple straightforward way of working down the tree of *distinguished names* to get to an entry with information about an object, X.500 allows other leaf entries to point to an object. An example of such an *alias* is shown in Fig 11.3. The route to get to such an alias entry gives an alternative name for the same object. One of the more interesting applications of such aliases is the possibility of having a parallel tree to the normal naming tree, but which is set up specifically to categorise information rather than to name it. Thus, if we think of the normal tree as corresponding to the tree of telephone directories, country, city, name..., then the alias tree might be set up like the Yellow Pages, with lists of specific services and suchlike. Then the user browsing in such a namespace would get a quite different view onto exactly the same ultimate database. The standard envisages such directories as perhaps being maintained by third parties as an added value service.

One kind of operation is *compare* (and tell me if it matches). This is intended for the storage of passwords. The idea is that a computing service of some sort may wish to authenticate a user by asking the Directory Service to compare a password that he offers with that stored in the database. However, this sort of authentication is clearly fairly weak, and is recognised as such in the standard. X.500 also supports so-called *strong authentication*. However, this is based on public key encryption, and we shall see in Chapter 14 that some question marks hang over such mechanisms.

We have seen that one useful aspect of computer mail is the concept of mailing lists. X.500 supports the notion of groups, where an entry can contain a list of objects. This list can be interpreted as a mailing list.

Finally, of course, there are provisions for the owners or administrators of information in the database to alter the information.

11.5   Maintaining the Database

We have seen how directories are useful in allowing the late binding of information by allowing a symbolic token, the *name* to be stored in a directory, and the corresponding addressing information to be retrieved when required. This is useful if it can be arranged so that the names change less frequently than the addresses.

In addition, we have seen how the hierarchical structure of the name space allows two desirable conditions to be met. One is that the responsibility for allocating names can be delegated by recursively delegating administrative responsibility for sub-trees of the overall naming tree. Another advantage is that it is not necessary for the whole of the database to be stored in one place. It can be decentralised along administrative lines, and servers supporting parts of it can refer requests onto other parts by traversing the naming tree and its associated servers in a fairly obvious way.

In the ARPANET scheme, servers that retrieve such information from other servers are expected to cache such information so that future requests can be answered without making an ongoing call. The information so cached is discarded after a certain time. In this way, changes made in a local server supporting part of the overall tree eventually percolates out amongst all servers as the old information dies out. This kind of chaching of information that may temporarily become outdated is commonly thought acceptable because of the performance and traffic improvements resulting from the caching operation. However, there is the implication that the canonical form of the information is kept in one place only and is thus vulnerable to this single point of failure. The *Grapevine* system (Birrel et al,1982) allows the elimination of such a point of failure by full duplication of the database.

One of the essentials of Grapevine was that the database must be available both for query *and update* independently of the failure of any component. Thus, it must be possible to update the data in one copy of the database even when another copy of the same data is not available for whatever reason. This implies that the database may contain inconsistent data, and the database is designed in such a way that the inconsistencies will be automatically eliminated by mechanisms in the database itself. The design took the view that these temporary inconsistencies, coupled with an automatic correction mechanism were preferable to the alternative in which *all* copies of the data involved must be simultaneously available, and may only be updated by a single atomic action—perhaps by using some version of the CCR protocol mentioned earlier in this chapter. The problem with this latter approach is that updates will depend on the simultaneous availibility of *all* copies of the data, and thus may be difficult to perform in the face of unreliable machines.

The elimination of inconsistencies is achieved by a system of time stamping. Each update to the database carries a timestamp, and while duplicates of the same part of the database are active they communicate, and propogate these updates. Thus, the same part of the database can be updated at *different* times by interacting with *different copies* of the database. It is assumed that the different parts of the database keep clocks that are sufficiently well synchronised that as the copies of the updates are distributed, the times stamps will order the updates correctly, and all the copies of the data will eventually become consistent. It is further assumed that incompatible updates will not "simultaneously" be made to the same data. However, if they are, then the accidental variations in the clock settings will resolve the conflict, but it is up to the human "owner" of the data concerned to ensure that such race conditions do not occur in the first place. In practice this should not occur otherwise the value of the information itself is in doubt.

Note one interesting point about this algorithm. If entries are deleted, it is not sufficient merely to remove the entry from the database. The fact that an entry has been present, and has been deleted must be retained. If it were merely deleted, then the undeleted copies in other parts of the database would merely be copied across, and the entry would reappear. In addition, an update to add the same entry might arrive. If this instruction to add the entry was timed *after* the removal, then the net result is that the entry is present. On the other hand, if it was timed *before* the deletion entry, then the final result is that the entry is deleted. In Grapevine, the database is in the form of *groups* or lists containing *entries*. Once an item has been an entry in a group, it is not *removed* from the group by an incoming delete message, it merely moves between two lists—Members and DelMembers depending on the timestamp on the most recent update message, and this timestamp on the latest update message is retained in order to be able to process incoming updates. In Grapevine, each member of a group is represented by the text of the member, the timestamp, and the Member/Deleted flag. Such entries are exchanged amongst the servers supporting the specific group, and new incoming messages are merged with existing knowledge about that string. The result is always one entry for the given string—that with the latest time—and membership of the Member or DelMember group.

In order to avoid the system silting up with deleted entries, an arbitrary time limit is declared on data in the deleted group. After fourteen days it is assumed that no earlier membership entries will appear, and the entry is purged from the deleted list.

11.6   Summary

The ISO standardisation process has also produced standards for use in the application layer as well as communication standards for the layers below. These are classified as CASEs and SASEs according to their perceived popularity. We have looked at *Association Control* and *CCR* CASEs. In addition, we have examined the generalised tools provided for generating general remote operation protocols—ROS and we studied the way in which the four upper layers co-operate to support application programs.

Finally we looked briefly at directory services, which are rapidly becoming important services for the network user. We briefly returned again to the ARPANET Domain system, glimpsed a few of the features of the X.500 directory service, and looked at the way in which the Grapevine directory manages the completely distributed maintenance of the directory database.

12

Performance and System Issues

This chapter looks at some of the ways in which the performance of communications systems depends on many complex interacting factors, both of the protocols themselves, and of the hardware and software upon which they are implemented.

We look at some so-called "lightweight" protocols as an alternative to the more traditional "heavyweight" protocols. The point of these protocols is to provide a service in a simpler way that should be quicker and cheaper to implement, and cheaper and more reliable in service. We see how far those targets are achieved in reality. We also look at some of the detailed techniques of both software and hardware that can be used to improve performance and reduce the "cost" of handling protocols. In the latter part of the chapter we discuss various aspects of "performance" and "efficiency" in implementing protocols in general. We examine various techniques and concepts that are employed, and take some time in a philosophical discussion of what the term "efficiency" and "cost" actually mean. We find that the concepts of "efficiency" and "cost" are themselves seen to be somewhat elusive and dependent on the perception of the observer.

12.1 Lightweight Protocols

So far we have looked at communications in a very traditional manner. Various issues have been identified, such as errors, flow control, routing, and so forth. These issues have been assigned to a layered structure, and treated, one by one, with a tower of protocols. The result is a very general structure that has wide applicability. There are several existing architectures that follow this structure, including the ISO model.

One of the biggest criticisms of such an arrangement is its sheer complexity. In our examination of the various layers, we have seen some hints of this. By the nature of the structure, several issues crop up in more than one layer—for example flow control and addressing—and must be allowed for in the protocols and their implementations. Indeed, this complexity is such that it has been said that few people are capable of being experts in more than a subset of the levels in the ISO model!

There are many consequences of this complexity. One is the sheer difficulty, and thus expense, of implementing such a complex set of protocols. Often teams of people are involved, and the cost and time required means that not only are implementations a long time coming, but they are difficult to debug. Even when an implementation is written, debugged, installed and paid for, it can still be expensive in terms of the machine resources required to run it. Maintenance of such complex software also requires a substantial team of skilled people. It is a truism that no program is ever finally "debugged", and in general, complex programs such as those required for complex protocols, will suffer more from bugs than will simpler ones.

We illustrate the topic of lightweight protocols by returning to the concept of the "remote procedure call" that we introduced in Chapter 2 as an alternative way of understanding a simple error recovery protocol. The reader will remember that there we introduced the idea of executing a write procedure remotely rather than locally. Thus, each record is dispatched down a link and an acknowledgement of its safe arrival is awaited, and we reinterpreted this as the execution of a write procedure remotely at the other end of the link—each record transmission was reinterpreted as the sending of a bunch of procedure parameters (including the record itself) to a remote location, and each acknowledgement became the subsequent return of the indication of the success or failure of a remote procedure execution. We saw that the understanding of the process in terms of the repeated attempts at executing the procedure until it was successful, was somewhat simpler to understand than the equivalent protocol with its messages passing back and forth.

12.2   Remote Procedure Calls

A remote procedure call (RPC) can be implemented in several ways. We look at implementing it first over a reliable transport service, and then over an unreliable datagram service.

Given a reliable transport service, the implementation of the RPC is trivial. The sender merely bundles up the parameters of the procedure call and sends them down the connection. The receiver unbundles the parameters, executes the procedure, and returns the result. In our simple case of writing a series of records onto the end of a file, the parameters of the procedure call are simply the data to be written, and the result returned is merely an indication of the success or failure of the attempt to add a new record to the end of the file. While we shall only examine the data transfer phase, the stages of opening the file, checking access, and so forth, all carry through in a similar fashion.

When we compare this method of working with using a file transfer protocol as described in Chapter 9, we are at first struck by the considerable simplification that has taken place compared with using the file transfer protocol. How is it that all this complexity has disappeared, and yet we can still work, and transfer files? If we look back at the discussion of file transfer protocols, we shall see that many of the features of those protocols are just not represented in any form at all. For example, if two machines work with different character sets, and they are transferring a text file, then the characters had better get translated sometime into the right code otherwise the file transfer is pointless. Similarly, if one machine views a file as an array of characters that has internal structure because of the presence of the carriage return character, and the other machine's filing system has an inbuilt record structure, then somewhere the mapping needs to be made. Simple RPCs ignore these issues and thus cannot be used in heterogeneous situations.

Is the RPC method, then, an irrelevance? Well, firstly, there are a great many occasions when transfers need to be made between machines of the same type. This is especially true in a local context where there is likely to be a concentration of similar machines, perhaps microcomputers, or high-powered personal computers. Then we can expect that a group of machines all running the same system, say PC-DOS, could usefully employ an RPC mechanism to communicate between themselves. Indeed it is likely that such a user community would need to exchange much larger amounts of such machine-specific data locally than they are likely to want to exchange more remotely with more markedly different machines. The need for full internetworking is still present, but is relatively of much less importance than a more closed local networking.

It is also possible to apply the RPC type of communication more widely than just between similar machines and operating systems. The first method is to realise that any specific RPC file access method implicitly contains the semantics of some particular file system. The file system may be that of one particular actual operating system such as the PC-DOS mentioned above, or it may be a more abstract system such as the Sun Network File System. Each system that wishes to talk using the file system embedded in the RPC must map that system to and from its own file system. For example, if the file system on the network embodies the concept of ASCII characters structured by the presence of carriage return characters, and a user has an EBCDIC filing system with built-in records, then the interface to the RPC protocol must internally map between these two structures. The implementor might choose to buffer incoming characters up to a carriage return, translate from ASCII to EBCDIC, and write the record into its file. Note that certain assumptions have been made. The main one is that data on the network is all text. It is quite possible that some files are actually binary numbers representing the shape of a new motor car, or the doses of a new drug to control epileptic fits. We have looked at such presentation issues in some depth in Chapters 8 and 9. The main point here is that the simplest RPC protocols ignore this type of issue, and can thus only be used successfully when the consequences of this ignorance are unimportant.

Of course, some RPC systems do not ignore such presentation issues. For example, the ISO Remote Operations Service addresses these problems in a fairly complete way (see Chapter 11).

We started out on our study of RPC protocols by assuming that a reliable transport service was available. However, further overall simplification may be made by building the remote procedure call mechanism on top of an unreliable datagram service. In this case, the originator of the RPC bundles the parameters of the RPC into a datagram and sends it off to the far end for execution. There a server of some sort processes the RPC request and returns the response in another datagram. The originator receives the response in the datagram, and completes the RPC execution. At a stroke we appear to have dispensed with the need for a reliable transport service. All we appear to need is a simpler unreliable datagram service. If we look a little more closely at this implementation of RPCs upon unreliable datagrams, we shall see where the features of the transport service have gone to.

Most basically, how does the RPC service work in the face of the unreliability of the datagram service? If we go back to our introduction of the RPC concept in understanding a simple request/response error recovery protocol in Chapter 2, we can see the mechanism at work. In that protocol, the packet was repeatedly sent until a suitable response was received. In the early versions of the protocol, we had problems with duplicated records. These arose when the record was transferred successfully, but the response was corrupted. When this happened, the second transmission of the record resulted in a duplicated version of the record at the destination. We avoided this problem by attaching a cycle of labels A, B, A, B, ... to the records that were sent. We used these labels to avoid duplicated records by ignoring those that were not labelled as expected (assuming them to be duplicates of the last request) but nevertheless replying with a positive acknowledgement. With the remote procedure calls we have the same problem: If acknowledgements get lost and the originator resends the request to execute the procedure, how can we ensure that the second execution of the procedure does not have undesirable effects such as the duplication of records?

The way to avoid this type of trouble is to make the execution of procedures idempotent. In our introduction of the RPC concept in Chapter 2, we had already made our RPC idempotent in the limited circumstances in which it was expected to operate. Thus, we could interpret the RPC protocol there as *"Add this record to the file if its label matches the expected label (A or B), but otherwise ignore it. Reply* ACK *anyway."* This is idempotent, since we are implicitly assuming that the packets carrying the requests and responses cannot be unduly delayed, duplicated, disordered, and so on. We have discussed the need for time-outs to be of a suitable value so that when the timeout expires, there is no significant chance that the lost packet will turn up later. Generally, it is not difficult to come up with a timeout that works reasonably well on a point-to-point link. However, RPC protocols are often implemented over a general datagram service. Such a service may be realised over a small local network, such as the rings or contention media studied in Chapter 3. If such is the case, it is likely that datagrams will arrive either very quickly or not at all, and the timeouts can be chosen as simply as with the point-to-point links. However, datagram services are often implemented on much more complex and heterogeneous networks that involve mixtures of local and wide-area networks and complex gateways. There may be dynamic routing to avoid failed links or balance traffic across several busy paths. The result of all this is that datagrams may be disordered and subject to varying delays. In error or overload conditions, packets may be duplicated, lost, or subjected to exceptionally long delays.

With such a service, it is not practical to set the retry timeout to be longer than the longest delay that is likely to occur. If the timeout was set that high then the normal error recovery would be too sluggish. Thus it is normal to choose a retry time that is long enough so that it does not trigger because of the normal delays, but that may well be shorter than the exceptional, but not unusual delays that sometimes happen. In such conditions, it is necessary to have some other mechanism to control the effect of such abnormally delayed packets. The strength of the mechanism required depends both on the application and on the pattern of errors. Thus a simple numbering scheme may be sufficient. With such a scheme, each requesting datagram is labelled with a sequence number that does not repeat within the time a delayed datagram is likely still to arrive. The replies contain the same sequence number. Thus, request number 42 will be paired with response 42, and so on. If a requester is expecting response 42, and receives a response 41, say, then it will discard it as a rogue, and continue waiting for the correctly numbered response arrives, or until the timeout expires.

A further elaboration of the sequence numbering may be necessary if it is required to protect against a possible problem when the machine restarts. This is caused when a machine, or process starts up again, perhaps after a software or hardware fault, and re-initialises its sequence number. Under such circumstances it is possible that the same sequence number will be re-used on a request datagram within a short period, and the response to the request that was emitted before the crash arrives while the response to the later request (after the crash) is still awaited. We have seen how HDLC handled this problem by having the notion of a "connected phase". With RPC it is normal not to rely on this device but to eliminate the problem either by keeping the sequence numbers in some sort of non-volatile storage, or by using the time from an external clock in place of the sequence number (which is actually a very similar thing to do). Whatever the detailed method, the basic aim is to ensure that the labels on any returned responses enable the unequivocal identification with a specific request.

These techniques, coupled with idempotent requests, allow a reliable RPC service to be constructed on top of an unreliable datagram service.

Now we can see why it is not necessary to have a reliable transport service to implement a reliable RPC service. This is because we have error recovery and sequencing at the RPC level itself with the combination of idempotent requests and sequence numbering taken together with the persistent retrys until the desired result has not only taken place, but has been seen to have taken place. The necessity for these elements of a transport service have not disappeared, but have been re-implemented in a different place and at a different level.

Exercise 12.1 Compare and contrast this method of implementing reliable RPCs upon an unreliable datagram service with the TCP protocol's use of sequence numbers (see Chapter 6).

Similarly, we can find the majority of the other features of the transport service. Certain of the transport service elements, in particular addressing and fragmentation, have been loaded onto the datagram service. The addresses used by our datagram service are clearly at the transport service level. In any actual implementation they will be mapped firstly onto any available network services, including any multiplexing that might be done for economic reasons, and then on down to any local MAC-level addresses that are being used internally. The addresses, and the way they are handled, are clearly just as complex in the datagram case as with the connection-oriented transport service. Indeed, the handling may be more complex and expensive in that addresses need to be mapped for every datagram (see Chapters 5 and 6), possibly involving a directory lookup function, whereas with the virtual call this needs only to be done once at call setup time. Next, there is the fragmentation issue. It is important that an RPC mechanism should be free to transfer blocks of data that are of a size that is convenient for the application. Indeed, to increase throughput on such operations as a file copy, it is important to be able to send large blocks of data. This implies that the datagram service must provide possibly large datagram sizes. To do this, it is necessary that underneath there be fragmentation and reassembly mechanisms that are just the same as those provided in the connection-oriented service. We can go though all the other features provided by a connection-oriented transport service, such as multiplexing, and see that our only saving is that we no longer maintain a virtual call, and thus do not provide an ordered sequence of records with the errors recovered by lower level mechanisms. Otherwise, all the other elements are either still present (such as addressing and fragmentation) or have deliberately been omitted (such as presentation issues, or multiplexing). The properties of sequencing and error recovery—those normally associated with a connection—have been moved upwards in the hierarchy of protocols, and mixed in with the RPC mechanism itself when idempotent procedure executions and a non-repeating labelling scheme were specified.

Thus, we see that if we look closely enough, the RPC over datagrams type of scheme has not actually eliminated a transport service at all, but merely moved its components around. Looked at in this way, how have we saved anything over the more traditional approach? The major saving is in the form of simplification, since an RPC service over datagrams can be viewed as a fairly straightforward single-thread process. On the other hand a connection-oriented transport service is a full-duplex process, and is typically represented by several communicating processes that must be synchronised by some means or other. Handling asynchronous processes, be they interrupts in a single system, or a system with multiple processors, is a notoriously difficult intellectual task. Even at the simple link level we saw in Chapter 2 that the intellectual complexities were difficult to handle. Most programming environments to implement protocols try to reduce this sort of complexity for the programmer by some means or other. Indeed the programming task is similar to the sorts of task that are found in operating system design, and it is normal to use similar tools to handle the similar problems. A popular structuring tool is the model of multiple processes, each of which is a single-thread process, and which communicates with other processes at carefully controlled places and in carefully controlled ways. For descriptions of various process synchronizing tools see Dijkstra (1972), Hoare (1974), Wirth (1977), and their various references. An alternative structuring tool is the concept of an object which implements a protocol entity with messages passing from object to object. Smalltalk, and the Apple Macintosh and Microsoft OS/2 operating systems are examples of this approach. Clearly, this latter environment more closely matches the common descriptions of protocols. In fact the message-oriented environment is a much superior to the multi-process environment for implementing protocols for this and other reasons. Sadly, we have no space to pursue this question in the present work.

In a full-duplex transport service there is a two-way flow of messages, and the implementations must be capable of handling this flow. With the RPC approach, this world of asynchronous events has been reduced to a single sequential flow. The requesting program bundles up the request into a datagram, the datagram may then be transformed and fragmented as it descends the levels of protocol until it is finally sent out on some physical medium. The sending process then waits until the response arrives back, possibly fragment by fragment. The fragments are gathered and reassembled, and then the process finally continues when the response is complete. The closest we get to an asynchronous event is when a timeout expires or an orphaned datagram arrives and is discarded, and even these events are handled in a synchronous way.

One of the advantages of a full duplex transport service is that it is possible to achieve a high throughput on a bandwidth-limited link by keeping one or other direction of transmission operating continuously. Thus, if we are transferring a file, say, it is possible to keep one direction of flow fully busy with the file transfer without any pauses, while the return leg carries acknowledgements from time to time. To do this properly, it is necessary to overlap the sending of later file records with the receipt of earlier acknowledgements using some variation of the sliding window flow control mentioned in Chapter 4. This gives a full-duplex process that needs the appropriate programming environment support.

On the other hand, an RPC approach will not in general be able to keep such a channel fully loaded. This is because the sending process will transmit a record, and then wait for a reply (see section 4.6). The reply will be delayed by the round trip delay of the network and the response times of the computers involved. (We shall examine such delays in more detail later.) The sending leg will thus see pauses between the transmitted records because of the single-thread way in which the process works. We see, then, that the single thread way of working can reduce the throughput in certain circumstances. However, this disadvantage can be reduced by increasing the amount of data transferred at one time. Thus, on a file copy for example, it is advantageous for throughput reasons to transfer as large an amount of data as possible in each transfer. By increasing the amount of data per RPC, the use of the transmit leg may be increased asymptotically towards 100%. As always, there are penalties to consider. If the error rate is significant, then each time there is an error, a complete large block of data must be re-sent. The longer the block, the greater will be the impact on throughput. To paraphrase the old adage *"don't put all your data in one packet"*. In addition, the RPC method will recover from errors by timing out, whereas if records do not get reordered, the window type of operation is likely to be able to use the fact that records are missing from a sequence to react more quickly.

One other way of exploiting the full capacity of the channel using RPC is to use several simultaneous transfers. Thus, it would be possible to divide a large file into, say, five equal parts, and then to start five simultaneous transfers, each using an independent RPC. In this way the file transfers will interleave, one with another, and thus use more of the available channel. This assumes some sort of use of low level multiplexing and de-multiplexing between the five tasks implementing the simultaneous transfers. Whether or not such a procedure is sensible in practice is another matter of course.

Most of the other simplifications that are claimed by the proponents of the RPC style of protocols can be attributed to the fact that such protocols are often more or less special purpose, such as UNIX to UNIX, or MS-DOS to MS-DOS, and have thus deliberately omitted certain functions, such as presentation images, transport service multiplexing, or even fragmentation. Obviously, tailor-made specialist protocols of such types should outperform general purpose protocols. This is not in any way a criticism, quite the contrary. There is a strong tendency for the holy grail of universal interconnection to be sought at whatever the cost. It should be more widely recognised that full general purpose protocols do have costs in both machine resources and money, and that special purpose protocols, such as RPC between similar machines, do have an important role to play.

12.3   General Performance and Cost Issues

Having compared some different types of protocol, and discussed some of the efficiency issues when comparing "lightweight" protocols and what we must now presumably call the "heavyweight" connection-oriented protocols, we now turn our attention to some other aspects of performance and cost.

12.4   Packet Handling Costs

All packet protocols will eventually involve the transmission and reception of individual packets of data. It is often critically important to the overall cost of the protocol to transmit and receive these packets in the most efficient way. To illustrate what we are talking about, we shall take several specific examples.

Imagine that we have a computer system that is attached to a communications line by means of a simple byte-by-byte interface. Typically, such an interface transmits a single byte, and then causes an interrupt when it is ready to accept the next byte. On input, an interrupt is requested as each byte arrives and is ready for processing by the host computer system. The important attribute of such devices is the interrupt load that they generate in the host computer system, one for each byte transmitted or received. The main consequence of such a rate of interrupts depends both on the byte rate, and on the cost of each interrupt.

In some operating systems, the only way of handling an interrupt is by assigning a process of some sort to it and then requesting that the interrupt send a signal to this process to cause it to be dispatched. This type of structuring is conceptually very powerful, and leads to a comparatively friendly programming environment. The problem is that it is also quite expensive in machine resources. When a machine interrupt is taken, a typical sequence is that the current state of the machine is stored away, and then the environment for the interrupt routine is set up. Typically, this involves storing the working registers of the CPU, and loading a new set, though the details depend strongly on the machine. On some machines registers must be saved and restored one by one, on others a single instruction will save or restore a full set of registers, or they may automatically get saved and restored as part of the hardware interrupt process. Some machines have duplicate sets of registers to allow fast interrupt response. In whatever way the interrupt is taken, some time later, the interrupt routine is in operation. It then needs to identify both the source of the interrupt (there may be several similar interfaces active at any time), and the process that is waiting for the signal. The signal is sent appropriately, usually involving some significant interaction with the kernel that is controlling the operating system. Finally, the interrupt routine terminates and the original environment is restored. Though the interrupt routine is now done, the destination task still needs dispatching. This may take place immediately on the termination of the interrupt routine, or possibly some time later. Whatever, the detailed process, eventually some sort of kernel will get around to dispatching the process that has been assigned to handle the interrupt, and thus to handle the byte that has just arrived or get another byte to send after the last one.

This whole process is clearly a long and involved one, and involves considerable overhead for each byte handled. Suppose, for example, that each such interrupt plus dispatch of a task involves a machine overhead of $1mS$. A mere 1000 bytes per second will absorb all the CPU resources just in switching tasks, and without even doing any processing of the bytes at all!

There is another variation on this theme that involves teaching the interrupt routines to handle packets rather than single bytes. Thus, for example, rather than the interrupt routine passing the data byte-by-byte to the process handling the device, and receiving single bytes to be output, complete packets are passed to and from the interrupt routine. A typical implementation of this is for the process and interrupt routine to exchange a pointer to a region of storage together with a length of the region. The device driver stores the pointer and the count and sends the first byte out to the device. When the interrupt signalling the readiness of the next byte is taken, the interrupt routine first looks at the pointer and count. If there is more data to be sent, then the next byte is sent directly, rather than needing to interact with the controlling process. This cycle is repeated until the whole of the block of data has been output. When all the data has gone then the controlling process at last needs to be told that transmission is complete.

Similarly for input, the interrupt routine receives a buffer that it may use (again passed as a pointer and a count). Input interrupts cause bytes to be inserted in this buffer one by one until the buffer is complete. Input may be complete perhaps because the buffer is full, or because the input routine has just found the appropriate terminating sequence—"DLE, ETX" for example. At this point the controlling process is finally signalled.

What have we gained by this method? Well, we still have the same number of I/O interrupts. However, most of these interrupts now merely transfer bytes to and from buffers. Only the occasional interrupt that coincides with the end of a buffer interacts through the kernel with the controlling process. Thus, we have eliminated the task signalling and switching overhead for the vast majority of bytes. Since the task switching overhead is usually much more expensive than the interrupt overhead, sometimes by a large factor, we have achieved a considerable improvement in system performance. The cost of this improvement is that the interrupt routines themselves significantly more complex and special purpose.

The third variation on this theme is to put the handling of the full buffer into the hardware of the device itself. Thus, instead of sending the data across to the device a byte at a time, and handling an interrupt for each one, the data is passed a full buffer at a time. As usual, there are many ways of doing this. Perhaps the simplest from the programmer's point of view is to pass a buffer to the device in the form of a pointer and a count in much the same way as earlier we passed the buffer between the controlling process and the smart interrupt routine. The device then accesses memory directly without needing the intervention of the processor. Since the device accesses memory directly, this type of access is frequently termed *Direct Memory Access*—DMA. (And thus also, the previous method of getting the interrupt routine to handle whole packets is sometimes referred to as "pseudo-DMA".)

We have now managed a very large improvement in system performance and efficiency. We have eliminated all the byte-level interrupts, and are left with only the packet-level interrupts. To a first approximation we have reduced the overhead in terms of machine cycles needed to handle a packet by a factor of something like the number of bytes in a packet compared with the original byte-by-byte method. To set against this, we have introduced two new types of cost. One is the fairly obvious one of complexity and cost in the hardware device itself. While such costs are significant, they are generally an excellent investment in terms of the saving in overall system overhead or, conversely, in terms of increased throughput. The second cost is less obvious, and somewhat dependent on machine architecture. DMA can be thought of in terms of a bus architecture. Thus, in Fig 12.1, we see that the processor, memory, and the device all share the same bus.

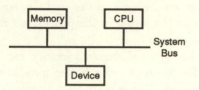

Fig 12.1. DMA on a Bus Architecture

The device, in performing I/O operations, accesses the memory directly via the bus, avoiding the processor. This is often the same bus that is used by the processor itself in accessing memory to fetch instructions, and to fetch and store operands. Any other devices will also share the same bus. The memory and bus will have a certain limited bandwidth. Normally, this will be more than sufficient for the operation of the processor. However, if there are one or more fast DMA devices active they can significantly affect the bandwidth available for the processor and thus reduce the performance of the processor without directly interrupting it. Moreover, the devices can interfere one with another. When there are too many fast devices, they can even interfere with each other sufficiently so that they cannot meet their own time constraints. In serious cases this may lead to incoming data being lost before there is an opportunity to transfer it into the DMA buffer—"overrun"—or lead to transmitted data not being read from the buffer soon enough to be transmitted—"underrun".

There are two other ways of avoiding the byte-by-byte interrupt overhead. In the first of these, the device has an internal buffer that is big enough to hold the biggest packet that will be handled. Each block is then transferred to the device at the start of transmission (or from it at the end) in a tight loop of program that copies the bytes from (or to) a buffer in memory to (or from) the internal buffer in the device.

At first sight, this may seem just as costly as the interrupt per byte method—every byte has to be handled individually after all. However, despite the fact that each byte is handled individually, the overhead per byte is much lower if the handling is in a tight loop of program rather than also incurring the full-blown invocation of a machine interrupt. Interrupts vary in their expense depending strongly on machine architecture, but are never cheap compared with a single step in a tight loop of program.

The other way of communicating between a device and a host processor is by means of shared memory. As a typical example of this, we may have the device's buffer appearing in the processor's memory at some specific position. The data is then copied to or from this area of memory in much the same way as we have just described for a hidden internal buffer. The effect of such an arrangement is very similar to previously except that the presence of the buffer in the processor's memory space can be an inconvenience.

We should note that this type of shared memory can be implemented in different ways. For example, the buffer may in fact be inside the processor's actual memory. If this is so, then the device must still perform the DMA to transfer the data between the buffer and the actual device. There is still the possibility that the DMA process may significantly degrade the performance of the rest of the system—and the buffer has already had to be copied. The other way is for the buffer to be implemented physically inside the device itself. Thus a "hole" of some sort must appear in the main memory to accommodate this. The clear advantage of this latter method is that since the buffer is internal to the device, then transferring data to and from the buffer does not involve the main system bus and thus does not impact the memory bandwidth available in the rest of the system.

It can be seen that full-blown DMA is a logical extension of the shared memory concept where the device and processor both share the same total memory space. The buffer no longer needs to be in a fixed position, and the copying stage is eliminated. Indeed, one can imagine many other shared memory schemes where each of the processor and the device has its own address space, and each address space overlaps the other to a greater or lesser extent. Many of these schemes are actually implemented by so called "intelligent" devices that implement several layers of protocol within the device itself. Such schemes need to be designed and implemented carefully otherwise data will need to be copied back and forth to be in the right place for I/O.

12.5   Single Byte Interactions

We have just examined in some detail how it is advantageous to deal with data in large blocks and thus reduce the overheads of byte-by-byte interaction as far as possible. Unfortunately, there are not infrequent occasions when this is made more or less impossible by the way in which the users of the network choose to work. The prime example of this is when host operating systems choose to work with single character interactions. Thus, there are several popular operating systems whose normal mode of operation is one input character at a time. As the user presses each key on his terminal, the byte representing the character is handled individually by the host. The host dispatches the task that is handling the terminal, and then decides what action to take depending upon the character and the state of the process. The response is frequently merely to echo the character back onto the terminal's screen, but once in a while quite a large amount of traffic may be emitted by the host.

The problem with such modes of working is that they make it impossible to optimise the treatment of input bytes by blocking them together. With a small machine and a few locally attached terminals this does not matter. Indeed it is often from such small scale local configurations that such modes of working have evolved. However, the costs cease to be negligible when the terminals are no longer local but connected to a large network, and the host is scaled up from a small scale configuration with a handful of terminals to a large mainframe supporting several hundreds of terminals. In this case few large scale hosts switch processes sufficiently cheaply, and the end-to-end delay in echoing characters across large networks soon becomes irritating and obstructive to the work of the terminal user. Clearly, it is possible to forward single characters one to a packet, but the efficiency of such a method of working is low. In addition, the delay in echoing single characters from the host, one by one, can mean that as a user types on her terminal, the echo onto her screen may be delayed by several characters. Such a mode of working over a packet network has many disadvantages, including inefficiency and cost. It is depressing how often such a mode is forced by the host system involved.

12.6 Multiple Packet Interactions

In the last section we looked at how some hosts would force single character interactions and cause the overhead in both the host and the network to increase. In this section we will look at the other extreme—where we can reduce the overhead per packet by handling several packets at once.

With low speed communications, that is up to say 1000 bytes per second or so, there is little incentive to reduce the packet overhead much. This is because the overhead per packet is usually relatively small—provided we are working with packet-by-packet hardware and reasonably sized packets. Thus the total machine resources to keep, say, a 1000 byte per second line busy are often fairly modest. However, 1000 bytes per second has now become a fairly slow speed. It is commonplace to obtain links of five or ten times this speed from public utilities, and speeds of over a million bits per second are available for those with the money to pay.

However, the most dramatic improvements have taken place locally with the sorts of shared media that we studied in Chapter 3. On such local networks, speeds of 5 or 10 million bits per second are normal, and 100 million bits per second networks are appearing. The main impediment to this further increase is the ability of machines to be able to use what is already available. To see why, it is merely necessary to think of the overheads associated with handling each packet.

Suppose, for the sake of an example, we are sending data across a 10Mbps local network in packets of 250 bytes. To keep the medium fully occupied with the one transfer (assuming there are no other contenders for the medium), we need to send out about 5,000 packets per second across the network, or about one every $200\mu S$. Even if we ignore the overhead of handling any protocol itself, the demands upon an operating system of handling an interrupt, dispatching a task, and then swapping back to some other task to continue their work, is clearly beyond the regular everyday type of work for which such systems were designed. $200\mu S$ is just not enough. The result is that if we try to transfer data at maximum speed across a high speed *Local Area Network*—LAN using the normal protocol techniques that are designed to work reasonably for slow speed links, then the performance will be very poor, and the overheads high.

However, there are two main techniques that we may use to improve matters. The first is to increase the size of the packet very substantially. In our example we deliberately chose 250 bytes as being at the larger end of what is commonly employed in wide area packet networks. This can be increased substantially with corresponding increases in throughput.

The other technique is to avoid most or all of the task switching overhead. One way to achieve this is to arrange for the process sending or receiving data to do a "busy wait" rather than the more normal "system wait". The normal "system wait" in a multiprogrammed system is for the process that is to wait for an event to communicate with the operating system with some parameters that say in effect *"Here is an event X. Awake me when it occurs, but in the meantime dispatch someone else."* This works fine when the expected time to event X is much greater than the dispatching time for some other task, but when the expected time to event X is much less than the task switching time, then switching tasks is not really useful.

It is much more useful for the process to do a "busy wait"—that is to loop, polling for the event X. This is against much of our training in operating system design, where the normal wisdom is to arrange for an interrupt and then find something else to do. Now we can see that this approach is predicated on an assumption that is invalid for fast communications. It may seem wasteful to spin in a loop waiting for an event to occur, but in the circumstances we have described, this is actually the more efficient thing to do.

Another way of achieving a reduction in task switching is to alter the protocol so that fewer waits need to be done by either sender or receiver. The "blast protocol" described later is one way of achieving this.

12.7 Hardware Checksum Calculation

We have seen how the efficiency of transmitting blocks may be increased by employing DMA or related techniques to offload the low level "clerical" tasks from the CPU onto specialised hardware. At the same time, it is quite usual for the specialised hardware also to perform the packet framing (with a DLE mechanism, or perhaps flags and bit stuffing, or by whatever method). The other function that is also usually delegated to specialised hardware is the generation and checking of CRC checksums. Indeed, it is fairly normal to have a single integrated circuit that on the computer side deals with blocks of raw data bytes together with the control signals such as start-of-block, etc, and on the communications side produces a serial bit stream suitable for driving a modem. The bit stream will have DLEs inserted or bits stuffed as appropriate, have the correct CRC generated on transmission and checked on receipt have the framing bracketing the data, produce either raw bits, or optional NRZI format, etc. Such a chip corresponds in function to the UART that we mentioned in Chapter 1.

So we see that with such a package, we have offloaded the function of generating and checking all of the lowest level of data framing onto the hardware itself.

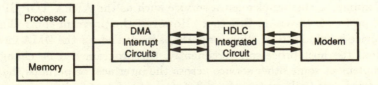

Fig 12.2. HDLC on a Chip

Fig 12.2 shows the general schematic block diagram of such a device. Here the HDLC chip performs the low level front end tasks, and the DMA circuitry transfers the raw packets of data into and out of the computer's memory. In this case, we specifically have the HDLC protocol implemented. However, with the correct chips, we could have the similar frame level of communication for other types of communication. Indeed, such devices do currently exist for implementing the lowest levels of most fast local area networks, and will be produced for any other type of medium that becomes sufficiently popular. In fact, such packages are essential for the higher performance shared media, since the time constraints cannot usually be met, even by dedicated microprocessors, and specialised hardware is required. A large amount of "random logic" becomes uneconomic for other than a very small number of implementations, and integrated circuits are essential for the mass market.

This notion of a special purpose package connected by DMA circuitry can be extended to cover higher levels of protocol, rather than just the framing of individual packets. Thus, consider Fig 12.3.

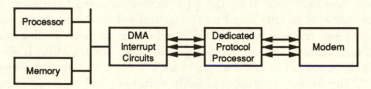

Fig 12.3.   A Specialised Communications Processor

This arrangement is identical with the previous figure, with the exception that the box between the DMA circuits and the modem has been relabelled. The point of such an arrangement is that the "dedicated protocol processor" contains a dedicated microprocessor and program to implement a stack of protocol layers up to some given level, and then to present the service corresponding to this stack of protocols across the DMA interface to the host processor. The level of service offered will vary, but it is often at the X.25 network level, or the transport service level. There is now an increasing number of such devices on the market. Commonly, they implement a service such as the ARPA TCP/IP suite of protocols across an Ethernet. However, the program controlling the device is held in ROM chips, or perhaps loaded across the DMA interface from the host processor. Frequently, the program can be changed to implement some other service across the interface, or perhaps the same service, but built on top of a different suite of protocols.

There are many advantages to such devices. The two major ones are firstly that the overhead of implementing several layers of protocol are offloaded from the host and put into a special purpose processor, and secondly that it is much easier and quicker to implement an *interface* to a high level protocol, such as TCP or ISO transport, that is provided by one of these devices, rather than re-implement the *protocol stack* itself. One of the disadvantages of such packages is that they do tend to be rather expensive. "Expensive" is a relative term of course, and must be balanced against what other costs would be involved in providing the same service by other means. Host software in this area is also frequently expensive, and the costs of host resources enter the equation too.

This type of package is very effective at relieving the host system of mundane low level tasks concerned with a given stack of protocols. However, there are some architectural criticisms that can be made. It is indeed often true that in communications systems the communications lines are the primary source of errors. However, there are other important sources of error. It is the author's experience that some types of error can be introduced by this type of device. One of the more insidious types of error is when a frame of data is received correctly from the line by the device, and the device signals that the packet was correct. However, if something goes wrong, say with the DMA circuitry, the data may be corrupted between the computer memory and the device. In this way, errors are introduced which are very difficult to trace, particularly if the error is intermittent. In general, the hardware from which such systems are constructed is not of the same level of reliability as that from which large scale mainframes are built. For example, large mainframes often employ memory with Hamming Code error correction, and can continue to provide reliable user service in the face of memory faults. At the other extreme, the memory inside such a communications device may not even have parity error detection on the memory. A failing bit in memory may "merely" corrupt one data bit, or may perhaps corrupt pointers or machine instructions, with unlimited consequences.

As well as the various sorts of hardware error that can strike such devices, their increasing complexity means that bugs in either the hardware (such as the LSI chips) or in the firmware controlling any microprocessors inside the device are that much more likely.

As we have seen in Chapter 6, the ISO Transport protocol provides an end-to-end error checking option (class 4) when the underlying network service is of insufficient quality. There seems to be good reason to run such a protocol end to end, that is, not implemented in such front-end devices, since in this way many of the errors introduced by either the hardware or the software of these devices can be eliminated. Of course, the level of reliability of service that is required depends on the application, and in each case a decision must be made as to whether such an enhancement is necessary. The point is that the increasing complexity of communications devices and their architecture can introduce a new type of error at a rate which may be too high for some applications.

12.8   The Cost of Heavyweight Protocols

This discussion of offloading protocol support onto specialised microprocessors leads us into a consideration of the costs of heavyweight protocols. We started this chapter with a discussion of lightweight protocols as exemplified by the RPC approach to providing services across a network. We saw that various economies were indeed possible compared with the fully open heavyweight protocols. Now that we have examined some of the ways of implementing various levels of protocol in specialised hardware, it is time to return to the comparison between heavyweight and lightweight protocols.

One of the arguments against heavyweight protocols concerned their cost in terms of system resources. The underlying assumption was that the resources were taken from the host computer itself, and could otherwise be employed doing useful work such as running applications programs. However, if a protocol is implemented within a "black box" that is a fixed modest price, and gives a straightforward, simple, reliable interface to a host, then who cares what goes on inside? Few TV viewers care about the internal complexities of a TV set, TV studio, or international TV network bringing the latest live sports events from across the world. Similarly, why should we care that a new interface that has just been plugged into our favourite computer actually contains a specialised processor and hardware that is executing a huge program for a horrendously complex stack of protocols, and is actually consuming more internal resources than the host computer has directly available to itself? We see that the meaning of the word "cost" has suddenly become somewhat elusive.

However, there are still good reasons for wanting protocols to remain as simple as possible. As we have commented before, simpler devices are in general more reliable and bug free than more complex ones. It is all very well for chip designers to say *"Well, if we put it into silicon, why should you care about its complexity?"* Some of us have had to live with comparatively simple processes that have been put into silicon, such as the frame level of HDLC. The chip designers are onto new, more complex and exciting things. This is not merely a matter of chip design either. Software is at least as susceptible to bugs, and is just as frustrating to live with when blown into ROMs as is faulty hardware. Software in ROMs is sometimes referred to as "firmware", but a better word that is sometimes heard is "rigidware". There seems to be an inevitable human tendency to attempt to construct computer systems that are just beyond the capability of the tools that are to hand. This is not a new phenomenon. Parkinson's notorious laws were published many years ago, and this urge is clearly the manifestation of the same human trait in the computing environment. However, if the aim is to produce a reliable service rather than an elaborate one, then the moral is absolutely clear.

12.9   The Task Switching Overhead—Back-to-Back Blocks

We have studied at some length the performance implications of handling data in various sized pieces—byte, block, etc, and the various ways of minimising the system overhead. In discussing this we have been concerned with the total overhead in the system, and the cost in terms of the system resources consumed. Important though these considerations are, there is yet another aspect to the system overhead that is concerned with the reaction time of systems and the time constraints that need to be met.

To be more specific, let us consider the design of a device to handle fast input. Since the input is going to be fast, we may decide to construct a DMA device. For each input block the host processor loads up the device's control registers with the size of and a pointer to the input buffer. The hardware implements the frame level of the protocol, HDLC for example, and when an incoming packet is complete an interrupt is requested. The processor responds in some suitable way, and processes the incoming block. Eventually, the device will be supplied with a new size and pointer ready for the next block. The same buffer may well be re-used since the data it contained has now been processed. So far we have been concerned with the total system overhead per block. Naturally, we were keen to keep this as low as possible, but provided that the system overhead per block is less than the time between the arrival of the blocks, then we assumed that we would be able to keep up with the traffic flow. If we look a little more closely at handling our DMA device, we can see that there is still plenty of scope for trouble.

The way we have described the sequence of events for handling incoming frames has an inbuilt assumption that providing that the input buffer is ready for the end of an incoming frame, then we should be OK. In fact, of course, we must be ready for the *start* of the incoming block. Suppose that we have an incoming data rate of 9,600 bits per second. With HDLC, frames are separated by a sequence of one or more "flags": 01111110. Thus, the incoming data is assembled until the flag pattern is seen, at which point the interrupt is requested and the input DMA transfer is suspended until the control registers indicate that the next input buffer is ready for the next frame. In the meantime, input from the communications line may continue unabated. If we are lucky, then only flag bytes will be seen, and the line is effectively idle. However, in the worst case the blocks may arrive "back to back" with only a single flag between them. If we assume that the circuitry implementing the HDLC frame level will want to do byte-by-byte DMA transfer, then from the end of the flag terminating the last input block to the time that the first byte of the next frame is ready for DMA transfer is only a single byte time—$0.8mS$ at a speed of 9,600 bps. If we assume that the HDLC circuitry has storage for a few, say two or three, bytes, then the host processor will only have two or three mS to react to the interrupt for the last block complete and load up the DMA registers ready for the next frame. For higher speeds the required response time is proportionally shorter.

This is indeed a severe constraint. Remember that when we were discussing handling input data one byte at a time, we could only expect to handle a modest data rate because of the overhead. Well, now it seems that even when using a simple DMA device, the constraints are nearly as bad. Even though we have reduced the block-on-block processing time by putting the frame handling into hardware, the time constraint imposed by having to handle back-to-back blocks seems about the same.

Well, what are the consequences of missing occasional blocks in a back-to-back sequence? The most likely result of a device being unable to react in time to catch blocks coming in back-to-back is that it will receive alternate blocks correctly, and lose the other ones in between. *"Well, what does this matter?"* we might ask, *"Error recovery procedures will cause the blocks to be re-sent, so they will get through eventually."* That is true enough. Data is unlikely to be lost. But, consider an HDLC link for example. If blocks 1, 2, 3... are sent back-to-back, then block 1 will get through, block 2 will be lost, and block 3 will get through OK. At this point the receiver will see the gap in the sequence numbers, and respond with a Reject that requests the retransmission starting back at block 2. In the meantime the transmitter may well be on to transmitting blocks 4 or 5. On receipt of the Reject it backs up and transmits the sequence 2, 3, 4, ... This time 2 gets through, 3 gets lost, and 4 triggers the reject. The transmitter backs up from block 5 or perhaps 6, and resends 3, 4, 5, ... Thus, we see that for every packet that gets through several others are transmitted and retransmitted several times.

Indeed, the problem may be even worse. Suppose that when the transmitter receives a reject, it is transmitting a block, n. The transmitter may either abort the transmission of this block, or it may just complete the transmission of this block, and then follow that transmission immediately with the retransmission of the block requested in the reject. Now, if block n was one that the receiver was receiving correctly, then it will miss the next block because of its slow reaction time, and a further reject and retransmission may be required before the block finally gets through. Of course, a second Reject is not allowed in HDLC until a rejected frame has been received correctly, and thus the transmitter must time out and retransmit the packet—an even longer delay. In severe cases the link may loop and never get the rejected packet through. In this case, the link will time out and need to reinitialise. One other way in which the system may be worse is if the traffic is very busy in both directions, then the transmitter may well miss a reject packet. In this case the error recovery will fall back on the timeout. This will of necessity waste a long time—equivalent to the transmission time of many packets on the link.

Datagram networks are not necessarily any better, and can be worse. Suppose a network is transmitting an IP datagram, and that the IP datagram has been fragmented into, say, seven fragments because it is rather larger than the transmission medium can comfortably handle. If *any* of the seven fragments is lost, then the reassembly of the IP datagram at the receiver will fail, and the *whole* IP datagram—that is, all the seven fragments—will be retransmitted. It is not difficult to see that problems in receiving back-to-back blocks may mean that IP datagrams may *never* get through.

On the other hand, if recovery is at the same level as the packet that is lost (i.e. that there is no fragmentation at this level) then the datagram approach may, with suitable recovery techniques, be less impacted by this kind of error than than other forms of data transmission since the successfully transmitted packets are not delayed behind the packets that have been lost and need retrnsmission.

Whatever the reason, it is clearly extremely undesirable to have a system that misses packets, since the impact on the throughput of the link can be disasterous.

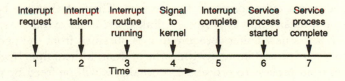

Fig 12.4.   The Anatomy of an Interrupt

There are several techniques that can be employed to enable us to meet these time constraints. Firstly, consider Fig 12.4. This is a schematic diagram of the sequence of events when an interrupt occurs. There is no implication that the diagram is to scale, and indeed, the time between events 1 and 2 and between events 5 and 6 may sometimes be very short.

In our discussion above, we have assumed that the DMA device is not re-enabled until late in the period 6 to 7 when the process that services the interrupt is running, possibly immediately before it terminates at 7. It may be necessary to work this way if only a single input buffer is available, since the contents of any buffer must be completely processed (or moved elsewhere) before any further input DMA is enabled into the same buffer. By looking at it in this way, we see the obvious method for improving things—use more than one buffer. If a second buffer is allocated to each input device then a considerable improvement can be achieved, since before one buffer is processed DMA can be enabled into the other buffer. When the processing of the first buffer is complete, it is then ready for use after the next interrupt. Thus the two buffers get used alternately, and are sometimes referred to as "swing buffers". The clear advantage of this method is that the DMA into the next buffer can be enabled much earlier, and the earlier the better. The best time of all is as soon as possible after point 3 when the interrupt routine gains control, though even if the interrupt routines cannot be altered, and only the service process can be changed, then enabling DMA into a swing buffer soon after the start of the service routine is much better than just before the end.

Note that we have been assuming that when we get an interrupt for input DMA complete, that the processing of the other buffer to which we are about to swap will be complete, and it will be free for reuse. This may not always be so, and it is important to ensure by some means that buffers do not get reused too early. There are many obvious ways of doing this by setting flags and suchlike, and the details will be strongly dependent on the individual hardware and software systems in use.

However, one method has wider possibilities. This method involves keeping a queue of free buffers. The available free buffers are arranged into a queue or pool of some sort. The fact that the buffer is in the pool means that it is free. A linked list is an excellent arrangement. When a new buffer is required, it is obtained from the pool. The buffer may be passed around within the system, for example by passing pointers from process to process. Eventually, it will be freed by putting it back into the free pool or queue. This method of keeping all the free buffers together has several advantages. Firstly, the fact that the buffer is in the pool means that it is free for reuse, and thus no further flags are needed to ensure this. Secondly, several processes may share the same pool of buffers, and thus the profligate allocation of two buffers per device (with the swing buffer arrangement) is avoided.

As always, there are drawbacks. The buffer pool must be allocated in some suitable way. This is not straightforward, since buffer allocation and freeing must in general be done from asynchronous processes such as interrupt routines. In the worst case, this will have to be done with some kind of kernel assistance. This is called "worst case" since any sort of kernel assistance is usually comparatively expensive, and thus to be avoided if possible. However, the cost may still be justified depending on circumstances. Often the buffer allocation may be handled much more efficiently. In small dedicated processors it is often possible to code tight routines that "seize" the processor by some means (perhaps by masking off all interrupts for a few critical instructions) while the allocation is performed. Some machine architectures have recognised this basic need by providing special machine instructions that can be used for this purpose. Thus the IBM 370 architecture has the set of *Compare and Swap*—CS instructions, and the DEC VAX has specific instructions to manipulate linked lists.

There is another possible problem with several processes sharing a pool of buffers. We said earlier that *"The fact that the buffer is in the pool means that it is free."*. The problem arises when one or more of the group of processes sharing the buffer pool has bugs. Two types of bug are troublesome in such a shared pool environment. One is when a process "frees" a buffer, but accidentally keeps a pointer to the buffer. It then later continues to use the buffer. In the meantime, another process gets the "free" buffer from the pool and starts to use it. Multiple use of the buffer in this way can lead to all sorts of challenging errors including corrupted data, and corrupted buffer chains (when an already "free" buffer is "freed" a second time). The other variant on this theme is when a process forgets to free a buffer when it is finished with it. The most frequently used paths through the code are usually correct, and this sort of error will tend to occur in the infrequent exceptional cases. This leads to a gradual "leakage" of buffers, and the system will eventually grind to a halt as it runs out of buffers. There are programming techniques available to enable the elimination of such errors, but they are beyond the scope of this book.

There are other techniques that can enable us to catch back-to-back blocks arriving at high speed. One is for the device itself to have a built-in silo for received data. A grain silo is a vertical tower where grain is added at the top, and is taken out at the bottom. In computing, this is a first-in, first-out device—a FIFO—in contrast to a stack which is last-in, first-out—a LIFO. An electronic silo takes data in and stores it internally. The data can then be removed some time later, but in the same order. This is a hardware implementation of an elastic queue.

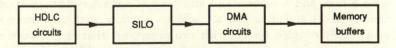

Fig 12.5.   An Elastic Buffer for Fast Input Blocks

Fig 12.5 shows a silo being used to buffer data between the

HDLC circuitry and the DMA circuits. The silo needs to store both input bytes and the control signals (such as end of block, valid checksum, etc). When the DMA circuit is enabled, it can work at very high speed until the silo is emptied. Then bytes fall through one by one until the end of the next frame. Of course, very short frames may be stored in the silo in their entirety, particularly if the reaction of the host is momentarily sluggish for some reason.

In this way, we can see that the silo allows the DMA circuitry more time to be set up for the next incoming frame before the incoming data starts to get lost. For example, if we used a silo that could contain 40 bytes together with the corresponding control signals, then the required reaction times have been increased by a factor of 40.

Fig 12.6.   An Elastic Buffer for Fast Input Bits

Another variation on this theme is to put the silo between the HDLC circuitry and the bits coming in from the modem, as in Fig 12.6. For this scheme to work, the output from the silo into the HDLC chip must be held up when the DMA is not enabled, and then must run faster to catch up when the next buffer has been set up. The external effect is much the same as using the silo to buffer the bytes that have been stripped out of the frame in the last section.

Other hardware variations are also possible, such as being able to supply the next buffer to the device before it is needed. In this way, the device can itself set up the DMA for the next buffer immediately the last input has finished. An obvious extension is to have not just one buffer, but a silo for more buffers. Such an arrangement can only be justified in the most extreme performance environments.

As a final variation, the device and the host processor can share memory. The device will probably then contain its own dedicated processor. With such an arrangement, almost any buffer strategy may be implemented, even to the extent of the device accessing the common buffer pool directly. It is not clear any longer that we are really working with a host and a device (and still have the master–slave relationship that implies) and it is just as valid to consider such an arrangement as a closely coupled system with two processors sharing the same main memory. However, it is normal with a multiple-CPU system to have processors all of the same type. On the other hand, with a system of the type we are describing, it is normal to have the host and the device containing quite different processors. In addition, there may be wide differences in power between the two processors. Sometimes the communications adaptor has the slower processor, but sometimes it may be more powerful than the "main" CPU. As usual, there is a cost. One of the costs that is most difficult to quantify is the fact that an error, hardware or software, in such a tightly coupled system can affect any other processor system directly. Eliminating software bugs or chasing hardware faults can be very difficult indeed.

12.10   The Impact of Transmission Errors on Throughput

It is easy to fall into the trap of assuming that if, say, one packet in 100 suffers a transmission error, then the throughput of a transmission link will be reduced proportionally, i.e. by about 1% in our example. However, if we merely look back to our discussion of the impact of missed blocks when running back to back to realise that the same considerations apply here too. Suppose that the round trip delay on an HDLC link is about n packets long (necessitating a window size of n for continuous operation). If a single packet is lost, and its loss detected at the receiver by a gap in the received sequence numbers, then the activation of the reject mechanism will not be able to initiate a retransmission and successful reception in less than n packet times, resulting in the loss of at least n packets. As the length of the link (in units of packets) increases, this loss becomes more important.

Of course, average throughput is only one measure of this impact. Another is the extra delay introduced. It may be that this delay becomes excessive for the application. There are several possible responses to this problem, should it arise. One is to abandon the HDLC type of recovery in which packets after a gap are discarded and the sender backs up and retransmits the missing packet and everything after it. Instead we need a mechanism for requesting the selective retransmission of the missing packet alone. Indeed some of the earlier and more complex versions of HDLC had just such a mechanism. Such a method still causes some hesitation in the flow, but the hesitation is only for the missing packet, rather than for all the other retransmissions too.

Another strategy is to implement several independent flows interleaved on the same link. Thus, we could imagine that each of the packets in the HDLC window instead of being strictly sequenced becomes part of a separately controlled flow, independent of all the other packets in the window. Thus, an error in one packet affects only the one multiplexed flow—since all the flows are decoupled then the other flows may proceed in full flood. A good example of this is a multiple parallel set of RPC operations that we described earlier. Of course, for this sort of approach to be valid, it places some constraint on the type of application that may use it. Thus, a single application cannot easily use all the bandwidth of a link with such an approach unless it is prepared to abandon the requirement that the data arrives in sequence. An interesting example of such an application is the blast file transfer protocol that we describe below.

Finally, if the delay must be avoided at all costs—for example with a deep space probe—then we must abandon reverse error correction altogether and resort to forward error correction as described in Chapter 2.

12.11   Non-Sequential Protocols

In the main in this book we have concentrated on flows of data that are in sequence and subject to flow control. However, let us now look at a particular type of flow that is subject to neither of these constraints, and challenges the traditional approach to transmitting data.

The blast protocol was invented for use on local area networks. These networks are usually based on some sort of shared medium such as the rings and buses that we described in Chapter 3. For our purposes now, the important points are:

1: They are fast, 1 to 10 Mbps or more, and
2: They have very short access times and end-to-end delay times (of the order of a few tens of microseconds because of their small geographical extent of typically a few Km).

Thus these networks are of comparable speed to the raw processor of many machines, and are faster than the reaction of most existing peripherals and of most operating systems.

It seems that on such networks, the "traditional" ordered flow of data with flow control limit the bandwidth available to a single user to a small fraction of what one might expect. For example, a pair of processes operating across a 10 Megabit ring may be able to obtain only a few hundred kilobits—a few percent of the total apparently available bandwidth.

The reasons for this are complex, and woolly statements like *"The protocol gets in the way"* are often made. One response to this has been to design a new breed of protocols sometimes referred to as "non-FIFO" protocols. For example the so-called "Blast file-transfer protocol" was designed at MIT. In the Blast protocol, the sender and receiver agree on the transfer, and settle on a rate which they expect to be able just to maintain. The sender then "blasts" the whole file to the sender at this agreed rate, with no responses from the receiver. The receiver "catches" whatever it can, possibly losing the odd block that arrives too fast. The sender finally transmits the end of file marker. The receiver then responds with a bit map to indicate those records that it missed. The sender then re-transmits the missing records, and the process is repeated until the receiver has all the blocks. Note that since this protocol allows for the receiver to lose the odd block, then it can be used on a medium that is subject to occasional losses too. The same recovery mechanism will suffice to recover from both sorts of loss.

Clearly, the blast protocol manages the flow in a way quite different from the methods of flow control we have discussed so far. In practice, a large fraction of the available bandwidth is obtainable by such methods, and the protocol functions much better than traditional sorts in such limited and rather specialised environments. It remains to be seen just where such techniques become necessary in the future.

Why do such radically different protocols seem to work so well? As yet this is a research question, but we may perhaps be able to see some inkling of the reason if we just think about the philosophy and design of the protocols. The "traditional" protocols have as their main aim the transfer of data in order, and without error or loss, and the prevention of the source overrunning the sink. The assumption is that overrun is *A Bad Thing*. In addition, the protocols are mostly designed either explicitly for slow networks, or with slow networks being the background in which the designer has always worked. Many links to public networks operate at 1000 characters per second or less, and such bandwidth may be shared by many users. The expensive, unusual 50 Kbps link is still commonly referred to as "wideband". It is only comparatively recently that higher speeds have started to become more widely available. Again, ignoring any other considerations, light takes over a millisecond to travel 200 miles, and the delay in satellite links is painfully obvious even inserted into a human telephone conversation, or live TV interview conducted via a satellite link. Thus all the speeds and times are much slower than those within most computer systems, even cheap personal micros. As an example of this assumption, look at Figs 4.4 and 4.5 describing M and N pacing: there the only times shown are communications delays—the delays within the operating systems are assumed to be so small by comparison as to be negligible.

On the other hand, the fast local area network is a different kind of computer peripheral—one whose response times are comparable to or shorter than those of the computing systems. With a 10 megabit LAN, a packet of a few hundred bytes may well take much less than a millisecond from start to finish. Thus, this time is less than the process switching time within many machines. Clearly, such fast devices will interact with the computing system in a way that is fundamentally different from the way in which devices a thousand times slower interact. For example, the question arises *"If a task is waiting for output completion on such a fast device, is it better to switch tasks in the traditional manner, and to switch back when the completion interrupt occurs, or is it better to wait synchronously, polling for the completion of the operation?"* In contrast to common practice, it is almost certainly better to do the latter. Here we have returned to one of the techniques of section 12.6 when considering multiple packet interactions.

> **Exercise 12.2**   Under what circumstances might the "blast protocol" perform well, and when poorly? When might there be undesirable side-effects?

12.12   Error Recovery and Network Congestion

There is yet another way in which the impact of errors may have a disproportionate effect on overall network performance. This is because either a transmission error, or an error caused by a discarded datagram may trigger increased network traffic causing congestion and thus an increase in the rate of discarding packets. This then feeds back as increased errors, and thus more traffic. This feedback may cause serious network problems, and so we shall study it a little more deeply

Suppose that the datagram network is being used to support many bilateral connections, and that these connections are being supported by some window protocol to recover from lost datagrams. Further suppose that one end sends a series of datagrams A, B, C, D, E, and, say, datagram B is discarded because of congestion. When it is realised that packet B has been lost, the normal recovery action is to "back up" and retransmit the sequence, starting with the packet that has been lost. In this way datagrams B, C, D, and E will be retransmitted. If this is done rapidly, then there will be an increase in network traffic because of the retransmissions. If the congestion is caused by the combined traffic of many users, and each of them starts to lose odd datagrams, then all users will start retransmitting datagrams, and a network that was previously just nudging up to the overload limit with the odd datagram being discarded will suddenly be pushed over the edge. There will be a sudden feedback, with more datagrams being discarded, causing more retransmissions causing more traffic causing more datagrams to be discarded. This is sometimes referred to as "congestion collapse".

In order to avoid this type of problem, the users of a datagram network need to recognise that a likely cause of lost datagrams is due to them being discarded because of congestion, and that increasing the offered traffic is only likely to make the matters worse. Thus, all datagram producers should voluntarily reduce the rate at which they feed new packets into the network when they start to see lost packets. In this way, the overall network benefits, and so do all the network users.

It is not difficult to see a parallel here between a datagram network and contention access to a shared medium such as an Ethernet or Aloha channel as examined in Chapter 3. In these cases, we saw that as the load increased there was an increased probability of a collision leading to a loss of packets or a delay in network access, and that the users of this shared medium needed to cooperate to keep the load low enough so that the collisions were kept within bounds. The parallel with a datagram network where the traffic needs to be kept low enough to avoid the need to discard datagrams is compelling.

As a final example of the complex interactions that can take place between congestion and throughput, consider a gateway that, for example, connects a fast network via a slow link to another fast network. Suppose that a large packet, say an IP datagram is sent from one network to the other, and is fragmented into, say, eight fragments before being sent off. When the eight fragments arrive at the slow gateway in rapid succession, they may well cause congestion. If the gateway has a small buffer space, it may only be able to handle the first seven fragments and will have to discard the last one. At the receiving end the fragments are re-assembled into the IP datagram, but because one is missing, the whole datagram will be discarded. The error recovery is to resend the whole large packet, and again, only $^7/_8{}^{ths}$ will get through. Even though the gateway is functioning, the data flow is effectively blocked. We see here one case (which actually occurred in practice—the IP datagram *was* rather large) where the protocols and the gateway's handling of congestion interacted in a very unfortunate way.

12.13 Summary

We have compared lightweight and heavyweight protocols, and seen that while considerable savings may sometimes be had by using lightweight protocols, there may be severe problems in terms of generality and openness. We have also looked at the interaction of protocols with operating systems and specialist hardware and seen some of the many varied divisions of labour that may be made.

We have seen how some kinds of transmission errors may have a disproportionate effect on throughput, even resulting in complete stoppage, and have looked at ways of reducing this kind of effect. A non-sequential protocol was also examined, and its contrast with more usual sequential protocols helped our understanding of both kinds of protocol.

13
Network Management

The subject of this chapter is the management of a network. By this we do not mean the administration involved in the human side of affairs, but in the internal maintenance of the network. Networks often consist of many machines that co-operate together to provide a service. In the case of a basic network service, these machines are usually dedicated switches of some kind, joined together by links that may be point-to-point or shared in some way. A network may involve tens to thousands of linked machines. If a network is of a "higher level" kind, say a mail network, then the main difference is that the nodes of the network are more likely not to be dedicated machines, but to be processes running within a host system whose primary function is, say, providing a time-shared interactive service. A prime example of such a higher level network is the BITNET/NETNORTH/EARN mail network

With all of these networks there are some common operations that need to be performed in similar ways. The sorts of operation are the monitoring of the operation of the network, the incidence of errors, the traffic pattern, congestion and delays, reliability and so on. Related to this is the reaction to problems—when things break do we just wait until lines or machines are fixed, or do we try to find an alternate route around the problem? How do we manage the network to include new destinations or routes to these destinations, and how do we remove destinations when they are decommissioned? On a day-to-day basis, how do we chase bugs in the network? Bugs always occur in real operating systems of course, never in test situations.

We need special tools to deal with the problems. When we have found software bugs, we need to fix the software. How do we then install it across our tens or thousands of machines without disrupting service? These, and a host of related problems in the technical management of networks, are the subject of this chapter. Mostly, the methods employed are specialised to the particular environment, and generalised methods of managing are still in their infancy. However, an examination of some of the ad hoc techniques should better prepare the reader for the general kinds of problem that she may encounter.

13.1   Error Monitoring

It is fairly common to log the occurrence of transmission errors. These are usually kept as counts of some sort. This is the easy part—it is much more difficult to do something useful with the figures produced. First, we need some suitable means of retrieving the counts and processing them. Any processing is most usefully done at some one place where the various counts from the network machines are gathered together and compared in some way. The counts will need to be transferred across the network itself as data and gathered together as a preliminary to the analysis.

This in itself means that if we are retrieving counts from some isolated stand-alone machines, then those machines must be capable not only of their normal task switching traffic between other places, but also of being the source and the sink of at least this specialised type of traffic. Purpose-designed switches are designed only to switch traffic for others, and being able to understand requests for data from themselves and respond appropriately with results is a significant extension of their function.

Once the error statistics have been gathered, how should we process them? Indeed, the question needs inverting—what processing do we want to do, and thus what raw statistics do we need to gather? Transmission errors can be caused either by interference of some sort "on the line" or by faults in the modem or the computer interface. In general, interference has a fairly random pattern with the exception of bursts of errors that we have often noted. Faults caused by equipment, however, follow a fairly definite pattern. Firstly, there is a low level of random errors that correspond to normal healthy operation. This level is normally extremely low, and may be undetectable.

Sometimes, though, the level begins to rise, and often such an increase is a sign that the device is about to fail. Thus, if we monitor the error rate on a network and follow the error rates link by link, we have a tool for diagnosing places where more serious failures are likely to develop days or weeks into the future. By this means, it is possible to use the next scheduled maintenance period to test or replace the suspect equipment, and thus avoid the consequences of failure at a less convenient time. Of course, not all failures are considerate enough to give such warning, but enough follow this pattern of onset to make this a method of great practical value.

To implement such a process, we need to collect both the error count and the traffic count periodically, and compare them with historical values. This is most usefully done by some program that is run periodically, and which brings changes of potential interest to the attention of some human operating staff.

This general class of error mechanism is important enough that various provisions have been built into the slotted and token ring architectures to gather and process such error data. Indeed this is one of the clear operational advantages claimed for ring architectures compared with bus architectures for local area networks. Since a ring is essentially a set of point-to-point links, then any errors are clearly concerned with a small set of equipment attached to that segment of the ring. On the other hand, errors seen on a bus network are much more difficult to ascribe to a small amount of equipment and thus the maintenance problem is that much more difficult.

13.2   Traffic and Congestion

Traffic and congestion also need regular measurement in order that the network may be tuned to give good service. Traffic in a network is notoriously "bursty". For example, a network whose prime function is to connect interactive terminals to a time-sharing mainframe has a traffic pattern which corresponds with the user pattern—one peak in late morning, and another in mid afternoon. As another example, it has been noted that a local network of personal workstations, each with its own working disc but with a network file server for archive and backup, sees a large peak at the end of the working day as everyone backs up the day's work before going home. Networks, like roads, need to be able to manage the worst traffic of the day, and the traffic at quieter times will take care of itself.

In the early days of computer networks, there was a strong emphasis on designing networks so that they matched the expected traffic flow with some precision. The techniques required for this type of analysis are well known from other branches of engineering, including the telephone network. For an introduction, see, for example, Tanenbaum (1981). We have chosen not to look at such methods partly because they are treated elsewhere, and partly because they are of less importance now than they used to be.

Precise network sizing is of less importance today because the economics of bandwidth have changed dramatically. In the early days of networking, both bandwidth and machine resources were very expensive. To a very large extent, this has now changed. In the late 1960s, a point-to-point link of 1200 bits per second was good, and 2400 bps was really something. Front-end machines to match would cost tens of thousands of dollars. In the late 1980s long haul links of 9600bps are normal, of 64,000 bps are commonplace and speeds in the megabit range are available from many public utilities. Not only are these vastly increased speeds available, but the cost of bandwidth is strongly non-linear. It is normal to be able to increase the speed of a link by a factor of five or ten but with only a very modest increase in the cost. This is of course because the faster links, say 64,000 bps or 2,040,000 bps are the internal speeds that the PTTs are using for voice anyway, and producing slower links means using expensive multiplexors.

Speeds on local networks start at hundreds of kilobits per second, and go up through 100 megabits or more. The upper limit tends to be set by the attached computers rather than by the links.

In addition, the advent of the microprocessor has meant that processor power has seen an even more dramatic rise in availability, and fall in cost.

The result of all this is that it is generally possible in some sense to throw resources at performance problems. Thus, if some link in a network becomes congested at a peak period, then it will typically be upgraded from say 9,600 to 64,000 bps in one jump, since any more modest increase is probably not even available. So while in the past the delay on a particular link would be monitored carefully, and individual links would be upgraded by a modest 50% or so as the traffic demanded, we now see the change in the speed of the links being much greater. It is as if the road system was upgraded in one step by replacing a dirt road by a four lane divided highway.

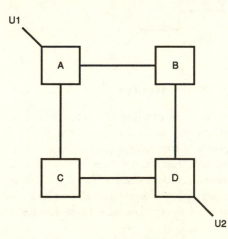

Fig 13.1. Simple Network

Indeed, with this type of availability of bandwidth, we sometimes see another trend in that we are able effectively to change the topology of networks in response to traffic demand. Consider, for example, Fig 13.1. Here we see a simple four node network. When user U1 communicates with user U2, her traffic must go via either nodes B or C, as well as the nodes A and D. As the link speeds increase, the delay time across the network decreases, until we reach a point where the major delay in travelling across the network is not due to the transmission time down the internode links, but is caused by the processing delays in the machines on the route.

Suppose that with the network in Fig 13.1, we have just upgraded the line speeds by some large factor—perhaps going from 64Kbps up to 1,000Kbps. It may well be that beyond a link speed of, say 200Kbps the processing delays dominate, and the effect of further increases in link speed is negligible.

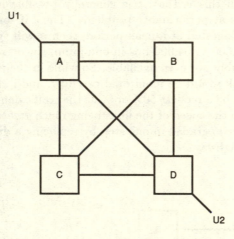
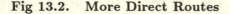

Fig 13.2.   More Direct Routes

Suppose that instead of upgrading the speeds of the links to 1000Kbps, we could instead modify the topology of the network to that of Fig 13.2, but with the speeds of the links upgraded to 200Kbps instead of the faster speed. We can see that traffic from U1 to U2 will traverse the network in Fig 13.2 faster than network in Fig 13.1. This is because the delays on the links are negligible, despite the slower link speeds, but there are less store and forward delays because there are less nodes en route.

This may seem all very well, but it seems to imply that more slower links need to be rented, and thus higher costs incurred. However, Fig 13.3 shows that this is not necessarily the case. This is because the two diagonal links in the network can be constructed out of the raw speed of the higher speed links by using multiplexors and connecting the subdivided links across from one multiplexor to another, thus avoiding the extra step through the node.

The multiplexors have been used to subdivide the very high speed communications lines into a more useful and convenient size. The fact is that it is easy for the user to subdivide the raw communications bandwidth into these convenient sized chunks, and connect them

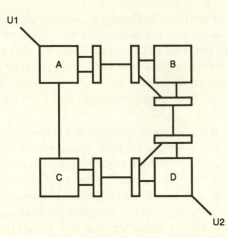

Fig 13.3.   Actual Implementation of Direct Routes

together in this useful way. It is seldom so convenient for the PTT providing the lines to be able to exploit such convenience on a large scale, and thus its tariffs must be pitched accordingly.

13.3   Dynamic Reconfiguration

Any network will suffer from faults from time to time. Two of the most common are that a node or a link will develop a fault and be out of action for some time. In Chapter 5 we have studied various routing strategies, including adaptive routing. With adaptive routing, a network can adapt automatically using alternate routes around a failing node or link—providing such alternate routes are available of course. However, some networks do not have adaptive routing for one reason or another, and in this case some sort of manual intervention is required. We saw in Chapter 5 that routing was usually performed by some sort of routing table. Establishing a different route manually involves altering the routing tables to establish a new route around the obstruction. It is possible that such alterations may be facilitated by explicit tools to allow the alteration of the routes. However, it is more likely that the tools described below to patch working systems will be employed to patch the tables themselves.

13.4   Distributing and Loading New Network Software

"Ordinary", or non-network software is distributed by various means. Discs or tapes are the most common, though much code is installed in *read only memory*—ROM chips, and software is increasingly sent across computer networks. From time to time, new versions of such software are produced, either to fix problems or to enhance facilities. The software is usually loaded into a machine for execution except for ROM software, which stays permanently loaded. "Network software", or software that runs in the machines that provide the network service has a significantly different pattern of maintenance. We shall see why this is by first considering the use of ordinary software, and then comparing this with network software.

Ordinary software is loaded usually under the control of a person operating the machine. The operator may be loading and tending a shared machine if it is a medium to large scale interactive time-shared system, or she may be doing the loading just for herself if the machine is a dedicated single-user system. The loading or "booting" process usually takes place at the start of the user's working day, though shared systems tend to run continuously for days or weeks without being restarted. Any booting of software not already in ROM is usually from an attached disc.

Machines that constitute a network tend to have a different pattern of use. Networks are a resource that is expected to be available whenever anyone or any user machine feels inclined to use it—something like the mains electric power or the telephone. Networks have become utilities. While personal machines may work for 10, 20, 40 hours or more per week, and time-shared systems work 100 up to perhaps 168 hours per week, networks are expected always to be available 168 hours week in and week out. A time-shared machine may have a scheduled maintenance period each Wednesday morning (or whenever), but networks, because of their general service nature, are expected to run with as little interruption to service as possible.

In addition to this, personal machines are operated by their users, and shared machines by dedicated operators who also service such devices as printers and tape drives. Sometimes networks are also serviced by operators. However, network machines are often expected to run unattended, with only the absolute minimum of human intervention. One further difference between user service machines and network machines is that normal network switches have little use for disc storage. Discs may be of use in loading the initial program, but then most switches have no further need of discs—packets must be switched in and out as fast as possible, not stored on disc. Some gateways may need disc storage for accounting and authorisation purposes, but these functions are not common compared with the simpler switch machine. One other reason for wishing to avoid the use of discs as an essential part of the operation of network switches is the need for regular maintenance with discs. This is incompatible with the very high duty cycle that we have just seen is expected of network components.

Finally, users tend to see shared or personal machines as direct services in themselves. The users often need to identify a particular machine—either the thing cluttering up their desk, or the specific time sharing service that they need to log on to. On the other hand, networks are seen rather as necessary impediments in between—even worse than Victorian children, they are preferably neither seen nor heard.

All of these differences between service and network machines conspire to make them broadly different. There is a much higher tendency for network machines to have no discs, to start up automatically whenever they are powered on (the ultimate "turnkey" systems), normally to run continuously for weeks on end, and to be hidden in unattended rooms with only a fire detector for company.

Such arrangements bring their own specific problems. For instance, must the machines have their program in ROM, since the normal alternative of a disc is not present? What happens when a serious fault develops? Must an operator be dispatched to the remote hiding place of the machine with a key to the locked door, or can some other action be taken? There are some challenging problems here both of a technical and a managerial nature.

Let us first take the loading of the program. ROMs can be used, but they have several serious drawbacks. In the early days of networking they were not usually large enough to contain the large amount of code needed to operate the machine as a full-blown switch. In addition, once a program is "blown" into a ROM, then the way of changing the program is to blow a new ROM, and then physically to visit the machine, switch it off, and install the new chips. Such intervention is not only cumbersome in the extreme, but also impacts seriously on the availability of the network. In addition, disturbing the hardware is a sure way to invite hardware problems and reduce reliability.

An alternative that has found fairly wide favour is that of downline loading. With this technique, only a small stand-alone loader program is blown into ROM. When the machine first starts up, it automatically enters this stand-alone loader program. It is the loader's task to communicate via the network to some network management machine. The network management machine has a full-blown file system in which is stored the program to be loaded, down the line, into each of the network machines. The network management machine identifies the empty machine and selects the appropriate program to load into it. The program is then transferred across the network and loaded into the target machine. Finally, the loader starts the loaded program.

It is normal for the down-line loading process to be done using a very simple specialised protocol. The main aim must be to make the loading process both simple and robust. In this way the small ROM program can be made simple and small, and thus be much less likely to suffer from errors that might require the replacement of the ROM.

Using a more generalised protocol, such as X.25, would not be appropriate here. X.25 is sufficiently complex that its implementation may well go through several releases before it is "right". In addition, the need to support, say, national options or new versions (such as the move from the 1980 version to the 1984 version), all mean that a simpler protocol is preferable for the down-line loading process. There is another reason for not using the full-blown protocol for the down-line loading process itself. If the ROM loader is implementing the full-blown protocol then it can only be importing more or less a different version of itself. Unless the down-line loader is much simpler than the full-blown program it loads, there is little point in the process, and we might as well put the full-blown program into ROM and be done with it.

By such a down-line loading process, a network of many nodes can be loaded from a central machine. Only the central machine itself needs to have a proper file store. The attached network can be loaded machine by machine working outwards from the central machine. Once the whole network is loaded, individual machines can be reloaded as necessary after a software failure.

Clearly, the fact that the central machine must have discs means that it is itself subject to the reduced duty cycle and increased main-tenance requirements that we said that we wished to avoid for network components. Making discless machines dependent on the less available network management machine apparently violates this desire. However, to miss-quote the song *"This 'aint necessarily so"*. Once network ma-chines are loaded, they can be expected to continue to operate over long periods, and only occasionally need reloading after some failure. With a single network control machine, this failure only impacts reliability when the failures coincide with the times when the network control machine is itself unavailable. If even this level of reliability is insufficient, then the network control machine can be replicated as needed until the required level of availability is achieved.

With such an arrangement of network control machines and downline loading, releasing new versions of network software becomes comparatively easy. First, the new software is set up in the one or more control machines. Then, at some prearranged time—probably at dead of night when traffic is minimal or perhaps when the last virtual call through the node is cleared—the network control machine forcibly reloads the network machines with the new software. Such a process can easily be made completely automatic, and it is easy—and routine—to reload a large network more quickly than a person can replace the ROM on a single machine—and while that person is asleep in bed too.

Network control machines typically serve other functions besides loading and reloading a network. When serious errors occur in any computer program it is often useful, as with any accident, to pick over the wreckage and try to obtain some clue as to the cause of the problem. This information can then be used to eliminate future errors of the same sort. With computer programs, this often involves "taking a dump", since the whole of memory is "dumped" into some filestore for future examination with whatever tools are available. With isolated network machines, there is no local file store where the dump can be put, so clearly if the network control machine loads "downline", then it must also dump "upline". Since this process is so similar to downline loading, only a small extension of the ROM loader program and the specialised protocol is necessary to allow upline dumps.

To complete the picture, we note that service machines with operators sometimes have facilities for displaying and altering the memory of the running system. The facilities may be very raw in that they may only allow the reference to absolute addresses in memory, or they may be arbitrarily more sophisticated and allow the reference to certain named system variables, and so forth. Such facilities may be used by skilled system programmers for a variety of purposes. Since isolated switches do not have an operator console, then any such facilities must be available downline from the network control machine. However, just as patch facilities are very dangerous tools in a normal service environment, they are doubly dangerous in the network environment. The patch facility itself is dependent on the network services provided by the system that is being patched. Nevertheless, the author has witnessed remote patching taking place across a distance of several thousand miles on another continent—perhaps the hallmark of a "Real Network Programmer"?

Of course, more sophisticated tools are sometimes available. Clearly, a display and modify facility is a very general tool. Providing the user has a detailed knowledge of the system, and has up-to-date listings of the code available, then many things can be done. However, the display/modify tool is not completely general. For example, if there is a dynamic linked list of buffers, then a series of displays will not safely be able to link down the chain, since the chain may well change substantially between individual displays. In addition, patching memory is a notoriously high-risk operation because of the possibility of typing errors, etc.—hence the reference to "Real Programmers" above. Much more satisfactory are more specific tools. Thus, a primitive operation for changing routing tables that says something like *"Route packets for destination* X *along link* Y*"* is much less error-prone than finding the location of the routing table, calculating the position of the entry for destination X, and patching the appropriate byte, word, or whatever to the internal representation of Y. Further, such operations as removing the last element from a specific buffer queue can only be done properly by having the right primitive operations available.

Now that we have seen how we might arrange the loading, dumping and installation of new versions of network software from network control machines, let us turn to a consideration of the remaining types of management facilities that we need. When a service machine is started there is typically some button to press that causes the machine to "boot" or otherwise reinitialise and load the appropriate control program. When a network machine is switched on this process must be started automatically. Usually, this is no problem, since many machines have some suitable automatic startup facility that allows the machine to enter the ROM downline loader immediately after switching on.

It is potentially much more of a problem to make sure that every possible type of error is trapped in the machine. Depending on the specific machine, various types of error may be trapped, such as invalid memory address, overflow, invalid instruction, etc. It is usually fairly straightforward to trap these errors with some appropriate software routine and take some appropriate corrective action. The appropriate action will vary depending on the error and the structure of the system. In all cases, some attempt should be made to report the error so that the problem may be fixed in the future. After reporting, the error should be handled, preferably with minimal damage to the network. Such handling may at best cause the loss of a packet that is later recovered by some recovery protocol, through a RESET for some virtual call, to at worst the complete reload of the node downline from the control centre, and the loss of all calls in progress through the node at the time of the error.

Whatever the precise action, the reporting and handling of the error should normally be done as expeditiously as possible to minimise the impact on the network service. The worst thing that can happen is for the node to hang indefinitely and need direct human intervention. This is as bad as the deadlock that we discussed in Chapter 5, since it has a major impact on network operation, particularly if the machine is inconveniently located and the access is correspondingly difficult and delayed.

As a real example of this type of problem from the author's own experience, consider the following. (The names have not been quoted in order to protect the guilty.) A node program contained trap routines for all the errors that were trappable on the machine. However, there was one instruction, the "HALT" instruction, which was not trappable. The effect of this instruction is that normal CPU operation is halted, and a small monitor microprogram is entered. This microprogram tries to talk to a specific attached terminal, and the intention is to allow the human user to display and modify memory or registers, and then restart the program. With a directly attached terminal, this is often an extremely useful debugging tool.

However, with a remote machine there was no console to talk to. The control program tried to send data to the console, got an invalid address error because it wasn't there, trapped back into the control program that tried to access the console... The worst has happened. The machine has gone into an infinite loop and will sulk there until some action is taken to kick it back into the ROM loader. How can we manage to live with such an awkward machine?

Well, due to a lack of vision or foresight, the facility could not be disabled. The solution seems simple and obvious—just don't execute a halt instruction. Well, obviously, we tried not to. The code contained none. The problem was that the code for a HALT was binary zero. Just now and again perhaps the use of a faulty buffer pointer could cause a zero to be written into the middle of code, or sometimes a peripheral device can malfunction and write a zero where it shouldn't. A branch index can have a bad value and jump into the middle of data, or an intermittent memory fault can start to develop. We managed to reduce the incidence of the error, but it is always impossible finally to eliminate the last error.

However, our "final solution" came close enough to elimination for our purposes. This was a hardware solution. A small amount of circuitry was added, actually on the ROM loader card, that sensed the bus of the machine for the address of the control register of the console. If this appeared on the bus, then either the control microprogram had just got control, or the software was trying to access something that it shouldn't. The circuitry responds to this by giving the processor an external signal that causes it to execute the power-on sequence and enter the ROM loader. This thus avoids the troublesome console support in the microprogram. Whilst we felt pleased with the eventual fix for this problem, much time and trouble could have been saved if the useless HALT facility could have been disabled in the first place.

In our anecdote, we have touched on some of the considerations that we must make in the "real world". Many of these considerations are the dirty end of programming that systems must handle on any real hardware. With a reasonable operating system the everyday applications programmer is protected from such considerations. However, network software is normally run on systems that do not have the friendly support of elaborate operating systems, and need to interface directly with the hardware in its raw state. Network programming is firmly in the "systems programming" sphere. Coping with hardware failures should be the expected everyday norm.

When writing software there is a host of tools and techniques that are available to improve the quality of the code produced. However, we are still a long way from being able to produce perfect code for other than toy systems. Thus, we need to allow not only for code that is faulty in the first place, but also for obscure errors that may cause code to become corrupted either because of its own faulty operation (via bad data pointers for example) or because of faulty hardware. Hardware can fail in the most creative of ways. Memory failures can corrupt pointers and change code itself to do surprising things. DMA devices can run amuck. When things go seriously wrong very quickly, the errors are detected very quickly, but the most insidious type of error is the occasional DMA error, or the single memory bit fault that changes say a byte operation into a word operation.

Thus, while we can try to eliminate a certain class of error by various techniques, we should never assume that we have completely succeeded. The techniques may not be perfect, and in any case neither hardware nor software is ever 100% trustworthy.

13.5   Software Integrity

We have looked at some of the facilities that are needed for the technical management of a network. Many of these facilities involve the recognition of the network as an object in itself. This view of the network by the manager is quite different from that of the user. To the user the network is merely a connection service to get her to wherever she wants to go. In order to use this service, the primitives available to her are very simple and limited. Thus, there are typically something like *Connect, Accept, Data, Reset, Disconnect*, etc for a virtual call network, or perhaps only *Send* and *Receive* for a datagram network. We shall see in the rest of the Chapter how various aspects of the normal network service can be used to access or corrupt data belonging to other network users. However, we should note here in passing that the existence of management tools on the network itself provides the possibility of security breaks.

Security breaches are often caused by foolish negligence. Thus, one recent notorious set of system breaches was caused by the fact that the operating system of a major computer manufacturer had a special account for the use of the service engineers. All instances of the system worldwide had the same account and password built into them. Naive as this was in itself, the problem was compounded first by the fact that the account had special managerial privileges, and secondly by the widely available X.25 software for that machine. Several systems worldwide were compromised before the break was discovered. Fortunately, most of the access were the usual curious probing and little real damage was done—no thanks to the manufacturer.

Worldwide networks are an irresistible temptation for the curious "hacker". One very powerful tool that network managements can use to protect themselves and each other is a detailed call log. When the author's home system was first joined to a public network it was the subject of a deliberate attack within a few days. The person attempting the break-in tried to cover her tracks by making the call in through several other systems. If the attack had been direct, then she would have needed a charged ID on the public network, and this would have immediately identified her—unless that too was stolen of course. However, the attack was indirect, first using a public dial-up access to a network, and then making a call into a host. Here a "stolen" account was used to call out across another public network to the eventual target. Each of these steps made it that much more difficult to trace back to the originator. Fortunately, most of the machines involved kept a detailed log of all network calls. Thus, we could trace the call back to the intermediate host via the X.25 address. This in turn was traced to the stolen account, and to the previous X.25 call. Unfortunately the phone company did not keep similar call records, so the trail became cold. However, the fact that the attempt was traced back to the originating city across two continents, and three public data networks in three countries within 24 hours shows the value of such call logging in deterring the international hacker and containing this increasing threat.

13.6   Topology of Shared Media
"Life! Don't talk to me about life!"
—Marvin the Paranoid Android.

We examined a wide range of ways of sharing a medium in Chapter 3. We have seen that while contention access is traditionally associated with bus media, and token access with ring media, it is quite possible to have contention rings and token buses. In this section we shall look at the topology of buses and rings, and try to assess what other similarities and differences there are between them. Let us first look at the inherent reliability in the face of certain sorts of failures.

In Fig 13.4 we see a schematic bus and a schematic ring. Let us emphasise that we are here talking about the physical topology of the medium. Thus the bus may be an Ethernet or a token bus. The token bus may be operating with a logical ring, but it is still a physical bus. The ring may be slotted, token, or contention, but physically the data flow in a single direction from station to station along the wires constituting the ring.

Much has been made by enthusiasts of the Ethernet, particularly in the early days, that with the bus architecture the medium was passive.

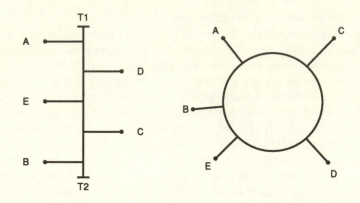

Fig 13.4. Schematic Bus and Ring Networks

This meant that the medium itself does not have logical circuits to go bad or power supplies to fail, and so on. It was even claimed that physical damage to a bus network might merely separate it into two pieces, each of which could continue to function independently of the other with no worse consequences than transient errors when the bulldozer broke through the cable. On the other hand, went the claim, users of a ring rely on the correct operation of all other ring stations, and in particular, the famous bulldozer which breaks one ring segment obviously immediately disables the whole ring.

Alas, Life, as Marvin loves to tell us, is not as simple as that. Let us look in detail at the bulldozer test. With the bus it is not necessarily true that the break merely leaves two smaller functioning buses. As we saw, an Ethernet detects collisions by listening to the Ether as it transmits, and detects the small disturbance due to the comparatively weak signals of other stations transmitting on the Ether at the same time. If the end of an Ethernet cable is not carefully terminated, then the electrical signal will be reflected from the end. This reflected signal can look like another station transmitting, and thus cause the whole Ethernet to cease to function. Again, the Ethernet cable segment must be earthed in one and only one place. If the earth is on the other side of the bulldozer, then this section of cable will probably not function.

(As a true, but sadly unattributable story, the author was once told of a pre-release Ethernet that was installed by a specialist communications company in the headquarters of a very large and internationally famous computer company. Apparently, the Ethernet worked fine most of the time, but now and again there was a huge burst of errors for a period of seconds or longer. The installers were repeatedly called in to fix the problem, but could find nothing wrong. This process continued for some time with increasing feeling on either side. Eventually the installers were given an ultimatum— *"Fix it or else!"*. The problem was eventually traced to the terminator at the end of the Ethernet cable that was physically in the office of one of the Vice-Presidents. It turned out that, when entertaining important visitors, the Vice-President liked to brag about the prototype Ethernet. *"...and look"* he would say *"Even when I remove this terminator, the Ethernet continues to work!"* Once he had been disabused of this misconception the Ethernet behaved itself, and that company has gone on to be a major user and supplier of Ethernets worldwide.)

While the necessity for proper termination is vital for Ethernets to the standard specification (IEEE 802.3 or ISO 8802/3), some forms of CSMA/CD network are less prone to this problem than others. The CSMA/CD network that was installed at Ford in Detroit, for example, has been claimed to continue operation even when physically broken. However, its electrical specification differs substantially from the standardised Ethernet. The token bus does not generally need the same careful examination for distortion by the *transmitting* station, and thus is claimed to be less critically susceptible to reflected signals than the Ethernet.

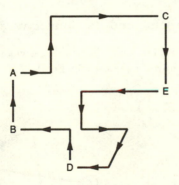

Fig 13.5.   The Geography of a Ring

Well, then, the ring must be worse, mustn't it? The implication of the ring diagram in Fig 13.4 is that the ring cable threads fairly directly from station to station. Geographically the wires will form some sort of loop. The loop will probably be of some odd shape, but, topologically, it will be a loop nevertheless. In such a case, a break in the ring in one place will cause a total ring failure. Such a "single" geographical ring is shown in Fig 13.5. The locations could be machines in a factory, divisions in an industrial complex, or laboratories in a research park.

Fig 13.6 shows a superficially similar ring. However, here the cable routes are filled with a pair of ring cables. For this reason we shall refer to such a ring as a "double" ring in distinction to the previous "single" ring. We see immediately that twice the amount of cable is used as with the single ring. In addition, the ways in which the cables are connected at the stations means that the "logical ring" is somewhat different, as shown on the right of Fig 13.6.

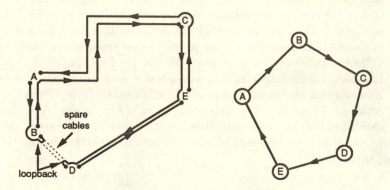

Fig 13.6.   A Double Ring and its Connectivity

Suppose a bulldozer severs the twin ring cable between E and C. The ring may quickly be reconfigured as shown in Fig 13.7.

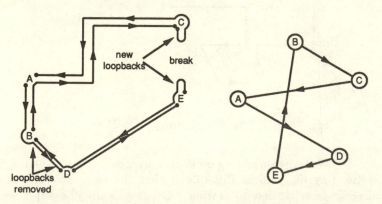

Fig 13.7.   A Broken and Reconfigured Double Ring

The use of the word "quickly" here requires some explanation. Note that if the open ring is broken, then the rejoining of the ring means in general that new replacement wires must be laid to replace those damaged. The reconfiguration for the double ring shown in Fig 13.7 is topologically more complex than merely mending a broken open ring. However, it can be achieved by replugging existing wires that make up the double ring and all this can be done in the controlled environment where the stations live, rather than down the bottom of a dirty manhole during the inevitable snowstorm. The changes have been made in only four places. The ring ends have been connected together on either side of the break (or, more likely, at the point where they used to leave the stations which they connect), and the loopback point has been removed. The existing connections at all other places have been preserved, including the direction of data travelling through each ring station. However, the topology of the ring—that is, which station is neighbour to which others—has been considerably changed as an examination of the equivalent logical rings shows. The resulting ring will continue to function until the broken cables are repaired.

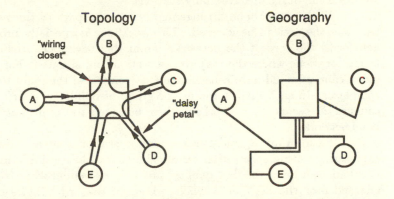

Fig 13.8.   A "Daisy-Petal" Ring

There is an alternative strategy in which each of the stations is wired back to a connection centre, sometimes known by the poetic appellation of "wiring closet". This is shown schematically in Fig 13.8. (The way in which the wires in Fig 13.8 outline the petals of a daisy flower gives a new twist to the phrase "daisy chaining".) Clearly, such a configuration will give resilience against the errant bulldozer damaging one of the petals, as a petal may be disconnected in a single location in the wiring closet. To facilitate this the closet could be equipped with a plugging board where all the petals are connected. Alternatively an electronic switch could perform the replugging in an even shorter time. The advantage of this over the double ring is that reconnections are only required in one place. However, the petal approach may well use a considerably larger amount of wire than the double ring, especially with increasing numbers of stations (and thus petals) on the ring.

However the resilience apparently offered by the daisy petal arrangement needs some planning for complete realisation. For example, if the ring extends over a small group of buildings, and uses existing tunnels for the cables, then Fig 13.8 also shows one possible geographical realisation of the topology. Several petals may well share the same tunnel for some distance. In this case the proverbial bulldozer, vandal's axe, or janitor's boot may well knock out several petals at once. Nor should it be forgotten that a vandal or a flood in the wiring closet could disable the whole of the attached daisy ring. Clearly, careful physical planning is vital for realising a resilient network.

13.7   Backbones
The resilience of both buses and rings can benefit from a backbone arrangement. This is particularly appropriate for networks that are physically large or have many stations.

With a backbone arrangement, a special part of the network traverses the area to be covered. This backbone is specially protected and forms the core of the network. From this backbone, ribs extend to the locations where the majority of stations are situated. For example, a campus could have a backbone that connected the main building complexes. In each main building, or group of buildings, a link would connect the secondary networks in these buildings to the primary backbone network.

Such an arrangement has several operational advantages. The engineering, siting, protection, and redundancy that is built into the backbone can be of the first quality, probably exceeding what could be afforded over the LAN as a whole. Each of the "rib" LANs can be engineered to a quality appropriate for its specific location. Typically, the only stations on the backbone are the connections to the ribs, and possibly a few important main service machines. However, the majority of stations will be only on the secondary networks. Thus, if a secondary network is disabled for any reason, the backbone can be isolated by disconnecting it from the secondary network at the bridge. Again, if much of the secondary traffic is within the area of the secondary network, then this need not go through the bridge into the backbone network. The bridges will allow the mixing of various technologies, particularly when the IEEE 802 architecture is adhered to. For example, a token ring backbone network could be bridged to Ethernets in most buildings, but with a slotted ring in one special location.

13.8   General Discussion

In the last few sections we have seen how the topology of buses and rings affects the reliability and maintainability of the network. At first sight it seems that a bus is a far better arrangement, but by careful arrangement, the ring topology can be made more resilient. In addition, the ability with rings to locate faults, and with suitable reconfiguration, to isolate them, means that rings are fundamentally superior to buses.

Whilst buses are fundamentally passive, and should be basically more reliable than an active medium, when faults do occur they can be very difficult to locate. Anecdotes indicate that the obvious faults, such as a broken Ethernet station whose transmitter jams on and brings down the network, are less trouble than the more subtle ones, such as a bad component or a bad connection that causes errors that apparently emanate from other stations! More than one Ethernet has developed a fault that could eventually only be traced by taking everything off the network, and putting each station back, one by one. On the other hand there is as yet no wide experience of the effectiveness or otherwise of the token ring maintenance protocols in practice. There is as yet no general consensus on the comparative reliability of the various types of LAN.

13.9   Size

With the Ethernet it is essential for the operation of the protocol, that the minimum size packet "fills" the bus. When the packet falls below this size, then the bus ceases to work in Ethernet mode and starts to operate in Aloha mode. The size of the packet compared with the network is

$$R = k\frac{s}{bL} \quad \text{where} \quad s \ \text{is packet size in bits}$$

b is network bit rate

L is physical size

k is a constant, including the speed
of light

The ratio R must stay above unity. As the bit rate or the physical length increases, a stage is reached when the packet size must be increased to keep R high enough. In order to ensure that Ethernets work in practice, the IEEE 802.3 standard specifies a fixed bit rate of 10 Mbps and minimum packet size of 512 bits, together with very strict limits on the size of the cables making up the network. Other Ethernets could be designed with a faster bit rate, but then either the packet size would have to be increased or the physical size decreased.

With the slotted ring the mini-packets are very small, and the ring must be big enough to contain a complete slot—that is a station must not see the leading bits returning before it has transmitted the last bit of the packet. Some slotted rings are big enough so that the ring can operate with several complete mini-packets. However some are so small that artificial delay must be introduced in order to contain just one slot.

The situation with token rings is more complex because of the variable packet size. The possibility of quite large packets means that the designers have not generally allowed the possibility of multiple packets (or, more precisely, multiple tokens) on the ring at one time. This matters little while the average packet length is longer than the perimeter of the ring (R above is > 1). However this ratio can fall below 1 as the bit rate and the perimeter of the ring increase for a given packet size. When this happens, the ring will still function properly except that its bandwidth will not be fully utilised. Given the same geographical set of stations as that covered by a bus, a daisy petal will in general have a greater length round the perimeter of the wire than the end-to-end distance across a branching Ethernet. It is often claimed that rings scale up to higher frequency operation better than do Ethernets, however, the wiring strategy needed for resilient operation negates some of this advantage. The multiple packets possible with the slotted ring allow some avoidance of this problem despite their fundamentally smaller size.

The FDDI ring, and later versions of the token ring address this problem by allowing the empty or free token to be transmitted before the header of the transmitted packet returns round the ring. This *early token release* allows multiple packets to fill large rings.

In addition to the limits on physical size there are also limits on the number of stations that may be attached to either an Ethernet or a ring.

With the Ethernet the limit arises because of the electrical disturbance of each of the taps onto the bus. Each electrical disturbance of the cable, be it a join or a tap, introduces a point where electrical signals will be reflected. Since the detection of collisions on the Ethernet depends on detecting the weaker disturbance of other stations transmitting at the same time as the sender is also transmitting, any reflections of this sort will make the detection of these collisions that much more difficult—when a signal is coming back, is it merely a reflection or actually someone else transmitting? The Ethernet specification sets a maximum of 100 connections to each part of the bus to avoid this problem.

One of the advantages of the token bus is that since its operation depends on orderly access via the token, it does not need to detect the simultaneous transmission of another station, and so does not need to impose a similar limit.

The limit on the number of stations on a ring is different in nature. Each station regenerates the signal received from the last station, and thus we might expect that an unlimited number of stations could be connected in series. The problem is that the input circuits lock onto the bits coming in from the previous station in the ring. As they do this, there is a small uncertainty about the phase—or the exact time at which the bit arrives. This is the "phase jitter". With a cascade of such amplifiers each one feeds on the last, with an increase in the jitter. This problem is not severe unless the cascade is closed into a ring, at which point the whole setup can become unstable if the jitter is too high. The limit this imposes in practical rings is a complex matter, and perhaps the most extensive treatment is by Cash (1984). However, practical rings do seem to be limited to perhaps 100 stations or less because of this problem.

The problem of accumulating phase jitter can be avoided if each station maintains its own clock independently of each of its neighbours rather than trying to lock onto the bits as they arrive. If the clocks are independent, then any jitter cannot accumulate. However, the problem has then been replaced by another. If the clocks are not locked together then they will drift one with respect to another. Thus, if the downstream clock is slightly slow, then bits will accumulate gradually. On the other hand, if the clock is slightly fast, then the station will run out of bits to process. Thus, we have a different set of problems with which we have no space here to deal.

13.10 Summary

Networks of both the "local"—LAN and "wide-area"—WAN kinds are large and complex entities. We have given only an inkling of the many and complex ways in which the technology of a network interacts with the way it is managed to provide a service for its users. The proper management of any entity is necessary so that it gives the required service, and the very nature of networks—that they are shared by many users—places that much greater requirement on their correct management. Management can be greatly helped by the appropriate technology, and this places requirements on the technology as we have seen in this chapter. In designing a network and assessing the available technology, aspects that lead to improved management are at least as important as the "traditional" measurements of throughput, delay time, purchase price, etc. Sadly, they are seldom given their fair share of attention, though this is now changing.

14
Security and Authentication

As computers become ever more pervasive and important, the information that they process and pass from one to another across networks becomes ever more critical. The information can be of immense value, particularly that passed between financial systems around the world. It is thus quite natural that there has been a huge increase in the volume of data that is protected by encryption so that even if the transmitted data falls into the wrong hands it is useless without the appropriate decryption. In addition, always hovering in the shadows in any discussion on such matters, are the military and diplomatic arms of government. Indeed, this latter connection is interesting because it has become clear that the first major application of practical computers was during the second world war where they were extensively employed in breaking codes (see e.g. Randell (1977, 1984)), and code breaking is still one of the most voracious consumers of computing power today.

14.1   The Need for Security
However, before we proceed to this interesting area we shall first look at some more mundane aspects of security. Let us take it as read that when information is transmitted between two people, or between two computing devices, there are some classes of information which it is necessary and desirable to keep secret. If my password is known abroad, then despite the fact that nothing I do is secret, some joker will try to use it either to disrupt my work, steal the text of the best seller that I'm writing, or to use (that is, steal) the computing resources to which it gives access.† All sorts of other information are much more desirable and potentially profitable, and thus subject to keener attentions from would-be thieves. The problem with communications is twofold. When information is transmitted there arises the possibility that it can be intercepted, and even if secret information is not itself transmitted, widespread communications makes access to distant computing resources that much easier. "Hacking" has become a significantly worse

---

† Despite the use of words like "steal" and "theft" we are not attempting to define the legal position in any country. We are merely indicating the attitude that most legal laymen would take to such actions. The legal position on such matters is complex, varies from country to country, and is quite outside the scope of this book.

problem with widespread computer networks. Interception of transmitted data constitutes "passive intrusion", while generating "false" data, or unauthorised access to a computer system is "active intrusion" or "hacking".

14.2 Physical Security

The first line of defence is of course to stop information being intercepted. If that can be achieved—i.e. the information can be prevented from falling into the wrong hands—then it need not be encrypted to protect it. With point-to-point links that are carefully controlled, a high level of security can be achieved. Thus, if a network is constructed of point-to-point links, there is little danger of "wire tapping" by amateur snoopers. It is impossible to quantify this in a simple way of course. The determined and knowledgable snooper could crawl into a manhole with his equipment and tap into the passing data. Whether this is likely in any specific case depends on the motivation of the snooper and the difficulty, unpleasantness, danger, and so on of the snooping process. Thus, it is probably unlikely that anyone but the mentally unbalanced would descend a black, wet, cold manhole to tap wires with complex and awkward equipment just "for a lark" (but when did a sense of proportion stop the dedicated practical joker?). However, if millions were at stake fierce dogs and armed guards on the manhole and piranhas in the water would be no guarantee against intruders.

There are countless examples of "hackers" prepared to face intractable intellectual puzzles to gain entry to computing systems just for the challenge. Indeed, the challenge itself is often the main motivation. This is innocent enough, but once "inside" the intruders could vandalise the system or be tempted to steal or otherwise gain remuneration for their efforts. Vast resources of money and brains are poured into electronic monitoring and cryptology in an attempt to keep one step ahead of the "enemy"—be she friend or foe. This area is so secret that only in the 1980s is a corner of the security covering the wartime activities in the 1940s being hesitantly lifted.

It is the case that between the extremes of complete openness and government paranoia there are many reasonable and pragmatic steps that can be taken. A computer operation can choose to site communications cables in such a way that they are unlikely to be tapped by eavesdroppers. In the previous chapter we have noted that the siting of cables constituting a network is a non-trivial management matter since it is influenced by considerations of the bulldozer effect—how resilient should the network be if some part of it is damaged by a mythical errant bulldozer? To this type of "security" we must add the "security" concerned with the prevention of tapping into sensitive communications to steal data or computing resources or even to falsify data. Tapping into copper cables can be of various levels of difficulty, from fairly easy for simple unshielded twisted pair cable; up to fairly difficult for shielded or coaxial cable. In addition it may be possible to listen to some signals not by physical intrusion, but by detecting the small amounts of electromagnetic radiation emitted by such cables. Thus, placing a pickup of some sort close to the cable may enable the signal to be received quite easily. One of the attractions of fibre optic transmission systems is that it is both very difficult to tap into them without completely breaking the cable, and the electromagnetic radiation emitted by such systems (i.e. the light escaping) is completely negligible.

Clearly the actions taken depend strongly on the assessments of the risk. Thus, a commercial company may not need to protect some operations within a factory at all. Any potential tapper would have the threat of dismissal as a deterrent, and the data may be widely available within the factory anyway. With a development company, the position may be completely different. The information within it may be worth many millions, and industrial competitors may be keen to use any means to access the information. Financial information might well fall into a similar bracket. A university falls somewhere in the middle. Often the sanctions against someone who eavesdrops may be minimal, and the culture of a university encourages inquisitive investigation. The motivation is often the challenge, though there is sometimes a malicious motivation too. If this is fuelled by a grievance, then the scope for damage can be considerable, though the potential for personal profit is mostly modest. In this case, intellectual barriers need to be insurmountable otherwise they will merely be an inducement. However, physical security rarely needs to be more than minimal. Thus, access to a shared Ethernet is a wide open invitation, whilst the physical tapping of wires is rarely seen as much of a risk.

Mention of the openness of Ethernets brings us to the special problems of shared media. All sorts of shared media have the property that all data can be heard by everyone, or at least passes through the hardware in every station on the medium. Normally a recipient chooses to receive only the data addressed to her personally. However the equipment is usually capable of operating in "promiscuous mode" where everything can be received. Devices and programs that monitor a network for traffic analysis, protocol debugging or other reason, work in this way. A snooper can set his apparatus into such a mode and sift through all the traffic flying by for the pieces of information in which he is interested.

A similar problem obviously exists with satellite or radio channels whether operating as a shared medium or merely being intercepted by third parties. To a greater or lesser extent, any communication will be subject to such interception depending on how difficult it is and the desirability of the information to the interceptor. Satellite channels are open to anyone with a receiving dish, and microwave links are almost as easy to intercept. The major powers operate powerful satellite monitoring systems whose function is to intercept the radio emissions of "the enemy", including military communications and domestic microwave links in telephone systems. Thus, there is an extensive interest in making any intercepted data useless to the unintended recipient. Cryptology is the study of just this.

14.3   A Potted History of Cryptology

Cryptology is a large field in itself, and the interested reader cannot get a better introduction to the subject than David Kahn's book *The Codebreakers*. This gives an excellent introduction to the principles of code making and code breaking, and also illustrates the subject with copious real life stories. That the book is now slightly dated by the revelations that have since been made about wartime codebreaking activities does not invalidate its pre-eminence.

In order to understand a little about the application of cryptology, we need to spend a little time studying its history. One of the earliest forms of secret writing is the Cæsar cypher. In this the alphabet is written out twice:

```
a b c d e f g h i j k l m n o p q r s t u v w x y z
D E F G H I J K L M N O P Q R S T U V W X Y Z A B C
```

Then to send a secret message, the letters of the message are taken one by one, and the letter appearing below is written in its stead. So the message "Send spears" would be encyphered as "VHQG VSHDUV". Apparently this was sufficient secrecy in Cæsar's time, but it is a trivial cypher to break these days, and cyphers of this type regularly appear in puzzles in children's periodicals.

The vital point that we should notice is that the Cæsar cypher is completely secure if the reader is not familiar with the simple *concept* of a cypher. Time and again in the brief history that follows we shall see the cycle repeated in which the cryptographer produces a "completely secure" form of encryption and sometimes even "proves" its security, and then the cryptanalyst finds a new way of cracking the cypher, either through a loophole in the original method, or by attacking the problem from an entirely novel angle outside those considered by the cryptographer. There is no reason to believe that this cycle will not continue.

Should the code be strictly a Cæsar cypher, then merely knowing that is sufficient to be able to read any encoded messages. All Caesar cyphers have the second alphabet written under the first, starting with D and cycling round with A following Z as above. The term is more widely applied to any similar arrangement, but starting with a given arbitrary letter. This latter case can be thought of as a cypher with a "key"—the letter at which the substitution alphabet starts. Thus, cracking the code consists merely in finding this key. Clearly, a simple computer program to "crack" this code would just cycle round the 25 possibilities, displaying the message on a computer screen each time for the human to glance at to see if it makes sense. On average twelve or thirteen tries would be sufficient to find the message. If this is thought too tiresome, then a simple device can speed the process: since spaces are not encoded, words can be seen. This could be exploited to pick a short word and try first only those keys that give a vowel. In general, it is a good idea either to encode spaces or to omit them altogether. Obscuring all patterns is a necessary part of designing secure codes.

The fact that Caesar cyphers are regularly solved by children with pencil and paper shows that they are not suitable for serious work today. The next generalisation might be to shuffle the letters in the substitution alphabet into a random order. Now we are suddenly faced with finding a "key" of length !26—a very large number. Clearly, our strategy of trying all the possible keys at random is now infeasable. Even with the fastest computers, such a method would take a very long time. A simplistic "proof" of the invulnerability of such a system could easily be constructed by claiming it would take too long to try all the possible keys. However, there are two very effective ways of attacking such a method of encypherment, both of which can be extended to much more complex encoding methods.

The first is by means of frequency analysis. The cypher is called a mono-alphabetic substitution cypher, which means that each letter is always represented in code by the same code letter. Now it is a fact that normal English text has the letters of the alphabet occurring in a very definitely non-random distribution. Thus, the letter "e" occurs about 13% of the time, "t" about 9%, "o" 8%, etc. So, by analysing the frequency of the encrypted text characters, the most frequent can easily be picked out. Just how far this can be taken depends on the size of the piece of text, and whether it is truly statistically representative. However, once the most frequent letters have been divined, then the rest are easily filled in by a human reader. Of course, the frequency of occurrence of pairs of letters (such as "th" the most frequent at about 3%) can also help in this process. An extension of this process is to guess a probable word or phrase. Depending on context, this might be perhaps "dollars", "Dear Sir", or "your most humble servant". In addition, the position of the phrase might be guessed if it is a regular form of greeting or of signing off, or suchlike—some military and diplomatic communications are particularly prone to such patterns—then, matching the word across the coded message, we would look for patterns such as the "ll" in "dollar". Given this, we might assume the encoding of the other letters "doar" and apply all of them to the rest of the message. Should this look promising, then good guesses can be made about the other letters, and the message is quickly decyphered.

The other method, which might be viewed as the ultimate extension of this word guessing technique is if a decrypted message is eventually seen—for example a diplomatic message that is later delivered by an ambassador—it can be compared with its previously intercepted encrypted version, and the method of decoding can be divined and applied to future messages. Clearly, if an encyphered message can be compared, character by character with the "plaintext"—the un-encyphered message, then deriving the substitution alphabet is trivial. Indeed, this type of analysis is also useful to the cryptanalyst for other much more complex methods, and it has often been the practice that when diplomatic messages are sent via an embassy to a foreign country, the embassy paraphrases the decoded message before delivering it to the host government in order to thwart such methods.

Possibly the most extreme extrapolation of the mono-alphabetic cypher is the code book. Here each and every word has a substitution rather than each letter. Thus, the code book is the size of a translation dictionary with one code entry for every word, (and one word for every code entry in the decoding section). To crack such a code completely a very large number of entries needs to be discovered.

Codes come in two flavours—one-part codes and two-part codes. In one-part codes both the plaintext words and the corresponding code symbols are looked up in the same ordered index. Thus, in a one part code we might have two columns thus:

```
              ⋮
    cordite    defwx
    cordon     degac
    corduroy   degpq
    cordwain   dehbc
              ⋮
```

The advantage of this is that since the plaintext words in the left column and the code words in the right column are both in the same order, the same table can be used both for encoding and decoding. The grave weakness is that the order of the words gives a clue to the code-breaker. Thus, if she knows already that "`defwx`" stands for "`cordite`" and that "`degpq`" stands for "`cordwain`", then she can be sure that "`degpq`" stands for a word starting with "`cord...`". The two-part code avoids this problem by decoupling the order of the plaintext and code words. Thus, the encoding part of the dictionary might look something like:

```
        ⋮
cordite   defwx
cordon    abqyp
corduroy  xawqy
cordwain  gsleo
        ⋮
```

Strictly, this is all that is needed. However, for practical decoding, there needs to be another part with the codewords in order. This is just the same set of entries, but sorted on the codewords rather than the plaintext words. Part of this might look like:

```
        ⋮
cordite   defwx
zebra     deghi
aardvark  demna
gunpowder depwq
        ⋮
```

The disadvantage of this is that twice the space is needed to store the two parts of the code. This could be a problem if only a hollow tooth is available.

Such codes must be, by virtue of their size, comparatively difficult to change, and the interception and decoding of just a few messages would lead to rapid divination of the more common words. Indeed, they are also open to attack by frequency analysis of word occurrance—"`the`", "`in`", "`general`", "`attack`" and so on would soon become well-known. One elaboration of code books to make them more difficult to crack would be first to look up a word to find, say, a number. Then some manipulation could be performed, such as adding the day of the month and a personal key number and then looking up the number in a second part to produce another word. There are all sorts of techniques available that we shall see on a character-by-character basis soon.

Strictly, codes at the letter or character level are known as "cyphers", and at the word or phrase level are known as "codes". The distinction is in terms of the size of the linguistic unit that is subject to processing at one time. However, we shall merely assume that codes are in principle really just very large mono-alphabetic substitutions, and proceed to consider only cyphers. In addition we shall use the terms "cypher" and "code" interchangably.

We have seen that mono-alphabetic substitutions are susceptible to rather simple methods of attack. The next natural extension is to use *poly-alphabetic cyphers*. Thus, we might take not just one cypher, but several together, and apply the different cyphers to successive letters in some sequence known to the encoder and the decoder.

This notion can be traced back to an idea first mentioned by Alberti in about 1467. Slight paraphrasing his method, he enscribed the alphabet in equal sectors around a fixed disc. Another concentric disc had the letters in a different scrambled order. The encoding method was started by setting the discs in some well-known arrangement—say with the inner "w" against the outer "c". Then the letters are taken one by one and encyphered by reading off the outer letter opposite the letter to be encyphered in the inner disc. So far we have just a mono-alphabetic cypher. However, Alberti then suggested that every few words the inner ring would be rotated by a variable amount before proceeding with the encryption. This would be communicated to the recipient by transmitting the index of the wheel's rotation as part of the message. Thus, we might agree to specify the index as the inner letter opposite the outer "a". Then, setting the inner "w" against the outer "a" we would encypher a few characters, then turn to the inner "m", and encypher a few more. The "w" and the "m" would be transmitted so that the recipient, with his similar wheel, would be able to decypher the message easily.

If we know the method of encoding, then attacking this method of encryption is, in principle, only a matter of deducing the basic arrangement of the wheel, and spotting those characters that indicate wheel rotation rather than actual data. There are other weaknesses in Alberti's method. One is that the same mono-alphabetic substitution is used for a period before switching to another. For example "Alberti" might all be encyphered with the same substitution before switching. Spotting *patterns* is the analyst's game, and any pattern can be exploited to help to break a cypher. Another weakness is that the encypherment key itself is transmitted as part of the message. Once this is known then the decryption becomes just as easy for the analyst as for the intended recipient.

However, Alberti's basic method of adding complexity by changing the substitution alphabet is the root of much of the work that followed. Trithemius in 1518 described an encyphering method that used a new Caesar alphabet for every new letter. The basis of this method was his "tabula recta" which was a square matrix of 26 Caesar alphabets.

```
a b c d e f g h i j k l m n o p q r s t u v w x y z
b c d e f g h i j k l m n o p q r s t u v w x y z a
c d e f g h i j k l m n o p q r s t u v w x y z a b
...
y z a b c d e f g h i j k l m n o p q r s t u v w x
z a b c d e f g h i j k l m n o p q r s t u v w x y
```

The first letter would be enciphered with the first row, the second with the second, the third with the third, and so on. The advantage over Alberti's method is clearly that the substitution is changed for every letter, thus eliminating the patterns showing through Alberti's encypherment. In addition, the key is not part of the transmitted text. The difficulty is that once the method is known, perhaps by reading Trithemius' book, then all such enciphered messages are easily decyphered. However, a practical method might thwart such an attack by using 26 (or some other number perhaps) general jumbled alphabets rather than the merely shifted Caesar alphabets.

Belaso made the next improvement in 1553 by inventing the concept of a key. Along with a table of substitution alphabets, a short, easily remembered key is provided. This is written out repeatedly above the message. Thus, if the key is "ZAPHODBEEBLEBROX", and the message "we shall invade his country in the spring of next year", the two are written out:

```
ZAPHODBEEBLEBROXZAPHODBEEBLEBROXZAPHODBEEBLE
weshallinvadehiscountryinthespringofnextyear
```

Then the letters of the repeated keyword are used to index into the tabula recta to obtain the Caesar alphabet to be used. Thus, the first letter is enciphered using alphabet Z, the next using alphabet A, the next with P, and on and on. In addition, Belasio specified that rather than the set of Caesar alphabets specified in Trithemius' tableau, the substitution alphabets should be general substitution alphabets as used by Alberti on his wheel.

In addition to making the cypher much more difficult to break, the introduction of the key in the form of an easily remembered word gives a huge flexibility to the method. Thus, each of the Papal Legates could be assigned his own keyword. Even if the complete method is known, including the details of the tables of substitutions, then changing the key would make the method unreadable.

The final variation on the theme is due to Vigenère in 1586. Vigenère dispensed with the keyword, and instead used the message itself an an encryption key. Thus, the encypheror would start with some given letter and use this to choose the substitution alphabet from the tableau for the first letter. Then the first letter was used to choose the substitution for the second letter, and so on. Thus, if we were to encrypt "there are three thousand soldiers...", we would first choose some starting key letter, such as "w", say. Then alphabet "w" is used to encrypt the first letter, "t". Next, alphabet "t" is used to encrypt letter "h", then alphabet "h" for the third letter "e", and so on. The value of this method is that the "key" is long and does not repeat. However, if the method is known together with the tableau, (via a spy or a traitor) then deciphering the message is merely a matter of trying all 26 initial possibilities until the message starts to make sense. The encypherment is in some ways more complex in that the "key" never cycles or repeats. However, it is weaker in that the key is transmitted along with the message itself, and can easily be derived from it and it is thus not really a key at all.

What is commonly referred to as the Vigenère cypher is really Belaso's method with a secret keyword, but using a set of tables that is an ordered set of Caesar alphabets as used by Trithemius.

It is interesting that the methods of enciphering messages that we have just described were completely unbreakable for several hundred years after their invention. Unfortunately, these methods are impractical when implemented with quill pen on parchment. The problem is that a single error can garble the rest of the message. Clearly this would be an irritation even today with instant global communications. However, in the days of sailing ships, we can see that forward error correction clearly has advantages over reverse error correction (See Chapter 2). Thus, the unbreakable methods were both slow and cumbersome.

For this reason the so-called *nomenclators* were used instead. Nomenclators consist of two main parts. Several hundred words or phrases had associated codewords—it was a code in the strict sense of the word. The rest of the message would be encoded using a cypher. However, rather than a simple mono-alphabetic substitution cypher, a set of homophones would be used—each and every letter would have not one, but several possible substitutions. So, for example, the letter "a" might be represented by any of 23, 44, 567, 599, or 902. "b" might be represented by 77, 85, 128, 542, or 789. The encodings would be chosen at random, but the decoder could always be sure independently of context that 599 represented "a". While such schemes were fast, convenient, and forgiving of errors, and were thus in general use from 1400 to 1850, they were also often decoded.

A further technique is "super-encypherment". With this technique a message is first coded using an extensive code table or code book. The resulting codewords are then encyphered. Apart from the obvious improvement of combining two sorts of complexity, the coding and encypherment interact together in the sense that the use of the code table to represent words and common phrases results in codewords that do not have the frequency patterns which we have seen to be useful in attacking cyphers. Thus the combination of the two methods in super-encypherment can be thought of as a geometric rather than an arithmetic increase in complexity and difficulty.

In the 19th century, the drawback of human errors was reduced by the introduction of the telegraph. Thus, if a message was corrupted and undecypherable, a new message could be sent within a short time. Reverse error correction had enabled the adoption of the old and more secure methods. The so-called Vigenère cypher was soon became widely used. However, a method of solution was also soon found.

The technique attributed to Kasiski is to guess the length of the encryption key, and then to write out the encrypted text in rows of the length of the guessed key. The guess need not be a wild one since the repeated application of the same fixed length key interacts with patterns in the plain text to produce interference patterns in the encyphered text. By analysing these frequency patterns some clues can be gathered about the possible lengths of the key. Once the length of the key has been guessed and the text arranged in rows, frequency analysis can then be applied to each column to solve the substitution used for that column.

Clearly, in general this will be a formidable task, even if the general technique of encoding and the format of the coding tables is known. However, in practice the cryptologist is aided strongly by the human frailty of those who encypher and decypher the messages. Thus, the keys will tend to be short and mnemonic so that they may more easily be applied, and thus also more easily be broken. They will not be changed regularly enough, or the change will follow a pattern—perhaps the key will always be the same length for example, or always be the name of a flower or river. Sometimes the same message, with such minor alterations as the name of the recipient only will be sent out with different codes. Cracking one will allow the quick solution of the other. In addition rigid adherence to a strict format can give vital clues. Any military force that insists on starting all messages to a general with some such phrase as "Most honourable Sir, may I draw your attention..." is giving an enormous help to the cryptanalyst.

14.4   Rotor Machines

Coding and decoding are tedious and error-prone. The use of machines for this process increases the speed and accuracy of the process, and also allows the use of much more complex cyphers. Several cypher machines were produced in the early part of this centuary. We shall concentrate on the rotor machines.

Perhaps one of the most important cypher machines was the Enigma machine that was widely used by the German forces during World War II as part of their battlefield communications system. The encryption part consisted of three rotors, a reflector or *Umkerwaltze*, and a plugboard or *Steckerboard*. The plaintext was entered on a keyboard and the encrypted text was displayed on a set of lamps. The device had 26 keys for the letters of the alphabet. There was no allowance for spaces, punctuation, or other special symbols.

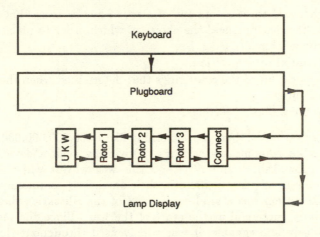

Fig 14.1. The Enigma Cypher Machine

The logical structure of the machine was as shown in Fig 14.1. The keyboard was connected to the Steckerboard or plugboard that normally mapped letters through directly. However, when plugs were inserted, one letter would be mapped to another depending on the position of the plugs. The three rotors were constructed so that they each had 26 segments, one for each letter. Each segment had a plate on one side and a spring-loaded contact on the other. Internally, each wheel was wired so that each plate on the one side was wired to a contact on the other. If each plate corresponds to one plaintext letter, the contact on the other corresponds to an encyphered letter. The whole wheel constituted a mono-alphabetic substitution cypher.

However, since three wheels could be stacked together with the contacts on one side passing the electrical current onto the segments of the next wheel, this implemented three such cyphers in series. The current then flowed through the umkerwaltze and back again through all three wheels, giving seven substitution cyphers in series, plus the steckerboard. Finally, of course, the wheels rotated. This was arranged so that as each new key was pressed on the keyboard, the rightmost wheel rotated by one letter position. On each full rotation this caused the next wheel to move by one position, and this in turn, like the odometer on a motor car, moved the next wheel on one position every turn. The wheels could be started in any one of 26 positions at the start of a message, and they were equipped with rings that could be moved round to any of 26 positions. This ring position varied the point at which the next wheel was moved on by one letter—the turnover position. Thus, the total encryption key consisted of four parts:

a) A choice of three rotors out of a set of five or more that came with the machine, and the choice of which order to place them in the machine.
b) The initial rotor positions.
c) The positions of the rotor rings that determined when the next rotor turns.
d) The Steckerboard settings.

With all these variables, there are something like 1,000,000,000,000,000,-000,000 possible different key settings. Obviously such a device was completely unbreakable (isn't it?) and this was why it was used by the German forces as a key element in their battlefield communications system. This system was a vital component of the Blitzkrieg that was so spectacularly successful at the start of the war. Since the method was so obviously impregnable, it was widely used throughout the war for all sorts of communications. Since everyone knew it was perfect, it was treated as a casual part of the apparatus of war.

In fact, of course, the Enigma machine was regularly and comprehensively decyphered by the teams that were assembled for just that purpose at Bletchley Park in England. The story is a long, complicated and fascinating one. It involved large teams of inspired minds, and it has been argued that the modern electronic computer was to a large extent developed in order to crack just this cypher machine. The effort was spectacularly successful. For accounts of this story the reader may read Winterbothm (1974) for the intelligence aspect, Welchman (1982) for an account of the details of how the cyphers were cracked, and Randell (1977) for the genealogy of the computer. We have insufficient space to describe the method of solution in detail, however some brief indication of the methods used should provide food for thought.

The Enigma machine would have been completely insoluble if it had been used correctly but there were serious errors in the way in which the machine was used that allowed the analysts to solve the cyphers.

Firstly, the analysts had a complete knowledge of the machine itself, indeed they had a complete machine (either replica or prototype depending on the author) that was supplied by the Poles at the start of the war. In addition they had a fairly detailed knowledge of the operating procedures. The machine itself was constructed in such a way that by using the same key, it could be used both to encypher and decypher a message. Thus, at any instant, if letter X on the keyboard enciphered to letter Y on the lights, then at the same time letter Y on the keyboard would encypher to letter X on the lights. This was obviously very convenient operationally since it allowed the machine to be set up with the same key and used either for enciphering or deciphering. However it also meant that the transformations of the machine could be subjected to certain analyses that allowed for special kinds of attack.

Keys were issued to the operators for use over a specific period. They were changed at midnight. There would be a set of keys, each key to be used for a different set of traffic. Each such key would be allocated a three letter "discriminant". So that the receiver would know which deciphering key to use, the three letter discriminant, say "HUT", was transmitted unenciphered as part of the header of the message.

Next, an extra little obstacle was added. The transmitting cypher clerk was allowed to choose the initial positions of the rotors. Thus, he might choose "SIX"—Welchman (1982) calls this the "text setting". Of course, this needed to be transmitted to the other end for the deciphering clerk to use. To do this, the enciphering clerk chose another three letters, say "GOW". He then set his machine up with the current key, set the wheels to "GOW" and typed out the three letter text setting twice, producing perhaps the six enciphered letters "SWEJWU". He would then reset his machine to his personal setting of "SIX" and encypher the message, perhaps producing the enciphered message "SE-HUEWGINGAE...". The actual message transmitted would then be:

> HUT
>
> GOWSWEJWU
>
> SEHUEWGINGAE...

Note that although the cypher discriminant "HUT" and the setting "GOW" are transmitted in plain, the personal setting "SIX" is not. The receiving clerk uses the discriminant to choose amongst his codes for today, sets the wheels to "GOW", and taps out "SWEJWU" to produce the secret "SIXSIX". He then resets the machine to "SIX" and deciphers "SE-HUEWGINGAE...".

Welchman describes how the early attacks concentrated on the encypherment of the personal key "SIX" being done twice. Analysis of the machine showed that when the double encypherment of the key such as "SIXSIX" produced code with a letter repeated twice at the interval three—in our example "SWEJWU" has the letter "W" appearing twice for the same (so far unknown) letter "I"—this allowed certain constraints to be placed on the set of possible keys. With a sufficient volume of messages, and enough such examples of repeated letters (referred to as "females") the possible set of keys could be narrowed sufficiently so that the remaining set of keys was small enough to be attacked by other means.

In addition to this exploitation of the double encypherment of the personal key, ingenious ways were devised for performing specialised parallel processing on the possible set of remaining keys by stacking sheets of paper with holes in specific places one on top of another in such a way that light shone through only in places corresponding to the possible keys. In this way, by exploiting the operational error of encyphering the cypher clerk's key twice (when once would have done) and performing certain "calculations" by ingenious and effectively very fast methods, an apparently "impossible" problem was solved regularly and frequently.

Later, the double encypherment was discontinued, but by this time the decoders had sufficient knowledge of operational procedures to be able still to break the codes regularly. They exploited a mass of detailed knowledge, no one part of which would of itself have been sufficient. For example, lax operational procedures by cypher clerks meant that they sometimes chose the same text setting and initial key. Thus, they might choose a text setting of QAZ, and use this to encypher itself twice. There was a strong tendency to choose the "random" setting as the top three letters on the keyboard, and so on. Later on, specialised electronic apparatus, referred to as the "bombe", allowed extremely fast analysis of the encrypted message traffic.

Such patterns, the product of lax discipline, or perhaps of misplaced confidence in the impregnability of the cypher machine, enabled the Allied forces to tap into enormous sources of incomparable intelligence. Welchman's book can be read at many levels for tips on how not to run an encypherment system, how to look for and exploit human weaknesses, how to glean small parts of an overall system and build it into a staggeringly successful whole, and so on. For our purposes here the moral is clear—any system, however secure it is believed to be—can be severely compromised if it not operated correctly. Making a system that still works correctly even when operated improperly is very difficult. As someone once remarked, *"The main problem with making a system foolproof is the inventiveness of fools"*.

14.5   The DES Standard

In 1977 a standard encryption method was adopted by the U.S.

government, the so-called *Data Encryption Standard*—DES (NBS 1977) to be used for non-classified information. We shall first outline the basic algorithm, and then discuss some of the issues surrounding it. We shall start from the basic building blocks and work upwards. Overall, the DES algorithm takes 64 bits of input data and uses a 56-bit key and the specified steps of the algorithm to produce 64 bits of encrypted data. The algorithm is such that the resulting 64 bits may be taken together with the same encryption key, and, running the stages in the reverse order, the original set of 64 bits is the result.

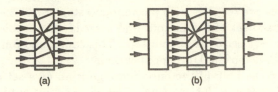

(a)   (b)

Fig 14.2.   DES Building Blocks—the S-function

The most elementary building block of DES is very similar in function to that of the rotor of the Enigma machine. If we have the box in Fig 14.2(a), we see that each of the eight inputs is wired to a different output. This, like the Enigma rotor, is an implementation of a mono-alphabetic substitution with an alphabet of size 8. If we input on exactly one input, then exactly one output will be activated. Of course, circuits tend to work, not with eight wires in parallel, only one of which gives the signal, but with a smaller number of wires in parallel carrying the binary equivalent of the signal. Thus, rather than the one-out-of-eight operation as shown in Fig 14.2(a), we would have three parallel wires carrying the equivalent eight combinations. This would be fed through a three-to-eight decoder to give a one-out-of-eight output. The result of the transposition would be fed into a eight-into-three encoder to give the three wire result as in Fig 14.2(b).

So, with this simple circuit, and the appropriate wiring in the centre box, such a piece of hardware can be set up to perform any mono-alphabetic substitution on the input. The S-function in DES is very similar to this, except that four bits are input in parallel, rather than three, giving a substitution from an alphabet of 16 symbols. In addition, DES has another elaboration—two extra bits in parallel with the four bits select which of four possible substitutions are to be used. Thus, six input bits result in four output bits for each S-function.

Eight S-functions operate in parallel in DES, taking 48 input bits and producing 32 output bits. Since this process has no "memory" this can be thought of as another particular mono-alphabetic substitution.

However, because of its construction, not all possible substitutions of 32-bit results for 48-bit inputs can be constructed—only those that are specified by choosing the elementary S-functions. In particular, there is no way that any of the inputs of any one S-function can directly affect any of the outputs of any of the other seven S-functions. However, we still have several levels of complexity to add.

The 48 bits of input to this set of eight S-functions are formed by taking 32 bits of data (call them R) and expanding them to 48 by spreading them out, and duplicating some of them. This set of 48 bits is exclusive-ORed with a set of 48 bits (call them K) taken from the 56-bit encryption key. Thus, we see that such a compound stage takes 32 data bits, and, using a fixed set of S-functions and a set of 48 settable bits from the key, produces a set of 32 output bits. This compound function is referred to as $f(R, K)$ in the DES specification.

DES defines the bulk of the encoding algorithm as a set of 16 steps. At each step a 64-bit input is transformed into a 64-bit output by dividing the 64 bits into two lots of 32, called L and R. If the resulting 64 bits are called L' and R', then

$$L' = R$$
$$\text{and} \quad R' = L + f(R, K)$$

Each of the 16 steps takes the output of the last as input, and the function $f(R, K)$ is different at each step because a different set of S-functions is specified each time. The 48 bits used from the key at each step are chosen from the overall 56 bits of the main encryption key for the whole process according to a set of shifts and selections specified as part of the algorithm.

Finally, the input to the first stage is constructed by permuting the 64 bits of input data, and the output from the last of the sixteen steps has its two halves swapped; the resulting bits are permuted with the inverse of the initial permutation.

The original standards document is very readable. Tanenbaum (1981) published a Pascal algorithm, and Aruliah et al (1985) have extended this work. Their Pascal implementation can be obtained from Grey Matter (1985).

As a final note, we can see that if the DES is operated by taking the input data 64 bits at a time, then it is simply a mono-alphabetic substitution cypher which is 64 bits wide. The actual substitution is controlled both by the inbuilt structure and constants of the DES algorithm itself, and by the choice of the 56-bit key. Note that not all possible 64-bit wide mono-alphabetic substitution cyphers can be represented in this way. The range of possibilities is first restricted by the logical structure of the DES algorithm, and second by the specific choices of S-functions, selections of keys for each of the steps, and choice of permutation. Thus, DES offers a choice not of $!2^{64}$ such alphabets, but a specific subset of 2^{56} of them.

14.6   The DES Controversy

Ever since its introduction, DES has been surrounded with controversy. The standard was based on some original work done by IBM on the Lucifer encryption algorithm in the early 1970s. That work has never been made public. The U.S. National Security Agency requested that the key size be reduced from 128 bits in the original design to the 56 bits in the standard. Again, the reason was never made public, but there have been persistent rumours that this was so that the NSA could break the cypher easily. The design principles have been kept secret too, leaving the nagging doubt that somewhere in the specific set of S-functions, etc, some sort of trapdoor has been built in that would let those in the know read encrypted messages easily. Fully to appreciate the significance of this, the reader should realise that though the algorithm is elaborate to describe, and expensive to run in a high-level language implementation, it is easy to implement in hardware. It is likely that it will be widely available to encrypt digitised voice in real time or to keep computer mail to and from home micros truly secret. Governments would hardly welcome such developments, and would be much more likely to support a system that was safe from everyone but themselves.

The complexity of DES as we have described it, is daunting indeed. But then, so was the complexity of the Enigma machine, and we have related how ingenious people achieved what was combinatorially "impossible".

Several ways of attacking DES have been proposed. If users are allowed to choose their own keys, then, as with passwords, simple names, such as those of spouses, friends, babies, football teams, flowers, and so on are much more likely than "$;%7*d"Gb}[". Indeed, as illustrated in the film "War Games", if the key setter is known, then personal knowledge of her, such as her husband, favourite colour and suchlike gives a fertile field for first attempts. Lest the reader think this is flippant, she should refer to Welchman's book on the wartime solution of the Enigma codes. Recently one sustained attack on a major time-sharing system used personal information such as name, address and telephone number stored in a database on that system to guess passwords for user accounts. The success rate was several percent. Many studies of the passwords users actually use show that a large fraction can be guessed just by trying common names and words.

A list of such probable keys can easily be constructed by taking the names from a telephone book, some books of first names for your baby, flower names, a reasonably sized dictionary, etc. Tanenbaum (1981) suggests that such a list is unlikely to exceed a million entries. If trying each such key takes x microseconds, then trying all of them will consume just x seconds. Even if the keys are chosen truly randomly, then the 56-bit key is still not safe against the determined and well-backed intruder (like the NSA?), and Hellman (1980) has devised a way of speeding up an exhaustive search of the key space providing certain information is prepared in advance and stored on mass backing store. Can anyone doubt that such preparations have been made by the security agencies?

There are other ways to improve the security of the DES algorithm. As we have said before, the straightforward way of encyphering 64 bits at once produces the effect of a (large) mono-alphabetic substitution cypher. Sometimes this is referred to as "code-book mode". If instead of the simple DES operation, the output of the encryption is exclusive-ORed with the next block of 64 bits before encrypting that, and so-on, then we have a simple variation on the Vigenère cypher. The process is easy to reverse by taking the output of the decryption, and exclusive-ORing a block of 64 bits at a time with the *next* 64 bits of incoming cypher text. (Note carefully the choice of which block of 64 bits to use each time.) This simple and cheap elaboration makes the use of DES much more secure. This mode of working is the "stream-cypher mode".

Fig 14.3.   DES à le Vigenère

14.7   Public Key Encryption

Recently there has been a revolution in the way in which we think about cryptology. This was sparked off by the introduction of the concept of *public key encryption* by Diffie and Hellman in 1976. Until their paper, it had been widely assumed that the key needed to encode a message, and the key needed to decode it were one and the same, or at least trivially related one to another. Thus, our key "ZAPHODBEEBLE-BROX" (and the encoding algorithm of course) is sufficient both to encode a message using the Vigenère cypher, and to decode it. Diffie and Hellman suggested that this was not an immutable law of cryptology. They proposed a class of encryption techniques in which two keys would be used rather than just one. One key would be secret, and known only to the intended recipient—the eventual decoder, and the other could be published abroad for anyone to use. The plan is to choose the keys in such a way that even if the public key is known, and also the method of encryption, it is not possible to derive the decryption key from them, and so break the code. Nor should it be possible to break the method by "plaintext attack"—feeding in various pieces of known text into the algorithm, and trying to break the method by looking at what results.

Since the method of public key encryption is such a conceptually important method, and also a rather surprising one, it is worth going through the method in enough detail to convince ourselves that it does indeed make sense. If we represent the encryption process as the function E, and the decryption process by the function D, then

$$Encrypted\ Message = E(Plain\ Text)$$
and
$$Plain\ Text = D(Encrypted\ Message)$$
i.e. that
$$D(E(P)) = P.$$

Note that E is a combination of the publicly known encryption algorithm and the publicly known key, and D is a combination of the secret key and the (probably) publicly known decryption algorithm. While we have said that D must not be derivable from E, this is not strictly true. What we must ensure is that D cannot be derived from E within a "reasonable" time. The sort of assertion that is usually made is

"Take a computer operating at several million operations per second. If decoding would take millions of years, then we shall assume the method is safe."

The function E is a *one-way function*. However, to be useful for cryptology, the function must be reversible by the intended recipient. There must be some way, probably with secret knowledge, of reversing the encryption to reveal the plaintext. This is usually referred to as a *trapdoor* that is built into the one-way function. The two main algorithms that have been put forward to satisfy these constraints are the so-called *Knapsack algorithm* and the *RSA algorithm*.

The knapsack algorithm is based on the "knapsack problem". In this problem the task is to take a well-specified space, such as a knapsack or the back of a truck, and a collection of variously sized objects, and choose a subset of them to fit into the space given. All the known methods for doing this get rapidly more difficult with the size of the problem, and in fact none are significantly better than just trying all the possible combinations one by one. Such a method is fine for small numbers of objects, but the number of operations increases as the factorial of the number of objects. Thus, for ten objects we need a thousand or so trials, but for 50 objects hundreds of millions of trials will be needed. For a thousand objects the number of trials exceeds the estimated number of atoms in the universe.

Problems of this type are known to mathematicians as "nondeterministic polynomial-time complete" or "NP-complete". The important property is that the time required to solve such problems increases faster even than any power of the size of the problem. Thus, the "try every possibility" approach increases as the factorial of the number of objects in the knapsack, which is worse than any finite power of the size of the problem. These problems are attractive in this context because merely by making them bigger (i.e. by making the key bigger) the difficulty of solving the problem (i.e. finding the key) can rapidly be made arbitrarly difficult.

14.8   The Knapsack Algorithm

Merkle and Hellman (1978) suggested turning the knapsack problem into a trapdoor function by choosing an ordered set of n random numbers (all different) and publishing them as the public encryption key. Then the plaintext message is represented as a set of bits. These bits are taken in groups of n, and matched against the published numbers. A sum is taken of the numbers corresponding to one bits in the message to be encrypted. Thus, if we had the (trivially inadequate) public set of numbers $\{2, 8, 4, 5\}$ and the four bits (1101) to encypher, we would take the so-called "dot" product of the two: $2 \times 1 + 8 \times 1 + 4 \times 0 + 5 \times 1 = 15$. Then 15 is the encrypted version of the four bits. To find the four bits, various combinations of the public key numbers can be tried until one gives the correct answer. (Clearly, to make this process unique, no two disjoint subsets must have the same sum.)

With a small number of bits at one time this process of trying all the possibilities is simple and quick but with 50 or 100 bits this is not feasible. The method is simple and straightforward in that it merely involves trying all the possible combinations, but the number of possible combinations is so huge that the time required is far too large.

Now we need to see how a trapdoor can be built into the set of numbers making up the public key. If the set of numbers is chosen so that each number in the ordered set is more than the sum of all the preceeding numbers (a super-increasing set), then the process is trivial. Thus, suppose we had the set of numbers $\{2, 3, 6, 13\}$ and we needed to see what subset of these made up the number (knapsack) 16. First we try the biggest, 13. If 13 is less than or equal to the offered sum, then it must be part of it. This must be true, since 13 is larger than the sum of all the other numbers, and so cannot be replaced by any combination of the others. This process is repeated recursively with the other numbers in descending order of size and so on until the entire set is found. Obviously this process is not exponential in the number of components but linear, and thus the process is easy to do for 100 numbers (binary digits) or many more. Note that this process also produces numbers that satisfy our earlier requirement of no two disjoint sub-sets having the same sum.

Of course, such a set of numbers is not a useful encryption key since others could perform the same trivial manipulation. Thus, we need to disguise the easy set and make it into an apparently difficult set. To do this we choose two large random numbers p and q and use modular arithmetic. Thus, we take each number in the easy set, $\{a_1,\ a_2,\ a_3,\ \ldots\ a_n\}$ and multiply it by $p \bmod q$ to give the new set $\{a_1',\ a_2',\ a_3',\ \ldots\ a_n'\}$. This operation has the very desirable property that it obscures the regular nature of the set of numbers. As an illustration of the utility of modularity, consider the problem of trying to figure out the value x for which $f(x)$ is some given value. If we want to try it for, say, $f(x) = 2x + 1 = 5$, we might try $x = 0$ giving $f = 1$, $x = 1$ giving $f = 3$, $x = 3$ giving $f = 7$, so obviously we should try $x = 2$. The pattern of $f(x)$ is simple and gives hints for its solution. However, consider a similar looking function $f(x) = (3x + 2) \bmod 5$. Here $f(0) = 2$, $f(1) = 5$, $f(2) = 3$, $f(3) = 1$, $f(4) = 4 \ldots$ The function leaps about apparently haphazardly and gives little clue for its solution.

Thus, the published set of apparently random numbers has an associated set of simple numbers that can be derived by knowing the two secret numbers p and q. Indeed, it is a simple matter to derive the easy set from the difficult set given these two integers. Perhaps more importantly, p^{-1}, the inverse of $p \bmod q$ can be found from p and q. Now, if the encyphered message is C, then

$$C = a_1 x_1 + a_2 x_2 + \ldots + a_n x_n$$

thus $$C' = C p^{-1} \bmod q$$

$$= (a_1 x_1 p^{-1} + \ldots + a_n x_n p^{-1}) \bmod q$$

Of course, $$a_i = a_i' p \bmod q$$

so $$a_i p^{-1} = a_i' \bmod q$$

thus $$C = a_1' x_1 + a_2' x_2 + a_2' x_3 + \ldots + a_n' x_n$$

14.9 The RSA Algorithm

Another public key system is based on the difficulty of factoring very large numbers. This problem has been studied since the time of the ancient Greeks. No "efficient" solutions have been found, and factoring a 200-digit number would take the most powerful computers hundreds of millions of years. However, once the factors are found it is a simple matter to confirm that the factors do indeed make the original number when multiplied together. As an example, Hellman (1979) suggests that factoring the number 29,083 by hand would take perhaps an hour, but confirming that the factors are indeed 127 and 229 takes only about a minute. The disparity between these two operations widens as the numbers involved get larger and larger. Rivest, Shamir and Adleman devised a way of using this as the basis for a public key encryption system—the so-called RSA algorithm. We shall outline this method, but for details the reader must consult either the original works cited in the references, or a specialised work such as Denning's book "Cryptography and Data Security" (1982).

Two large prime numbers p and q are chosen at random, together with a third random number E. The public encrypting key is then the product n of p and q, and the number E. The primes p and q form the basis of the secret key. While p and q can in principle be derived from the publicly known product, n, it is not feasible to find them in reasonable time.

To encrypt a message, it is first represented as a set of numbers in the range 0 to $n-1$. Typically this might be done by splitting up the binary representation of the message into equally sized blocks of bits, though any other numerical factoring of the message—binary or not— will do. Supposing these numbers are P_1, P_2, $P_3 \ldots$, the cyphertext numbers are then calculated by raising P_i to the power E mod n:

$$C_i = (P_i^E) \bmod n$$

To reverse this process the receiver uses her private knowledge of the secret key p and q, and some results from number theory. In outline, this depends on a quantity known as Euler's totient function $f_i(n)$. This is the number of integers between 1 and n that have no common factor with n:

$$f_i(n) = (p-1)(q-1)$$

The importance of $f_i(n)$ is that when arithmetic is performed mod n, then arithmetic in the exponent E can be performed mod $f_i(n)$ rather than mod n. As an homiletic example consider 2^{13} mod 10. This corresponds to encrypting the value 2 by using a public key ($E = 13, n = 10$). $2^{13} = 8192$. 8192 mod 10 = 2. However, 13 mod 10 = 3, and clearly, $2^3 \neq 2$. On the other hand, 10 is the product of two primes, 2 and 5. Thus, $f_i(10) = (2-1) \times (5-1) = 4$. The exponent mod $f_i(10) =$ 13 mod 4 = 1, and $2^1 = 2$, the correct answer. The reader will find that this works as long as the power is not divisible by $f_i(n)$. However, while we have demonstrated that $f_i(n)$ could be useful in the encrypting part of the process, $f_i(n)$ is the basis of the secret key. Thus, $f_i(n)$ is used by the receiver to decrypt the message as described below, but cannot be used by the encryptor to speed the encrypting process.

Now, the properties of $f_i(n)$ guarantee that there is always an inverse, D, of E mod $f_i(n)$, i.e. a D that satisfies the equation

$$ED \bmod f_i(n) = 1$$

and in fact there is a fast and efficient easy way of calculating D from p, q and E. This inverse is the secret decryption key. Since it depends on the hard-to-derive p and q, the hypothesis is that it is safe from the cryptanalyst. The receiver uses D by computing $Ci^D \bmod n$ for each encrypted number:

$$
\begin{aligned}
Ci^D \bmod n &= (P_i^E)^D \bmod n \\
&= P_i^E \times D \bmod n \\
&= P_i^{(E \times D \bmod fi(n))} \\
&= P_i
\end{aligned}
$$

The method of encryption and decryption must be computationally efficient in order for the method to be affordable. Much of the discussion of the RSA system considers that p and q are prime numbers of something like 100 decimal digits each (giving n some 200 digits and thus a problem in finding the factors p and q that would take of the order of 1,000,000,000 years on a fast computer with a following wind). On realistic RSA systems, D would also be a large number. Calculating a large power of P or of C by repeated multiplication would be a long process. A much faster algorithm can be constructed by breaking the exponent down into its binary representation. This is used to decompose the function into the product of binary powers of the number. These are calculated upwards from the lowest ones, and in addition, each of these powers is modular calculation. As an example, consider the earlier power $2^{13} \bmod 10$. Express 13 as binary, with the bits reversed starting with 2^0, 2^1, ... and calculate the powers of 2:

$$
\begin{aligned}
13 \quad &= \quad 1011 \\
2^0 \bmod 10 &= 1 \bmod 10 \ = 1 \\
2^1 \bmod 10 &= 2 \bmod 10 \ = 2 \\
2^2 \bmod 10 &= 4 \bmod 10 \ = 4 \\
2^3 \bmod 10 &= 8 \bmod 10 \ = 8
\end{aligned}
$$

(the mod 10 has no function in this small example, but would in the next step)

$$1 \times 4 \times 8 \bmod 10 = 32 \bmod 10 = 2$$

Not only is such a method efficient for large numbers, but it also contains all intermediate results within the modulus since all intermediate steps are mod n too.

> **Exercise 14.1**   Despite what was said earlier, the plaintext should be split up into blocks of a similar size to n otherwise the method is significantly weakened. As an example of this, suppose that the plaintext is enciphered, not 200 digits at a time, but one ASCII character at a time. This makes the cypher not only grossly inefficient in terms of bandwidth utilisation, but trivially easy to break, quite independently of the safety of the public key encryption method itself. It is left to the reader to discover why this is. Lest this seem a stupid way of using such a cypher, or any cypher (which it is), the reader should suspend judgement until he has read the account of human frailty in cryptography in Kahn's or Welchman's books.

14.10   Digital Signatures

One of the intriguing aspects of public key encryption systems in general (Merkle and Hellman 1978) and the RSA system in particular is the possibility of providing authentication in the form of digital signatures. Passwords are a well-known way of users verifying their identity to a time-sharing system. However, passwords need to be kept secret, and once they become well-known they are worthless. Thus, passwords are of no use in ensuring that a message came from a particular person— once the password becomes known, anyone can use it to gain entrance to an operating system, and clearly anyone could type a password onto a computer message. For this reason, signatures on documents are never typed, but are handwritten. The authentication lies in the pecularities of everyone's handwriting. In addition, only the original handwritten documents are valid—photocopies are normally not accepted. This is so that it can be verified that the signature is indeed an original done with a pen of some sort and not, say, a cut and pasted photocopy (or, today, a digitised signature on a laser printer as we are sadly wont to receive on upmarket junk mail). Should the authentication be important, then further checks may be required, such as witnesses to the signature, perhaps in front of a public notary. Other authentication devices may also be employed, such as photographs, fingerprints or company seals. The public key encryption system has provided a digital version of this in the form often referred to as digital signatures.

The two main properties of a signature are:

- The receiver can use it to reassure herself and perhaps others that the identity of the sender is as claimed.
- The sender commits her identity by signing the document—she cannot later disavow the document.

Encryption methods have the property that $D(E(P)) = P$. Some public key encryption methods and many secret key encryption methods also have the commutative property that $E(D(P)) = P$. One such example is the RSA method. Thus, to "sign" a message, a sender "decrypts" the message using her secret decryption key before sending the message. The receiver (or anyone else) can use the public encryption key to "encrypt" the message. Since the two operations are commutative, then the original message is revealed by the "encryption". The message is "signed" because only the sender knows the secret encryption key and thus only she (or someone knowing the key) could have constructed the message, but anyone knowing the public key can verify this. The sender cannot disavow the message without claiming that her private key has been compromised.

There is some parallel here with the use of a company seal—a company could try to disavow its company seal if it had been stolen or given away, or copied. Similarly, a dishonest digital signatory to a message could claim its secret key had been stolen or given away or copied. With the exception that a digital key is easier to copy than a physical seal, the two situations are really very comparable. A dishonest company could disavow its key by publishing its key and then claim that the key had been stolen. In principle the situation there is plainly fraud, and just the same as throwing the company seal away and claiming that it was stolen. However, proving such a comparitively abstract notion in front of a jury might be difficult. As with all real world situations there are no mathematical certainties, and extra evidence such as time and date stamps, network addresses, audit trails, and common sense need to be applied to reach acceptable levels of confidence. Davies and Price (1980) discuss digital signatures.

Public key encryption systems have revolutionised the way in which we think about encryption systems, and provided the possibility of signing documents digitally. However, all is not as black and white as may at first seem. Even if the mathematical foundation upon which an encryption system is based can be proved mathematically to be "insoluble" then this does not prove that the method itself will in practice be insoluble. This is because the real world, complete with human failings, is never completely captured by the mathematical abstraction upon which the proof will be based. One aim of our potted history of cryptology earlier in this chapter was to emphasise this point.

14.11　Weaknesses of Current Public Key Algorithms

It seems that the knapsack problem itself is still insoluble. However, Shamir (1984) showed that the particular type of knapsack problem proposed by Merkle and Hellman could be solved fairly efficiently. The weakness is that Merkle and Hellman actually use a trivial super-increasing knapsack problem and disguise it as a difficult one by using modulo arithmetic. Shamir showed how to apply some work by Lenstra in integer programming to retrieve the original super-increasing trap-door set and thus break the cypher. As Shamir points out, an important property of his attack is that it is based not on a specific encrypted message, but on the public key itself. Thus, the cryptanalyst can be performing her analysis of the key in anticipation of the first message, and the method is claimed to be easy to implement, and *"Efficient, even on a microcomputer"*.

Recently, doubts have begun to surface about the security of the RSA method (Lenstra 1986, Stewart 1987). Lenstra has extended some work of Pollard (see Riesel 1985). Pollard's method looks for prime factors p of a number N such that p is a "nice prime". A nice prime is one such that the number $p-1$ factorises into lots of small primes. This, together with some results from number theory allows the prime factors of a large number N to be found if the factors are nice. Lenstra has extended Pollard's method using some subtle results concerned with the group theory of elliptic curves. So, even if $p-1$ is not nice, then $p-2$ can be tried, and in turn, $p-3$ can also be tried. This method enables prime factors to be found in a time that depends on the "distance" of the nearest number that can be factored into small primes. It seems that most primes are fairly close to numbers with many small factors. Stewart quotes the example of using Pollard's method to find the factor $p = 2670091735108484737$ of $3^{136} + 1$. The factor p is itself large, but $p - 1 = 2^7.3^2.7^2.17^2.19.569.631.23993$—all small primes.

The running time of the algorithm depends on how close a "nice" number is, and so varies widely. However, it appears that for the 200 to 250 digit numbers that are usually considered, the running time on a top of the range computer has been reduced to minutes or hours, with the worst cases of a day or so. This is enough of a reduction from the "age of the universe" type of running time that, as this is written in the late 1980s, the security of the RSA algorithm is seriously in question.

Even without these methods of attack on the basic RSA cryptosystem, the use of RSA cryptosystems for providing digital signatures is vulnerable to attack if the cryptanalyst can cause arbitrary messages to be signed. Denning (1984) analyses this weakness and points out that not only must the cryptosystem itself be secure, but so also must the protocols for using it. There is a parallel here with the wartime use of the Enigma system that we looked at earlier. The basic system was for all practical purposes uncrackable, but the system was compromised first by the operational procedure of starting the message with a repeat of the three letter discriminant, and later by the allocation of foolish keys. There were other factors in the wartime Enigma story, but the protocols of use were a major compromising factor, and still can be—as Denning's study of digital signatures shows.

14.12   Network Applications of Encryption

So far in this chapter, we have concentrated on the techniques of encryption, on what can be achieved, and in which ways the user should take a lesson from history and proceed with caution. We have implicitly assumed that the security and confidentiality of communication between two network users will, of necessity, be improved if encryption is employed, and we have concentrated on the way in which the encryption methods work, and the way in which they may be compromised. Now we shall take a step back, and see how encryption techniques can be used in a network environment to achieve some, sometimes surprising, results.

14.13   Equivalence of Secure Channels and Authentication

First we shall make the observation that, assuming the encryption *method* to be secure, if two users share a secret *key* and use it for single-key encrypted communication, then the shared possession of the secret key is equivalent to having shared access to a secure communications channel. Since one of the attributes of this shared channel is that it is secure from access by everyone except those who have authorised access by virtue of the secret key, then the posession of the shared channel is also a verification that the other user is who you think it is. That is, the channel *authenticates* the identity of the two channel users to each other. Thus, we observe that these different aspects of the communication—the *key*, the *channel*, and *authentication*—are but different views onto the same logical process. In this way, key distribution is equivalent to authentication in a network environment.

14.14   Key Management

As we said above, it is fairly clear that if two parties communicate over an insecure network, then their communication can be made more secure and secret by the two agreeing to use a certain encryption method together with a specific key. This is fine for small numbers of parties wishing to communicate. The problem comes when the numbers get larger and larger. For a total population, N, of objects that might wish to communicate, the total number of keys required will be

$N(N-1)/2$. Because this increases with the square of the number of communicating objects N, this rapidly becomes unmanageable. Still worse is the fact that, for security, the keys should be changed frequently, and we see that the security of the system will be compromised because of the difficulty of managing the keys.

Needham and Schroeder (1978) observed that this problem can be alleviated by having trusted *authentication servers* in the network. With such servers, each potential communicating entity need only maintain a shared secret key with the authentication server. Then if two such entities wished to communicate they could use their keys to communicate with the Authentication Server, and the authentication server could issue a new key that could be used for that session.

In outline, the protocol is as follows: Entity A wishes to communicate with entity B. A and B do not share a key, and so cannot yet communicate securely. However, entities A and B each have their own key that is a secret between them and the authentication server, AS. A uses this secure channel to ask the authentication server for a new, temporary, key for a session with B. AS generates the new key and sends it along the secret channels to both A and B. Thus, the new key is known only to A and B (and to the trusted AS of course). In this way new keys are generated and distributed by the Authentication Server as the need arises for communication. Each communicating entity needs only to maintain a single key with the authentication server, rather than $N-1$ keys with the (potential) entities with which it might sometime communicate. The initial allocation of the keys, by some administrative mechanism outside the system is that much simpler, and the regular changing of keys that is so essential to security, is simplified.

Since this result is of such importance, it is worth looking at the protocol in detail. Let us assume that some suitable single-key encryption algorithm is chosen. We shall denote encrypting the piece of data X using the key K by the notation $\{X\}^K$. We have described the process as if the entity wishing to obtain a new key sent a message to the authentication server, and the authentication server just sent the new session key in a message separately to each of the new entities. This is unsatisfactory, since it is quite possible that the initiator would receive its new key and try to use it before the responder had received its copy of the session key. Needham and Schroeder neatly solved this synchronisation problem by having the server send the key to both ends via the initiator. The initiator A first sends a message *in the clear* to the authentication server AS requesting a new session key for use with B:

$$A \rightarrow AS: \quad A, B \tag{M_1}$$

AS looks up both secret keys K_A and K_B, and computes a new session key K_S. It then sends a complex message back to A:

$$AS \rightarrow A: \quad \{B, K_S, \{K_S, A\}^{K_B}\}^{K_A} \qquad\qquad (M_2)$$

Because the message M_2 is encrypted with A's secret key, only A can read the message and obtain the session key from inside. The presence of the label B is needed to make sure this is not confused with any other message concerning communication with another entity. In addition, since the message M_1 is not encrypted, an intruder could have changed the identifier B to another value. Were it not for the confirming presence of the identifier B under the authenticating seal of the encryption key, then the unsuspecting user A might be about to communicate with something entirely different to the intended B. A also obtains the odd value "$\{K_S, A\}^{K_B}$". Since this is encrypted with B's key, A cannot read it. However, it is not useless to A as this *authenticator* is now sent on to B:

$$A \rightarrow B: \quad \{K_S, A\}^{K_B} \qquad\qquad (M_3)$$

B and only B (apart from the trusted AS) is able to decrypt this and obtain the session key. Since the data comes under the protection of the key, and also contain A's identification, B knows this is a message from AS and thus that it can trust the new key K_S.

Note that although the key arrived at B via A, it was protected by B's private key K_B. In other words, it was transmitted to B from AS through the secret channel with B. The actual route through A is unimportant in this respect. The route through A *is* important in that it synchronises the arrival of the new key at B with the expectations of A.

Let us think about the use made of the three keys. K_A and K_B are both used in the exchange to encrypt data, but K_S is merely passed as data. From now on, though, only K_S will be used to encrypt the session, and K_A and K_B will not be used again until the next authentication exchange. In a very high security environment where lots of data will be passed, K_S is the most likely to be broken by cryptanalysis merely because of its more intensive use. Also, since K_S will be kept around in the computer systems A and B, it is more likely to be compromised be penetration of those systems themselves. K_A and K_B need not be, and should not be retained.

On the other hand, the lifetime of K_S is for the session only, whereas while the private keys of the two entities may be used only in the authentication phase, they will be used in several—possibly many— authentication phases over a long period. Indeed, the session key may be used with a different encryption algorithm from the authentication phase. It might be that the two principals A and B don't care too much if others can see their session as long as they know that their session is definitely with the intended entity and not an imposter. (That is, they are only concerned to prevent active intrusion and are not concerned with passive intrusion.) The ultimate variation on this theme might be an interactive user establishing contact with a service machine. If it is assumed impractical for someone to "take over" an X.25 call, say, once it is in progress, then many users would settle for a securely authenticated login session and not be too worried about others watching them, say, compiling and debugging a computer program. (Of course, this does not mean that any stage of encryption can be dispensed with during the authentication exchanges themselves.)

If we assume that the session key will be more vulnerable than the private keys, then we need to elaborate the protocol somewhat. In addition, intruders can wreak havoc, even if they cannot decrypt messages, by recording messages and re-playing them later.

To guard against this, the notion of a *nonce identifier* is sometimes used. *Nonce* means *used only once*. The idea is that to make sure a certain message is actually a reply to the one you sent out, the outward message is labelled with a nonce identifier, and the presence of the same identifier on the reply re-assures the receiver that the reply is current rather than a replay, and that other associated data are thus up-to-date. If we denote nonces as I with various subscripts, then the first two messages in Needham and Schroeder's protocol become

$$A \rightarrow AS : A, B, I_A \qquad\qquad (M_1)$$

$$AS \rightarrow A : \{I_A, B, K_S, \{K_S, A\}^{K_B}\}^{K_A} \qquad\qquad (M_2)$$

If the nonce I_A is fresh and unique, then its presence in the reply re-assures A that the new key K_S and the authenticator $\{K_S, A\}^{K_B}$ are fresh and new.

The third step in the protocol, M_3, remains the same. Needham and Schroeder pointed out that while the presence of the nonce I_A reassures A of the currency of the new session key, B has no such reassurance. They added two further steps to their protocol in which B generated its own nonce I_B and used it in a further interaction with A:

$$B \rightarrow A : \{I_B\}^{K_S} \qquad\qquad (M_4)$$

$$A \rightarrow B : \{f(I_B)\}^{K_S} \qquad\qquad (M_5)$$

(The actual form of the function f is not important as long as the messages M_4 and M_5 are different, and thus demonstrate the use of K_S.

Needham and Schroeder suggested that $f(x) = x - 1$ was suitable.) This extra exchange has given B confidence in K_S in that it assumes that A has checked the currency of the new session key via the use of I_A, and is passing on the notice of this freshness under the protection of the new session key.

A little later in 1981 Denning and Sacco pointed out a flaw in the protocol. They observed that the final exchange between A and B is carried out under the protection of the very same key that the exchange is validating. Suppose that an intruder has recorded all the messages, and then watched a long session and by analysis or other means it has obtained the session key K_S. The intruder can then replay message M_3, the authenticator message, and partake in the final exchange M_4, M_5 masquerading to B as A. Note that it can use the authenticator message M_3 without needing to decrypt it—that is there is no need to obtain K_B. All the intruder needs to do is to obtain the session key K_S itself to be able to impersonate A indefinitely. We have made comments above about the relative security of K_S compared with K_A and K_B.

Denning and Sacco suggested that the participants in the exchange should each maintain time of day clocks. They then eliminated the handshake, and solved the problem of the re-played message by specifying the protocol with a timestamp T:

$$A \rightarrow AS : A, B \qquad (M_1)$$

$$AS \rightarrow A : \{B, K_S, T, \{K_S, A, T\}^{K_B}\}^{K_A} \qquad (M_2)$$

$$A \rightarrow B : \{K_S, A, T\}^{K_B} \qquad (M_3)$$

The value of the timestamp is that both A and B can check their timestamps against the clock. Obviously, some allowance has to be made for clocks that are out of synchronisation, and for the delays in traversing the network. However, Denning and Sacco suggest that an allowed interval of a minute or so would suffice.

Needham and Schroeder (1987) returned to this question, and modified their protocol to solve the same problem using nonces. Needham has proposed the principle that *"The suspicious party should always generate the challenge"* (Otway and Rees, 1987). Thus, B needs to be given the opportunity to insert a nonce identifier into the authenticator. This can be achieved by the two preliminary steps:

$$A \rightarrow B : A$$

$$B \rightarrow A : \{A, I_B\}^{K_B}$$

The quantity passed to A is then sent onto AS as an additional parameter on the request from A. Since AS can read this quantity, it can generate the more complex authenticator $\{K_S, A, I_B\}^{K_B}$. This is sent back to A, and then from A onto B as before. Since this new style of authenticator contains B's nonce, it reassures B of the freshness of the whole authentication process, including the new K_S.

> **Exercise 14.2**   Compare and contrast Needham and Schroeder's use of "nonce identifiers" with the use of "Initial Sequence Numbers" in connection management in the TCP Protocol described in Chapter 6.

> **Exercise 14.3**   Compare and contrast Needham and Schroeder's use of "nonce identifiers" with the method of implementing reliable RPCs on an unreliable datagram service in section 11.2

14.15   Formal Protocol Analysis

The fact that an error appeared in Needham and Schroeder's protocol, should warn the reader that authentication protocols are perhaps even more subtle than other protocols. Throughout this chapter we have been emphasizing caution in the use of encryption. Now we are doing the same for encryption protocols independently of the quality of the encryption methods themselves.

Burrows, Abadi, and Needham (1988) have developed a formalism for analysing authentication protocols. This enables them to examine real authentication protocols, and to expose weaknesses such as the one pointed out by Denning and Sacco. This has been applied to the original Needham-Schroeder protocol, and clearly shows the problem. In January 1987, two papers were published in the same journal (Needham and Schroeder (1987) and Otway and Rees (1987)) concerning authentication. Needham and Schroeder revised their 1978 protocol as described above, and Otway and Rees suggested a new protocol to achieve the same result. Burrows *et al* have applied their formalism to both of them. Interestingly, it turns out that the revised Needham-Schroeder protocol achieves the job, but the Otway and Rees protocol not only has redundancy, but is also incomplete in that while the two parties end up with the secret session key K_S, neither has sufficient knowledge about whether the other possesses the key. However, the two suggestions are very similar, and Needham (1988) has remarked that the need for a formalism is indicated by the fact that none of the parties involved in writing the papers nor in editing the publication realised the similarity of the two suggestions. We can only hope that the availibility of the new formalism will improve matters in this area.

14.16   Confidentiality Using Public Key Encryption

Suppose that the two parties A and B each have public and secret keys, PK_A, SK_A, PK_B, and SK_B. Given this, A can communicate in safety and confidence with B by sending messages of the form $\{\{M\}^{PK_B}\}^{SK_A}$ or $\{\{M\}^{SK_A}\}^{PK_B}$—and similarly for messages from B to A. Both kinds of messages can only be read by B and could only have been made by A. (Needham (1988) has pointed out subtle differences in meaning between the two types, but these need not concern us here.)

The need for an authentication protocol is thus apparently eliminated. Public key encryption seems to offer a solution to the key distribution problem in that the public key of various servers can be published in some way. However, Kline and Popek (1979) have pointed out that this assumption is superficial. For a start, each *user* must in general also be authenticated to the server.

14.17 Public vs Private Key Authentication

Kline and Popek compared public and conventional key encryption methods and concluded that the two methods have the same complexity of protocol. The problem lies with the "publication" of the public keys for everyone—server and user alike. In a static situation, something like a telephone directory could be published, and the contents of this book could be trusted to a large degree. There would be error from time to time, but deliberate errors inserted by an hostile intruder would immediately come to light. However, in a realistic situation on a large scale, this arrangement would not suffice. Encryption keys, whether public or private, need to be changed regularly to limit and contain the damage caused by the keys being compromised for whatever reason. Keys of any sort should not be used for very long. In addition, a large population of entities will be in constant change, and a static published directory will be inadequate. Just as a printed telephone directory is backed up by a directory enquiry service of some sort, a "published" key directory would need to be backed up by an electronic key server. Once this need is recognised, then the electronic key server might as well be the only service that is used.

Needham and Schroeder (1979) defined protocols for such a server, but we shall use the timestamped protocols of Denning and Sacco for a more equitable comparison:

$$A \rightarrow AS : A, B \qquad\qquad (M_1)$$

$$AS \rightarrow A : C_A, C_B \qquad\qquad (M_2)$$

$$A \rightarrow B : C_A, C_B \qquad\qquad (M_3)$$

where $C_A = \{A, PK_A, T\}^{SK_{AS}}$, and $C_B = \{B, PK_B, T\}^{SK_{AS}}$.

Now, C_A and C_B are *certificates* containing the public keys of A and B. The certificates have the identifying label, and the timestamp so that old messages may not be replayed. In addition, they are *signed* by being encrypted with the secret key of the authentication server. Note here that anyone can decrypt these certificates, and the contents are public knowledge. The point of the encryption is to *authenticate* the contents as being from the authentication server, not to keep the keys secret.

The surprising thing about these protocols is that they have exactly the same complexity as the conventional or private key protocols. The reason is that the user and the server must each be sure that the other is who she purports to be by suitable use of the encryption keys. The protocols would only be simpler if the server could be dispensed with. This would only be possible on a very small and stable network where the public keys could really be well-known and no server would thus be required. However, on realistic networks, which are usually large and dynamic even if they start out small and static, servers will be needed. Kline and Popek make the case that there is thus no advantage to the use of public key encryption. Perhaps this is fortunate when one thinks of the twin disadvantages of the computational expense of currently known public key algorithms and of the doubts over their security.

14.18 Summary

We have seen how the study of cryptology has progressed from stage to stage. With the Cæsar cypher the security is entirely in the fact that the jumble of letters has no apparent meaning. As soon as the eavesdropper knows that she is looking at a Cæsar encyphered message, then the solution is trivial. Later developments made the process much harder to reverse and thus it became permissible for the "enemy" to know that the message at which she is looking is encoded because she is assumed to be unable to reverse the hard encyphering process. However, once the method of Alberti, for example, is known, including the arrangement of Alberti's encoding wheel, or of Trithemius's "tabula recta", then the whole method becomes worthless. To make it useful again, the whole method has to be changed, or at least the wheel or tables used must be changed.

Belaso introduced the concept of the key. With this, the safety of the method becomes primarily dependent on knowing the key. The basic assumption of modern cryptology is that "the enemy" knows the method, and the security of the encryption lies with the key. Thus merely changing the key restores the security of the method. This is a dramatic improvement in that keys are much more easily managed—and in particular changed—than complete methods. However, even this has some drawbacks. Transporting and distributing keys is a large problem in some circumstances. Often it involves trusted couriers and the like, and may even involve resisting tempting liasons during overnight stops. In addition to being clumsy and slow, it is very expensive and it may sometimes be impossible. For example, if a forward unit is surrounded on a battlefield, then its only means of communication may be via the very radio channel that it is trying to protect.

We have seen how the concept of public keys has changed the way in which we look at cyphers, and appears to obviate the need to distribute secret keys. However, the protocols for managing the distribution of keys from authentication servers are of equivalent complexity.

Throughout the history of encryption there has been a constant swing between the advantage gained by the maker of codes and the advantage gained by the breaker. Constantly the story has been one of the ingenuity of the cryptanalyst exploiting the smallest chink either in the encryption method itself or in the encryption process as a whole— including the human weaknesses of the operators. The recent surge of activity in cryptology and in communications protocols that exploit cryptology only serves to reinforce this lesson, and we have tried to point out some of the pitfalls awaiting the naive who trust too readily in cryptology to solve their problems. *Caveat emptor* should be applied in this area, perhaps even more than when, say, buying a second-hand car.

Needham (1988) has reported the remark that whenever anyone says *"Oh, you solve that easily by encryption"*, the speaker has not understood the problem. Protection problems *can* be solved by encryption, but this chapter is intended not only to point out some of the techniques that may be employed, but, perhaps even more importantly, to point out the mass of ways in which the attempt may fail.

As we have tried to emphasise, it is the security of the *whole system* that matters. For example, in his book *Spy Catcher*, Peter Wright (1987) relates the tale of how the British security services tapped into the messages to and from the French embassy, not by breaking the codes used, but by installing listening devices that revealed the messages by listening to the teleprinter machines in action in the embassy. The modern equivalent of this must be the amazing simplicity with which the electomagnetic emissions of video displays may be picked up by inexpensive equipment outside the building in which the display is operating. Word processors, microcomputer screens, and so on can be simply watched. This is quite independent of any security in either the operating system of the computer or the networks to which it might be connected. It even violates the security of a locked door in which some people have a quite unjustified faith. Only electronic screening can prevent such interception. All communication security is as nothing if the data displayed on a screen can be so easily intercepted.

15
Gateways

So far we have studied the various elements that constitute a network, and it will be clear that there is a multitude of different ways in which networks can be constructed. In this chapter we shall study how whole networks can be connected one to another, allowing users to communicate not just within one network, but across several networks.

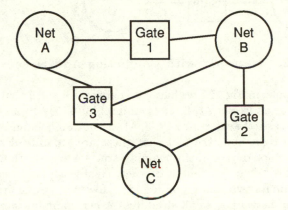

Fig 15.1.   Networks Joined via Gateways

Fig 15.1 shows three networks that are interconnected. The devices that interconnect the networks are usually called gateways, and this chapter is devoted to the study of the problems that these gateways need to solve for successful interconnection. In Fig 15.1 there are three gateways. Gateways 1 and 2 are simple gateways that interconnect two networks. Gateway 3 connects all three networks. We can see that we have formed a network of networks. This is often termed an internetwork, and we could equally have entitled this chapter "Internetworking".

At first sight it might seem that gateways are mere electrical connections. After all, a store and forward network consists of a set of nodes connected by links—if we have two or more networks, then merely adding another link from a node on one network to a node on the other serves to connect the two together. So why do we need to call such links "gateways" and the combined network an "internetwork"? The problems that gateways face and sometimes solve are many and varied, and stem from the fact that different networks almost always differ in some way or another. It may be because of the networks having different technologies or different sets of addresses, or may merely be because they are run by different organisations that have separate budgets and philosophies. Some of the problems and some of their solutions are the subject of this chapter.

15.1   Addressing Domains

One of the important functions of gateways is to allow communication between two networks that have different sets of addresses.

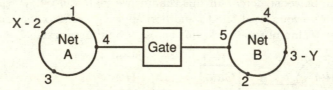

Fig 15.2.   Networks with Conflicting Addresses

For example, in Fig 15.2 we have two networks A and B that have overlapping sets of addresses $\{1, 2, 3, 4\}$ and $\{2, 3, 4, 5\}$. In a global, or internetwork sense, the addresses $\{2, 3, 4\}$ are not unique, and while 1 may be unique right now, the fact that these are separate domains means that we cannot rely on this remaining true since network B may allocate an address "1" at any time it chooses. Really, any address only has meaning within its own context or domain. However, we can arrange it so that a user of network A, say X at address 2, can communicate with a user Y at address 3 on network B, and we can do it by using only the domain addresses above. Obviously, the user at X cannot merely feed address "3" to network A, or she will get it interpreted locally within A's addressing domain, and get the local destination, not the remote one that is intended. We need some mechanism for saying *"address 3, but on network B"*. One fairly straightforward way is to form a compound address, first the address of the gateway within the local domain, and then the other address on the other side of the gateway. Thus the user at X will generate an address something like "4,3" and feed this to network A. The first part of the address, "4", will be used to reach the gateway. The gateway then retrieves the rest of the address, "3", for use on the network B.

Note that the reverse address from Y to X is "5,2". The important thing about this address is that it again contains the address of the gateway G, but from the other side, in the other domain, and in general this is different. This point is an important one because a common useful feature of networks is the provision to the callee of a reverse address by which the caller may be reached. This is often used as part of an authorisation process. If an internetwork gateway is to participate in providing such a facility, then it must be careful to perform the correct manipulations. For our example, user X feeds the call request to network A with a "To Address" of "4,3", and a null "From Address". Network A takes the first part of the address, "4" and passes the call request to the gateway at address 4, where it arrives with the remaining "To Address" of "3" and a "From Address" of "2". The gateway G passes the request through to network B. Here the remaining "To Address" of "3" is used to place the final leg of the call. In the meantime the "From Address" gains the address of the gateway, but in the new domain, and becomes "5,2".

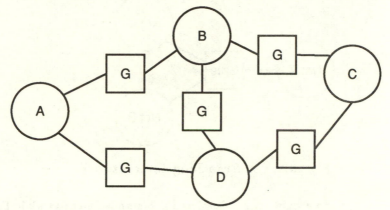

Fig 15.3. Multiple Gateway Connections

Such a mechanism is perfectly general. For example, in Fig 15.3, where we have four networks interconnected by five gateways, any user on any network can connect with any user on any other network. This is possible, even when all four networks have entirely different addressing structures. However, there are some problems. Firstly, since the address that the caller must construct is essentially a specific route through a nominated set of gateways, the caller must have some knowledge of the topology of the connected networks and gateways to be able to construct this route. This knowledge tends to be a topological map on someone's office wall, and the routing address tends to be constructed by hand. Of course, such information rapidly gets out of date, and monitoring the changes in any other than a simple structure is a very onerous job. What invariably happens is that anything that works is left untouched until it ceases to work. This may be despite the availability of more direct routes, routes that are less congested, or routes that are cheaper.

Exercise 15.1   Consider the internetwork in Fig 15.4. What address is needed to communicate from address X on network 1 to address N on network 3? Trace the transformation of the to-address

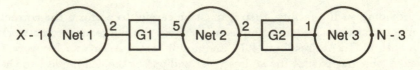

Fig 15.4.   A Linear Internetwork

and from-address at intermediate points in the establishment of the call.

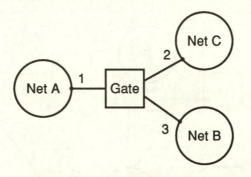

Fig 15.5.   A Branching Internetwork

Exercise 15.2   Consider the branching internetwork in Fig 15.5. Three networks are all interconnected through a single gateway, G. This gateway has a unique address on each of these three networks. Our routing address scheme will not work for this type of network. Why not? Devise and explain a modified scheme to overcome the difficulty.

15.2   Third Party Addressing

One of the problems with specifying internet addresses by routes is the problem of referring to third parties. Consider the internetwork in Fig 15.6.

In some of the more complex applications, for example, transferring a batch job, it is desirable to say something like *"here is a piece of work, and by the way, use that file over there"*. For example, a user at X may wish to create a job that uses a file at Y, and transfer the job to Z to be executed. The job may start at X as something that is schematically like

> **begin** $< Job >$
> ...
> *execute fertang input* $= file@[4,3]$
> ...

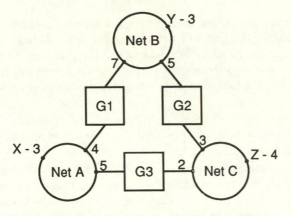

Fig 15.6. Third Party Addressing

end $< Job >$

Clearly, when the job gets to Z, the address [4,3] is invalid because it is now in the wrong domain. However, the address can be modified in the same way as the "From Address" as it goes through a gateway. Thus, as it passes through gateway G3 on the way to Z, the reference address [4,3] is prefixed with G3's address in the domain of network C, giving a new address [2,4,3]. The new job has now been transformed to

begin $< Job >$

...

$execute\ fertang\ input = file@[2,4,3]$

...

end $< Job >$

Now, this will clearly work, with the program "*fertang*" happily referencing the correct file at Y. However, the route is not optimal, avoiding the obvious gateway G2. We would clearly prefer to use the more direct routing address of [3,3]. Indeed, much more pathological examples can easily be devised.

There are other, more intractable, problems with this routing style of addressing. The job containing the reference to a file could be transformed because the address field within it was identified as such to the gateway, and the gateway transformed it into something that was valid on the next domain. The transformation was not necessarily optimal, but at least it would work. However, imagine two users interchanging computer mail concerning access to a file. Perhaps a user at X may be trying to help a colleague at Z to access a file at Y, referring to it in her message as "...*at the address 3 through gateway 4*". Since this is just human readable text rather than a protocol element identified as an address to transform, the text will not be flagged as an address, and will be passed through by the gateway unchanged. The piece of text will thus not directly be useful to the recipient. Similar comments apply to other forms of communication, such as printed documents or telephone conversations.

There are two types of solution to this sort of problem. One is to have an overlayed naming scheme, and the other is to merge the separate addressing domains.

An overlayed naming scheme is essentially the process of allocating each user of the internet a unique identifier or name. There is usually a notion that a "name" is in some way more absolute than an internet "address" (and we have looked at the kinds of names that appear in directories in Chapter 11). Thus, for example, *"Gargleblasters Inc"* may cease its connection with network 1 and subscribe instead to network 2—perhaps because it is cheaper, or faster, or more reliable. Thus, its internet address might change, but its internet name, *"Gargleblasters Inc"* should stay constant. Users of the internet would refer to each other by name for as long as possible. When it comes to the final moment and an internet address is needed, then some sort of name server is consulted. The resulting routing address is the most up-to-date route from the present location and through the available gateways.

In an ideal world, the server would know about faulty or overloaded routes or gateways, and adjust the routing address accordingly. Looking back at the chapter on routing and congestion control, we can see that we have reinvented the same structure, and are facing the same problems, but at a higher level where the nodes have become gateways, and the links have become whole networks. In practice, not only have we "gone up" a level, but we have also slowed down the rate of adaption. The routing through the gateways obtained from the name lookup service is fairly static and is frequently administered by hand.

15.3   Hierarchical Naming

The other way to handle the separate domains is to eliminate them. An early attempt at this was the CCITT X.121 standard. In this standard, each country is allocated a three digit country code, another digit is used to identify a network within that country, and a further eight digits identify an "end user" within the country. Finally there can be an optional subaddress of two digits that the "end user" can use for further selection. The scheme is thus a simple hierarchical addressing scheme of country, network, address, subaddress. In this way, all the addresses used by the PTTs are made unique, and the advantages of having a structured address allow it to be used for routing purposes too.

The main failing of the X.121 scheme is the limited way in which it was devised for the use of the PTTs only. It ignores the fact that the "end user" connected to a single address on the public network may be not merely one person or one service, but may be a gateway to a large local network with tens of hosts and hundreds or thousands of users. The network may not even be local, but may span hundreds or thousands of miles. Thus, for example, an X.25 network like Telenet that spans the USA connects to the Merit network in Michigan. The Merit network spans the state of Michigan with tens of hosts, a hundred or more nodes and thousands of users. The two digits of subaddress left over by the X.121 scheme are quite inadequate to cover this network.

The way in which X.121 is designed for use by PTTs only is also reflected in the way in which only one digit is reserved for a network number within a country. This is not even sufficient to cover the expected use by the PTTs, and countries such as the USA that are expected to have more networks than can be encompassed by one digit have been allocated a range of country codes as a classic "kludge"†to avoid the problem. Such a system cannot possibly extend to cover private X.25 networks too. Thus, JANET the network covering the Universities and Research Establishments in the UK is outside the X.121 scheme even though it is an X.25 network of country-wide extent. Again, the ARPANET is also outside this scheme, only partly because it has a different addressing structure.

With the OSI effort, an expanded scheme similar to X.121 has been set up. This has had most of the limitations of X.121 removed. Most importantly, it is an hierarchical scheme in which all organisations, not just the PTTs, may register a range of addresses. The whole of X.121 has been included in this new system.

15.4   Administrative Gateways

Another function of a gateway is to join (or separate!) two networks that are administered separately. The most important aspect of this is when the two networks have different charging structures, or perhaps different policies about who may use the network.

A very common instance of this is a private network within an organisation that is centrally funded for use by anyone within that

---

† The word "kludge" is commonly used in computing circles to indicate a "fix-up" or a "work-around" for a problem. There is a connotation that the fix is at least aesthetically objectionable or "impure", and sometimes also, as in this case, an implication that the problem should have been anticipated and then the kludge would not have been necessary.

organisation without charge. The private network is joined by a gateway to a public network where all calls are charged by duration and volume of data. It is usual for only a subset of the organisation's users to be allowed to incur charges on the public network, and each organisation has its own policy on whether such charges are billed back to individual users, to a central fund, or some other arrangement.

There is another somewhat similar reason for wishing to identify specific users of gateways to other networks. The destination network may not be a charged network in the public data network sense, but it may be a network that is funded centrally, but only for a specific set of users. Thus the ARPANET is funded by the US Department of Defense for military research. Gateways into this network are intended to block users that do not have Defense Research contracts. Similar considerations apply to the JANET network, which is funded for academic research purposes, and should not be used for commercial purposes. In a similar vein, the gateway may need to filter out all those not satisfying certain security criteria.

Thus we see that what we have called administrative gateways have to perform several operations. They must bar unauthorised use, depending on the organisation's policy. They probably need to identify individuals on a name and password basis, or on the basis of the originating network address, and may need to prepare billing information. They also need to give users the tools to protect their accounts, particularly with respect to the changing of passwords, allowing passwords to be entered without being displayed, and in keeping password and billing information confidential.

Incidentally, while it is well known that passwords should be changed both regularly and often to increase security, it is depressing that both banks and PTTs rarely offer the ability for users to change their own passwords, thereby weakening the users' security (but not their own!) significantly.

Many of the functions that we have just described have been implemented in time-sharing systems for many years. Users have been identified by identifiers of some sort—even their names on occasions—have protected their resources with passwords, and been billed for machine resources used. Thus, the techniques for building such billing and authorisation systems are well-known. Indeed, it is frequently possible, by building a gateway on top of a time sharing system, to exploit already existing mechanisms rather than starting over from scratch. Thus, we shall not concern ourselves with this end of the matter, but with the networking and protocol implications.

An administrative gateway is often "non-transparent". What this means is that when such a gateway is used special actions have to be taken, such as entering identifiers or passwords of some sort. This is particularly true of terminal connections. Thus, for example, a terminal user on a local network will first call a gateway, and will enter into a dialogue with it. After a suitable exchange of identifiers and passwords, the gateway will then allow a request for an onward connection. The gateway then monitors the connection for the appropriate billing statistics, and passes them on to an accounting agent as necessary. In the case of the human terminal user, this method is quite satisfactory, and is widely used.

However, if the "user" is not human, but a program of some sort, then the method of entering into a dialogue with the gateway is much less satisfactory. For example, if a process on a local network needs to transfer a file across a local network, though a gateway, and out across a public network that charges money, then the program is unlikely to be capable of entering into an identifier/password type of dialogue. There are several reasons for this. Firstly, the program is probably implementing a well-defined file transfer protocol. It is very unlikely that this protocol, or any of the other supporting network, transport, etc. protocols include facilities to enter into such a dialogue with the intermediate gateway. Secondly, the process will need to have identifiers and passwords available to use during the dialogue. This is in itself a danger to security. The more widely that passwords in particular are stored, the more accessible they are to the growing threat by hackers.

However, there are ways of handling these problems to a certain extent. Firstly, if it is decided that the programs can have the identifier and password available, then these two items can be added into the address field even though they are not strictly elements of the address. For example, suppose the gateway address on the local network is GATE, and the public address is 311031300062. Then, we might construct the address through the gateway as the compound "GATE+311031300062". Suppose, further, that the identifier and password pair needed by the gateway are "Zaphod" and "Beeblebrox". The overloaded address string might then look something like

GATE(Zaphod,Beeblebrox)+311031300062

Here the address has the extra inserted part which is intended for authorisation at the gateway, and will be stripped out by the gateway before connecting the call on across the public network. It is also necessary that other local network users should not be able to see the password as it traverses the local network. However, this is true of all password schemes, and alternative authentication mechanisms are examined in the last chapter.

The second method depends on the gateway being able to trust certain local users or agents. Thus, if the gateway receives an address like "GATE+311031300062", it looks at the originating address. If the address is one at which a trusted agent resides, then it can permit the call to proceed. The agent is trusted to have performed the correct authorisation checks on the original user, and in addition the agent is also trusted to be generating the appropriate billing and statistical information. Clearly, the gateway also needs to be able to trust the local network to supply it with reliable addresses that could not be forged by untrusted agents. For example, assume that on some local network the gateway knows that it can trust calls from addresses A and B. At addresses A and B will reside perhaps interactive systems that will have validated their users and will be monitoring the outgoing calls and preparing the bills. Obviously there needs to be some arrangement by which the trusted agents reimburse the costs incurred at the gateway.

One of the important benefits of this type of scheme is that the number of places where password information is stored and where users are checked is reduced with a corresponding improvement in security.

An extreme case of this type of gateway with trusted agents is a network where *only* trusted agents are able to make a call to the gateway, and thus *all* outgoing calls are valid and no further checking needs to be done.

A final variation on this theme is the possibility of handling the user authorisation by means of a second virtual call that is independent of the main call. For example, when an outgoing call arrives at a gateway, the gateway may establish a separate call to a server, or perhaps back to the originator of the call. The authentication is then conducted on this second call. The main advantage of this type of approach is that the original call does not need to have such information "overloaded" onto it, neither by tweaking the address nor by any other means. The main disadvantage is the extra complication of establishing the second call, and of linking the two calls together to ensure that the authorisation is of the call intended, and not of some other.

15.5   Transparent Gateways

Some gateways between different billing authorities are transparent to the user because the administrations of the two networks have come to an agreement. Such arrangements parallel the situation with the telephone network. Thus, for example, the British PSS and the US Telenet share the same X.121 addressing scheme with the rest of the world's public X.25 networks. Calls within PSS are charged at one rate, and calls within Telenet are charged at another. Calls originating in one network and destined for the other network are charged at considerably higher rates. However, the gateway joining the networks is completely transparent, and does not ask the originator of the international call for any further authorisation. This is because the PSS and Telenet authorities have established some financial agreement on the operation of the gateway and associated links, and for each's use of the other's network. One possibility is a joint agreement where a single block payment is negotiated each year on the basis of projected traffic. Then each of the administrations can decide on its own charging structure and rate for international calls that it feels is most suitable for making a profit.

Technically, it would be quite possible for an entirely separate company to use, say, a satellite link, and a connection in the USA to Telenet, and in the UK to PSS, and to offer international links between the two networks at a different rate to that charged by Telenet or PSS. In this case the gateway would either have to be non-transparent, and involve itself in one of the methods of gateway authorisation described above, or possibly just rely on the originating network address as it's form of authorisation. At the very least, the user would expect to be able to choose the gateway if there were charging implications.

15.6 Protocol Mapping

Gateways may be used to join networks that run different sets of protocols. For example, a gateway may be used to interconnect a datagram network on one side to a virtual-call network on the other. At another level, a gateway may attempt to map two higher-level protocols to each other, allowing file transfer, for example, to take place.

This type of gateway is potentially extremely useful, allowing the interworking of the different types of technology available for local and wide area networks, and allowing a wide variety of different networks to work together. However, this type of gateway is also potentially the most complex type of gateway, since it requires an intimate knowledge of the different protocols that are being mapped. We shall see that there are some sets of protocols that are unmappable, giving rise to some types of gateway that are either imperfect or impracticable.

Protocol mapping functions may take place at many levels. We shall examine some of the problems by starting at the bottom and working upwards.

15.7 Mapping at the Packet Level—Packet Sizes

It is generally easy to map at the packet level. As we have seen, most of the technologies that we have studied work with a transparent packet of data that is transmitted via the physical level. Thus, if we have two different types of technology that we wish to gateway together, it is generally straightforward to take a packet from one type of technology and transmit it onwards across the other.

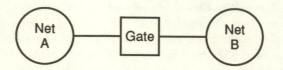

Fig 15.7.   Networks With Differing Packet Sizes

However, there are still a few possible problems, even with such an apparently trivial task, for example, packet sizes and addressing. Consider Fig 15.7. Suppose that network **A** is capable of working with packet sizes up to 128 bytes, but that network **B** can handle packets up to 512 bytes long. There is no problem with sending a packet from network **A** to network **B**, but suppose a packet from network **B** that is 350 bytes long arrives at the gateway destined for network **A**. Obviously, the 350-byte packet will not fit into the smaller 128-byte packets in network **A**. It is almost certainly not acceptable just to put the first 128 bytes into a packet on **A**, and discard the remaining 222 bytes, so what is to be done?

There is a range of possible solutions, but most of them depend on the amount of "control" or "influence" that can be exerted on one or other network. Thus, if a network is entirely "under our control", this means that we can change the protocols in use on the network. This may be the case if a private network has grown up and the time comes to interface with a public network. The incentive may be sufficient that the internal protocols on the private network get changed in some way in order to facilitate interworking. It may be that the control is less. For example, the manpower or expertise to change the protocols may not be available, or perhaps some large investment in specific hardware means that a suitable change cannot be made. Again, we may not even own the network, or perhaps the network runs a set of protocols supplied by some manufacturer, and he is unwilling to change them. If this is the case, then we may have no control over the situation, and some of the technically possible gateway solutions are unavailable. In between these two extremes, we may be able to "influence" the situation. Thus, there may be certain parameters that control certain aspects of the situation. For example, it may be possible for users of the network **B** to make a call through the gateway, and to supply a parameter that forces smaller packets to be made for this particular call.

Another solution is possible if we have sufficient control over network **A**. We may take the long packets from network **B** and split them up into smaller fragments that will fit the packets on network **A**. Of course, not only must the gateway be capable of doing this, but the users of network A must be able to use the fragmented packets from the gateway. If the packet boundaries on network B are not significant, then there is no problem. However, if the packet boundaries are significant, and they usually are, then this information must be preserved in some way in the fragmented packets on network A, and the users of the network must interpret these boundaries correctly. Conversely, a user of network A wishing to generate a long packet on network B must use the fragmenting protocol to transmit the packet across network A. All this will be satisfactory as long as there is a pre-existing fragmenting protocol on network A that can be used. However, if a new protocol needs to be invented, then all the users of A that want to gateway across to B need to implement this new protocol.

We can see that the approach of transmitting the long packets from B over A using a fragmenting protocol is really a matter of taking the long packet service of network B and extending it across A by means of a special purpose protocol. This type of gateway solution—using one network service to carry and extend another service at the same level—is one that is possible at various levels.

In practice, packet size mapping is not often a problem. Most networks can either carry a basic packet as long as is ever used in practice, or have a built in fragmentation mechanism at this lowest level. The trend is that most networks do both—have a large basic packet size, and a fragmentation mechanism. If both networks A and B had such a fragmentation mechanism, then a 2000 byte "meta-packet" could traverse both networks by being split into 128-byte fragments on network A and 512-byte fragments on network B. The gateway would then be responsible for packing and unpacking the fragments as required. One possibility is for the gateway to allocate a 2000-byte buffer and assemble the whole 2000-byte packet before forwarding it onto the other network. Clearly this type of approach has practical problems if the fragmentation mechanism allows "meta-packets" of unbounded size. However, there several other possible choices. It could be that the gateway only made packets smaller on moving from network B to network A, and merely passed small packets from A to B without trying to reassemble larger fragments for transmission across B. However, there are some problems with the latter approach. Some fragmentation schemes, such as that in X.25, insist that all fragments but the last one be of maximum size ("full"). There may also be strong charging reasons for using maximum sized packets (if data is charged by the packet rather than the byte), and the performance is almost certainly improved by using larger rather than smaller packets. To achieve this we must buffer the smaller fragments in the gateway to assemble larger ones.

15.8   Packet-Level Addressing

Addressing is a function that is needed at virtually every level of protocol, including this basic packet level. On a point-to-point link the addressing is null—the only possible destination is the other end. However, on networks that share a medium amongst many users, the addressing is very important. If we are trying to interconnect two networks with quite different addressing structures, then there may be problems.

Suppose that we are connecting a point-to-point link with an Ethernet. Packets across the Ethernet that are addressed to the gateway are clearly destined for the other end of the line, but packets flowing the other way need to contain some onward addressing information for use on the Ethernet.

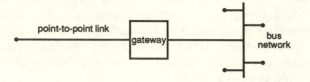

Fig 15.8.   Gateway Addressing—The Simplest Case

For example, an X.25 point-to-point link does not contain the right addressing information at this level for onward travel. This does not mean that an X.25 network cannot be gatewayed to an Ethernet, but that it cannot be gatewayed at the packet level. Instead, it must be gatewayed at the network service level, as we shall see below.

In the IEEE 802 scheme, all the packets at the MAC level contain the same type of 48-bit address. In addition, all IEEE 802 networks understand the same set of addresses. Thus, if we have an Ethernet and a token ring joined together by a gateway, then a packet can be sent across the Ethernet with an address of a station on the token ring, and vice-versa. The gateway used in this type of application is called a "MAC-level bridge" and can work in either of two rather simple ways. The simplest way is for the bridge to accept all packets from either side, and retransmit every one onto the other network. This allows all users of both networks a full capability of interworking with all other users. A much more useful sort of bridge is one that "learns" where certain destinations are. To do this it monitors all traffic from both sides and builds up a picture of where each originating address is. This list can now be used to decide whether a packet needs to be retransmitted onto the other network to reach its destination, or whether it is already on the right side of the gateway.

In the beginning, when its list of known destinations is small or empty, then most packets will be forwarded because a decision not to forward cannot be made in the absence of knowledge of where the destinations are. As the picture of the destinations becomes more complete the packets will mostly only be forwarded as necessary.

Such MAC-level bridges are extremely useful, not only in bridging between different IEEE 802 technologies, but also for localising traffic in a large network. It has often been observed that traffic has a strong tendency to be local. It is very advantageous to split up a large network, say an Ethernet across a university campus, so that the bulk of the traffic stays within small subnetworks, and only a comparitively small amount reaches other parts of the network as necessary. This has the twin advantages that the total traffic at any point is decreased, and that sensitive traffic, including especially passwords, private mail, and suchlike, is much less widely distributed, and is thus not so available to snoopers.

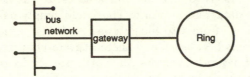

Fig 15.9.   Gatewaying a Bus to a Ring

15.9   Network-Level Gateways
With network level gateways we re-encounter some of the same problems that we did with packet-level gateways, including packet size and addressing. However, we also have the extra problems of the datagram versus virtual call type of network service.

15.10   Network-Level Packet Sizes
This is just a repeat of the problems that we looked at with packet level gateways. We merely need to note that the fragmentation and reassembly mechanism that we discussed at the packet level are applicable here too, and are mostly available. Beyond having to buffer data to fill packets, there is unlikely to be a problem in this area.

15.11   Datagram or Virtual Call?
In Chapter 5 we examined the two approaches to the provision of a network service—virtual call and datagram, and we have seen in particular how a virtual-call service can be built on top of a datagram service. If we have a need to gateway between a network providing a datagram service and one providing a virtual-call service, then the difficulty of building the gateway will depend on what is required by or

is acceptable to the end users. Suppose there exists a datagram network and a virtual-call network, and we need to provide a service to user X on the virtual-call network whereby she can access destinations A, B, and C on the datagram network.

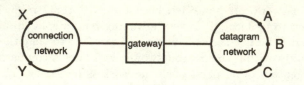

Fig 15.10.   Gatewaying Datagrams and Virtual Calls

There are at least two radically different services that we can think of supplying. The first is to give the user X access to the normal datagram service on the datagram network. This could simply be done by establishing a virtual call from X to the gateway, and then using this call to transport datagrams between X and the datagram network. We are using the virtual-call network to extend the datagram service out to all its users. (This is the same technique, of extending one service out across another network, using its different service as a carrier, that we mentioned when discussing packet fragmentation.)

It is also possible to use the inverse of the technique, but driven from the side of the datagram network. Thus, a datagram intended for someone on the virtual-call network could be intercepted by the gateway. The gateway could then establish a virtual call to the intended destination, transmit the datagram along the call, and then clear down the call. This might be somewhat expensive in terms of the call setups and cleardowns that were necessary, and it is likely that economies could be made if the gateway maintained "sticky" calls. Such calls would be established as required, but not cleared down until they had remained idle for some chosen period. As new datagrams arrive, pre-existing calls would be used in preference to setting up a new call. In this way many calls would be reused by bursts of datagrams, and the need for setting up and clearing down calls would be much reduced.

Exercise 15.3   Consider what types of traffic favour a "sticky" call type of approach, rather than the "use once" type of approach.

Exercise 15.4   Suppose a datagram fits into one packet on the virtual-call network. Suppose that one packet costs 1p, one minute duration time costs 7.5p, and a virtual call takes 6 packets and 10 seconds to establish, and 4 packets and 5 seconds to clear. What influence does this have on the best (most economic) strategy to choose for various datagram traffic patterns?

Let us suppose that rather than extending the datagram service across the virtual-call network, we wish instead to extend the virtual-call service out across the datagram network. We have seen in Chapter 5 how to implement virtual calls on top of a datagram service. We can use this technique to implement a call between the gateway and the intended respondent on the datagram network. Thus, in Fig 15.10, if a virtual call from X, say, is intended to reach B it would first be directed to the gateway. The gateway would establish an onward call to the destination, and join the two calls together forming an internetwork call from X to B.

None of the gateways between datagram and virtual-call networks that we have looked at so far is transparent. In a real sense it is not possible to make such a gateway truly transparent. The gateway can be made transparent from one side or the other, but not from both at once. Thus, it can extend the virtual call across the datagram network, and even do it transparently to the user of the virtual call, or it can extend the datagram service out across the virtual-call network transparently to the datagram user. The point is that either one or the other network carries the "foreign" service on top of its normal service, and that cannot be done transparently because of the semantic mismatch. When there is such a semantic mismatch, then one or other protocol must be enhanced with some adaption or "bridging" protocol to accommodate the different semantics of the other.

However, it is possible to connect two virtual calls together transparently across an intermediate datagram network.

Fig 15.11.   Calls to Datagrams to Calls

Exercise 15.5   Consider how to do this.

Exercise 15.6   Consider joining two datagram networks together across an intervening virtual-call network.

15.12   Internetwork Services

Thus far we have looked at using gateways to extend one type of service across a network providing another type of service. One of the problems with this type of approach is that we must choose one of the technologies to favour. Sometimes this is forced upon us by one network being immutable for some reason. However, an alternative approach, where change is possible, is to choose a certain type of service that we wish to use across all the networks, and to map this service onto the facilities provided by each of these networks. This can be thought of as a "Network-Independent Network Service" or it is sometimes termed an "Internetwork Service". We shall look at two types of such a service.

The first is the so called "Yellow Book Transport Service" (Linington (1980)), though it has several other names. This grew out of the early experience with the *Experimental Packet-Switched Service*—EPSS experiment run by the then British Post Office in the mid-1970s, and the "Bridging Protocol" that was designed to run on top of that network. It was recognised early on in the EPSS experiment that there were problems in tying oneself down to a particular network technology, such as EPSS, and that many of the problems came precisely at the point where EPSS was connected to a local network that ran with a different network service. The bridging protocol was an attempt to come up with an abstract network service (though the term "transport service" was used) that was independent of the specific underlying service, but that could easily be provided on top of many underlying network services, and could be connected easily together at gateways. Moreover, implementations across networks could easily be plugged together at the gateways to form long strings of dissimilar networks that were interworking at this new abstract level. Essentially, this approach is that we should enhance each network service up to the YBTS level, and then plug them all together as in Fig 15.12. This has all the advantages and problems of being a virtual-call approach.

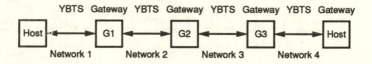

Fig 15.12.   The Virtual-Call Way of Internetworking

The so called "Internetwork" approach is just the opposite. Here, we choose the datagram service as the lowest common denominator, and join the networks together by gateways that transmit and receive datagrams across the available network service. This approach is perhaps best exemplified by the ARPANET *Internet Protocol*—IP (RFC 791), and the related Xerox work with the PARC Universal Packet (Boggs (1980)). Each datagram is released onto the Internet, and may be fragmented and reassembled as requested at the intermediate gateways.

There are two main advantages to this type of approach. Firstly, a datagram service is commonly seen as just about the simplest type of service at the network level. It may be provided across both existing datagram networks and also across virtual-call networks by the types of techniques mentioned above. Thus, the implementation of the IP service should be simple compared with enhancing a network service up to a given level. Secondly, the service should be more reliable than a hop-by-hop method. With the hop-by-hop method, any failure in the chain causes the whole chain of virtual calls to fail. It is possible to reconnect the chain of virtual calls, but this is a rather heavyweight process. With the datagram method, any failure en route can at worst corrupt some datagrams. Such failures are expected, and allowed for in the higher level protocols. All this is a restatement of the classic datagram versus virtual call arguments that we discussed in Chapters 5 and 6, and we shall not repeat them here.

15.13 Higher Level Gateways

So far we have looked at the various problems that may be encountered in constructing gateways between the lower levels of protocol. Less tractable problems appear at the upper levels. Indeed it is possible to find pairs of protocols at the same level that are unmappable.

As an example of an unmappable pair of protocols, let us look at two real file transfer protocols that have both been in use on the research networks at MIT. We shall refer to them as the "sequential protocol" and the "blast protocol". With the sequential protocol, a file is transferred sequentially, record by record. As each record is transferred, it is checked, and if it is in error it is retransmitted. At the end of the transfer an end-of-file marker is transmitted. When the the recipient responds positively to the end-of-file marker, the file transfer is complete. The meaning of "complete" is that the file has arrived safely, is residing in the backing store, and in now available in the filing system. Machine failures will not cause the file to be lost, as they might if it was still being held in volatile memory. Thus, the sender may now modify or delete its own original copy of the file, safe in the knowledge that the transferred file is safe at its destination.

The blast protocol works quite differently. Right at the start, the sender specifies the size of the file it is about to send so that the recipient may reserve the space for it. Next the numbered records of the file are blasted out across the network as quickly as possible, with no acknowledgements or flow control. At the end, an "end of transfer" marker is sent. The valid responses to this are either "all received OK", or "the following records are missing" followed by a bit-map of the missing records. The sender blasts across any missing records, and repeats the "end of transfer" message. The loop is repeated until all of the file is received correctly, and the receiver finally replies "all received OK".

There are some interesting comparisons between the performances of the two protocols that we discussed in Chapter 12. The aspect that is of interest just now is the question, *"Can we build a gateway between these two protocols?"* Imagine a sender working with the sequential protocol, a gateway sitting in the middle, and a destination that is talking the blast protocol—Fig 15.13.

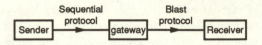

Fig 15.13.   Two Unmappable Protocols

Since the blast protocol requires the size of the file in the initial negotiation, the gateway must acquire this from the sequential protocol. However, the sequential protocol only gives this information implicitly by sending the end-of-file marker. Thus the gateway must store up the whole file transferred across the sequential link before it can even start the initial negotiation for the blast protocol. Even worse than this need for unbounded storage in the gateway is the meaning of the final exchange in the sequential protocol—that the file has arrived safely. The gateway can hardly say "yes" if it hasn't even started the onward transfer yet.

We might think that the gateway could prevaricate at this point, putting off the response to the final end-of-file indication from the sender of the file until the onward blast transfer was complete. However, this sort of delay would not be acceptable to the sender, which would time out and abort the transfer. The gateway cannot say "yes" because the onward transfer may fail for any of a host of reasons including a refusal be the recipient even to start the transfer, and a failure of any of the machines or communications media involved. In any case, if it did send a positive response to the sender, it would be violating the semantics, that the file *was already present and available in the destination system.* While this might not matter sometimes, there are several situations, particularly in real time distributed processing, where this deviation from the precise semantic meaning could be disasterous.

We have thus seen that the two protocols are unmappable in principle. It is possible to gateway the two by violating the protocol— the gateway could reply positively to the end of the sequential request, and then cross its fingers and hope that the onward blast transfer would succeed. Providing that the users of this gateway were warned, then such a change in the semantics of the protocol when used through the gateway could provide a useful service. However, the gateway has now become visible in the sense that users of such a gateway need to be warned to check by other means that their files have arrived rather than relying on the semantics of the protocol. It is also true that the problems of storage in the gateway for temporary storage of files in transit still need to be faced.

15.14   Store and Forward Gateways

All the types of gateway that we have studied so far have been "store and forward" in a certain limited sense. That is, that packets are received, one by one, and stored in memory. They are possibly then modified to a greater or lesser extent, and queued for onward transmission. The storage time is usually of minimal duration, and may be milliseconds or microseconds. Only in times of severe congestion or other malfunction does the storage time exceed a second or so. Indeed, when storage times exceed a few seconds it is not unusual for gateways to discard packets. Unduly delayed packets can cause worse problems than packets that are not delivered at all.

However, some gateways function mainly at a file or a computer mail message level—storing the file in a file store on disc for minutes or even days before onward transmission. It is this type of gateway that we refer to as a "Store and Forward Gateway" and which we shall now discuss.

In the previous section in this chapter, we took two specific file transfer protocols and showed that they could not be mapped perfectly, one to the other. The main reason for this was the detailed specific meaning of one of the protocols used—that when the sender had received a completion signal, then the transfer was complete, and the file was safely at its destination. Most file transfer protocols are less awkwardly pedantic about this point, and it is often perfectly reasonable to gateway different file transfer protocols together by staging the file through intermediate storage in the gateways.

There are several reasons why we might want to do this with files. We can see that our example pair of sequential and blast protocol could be gatewayed together with an intermediate storage of the complete file providing that we can remove or ignore the troublesome meaning of *"it has now arrived safely in real time"*. Many pairs of file transfer protocols become easier to map if such an intermediate stage of storing the whole file is permitted.

A second advantage of intermediate storage is to bridge a difference in operating time between the sending and receiving machines. For example, networks now span the world, and regular intercontinental file transfer is an everyday tool for many people. Sometimes machines, particularly the growing population of purely personal machines, are only operational for a normal working day. Without intermediate relaying gateways to store and forward the files, such machines could never exchange files with others in time zones so distant that the working days do not overlap. As a specific example of this, consider the nine-hour time difference between Europe and Western North America.

While file transfer itself is very important, even more important is the global traffic in computer-based mail. Here intermediate gateways regularly store mail in transit for varying periods. The parallel with sorting offices in more traditional postal operations is quite strong. Indeed, it becomes quite difficult to separate a node in a computer-based network mail system from a gateway, and making a distinction is perhaps a little pointless.

We have looked at some of the characteristics of mail networks in Chapter 10. The important point right now is that a node may sit simultaneously on more than one type of network. If it allows messages to travel to it across one network, and will then send them out across another, then it is a gateway in some sense of the word. We have seen how mail networks are frequently arranged orthogonally on top of other networks. Thus, they may coincide with the domain of a network—as does ARPANET mail—and so become closely associated with that network, even seen as part of it. On the other hand the mail network may be formed from a collection of nodes that communicate together using communication services as available and required. Thus the BITNET/EARN network uses mainly leased lines plus some X.25 connections; before its demise MAILNET used both X.25 connections and dialup asynchronous lines; and UNIX UUCP mail uses a majority of dialup asynchronous lines. Each of these mail networks is made up of a network of hosts. In the cases of BITNET/EARN and UUCP networks the network is mainly held together by one type of operating system (IBM's VM, and UNIX respectively) while MAILNET was a hub network based on and administered by one host, but having a wide variety of different hosts on the mail network.

With the various mail networks that exist, there is a danger that users will end up as several disjoint sets that are unable to intercommunicate, one set with another. However, there are several gateways between these mail networks. In practice, just about any user of one network may be reached by any user of any other network. However, some experimentation, knowledge, good luck, and a following wind are required. Many years ago, in the days of sailing ships, mail was sent by giving it to passing ships and hoping they would pass it on at the next port. Letters did often get through, frequently after adventures of their own. The parallel with much of present day computer mail is compelling.

One of the most ingenious, and perhaps the cheekiest network is an amateur mail network in the USA. This transfers mail messages from personal computer to personal computer in a multitude of small local hops each using a dialup telephone connection until the eventual destination is finally reached. The cheeky part is that each hop is short enough so that it is a local, and thus free call, giving a long distance free message service.

15.15   Gateway, Router, Switch, Bridge, or Repeater?

Throughout this chapter we have used the generic term "gateway" to cover the functions for which some writers prefer the terms "router", "bridge" or "repeater", and a few words are in order to explain this. Working from the physical level upwards, the term "repeater" usually refers to the physical level, "bridge" refers to the link level, "router" refers to the network level.

A repeater is most commonly encountered when joining segments of Ethernet together. It usually involves a very simple regeneration of the signal onto the next segment of cable or fibre, though sometimes the repeater can isolate faulty segments one from the other. We have met "Mac-level bridges" that may be used to take frames of data off one local network and transmit it onto another. These may be used to join together differing technologies, to extend networks, and to localise traffic within parts of those extended networks. "Routers" are similar to bridges except that they work at the network level. They are most commonly met in IP networks where the routing is performed on the basis of the IP address. In X.25 networks the corresponding function is performed by the X.25 switch.

The term "gateway" is sometimes relegated to covering the similar functions at the higher levels, or just at level 7. We have chosen to use the term generically to cover all levels, not least because of the way in which some of the issues recur at several levels.

15.16   Summary

We have thus seen that the functions of gateways between networks are many and varied. Indeed, there are various other functions that we have not had time to investigate. The gateways that we have looked at range from almost literally an electrical plug and socket, to a complex accounting and authorisation server, or complex protocol and address mapping gateways. Of course, one actual gateway may need simultaneously to serve several of the functions that we have studied, and perhaps store considerable volumes of data to boot. Such gateways vary from the mundane forwarding of packets onto another similar network (the MAC-level bridges) to varied and sophisticated functions which need a combination of very clever understanding and complex heuristics. A challenge indeed!

16
Standards

Throughout this book, we have made many references to standards of various sorts. Standards are important in life in general, but are doubly important in communications because of the nature of the subject. The study of computer communications is about having a "conversation" with another machine, and only by talking the same language or protocol can the two machines have meaningful interaction. Standardisation is the process by which the two parties to the conversation agree to use the same protocol. However, belief in standards, and in a particular suite of standards is one of those odd things that attracts violent passions of love and hate that are commonly associated with romantic love or religion. In this chapter, we shall discuss various aspects of the standards game.

16.1   The Need for Standards

Firstly, what are standards? Standards are agreements to produce, arrange, or design things in a particular way for some purpose. For example, the mains electrical supply within a country is normally supplied at a standard voltage, and through plugs and sockets of a standardised design. Thus, we normally expect that when we move house, a table lamp that we take with us should plug into a socket in the new house, and work when we switch it on. We don't even bother to check the voltage in the new house to make sure that it will work, and we expect not to have to change the plug. The same does not necessarily hold true when we move from country to country. Voltage levels through Europe are mostly similar enough that most things will work, but plugs and sockets vary widely, leading to a market in elaborate plugs with multiple retractable pins of varying shapes and positions to allow hair driers to be taken on holiday. The position is more radical when moving between Europe and North America, with a change in voltage from around 220 to 250 down to 110, a change in frequency from 50 *cps* to 60 *cps*, and a radically different plug. Only unusually forgiving equipment will accommodate such a change of standards.

The point here is not whether 110 volts is better or worse than 250, whether one sort of plug is grossly over-engineered and thus too bulky and expensive or the other so flimsy that it always runs hot for all but the lightest duty applications. The point is that they are *different*. There is no doubt that the long-term interests of the users would be best served if just one standard were chosen and then all electrical equipment could be made to the same standard and the users would have the widest possible choice. And for the user, which is chosen is a mere bagatelle compared with a single uniform standard being available rather than a morass of different "standards" being used.

Of course, there is a problem with such a Utopian view. Firstly, if one existing standard is chosen, then that gives the manufacturers that already produce equipment to that standard an "unfair" advantage. This advantage would be worth many millions in whatever currency it was calculated. The other disadvantage is what happens during the transition period? If the electrical supply within a country is changed from one standard to another, what happens to all the electrical equipment that already exists? If there is previously existing equipment, then this will no longer work on the new standard. What should everyone do—throw away all the old equipment and buy new? No doubt the electrical goods suppliers would be happy, but no one else would. Another possibility would be for two supplies to be laid side by side. However this is also a very expensive solution, as is the possibility of each household installing its own transformer to run the old equipment. Yet another possibility is to have a changeover period during which all new equipment is manufactured to dual standard—able to work on both the old and the new standard. Then on some day when most of the equipment is ready for the new standard, the changeover can be made.

It must now be clear why such a change has not been made—the pain and expense of the change outweighs any benefit that will accrue within a reasonable time. Things are made to different standards in different countries. This in itself is not too expensive, since it means supplying a different plug, and perhaps a different transformer for each different country. The volumes per country are large enough so that large international companies are not severely affected. Those who are affected are the ones who wish to move house across international boundaries. Their vote is insignificant enough to be ignored by governments, and they tend to have other problems to cope with that are more pressing than taking the fridge along with them.

The position with communications standards has some parallels with this. Thus, it is important that a computer terminal, say, can be plugged directly into a modem supplied by anyone, not just the special model that is only sold by the terminal manufacturer to go with that terminal, and which thus costs ten times as much as it otherwise would. In addition, the adoption of specific standards for modems means that any two modems operating to, say, the V.21 standard should be able to interwork. So a time-sharing service, for example, should be able to offer dial-up slots with V.21 modems, and anyone with a V.21 modem should be able to use this service. In addition, anyone with a V.21

modem should immediately be able to use any service offered using V.21. The communication standard is what matters, and the user is able to look around the market for the V.21 modem that suits her best—the cheapest, the most reliable, the neatest box, whatever.

Just as with mains electrical supply the standard combination of plug, voltage, frequency, etc allows the free movement of table lamps, so the communications standards, such as V.21, bit rate, and so on allow the free interconnection of equipment from different suppliers. This opens up a free market. Of course, some governments or other agencies may not want a free market. A government with a fledgling telecommunications industry may fear that opening up its market to free foreign competition will lead to immediate collapse and thus to foreign domination. It may thus feel justified in imposing national standards that are out of line with accepted international standards in order to protect its national interest. Other possible strategies to protect the domestic market are blatant protection via regulated telecommunications services.

One of the truisms about standards was set out in a standards working document that, sadly, the author now cannot find and thus can neither quote verbatim nor attribute properly. In essence it said *"Standards are only required when there are viable technical alternatives from which to choose. The process of standardisation is thus, by its very nature, one of compromise."* Once digested, this statement seems blindingly obvious. However, it tends not to be appreciated in some quarters. The problem seems to be that people seem to be oblivious to the fact that others can do the same thing in different ways, and might also believe that their own way is the one and only method of doing things. Then again, compromise is something that we always expect others to be better at than we are, and it always hurts to move to a standard that gives less function than we are used to merely because that will allow us to talk with someone else. Why can't she compromise and do it our better (of course) way?

Currently in the late 1980s there is a trend in the western world to a more open and competitive market. However there are wide differences between countries, and sometimes between the stated aims of a country and the reality of its domestic policy. Whether such policies are "right" is partly a matter of political belief, and partly a matter of whether the person considering the rightness of the policy is more likely to benefit from such policies. Thus, such value judgements are outside the scope of this book. However, it is impossible properly to understand the international standards process without being aware of such political pressures on what superficially appear to be purely technical matters.

As well as national interests it should not be forgotten that there are also very large commercial interests at stake. It has frequently been the case that a manufacturer has tried to lock its users into its own products. As well as the common ones of languages, and dependencies on operating system idiosyncrasies, a proprietary communications architecture has been a prime tool in such marketing strategies. Thus, all the large computer manufacturers had their own communications architectures that were different from each other. Naturally, each was "better" than anyone else's, but as long as the architecture was adequate, the main attribute was that it was *different* from that of other people. Thus, once a user had installed computers from company Y, and then installed their terminals, and a little more equipment, she found that she had a system that hung together quite well. The problems started to appear when she came to upgrade time. Now, not only would her applications programmers tell her that the pain of moving to a new operating system would be such that she could only contemplate another box from Y, but her operations staff would also inform her that if she installed a new machine from company Z, she would also have to junk all her terminals and buy a new set of them from Z too.

Perhaps even worse would be if she needed a box from company Y because of an important database package, and another from Z because of its ability to run certain graphics packages, she would suddenly realise that she needed two sets of terminals and two networks to connect them to the two sets of boxes; one set from Y and one from Z. In addition, should she need to use a remote database, perhaps via a direct leased line, then it is almost certain that she would need yet another terminal that was necessary to access that database, and useless for anything else. The reader may think the example a little strained. On the contrary, reality is sometimes far worse.

Thus, companies Y and Z would attempt to lock in their customers by providing them with a complete architecture of both machines and communications. As with the investment in a particular forms of electrical supply, the hope of the company was that once locked into his architecture, the pain of movement would be such that the user would not desert to another company.

However, apart from the problems that we have outlined above for the user, there were also problems for the companies themselves in this strategy. One is that the company must supply a complete solution for the user. As time went on the scale of the complete solution, terminals batch stations, mail, database, and on and on, became ever greater and outstripped all but the largest most capable companies. The companies became aware that just as it was to the users' advantage to be able to shop around, it was also to its own advantage to be able to rely perhaps on specialist terminal makers to supply terminals, or network specialists to install local networks. It is thus the case that companies are coming to recognise that non-proprietary standards can work to their advantage as well as to that of the user.

Of course, the largest companies come to this point later (if at all). As this is written there is hot debate as to whether the largest, IBM, really believes in international standards and supports them properly, or only pays lip-service and is really trying to play the old game with its own architecture SNA. IBM watching is of course a compulsive pastime in the computer industry. IBM is in such a dominant market position that its products, be they computer architecture or communications protocols, form a *de facto standard*. Just as IBM is able to flaunt standards more than any other organisation, so also is all its architecture copied by other companies as an industry standard. This applies also to its SNA communications architecture.

However, apart from industry standards, important though they are, there is a mass of interacting bodies that co-operate to a varying extent in generating communications standards.

16.2   The Standards Makers

One of the most important is the CCITT (the *Comité Consultatif Internationale de Télégraphique et Téléphonique*). This is one of the divisions of the United Nations agency, the International Telecommunications Union. The members are the various national bodies that run the telephone and telegraph services (*Post, Telegraph and Telephone administrations*—PTTs) in the various countries. These may be national government-run monopolies, or private companies run under varying degrees of government control. Over many years the CCITT has been responsible for the plethora of standards that is needed to operate Telephone and Telegraph services in the various countries around the world. This body addresses the questions that need to be resolved for those services to interwork in the dramatically effective way that they do. The work of the CCITT has enabled the miracle of international dialling from the majority of the world's telephones.

In the computer communications field there are several series of recommendations (this is CCITT jargon for a standard—all sub-cultures generate their own sub-languages) for various aspects of communications. These standards cover all sorts of aspects of communications, from the details of the signalling systems by which telephone exchanges talk to each other over intercontinental links, though the specification of the signals emitted by various classes of modem, international character sets of bewildering variety, communications standards such as the X.25 packet network protocol, the X.3, X.28, X.29 character terminal protocols, the X.400 series of message exchange protocols, and so forth.

The CCITT works on a four-year cycle. In each cycle a new set of recommendations is produced. Sometimes the recommendations are substantially unchanged for many cycles, but sometimes there are radical changes at a new cycle. For example, X.25 was introduced in the 1976 cycle, and revised substantially in 1980 and 1984. As this is written the 1988 version is expected only to suffer minor changes. There have been many substantial changes in the data communications recommendations since 1976, and this activity shows no signs of diminishing.

Another prime player in the communications protocol field is ISO, the International Standards Organisation. ISO's members are the national standards bodies of the various countries in the world. So ANSI in the USA, AFNOR in France, BSI in the UK, for example, all contribute to the standards making process in ISO. ISO is a very democratic body, and standards are formulated by a rather longwinded process of forming working groups that come up with proposals. These are put out to ballot by the member countries, and only progress towards standards as a consensus is gradually achieved. Obviously, this is a long and prolix process, and keeping track of the details of the huge volume of work that is handled by a combination of working groups, meetings, published proposals, postal votes, and so forth is a major task. That anything ever comes out of such a cumbersome process is surprising, so some of the innovatory work that actually results is a miracle. That some of the results are more complex than might be desired is an inevitable result of the process of compromise that is the reality of such a political process.

One of the most important aspects of recent ISO work in communications is the ISO model of communications. We shall return to this briefly in a little while. Because of the strong overlap between the work of the CCITT and ISO in this area, the two bodies have come to an agreement that certain areas of standardisation will be allocated to each. Thus, the ISO model has been adopted by the CCITT—international standard ISO 7498, the ISO model itself, is also CCITT recommendation X.200. The texts are identical. There is also an "alignment" of many other standards in this area. To a great extent, this amounts to the CCITT taking most of the standards arising out of the ISO model and producing them as CCITT recommendations. However, the adoption is not merely a matter of CCITT putting new covers on the same standards and changing the word "standard" to "recommendation". There is a technical review of the standard, and sometimes there is a period of discussion where further revisions are made before final adoption of a standard.

This procedure is not all one-way. Thus, the Abstract Syntax Notation—ASN.1—that we studied in Chapters 7 and 8 originated as CCITT X.409—part of the X.400 series on message-transfer protocols in the 1984 CCITT cycle. This was adopted and developed by ISO in their work on presentation specification, and has become IS 8824 and 8825. Because of this elevation from a specialist tool to being part of the general OSI toolkit, the revised version will appear in 1988 as one of the X.200 CCITT recommendations, and X.409 will be withdrawn.

Another player in this arena is the *Institute of Electrical and Electronics Engineers*—IEEE. The IEEE started a program of making standards for various forms of local-area network. Originally, this addressed only the physical and link levels—the modulation techniques, medium access control, and the error recovery level. However, the work was gradually realigned so that it fitted into the ISO model. Originally, the ISO model of communication was concerned with an X.25-like world of long-haul communication. With the integration of the IEEE work at the bottom level, the various forms of local network have been integrated into the model. The IEEE work is organised as a set of standards called IEEE 802. There are general overview standards, plus one each for various specific types of network, such as Ethernet, token ring, token bus, slotted ring, and some glass-fibre standards. Thus, for example, the standard IEEE 802.3 refers to the Ethernet local network. This is also the same as international standard ISO 8802/3.

As side players on this scene are such bodies as the *European Computer Manufacturers' Association*—ECMA. Despite its name, most of the large American manufacturers are members of this body and so it is more of an international body than its somewhat continental name implies. This does much co-operative work in studying and encouraging standards development. So, for example, the ISO Transport protocol owes much of its form to the preparatory work done in developing the ECMA transport protocol. In addition the ECMA work on using the Remote Operations derived from X.410 for their distributed systems work has been a very strong influence on similar work in both the CCITT and ISO. Of course, the influence is spread not only by the work itself, but by the fact that the participating experts frequently belong to several overlapping working bodies.

In addition to all this is a bewildering collection of other bodies with various influences on standards and their adoption. For example, there are several interrelated bodies in the European Community concerned with the development and acceptance of communications standards.

In parallel with all this is the work done in the ARPANET community. The ARPANET is a computer network that is financed by the US Department of Defense. It serves a dual role in that on the one hand it is used as a service to connect agencies of the US Government and research establishments, principally in universities that are engaged in defence work, and on the other hand the network itself and the services around it are a large scale experiment into the technology of packet switched networking. Over the years, pioneering work has been done on the ARPANET, and, to pick out just one example, the studies of Klein-rock (1976) and his co-workers in many aspects of congestion control, routing, and so forth form the bulk of the accepted work in this area.

The ARPANET community is a co-operative set of users that develop their own protocols by means of a special method of publishing commonly referred to as RFCs (for *Requests For Comments*). These are available across the ARPANET via file transfer or computer mail (or even on paper if you really must—see the glossary). Some RFCs are only discussion papers, but some achieve the status of accepted standards for the ARPANET. We have studied several of these in this book, for example RFC 793 (TCP), RFC 791 (IP) RFC 854 (TELNET), RFC 733, RFC 822 and RFC 823 (Mail), RFC 959 (FTP) and so on. Not only are the ARPANET standards used on the ARPANET itself, but the "ARPANET Suite of protocols" is widely implemented in UNIX systems. Thus, for computers ranging from modest machines of the IBM PC size through to mainframes, the most common method of communicating locally on an Ethernet is by using the ARPANET suite. We have also indicated the use of the ARPANET mail protocols independently of the other ARPANET protocols.

The relationship between the ARPANET community and the ISO/OSI world is characterised more by heat than light. The ARPANET community sees itself as operating a large, open, successful operation that is independent of any specific manufacturer (because of its devel-opment of its standards via the RFC mechanism), that has pioneered packet switched networking. Other organisations and individuals tend to be seen as naïve or inexperienced. In particular, the whole OSI cum CCITT process sometimes receives vitriolic comment (see e.g. Padlipsky (1987)). The tone is perhaps *"We invented it, why do you ignore us"*. This is despite the fact that the same reference makes only grudging acknowledgement of the even earlier work in packet switching done at the NPL (see, e.g. Davies and Barber (1973)—widely referenced in the literature). Of course, whether the ARPANET is itself "open" depends on whether you are one of the acolytes, or outside the door having a problem gaining entry to an exclusive network.

We have mentioned above the possible commercial problems of taking up a standard that is already actively and effectively exploited by others. We have tried to indicate that there are things to be said on both sides—whether it is better to join an existing standard and meet already entrenched competition, or go for a new standard that is equally much work for everyone (and more in total). Whichever way you decide, it is commercially naïve to refuse to recognise the problem is a real one. Of course, the consequences of commercial naïvity are more tolerable if the naïvity lands one on the "winning" side.

An extra spice in the recipe is the other semi-religious argument of whether a network service should be a datagram service as with the ARPANET IP service, or virtual circuit as with X.25 networks. We have already looked at the arguments about this one in Chapter 6. Suffice to say at this point that there must be a certain difference in emphasis with the ARPANET being on the one hand slanted towards the military establishment, and therefore emphasising the reliability and recoverability features of a datagram subnetwork, while the X.25 service arose out of the telephonic background of the CCITT with its culture of circuits and its emphasis on saving transmission bits.

On the other side, the ISO camp is spreading its new religion with the fervour of the reformed atheist, and is thus just as likely to offend with its born-again enthusiasm as anyone in the ARPANET camp. That work on the ARPANET is frequently dismissed out of hand hardly calms matters—though the fact that notice has been taken of the ARPANET (and other) work is as undeniable as the fact that complete solutions are being prematurely claimed by the ISO camp. It is also true that at the higher levels in particular, new ground is being broken. For example, the presentation work has no real parallel in most other major communications architectures, and those architectures are the poorer for that.

What a pity that the two camps cannot lower the decibel count and listen as well as speak. They have so much to teach, and learn from each other. Still, perhaps Bronowski is right that great science is driven by ego rather than the quiet diligent reflective work that we traditionally visualise as the scientific process.

16.3   Communications Models

We have seen in this book the way in which communications architectures are structured into layers. Typically there are lower layers containing the detailed means of communication, middle layers containing the means of shifting data from end to end, and upper layers responsible for enabling applications programs to make use of the communications provisions. The earliest communications architectures were much simpler, and had little separation into layers. For example, the HASP multi-leaving protocol ran over a simple point-to-point link. There was a lower level where framing and error recovery were strongly intertwined. Since the link was source to destination there was no network layer to handle routing, and the end-to-end functions of the transport layer were served by the error recovery across the link. There was a session layer only in the sense of a connection being established (or was this the transport layer?). Most presentation issues were dealt with by having the same representation at both ends, but there was residual presentation function in the form of data compression.

Many modern communications architectures have an elaborate layered structure. We shall briefly describe but two—the ARPANET model, and the ISO/OSI model.

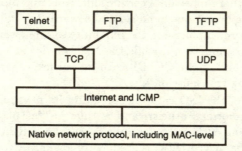

Fig 16.1.   The ARPANET Model

The ARPANET model consists of the "roughly" four layers shown in Fig 16.1. The diagram clearly shows four layers, however, ARPANET gurus insist that this is a three-layer architecture. This is because they wish not to become involved in the specification of the lowest layer—what we have termed the "Native network protocol". This lowest layer may consist of an Ethernet with the internet datagrams being carried one by one in an Ethernet frame, or it may be a point-to-point link, running perhaps HDLC. For the agnostic operator it could be an X.25 virtual circuit along which internet datagrams are sent one by one in complete packet sequences. The lowest "proper" layer is the internet datagram. This is carried end to end across the internet. The internet datagram is the basis upon which all ARPANET applications are built. In addition to the Internet datagrams that are sent end to end, the ICMP protocol allows the switches constituting the network to communicate one with another. In this way they can react dynamically to failures of parts of the network. The IP datagrams are used in two main ways—either to support a TCP connection as described in Chapter 6, or to support a user-level datagram protocol, UDP. TFTP is the trivial file transfer protocol.

A layered communications architecture, such as the ARPANET suite of protocols has the general abstract structure that each layer provides a service to the layer above. It provides this service by communicating with a peer-level entity across the network, and it does this by using the services provided by the layer below. In general terms this is illustrated by Fig 16.2. This diagram is meant to show two entities at the same level communicating with each other using the protocol of this layer. They provide a service to the layer above. The entities are in different machines, and so they cannot communicate directly, but must use the services of the layer below in order to exchange their protocol messages.

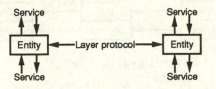

Fig 16.2.   Layers of Protocol

This is a rather abstract notion, so to make it more concrete we shall take the TCP service that we examined in Chapter 6. Thus (working bottom up), the service offered by the layer below is the IP datagram service. The two entities in question are the processes in the two communicating computers. These entities co-operate with each other in offering the TCP connection service to some higher-level pair of users (or entities), one in each machine. For example, these may be other processes that are conducting a TELNET terminal connection. They offer the TCP service, of a full duplex, sequenced, error free stream of bytes by communicating with each other using the IP datagrams to carry the TCP protocol messages. They enhance the service underneath, the IP service, to give an improved service, the TCP service, to the TELNET entities above.

Since the ARPANET suite of protocols recognises only three layers, this generalised abstract notion of layering is not fully developed as a separate notion in that model. However, the ISO/OSI model has seven layers in all and thus this abstract notion is well developed. Indeed, the document specifying the OSI model itself spends a considerable time developing the principles of layering. The general model looks something like Fig 16.3.

This model specifies seven layers. As we work up the tower the service provided by each layer gives an enhanced service to the next layer above. This builds up from the elementary service provided by the physical layer at the bottom right up to the application layer where the real work for the users is actually performed. We have covered all the elements in this tower of protocols as we have worked through this book, so examining the OSI model is a convenient review of much of the ground covered in the chapters of this book. The model provides

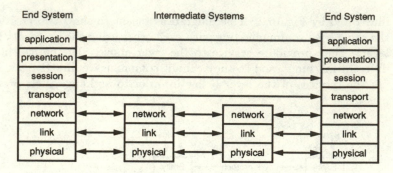

Fig 16.3.   The ISO Seven-Layer Stack

a good conceptual framework in which to organise our mental view of communications architectures.

At the physical level, various different sorts of medium can be used to shift bits from one place to another. We have looked at several of these in some detail, varying from point-to-point links, through shared radio channels, to shared media of various access disciplines and topologies. In Chapter 1 we examined point-to-point media, modem interfaces, and suchlike, and in Chapter 3 we looked at various forms of shared media. The next layer up is the data link layer. This corresponds to the HDLC error recovery procedures that we studied in detail in Chapter 2. The OSI model was primarily developed as a description of wide area networking over long distances. The IEEE 802 work covers these two layers for the case of local networks, and we shall return to this again below when we discuss the architectural relationship of the IEEE 802 work to the lowest layers of the OSI model.

Continuing upward, the network and transport layers come next. These were the subject of Chapters 5 and 6. We see that we have now built up from the basic raw communications facility provided by the physical medium through error control, network routing and congestion control, until the transport layer has been reached. This provides a two way "bit pipe" from end-to-end with assurance that bits have actually been delivered at the other end. This latter point is the reason for the change in the schematic diagram at the transport layer. At lower layers it is permissible for there to be intermediate relay entities. Thus, one leg of an end-to-end call might be via X.25 across a public network, and another might be across a local network using token bus for example. This is illustrated by an intermediate entity that sits at the junction between the X.25 network and the local network, and is one of the forms of "gateway" that we looked at in the last chapter. However, the transport connection is end-to-end, from the entity in one end system to the corresponding entity in the other system. The transport service has as one of its attributes the property that the sender can tell when certain data that has been sent has actually arrived. This is not the case with any lower layer.

Above the transport layer, the character of the communications services changes. Some authors claim that the transport service is the end of "traditional communications services"—presumably referring to the fact that communications are "traditionally" concerned with providing just the bit-pipe sort of service that the transport service is. However, the session service can be seen as an extension of the transport service notion to a more extended timescale. The presentation service is something that is much more radical in communications architectures. However, it can be seen as an abstraction and generalisation of exactly similar pre-existing notions that have long been present in earlier higher level protocols such as terminal support and file transfer protocols.

At the top of the model come the application level services. We have looked at FTP as perhaps the most important example of this. There is also the CASE standardisation that is taking place at this level too.

The reader may wonder where a service such as messaging fits into the OSI model. The answer is that it doesn't fit *into* it, but *on top* of it. Thus, if we look back at the X.400 set of protocols, we see that the link between one MTA and another, or between a UA and an MTA is an application level association. Thus, the delivery of a message from a source UA to a destination UA involves a series of OSI associations between "end systems". X.400 is a good illustration of what OSI end systems are. They are the co-operating systems for a particular interaction. They are not necessarily the highest conceptual level of connection that can ever be distinguished. Indeed, should this have been the case, then severe conceptual difficulties would have arisen.

Let us pursue this for messages to illustrate the point. Suppose that an application association was required to deliver a message from one UA to another. Then either many of the functions of MTA agents (such as storing mail at a relay point for hours or perhaps days) would have to have been discarded, or the end to end application association would have needed to be expanded to cope with the functions that we expect of MTAs.

The problem is that this process, once begun, never stops. Suppose the X.400 messages constitute the moves in the chess game that we used to illustrate the conceptual difference between datagrams and virtual calls. Since this is a higher conceptual level our insistence that the application association must cover it means that the chess game must be reflected in the application-level protocol. Of course, the ability of the human mind to detect ever further logical associations, such as a message sparking an idea in someone's mind, leading to another message to a colleague that results in a terminal session that causes a file to be transferred that... Making an application association correspond with *every* such notion is clearly as absurd as it is impossible. OSI does not insist on such a notion, but merely identifies the interaction between "application entities" as the ambit of its applicability.

16.4   IEEE Project 802

We have briefly mentioned the IEEE 802 work on local networks. Originally, this was started in parallel with and independently from the ISO/OSI work. IEEE 802 is an attempt to standardise *Local Area Networks*—LANs. Thus, IEEE 802.1 constitutes a general description of local networks, IEEE 802.2 describes link-level error recovery procedures that are closely related to HDLC, and IEEE 802.3 defines the standard "Ethernet". Other IEEE 802 standards cover token bus, token and slotted ring, and some glass-fibre issues. Clearly, these align closely with the bottom two layers of the OSI model, and steps have been taken to harmonise the IEEE 802 work with the OSI effort.

Layer 2: Data Link		LLC
Layer 1: Physical		MAC: Medium Access Control

Fig 16.4.   IEEE 802 and the ISO Model

It is instructive to examine the way in which project IEEE 802 relates to the ISO model. The relationship is quite straightforward. The lowest layer is the physical layer in both cases. In the case of straight OSI this will normally take the form of some specific modulation technique on a point-to-point wire of some sort. There are several of these in the V-series of CCITT recommendations. The corresponding layer in the IEEE 802 LAN is the specific modulation technique and access method for the particular sort of LAN in question. For example, IEEE 802.3 specifies a CSMA/CD network implemented on top of a physical medium that is a coaxial cable of a very specific type using a very particular modulation technique. On the other hand, the IEEE 802.5 token ring specifies the use of twisted-pair cable with a quite different way of transmitting the bits. In addition, just as there are several alternative V-series recommendations that can be used on point-to-point links (depending mainly on the transmission rate), so there is also a growing number of alternatives in the IEEE 802 LAN specifications. For example. IEEE 802.3 also specifies a cheaper coaxial cable option that can be used in place of the full specification cable (but which has more restrictive conditions on length and number of connections), and other possibilities of transmitting the bits (and detecting the collisions) over glass fibre and twisted pair are also being standardised.

The next level up in the ISO model is concerned with framing the bits into packets, and calculating checksums to detect errors. We have examined some of the techniques in this area in Chapter 1. In the same layer are the error recovery procedures, and here variants of HDLC are by far the most important technique for recovering from the errors detected by the cyclic redundancy checksum. On the IEEE 802 LAN side, the various sorts of shared media each have their different ways of delimiting packets. In addition, they have specific procedures for accessing the shared medium that are not normally needed with HDLC since it usually works on a point-to-point link.

Some varieties of HDLC actually support multiple access to a shared circuit. The technique used is for a master station to poll round the several slaves in turn to see if they have anything to send. This technique is much like the token access in a token controlled LAN, except that it is much more static than the decentralised token management that we see in token rings and buses. The ultimate degeneration of this is the "half-duplex" or more precisely the "two-way alternate" point-to-point link. Here there are just two stations on the circuit, but only one can transmit at a time. This is managed by the master polling the one other station to allow it a turn at transmitting.

All shared media need some such way of controlling access to the medium, and thus the varying procedures for doing this are termed MAC procedures, for "Medium Access Control". Depending on the specific LAN these can vary from the protocol used in detecting a signal already on the medium, or detecting a collision as with CSMA/CD networks, to an elaborate exchange of packets such as takes place when setting up either a token ring or especially a token bus. As well as the detailed format of the packets, token management, and monitoring of the ring, this level includes a CRC checksum. Interestingly enough, even though the basic bit error rate on local networks is usually much less than on long haul circuits, the checksum used on local networks is usually specified as a 32-bit checksum rather than the weaker 16-bit checksum that is used on point-to-point circuits. This is partly explained by the fact that data packets on local networks are often much longer than on long haul circuits. However, since link-level checksums are invariably calculated in hardware on high speed LANs, the overhead in processing is minimal and thus the extra security is affordable.

In addition, point-to-point links have only vestigial addressing (since the only place a frame can go is to the other end), but shared media have a large address that has been standardised at 48 bits long.

48 bits may sound somewhat excessive, but the intention is that all stations on all LANs in the world should be capable of being allocated a globally unique address. To ensure this a central register of such MAC addresses is maintained, and all new equipment should have addresses allocated from this registry. While this ensures that equipment bought from different sources may be mixed without the problems that might be caused by duplicate addresses, it does not ensure that these addresses are useful for routing packets from one network in one part of the world to another network in another part of the world. This is because the addresses are not suitably structured to aid the routing process.

16.5   TOP and MAP

TOP and MAP are not really standards generating efforts at all, but movements towards the adoption of certain specific sets of OSI/IEEE standards in two industrial areas. MAP stands for *Manufacturing and Automation Protocol*. This arose from the recognition by the car making giant General Motors that an increasing fraction of its spending on industrial equipment involved devices that needed to communicate one with another. Thus, milling machines, robots, stock control computers, and suchlike needed to communicate with each other using some common medium and set of protocols so that the whole mass production operation could be tied together in the most efficient way. The use of communications standards would allow the same benefits on the factory floor that they give the user of more traditional computing equipment. GM decided to use its unrivalled purchasing power to enforce an agressive standardisation effort. It set up a MAP study group that came up with a selection of the emerging OSI standards. The aim was to select a subset of the full range of protocols and to move this progressively towards eventual full conformance with the ISO model.

MAP chose a specific type of local network for use on the factory floor—the token bus. This was chosen because its various properties were thought to be most suitable for that environment. On top of this MAP specified no link-level error recovery (since the LAN was fairly reliable and error recovery would take place at the transport level), a null network layer (routing was not needed on a single local network), transport protocol class 4 (full error checking and recovery), and null session and presentation layers. At the top came the FTAM protocol. The session and presentation layers were specified as null because they could manage without the corresponding services, and also because the standards were somewhat premature at the time.

Later versions of MAP have replaced the network layer with the connectionless network service (similar to the ARPANET IP service), and elementary versions of the session and presentation layers. In addition, MAP is now supported by many other automobile companies and by increasing number of other manufacturing industries.

TOP is a corresponding effort in the area of office automation. The most striking difference from the MAP set of protocols is the selection of the Ethernet (IEEE 802.3) as the lowest level carrier. This should perhaps not be surprising considering the history of Ethernet in this area, and its origin in the research labs of Xerox PARC. Here the fact that the access to the Ethernet is statistical, and thus non-determinate is less critical than on the factory floor. The determinism of the token access weighs heavily in favour when operating robots in a time-critical environment, as do the electrical characteristics of the bus architecture.

16.6   Functional Standards

TOP and MAP are examples of what has come to be known as *Functional Standards*. The reader will now be aware that there is a huge set of protocols from which to choose, and in addition, many of the protocols have a whole series of parameters—such as timeout values, the number of times to retry before signalling an error, etc—which are not specified in the protocol definition. A *Functional Standard* is a specification of a set of protocols that will work together, including the specification of timers, retry counts, etc, and will deliver a particular service. There are various groups at work specifying functional standards for various services, such a mail, dumb terminal access, FTAM, and so on. The aim is to provide a specification of a useful set of protocols to which implementors may work.

16.7   Protocol Description

In this book we have looked at many protocols. We have described them in very informal terms. However, this informal description is not satisfactory, and a more precise specification of protocols is necessary.

The reader will doubtless be familiar with the similar concepts in connection with computer languages. It is normal to teach computer languages in a very informal way using chalk and talk in a classroom, or text and examples in a textbook. However, such methods are insufficiently precise when it comes to defining the language well enough so that compilers may be written, and so that a source program may, using two different compilers, compile and run and produce the same result. Typically, a human learns to program in a particular language by a combination of classroom and textbook, plus practical exercises using a particular compiler on a particular machine. However a language definition, for Pascal, or C, must be more abstract than a particular implementation.

For computer languages, the most common definition techniques are based on the *Backus-Naur form*—BNF that was first used in the definition of Algol 60. Indeed, this technique has spread and is used in various forms in the definition of many computing concepts. We have seen that one of its applications is in the area of presentation-level definitions, and the ASN.1 notation that we discussed in Chapter 8 is closely related to the original BNF notation. This should not be surprising, since the presentation level is concerned with the abstract representation of data and is thus closely related to the very similar issues in strongly typed languages, including Algol 60 and its multitudinous descendents.

In addition to their use in the formal definition of a language, such forms can be used directly by computers in the processing of the language. Thus, there are many automatic tools (i.e. algorithms and implementations of these algorithms as useful programs) that allow the investigation of the grammar of a new language to see whether it is self-consistent, and will ensure that valid programs can only be parsed unambiguously, and so on. Further, the grammar may be used directly by a general purpose parser so that it is not necessary for a new parser to be written by hand for each new language. This both eases and speeds the implementation of a new language, and ensures that errors are prac-tically eliminated—that is that the implementation actually corresponds to the definition. We shall see that there is a large correspondence here with what is possible with protocols in the most favourable circum-stances. However, in general, protocol implementations fall somewhat short of what has been achieved with languages.

However, the lower layers of protocols have a different nature in that they are concerned with a sequence of events in time. In particular, they are concerned with two (or more) entities that communicate with each other by sending messages. The messages have a finite transmission time, and, just like traditional letter post, the messages can "cross" in transit. This type of behaviour is difficult to model using many tech-niques. To date, by far the most successful technique is that of the finite state machine. We shall concern ourselves almost exclusively with this type of description during the rest of this chapter.

As an illustration of the description of a protocol by means of states, let us consider the protocol exchanges involved in establishing a connection. We have come across well-developed versions of connection establishment protocols first when looking at the link-level HDLC pro-tocol in Chapter 2, and again when considering network and transport connections in Chapter 6. Rather than modelling one of these well-developed protocols, let us develop a much simpler connection protocol and show how the finite state machine approach helps to point out some of the traps that await the protocol designer. Suppose that we first design the protocol so that it has two states, disconnected and connected. An entity moves from one state to the other either by emitting (−) or receiving (+) a connect message—Fig 16.5.

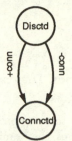

Fig 16.5. A State Transition Diagram

The value of this diagram is that it shows pictorially the way in which the states of the entities change as messages arrive. It also shows other things fairly easily. For example, once an entity has moved from the disconnected to the connected state, there is no way back. This can be seen from the fact that there are two arcs from the disconnected state to the connected state (corresponding to receiving or emitting a connect message) but there are none pointing back to the original state. This much would be pretty obvious from an examination of the corresponding rules expressed in everyday prose, but only because the set of possible states is very small and easy to hold in the mind at one time. However, for bigger sets of states it becomes much more difficult to visualise the possibilities. In that case a pictorial representation becomes much easier to follow.

Our deliberately oversimplified example above illustrates the fact that a protocol may be "invalid". This may happen for several reasons. The one we have illustrated is that it may be possible to reach some state and then never to escape that state again because there is no event that can happen to cause the state to move to anything else. This is almost invariably a design error, and analysis of such a state transition diagram can enable the protocol designer to build in escape routes. Obvious ones for the specific example we have given are the emission or reception of a disconnect message that allows the state to return to the disconnected state.

However, the diagram still does not specify the full protocol, or rather the protocol that it does specify is not correct in the sense that it does not allow for all possibilities. In particular it does not allow for "connection collision". Connection collision is the classic example of the

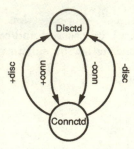

Fig 16.6.   An Example State Transition Diagram

sort of complexity that occurs in protocols because the two parties to a conversation are not synchronised, and the messages they emit take a finite time before arriving. Thus, it is quite possible for one entity to emit a connect message and change its state to connected, and while that connect message is in transit for the other entity to do the same. The result is that both entities receive a connect message when they are in a state in which they do not expect it. The problem is that it is all too easy for protocol designers to have an "instantaneous" system in mind. In an instantaneous system, there is no such transit time between the sender sending a message and the receiver receiving it. (This occurs for example when the communication is by means of subroutine calls from the one entity to the other.)

There are two possible sorts of fix for this problem. The first is to specify that in the connected state, the reception of a further connection request is merely ignored and the state remains connected. A similar rule can be made for disconnects crossing in the network and arriving when the entity is already disconnected. These are usually shown as loops on the diagram—Fig 16.7.

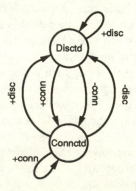

Fig 16.7.   A Modified State Transition Diagram

This method allows for the arrival of protocol messages when they are not normally expected. There are many cases when the state transition diagram of a protocol needs to have such loops added as incoming redundant messages are ignored. Another way of handling the immediate problem of call collision is to add new states, and to make the connection process altogether more complex. This approach has the value of handling the problem of lost messages in a simple way. The protocol that we have illustrated so far has the problem that if the outbound connect message is lost, then it will remain connected, but its intended interlocutor will never respond, and there is no mechanism for recovery from this erroneous state. In our studies we have seen that one cure for this is for the initiator of the conversation to persist in attempting to set up the conversation until it receives a satisfactory response.

In the finite-state model this type of behaviour can be modelled by inventing a new halfway state. Thus, the initiator of a connection moves from the starting state disconnected to an intermediate state calling destination as it emits the first connect message. Normally it expects to receive a connect accept from the respondent, and it then moves from the intermediate calling destination into the connected state as this message arrives. Alternatively, an incoming call causes a transition from the initial disconnected state to the other intermediate state incoming call. The entity will then remain in this state while it decides whether or not to accept the call (possibly communicating with some higher-level entity in the process) and then it will normally move from the incoming call state into the connected state by emitting connect accept. This gives the symmetric four-state diagram in Fig 16.(8).

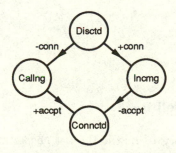

Fig 16.8.   A Connection—Disconnection Diagram

So far there is little apparent value in the new arrangement with the extra states. However, the problems of call collision and lost call packets can be neatly handled. The call collision is handled by adding rules for recognising the collision messages in the intermediate states. Thus, if an entity has sent out a Call Request and is sitting in the Calling

Destination state expecting an Accept message in response, then, a call collision occurs when it gets an incoming Call Request instead of the more usual Accept message. If this Call Request is from the entity to which it was trying to make the call in the first place, then the incoming Call Request can be treated like an Accept, and the connection completed—Fig 16.(9).

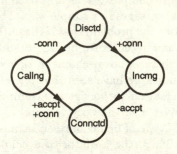

Fig 16.9.   Handling Call Collisions

Of course, such fixes can be made to a protocol by other means. However, we have described them in this context since similar design errors were found in the early versions of X.25 by precisely this type of analysis. These errors have long since been fixed in more recent versions of the protocols.

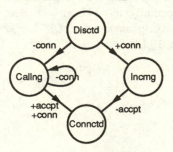

Fig 16.10.   Repeated Call Request

In addition, if it is necessary to repeat the Call Request after a timeout until it eventually elicits a reply, then this can be shown as a loop out of the intermediate states and back into the same state. This loop is taken, together with the re-emission of the corresponding request packet, as the timeout expires and the call is reattempted.

Exercise 16.1   The state diagrams are still incomplete in that they do not show the disconnection process. Complete the diagram with intermediate disconnecting states. In addition, represent the use of the Disconnect message to refuse a call.

Exercise 16.2 Invent a set of states and draw the state diagram for the RESET process in X.25.

State diagrams such as the above are used to describe fairly elaborate protocols. For example the definition of X.25 contains several state diagrams defining various aspects of the protocol. In general, protocols are described in terms of several state variables rather than just one. For example, in Chapter 6 we described the RESET mechanism in X.25. The RESET mechanism can be described in terms of a separate state variable with three values. Once a Reset packet has been transmitted, this state variable changes from No Reset to Expecting Reset Response until a confirmation is received from the network. Similarly, incoming Resets cause the reset variable to change to Received Reset until the Reset Response is finally sent out.

This mechanism is normally represented by a specific state variable that is separate from the main connection state variable. The *Reset State Variable* is only valid when the *Connection State Variable* is Connected. Thus, Resets have no particular meaning unless a connection is in progress. This allows a simple state diagram for the reset process that is contained "within" one of the main connection states. It is quite possible to merge the two states into one larger state. Thus, we might replace the one value of the main connection state variable by three new connected states that correspond to the reset-specific states above. In this way we have combined the two states, and the two state diagrams.

The disadvantage is of course that we have one larger and more complex diagram instead of two smaller and simpler diagrams. In particular, all three new connected states will have all the incoming and outgoing arcs of the single old connected state in the connection-disconnection state diagram. This will in itself be bad enough, but in addition, all three new substates will also have the arcs connecting them that correspond to the reset state diagram. (In fact things are slightly less regular than this since the initial state reached, as a connection is completed, can only be the No Reset state.) Such combined diagrams becomes quite impractical either to draw or to follow. It is for this reason that the total state space is usually structured in such a way that each of the several resulting state variables has a smaller and more easily managed state space. Really, this is just an example of the way in which it is always desirable to decompose a large complex structure into several smaller and simpler structures.

There is another, similar way in which the potentially large state space of such a finite state machine can be simplified. This is by the use of other auxiliary variables. The prime example of this is of course with flow control with multiple credits. We could model such a flow control process by having a series of state variable values corresponding to the possible window sizes or outstanding credit numbers. The problem is that with a moderately sized window there is a new state variable value for each possible size of the window or for each possible additional credit that may be sent. With TCP the window size can vary from 0 up to $2^{32} - 1$. The corresponding state diagrams would be very regular but completely unmanageable. It is very unusual to model the flow control in this way, and it is more usual to have arithmetic variables that correspond to the number of credits, etc, and to increment and decrement these according to data sent and received. What is common however, is to have special states (such as Flow Stopped) that correspond to extreme values of these flow control variables.

While state transition diagrams are useful in visualising the behaviour of a protocol, they are not directly useful as input for computer programs. However, an equivalent representation is by means of a state transition table. This is often displayed as a rectangular matrix. Each row of the matrix is labelled with one of the states of the state variable, and each column is labelled with the event that is to be described. The elements in the matrix give the next state. As an example of this type of representation, consider Fig 16.11 showing the simple two-state connected/disconnected machine, with the four events +conn (receive connect), +disc (receive disconnect), −conn (emit connect) and −disc (emit disconnect). This can be represented by the matrix in Fig 16.11.

		+conn	+disc	-conn	-disc
Old State	Disconnd.	Connected	(Disconnd.)	Connected	[Error]
	Connected	Connected	Disconnd.	[Error]	Disconnd.

(above the event columns: ← Event →)

Fig 16.11.   The State Transition Table

In the cases corresponding to the arcs shown in Fig 16.11, the next state is shown. There are two entries shown as [Error]. These correspond to the entity emitting (−) a particular packet that does not make sense in our specific protocol. (However, note that the HDLC connection protocol does indeed emit disconnects in the disconnected state, and thus the entries would not in that case be [Error]). There is one extra entry corresponding to the case when an entity in the Disconnected state receives a Disconnect. Though the action to be taken—just stay disconnected—is trivial, we had not allowed for it in our state transition diagram. Using a matrix of this sort allows us the opportunity to ensure that there are no null entries. Thus it is a simple and effective way of ensuring that every state and event combination has been allowed for. This is less easily done when working with the diagram.

As well as a matrix indicating the next state, the protocol definition can also contain a similar matrix where each of the entries specifies the action to be taken in this particular state-event combination. For example, the receipt of a Reset packet in the Data state will cause the protocol entity not only to go into the Reset Received state, but will also in general initiate some response, such as the discarding of queued data, and the resetting of flow control parameters. This action can be represented as an entry in an action matrix that has exactly the same shape as the state transition matrix. As an example of such a definition, the ISO transport service protocol definition contains a large transition matrix. Each of the entries specifies both the next state and the action to be taken.

The author has implemented a protocol entity for a protocol (the *Yellow-Book Transport Service*—Linington (1980)) that was defined in this way by using the transition matrix directly in the software implementation. The protocol state was represented by a Pascal-style enumerated type, and the events were converted to another enumerated type. These two enumerated types were used to index two rectangular arrays. One array had as its values the next state (an enumerated type) and the other array had a set of action procedures as its values. The core of the implementation merely consisted of the double index to obtain the two values from the two arrays. Of course, the action procedures themselves still needed to be programmed appropriately, and the events needed correct conversion into the enumerated type. However there was no problem with making the action of the protocol implementation coincide precisely with the transition matrix protocol definition—flaws and all. This was much more direct than the normal implementation as **if-then-else** or **case** statements, and was in fact extremely efficient. Part of this efficiency involved the use of a strongly typed language that allowed the definition of arrays of procedures.

This matrix form that can be directly represented in the machine can also be used to investigate the protocol itself. Thus, consider a state vector that consists of an array of Boolean values indexed by the state variable. If the state under consideration has, say, four values, then the state vector will have four Boolean variables, each one corresponding to one of the four possible states Suppose we start with an initial state vector that has a single 1 bit (or "true"). We may then multiply this by the transition matrix to produce a new state vector. This state vector has as its values Boolean "true" in the positions where it is possible to have reached the corresponding state after just the one interaction. Since all possibilities have been considered, then this vector will express all possible results. Another multiplication will produce all possible states after two events, and so on. We can see that this is the equivalent to building up the tree of all possible resulting states starting with the initial state. The tree will in general be infinitely "tall", but to keep the representation finite, growth stops when no new states are reached. Each "leaf state" points to the possible successor states which will already have been defined.

Once this tree has been obtained it can be analysed. Firstly, and trivially, it can be determined whether all states are reachable. If some are not reached by the tree, then those states are clearly useless. Secondly, the tree can be analized to see whether there are states from which there are no routes back to an acceptable terminating state.

It is even possible to use the state tree in estimating the performance of protocols. This can be done by estimating the "cost", in CPU cycles perhaps, or in elapsed time delay, of each branch in the state tree. Then the average cost from one state to another (for example from an error state back to the error recovered state, or the cost from receiving one packet correctly to getting the next one) can be estimated by taking all possible paths and summing the costs along each of these paths. These costs on each path are then weighted according to the probability that that path is being taken.

16.8   Testing Protocol Definitions and Implementations
We have pointed out how the formal description of a protocol in terms of its state table transitions can be used in its implementation, thus reducing development time and increasing the confidence in its correctness. However, we are some way from being able to compile a protocol definition directly into a complete implementation. Apart from the protocol description tools not being adequate for this, there are other reasons why this has not yet been (and might never be) achieved. One is that protocol specifications are not complete in several ways. For example, they do not normally specify buffer handling or flow control strategies. In large measure this is deliberate since these will be dictated by the design constraints within the implementor must work. Thus, if a protocol allows a flow control window to become very large it does not necessarily mean that a particular implementation must always take full advantage of that. There may not be sufficient buffer space available for a large window to be specified. Alternatively, if the application being served is, say, a human user on an interactive screen, there is little point in allowing the flow of data to her display getting more than a screen full or so beyond where she is looking even though there might be enough space for the flow to get hundreds of screens beyond where she is looking. Indeed this would be thoroughly undesirable as she would get a quite wrong picture of where the process she is watching has got to.

In addition, specific implementations must live in fairly specific programming environments, with very particular, perhaps even peculiar constraints. It is the task of the implementor to accommodate such strangenesses. However, it is still possible that implementations of protocols may in the future be compiled from formal protocol definitions, with issues being settled not by a person coding the protocol, but by supplying supplementary parameters or rules as required for the specific implementation.

Since much of the actual implementation is still done by hand coding, with only limited direct use of the formal definition itself, much work has to be done, as with any programming endeavour, in making sure that the implementation is "correct". Traditionally, the major part of testing a protocol implementation to see whether it was "correct" consisted firstly in various *ad hoc* testing procedures, such as exercising the implementation with manually generated data and looking at the results to see whether they were as expected. Sometimes the test data was systematically generated. The next stage would frequently be to test the implementation against itself (if the protocol in question was sufficiently symmetrical to make this approach sensible). Finally, the implementation would be tested against some other implementation elsewhere across a network connection. In some sense, this latter test is the ultimate. After all, the point of a protocol implementation is for it to work with other implementations to give interconnection services. As long as it works, then that is all (apart from performance, efficiency and reliability) there is to it.

However, this type of testing is no more satisfactory than just trying any other piece of software and just accepting it providing that it "works". For the testing to be of any real use, it has to cover the types of use that it is likely to encounter in real life. For example, an X.25 implementation might work satisfactorily providing that the RESET facility is not used, or it might crash if the window size is opened up. There are implementations of certain protocols on the market as this is written that cost good money but that appear to crash when a certain number of thousands of packets have passed through them (could a counter be overflowing?). To give an acceptable assurance of quality, testing has to be carefully designed so that out of the extremely large set of combinations of possible events, a sufficiently diverse and carefully chosen set has been exercised that the chance of errors happening in the other untested combinations is acceptably small. Thus, a large area of study and work has grown up around this area of testing implementations of protocols to ensure that they work as expected.

Some of the early attempts at testing implementations of X.25 involved a portable reference tester. This consisted typically of a minicomputer that could be connected to the other end of the communications line and used to exercise the implementation under test. Typically the tester would run through some prearranged set of tests of usual and unusual conditions, and would perhaps introduce errors of various types to make sure the error recovery mechanisms worked correctly. This type of device was extremely useful, and was often a prerequisite before an implementation could be connected to a real live public network.

Much of the later development work on testing ISO protocols is a logical development of this. However, the concept of an actual physical portable tester has tended to be replaced by the concept of remote testing. Thus, it is assumed that most of the testing required in the future will not be of network services corresponding to X.25, but will be of higher level protocols. In addition, the assumption is made that the basic network service will be in place, and thus the tester need not physically be brought on site, but can be used remotely across the network connection.

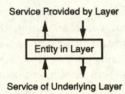

Fig 16.12.   Inter-Layer Relationships

The things that are to be tested may either be a complete stack of protocols right from the physical layer up, or may be a protocol entity that exists in a single layer. Consider the abstract form of an entity in a protocol layer in Fig 16.12.

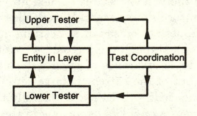

Fig 16.13.   Testing Protocol Entities

The problem is to ensure that the entity under consideration supplies the correct service to the layer above and makes proper use of the service below. In the general abstract case, these types of test can be carried out by supplying abstract test entities above and below that are co-ordinated in some way. Thus, we have a structure something like Fig 16.13

Given such an abstract arrangement, the protocol entity can be tested by feeding in suitable messages at the top and bottom, and examining the messages emitted, both top and bottom. However, this is an abstract setup. In practice, some acknowledgement of reality is needed. The problem is that specific implementations live in quite specific environments. In addition, while protocols are described in layered terms with stacks of entities communicating by means of message interchanges, it is by no means required that actual implementations be structured in this way. Indeed protocol definitions specify only the patterns of bits on the communications medium, and details of implementation are very carefully not specified. Thus it may not be possible to isolate specific implementations in such abstract testing surroundings. What is tending to happen is that protocols are implemented, and tested from the bottom up. Thus, the "lower tester" tends to be separated from the actual implementation by means of a communications line.

The upper tester may be a program of some sort living in the host system and somehow accessing the service interface that it is supposed to be testing. The sort of arrangement that has been tried is to write a program in some fairly portable language, such as C or possibly Pascal, and to drive it from a script in a file. However, such a program needs some specific interfacing both to the actual service under test and to the host operating system. This interfacing may itself be a significant programming task and brings with it its own possibilities for introducing errors into the testing process. However, while this increases the cost of this sort of testing, it is not too likely that errors introduced by the customising of the tester program cancel errors in the implementation. (But as we all know, in computing the unlikely always happens, especially if we don't want it to.)

16.9   Summary

This final chapter has indicated why standards are especially pertinent to communications, and has briefly summarised some of the main standards bodies and processes. Of course, standards agreements are worthless unless they are correct, precise and unambiguous, and unless implementations conform to the standards, and this conformance can be demonstrated.

We have seen how a formal protocol specification can allow the analysis of that protocol for certain types of error. These types of analysis have been used on pre-existing protocols and shown up design errors that the earlier manual methods did not detect. The analysis can also make performance estimates about the protocol. The description can also be used in the implementation itself. Currently the extent of the direct use in the implementation is limited, but this will necessarily increase with time. Finally, the specification in terms of messages to and from a protocol entity can be used in the testing and certification of implementations of various protocols.

Glossary

Abstract Syntax Notation One—ASN.1: A method of describing precisely the syntax of protocol and data formats in a machine independent way.

Addresses and Routes: A computer communications network is used to connect a set of entities together. The entities are usually distributed geographically, though several may coexist within one computer system. A network *address* is some form of identification of the network entities, and the *route* is the path that the data uses to traverse the network from the source entity to the destination entity.

Application Layer: The topmost layer of protocol in the ISO Model. This is the level that is seen by user or Application-Level programs.

ARPA: The *Advanced Research Projects Agency*, now called DARPA for *Defense* ARPA, is a US Government body that funds research projects. ARPA funded the original ARPANET (among various other projects), and later the DARPA Internet.

ARPANET: The wide-area network, mainly in the USA, funded by ARPA.

Association Control Service Element—ACSE: An entity or piece of program in the application layer that controls associations or connections with other application programs.

Asynchronous Transmission: A particular method of transmission of data, normally indicating the transmission on a character-by-character basis.

Bandwidth: A measure of the information-carrying capacity of a communications medium.

Baseband: A method of transmission in which the data signals are carried directly rather than first being used to modulate another signal.

Baud Rate: The rate at which the communications medium transmits changes in signal. This is *not* in general the same as the bit rate.

Big-Endian:　Characters in Swift's *Gulliver's Travels* who held the fanatical religious belief that boiled eggs must only be eaten starting at the big end. Also a term indicating that the most important or significant part of a data entity is transmitted first. See also *Little-Endian*.

Bit Rate:　The rate at which bits are transmitted. Usually measured in bits per second.

Bit Stuffing:　A method of framing data blocks with two flag-sequences of bits and "stuffing" or inserting zero bits into the data stream to avoid the same flag pattern in data confusing the framing process.

Bitmapped Terminal:　A kind of video-display terminal in which each point or pixel (q.v.) on the screen is mapped into one or more bits in a computer memory. In this way complete control of the display is possible, and—subject to screen resulution— any arbitrary picture may be displayed by suitably changing the pixels.

BITNET:　A network that originally linked IBM computers together across the USA using IBM-specific protocols. The network used point-to-point links to link mainframes together. The main traffic is file transfer, but some of the file transfer traffic contains computer messages. The network has spread to other kinds of machines that use the same protocols, and has also spread to Canada (NETNORTH), and Europe (EARN), and is linked to other networks.

Broadcast:　A method of broadcasting data to many destinations simultaneously rather than sending to just one destination.

Burst Errors:　Errors often occur in groups or *bursts* rather than randomly and singly.

Bus:　The topology of a shared medium in which all stations connect to a common passive medium as opposed to a ring in which data is forwarded from station to station.

Byte:　A byte of data contains eight bits, and is usually the smallest unit of data separately addressable in the memory of a computer. Text characters are usually represented by a single byte. Bytes in protocol messages are often called "octets".

Carrier:　The signal that is used to carry the data. The carrier is *modulated* by the data signal.

Carrier Sense, Multiple Access—CSMA: A method of controlling access to a shared medium in which the medium is first sensed for a pre-existing signal. When *Collision Detection—CD* is added the protocol becomes CSMA/CD, the method of controlling shared access to a medium that originated on the Ethernet.

CCITT: (Comité Consultatif Internationale de Télégraphique et Téléphonique) A division of the International Telecommunications Union, a United Nations agency. The members are the various national PTTs or similar bodies.

Channel: Some means of communication, such as a wire carrying an electrical signal, or a radio wave, or a light beam in an optical fibre, that is used to convey information between two or more entities.

Checksum: Checking information that is added to the end of a frame or packet of data in order to check for transmission errors. See also *code word* and *data word*.

Circuit: A direct or indirect connection between two entities that can be used to exchange data. A "real" circuit (as opposed to a "virtual" circuit (q.v.)) usually has a fixed bandwidth and end-to-end delay characteristics independently of use.

Circuit Switching: A method of moving data between two entities by establishing a circuit between the two entities for the time during which they wish to communicate.

Clock: When a set of data bits is transmitted, the bits are usually serialized and transmitted one-by-one at regular time intervals along a tranmission medium. The regular time intervals are supplied from a *clock*. At the receiving end the times or pulses of clock signal must be known in order to interpret the incoming data signal. This clock signal is usually either encoded along with the data in some form or transmitted in parallel along another channel. There are many different ways of doing this.

Coaxial Cable: A particular kind of cable where one conductor is surrounded by a coaxial sheath.

Code Word: A unit of information that includes some error checking information. See also *data word*.

Collision Detection: See *Carrier Sense, Multiple Access*.

Committment, Concurrency and Recovery—CCR: A kind of protocol for accessing distributed data. It provides a way in which mutually exclusive operations and atomic operations can be implemented.

Common Application Service Element—CASE: Protocol services at the application level that are sufficiently common across different applications that they are standardised.

Cryptography: The art of secret writing. Cryptology is the study of cryptography, and cryptanalysis is the study of the encrypted information, primarily with the aim of "breaking" the code and obtaining the "plaintext" or original information.

Cut and Paste: Documents may be edited by cutting pieces of paper with the text or diagrams on them and pasting or gluing the pieces back together in a different arrangement. Many electronic systems have the anologue of this where sections of a document—text or pictures—may be "cut" from and "pasted" into different parts of the same or other documents. The terms "cut" and "paste" are still used.

Cyclic Redundancy Check—CRC: A certain kind of checking information that is normally calculated over a block or frame of data and transmitted with the frame. The aim is to detect transmission errors.

DARPA: See *ARPA*.

Data Circuit-Terminating Equipment—DCE: The equipment that is supplied by the network provider for the attachment of user equipment. Primarily a term used in conjunction with PTT or public utility networks.

Data Encryption Standard—DES: The standard endorsed by the US National Bureau of Standards for the encryption of data.

Data Link Layer: Layer 2 of the ISO model. This is concerned with the transmission of data across the particular medium.

Data Terminal Equipment—DTE: Equipment that the user attaches to a network, particularly to a DCE provided by a public utility.

Data Word: A set or unit of data bits to which some checking information is added in order to detect transmission errors. The larger word, including the added checking information, is called a *code word*.

Datagram: A self-contained packet of data, including a destination address, that is sent through a network independently of any other packet of data.

Data Encryption Standard—DES: A standardised, private-key encryption method.

DCE: See *Data Circuit-Terminating Equipment.*

DeciBel—dB: A logarithmic measure of the strength of a signal.

Direct Memory Access—DMA: A way of constructing a computer system in which data is transferred directly between a peripheral device and the main memory of the computer without involving or interrupting the CPU. In this way the transfer can proceed faster under hardware control, and the CPU is not constantly diverted from its other work.

Directory Service: A network service that allows data to be associated with names, and retrieved by giving the name as a key. It corresponds loosely to the kind of facilities provided by a telephone directory.

DTE: See *Data Terminal Equipment.*

DXE: A generic term used to refer to both "DCE" and "DTE" when describing the symmetrical peer-to-peer aspects of X.25(1984)

ECMA: The *European Computer Manufacturers Association.* Since this includes most of the main manufacturers *active* in Europe, it encompasses most major manufacturers worldwide.

Ethernet: A local-area network that shares a cable between many users using the CSMA/CD access method (q.v.). Originally developed at the Xerox PARC Research Center, it was developed into an industry standard by DEC, Intel and Xerox, and then further elaborated to become the IEEE 802.3 standard.

Facsimile—Fax: A method of transmitting photographic images using the telephone network.

Fiber Distributed Data Interface—FDDI: A particular kind of token ring that runs on fibre optic cable at 100 Mbps over distances of up to 100 kilometres or so.

Flag Sequence: A special sequence of bits that is used to indicate the boundaries of frames of data

Flaming: Violent argument that is carried on by electronic means— say in a message exchange—in which the participants go beyond the norms of reasonable behavour

Flow Control: A method of controlling the flow of data between two communicating systems.

Footprint of a Communications Satellite: That area of the Earth's surface that can best receive the transmission of the satellite. This area might be everywhere within line of sight of the satellite, or possibly a smaller area if directional antennas are used to restrict it.

Forward Error Correction: The process of recovering from errors by adding sufficient and suitable redundancy so that errors can be corrected at the receiver without further reference to the source of the data. See also *reverse error correction*.

Frame: A block or packet of data that is sent across a network. Usually it is several bytes long.

Frame Check Sequence—FCS: Redundant checking information sent with a frame of data in order to detect errors. Often this is a cyclic redundancy check.

Framing: The method or process of marking the boundaries of a *frame* (q.v.) of data.

Frequency Division Multiplexing—FDM: A technique for combining or multiplexing a number of channels by allocating each carrier to a different section of the frequency spectrum.

Frequency Shift Keying—FSK: A modulation technique whereby the binary data is used to switch between two transmitted frequencies.

Full-Duplex: A communication channel is *full-duplex* if communication can take place in both directions simultaneously.

Functional Standard: There are many standards in existance. To interwork, two systems need to agree on an appropriate *set* of standards together with certain options and parameters for those standards. A *functional standard* is such a set of standards and options for a specific field of application.

Gateway: A connection between two networks, usually operating at a high level of protocol.

Generator Polynomial: The polynomial representing the particular checksum being used. See also *Checksum* and *Polynomial*.

Half-Duplex: Strictly this means a channel that can only operate in one direction, though it is often also applied to a two-way alternate channel.

High-Level Data Link Control—HDLC: A link-level error recovery protocol.

Idempotent Operations: An operation is said to be *idempotent* if each and every one of its applications is equally potent or effective—that is, gives the same result.

Integrated Services Digital Network—ISDN: A new, internationally agreed telephone and data transmission network.

International Standards Organization—ISO: The body responsible for getting agreement on international standards.

Internet: Generically, this means a combination of networks into a larger whole or *Internet*. More specifically, the word refers to the particular interconnected set of networks that is interconnected using the ARPANET Internet Protocol (q.v.).

Internet Protocol—IP: The specific ARPANET protocol that can be used to implement an Internet (q.v.).

ISO Model: More completely, the *ISO model for Open Systems Interconnection*. This is the model of computer communications which has seven layers. The ISO model describes the ISO OSI communications architecture. ISO communications standards fit into specific places in this model.

Kermit: A simple error-recovery protocol used over asynchronous character-by-character lines, or over terminal connections across a network. It is widely used to transfer files reliably between microcomputers and either other microcomputers or mainframes. It is widely used because the protocol is simple and easy to implement, is in the public domain, and implementations for most machines are available free.

Linear: A *linear* amplifier is one in which the graph of the output intensity versus the input intensity is a straight line through the origin. This means that the output is a constant times the input. The constant of proportionality—that is the slope or gradient of the curve—is the amplification or gain of the amplifier. The term "linear" is applied to many systems where this kind of straight-line proportionality applies.

Little-Endian: Characters in Swift's *Gulliver's Travels* who held the fanatical religious belief that boiled eggs must only be eaten starting at the little end. Also a term indicating that the least important or significant part of a data entity is transmitted first. See also *Big-Endian*.

Local Area Network—LAN: A network covering an area usually not larger than a few kilometers. It is characterised by very high throughput and low end-to-end delay time.

Logical Link Control—LLC: The protocol implemending a logical link between two entities. This may be across a shared medium of some kind.

Longitudinal Parity: If a sequence of bytes is imagined as being written in a column, line by line—one byte's bits per line—then *transverse parity* is the parity calculated across rows—a byte at a time—and *longitudinal parity* is the parity calculated one column of bits at a time—each parity referring to one bit out of each byte.

Manchester Encoding: A particular way of encoding both a data signal and clocking or timing information reliably in the same signal.

Medium Access Control—MAC: The particular method by which the access of several stations to a shared medium of some sort is regulated.

Mesh: A network with sufficient interconnections so that (as opposed to a tree) there is more than one route between some nodes.

Message Polynomial: The polynomial representing a frame or *data-word*. The checksum is derived by dividing the message polynomial by the generator polynomial. See also *checksum* and *polynomial*.

Modem: A *Mo*dulator-*dem*odulator—that is, a device for modulating a carrier with a data stream ready for transmission, and demodulating or extracting a data signal from a received signal.

Modulation: A method of transmission in which the data signals are used to vary or modulate another signal—perhaps its amplitude, frequency or phase—rather than being used directly as in baseband transmission (q.v.). The signal that is modulated is called the *carrier*.

Multiplexing: The method of mixing several signals together and transmitting them down some kind of channel.

Murphy's Law: The fundamental law of nature that states *"If anything can possibly go wrong then it will. It will still go wrong even if it's not possible to go wrong."* Many branches of human endeavor claim the particular application of Murphy's Law in their own field, and computers and communications are no exception to this rule.

Network Layer: The layer of protocol that provides the ISO level 3 service, or similar service on other networks. This is concerned with the transmission of data across networks.

NeWS: Sun's *N*etworked *W*indow *S*ystem is a way of supporting bitmapped terminals remotely across networks.

Node: One element—usually a switching element—of a network.

Noise: Electrical disturbance that is generated naturally by all electronic circuits and also picked up from outside interference. Sufficiently intense noise may corrupt data signals.

NRZ—NRZI: Two schemes for encoding data signals that have varying properties depending on the exact scheme and the need to be able to extract the clock reliably from the received signal.

Octet: See *Byte*.

Open Systems Interconnection—OSI: The ISO project and associated protocols to achieve open interconnection across diverse systems.

Opcode: An *opcode* or *operation code* is a general term in computing for a binary pattern or code that is usually placed at the start of a message. The value of the code indicates some operation that is to be performed by the recipient of the message. The rest of the message may be blank or it may consist of operands or parameters for the operation. Two common occurrences of opcodes in computing are in machine instructions that are read from instruction memory by a processor, and protocol messages that form part of a communications protocol.

Optical Fibre: It is common for the transmission medium to be either the traditional copper wire in various forms, a radio signal, or optical fibre. In the case of optical fibre the data is used to modulate a light wave by some means, and the light travels along the optical fibre. Optical fibres have potentially huge data carrying capacity, are immune from electrical interference, are difficult to tap unobtrusively, have smaller diameter than electrical wiring, and, since the medium is an electrical insulator, can be advantageous in some safety-critical applications.

Overrun: During the reception of data, the bits must be passed on, stored in a buffer, or otherwise dealt with by the receiver. If the bits arrive so quickly that the receiver cannot properly deal

with them then there is an *overrun* error condition. See also
underrun.

Packet Assembler/Disassembler—PAD: A device used to interface a packet switching network to a character-by-character terminal.

Packet Switching: The method of routing data through a network by
assembling groups of characters or bytes together into packets
and switching the packets from machine to machine until the
destination is reached. The particular value of packet switching
is that it allows the multiplexing of several *virtual calls* (q.v.)
across particular real circuits, and allows the statistical traffic demands of each of the calls to be averaged over those real
circuits.

Pacing: Some writers refer to *flow control* as *pacing*.

Parity: A simple method of checking for single-bit errors. A single parity bit is added to a block of data—usually just one character—
and is set to 0 or 1 in order to make the number of bits even
or odd depending on whether even or odd parity is being used.
This method is very weak since it will detect only an odd number of bit errors and is thus only useful where isolated single-bit
errors are expected.

PBX: A *P*rivate *B*ranch telephone e*X*change.

Physical Layer: The lowest layer—layer 1—in the ISO model. This
concerns the specific kind of transmission medium being used.

Piggyback: The method of *piggybacking* is used to combine data and
control information in the same packet in order to reduce the
number of packets transmitted. This is particularly useful in
full-duplex communication. The prime example is the piggybacking of flow control information on to data packets—each
stream of flow control information is piggybacked on the data
stream flowing in the same direction, and refers to the data
travelling in the reverse direction.

Pixel: For a digitised picture, one spot is represented by one pixel. This
representation may be as simple as one bit for a monochrome
picture or as elaborate as a set of intensities for the various
colours.

Plain Old Telephone Service—POTS: The name given to the
familiar, pre-ISDN telephone service by people working with
the new ISDN and extolling its virtues.

Polynomial: In communications, the algebra of a particular sort of polynomials is used to analyse the properties of cyclic redundancy checksums. The data block or codeword to be checked is represented as the coefficients of a polynomial, the specific kind of checksum is represented as a *generator polynomial*, and the codeword is divided by the generator polynomial to yield a *remainder*. This remainder forms the *checksum* and is concatenated on the end of the dataword to form the codeword.

Postal, Telegraph and Telephone Authority—PTT: The national authority that runs those services. The tradition that, except in the USA, these are the same single monopoly is beginning to break down in some countries.

PostScript: A language for describing the layout of pages of both text and pictures. This has become the de facto standard for this kind of application in the late 1980s. In addition, variations and extensions of the language are being used for screen support functions, including NeWS.

Presentation Layer: The issues and the set of communication protocols that are concerned with the representation of data in a machine-independent way.

Promiscuous Mode: A term that is sometimes applied to a station on a shared medium of some kind. If the station is operating in *promiscuous mode* then it receives *all* packets on the shared medium, not just those addresses specifically to itself. Monitor stations often work in promiscuous mde.

Protocol: A set of messages and the rules for exchanging those messages in order to provide some kind of service.

Protocol Data Unit—PDU: A message that is part of some protocol.

Public-Key Encryption: The process of encrypting data with a public or well-known key, and yet needing a different, secret key in order to obtain the secret data.

Public-Switched Data Network—PSDN: A switched-data network which is run by a public utility or PTT.

Public-Switched Telephone Network—PSTN: The public telephone system which is run by public utilities or PTTs.

Request For Comment—RFC: A particular kind of informal paper that is freely available across the ARPANET. A message may be sent to the ARPA address SERVICE@SRI-NIC.ARPA that has as its subject field "RFC nnnn". The number "nnnn" is either the RFC number or the string "INDEX". The service is automatic, and the requested document is returned promptly as one or several messages containing ASCII text. The information may also be obtained on paper by writing to the address NET-WORK INFORMATION CENTER, SRI International, Menlo Park, California 94025.

Remote Operations Service Element—ROSE: An applications-level service that allows applications to execute operations remotely.

Remote Procedure Call—RPC: A *Remote Procedure Call* is similar to a local procedure call except that the parameters of the procedure are exported across a network to some remote environment, and the procedure is executed there in the remote environment. Any results are then returned back across the network to the originating system.

Reverse Error Correction: The process of recovering from errors by adding sufficient redundancy to data frames so that errors may be detected, and then correcting the errors by causing a sufficient number of retransmissions so that the frame eventually is received without any (detected) error. See also *forward error correction.*

Ring: A network topology in which the participating stations are connected together in a topological ring.

Route: See *Addesses and Routes.*

Round Robin: A method of choosing which of several alternatives to take next. The list of alternatives is arranged in a logical ring, and each time a choice is needed, the next one in the ring is chosen.

Scrolling: When text data is shown on a video screen, the full extent of the data is frequently larger than can be shown on the screen all at once, and a mechanism is usually provided whereby the user can move the screen view around the data. This process of moving the view to show different parts of the data is referred to as "scrolling".

Serial Data: Data is usually transmitted along a communications line serially, bit-by-bit. See also *Clock.*

Server: In an environment of networked computers it is common for some machines to provide *services* for others. The service may be generalised—for example a time-sharing service—or it may be specialised—for example that provided by a print *server*.

Service Access Point—SAP: The term for the addressable point at which a service is accessed.

Session Layer: Layer 5 of the ISO model concerned with maintaining a connection or session between two entities that may transcend transport connections. This layer may also control the nature of the message exchange between the entities.

Signal-to-Noise Ratio: The ratio between the signal and noise on a circuit. Higher ratios correspond to better quality circuits.

Simplex: One-way-only communication is *simplex* communication.

Sliding-Window: A flow control strategy that uses the concept of a transmission window.

Slotted Ring: A particular kind of ring network in which the access is controlled by the availibility of a circulating fixed-sized slot, and the data is carried in that slot. The slot is usually quite small.

Specific Application Service Element—SASE: Protocol services at the application level that are sufficiently uncommon across different applications that they are unlikely to be standardised.

Standard: Protocol standards have been developed to allow inter-working between a variety of computer equipment and operating systems. Chapter 16 describes the standards process, and many of the standards issues.

Star: A kind of network topology in which every node is connected to a central switch that switches all the data packets for everyone. Sometimes a star network may be two or more levels deep. Its topology is then a multi-level star or tree (q.v.).

Subscriber: A term for a network user, particularly a user of a public, commercial network.

Switched Circuit: A telephone call involves switching in a circuit between the caller and callee that is available for the duration of the call. Data circuits many be similarly switched. *Virtial Circuits* (q.v.) are similar in effect to switched circuits.

Synchronous Data Link Control—SDLC: The IBM link-level protocol from which HDLC was derived.

Synchronous Transmission: A method of data transmission in which the transmitting and receiving stations operate with their clocks in synchronization. This method, in contrast to *asynchronous transmission* (q.v.), is characterised by the sending of frames of data rather than single characters.

TELNET: The ARPANET standard terminal support protocol.

Time-Division Multiplexing—TDM: A method of multiplexing in which a channel is shared amongst several subchannels by giving each of the subchannels a regular fixed time interval during which they may use the whole channel.

Throughput: The rate at which data is actually transmitted successfully across a link or a network. This is frequently much less than the apparent raw bandwidth.

Token: A logical entity that is used to control access to a resource of some sort that is shared by two or more entities. The most common communications resources for which a token is used are shared transmission media or a screen image.

Token Bus: A bus network, access to which is controlled by means of a token.

Token Ring: A ring network, access to which is controlled by means of a token. There are several kinds of token ring including the IEEE 802.5 cable ring and the FDDI fibre ring.

Transmission Control Protocol—TCP: The ARPANET standard transport protocol.

Transparent Channel: A channel which lets through *all* data unmolested, and does not add, take away, or change any bit patterns.

Transport Layer: Layer 4 of the ISO model. This is concerned with the reliable end-to-end transmission of data across possibly several networks. It marks the dividing line between the lower layers that are concerned with the shifting of bits, and the upper layers that are more concerned with data representation and meaningful communication.

Transport Protocol: The protocol that is concerned with providing the *Transport Layer* service.

Transverse Parity: The parity taken over a short set of bits—usually a single byte. This is the usual form of parity, and *transverse parity* is normally only so-called to distinguish it from *longitudinal* parity (q.v.).

Tree: A topology which can be represented by a branching tree. A multi-level star is a tree. On a tree network (as opposed to a mesh network) there is only one route between two entities. See also *Star*.

Twisted Pair: A pair of insulated wires that are twisted together to reduce the pickup of stray electrical signals. Sometimes such wire is shielded. Twisted pair is used extensively for local telephone distribution, and the same kinds of wiring can be used for distributing LAN signals and connections.

Two-Way Alternate: A channel that can operate in either direction, but only alternately rather than simultaneously as can a full-duplex channel.

Underrun: During transmission of data there will be certain time constraints on the rate at which bits must be made ready for transmission. This is particularly true of synchronous transmission. If the bits are not made ready in time for transmission then there is an *underrun* error condition. See also *overrun*.

Virtual Call or Virtual Circuit: This has many similar characteristics to a switched circuit. It is often implemented by dividing the data stream into packets and switching the packets rather than the circuit itself. The use of packet switching means that the statistically varying demands of many computer connections can be efficiently multiplexed down real circuits.

Virtual Terminal: An idealized abstract terminal that allows real diverse terminals to be accessed in a single standard way with the differences being isolated in the terminal driver rather than contaminating the host application.

Wide-Area Network—WAN: A network—public or private—that covers a wide geographical area. The dimensions are usually at least hundreds of kilometres.

Window: *Window* has at least two quite different meanings in networking. One refers to the management of video screens by dividing the screen up into various regions or windows. The other refers to flow control in which only data belonging within a particular window in the sequence of data may be transmitted.

Windows, Icons, Menus and Pointers—WIMPs: This designates the fashionable and easy-to-use kind of interface found on many personal computers. The ideas originated with Englebart in the 1960s and were developed at Xerox PARC research centre. They were first commercially successful with the Apple Macintosh computer.

X-Windows, or just X: A form of supporting bitmapped terminals remotely across networks.

Zero-Bit Insertion: See *Bit Stuffing*.

Further Reading and References

Further Reading

The following is a suggested list of further reading. In the main it consists of important textbooks or review papers, but there is a sprinkling of key papers in various areas of the subject. The treat of reading, for example, Hamming's original paper should not be missed by relying only on later textbooks. This list is followed by a set of references.

Abramson, N. "The ALOHA System—Another Alternative for Computer Communications" *FJCC* p 281 1970

Binder, R., Abramson, N., Kuo, F., Okinaka, A., and Wax, D. "Aloha Packet Broadcasting—A Retrospect" *AFIPS Conference proceedings* **44** p 203 1975

Clarke, Arthur C. "EXTRA-TERRESTRIAL RELAYS—Can Rocket Stations Give World-wide Radio Coverage?" *Wireless World* **LI** No. 10 pp 305–308 Oct 1945

Comer, D. "Internetworking with TCP/IP: Principles, Protocols, and Architecture" *Prentice-Hall ISBN 0 13 470188 7, 1988*

Currie, W.S. "LANs Explained—a guide to local area networks" *Ellis Horward Ltd ISBN 0 7458 0238 9, 1988*

Davies, D.W. "Tutorial: The Security of Data in Networks" *IEEE Computer Society Catalog Number EHO183-4 1981 (Very useful compendium of papers on Public Key cryptosystems, including the originals by Diffie, Hellman, Merkle, Rivest, Shamir, etc. Also an exposition of the Data Encryption Standard.)*

Davies, D.W. and Price, W.L. "Security for Computer Networks: An introduction to data security in Teleprocessing and Electronic Funds Transfer" *Wiley ISBN 0 471 90063 X, 1984 (Extensive coverage of various aspects of data security.)*

Denning, D.E.R. "Cryptology and Data Security" *Addison-Wesley ISBN 0 201 10150 5, 1983 (Good explanation of the mathematics behind many cryptosystems, including public key systems.)*

Diffie, W. and Hellman, M.E. "Privacy and Authentication: An Introduction to Cryptography" *Proc IEEE,* **67** p 397 Mar 1979

Diffie, W. and Hellman, M.E. "New Directions in Cryptography" *IEEE Trans Inf Theo* p 644 Nov 1976

Edge, S.W. "Comparison of the Hop-by-Hop and Endpoint approaches to Network Interconnection in Flow Control in Computer Networks, Eds: J.-L. Grange and M. Gien" *North-Holland* p 359 1979

Gerla, M. and Kleinrock, L. "Flow Control: A Comparitive Survey" *IEEE Trans Commun* **COM-28** 553 1980

Goldberg, A. "A History of Personal Workstations" *ACM Press ISBN 201 11259 0,* 1988

Hamming, R.W. "Error Detecting and Error Correcting Codes" *The Bell System Technical Journal* **XXVI** 147 April 1950 *(A Model of clarity.)*

Hamming, R.W. "Coding and Information Theory" *Prentice-Hall, Inc. ISBN 0 13 139139 9,* 1980

Hellman M.E. "Public Key Cryptosystems" *Scientific American* 1979

Hill, R. "A First Course in Coding Theory" *Clarendon Press. ISBN 0 19 853803 0,* 1986 *(An introduction to various codes, including cyclic and error-correcting codes.)*

Huffman, D. "A Method for the Construction of Minimum Redundancy Codes" *Proc IRE* **40** 1098 Sept 1952

Kahn, D. "The Codebreakers" *Sphere Books Ltd ISBN 0 7221 5152 7,* 1973 *("Popular" account of the history of code making and breaking, with many fascinating anecdotes.)*

Kolata, G.B. "Computer Encryption and the National Security Agency Connection" *Science* **197** 438 July 1977

Metcalfe, R.M., and Boggs, D.R. "Ethernet: Distributed Packet Switching for Local Computer Networks" *CACM* **19** p 395. July 1976

Peterson, W.W., and Brown, D.T. "Cyclic Codes for Error Detection" *Proc IRE* **49** p 228 Jan 1961

Pouzin, L "Virtual Circuits vs Datagrams—Technical and Political Problems" *Proc NCC* p 483 1976

Pouzin, L. "The Network Business—Monoplies and Entrepreneurs" *Proc Third ICCC* p 563 1976

Pouzin, L. "Packet Networks, Issues and Choices" *Proc IFIP Congr* **77** p 515 1977

Randell, B. (ed.) "Security and Privacy" *Proceedings of joint IBM— University of Newcastle upon Tyne Seminar 1984*

Randell, B. (ed.) "Network Protocols" *Proceedings of joint IBM— University of Newcastle upon Tyne Seminar 1986*

Rivest, R.L., Shamir, A., and Adelman, l. "A Method for Obtaining Digital Signatures and Public-Key Cryptosystems" *CACM* **21** p 120 Feb 1978

Scantlebury, R.A. and Wilkinson, P.T., "The National Physical Laboratory Data Communications Network" *Proc. Int. Conf. on Comput. Comms.* Stockholm p 223, Aug 1974

Shannon, C. "A Mathematical Theory of Communication" *Bell Syst J.* **27** p 379 July 1948, and p 623 Oct 1948

Shannon, C. "Communication Theory of Security Systems" *Bell Syst J* **28** p 656 Oct 1949

Sunshine, C.A., and Dalal, Y.K. "Connection Management in Transport Protocols" *Computer Networks* **2** p 454 1978

Swift, J. "Gulliver's Travels—1726" *Penguin English Library ISBN 0 14 043022 9 1967*

Tanenbaum, A.S. "Computer Networks" *Prentice-Hall International ISBN 0 13 164699 0*, 1981 (Also second edition, 1987)

Welchman, G. "The Hut Six Story—Breaking the Enigma Codes" *McGraw-Hill ISBN 0 07 069180 0*, 1982

West, C.H. "General Technique for Communications Protocol Validation" *IBM J. Res. Dev* **22** p 393 July 1978

Wright, P. "Spy Catcher" *Viking Penguin Inc. ISBN 0 670 82055 5*, 1987

References

Abramson, N. "The ALOHA System" in "Computer Communication Networks" *Eds Abramson, N. and Kuo, F. Prentice-Hall* 1973

Abramson, N. "Packet Switching with Satellites" *NCC* p 695 1973

Adobe Systems "PostScript Language Reference Manual" *Addison-Wesley ISBN 0 201 10174 2*, 1985

Aruliah, A.A., Parkin, G.I., Wichmann, B.A. "A Pascal Implmentation of the DES Encryption Algorithm, Including Cipher Block Chaining." *National Physical Laboratory Report DITC 61/85*

June 1985 *(Derived from Tanenbaum (q.v.), and available from a software company, Grey Matter Ltd., U.K.)*

Birrell, A.D., Levin, R., Needham, R.M., Schroeder, M.D. "Grapevine: An Exercise in Distributed Computing" *Comm ACM* **25** p 260-274 1982

Bochmann, G., and Sunshine, C. "Formal Methods in Communication Protocol Design" *IEEE Trans Comm* **COM-28** p 624 April 1980

Boggs, D.R., Shoch, J.F., Taft, E.A., and Metcalfe, R.M. "PUP: An Internetwork Architecture" *IEEE Trans Comm* **COM-28** p 612 April 1980

Boudreau, P.E., and Steen, R.F. "Cyclic Redundancy Checking by Program" *FJCC* p 10 1971

Cash, A.R. "Ring Local Area Networks: A Strategy for Choosing the Phase Locked Loop Class for Data Repeaters" *Report RL-84-081* Science and Engineering Research Council, Rutherford Appleton Laboratory, Chilton, Didcot, Oxon OX11 OQX, England. 1984

Cashin, P.M. "Datapac Network Protocols" *Proceedings of the Third International Conference on Computer Communication, Toronto.* p 150 Aug 1976

Christoffersson, P. "Crypto Users' Handbook" *North-Holland ISBN 0 444 70484 1,* 1988

Clipsham, W.W., and Glave, F.E. "Datapac Network Overview" *Proceedings of the Third International Conference on Computer Communication, Toronto* p 131 Aug 1976

Crowther, W., Rettberg, R., Walden, D., Ornstein, S., and Heart, F. "A System for Broadcast Communication: Reservation-Aloha" *Proc Sixth Hawaii Conf Syst Sci* p 371 1973

Cunningham, I.M., Older, W.J., and Trivedi, A.K. "Datapac Software Architecture" *COMSAC77, Chicago* 1977

Dalal, Y., and Metcalfe, R. "Reverse Path Forwarding of Broadcast Packets" *CACM* **21** p 1040 1978

Davies, D.W. and Barber, D.L.A. "Communication Networks for Computers" *Wiley ISBN 0 471 19874 9,* 1973

Davies, D.W. and Price, W.L. "The Application of Digital Signatures Based on Public Key Cryptosystems." *National Physical Laboratory Report DNACS 39/80* Dec 1980

Denning, D. E. and Sacco, G.M. "Timestamps in Key Distribution Protocols" *CACM* **24** pp 533–536 1981

Denning, D. E. "Digital Signatures with RSA and Other Public-Key Cryptosystems" *CACM* **27** p 388 1984

Diffie, W. and Hellman, M.E. "Extensive Cryptanalysis of the NBS Data Encryption Standard" *Computer* **10** p 74 June 1977

Diffie, W. and Hellman, M.E. "Privacy and Authentication" *Proc IEEE* **67** p 397 March 1979

Dijkstra, E. W. "Cooperating Sequential Processes" in "Programming Languages" *(Ed. F. Genuys) Academic Press* 1972

Euronet "Data Entry Virtual Terminal Protocol for EURONET" *Directorate General Scientific and Technical Information and Information Management, Luxembourg* November 1978. VTP-D/Issue 4

Haas, Z., Cheriton, D.R. " Blazenet: A Photonic Implementable Wide-Area Network" *Report STAN-CS-87-1185 (also numbered CSL-TR-87-346)* Oct 1987 Department of Computer Science, Stanford University

Hale, R.W.S. "File Transfer Protocols - Comparison and Critique" *National Physical Laboratory Report DNACS 48/81* July 1981

Halsall, F. "Data Communications, Computer Networks, and OSI" *Second edition Addison-Wesley ISBN 0 201 18244 0,* 1988

Hellman, M.E. "A Cryptanalytic Time-Memory Tradeoff" *IEEE Trans Inf Theo* **IT-26** p 401 July 1980

Hoare, C.A.R. "Monitors: An Operating System Structuring Concept" *Comm. ACM* **17** 10 pp 549–557 October 1974

Hopgood, F. R. A. et al (eds.) "Methodology of Window Management" *Springer-Verlag ISBN 3 540 16116 3,* 1986

Hunter, J.A. "The Simple Screen Management Protocol" *Published for the Joint Network Team by The Computing Laboratory of the University of Newcastle upon Tyne, Newcastle NE1 7RU, England* 1985

IEEE "Journal on Selected Areas in Communication" **SAC-1** May 1986

Kleinrock, L., and Lam, S.S. "Packet Switching in a Multi-access Broadcast Channel: Performance Evaluation." *IEEE Trans Comm* **COM-23** p 410, April 1975

Kleinrock,L., and Lam, S.S. "Packet Switching in a Multi-access Broadcast Channel: Carrier Sense Multiple Access Modes and their Throughput-Delay Characteristics" *IEEE Trans Comm* **COM-23** p 1400, 1975

Kleinrock, L., and Tobagi, F. "Random Access Techniques for Data Transmission over Packet-Switched Radio Channels." *AFIPS Conference Proceedings* **44** p 187. 1975

Kleinrock, L. "Queueing Systems, Vol 2: Computer Applications" *Wiley ISBN 0 471 49111 X, 1976*

Kline, C.S. and Popeck, G.J. "Public vs. Private Key Encryption" *AFIPS Conference proceedings* **48** pp 831–837 1979

Lenstra, H.W. "Factoring Integers with Elliptic Curves" *Mathematical Sciences Research Institute preprint, Berkeley 1986*

Linington, P.F. "A Network Independent Transport Service" *Prepared by Study Group 3 of The Post Office PSS User Forum.* Feb 1980 *(Commonly known as "The Yellow Book Transport Service"— not to be confused with the CCITT "Yellow Books" of the same year.)*

Merkle, R.C. "Secure Communications Over Insecure Channels" *CACM* **21** p 294 April 1978

Merlin, P.M., and Schweitzer, P.J. "Deadlock Avoidance in Store-and-Forward Networks I: Store-and-Forward Deadlock" *IEEE Trans Comm.* **COM-28** p 345, March 1980

Merlin, P.M., and Schweitzer, P.J. "Deadlock Avoidance in Store-and-Forward Networks II: Other Deadlock Types" *IEEE Trans. Comm.* **COM-28** p 355, March 1980

Metcalfe, R.M. "Steady-State Analysis of a Slotted and Controlled Aloha System with Blocking" *6th Hawaii Conference on System Science* Jan 1973

Mitrani, I. "Modelling of Computer and Communication Systems" *Cambridge University Press ISBN 0 521 31422 4, 1987*

National Bureau of Standards "Data Encryption Standard" *FIPS Publication 46* p 1, Jan 1977

Needham, R.M. and Schroeder, M.D. "Using Encryption for Authentication in Large Networks of Computers" *CACM* **21** p 993 Dec 1978

Needham, R.M. and Schroeder, M.D. "Authentication Revisited" *Op. Sys. Rev.* **21** p 7 Jan 1987

Otway, D. and Rees, O. "Efficient and Timely Mutual Authentication" *Op. Sys. Rev.* **21** pp 8–10 Jan 1987

Padlipsky, M.A. "The Elements of Networking Style and Other Essays and Animadversions on the Art of Intercomputer Networking" *Prentice-Hall ISBN 0 13 268111 0*, 1987

Peterson, W.W. and Weldon, E.J. "Error-Correcting Codes" *Second edition MIT Press ISBN 0 262 16 039 0*, 1972

Prange, E. "Cyclic Error-Correcting Codes in Two Symbols" *Air Force Cambridge Research Center Bedford Mass. Tech Note AFCRC-TN-57-103* Sept 1957

Prange, E. "Some Cyclic Error-Correcting Codes with Simple Decoding Algorithms." *Air Force Cambridge Research Center Bedford Mass. Tech Note AFCRC-TN-58-156* Apr 1958

Price, W.L. "Seventh Annotated Bibliography of Recent Publications on Data Security and Cryptography" *National Physical Laboratory Report DITC 64/85* Aug 1985

Randell, B. (ed.) "Colossus: Godfather of the Computer" *New Scientist* **73** 1038, 10 Feb 1977 (Also reprinted in "The Origins of Digital Computers - Selected Papers" Third edition p 349 Edited by B Randell, Springer-Verlag 1982 ISBN 3-540-11319-3.)

Reeds, J. "Cracking a Random Number Generator" *Cryptologia* **1** p 20 1977

Riesel, H. "Prime Numbers and Computer Methods for Factorization" *Birkhäuser, Boston* 1985

Rosenthal, D.S.H. "A simple X11 Client Program" *USENIX conf. Dallas* Feb 1988 Reprinted as *"Going for Baroque"*, Unix Review, June 1988

Saltzer, J.H. "On Digital Signatures" *Op Sys Rev.* **12** p 12 April 1978

Scheifler, R. W. and Gettys, J. "The X Window System" *ACM Trans Graphics* **5** No 2, pp79-109 1986

Shamir, A., and Zippel, R.E. "On the Security of the Merkle-Hellman Cryptographic Scheme" *IEEE Trans Inf Theor* **IT-26** p 339 May 1980

Shoch, J.F. "Packet Fragmentation in Inter-Network Protocols" *Comput Nets* **3** p 3 1979

Shoch, J.F. "Inter-Network Naming, Addresing, and Routing" *Compcon.* p 72 1978

Stewart, I. "Geometry finds factors faster" *Nature* **325** p 199 January 1987

Sun Microsystems "NeWS Preliminary Technical Overview" October 1986

Sunshine, C.A. "Formal Techniques for Protocol Specification and Verification" *Computer* **2** p 454 1978

Twyver, D.A., and Rybczynski, A.M. "Datapac Subscriber Interfaces" *Proceedings of the Third International Conference on Computer Communication, Toronto* p 143 Aug 1976

Watson, R.W. "Interprocess Communication: Interface and End-to-End (Transport) Protocol Design Issues" *in "Distributed Systems— Architecture and Implementation: An Advanced Course" pp140-174. Springer-Verlag ISBN 3 540 10571 9, 1981*

West, C.H. "General Technique for Communications Protocol Validation" *IBM J. Res. Dev* **22** p 393 July 1978

Winterbotham, F.W. "The ULTRA Secret" *Harper and Row* 1974

Wirth, N. "Modula: a Language for Modular Multiprogramming" *Soft— Pract. & Exper.* **7** pp 3–35 1977

Young, S.C.K., and McGibbon, C.I. "The Control System of the Datapac Network" *Proceedings of the Third International Conference on Computer Communication, Toronto.* p 137 Aug 1976

Index